The Complete
City Maps
of
Michigan

D0873617

CɪᴛMᴀᴘ Corporation
P.O. Box 37
Grawn, Michigan 49637
616-276-6937

CitMap Corporation
P.O. Box 37
Grawn, Michigan 49637

CɪᴛMᴀᴘ Table of Contents

I.   Introduction

II. Michigan State Map Upper Peninsula

III. Michigan State Map Lower Peninsula

IV. Michigan City Index

V.   Index Instructions and Map Key Guide

VI. Pages 1-482 Michigan City Maps 2000 or more in population

VII. Pages 483-527 Michigan City Maps 1000-1999 in population

VIII. Zip Codes for Michigan Cities

IX. Mileage Between Michigan Cities

CitMap
CORPORATION

A letter from the publisher

This Citmap publication represents many months
of research, meticulous planning and design . . . to produce
a product that helps you find your way easier
and more efficiently.

We use only the best and the most reliable sources to
confirm map details. However, even with the best of efforts,
errors can occur so we cannot guarantee absolute
accuracy for each map. Please let us know of any corrections
or comments you may have.

In the interest of saving time and conserving
energy, may this guide prove itself worthy of
the investment.

Safe and pleasant traveling from Citmap Corporation!

Sincerely,

Russell Madsen

Russell Madsen
Publisher

UPPER MICHIGAN

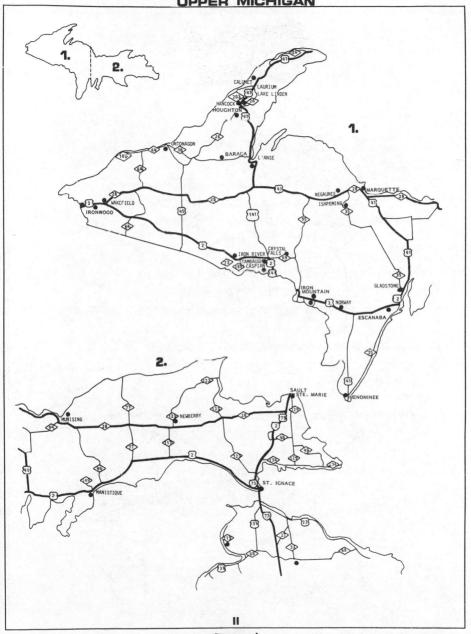

II

MICHIGAN

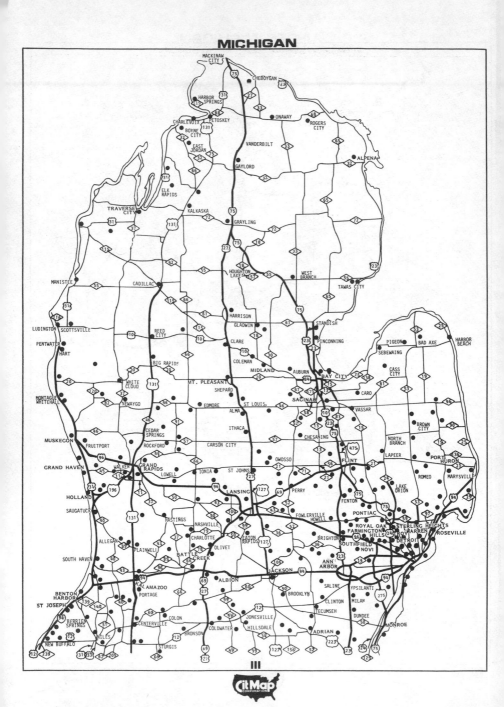

III

MICHIGAN CITY INDEX

CITY	PAGE
ADRIAN CITY	1
ALBION CITY	2
ALGONAC CITY	3
ALLEGAN CITY	4
ALLEN PARK CITY	B*
ALMA CITY	5
ALMONT VILLAGE	483
ALPENA CITY	6
ANN ARBOR CITY	7
ARMADA VILLAGE	483
AUBURN CITY	25
BAD AXE CITY	26
BANGOR CITY	27
BARAGA VILLAGE	484
BATTLE CREEK CITY	28
BAY CITY	36
BEAVERTON CITY	484
BELDING CITY	37
BELLAIRE VILLAGE	485
BELLEVILLE CITY	38
BELLEVUE VILLAGE	485
BENTON HARBOR CITY	39
BERKLEY CITY	43
BERRIEN SPRINGS VIL	44
BESSEMER CITY	45
BEVERLY HILLS VILLAGE	46
BIG RAPIDS CITY	47
BIRCH RUN VILLAGE	486
BIRMINGHAM CITY	48
BLISSFIELD VILLAGE	49
BLOOMFIELD HILLS CITY	50
BOYNE CITY	51
BRECKENRIDGE VILLAGE	486
BRIDGMAN CITY	52
BRIGHTON CITY	53
BRONSON CITY	54
BROOKLYN VILLAGE	487
BROWN CITY	487
BUCHANAN CITY	55
BURTON CITY	192
CADILLAC CITY	56
CALUMET VILLAGE	488
CAPAC VILLAGE	488
CARLETON VILLAGE	57
CARO VILLAGE	58
CARSON CITY	489
CASPIAN CITY	489
CASS CITY VILLAGE	59
CASSOPOLIS VILLAGE	60
CEDAR SPRINGS CITY	61
CENTER LINE CITY	62
CENTREVILLE VILLAGE	490
CHARLEVOIX CITY	63
CHARLOTTE CITY	64
CHEBOYGAN CITY	65
CHELSEA VILLAGE	66
CHESANING VILLAGE	67
CLARE CITY	68
CLAWSON CITY	69
CLINTON VILLAGE	70
CLIO CITY	71
COLDWATER CITY	72
COLEMAN CITY	490
COLOMA CITY	491
COLON VILLAGE	491
CONSTANTINE VILLAGE	492
COOPERSVILLE CITY	73
CORUNNA CITY	74
CROSWELL CITY	75
CRYSTAL FALLS CITY	76
DAVISON CITY	77
DEARBORN CITY	B*
DEARBORN HGTS. CITY	B*
DECATUR VILLAGE	78
DETROIT CITY	79
DeWITT CITY	177
DEXTER VILLAGE	492
DIMONDALE VILLAGE	493
DOWAGIAC CITY	174
DUNDEE VILLAGE	175
DURAND CITY	176
EAST DETROIT CITY	177
EAST GRAND RAPIDS	C*
EAST JORDAN CITY	178
EAST LANSING CITY	E*
EAST TAWAS CITY	179
EATON RAPIDS CITY	180
ECORSE CITY	B*
EDMORE VILLAGE	493
EDWARDSBURG VILLAGE	494
ELK RAPIDS VILLAGE	494
ELSIE VILLAGE	495
ESCANABA CITY	181
ESSEXVILLE CITY	182
EVART CITY	183

FARMINGTON CITY	186
FARMINGTON HILLS	184
FENTON CITY	188
FERNDALE CITY	189
FERRYSBURG CITY	190
FLAT ROCK CITY	191
FLINT CITY	192
FLUSHING CITY	216
FOWLER	495
FOWLERVILLE VILLAGE	217
FRANKENMUTH CITY	218
FRANKFORT CITY	496
FRANKLIN VILLAGE	219
FRASER CITY	220
FREMONT CITY	221
FRUITPORT VILLAGE	496
GALESBURG CITY	497
GARDEN CITY	B*
GAYLORD CITY	222
GIBRALTAR CITY	223
GLADSTONE CITY	224
GLADWIN CITY	225
GRAND BLANC CITY	226
GRAND HAVEN CITY	227
GRAND LEDGE CITY	228
GRAND RAPIDS CITY	229
GRANDVILLE CITY	C*
GRAYLING CITY	497
GREENVILLE CITY	263
GROSSE POINTE CITY	B*
GROSSE POINTE FARMS	B*
GROSSE POINTE PARK	B*
GROSSE POINTE SHORES	B*
GROSSE POINTE WOODS	B*
HAMTRAMCK CITY	B*
HANCOCK CITY	264
HARBOR BEACH CITY	266
HARBOR SPRINGS CITY	498
HARPER WOODS CITY	B*
HARRISON CITY	498
HART CITY	499
HARTFORD CITY	267
HASTINGS CITY	268
HAZEL PARK CITY	269
HIGHLAND PARK CITY	B*
HILLSDALE CITY	270
HOLLAND CITY	271
HOLLY VILLAGE	273
HOMER VILLAGE	499
HOUGHTON CITY	273
HOWARD CITY VILLAGE	500
HOWELL CITY	274
HUDSON CITY	275
HUDSONVILLE CITY	276
HUNTINGTON WOODS	277
IMLAY CITY	278
INKSTER CITY	B*
IONIA CITY	279
IRON MOUNTAIN CITY	280
IRON RIVER CITY	281
IRONWOOD CITY	282
ISHPEMING CITY	283
ITHACA CITY	284
JACKSON CITY	285
JENISON	481
JONESVILLE VILLAGE	293
KALAMAZOO CITY	294
KALKASKA VILLAGE	500
KEEGO HARBOR CITY	392
KENTWOOD CITY	C*
KINGSFORD CITY	307
LAINGSBURG CITY	501
LAKE LINDEN VILLAGE	501
LAKE ODESSA VILLAGE	308
LAKE ORION VILLAGE	309
LAKEVIEW VILLAGE	502
L'ANSE VILLAGE	310
LANSING CITY	311
LAPEER CITY	330
LATHRUP VILLAGE CITY	I*
LAURIUM VILLAGE	331
LAWTON VILLAGE	502
LESLIE CITY	332
LINCOLN PARK CITY	B*
LINDEN VILLAGE	333
LITCHFIELD CITY	503
LIVONIA CITY	B*
LOWELL CITY	334
LUDINGTON CITY	335
LUNA PIER CITY	503

MADISON HGTS. CITY	336
MANCELONA VILLAGE	504
MANCHESTER VILLAGE	504
MANISTEE CITY	337
MANISTIQUE CITY	338
MANTON CITY	505
MARCELLUS VILLAGE	505
MARINE CITY	339
MARLETTE VILLAGE	506
MARQUETTE CITY	340
MARSHALL CITY	341
MARYSVILLE CITY	402
MASON CITY	342
MATTAWAN VILLAGE	343
MELVINDALE CITY	B*
MEMPHIS CITY	506
MENOMINEE CITY	344
MIDDLEVILLE VILLAGE	507
MIDLAND CITY	345
MILAN CITY	347
MILFORD VILLAGE	348
MILLINGTON VILLAGE	507
MONROE CITY	349
MONTAGUE CITY	350
MONTROSE VILLAGE	508
MORENCI CITY	351
MOUNT CLEMENS CITY	352
MOUNT MORRIS CITY	353
MOUNT PLEASANT CITY	354
MUNISING CITY	355
MUSKEGON CITY	356
MUSKEGON HEIGHTS	F*
NASHVILLE VILLAGE	508
NEGAUNEE CITY	372
NEWAYGO CITY	509
NEW BALTIMORE CITY	373
NEWBERRY VILLAGE	373
NEW BUFFALO CITY	373
NEW HAVEN VILLAGE	509
NILES CITY	376
NORTH MUSKEGON CITY	F*
NORTHVILLE CITY	377
NORTON SHORES CITY	F*
NORWAY CITY	378
NOVI CITY	379
OAK PARK CITY	381
OLIVET CITY	510
ONAWAY CITY	510
ONTONAGON VILLAGE	382
ORCHARD LAKE VIL	511
ORTONVILLE VILLAGE	511
OTSEGO CITY	383
OVID VILLAGE	512
OWOSSO CITY	384
OXFORD VILLAGE	385
PARCHMENT CITY	D*
PAW PAW VILLAGE	386
PENTWATER VILLAGE	512
PERRY CITY	387
PETERSBURG CITY	513
PETOSKEY CITY	388
PIGEON VILLAGE	513
PINCKNEY VILLAGE	514
PINCONNING CITY	514
PLAINWELL CITY	389
PLEASANT RIDGE CITY	390
PLYMOUTH CITY	391
PONTIAC CITY	392
PORTAGE CITY	D*
PORT HURON CITY	402
PORTLAND CITY	404
POTTERSVILLE CITY	515
QUINCY VILLAGE	515
READING CITY	516
REED CITY	405
REESE VILLAGE	516
RICHMOND CITY	406
RIVER ROUGE CITY	B*
RIVERVIEW CITY	B*
ROCHESTER CITY	407
ROCKFORD CITY	408
ROCKWOOD CITY	409
ROGERS CITY	410
ROMEO VILLAGE	411
ROMULUS CITY	B*
ROOSEVELT PARK CITY	F*
ROSEVILLE CITY	413
ROYAL OAK CITY	414
SAGINAW CITY	416
ST. CHARLES VILLAGE	429
ST. CLAIR CITY	430
ST. CLAIR SHORES	431

ST. IGNACE CITY	432
ST. JOHNS CITY	433
ST. JOSEPH CITY	40
ST. LOUIS CITY	434
SALINE CITY	435
SANDUSKY CITY	436
SARANAC VILLAGE	517
SAUGATUCK VILLAGE	517
SAULT STE. MARIE	437
SCHOOLCRAFT VILLAGE	518
SCOTTVILLE CITY	518
SEBEWAING VILLAGE	439
SHELBY VILLAGE	519
SHEPHERD VILLAGE	519
SOUTHFIELD CITY	440
SOUTHGATE CITY	B*
SOUTH HAVEN CITY	444
SOUTH LYON CITY	445
SOUTH ROCKWOOD	520
SPARTA VILLAGE	446
SPRINGFIELD CITY	447
SPRING LAKE VILLAGE	448
STAMBAUGH CITY	520
STANDISH CITY	521
STANTON CITY	521
STERLING HGTS. CITY	449
STEVENSVILLE VILLAGE	522
STOCKBRIDGE VILLAGE	522
STURGIS CITY	453
SWARTZ CREEK CITY	454
SYLVAN LAKE CITY	G*
TAWAS CITY	455
TAYLOR CITY	B*
TECUMSEH CITY	456
THREE OAKS VILLAGE	523
THREE RIVERS CITY	457
TRAVERSE CITY	458
TRENTON CITY	459
TROY CITY	460
UNION CITY VILLAGE	523
UTICA CITY	464
VASSAR CITY	465
VERNON VILLAGE	524
VICKSBURG VILLAGE	466
WAKEFIELD CITY	467
WALKER CITY	C*
WALLED LAKE CITY	468
WARREN CITY	469
WATERVLIET CITY	524
WAYLAND CITY	473
WAYNE CITY	B*
WEBBERVILLE VILLAGE	525
WEST BRANCH CITY	525
WESTLAND CITY	B*
WHITE CLOUD CITY	526
WHITEHALL CITY	350
WHITE PIGEON VILLAGE	526
WILLIAMSTON CITY	474
WIXOM CITY	475
WOLVERINE LAKE	476
WOODHAVEN CITY	477
WYANDOTTE CITY	B*
WYOMING CITY	C*
YALE CITY	527
YPSILANTI CITY	A*
ZEELAND CITY	478
ZILWAUKEE CITY	H*

A*	SEE ANN ARBOR
B*	SEE DETROIT
C*	SEE GRAND RAPIDS
D*	SEE KALAMAZOO
E*	SEE LANSING
F*	SEE MUSKEGON
G*	SEE PONTIAC
H*	SEE SAGINAW
I*	SEE SOUTHFIELD

Index Instructions

Finding street names is easy with CitMaps new Quadrant system.

First, look for the desired street in the City Index. Behind the street name will be a page number and an indication of either a NW, NE, SW or SE Quadrant.

Go to the needed page number and look in the desired Quadrant for the street.

Quadrants are defined by the black triangles placed on each side of the maps that have been indexed.

Map Key Guide

ROAD SYMBOLS

══════ OR ══════
– LIMITED ACCESS HIGHWAY

────────────────
– FULL ACCESS HIGHWAY

────────────────
– MAJOR ROADS OF A CITY

─────────/\/────────
– SHORTENED STREET

+++++++++++++
– RAILROAD

OTHER SYMBOLS

– – – – – – – – – – –
– CITY LIMITS (ON OVERVIEW MAPS)

◆◆◆◆◆◆◆◆◆◆◆
– INDICATION OF MAP SEPARATIONS
  (ON OVERVIEW MAPS)

NW   NE   SW   SE
– LABELS OF QUADRANTS OF INDEXED MAPS

🇳
– NORTH INDICATOR

▲
– QUADRANT DIVIDER

HIGHWAY SIGNS

(96) – INTERSTATE HIGHWAY   {23} – FEDERAL HIGHWAY   ◇S◇ – STATE HIGHWAY

* POPULATIONS BASED ON 1980 CENSUS

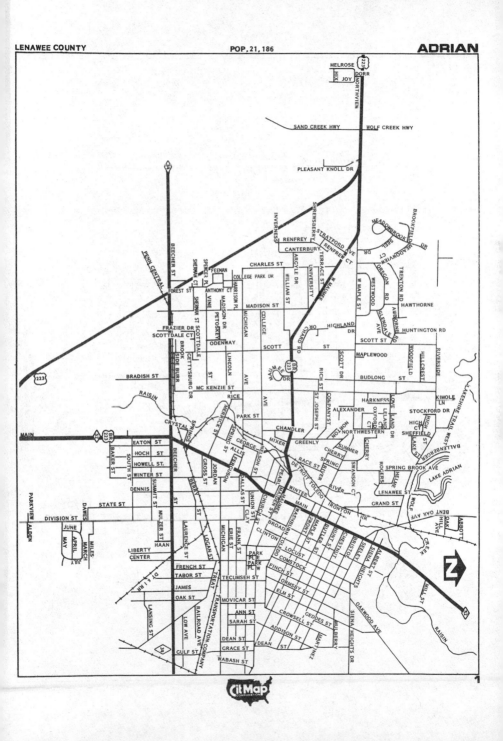

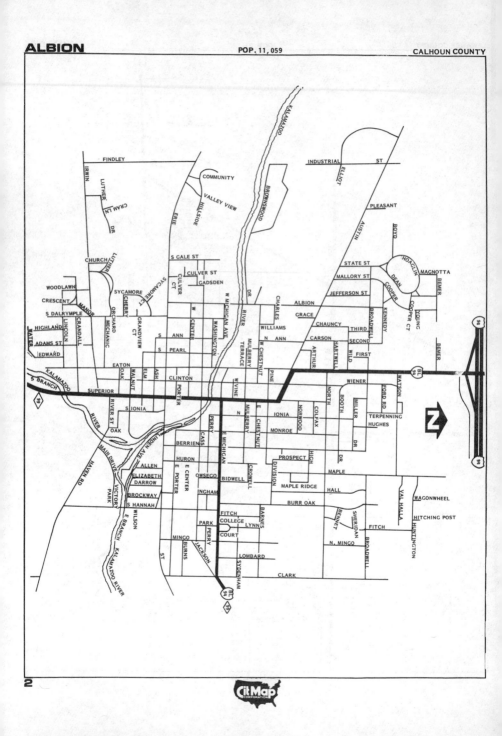

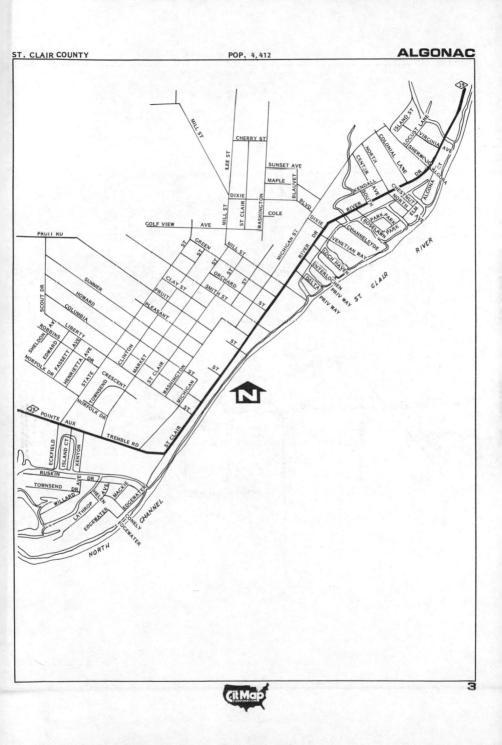

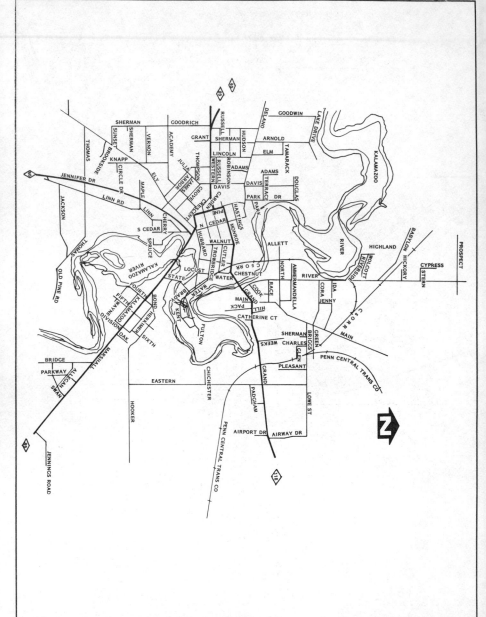

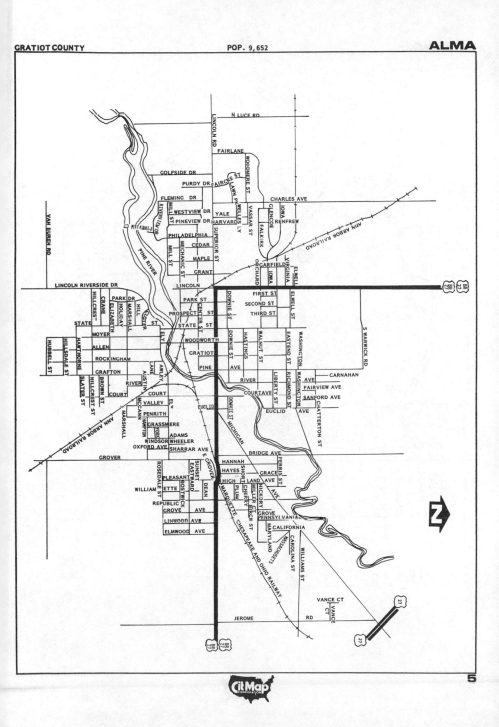

POP. 12,214

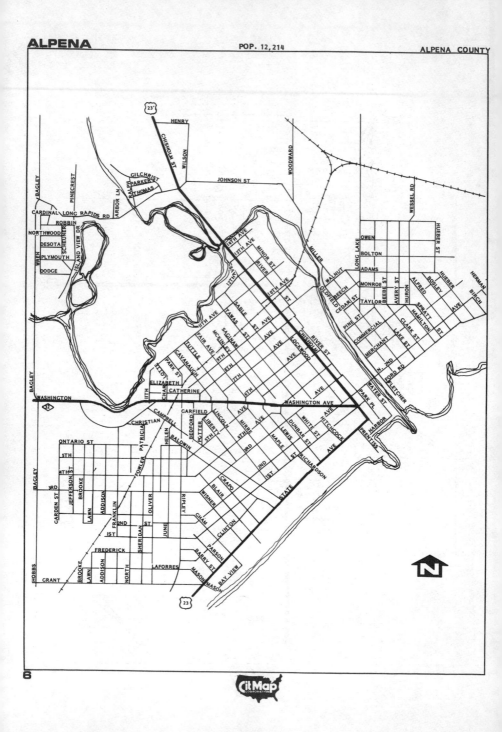

STREET	PG	DR
ABBOTT AVE	15	NW
ABERDEEN DR	16	SE
ADAMS ST	15	SW
ADARE RD	16	SW
ADARE RD	16	SW
ADRIENNE LA	14	NW
AINSLEY	22	NW
AIRPORT BLVD	20	NE
AIRPORT DR	20	NW
ALEXANDRA BLVD	12	SW
ALGONAC AVE	15	SE
ALHAMBRA DR	13	NW
ALICE ST	15	NW
ALLEN DR	15	NW
ALLISON DR	15	NW
ALLMAND ST	15	SW
ALTON CT	13	SE
AGINCOURT	15	SW
AMESBURY DR	15	SW
AMHERST AVE	15	NW
ANDERSON AVE	16	SW
ANDOVER RD	16	NE
ANDREA CT	14	NE
ANN ST	15	NE
ANN ARBOR SALINE	15	SE
ANN ARBOR SALINE	16	SW
ANTIETAM DR	13	SE
APPLEWAY	16	SW
APPLEWOOD CT	15	SW
APRIL DR	14	NW
ARBANA DR	15	NW
ARBOR	15	SE
ARBORDALE	15	NW
ARBORVIEW	15	NW
ARCH ST	15	SE
ARCHWOOD DR	15	NW
ARDENNE DR	15	NW
ARDMOOR AVE	15	SW
ARELLA BLVD	15	SW
ARGO DR	15	NE
ARGONNE DR	13	SE
ARGYLE CRESCENT	15	SE
ARLENE ST	15	SW
ARLINGTON BLVD	15	SE
ARROW WOOD TR	13	SW
ASCOT RD	15	SW
ASPEN	13	SW
ASTER AVE	15	SW
AURORA (WEBSTER)	13	SE
AU SABLE PI	16	NE
AUSTIN AVE	15	SE
AVALON DR	15	NW
AVALON PL	16	SW
AVON RD	15	SW
AVONDALE AVE	15	SW
AWIXA RD	16	SW
BAITS DR	16	NW
BALDWIN AVE	15	SE
BALDWIN PL	15	SE
BALMORAL CT	12	SW
BANDERA	14	NW
BARBER	14	NE
BARDSTOWN TR	16	NE
BARNARD	15	SW
BARRINGTON PL	15	SW
BARRISTER RD	16	NE
BARTON DR	16	NW
BARTON LANE	12	SE
BARTON NORTH DR	12	SE
BARTON SHORE DR	12	SE
BATH ST	15	NE
BAYLIS DR	21	NW
BAXTER RD	16	NE
BEACON HILL	12	SW
BEACONSFIELD DR	15	NE
BEAKES ST	15	NE
BEAL AVE	15	NE
BEDFORD RD	15	NE
BEECHWOOD	15	NE
BELFIELD CIR	15	NW
BELGRADE NOTCH	12	SW
BELLWOOD AVE	21	NE
BELMAR PL	15	SE
BELMONT RD	15	SE
BELVIDERE ST	21	NE
BEMIDJI ST	15	NW
BEMIDJI DR	15	NW
BENDING RD	15	NW
BENJAMIN ST	15	SE
BENS ST	15	SW
BERKLEY AVE	15	SW
BERKSHIRE RD	16	SW
BERNICE AVE	15	SW
BIRCH HOLLOW DR	21	NW
BIRD RD	15	SW
BIRD HILLS LA	12	SW
BIRK AVE	15	SW
BISHOP	16	NW
BLAIN CT	15	SW
BLAKELY CT	15	SE
BLAKEWAY	16	SE
BLANEY DR	15	SW
BLUEBERRY LANE	12	SW
BLUETT DR	13	SE
BOLGOS CIRCLE	13	SE
BOMBRIDGE	21	NE
BONISTEEL BLVD	16	NW
BOWENS ST	15	NE
BOULEVARD DR	15	NE
BRAEBURN CIRCLE	21	NE
BRAEBURN CT	21	NE
BRAESIDE PL	15	SW
BRAMPTON CT	15	SW
BRANDYWINE DR	21	NE
BRASSOW RD	20	SW
BRAUN DR	15	SW
BREDE	12	SE
BRENTWOOD CT	15	NE
BRIARCLIFF ST	13	SE
BRIAR GLEN	20	SW
BRIARWOOD	15	NW
BRIARWOOD CIRCLE	20	NE
BRIDGEWAY	11	NW
BRISTOL CT	16	NE
BROADWAY HILLS	16	SW
BROADWAY ST	16	NW
BROCK CT	16	SW
BROCKMAN BLVD	15	SE
BROOK	11	NW
BROOKLYN AVE	15	NE
BROOKRIDGE RD	15	NE
BROOKS	15	NE
BROOKSIDE CT	15	NE
BROOKSIDE DR	12	SE
BROOKWOOD PL	15	NE
BROWN ST	15	SE
BRUCE ST	22	NW
BRUCE ST	15	NW
BUCKINGHAM CT	15	SW
BUCKINGHAM RD	16	SW
BUENA VISTA AVE	15	SE
BUNKER HILL	13	SE
BURBANK DR	13	SE
BURGUNDY RD	16	NE
BURLINGAME CT	21	NW
BURLINGTON CT	16	SW
BURLINGTON ST	16	SW
BURTON	14	NW
BURSON PL	16	SW
BURWOOD AVE	15	NW
BUTTERNUT ST	21	NE
BYDDING RD	15	NE
BYINGTON BLVD	11	SE
CALUMET AVE	21	NW
CALVIN	*5	NW
CAMBRIDGE RD	16	SW
CAMELOT RD	16	SE
CANAL ST	15	NE
CANTERBURY	21	NE
CANTERBURY RD	21	NE
CARBECK DR	15	NE
CARDINAL	21	NE
CAREY ST	15	NE
CARHART AVE	16	SW
CARL CT	13	SE
CARLTON	22	NW
CARLYLE AVE	21	NW
CAROL DR	15	NW
CAROLINA ST	21	NW
CAROLYN ST	21	NE
CARMEL ST	21	NE
CARPENTER	22	NW
CARTER PL	22	NW
CATALINA DR	15	SW
CATALPA CIR	21	NW
CATHERINE ST	15	NE
CAYUGA PL	16	SW
CEDARBEND DR	15	NW
CENTER	15	NW
CENTRAL	14	NE
CENTRAL	22	NW
CHALMERS DR	15	NE
CHAMPAGNE DR	21	NW
CHANDLER RD	12	SE
CHAPEL CT	15	SW
CHAPIN ST	15	NE
CHARING CROSS	21	NE
CHARLES	15	NE
CHARLTON DR	15	NE
CHARTER PL	16	NE
CHATHAM WAY	16	NE
CHAUCER CT	15	SE
CHAUCER DR	15	SE
CHEROKEE RD	15	NE
CHERRY ST	15	NE
CHERRY TREE RD	21	NW
CHESTER DR	22	NW
CHESTERFIELD DR	15	NW
CHESTNUT ST	21	NE
CHRISTINE DR	14	NW
CHURCH	16	SW
CHURCHILL DR	15	NW
CLAGUE AVE	15	NE
CLAIR CIRCLE	15	NW
CLARENDON DR	15	NW
CLIMBING WAY	11	NW
CLOVERDALE AVE	12	NE
CLOVERLAWN	15	NW
CLUB DR	22	NW
COCHRAN	22	SW
COOLEY AVE	15	SW
COLE BLVD DR	22	NW
COLER RD	16	SW
COLGATE CIR	15	NW
COLLINGWOOD AVE	15	NW
COLLISTON	15	NW
COLONY CT	15	NW
COLONY RD	21	NW
COLUMBIA AVE	15	NW
COMMERCE DR	21	NE
CONCORD RD	16	NW
COOLEY AVE	15	NE
COPLEY AVE	15	NE
CORNWELL PL	15	NE
CORONADA DR	15	NW
CORRIE	12	SE
COTTAGE LANE	14	NW
COTTAGE GROVE	15	NW
COTTONTAIL LA	11	SE
COUNTRY CLUB	12	NW
COVINGTON DR	15	SW
CRAIG RD	15	NW
CRAM CIRCLE	16	NW
CRAM PL	16	NW
CRANBROOK RD	21	NE
CRANE	22	SW
CRAWFORD LA	15	NW
CREAL CT	15	NW
CREAL CRESCENT	15	NW
CREEK DR	21	NE
CREST AVE	15	NE
CRESTLAND DR	16	SW
CRESTLINE	11	NW
CRESTVIEW	22	NW
CRESSFIELD LN	15	NW
CROSBY CRESCENT	15	SW
CROSS ST	15	SE
CRYSTAL	22	NW
CULVER RD	15	NE
CUMBERLAND AVE	21	NE
CURLEW	11	NW
DALEVIEW	11	SE
DALTON	22	NW
DANBURY LANE	12	SW
DANIEL ST	15	NE
DARROW DR	16	SE
DARTMOOR DR	15	NE
DARTMOUTH CT	22	SW
DAWSON	11	NW
DAVID CT	13	SW
DAVIS	15	SE
DAY ST	15	NE
DAYTON	22	NW
DEAKE	22	NW
DEAN RD	16	NE
DECO CT	17	SW
DEERFIELD PL	11	SE
DELAFIELD DR	12	SE
DELAWARE CT	15	NE
DELAWARE DR	15	NE
DELLWOOD DR	14	SW
DELTA ST	15	NE
DEPOT ST	15	NE
DETROIT ST	15	NE
DEVOLSON AVE	16	SW
DEVONSHIRE RD	15	SW
DEWEY ST	15	SE
DEXTER ANN ARBOR	11	SW
DEXTER RD	15	NW
DHU VARREN RD	12	SE
DICKEN DR	15	SW
DIVISION ST N	15	NE
DIXBORO RD	17	SW
DONEGAL CT	21	NE
DORCHESTER RD	16	SW
DOREMUS ST	15	NE
DORSET RD	16	SW
DOTTY AVE	15	NW
DOVER CT	15	SW
DOVER PL	15	SW
DOWNING CT	21	NW
DOWN UP CIRCLE	12	SW
DRAPER RD	16	NW
DUANE CT	15	NE
DUFFIELD	15	NW
DUNCAN ST	15	SW
DUNDEE DR	15	SW
DUNMORE RD	21	NW
DUPONT CIRCLE	14	NE
EARHART RD	17	NW
EAST	15	SE
EAST BURY CT	13	SE
EAST DELHI RD	11	SW
EASTGATE	11	NW
E GREENNOOK	11	NW
E LIBERTY ST	15	NE
EASTOVER	16	SW
E WILLIAM ST	15	NE
EAST UNIVERSITY AV	15	NE
EASY ST	21	NE
EBERWHITE	15	NW
EDDY ST	21	NE
EDEN CT E	21	NW
EDEN CT W	21	NW
EDGEWOOD AVE	15	SE
EDGEWOOD DR	21	NW
EDINBOROUGH	15	SE
EDMUND PL	15	SW
EDWARD	15	NE
EIGHTH ST	15	NE
EISENHOWER PKWY	20	NE
ELDER BLVD	15	NW
ELI DR	21	NE
ELIZABETH	14	NE
ELLSWORTH PL	20	NE
ELLSWORTH RD	20	NE
ELM ST	16	NW
ELMCREST	15	NE
ELMWOOD AVE	21	NE
ELMWOOD DR	15	NW
EMERALD	21	NW
ENCLAVE DR	12	SW
ENGLEWOOD CT	15	NW
ESCH CT	20	SW
ESCH CT	21	NW
ESSEX RD	15	NW
ETON CT	21	NE
EVELYN CT	15	NW
EVERGREEN DR	15	NE
EVERGREEN PL	16	SE
EXMOOR RD	16	SE
FAIR ST	15	NW
FAIRLANE	15	SE
FAIR OAKS PKWY	16	SW
FAIRVIEW AVE	15	NW
FAIRWAY	11	NW
FARMBROOK CT	21	NW
FAUST CT	21	NW
FAYE DR	15	NW
FEDERAL BLVD	15	SE
FELCH	15	NE
FENWICK	15	NE
FERDON RD	16	SW
FERNDALE PL	16	NW
FERNWOOD AVE	21	NW
FERRY ST	14	NE
FIFTH AVE N	15	NE
FIFTH AVE S	15	NE
FIFTH ST	15	SE
FIRST ST N	15	NE
FLETCHER ST	15	NE
FOLKSTONE CT N	16	NW
FOLKSTONE CT S	17	NW
FOREST AVE	12	NW
FOSS CT	12	SW
FOSS ST	12	SW
FOSTER (ANN ARBOR)	12	SW
FOSTER (PITTSFIELD)	22	NW
FOUNTAIN ST	15	NW
FOURTH AVE N	15	NE
FOURTH ST	15	NE
FOXCROFT RD	16	SE
FRANKLIN CT N	15	NW
FRANKLIN CT S	15	NW
FRANKLIN ST	15	NW
FRANKLIN ST	15	NW
FREDERICK	16	NE
FRESNO LANE	22	NW
FRIEZE AVE	16	NE
FULLER RD	16	NE
FULLER ST	16	NE
FULMER CT	15	NE
FULMER ST	15	NE
GALLWAY CT	21	NE
GARDEN CIRCLE	15	NW
GARDEN HOMES CT	15	NW
GARDEN HOMES DR	15	NW
GENEVA PL	13	SW
GEORGETOWN BLVD	15	SW
GEDDES AVE	16	NW
GEDDES HEIGHTS DR	16	NW
GEDDES RD	16	SE
GETTYSBURG RD	13	SE
GILBERT CT	15	NW
GLACIER WAY	16	NW
GLADSTONE DR	16	NW
GLASTONBURY RD	15	SW
GLEANER HALL RD	13	NW
GLEN	15	NW
GLENBRIDGE	21	NW
GLENCOE HILLS	17	SW
GLENDALE DR	15	NW
GLENDALOCH CIR	16	SW
GLENDALOCH RD	16	SW
GLEN-LEVEN RD	15	SW
GLEN OAK CT	20	SW
GLENWOOD ST	14	NE
GLENWOOD ST	15	NW
GLOUCESTER WAY	21	NE
GOLDEN AVE	15	SW
GOLFSIDE RD	22	NW
GOLFVIEW LANE	15	SE
GOSS	15	NW
GRACE	15	NW
GRALAKE AVE	14	NE
GRANADA AVE	15	SW
GRANDVIEW DR	15	NW
GRANDVIEW DR	22	NW
GRANGER AVE	15	NE
GRANT	22	NW
GREEN RD	15	SE
GREEN BRIAR BLVD	16	SW
GREENHILLS DR	17	NW
GREEN KNOLLS LA	17	SW
GREENMEADOW BLVB	22	NW
GREENWAY CT	15	NW
GREENWOOD	15	SW
GREENVIEW DR	15	SW
HAISLEY DR	15	NW
HALL AVE	15	NE
HAMILTON PL	15	NE
HAMPTON CT	15	SW
HAMPSHIRE RD	21	NE
HANDY LN	17	SW
HANOVER RD	15	SW
HANSEN DR	15	SW
HARBAL DR	15	NW
HARBROOKE AVE	15	SW
HARDING RD	15	NW
HARDYKE	21	NW
HARPST ST	16	SW
HARTFORD ST	15	NW
HARVARD PL	15	NW
HASPER DR	15	NW
HATCHER CRESCENT	15	NW
HATCHER ST	15	NW
HAVEN AVE	15	SE
HAVEN AVE	15	NE
HAVERHILL CT	13	SE
HAWKS	21	NE
HAWTHORN	16	SW
HAWTHORN (WEBSTER)	11	NW
HAYES CT	15	NW
HAYWARD ST	16	NW
HAZELWOOD AVE	14	NE
HEATHERIDGE	16	SW
HEATHERIDGE E	16	SW
HEATHERWAY	16	SE
HELEN	22	NW
HELEN ST	15	NW
HELLNER	12	NW
HEMLOCK ST	21	NW
HENRY RD	14	NE
HENRY ST	15	SE
HERBERT DR	15	NW
HERMINA CT	15	NW
HERMITAGE RD	14	NE
HEWETT	15	SW
HIAWATHA	13	SW
HICKORY AVE	16	SE
HICKORY LANE	16	SE
HIDDEN VALLEY LA	20	NE
HIGH ST (SCIO TWP)	14	NE
HIGH ST (ANN ARBOR)	15	NE
HIGHLAKE AVE	14	NE
HIGHLAND LANE	16	NW
HIGHLAND RD	16	NW
HILLCREST DR	15	NE
HILLDALE DR	12	SW
HILLRIDGE BLVD	15	NW
HILLSPUR	12	SE
HILL ST	15	SE
HILLSIDE CT	15	SW
HILLSIDE DR	22	NW
HILLTOP DR	14	NE
HILTON BLVD	20	NE
HISCOCK	15	NE
HOAK CT	21	NE
HUCKLEY LN	15	NE
HOGBACK	17	SE
HOGBACK	17	SW
HOLLYWAY	11	NW
HOLLYWOOD DR	15	NW
HOLYOKE LANE	12	SW
HONEY CREEK	11	SW
HOOVER AVE	15	SE
HORMAN CT	16	SW
HOSPITAL DR	16	NW
HOWLEY CT	15	NE
HUBBARD ST	16	NW
HUDDY RD	16	NW
HUNTING ALLEY RD	16	SW
HUNTINGTON DR	16	NE
HUNTINGTON PL	16	NE
HURON	11	NW
HURON PARKWAY	16	NE
HURON PARKWAY	12	SE
HURON ST E	15	NE
HURON RIVER	16	NE
HURON RIVER DR	11	NW
HURON RIVER DR	23	SE
HURONVIEW BLVD	15	SE
HUTCHINS AVE	15	NE
INDEPENDENCE BLVD	16	SW
INDIAN RIVER PL	16	NE
INDIANOLA DR	15	NE
INDUSTRIAL HWY	15	SE
INGALLS ST	15	NE
IRONWOOD	14	NE
IROQUOIS PL	16	NE
ISLAND	11	NW
ISLAND DR CT	16	NW
IVANHOE ST	16	SW
IVYDALE AVE	15	SW
IVYWOOD	15	SW
JACKSON	14	NE
JACKSON AVE	14	NE
JACKSON PLAZA	14	NE
JAMES	16	SE
JANET ST	15	SE
JAY	21	NW
JEANNE ST	15	SE
JEFFERSON CT	15	SE
JEFFERSON ST	15	NE
JENNINGS	15	NE
JEWETT AVE	16	SW
JOANNE	15	NW
JOHN ST	15	SE
JOHN HOLMES RD	11	SW
JONATHAN	21	NW
JONES DR	15	NE
JORN CT	16	SW
JOSEPH ST	16	SE
JOSEPHINE DR	16	SE
JOY	15	SE
JUNIPER LANE	12	SE
KAY PKWAY	15	SW
KEARNEY RD	16	SW
KEPPLER CT	15	NE
KELLOGG ST	16	SE
KENDRICK RD	16	SE
KENILWORTH DR	16	SE
KENSINGTON DR	16	SE
KENT	15	NE
KENWOOD AVE	15	NW
KILBRENNAN CT	21	NW
KIMBERLY RD	21	NW
KING GEORGE BLVD	21	NW
KING GEORGE CT	21	NW
KINGSLEY ST	15	NE
KINGWOOD ST	14	NE
KIPLING DR	15	SW
KIRTLAND	15	NW
KNIGHT	14	SW
KOCH AVE	15	SW
KUEBLER	11	SW

7

Street	Pg	Quad
KUEBLER CT	14	NE
KUEHNLE AVE	14	NE
KUEHNLE CT	14	NE
LAFAYETTE RD	16	SW
LAFERE ST	21	NE
LAKE CT	11	NW
LAKE	15	NW
LAKE ST	14	NE
LAKEHAVEN DR	16	NE
LAKEHURST LA	13	SW
LAKE LILA DR	13	SW
LAKE PARK LN	14	NE
LAKE RIDGE WAY	17	SW
LAKEWOOD DR	14	NE
LAKEVIEW	14	NE
LAKEVIEW DR	14	NE
LAMBETH DR	15	SW
LAMPLIGHTER DR	11	SE
LANCASHIRE	13	SW
LANDSDOWNE	12	NW
LANS WAY	15	SE
LARCHMONT DR	14	NE
LARKSPUR ST	12	SE
LA SALLE DR	21	NE
LAS VEGAS DR	15	SW
LAUREL HILL	11	SW
LAURELWOOD	21	NE
LAURENTIDE	12	SW
LAWRENCE ST	15	NE
LEAIRD DR	16	NW
LENNOX ST	15	SW
LEONAR DR	15	NW
LEROY	19	NE
LEXINGTON DR	13	SE
LIBERTY RD	14	SE
LINCOLN AVE	15	SE
LINCOLNSHIRE LA	12	SW
LINDA VISTA	15	NW
LINDEN ST	16	NW
LINWOOD AVE	15	NW
LILLIAN RD	21	NE
LOCH ALPINE E	11	NW
LOCH ALPINE W	11	NW
LOCKHAVEN DR	16	NE
LOCKRIDGE	21	NW
LOGAN CT	21	NE
LOHR RD	20	NE
LONGMAN LN AVE	15	NW
LONG SHORE DR	12	SE
LONDONDERRY CIR	16	SW
LONDONDERRY DR	16	SW
LOOK OUT CIRCLE	21	NE
LORRAINE PL	16	SW
LORRAINE ST	21	NE
LOUISE DR	15	NW
LOWELL RD	12	SW
LOYOLA DR	15	NW
LUCERNE CT	21	NW
LUELLA	14	NW
LUTZ AVE	15	NE
MABEL	14	NW
MACGREGOR LANE	16	NE
MADISON PL	15	SE
MADISON	15	SW
MAIDEN AVE	15	NE
MAIDEN LA CT	16	NW
MALLORY DR	16	NE
MANCHESTER CT	21	NW
MANCHESTER RD	15	SW
MANHATTAN DR	16	SW
MANITOU CT	21	NW
MAPLE	22	SW
MAPLE BLVD	15	SW
MAPLE RD	15	SW
MAPLE RIDGE	15	SW
MAPLEWOOD AVE	21	NE
MARGARET DR	21	NE
MARIAN AVE	15	NE
MARIE AVE	22	NW
MARK HANNAH PL	15	NE
MARLBOROUGH DR	16	SW
MARSHALL ST	21	NE
MARTHA AVE	15	NE
MARTIN PL	16	SW
MARY ST	15	SW
MARYFIELD DR	15	NW
MASON AVE	15	NE
MAXWELL AVE	15	NW
MAYNARD ST	15	SW
MAYWOOD AVE	15	SW
MC COMB ST	16	SW
MC COTTER	14	NE
MCINTYRE	15	SE
MCKINLEY AVE	15	SE
MEADE CT	13	SE
MEADOWBROOK AVE	15	SW
MEDFORD CIR	16	SW
MEDFORD CT	16	SW
MEDFORD RD	16	SW
MELROSE RD	15	SW
MERSHON DR	15	SW
METROVIEW CT	15	SW
MICHIGAN	15	SW
MIDDLETON DR	15	NW
MIDWAY	11	NW
MILLER AVE	15	NE
MILLER RD	11	SW
MINER	15	NE
MINGLEWOOD WAY	15	NE
MINERVA RD	15	NE
MIXTWOOD RD	15	NE
MOHAWK CT	14	NE
MONROE ST	15	SE
MONTCLAIR PL	16	SW
MONTGOMERY AVE	15	NW
MOORE	15	NE
MOREHEAD CT	15	SW
MOREHEAD DR	15	SW
MORGAN RD	21	NW
MORNINGSIDE DR	15	NE
MORROW CT	11	NW
MORTON AVE	15	SW
MOSLEY ST	15	SE
MT.PLEASANT AVE	15	NW
MT.VERNON AVE	15	SW
MULHOLLAND AVE	14	NE
MUNGER	22	SW
MURFIN AVE	14	NE
MURRAY CT	15	NE
MYRON CT	15	NE
MYRTLE	14	NW
NANCY RD	14	NE
NAPLES CT	16	SW
NAVARRE CIR	16	SW
NEEDHAM RD	16	SE
NEWBURY CT	16	SW
NEWCASTLE RD	16	SE
NEWPORT	15	NW
NEWPORT RD	15	NW
NICHOLS DR	16	NW
NIELSON CT	16	NW
NINEBANK	11	NW
NIXON RD	13	NE
NIXON ST	11	NW
NOB HILL PL	15	SE
NOLLAR	13	NW
NONAME	14	NW
NORDMAN RD	21	NW
NORENFIELD CHURCH	12	NW
NORFOLK AVE	15	SW
NORMAN PL	15	SW
NORMANDY RD	15	SW
NORTH CIRCLE DR	15	NW
NORTH DELHI	11	NE
NORTHGATE	11	NW
NOTTINGHAM RD	21	NW
N. MAIN	15	NE
N. RAVENA BLVD	15	NE
NORTHSIDE AVE	12	SE
NORTH UNIVERSITY	15	NE
N. THAYER ST	15	NE
NORTH WICK ST	13	SE
NORTHWOOD ST	15	SW
NORWOOD ST	21	NE
NORWAY RD	16	SW
OAK DR	22	NW
OAKCLEFT DR	15	SW
OAKDALE	12	SW
OAKDALE	22	NW
OAKLAND	15	SE
OAKWOOD ST	15	SW
OBSERVATORY ST	16	NE
OHIO AVE	15	SE
OLD BOSTON CT	21	NE
OLDEN RD	15	NW
OLIVIA AVE	16	SE
ONAWAY PL	16	SE
ONONDAGA ST	15	NW
ORCHARD ST	15	NW
ORCHARD HILLS	16	NW
ORKNEY DR	15	NE
OSAGE DR	13	SW
OSWEGO ST	16	SW
OTTAWA RD	15	NW
OVERRIDGE DR	16	SE
OXFORD RD	15	NE
PACE AVE	21	NW
PACKARD ST	15	SW
PAGE	21	NW
PAGE CT	21	NW
PAISLEY CT	16	NE
PALOMAR DR	15	SW
PAMELA	15	NW
PARK DR	15	SE
PARK PL	15	SE
PARK RD	14	NW
PARK ST	14	NE
PARKCREST	15	NW
PARKRIDGE DR	11	SE
PARKVIEW PL	15	NE
PARKWOOD AVE	16	SE
PARKWOOD ST	14	NE
PATRICIA AVE	15	NW
PATRICIA CT	15	NW
PATTERSON PL	16	NW
PAUL ST	15	NW
PAULINE BLVD	15	SW
PEACH	15	NE
PEAR	22	NW
PEARL	15	SW
PEARL ST	15	NE
PEBBLE CREEK DR	21	NW
PENBERTON DR	15	NW
PENBERTON LA ONE	17	NW
PENBERTON LA TWO	17	NW
PENBERTON LA THREE	17	NW
PENBERTON LA FOUR	17	NW
PENBERTON LA FIVE	17	NW
PENBERTON LA SIX	16	NE
PENBERTON LA EIGHT	17	NW
PENBERTON LA TEN	16	NE
PENBERTON LA TWL	16	NE
PENINSULA CT	15	SE
PENNCRAFT	15	NW
PENNSYLAVANIA AVE	15	SW
PEPPERMILL WAY	15	SW
PEPPER PIKE	16	NE
PHEASANT DR	11	SE
PHEASANT RUN CIR	21	NW
PHOENIX DR	21	NW
PICADILLY CIR	15	SW
PINE BRAE	17	NW
PINECREST AVE	16	SW
PINE RIDGE	13	NW
PINE TREE DR	15	NW
PINE VALLEY BLVD	21	NW
PINEVIEW CT	16	NW
PINEWOOD	14	NE
PITCHPINE CT	22	SW
PITCHPINE LA	22	SW
PITTSFIELD BLVD	16	SE
PITTSVIEW DR	21	NE
PLACID WAY	13	SW
PLAINVIEW CT	21	NW
PLATT RD	16	SE
PLEASANT	15	NW
PLUM ST	15	SE
PLYMOUTH RD	13	SE
POMONA RD	21	NW
PONTIAC	15	NE
PONTIAC TRAIL	13	NW
PORTER AVE	14	NE
POTTER AVE	15	SE
POWELL AVE	21	NW
PRAIRIE CT	13	SE
PRAIRIE ST	13	SE
PRATT RD	11	SW
PRESCOTT AVE	16	SE
PRESTWICK CT	16	NE
PRINCETON AVE	15	SE
PROFESSIONAL DR	16	SE
PROSPECT CT	11	NW
PROSPECT ST	15	SE
PROVINCIAL DR	15	SE
PROVINCETOWN CT	21	NW
QUAIL HOLLOW CT	21	NW
RADCLIFF AVE	21	NE
RAILROAD ST	15	SE
RAVENWOOD AVE	11	NW
RAY CT	14	NE
RAYMOND ST	15	SW
REDEEMER AVE	15	SW
RED OAK RD	15	SW
REDWOOD AVE	21	NE
REGENT	16	NW
RENFREW ST	13	SE
RESEARCH DR	15	SE
RESEARCH PK DR	20	NE
REVENA PL	15	NW
REVERE CT	21	NE
RHEA	21	NE
RICHARD ST	21	NE
RICHMOND CT	13	SE
RIDGE AVE	16	SW
RIDGE CT	12	SW
RIDGEMOR DR	15	SW
RIDGEMONT LA	14	NW
RIDGEWAY	15	NE
RIVERBEND DR	12	SW
RIVERSIDE CT	16	SW
RIVERVIEW	16	NE
ROBERT	16	SW
ROBIN RD	15	NE
ROBINWOOD DR	11	SE
ROCK CREEK CT	16	SW
ROCK CREEK DR	16	SW
ROCKLAND CT	15	SW
RONDO CT	11	NW
ROOSEVELT AVE	15	SW
ROSE AVE	15	SE
ROSE DR	14	NE
ROSEDALE CT	15	SW
ROSELAND	11	SE
ROSEWOOD ST	15	SW
ROSS ST	15	NW
ROTHBURY CT	22	SW
ROXBURY RD	16	NW
RUGBY CT	15	SW
RUGBY DR	15	SE
RUNNYMEDE BLVD	15	SW
RUSSELL RD	15	NE
RUSSELL ST	15	NW
RUSSETT AVE	15	SW
RUTHVEN PL	16	SW
SALISBURY LN	12	SW
SANFORD PL	15	SW
SANTA ROSA DR	21	NW
SAUER CT	15	SE
SAUNDERS CRESCENT	15	NW
SAXTON ST	15	NW
SCENIC LAKE DR	22	NW
SCIO CHURCH RD	15	SW
SCOTT CT	16	SW
SCOTTWOOD AVE	15	NE
SECOND ST	15	SE
SEELEY	14	SE
SEMINOLE	22	NW
SEMINOLE CT	22	NW
SENECA AVE	15	SW
SEQUOIA PKWY	15	NE
SERVICE RD	16	SE
SEYBOLD DR	15	SE
SHADFORD RD	16	NE
SHADOWOOD DR	21	NW
SHADY LN	21	NW
SHADY OAKS CT	11	SW
SHADY OAKS DR	11	SW
SHANNONDALE RD	16	SW
SHARON DR	21	NE
SHEEHAN AVE	15	SE
SHEFFIELD CT	13	SE
SHELBY AVE	15	NW
SHERIDAN DR	16	SW
SHERWOOD DR	15	SW
SHERWOOD CIR	15	SW
SHETLAND DR	17	GW
SHEVCHENKO	21	NW
SHIRLEY DR	13	SW
SHORE	15	NW
SNYDER AVE	15	SE
SNYDER AVE	15	SE
SHREWSBURY AVE	16	SE
SIXTH ST	15	SE
SKYDALE DR	12	SE
SKYNOB DR	16	NE
SORRENIO	21	NW
SOULE BLVD	15	SW
S ASHLEY ST	15	NE
SOUTH BLVD	16	SW
SOUTH CIRCLE DR	15	NW
S. DIVISION ST	15	SE
S. FIFTH AVE	15	SE
S. FIRST ST	15	SE
S. FOURTH AVE	15	SE
S. INGALLS ST	15	SE
S. LOCH	15	SE
S. MAIN ST	15	SE
S. RESEARCH PK DR	21	NW
S. REVENA BLVD	15	SW
S. SEVENTH ST	15	SE
S. STATE ST	15	SE
S. THAYER ST	15	SE
S. UNIVERSITY AVE	15	SE
S. WICK CT	13	SE
SPRING	15	NE
SPRINGBROOK AVE	21	NE
SPRING VALLEY	12	SW
SPRUCE DR	16	SE
ST FRANCIS DR	16	NE
STADIUM BLVD	15	NW
STADIUM WAY	15	NW
STANLEY AVE	15	NW
STARAK LA	12	NW
STARWICK DR	12	SW
STATE CIR	20	NE
STATE RD	15	SW
STEERE PL	16	SW
STEIN RD	12	NE
STELLAR RD	16	NW
STEPHEN TERR	15	SE
STIMPSON ST	15	SE
STONE RD	16	NE
STONE HAVEN	16	NE
STONE SCHOOL RD	21	NW
STOWE ST	14	NE
STRATFORD DR	16	SE
STRATHMOOR	16	SW
STRATION CT	21	NW
STURBRIDGE CT	15	SW
SUE WAY	15	NW
SUFFOLK AVE	15	SE
SULGRAVE CT	16	NE
SULLIVAN DR	11	SW
SUMAC LN	16	SE
SUMMIT ST	15	SE
SUNDERLAND	15	SE
SUNNYDALE	22	NW
SUNNYSIDE BLVD	15	SW
SUNNYWOOD DR	14	NE
SUNRISE ST	15	NW
SUNSET	15	NW
SUNSET RD	15	NE
SUSAN DR	16	NE
SUSSEX CT	21	NW
SWIFT ST	16	SW
SWISS STONE LA	22	SW
SYBIL ST	15	SE
SYCAMORE PL	15	SE
SYLVAN	15	NW
SYLVAN AVE	15	SE
TACOMA CIR	21	NW
TAHOE TR	15	SE
TAPPAN AVE	15	SE
TAYLOR ST	15	NE
TERHUNE RD	21	NE
THALER AVE	15	NE
THIRD ST	15	SE
THOMPSON ST	15	NE
THORN OAKS DR	17	SE
TICKNOR CT	21	NW
TILSBY CT	15	NE
TIMBERLANE	14	NW
TORREY	22	NW
TOWNER BLVD	21	NE
TRAVER BLVD	15	NE
TRAVER CT	13	SW
TRAVER RD	15	NE
TREASURE DR	16	NW
TREMEL AVE	16	NW
TREMONT DR	16	NE
TREMONT LA ONE	17	NW
TREMONT LA TWO	17	NW
TRENTON CT	15	NE
TROWBRIDGE CT	21	NW
TUBBS RD	11	NE
TUDOR DR	15	SW
TUEBINGEN PKWY	15	NW
TUOMY RD	15	NE
TURNER PARK CT	15	NE
TWIN LAKES DR	17	SW
UNDERDOWN	12	SE
UNIVERSITY CT	16	NW
UNIVERSITY TER	16	NW
UPLAND DR	12	SW
VALHALLA DR	15	SE
VALLEY DR	14	NE
VAN DUSEN	15	SE
VARSITY DR	21	NW
VAUGHN ST	15	SE
VENTURA CT	15	NW
VERLE AVE	21	NW
VESPER RD	15	SE
VICTORIA	15	NW
VICTORIA CIR	12	SW
VILLAGE GREEN LA	13	SW
VINEWOOD BLVD	16	SW
VINTAGE VALLEY RD	16	SE
VIRGINIA	15	NW
VIRNANKAY CIR	15	SW
WAGNER CT	11	SE
WAGNER RD	14	SE
WAGNER RD	11	SE
WAKEFIELD AVE	15	NW
WALDENWOOD DR	16	NE
WALDENWOOD LA ONE	17	NW
WALDENWOOD LA TWO	17	NW
WALDENWOOD LA TH	17	NW
WALDENWOOD LA FOR	16	NE
WALDENDOOW LA FIV	16	NE
WALDENWOOD LA SIX	17	NW
WALDENWOOD LA SEV	16	NE
WALDENWOOD LA NINE	16	NE
WALDENWOOD LA ELV	16	NE
WALDENWOOD LA THR	16	NE
WALDENWOOD LA FIF	16	NE
WALDENWOOD LA SVT	16	NE
WALDENWOOD LA NIT	16	NE
WALL ST	15	NE
WALLINGFORD RD	15	SW
WALNUT	11	SE
WALNUT ST	16	NW
WALTER DR	15	SW
WALTHAM DR	15	NW
WARD CT	21	NW
WARNER PL	16	LW
WARREN RD	21	NE
WARRINGTON CT N	16	NW
WARRINGTON CT S	21	NW
WARWICK CT	15	SW
WARWICK RD	16	SW
WASHINGTON	15	NE
WASHTENAW AVE	16	NE
WASHTENAW CT	22	NW
WATER ST	11	NE
WATERMAN	14	NE
WATERSEDGE	16	NE
WATERS RD	20	NE
WAVERLY	15	SW
WAYNE	15	NE
WAYNE ST	16	SW
WAYSIDE DR	12	SW
WEBSTER CHURCH	11	NW
WEEKS CT	21	NE
WELCH CT	15	SW
WELDON BLVD	15	SW
WELDON BLVD	15	SW
WELLS ST	16	SW
WELLINGTON CT	16	SW
WEMBLY CT	15	NW
WENDY RD	15	NW
WESLEY ST	15	NW
WEST ST	21	NW
WESTAIRE CT	15	NW
WEST BURY CT	13	SE
WEST DELHI RD	11	SW
WEST GARE	11	NW
WESTGATE	15	SW
WESTERN DR	15	SW
WESTFIELD AVE	11	NW
W. GREENOOK	11	NW
W. JEFFERSON	15	SW
W. KACEK AVE	15	SE
W. MADISON ST	15	SW
WESTMINSTER PL	15	SW
WESTRIDGE	14	NE
W. SUMMIT	15	SW
WESTWOOD AVE	15	NW
W. WILLIAM ST	15	SW
WEXFORD CT	21	NW
WHALEY CT	15	NW
WHIPPORWILL	12	SW
WHITE ST	15	SW
WHITEWOOD ST	11	NW
WHITMORE LR RD	11	NW
WHITMORE LK RD	12	SE
WHITTIER	21	NW
WICKFIELD CT	13	SE
WILDER PL	15	SE
WILDT ST	15	SW
WILDWOOD AVE	15	NW
WILLARD ST	15	SE
WILLIAM ST	15	NE
WILLIAMSBURG RD	16	NW
WILLOW LN	16	NW
WILMOT ST	15	NE
WILTON ST	15	NW
WILTSHIRE CT	15	NW
WILTSHIRE DR	15	NW
WIMPOLE ST	15	SW
WINCHELL DR	16	SW

STREET	PG	DR
ABBEY LA	19	SW
ACCESS RD E	17	SE
ACCESS RD W	17	SE
ADAMS ST	23	NW
ADELINE AVE	23	NW
AINSLEY	23	NW
AINSWORTH BLVD	23	NW
AINSWORTH CIR	23	NW
AIRPORT DR	24	NE
ALLEN	24	NW
ANDREA	24	SW
ANN ST	23	NW
ANNA ST	24	NW
APPLERIDGE	19	SE
ARBOR DR	23	SE
ARCADE	23	SE
ARDITH	23	SE
ARLINGTON DR	19	SW
ARMSTRONG DR	23	NW
ARNET ST	23	NE
ARROYO DR	22	SE
ARTHUR	23	SE
ASCOT DR	23	NE
AUBURNDALE	23	NE
AUTUMN WOODS	23	SE
AVIS	24	NW
BABBITT	23	NE
BAGLEY	23	SE
BAILEY	24	NW
BALLARD ST	23	NW
BARBOUR	23	SW
BAZLEY	19	SW
BELL ST	23	NE
BELLEVUE AVE	22	NE
BERGEN AVE	22	NE
BERKLEY AVE	22	NE
BERKSHIRE BLVD	18	SE
BEVERLY	24	SE
BIG PINE DR	18	SE
BLOSSOM	19	SE
BLOUNT	23	SW
BLUEGRASS	19	SW
BOARDMAN	23	NW
BOMBER	23	NE
BORGSTROM	23	NE
BOSTON AVE	22	NE
BOSUN'S WAY	23	SE
BOYNTON	23	SE
BRADLEY	24	SE
BRIARDALE CT	24	SW
BRIAR HILL	24	SW
BRIDGE	24	SE
BRISTOL CT	19	SW
BROADMOOR	23	SW
BROOKS ST	23	SW
BROOKSIDE RD	22	NE
BROOKTREE CT	24	NW
BROWNING	23	NE
BUCKINGHAM DR	18	SE
BUD	19	SE
BUFFALO ST	23	NW
BUICK	24	NW
BUMBLE B	19	SW
BURBANK	24	NW
BURNS AVE	22	NE
BURTON	23	NW
BURTON CT	23	NW
BYNAN DR	17	SW
BYRON	23	NW
CADILLAC	24	NW
CALDER	24	NW
CAMBRIDGE RD	23	NW
CAMPBELL	23	NE
CANDLEWOOD LA	18	SE
CANTERBERRY CT	23	NE
CANTON	23	SE
CANYON	22	SE
CAROL S ST	23	SE
CAROL ANN	24	NW
CARRIAGE CT	22	NE
CARRIAGE WAY	24	NW
CARVER ST	18	SE
CASCADE LA	22	SE
CASLER ST	23	NW
CASS	23	SE
CATHERINE ST	23	NW
CAYUGA	24	NW
CEDAR CT	18	SE
CEDARCLIFF AVE	19	SE
CENTENNIAL	19	SE
CENTER ST	23	NW
CHARLES ST	23	NE
CHERRY ST	23	NE
CHESTNUT	17	SE
CHEVROLET	24	SW
CHIDESTER ST	23	NW
CLARITA	24	SW
CLARK RD	23	SE
CLIFFS DR	24	SW
CLOVER	19	SW
CLUBVIEW DR	22	NE
COLEMAN	22	NE
COLLEEN COMMON	24	SE
COLLEGE PL	23	NW
COLLEGEWOOD DR	23	NW
COLONY CT	23	NW
COLONY WAY	23	NW
COMMONWEALTH	19	SW
CONGRESS ST	22	SW
CONWAY	23	SE
COOLIDGE	24	SW
CORNELL RD	23	SW
COTTAGE	24	SE
COURTLAND ST	22	NE
CRESCENT LA	23	SE
CRESTWOOD	24	SW
CRITTENDON	24	SW
CROSS ST	22	NE
DAKOTA	24	NW
DAVID	23	NW
DAVIS ST	23	NE
DAWN AVE	19	SW
DAYTONA	23	SE
DEBBY CT	23	NE
DEERING	18	SE
DELAWARE	24	NW
DEPOT	23	NW
DE-SOTO	24	NW
DEVON ST	18	SE
DEVONSHIRE	24	NW
DEXTER AVE	23	NW
DISCOLL	23	NW
DODGE	24	NW
DON'S DR	24	NW
DOROTHY	23	NW
DORSET	23	NE
DOUGLAS ST	22	NE
DOVER CT	18	SE
DRAPER AVE	22	NE
DUBIE	23	NE
DUNCAN	24	NW
DURHAM CT	18	SE
DWIGHT ST	23	NW
E. GRAND BLVD	24	NW
EASTLAWN AVE	22	NE
EASTMAN DR	22	NE
ECORSE RD	23	NE
EDISON AVE	23	NW
EDITH	23	NE
EDGEWOOD	23	NE
EILEEN	24	NW
ELBRIDGE PL	23	NW
ELDER ST	23	NW
ELLIS	22	SE
ELM ST	23	NW
ELLSWORTH RD	22	NW
ELMHURST AVE	22	NE
ELMWOOD CT	17	SE
ELMWOOD DR	17	SW
EMERICK ST	23	NW
EMERSON	24	NW
EMERSON	23	NE
EMMET ST	23	NW
ESTERBROOK	23	NW
EUELYN	23	NW
EUGENE	23	NW
FACTORY ST	23	NE
FAIRFIELD RD	22	NE
FAIRHILLS DR	22	NE
FAIRVIEW CIR	23	NW
FALL RIVER	18	SE
FARM LA	23	SE
FARMER ST	23	NW
FERRIER	23	NW
FERRIS ST	23	NW
FIRST	17	SE
FIRST AVE	23	NW
FIRST CT	23	NW
FIRWOOD ST	23	NW
FLORENCE ST	23	NW
FOLLEY	23	NW
FOLLET ST	23	NW
FORD	23	NE
FORD BLVD	24	NW
FOREST AVE	23	NE
FOREST CT	23	NE
FOX	24	NW
FRANKLIN ST	23	NW
FREDERICK ST	23	NE
FURNACE ST	23	NE
GABLE AVE	18	SE
GAIL CT	23	NW
GALE	17	NE
GARDEN CT	23	NW
GARLAND AVE	23	NW
GATES	24	SW
GATTEGNO	24	SW
GAULT	23	SE
GEDDES	17	NE
GEORGE PL	23	NW
GEORGINA	23	SE
GILL	23	NW
GLENDALE AVE	22	NE
GLENDALE DR	23	NW
GLENWOOD	23	NE
GOLFSIDE RD	17	SW
GORDON ST	23	NW
GOTFREDSON	22	SE
GOUCHNOUR	22	SE
GRANT ST	22	NE
GRASSLAND DR	23	NE
GRAYFIELD CIR	23	NW
GREEN RD	18	SW
GREENLAWN	23	NW
GREENSIDE AVE	22	NE
GREGORY AVE	17	SW
GROVE DR	23	NE
GROVE ST	23	NE
HAMILTON ST	23	NW
HAMLET DR	13	SE
HANDY LA	23	NW
HARDING AVE	22	NE
HARMON	28	SW
HARRIET ST	23	NW
HARRIS (YPS)	24	NW
HARRIS	19	NW
HARRY	19	SW
HART PL	23	NW
HARVEST	19	SW
HAVEN	18	SE
HAWKINS ST	23	NW
HAWTORNE	23	NE
HAYES	24	NE
HAZEL CT	22	NE
HEARTHSIDE	24	SE
HEATHER DR	18	SE
HEATHER RIDGE	18	SE
HELEN ST	23	NE
HEMLOCK CT	18	SE
HEMPHILL RD	23	NW
HERITAGE DR	22	NE
HEWITT RD	22	NE
HIAWATHA ST	23	NW
HICKMAN	17	NE
HIGH ST	23	NW
HIGHLAND CT	23	NW
HILL ST	23	NW
HILLCREST BLVD	22	NE
HILLSIDE CT	23	NW
HILLTOP	22	SE
HOLLIS	23	NE
HOLMES	23	NE
HOYT	23	NE
HUBBARD	23	SE
HUDSON	24	NW
HULL	23	SE
HUNT PL	23	NW
HUNTER AVE	19	SW
HURON ST	23	NW
HURON RIVER DR	17	SE
HURON RIVER DR	18	NW
IDE	23	NE
INDIAN HILLS DR	17	SE
INTERNATIONAL	17	SE
IVANHOE	24	NW
IVY LANE	23	SW
JANET	23	SW
JARVIS ST	23	NW
JAY	23	SE
JEFF	23	SW
JEFFERSON AVE	23	SW
JEFFERY	23	SE
JENNESS	23	NW
JEROME	23	NW
JOHNSON ST	23	NE
JONES AVE	23	NW
JONES ST	23	NW
JUNE	23	NW
JUNEAU	23	NW
KANSAS	24	NW
KATHLEEN COMMON	24	SE
KENMORE PL	23	NE
KENNEDY	24	NW
KEWANEE AVE	23	NE
KIMBERLY COMMON	24	SE
KINGSTON CT	18	SE
KINGWOOD AVE	23	NW
KIRK ST	23	SE
KNOWLES	24	SW
KRAMER ST	23	NW
LAKE IN THE WOOD	24	SW
LAKEVIEW	23	NW
LAKEVIEW DR	18	SE
LAKEWOOD	24	NW
LAMAY	24	NW
LA PORTE	23	NW
LATHERS AVE	23	NW
LAVERNE	24	NW
LEAF CT	23	SW.
LEE	23	SE
LEFORGE RD	18	NW
LESTER	23	NW
LEVONA	23	SE
LEXINGTON PKWY	23	NW
LINCOLN	23	NE
LINDEN PL	23	NW
LIVERPOOL CT	18	SE
LOCUST ST	23	NE
LORI	23	NW
LOWELL ST	23	NW
LOUISE	17	SE
LUMBER DR	23	NW
LYMAN	18	SW
LYNDHURST DR	22	NE
LYNN CT	24	NW
LYNNE	23	NE
MAC ARTHUR BLVD	19	SW
MAC ARTHUR DR	19	SW
MADISON BLVD	23	NE
MADRONA DR	22	SW
MAIN	23	NW
MANCHESTER DR	18	SE
MANSFIELD AVE	23	NW
MAPLE CT	23	NE
MAPLE ST	23	NE
MAPLE WOOD	23	NE
MARCUS	24	SW
MARGARITA	24	SW
MARGERY ST	24	SW
MARION ST	22	NE
MARK	17	SE
MARTIN ST	23	NW
MARY CATHERINE	24	SW
MARY COMMON DR	24	SE
MAULBETSCH AVE	22	NE
MAUS AVE	23	NE
MAXINE COMMON	24	SE
MAYER CT	23	SW
MAYHEW	23	NW
McCARTHY	23	NW
McCARTNY CT	23	NW
MC CORTNEY	24	NE
MC GREGOR	24	NE
McINTOSH	19	SW
McKINLEY AVE	22	NE
MEADOW	24	NW
MELVIN	23	NW
MERRILL AVE	22	NE
MESA DR	22	SW
MIAMI	24	NW
MICHIGAN AVE	22	NE
MIDDLE DR	23	NW
MIDVALE AVE	22	NE
MIDWAY	23	SW
MILDRED ST	23	NE
MILES ST	23	SE
MILL	24	NE
MOELLER	24	SE
MOHAWK	24	NW
MOLLIE	24	SW
MOLNER	23	SE
MONROE AVE	23	NW
MONTREAL	23	NE
MORGAN	23	NE
MORRIS	24	SE
MOTT	19	SE
NANCY ST	23	NW
NASH	24	NW
NEVADA	24	NW
NEW MEADOW DR	23	SW
NEWTON ST	18	SW
NINDE ST	23	NE
NORFOLK AVE	18	SW
NORMAL ST	23	NW
NORRIS ST	23	NW
NORTH ST	23	NW
N CONGRESS ST	23	NW
NORTHLAWN AVE	23	NE
NOTTINGHAM	23	SE
NOTTINGHAM CT	18	SE
OAK ST	23	NW
OAKLAWN	23	NW
OAKWOOD AVE	23	NW
OHIO	24	NW
OLDS	23	NW
OLIVE ST	23	NW
ONANDAGA	24	NW
ORCHARD	23	NW
OREGON	24	NW
OSBAND	23	NW
OSBAND ST	23	NW
OSWEGO	24	NW
OTTAWA	24	NW
OUTER LA	24	NW
OUTER LA	24	NW
OWENDALE AVE	23	SW
OXFORD CT	19	SW
OXFORD RD	23	NW
PACKARD ST	22	NE
PAGEANT	23	SW
PARK ST	23	NW
PANAMA AVE	19	SW
PANAMA CT	19	SW
PARKWOOD	23	NE
PARSONS ST	23	NW
PASADENA	24	SW
PATRICK	24	SW
PEABODY	23	NW
PEACHCREST	19	SE
PEARL ST	23	NW
PEARSON ST	23	NW
PENN	24	NW
PERRIN ST	23	NW
PERRY AVE	23	NE
PHOTO	23	NE
PHYLLIS	23	SW
PINE CT	18	SE
PINERIDGE CT	24	SW
PINE VIEW DR	23	NW
PINEWOOD	23	NW
PLEASANT DR	23	NW
PONDEROSA CT	24	SW
POPLAR ST	19	SE
PRAY	23	SE
PRINCETON PL	23	NE
PROSPECT CT	18	SE
PROSPECT ST	18	SE
PUTNAM	23	NW
RAILROAD ST	23	NW
RAINTREE CT E	23	SE
RAINTREE CT W	23	SE
RAINTREE DR	23	SE
RAMBLING RD	18	SE
RAWLEY CT	18	SE
RAWSONVILLE	24	NW
RED LEAF LA	24	NW
RED OAK	23	SW
RIDGE	19	SE
RILEY CT	24	NE
RIVER ST	18	SW
RIVER ST	23	NW
ROSEWOOD	24	NW
RUSSELL BLVD	24	NW
RUSSELL CT	24	NW
RUSSELL BLVD	24	NW
RUSSETT	19	SE
RUTH	24	SW
SALEM CT	22	NW
SANTA ROSA DR	21	NW
SCENIC LAKE DR	22	NW
SCHOONER	23	NE
SEMINOLE CT	22	NW
SENATE	22	NE
SEWAL	19	SE
SHADY LANE	21	NW
SHARE	24	NW
SHARON DR	21	NE
SHEFFIELD	18	SE
SHELLY	24	SW
SHERIDAN	23	NW
SHERMAN	23	NW
SHETLAND DR	17	SW
SHIRLEY	24	SW
SHORT	23	NW
SKYWALK DR	22	SE
SMITH	24	NE
SNOW	24	SE
SOUTH	23	NW
SPENCER	24	NW
SPINNAKER WAY	23	NE
SPRING FACTORY MAUSE	23	NE
ST JOHN	23	NE
STAMFORD	19	SW
STANLEY	23	NE
S STATE RD	21	SW
STATE	23	NE
STEPHENS	18	SE
STEWART	23	NE
STOMMEL	18	NW
STONE SCHOOL	21	SW
STUDEBAKER	24	NE
SUNNY DALE	22	NW
SUNSET TR	23	SE
SUPERIOR	17	SE
SUSSEX CT	21	NW
SWEET RD	18	SE
SWEET GRASS	14	SW
SWISS STONE LA	22	SW
TAFT RD	23	SE
TERRACE LA	18	SE
THOMAS ST	23	NE
THRUSH	19	SW
TIMBER LA	23	SE
TIMOTHY	23	SE
TODD	23	NW
TOWN CT	22	NE
TOWNER ST	23	NE
TROY ST	28	NE
TUTTLE HILL	24	SW
TWIN TOWERS	23	NE
TYLER RD	23	NE
TYRONE	22	SW
UNIVERSITY	22	NE
UNIVERSITY CT	24	SW
UTAH	23	NW
VALLEY DR	22	NE
VERNA AVE	22	NE
VICTOR	23	NE
VILLA DR	18	SW
VILLAGE LA	24	SW
VINE ST	23	SW
VINEWOOD CT	23	NE
VIRGINIA PL	23	NE
VISTA DR	23	NE
VOUGHT ST	23	NE
VREELAND	17	NE
WALLACE BLVD	23	NW
WALNUT	23	NW
WALTON	23	NW
WARE CT	19	SW
WARNER AVE	23	NW
WASHINGTON ST	23	NW
WASHTENAW AVE	23	NW
WATER ST	23	SE
WATLING BLVD	23	NW
WATSON	24	SE
WELMAN DR	23	NE
WENDELL AVE	18	SE
W WARNER AVE	22	NE
WESTLAWN AVE	22	NE
WESTMOORLAND RD	23	NW
WHARTON	23	NW
WHITMAN	24	NW
WHITMIRE AVE	22	NE
WHITTAKER AVE	23	SW
WHITTIER RD	22	NE
WIARD BLVD	19	SW
WIARD CT	24	NE
WILDWOOD	23	NE
WILLIAM	24	SW
WILLOWBRIDGE	23	SE
WILSON AVE	23	SE
WINDGATE BLVD	23	NW
WISDOM CT	18	SE
WISMER	24	SW
WOODALE	24	SE
WOODCREEK CT	23	NE
WOODGLEN AVE	24	NE
WOODLAWN	23	NW
WOODBUFF	19	SE
WOODS RD	23	NW
WOODVIEW DR	24	NE
WOOLMAN	19	SW
WORDEN ST	23	NW
YOUNG ST	23	NE
ZEPHYR	24	NW

NOTES

POP. 107,316

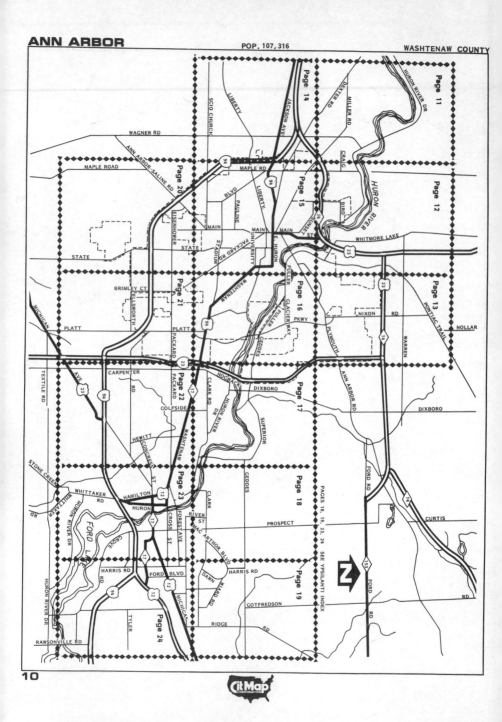

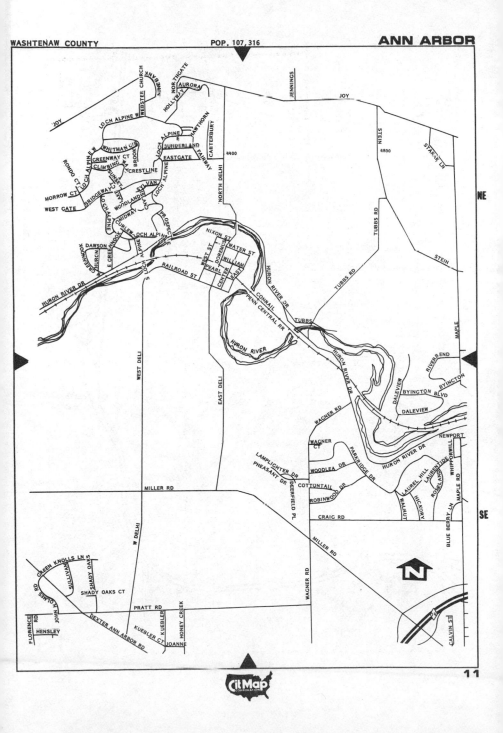

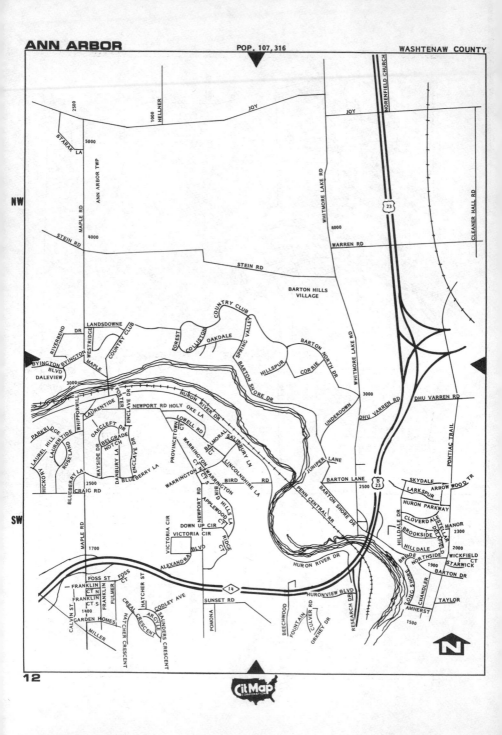

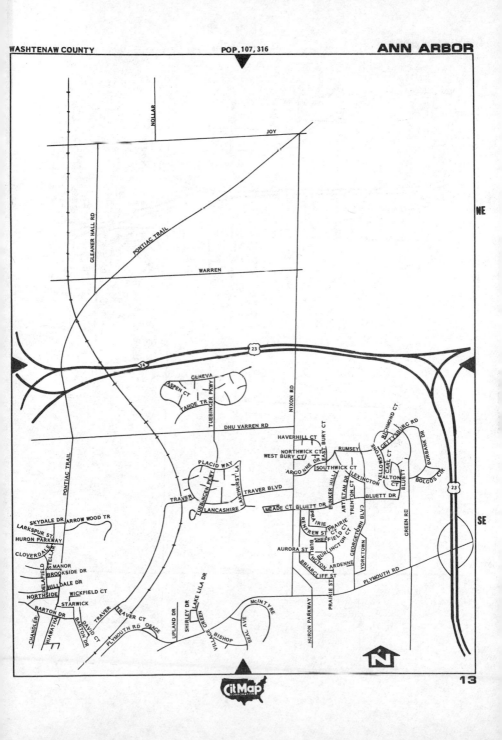

NE

SE

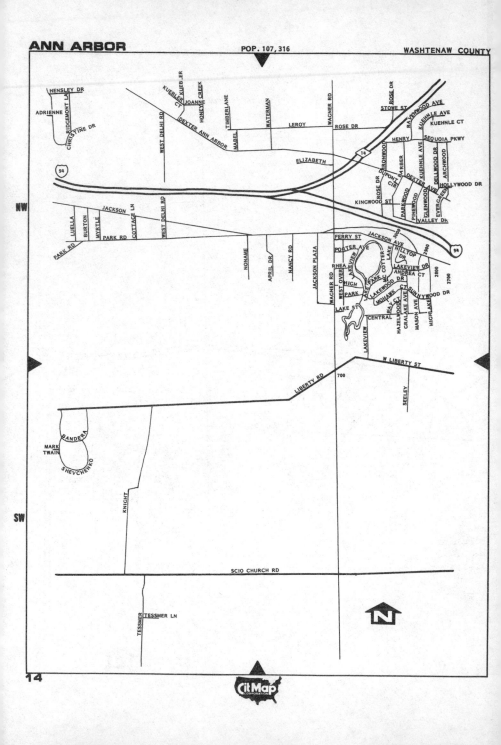

NW

SW

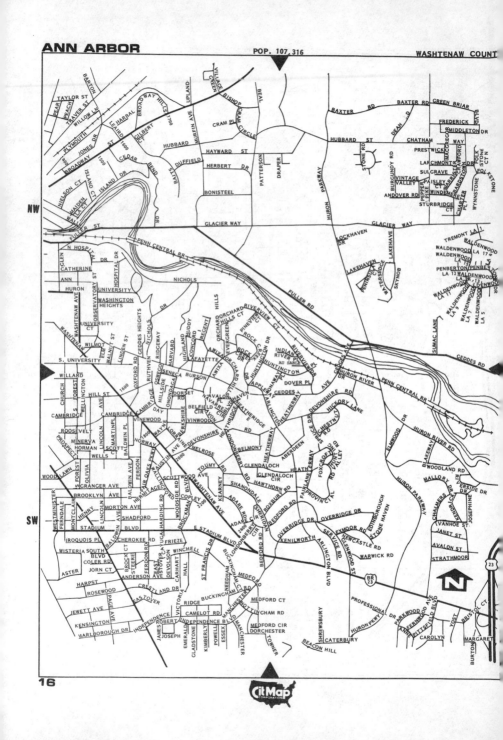

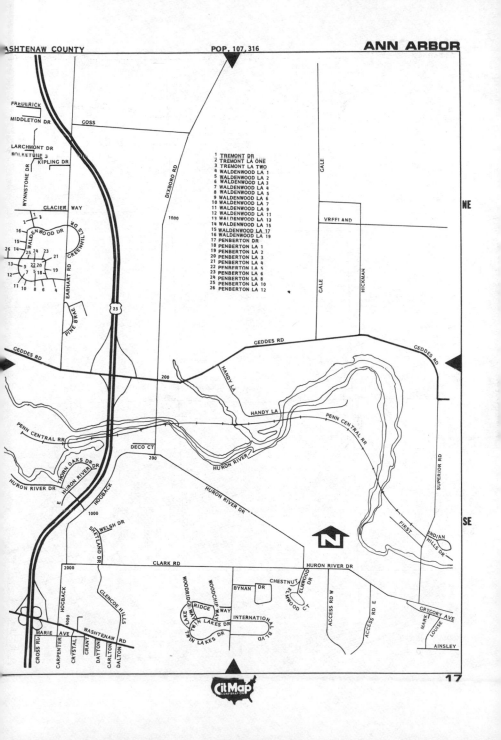

FREDERICK
MIDDLETON DR GOSS

LARCHMONT DR
BOLKSTONE 3
KIPLING DR
WYNNSTONE DR
GLACIER WAY

WALDENWOOD DR
GREENHILL ST
EARHART RD

PINE BRAE

23

1 TREMONT DR
2 TREMONT LA ONE
3 TREMONT LA TWO
4 WALDENWOOD LA 1
5 WALDENWOOD LA 2
6 WALDENWOOD LA 3
7 WALDENWOOD LA 4
8 WALDENWOOD LA 5
9 WALDENWOOD LA 6
10 WALDENWOOD LA 7
11 WALDENWOOD LA 9
12 WALDENWOOD LA 11
13 WALDENWOOD LA 13
14 WALDENWOOD LA 15
15 WALDENWOOD LA 17
16 WALDENWOOD LA 19
17 PENBERTON DR
18 PENBERTON LA 1
19 PENBERTON LA 2
20 PENBERTON LA 3
21 PENBERTON LA 4
22 PENBERTON LA 5
23 PENBERTON LA 6
24 PENBERTON LA 8
25 PENBERTON LA 10
26 PENBERTON LA 12

DIXBORO RD

GALE
VREELAND
GALE
HICKMAN

NE

1000

GEDDES RD

GEDDES RD   GEDDES RD

200

HANDY LA
HANDY LA

PENN CENTRAL RR
PENN CENTRAL RR

DECO CT

200

HURON RIVER

SUPERIOR RD

E THORN OAKS DR
HURON RIVER DR
HURON RIVER DR
HOGBACK

HURON RIVER DR

1000

WELSH DR
SHETLAND DR

FIRST
INDIAN HILLS DR

SE

CLARK RD

2000

HOGBACK

GLENCOE HILLS

WASHTENAW RD

MARIE AVE
CROSS RD
CARPENTER
CRYSTAL
GRANT
DAYTON
CARLTON
DALTON

WOODCHIP WAY
RIDGE
TWIN LAKES DR
TWIN LAKES DR

BYNAN DR
CHESTNUT
ELMWOOD CT
ELMWOOD DR
WOODCHIP

INTERNATIONAL BLVD

HURON RIVER DR

ACCESS RD W
ACCESS RD E

GREGORY AVE
MARK
LOUISE
AINSLEY

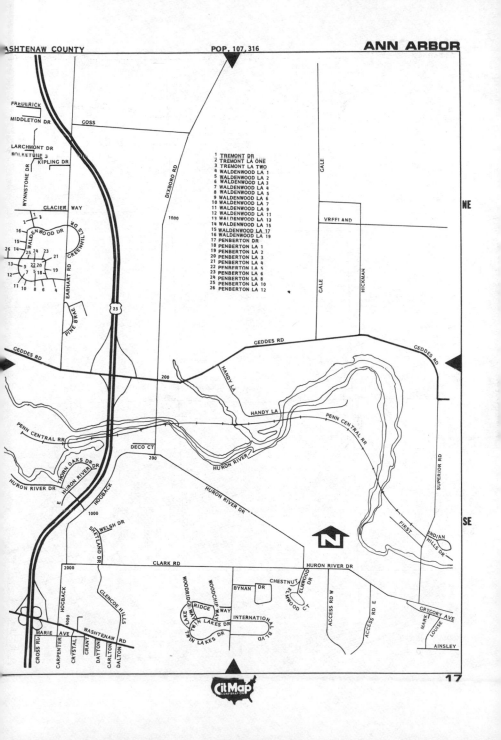

N

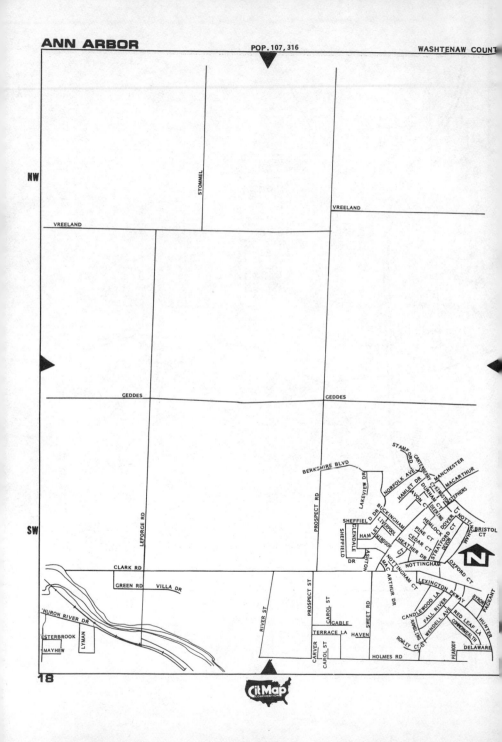

NW

VREELAND

STOMMEL

VREELAND

GEDDES

GEDDES

SW

BERKSHIRE BLVD

LAKEVIEW DR

PROSPECT RD

LEFORGE RD

STAMFORD
CANTERBURY
CLYDESDALE
Ct
NORFOLK AVE
HAMLET DR
DURHAM CT
AVON CT
DEERING
MANCHESTER
MACARTHUR
STEPHENS
CHRISTOPHER

SHEFFIELD DR
SHEFFIELD
GLENDALE
DR
HAM
WINDSOR
CT
BUCKINGHAM
LIVERPOOL
LEXINGTON
ASHTON
PINE CT
CEDAR CT
HEMLOCK
HEATHER DR
STRATFORD
DEVON
ODER CT
NOTTI
BRISTOL
CT
OXFORD CT

CLARK RD
GREEN RD
VILLA DR

NOTTINGHAM
MAC ARTHUR DR
NOTTINGHAM CT
NOTTINGHAM
LEXINGTON PKWY
BYRON
PAGEANT

HURON RIVER DR
ESTERBROOK
MAYHEW
LYMAN

RIVER ST
PROSPECT ST
CAROL ST
CARVER
CAROL ST
GABLE
TERRACE LA
HAVEN
SWEET RD

CANDLEWOOD LA
FALL RIVER
HAMLING
WENDELL AVE
RED LEAF LA
COMMONWEALTH
HUNTER
ROMLEY
CT
PEABODY
DELAWARE

HOLMES RD

18

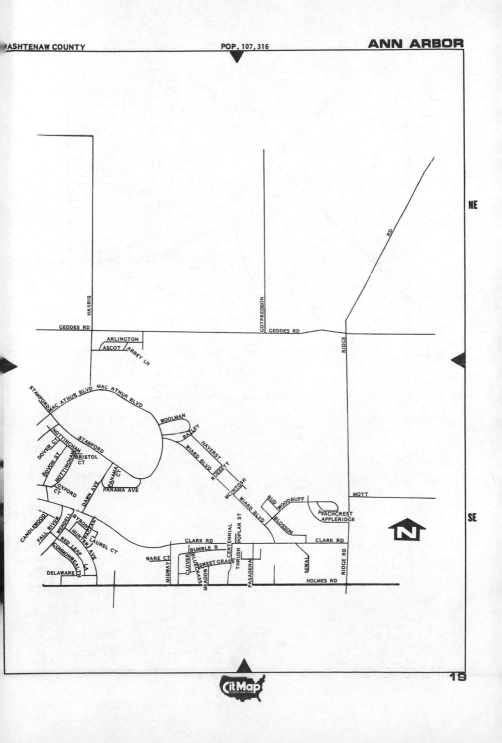

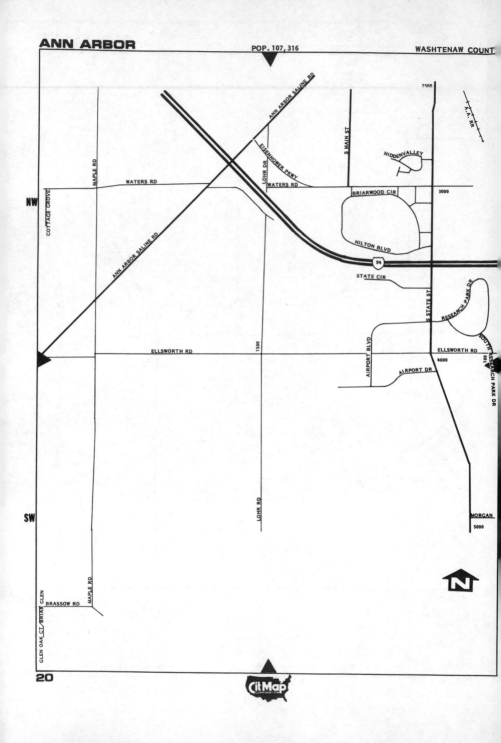

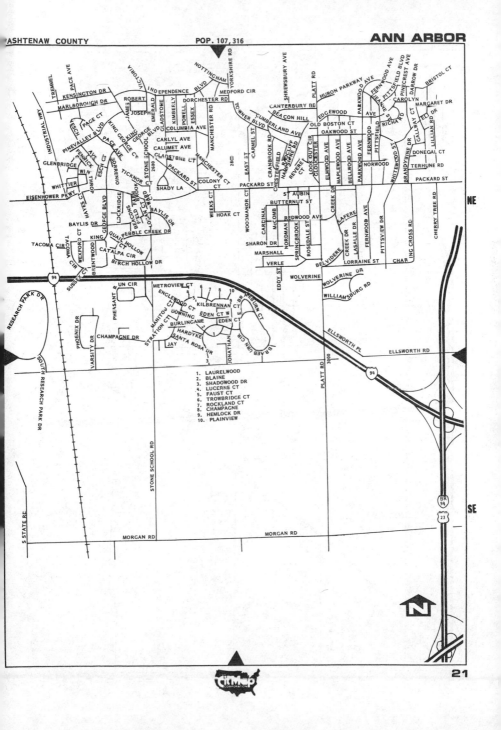

1. LAURELWOOD
2. BLAINE
3. SHADOWOOD DR
4. LUCERNE CT
5. FAUST CT
6. TROWBRIDGE CT
7. ROCKLAND CT
8. CHAMPAGNE
9. HEMLOCK DR
10. PLAINVIEW

NE

SE

N

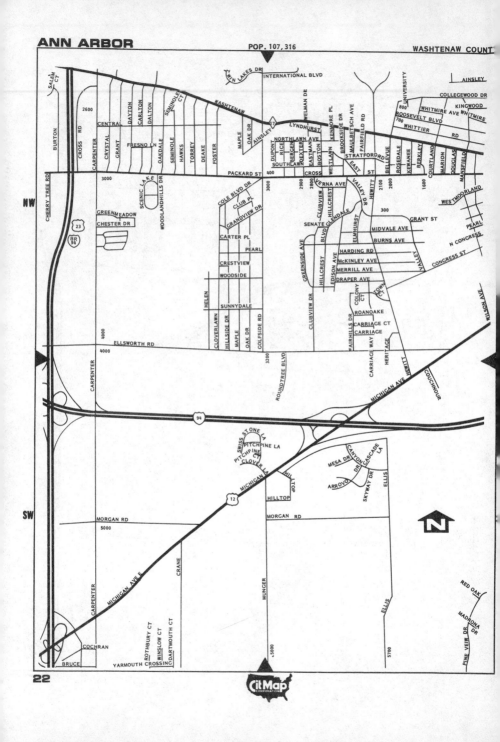

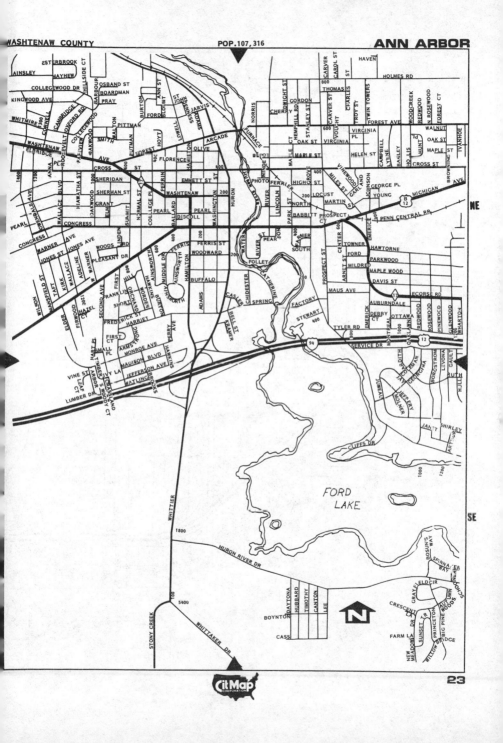

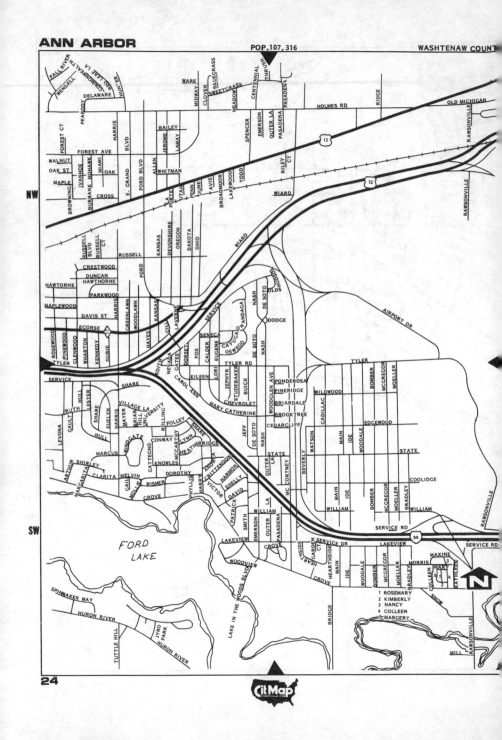

POP.107,316

FORD
LAKE

1 ROSEMARY
2 KIMBERLY
3 NANCY
4 COLLEEN
5 MARGERY

24

CitMap

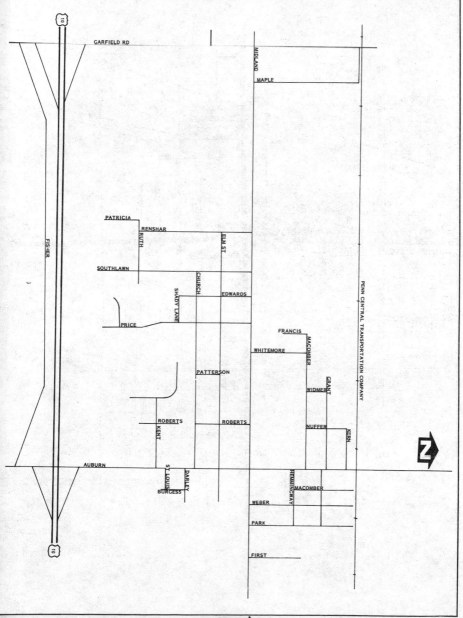

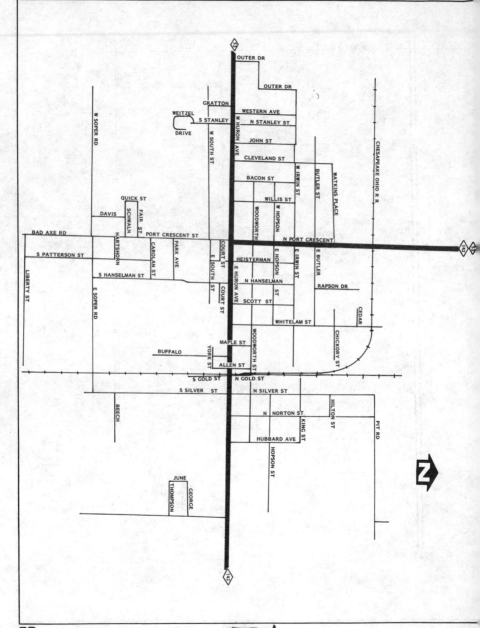

HASTINGS COURT

HASTINGS ST

KALAMAZOO ST

POND

NORTH ST

HIGH ST

ST

ST

ST

THIRD

BANGOR ST

SECOND

FIRST

MAIN ST

MILL ST

R.Y.

MILL

MONROE

WASHINGTON ST

LAFLER ST

AVE

AVE

AVE

MILL RACE RD

CEMETERY RD

OHIO

ST

CHERRY ST

CHERRY ST

JOY

AVE

ST

RAILROAD ST

EXCHANGE ST

PINE ST

ST

UNION

ST

CHARLES

MONROE

LINCOLN

CASS

HAMILTON

MORRISON

ST

ST

ST

ST

ST

ST

APPLE BLOSSOM

ALEXANDER

DOUGLAS

DIVISION

CLARK ST

WALNUT

MAPLE

ST

CHASE ST

OLIVER

RANDOLPH

ST

PROSPECT CT

PARK ST

ARLINGTON

CENTER

CHESAPEAKE

PARK

INDUSTRIAL

N

BATTLE CREEK

Street	Grid	Dir
ABERDEEN	32	SW
ACADEMY	31	SE
ACADIA E	33	NE
ACADIA W	33	NE
ACORN	33	NW
ADA	31	NW
ADALINE	31	NE
ADAMS	31	SE
ADMIRAL	30	SW
ALCO	33	NW
ALDEN	31	SE
ALDRICH	31	SE
ALEXANDER	31	NE
ALGONQUIN	31	NE
ALIDA	30	NE
ALLEN	31	NE
ALLISON	30	NW
ALOHA	31	NW
ALTAVISTA	31	NW
ALTHEA	31	NW
ALTON	31	NW
ALVENA	32	NW
ANDERSON	31	SW
ANDRUS	31	SE
ANGELL	31	SW
ANN	31	NE
ANNAPOLIS	33	NW
ANSTED	33	NW
ANYWAY DR	33	NW
APPERSON	33	NW
APPLE HILL LN	32	NW
APPLEWOOD PL	31	SW
ARBOR	31	SW
ARCADIA BLVD	31	NE
ARCHER CT	31	NE
ARDMOOR	31	NE
ARLINGTON	31	NE
ARMOUR LA	33	SE
ARMSTRONG	30	NW
ARMY	30	SW
ARTESIAN CT	31	SW
ARTHUR	31	NE
ASHLAND	30	NE
ASHLEY	32	SW
ASTOR	31	SE
AUBURN	33	NE
AVE A	30	SE
AVE B	31	SE
AVE C	31	SW
AVE D	31	SW
AVE E	31	SW
AVERY	30	NW
AVON DR	31	NW
B DR N	33	SE
BABCOCK	33	NE
BACH DR	33	SE
BAKER CT	31	SW
BALL	30	NW
BALDWIN	31	SW
BANSILL	30	NE
BARBERRY	31	SW
BARD	33	NE
BARNEY	31	SE
BARNEY BLVD	31	NW
BARTLETT	31	SW
BASE	30	SW
BATTLE CREEK	31	SW
BAUMAN	31	NE
BAY POINTE	33	SW
BAY SHORE DR	33	SW
BEACHFIELD	33	SE
BEACON	31	SW
BEADLE LAKE	33	NE
BEAUMONT	33	SW
BEAVER DAM	30	SW
BECKLEY	33	SW
BECKMAN	33	SW
BECKWITH	33	SW
BEGLIN CT	31	NW
BELL	32	SW
BELLEVUE	32	NW
BELTON	31	NE
BENJAMIN N	31	NE
BENJAMIN S	31	NE
BENNETT	31	NE
BERKLEY	31	NE
BERNARDO	32	SW
BERRIEN	32	SW
BETTERLY	31	SW
BEULAH	30	NW
BEVERLY	31	NW
BIBB LN	30	NE
BIDWELL E	31	SE
BIDWELL W	31	SE
BIGNELL	33	SE
BIRCH	33	NW
BIRCH HILL	33	SE
BIRCHWOOD	33	SE
BIRDSALL	30	NE
BITTERSWEET	33	NE
BLACKHAWK	31	SW
BLAIR	31	SW
BLAKE	32	SW
BLANCH	31	SW
BLENKEN CT	31	SW
BLUEBERRY LA	30	NW
BLUE SPRUCE LA	30	NW
BLUFF	31	NW
BOARDMAN	31	NW
BOND	30	SE
BONITA	31	SE
BONNY	30	NW
BORDEN	31	SE
BOULDER	31	SW
BOWEN	31	SW

Street	Grid	Dir
BOWERS	32	SW
BOWNE	30	NE
BOYD	31	NE
BOYER	30	NE
BOYES	31	NE
BRACE DR	31	NW
BRADEY	33	SW
BRADFORD	32	SW
BRADLEY	31	SW
BRADY	30	NW
BRAYTON	31	SW
BRENTWOOD	33	SE
BREWER	33	NW
BREWER S	33	NW
BRIAR HILL	33	NE
BRIARWOOD	33	NW
BRIDGE	32	SE
BRIGDEN DR	32	NW
BRIZSE	31	NW
BROAD N	31	SE
BROAD S	31	SE
BROADWAY ...LVD	30	NE
BROOK	31	SW
BROOKFIELD	33	SE
BROOKFIELD CT	33	SE
BROOKSIDE DR	8	SE
BROWN	31	NW
BROWN DR	31	NW
BRUCE	30	NE
BRUNSWICK	33	NW
BRYANT	31	SE
BUCKEYE	31	SE
BUCKLEY LA	33	SW
BUICK	33	NW
BURDGE	32	SW
BURNHAM	32	SW
BURNHAM W	31	SW
BURR	31	SW
BURTON	32	NW
BUTLER	31	NW
BYNUM	31	NW
BYRON	31	SE
C DR	33	SE
CADY	31	SE
CAINE	31	SE
CAKSIDE	33	SE
CALHOUN	31	SE
CALICO LA	31	NE
CAMBRIDGE	33	NE
CAMERON	31	SW
CAMPUS	30	SW
CANDY STRIPE	30	NE
CANDLEWOOD	32	SE
CANRIGHT	30	NW
CAPITAL NE	31	NE
CARDINAL	31	SW
CARL	31	SW
CARLETON N	32	NW
CARLTON S	32	NW
CARLYLE	31	NW
CAROLINE	31	NW
CARPENTER	31	SE
CASCADE	33	NW
CASCADE CT	31	NW
CASS	31	SW
CASTLE	30	SE
CATHEDRAL LN	33	SE
CEDAR	30	NE
CEDAR N	30	NE
CENTER	30	NE
CENTRAL	31	NE
CHALMERS	33	NW
CHAMBERS	31	SE
CHAMPION	31	SE
CHAPEL	31	SW
CHAPEL HILL	33	SW
CHAPEL HILL N	33	SW
CHAPIN	32	SW
CHARLES	32	SW
CHARLES E. PL	31	SW
CHARLESTON	30	NW
CHARLOTTE	31	SE
CHARLTON	31	SE
CHASE	31	SE
CHEROKEE	31	SE
CHERRY	31	NE
CHERRY LA	33	NE
CHESTNUT	31	NW
CHIPPAWA	32	NE
CHRISTOPHER LN	33	SE
CHRISTY DR	33	SE
CHRISTY RD	33	SE
CINDERELLA	30	SW
CIRCLE	31	SW
CLAIR	31	SE
CLARENCE BLVD	32	NW
CLARK	30	NW
CLAY	31	NW
CLAYTON	32	NW
CLERMONT	32	SW
CLEVELAND	31	NW
CLIFF	32	SW
CLIFTON	31	SW
CLIFTON PL	31	NE
CLINTON	31	SW
CLINTON E	31	SW
CLOVER LA	33	NE
COHASSET	32	SW
COLDWATER	30	NW
COLLEGE	31	NE
COLLIER	30	NE
COLONIAL	31	SE
COLORADO	30	SW
COLUMBIA E	31	SW
COLUMBIA W	31	NE
COLUMBINE LA	33	NW
COLVIN	31	SE

Street	Grid	Dir
CONCORD	32	SW
CONGRESS	31	NW
CONRAD	31	SE
CONVIS	31	SE
COOK	30	NW
COOLIDGE	31	NE
CORCORAN	32	NE
CORNELL	31	SE
CORNWELL	32	NE
CORWIN	31	SE
COUNTRY CLUB	33	SE
COUNTRY CLUB	33	SE
COURT	31	SE
COURT W	33	SE
COVE LA	33	SE
CREEKSIDE	33	NE
CREEK VIEW	30	NE
CRESCENT	32	NE
CREST	31	SW
CROCKET	31	SW
CROSS	30	NW
CROWN PL	30	NW
CULBERTSON	32	SW
CURTIS	31	NE
CUSTER	30	NW
CYNTHIA	31	SW
D DR. N	33	SE
DANKLEFSON	32	SW
DARLENE LA	32	SW
DAUGHERTY	32	NW
DELANO	31	SE
DERBY	31	SE
DEVOLL CT	33	NW
DEVON	31	SE
DEXTER	32	SW
DIANE	30	NE
DICK	31	SW
DICKMAN	31	SW
DIVISION N	31	SE
DIVISION S	31	SE
DOGWOOD TR	31	NE
DOUGLAS	31	SE
DOVERDALE LA	31	SW
DREAM	32	NW
DRIVE	33	NE
DULLES	31	NE
DUANE	30	NW
E DR. N	33	NE
EAGLE	31	SE
EAST AVE N	31	NW
EASTFIELD	33	NW
EAST HILL DR	32	SE
EASTLAND	32	SE
EAST S	31	SE
EAST WAY N	33	SE
EAST WAY S	33	SE
EASTWOOD DR	31	NE
EASY	30	SE
EATON	31	SE
ECHO	31	SE
EDEN	31	NE
EDGEHILL	33	NE
EDGEHILL PL	33	NE
EDGEMONT	31	SE
EDGEWOOD	31	SE
EDISON N	32	NE
EDISON S	32	NE
EEL	33	NW
EIFLER	30	NW
EISENHOWER	31	NE
ELDER	31	SE
ELDRED	31	SW
ELDREDGE	31	SE
ELECTRIC	32	SE
ELIZABETH	31	SE
ELLEN	30	NE
ELLIS	30	SE
ELM	31	SE
ELMSMERE	31	SE
EMBURY DR	33	SE
EMERALD	30	NE
EMMETT	31	SE
ENLOW CT	31	NE
ENSIGN	30	SE
ENWOOD	31	SE
ERSKINE	31	SE
EUCLID	31	SE
EVANS	32	SW
EVANSTON	32	SW
EVERETT	30	NW
EVERGREEN	31	SE
FAIRFIELD	31	SW
FAIRHOME	31	SW
FAIRVIEW	31	SW
FAIRWAY	30	NE
FELD	31	SW
FENTON	31	NE
FERNDALE CT	33	NW
FIFER DR	32	SW
FINLAY N	30	NW
FINLAY S	30	NW
FITZHUGH BLVD	30	NW
FLEETWOOD	31	NE
FLINT	31	SW
FLORAL	30	SE
FLORENCE	31	SE
FONDA	31	SE
FOOTE	31	NW
FOREST	31	SW

Street	Grid	Dir
FORTUNE	30	SE
FOSTER DR	31	SW
FOUNTAIN W	31	SW
FOX	31	NW
FRANK	31	SE
FREDERICK	31	SE
FRELINGHUYSEN	31	SE
FREMONT	31	SE
FRENCH LN	32	SE
FREY	32	NW
FRUIN	33	NE
FULLER	33	NE
FUNSTON	32	SW
GARDEN	31	NW
GARDENIA	31	NE
GARDNER	30	NW
GARFIELD	31	NE
GARRISON	31	NE
GEIGER	31	SW
GENERAL	30	SW
GENEVA	30	SW
GILBERT	31	SE
GLADYS CT	31	SE
GLEN	33	SE
GLENCROFT	33	SE
GLENDALE	31	NE
GLENURBAN	31	SW
GLENWOOD	31	SE
GOGUAC W	31	SW
GOGUAC E	31	SW
GOODALE	31	NW
GORDON BLVD	31	NW
GORSLINE	32	NW
GOULD	31	SW
GRAND	31	SW
GRAND CIR	31	SW
GRANDVIEW	31	SW
GRAND TRUNK	31	SW
GRANT	31	SW
GRAVES	31	SW
GREEN	31	SW
GREENFIELD	32	NW
GREEN RIDGE	33	NE
GREENVILLE	31	NE
GREENWOOD	31	NE
GREGG DR	32	SE
GRIFFIN	33	NE
GRIFFIN CT	33	NE
GROVE	31	SE
GROVELAND	31	SW
GUEST	31	SW
HAMLIN	33	SE
HAMILTON LA	33	SE
HAMILTON LA E	33	SE
HAMPTON	31	SE
HANCOCK CT	31	SE
HANNA	32	SE
HANOVER	31	NE
HANSON	30	NW
HARMONIA	30	SE
HARMONIE	30	SE
HARMONY LA	30	SE
HAROLD	31	SE
HARPER CREEK	33	SE
HARRIETT	31	NE
HARRIS	31	SE
HARRISON	31	SE
HARVARD	31	SE
HAWTHORNE	32	SE
HAYES BLVD	31	SE
HAYES RD	31	SE
HAYMAN	31	NE
HAZEL	31	SE
HAZELWOOD CT	33	NW
HEATH	32	SE
HEATHER RIDGE	31	NE
HELMER	31	NE
HENDRICKS	30	NE
HENRY	30	NE
HICKORY NUT	30	SE
HIDDEN LANE	31	NE
HIGH	31	SW
HIGHFIELD	30	NW
HIGHLAND	31	SW
HIGHWAY	32	SW
HILLIARD	32	SW
HILLBROOK	33	SE
HILLCREST	31	SE
HILLSDALE	31	SE
HILLSIDE	32	NW
HILL RD	31	SE
HILLS S	31	SW
HINMAN	30	NE
HOAG	31	SE
HODGSON	32	SE
HOFFMAN	32	SE
HOLLAND BEACH	33	SE
HOLT	30	NW
HOLT	31	NW
HOME PL	30	NW
HOMECREST	31	NW
HONEY	31	SE
HOOVER	31	SE
HOPKINS	33	SE
HORTON	31	SE
HOUSTON	31	SE
HOWLAND	31	SW

Street	Grid	Dir
HOYT	33	SE
HUBBARD	31	NW
HUBER	31	NW
HUDSON	31	NW
HULBERT	33	NW
HUMPHREY	32	SE
HUNTER	31	SE
HUPP	33	NW
HUSSEY	30	NE
HUYCK	32	SW
I	31	NE
I DR. N	32	SE
IDAHO	31	SE
IDEN	30	SE
ILLINOIS	31	SE
INDIAN RD	31	NE
INDUSTRIAL PK DR.	31	SW
INGRAM	31	SW
INN	31	SE
INTER URBAN AVE	32	SW
IONA	30	NW
IROQUOIS	33	NW
IRVING PARK	33	NW
ISLAND	30	NW
IVANHOE	31	SE
JACKSON	30	NE
JACKSON W	31	SW
JAMES	31	SW
JAMESON	32	SW
JANOAH	31	SE
JAY	31	SE
JEAN	33	NE
JENNINGS	33	NN
JERICHO	31	SE
JESSUP	32	NE
JEWELL	31	SE
JOHN BRIA	32	SW
JOHN R	31	NW
JOHNSON	32	SE
JORDAN	31	NW
JOY	32	NE
JUANITA	33	NW
JUNIPER	31	SE
K	30	SE
KALAMAZOO	31	NW
KATHERINE	32	SE
KEATHLEY	32	SE
KEDZIE CT	31	NE
KEITH	31	SW
KELLEY	32	SE
KELLOGG	30	NW
KELWOOD LA	33	NW
KENDALL N	31	SE
KENDALL S	31	SE
KENOSHA	31	SE
KERTSON	33	NW
KIMBALL	32	SW
KIMBER	31	SW
KINGMAN E	31	SE
KINGMAN W	31	SE
KING'S	32	SE
KIRKPATRICK	31	NE
KIRKWOOD	33	NE
KISTLER	33	SE
KNAPP DR	31	SW
KNOLL DR	31	NW
KNOLLWOOD	33	NW
KNOWLAND	32	SE
KULP	31	SE
L DR. N	32	SE
LACEY	31	SE
LAFAYETTE	30	SE
LAGRANGE	32	SE
LAKESHORE	33	NE
LAKESIDE	33	NE
LAKESIDE S	33	NE
LAKEVIEW	33	NE
LAKEWAY DR	31	NE
LAKEWOOD	33	NE
LAKE WOODS DR W	31	NE
LAMORA	30	NE
LANGLEY	31	SW
LANSING	31	SW
LARAMIE CT	31	SW
LAREDO	31	SW
LARK	32	SW
LA SALLE	31	SW
LATHROP	31	SW
LATTA	31	SW
LAUREL	31	NE
LAVERN	31	SE
LAVISTA	31	NE
LAVITA	31	NE
LAWLER	31	SE
LEAGUE CT	31	NE
LEE	32	NW
LELAND	33	NW
LELAND S	33	NW
LEMONT	31	SW
LENON	32	SW
LEONARD WOOD	31	SW
LIBERTY	30	SE
LILLIE	31	SE
LIMIT	31	NE
LINCOLN	31	SE
LINCOLN HILL	33	NW
LINCOLNWOOD	33	NW
LINDALE CT	31	NW

BATTLE CREEK

Street	Sec	Dir
LINDEN	31	NW
LINDON N	31	NE
LINDOW S	30	NE
LINDSAY	31	NE
LINN	33	NE
LIVINGSTON PL	33	SW
LOCH HAVEN LN	31	NE
LOGAN	31	SE
LOIS	32	SW
LOUISE	31	SE
LOUREL	32	SE
LOURIN CT	32	SW
LOWELL	32	SE
LOYD	33	NW
LUCILLE	33	NW
LUDLUM	33	NE
LUDWIG	30	NE
LYDA	31	SE
LYNWOOD	30	NE
LYNWOOD LA	33	NE
MADISON	31	SE
MAGNER	31	SW
MAGNOLIA	31	SE
MAIN	31	SE
MAJOR	30	SW
MAJORS DR	30	NE
MANCHESTER	31	SW
MAPLE CT	31	SE
MAPLEGROVE	31	SE
MAPLEHURST BLVD	32	NW
MAPLE PL	31	SE
MAPLE TERR	31	SE
MARCUS	32	SW
MARGARET	32	SW
MARIE	30	NE
MARION	33	NE
MARJORIE	31	SE
MARKHAM	30	NW
MARSHA	33	NW
MARTHA	33	NW
MARY	31	SE
MARYLAND	31	NE
MASON N	31	SW
MASON S	30	NE
MASSACHUSETTS	31	SE
MAURER	31	NW
MAXINE PL	30	NW
MAXWELL	31	SE
MAY	31	NW
MC ALLISTER	32	SW
MC ARTHUR	31	SW
MC CAMLY	31	SE
MC CORMICK	31	SE
MC GRATH PL	31	SW
MC KINLEY N	31	SE
MC KINLEY S	31	SE
MEACHEM	31	SW
MEADOW	31	NE
MEADOWLARK LA	31	NW
MEADOWLAWN	31	NE
MELODY	30	SW
MERRILL	33	NW
MERRITT	31	SE
MERWOOD	31	SE
MICHAEL	32	SW
MICHIGAN	31	SE
MICHIGAN AVE E	31	SE
MICHIGAN MALL	31	SE
MIDWAY CT	31	SE
MILITARY	30	SW
MILL	32	SW
MILLER	30	NE
MILTON	32	NW
MINERAL	31	SE
MINGES	33	SW
MINGES CIR	33	SE
MINGES E	33	SE
MINGES N	33	SW
MINT	31	SW
MOCKING BIRD CT	31	NE
MOFFITT	31	SE
MONROE	31	SE
MONTFORD	31	NE
MOORLAND N	33	NE
MORGAN	30	NE
MORLEY	31	SE
MORNINGSIDE	33	NE
MOSHER	30	NE
MOTT	31	SE
MURRAY	30	NW
MYRTLE	30	NE
N DR. N	32	NE
NAVY	30	SW
NELSON	31	SW
NETTLES	30	SE
NEVADA	31	SE
NEWARK	31	SE
NEWBURN DR	31	NW
NEW ENGLAND	31	NE
NEW MOON TER.N	30	NE
NEW MOON TER S	30	NE
NIBLETT	32	SE
NICHOLS	33	SW
NIXON	32	SE
NORAVE DR	31	NE
NORMAL	31	SE
NORTH	31	SE
NORTHFIELD	33	NW
NORTHSIDE DR E	31	SE
NORTHSIDE W	31	SW
NORTHWOOD DR	31	NW
N. P. DR	31	NE
O DR. N	31	NW
OAK	30	NE
OAK GROVE	31	SW
OAKHILL DR	31	SE
OAKLAND	33	SW
OAKLAND	31	SW
OAKLEY	31	SW
OAKWOOD	31	NE
OLIVE	32	SE
OLIVET	32	SW
O NEIL	33	NE
ONEITA	31	NW
ORBIT	33	NE
ORCHARD	31	SE
ORCHARD PL	31	SW
ORIENT	31	SE
ORIN	31	SE
ORIOLE	30	NW
ORLEANS	31	SW
OSCEOLA	31	SE
OVERLOOK LN	31	NE
OVERTON	33	NW
OXFORD	31	SE
P DR	30	NE
PAGE	31	SW
PALMER	32	SW
PALMITER	32	NE
PARISH	31	SW
PARK	32	SW
PARK PL	33	NW
PARKRIDGE	31	NW
PARKSIDE	31	NW
PARKVIEW	31	NE
PARKWAY	31	SW
PARROTT DR	30	NW
PARSONS	31	NW
PASADENA	31	NW
PATTERSON CT	31	NE
PAULINE	31	SE
PAWNEE	33	NE
PEACEFUL VALLEY	30	NE
PEACHTREE	33	SW
PEARL	32	SE
PECK	31	NW
PENN	31	SE
PENNBROOK	32	NW
PENNFIELD	31	NW
PENSACOLA	31	NW
PEPPERIDGE	31	NW
PEPPERIDGE LA	33	NW
PERRY	31	SE
PHELPS	31	SE
PICKFORD	31	SW
PINE	31	SE
PINE LAKE	32	NE
PINE TREE LA	31	NE
PINEVIEW CT	31	NE
PINEWOOD	33	NE
PIONEER	31	SW
PIPER	31	NE
PITMAN E	31	NW
PITMAN W	31	NW
PITTEE	31	SE
PLANTAIN	31	SW
PLEASANT	31	SW
PLEASANTVIEW	31	SE
PLYMOUTH	31	SW
PONY	32	NW
POPLAR	31	SW
PORTER	32	SW
POST	32	SW
POULSEN	32	NW
POWELL	31	NW
PRESIDENTIAL	30	NE
PRIMROSE TR	32	NW
PRINCETON	32	SW
PROSPECT	32	SW
PRUDENCE E	31	NE
PRUDENCE W	30	NE
PURDY	31	NE
PUTMAN	31	SE
Q DR. N	31	NW
QUIAL	30	NW
RADLEY	31	SW
RANDOLPH	31	SW
RAYMOND	32	SW
REBECCA	33	SW
REDNER	31	NE
REED CT	31	SW
REESE RD	31	SW
REVIEW	31	NW
REYN CIR	33	SE
REYNOLDS	31	SW
RHIMES	31	SW
RICHARDS PL	31	SW
RICHFIELD	31	SW
RICHMOND	31	SE
RIDGE	31	SW
RIDGEDALE	31	NW
RIDGEWAY	33	NE
RIDGEWAY N	31	NE
RIO GRANDE	30	NW
RISA	31	SW
RITCHIE LANE	30	SE
RITTENHOUSE	31	SW
RIVER S	32	SW
RIVERSIDE	31	SE
RIVERSIDE CT	31	SE
RIVERSIDE PKWY	31	SE
RIVERVIEW	31	SE
RIVERVIEW CT	31	SW
RIVIERA N	31	NE
ROBIN N	30	NW
ROBIN S	30	NW
ROBINWOOD	30	NW
ROCK CREEK LN	33	NW
ROCKFORD	31	NE
RODNEY	32	NW
ROE	31	SW
ROMANCE	33	NW
RONDALE	31	NE
ROOK	32	SW
ROOK CT	32	SW
ROOSEVELT	31	NW
ROSE	31	SE
ROSENEATH	31	NW
ROSEVELT CT	31	NW
ROTH	31	SW
ROXBURY LA	30	NW
ROYAL	31	SE
RUBLE DR	32	SE
RUSSELL	30	NE
RYE	31	SW
ST. JOSEPH LA	31	SE
SANATARIUM	31	SE
SANBORN	30	NW
SANDERSON	31	NE
SAN JUAN	30	NW
SANWOOD	33	NW
SARATOGA	31	NW
SASSAFRAS	31	NW
SAUNDERS CT	31	NW
SAWYER	32	SE
SCENERY	31	SW
SCHOOL	33	NW
SEEDORF	31	SE
SEIVOUR	31	SE
SELLERS	32	NW
SENATE	30	NE
SERVICE	31	SW
SHADOWOOD	32	SE
SHADYWOOD	33	NW
SHARON	31	NE
SHEFFIELD	30	NW
SHELLENBERGER	30	NE
SHEPARD	31	NE
SHERBROOKE	31	NW
SHERMAN	31	SW
SHERWOOD	33	NW
SHELTER	30	SE
SHIRLEY	32	SW
SHORT	31	SE
SHORTRIDGE	33	SE
SIGEL	31	SE
SILVER	33	NE
SIMMONS	30	NE
SISSON	31	SE
SLEEPY HOLLOW	31	SW
SMITHFIELD	33	NW
SNOW	30	NE
SOMERSET	31	SW
SONOMA	33	SW
SOUTH	31	SE
SOUTHFIELD	33	NW
SOVEREIGN	32	SW
SPARTAN	31	NW
SPAULDING	31	NE
SPENCER	32	SW
SPERRY	30	NW
SPRAGUE	32	SW
SPRING	31	SW
SPRINGFIELD	31	SW
SPRINGVIEW	31	NE
SPRUCE	31	NE
STAFFORD	33	NW
STARLIGHT	31	SE
STATE	31	SE
STATE E	31	SE
STEPHANIE	30	NE
STEUBEN	31	NE
STILLSON BLVD	30	NW
STONE	31	SE
STORKAN	32	NW
STRATFORD	31	NW
STRONGWOOD	32	SE
STUART BLVD	31	SE
SUGAR BEAR	30	SW
SUMMER	31	SW
SUMMIT	31	SE
SUNDOWN	31	SE
SUNNYSIDE	33	NW
SUNSET BLVD	31	NE
SUNWOOD	31	NE
SUSSEX	31	NE
SURRY	33	NW
SUSAN	30	NE
SUWANEE	31	SW
SWEDISH DR	30	NE
SYCAMORE	31	NE
SYLVAN	33	NW
TAFT	31	SE
TAMMY LANE	32	NW
TAYLOR	30	NE
TEAL	30	NW
TECUMSEH	31	NW
TEMPLE	31	NE
TENNYSON	31	SW
TERRACE	31	NE
TERRITORIAL E	31	SE
TERRITORIAL W	31	SE
TERRY CT	33	NW
THELMA DR	32	SE
THEODORE	32	SW
THORNAPPLE	33	SW
THORNCROFT	31	NE
THORNE	31	SW
TIMBERLANE	33	NE
TIMOTHY	33	SW
TOMPKINS	31	SE
TONY TIGER	30	NW
TRAVERSE	31	SE
TRCKOVIC	32	SE
TREE HAVEN	33	NE
TROY	31	NW
TRUTH	31	NW
TULIP TREE LA	30	NW
TURNER	31	NW
TYLER	33	NE
ULDRIKS	30	NW
UNION N	31	SE
UNION S	31	SE
UPSON LA	32	NW
UPTON	30	SE
URBANDALE BLVD	31	SW
VALE	31	SE
VALLEY	30	NE
VALLEYVIEW	33	SW
VANARMAN	31	NE
VAN BUREN W	31	SE
VASS	32	SW
VERMILLION	32	NW
VERNON	32	SW
VERONA	31	SE
VIKING CT	31	NE
VIKING DR	31	NE
VINE PL	30	NW
VINEYARD	31	SW
VIRGINIA	30	NE
WABASH N	31	SE
WABASH S	31	SE
WAGNER	31	SE
WAGNER DR	32	SW
WAGON WHEEL	31	NE
WAH WAH TAY SEE WAY	33	SW
WALKER	30	NW
WALLACE	32	SE
WALNUT	31	SE
WALNUT CT	31	SE
WALSH	31	SW
WALTERS	31	SE
WANONDOGER CIR	32	NW
WANONDOGER TR	32	NW
WARD	31	SW
WARFIELD CT	31	NE
WARREN	31	SW
WASHINGTON	31	NE
WASHINGTON N	31	NE
WATER	31	SE
WATKINS	33	SW
WATKINS LN	33	SW
WATTLES	32	SE
WATTS	32	SW
WAUBASCON	31	NW
WAUPAKA	30	NE
WAWEENORK	33	NW
WAYNE	30	NW
WEALTHY	33	SW
WEATON	33	NW
WEBBER	31	SW
WEEKS	33	NE
WELLINGTON	30	NE
WELLWORTH	31	SE
WENDELL	31	SW
WENTWORTH	31	SW
WEST	31	SE
WESTBROOK	32	SW
WEST HIGHLAND BOULEVARD	30	SE
WESTOVER	33	NW
WEST RIVER ROAD	31	SE
WESTVIEW CT	30	NE
WESTWARD HO	30	NE
WESTWAY	33	NW
WHEELER	30	NW
WHITE	31	NE
WHITE PINE BLVD	30	NE
WHITTIER	31	SW
WICKS	31	SE
WILBER	30	SE
WILDROSE LA	33	SW
WILDS	31	NE
WILDWOOD	32	SW
WILKES	31	SE
WILLARD	30	NE
WILLIAMS	33	SW
WILLIS	31	SW
WILLSON	32	NW
WILSON CIR	31	NE
WILTSHIRE	31	SW
WINDSOR	31	SW
WINDING WAY	31	SW
WINDY	30	SW
WINNIFRED	32	SW
WINSTON	33	NE
WINTER	31	NE
WOLVERINE	31	NW
WOODCLIFF	31	NE
WOODLAND	33	NW
WOODLAWN	31	NE
WOODMERE CT	31	SE
WOOD N	31	SW
WOODROW	31	SW
WOODS	33	NE
WOOD S	31	SW
WOODSIDE	30	NE
WOODWARD	31	SE
WOODWAY	33	NE
WOOLNOUGH	31	SE
WREN	32	SW
YALE		
YAWGER	31	SE
YORK	31	NW
YUBA	33	NE
1ST	31	SE
2ND	31	SE
3RD	31	SE
4TH	31	SE
5TH	31	SE
5TH	30	SE
6TH	30	SE
7TH	30	SE
8TH	30	SE
10TH	31	SE
11TH	31	SW
12TH	31	SW
12TH	31	SW
14TH	31	SW
15TH	30	NW
16TH	31	SW
17TH	31	SW
19TH	31	SW
20TH	31	SW
21ST	31	SW
22ND	31	SW
23RD	31	SW
24TH	31	SE
S. 24TH	33	NW
24TH CT	30	SE
25TH	30	SE
26TH	30	SE
27TH	30	SE
28TH	30	SE
29TH	30	SE
30TH	30	SE
31ST	30	SE
32ND	30	SL
33RD	30	SL
34TH	30	SE
2 MILE RD	30	NW
6 MILE RD	31	SE
6½ MILE RD	33	NE
7 MILE RD	33	SE
7 MILE RD	31	SE
8½ MILE RD	32	SE
10 MILE RD	32	SE

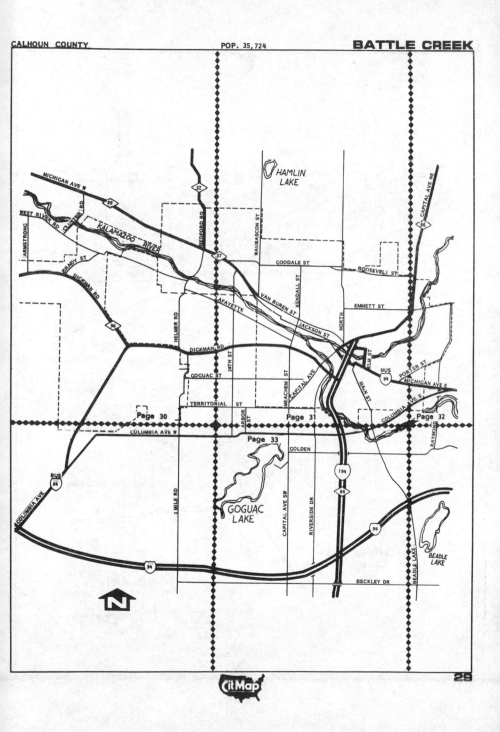

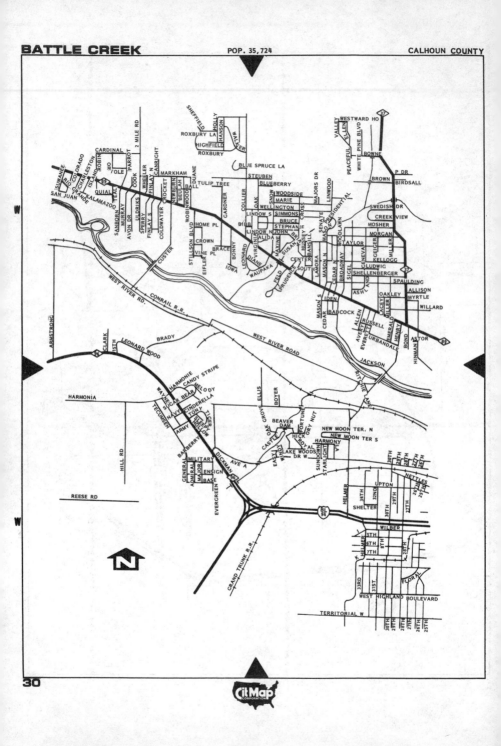

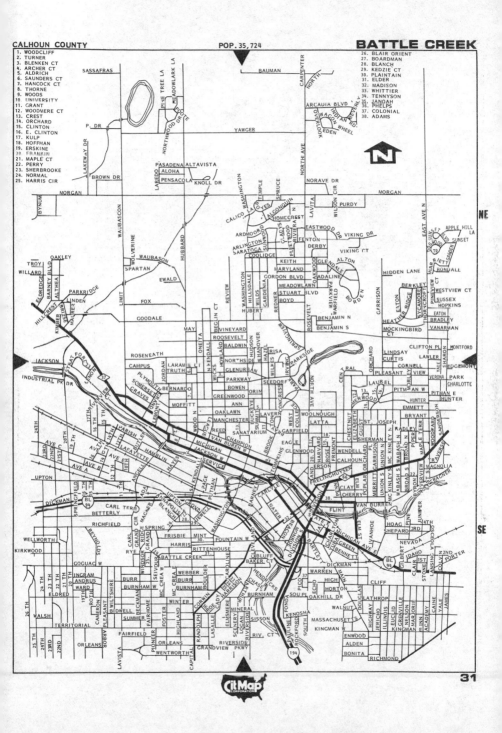

1. WOODCLIFF
2. TURNER
3. BLENKEN CT
4. ARCHER CT
5. ALDRICH
6. SAUNDERS CT
7. HANCOCK CT
8. THORNE
9. WOODS
10. UNIVERSITY
11. GRANT
12. WOODMERE CT
13. CREST
14. ORCHARD
15. CLINTON
16. E. CLINTON
17. KULP
18. HOFFMAN
19. ERSKINE
20. FRANKLIN
21. MAPLE CT
22. PERRY
23. SHERBROOKE
24. NORMAL
25. HARRIS CIR

26. BLAIR ORIENT
27. BOARDMAN
28. BLANCH
29. KEDZIE CT
30. PLAINTAIN
31. ELDER
32. MADISON
33. WHITTIER
34. TENNYSON
35. JANOAH
36. PHELPS
37. COLONIAL
38. ADAMS

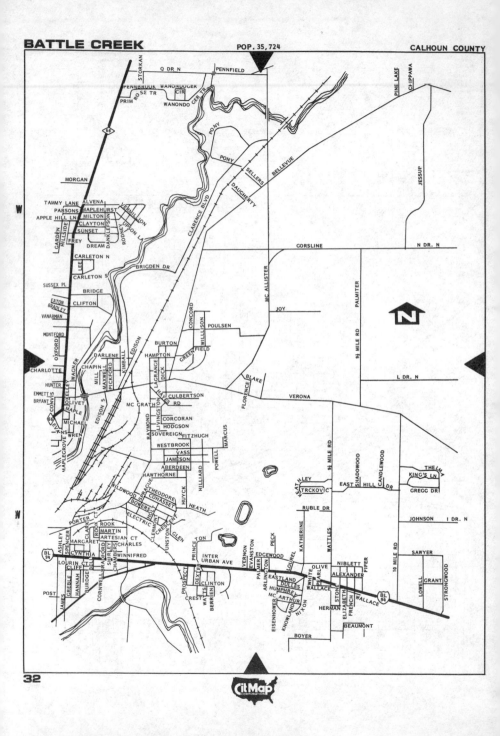

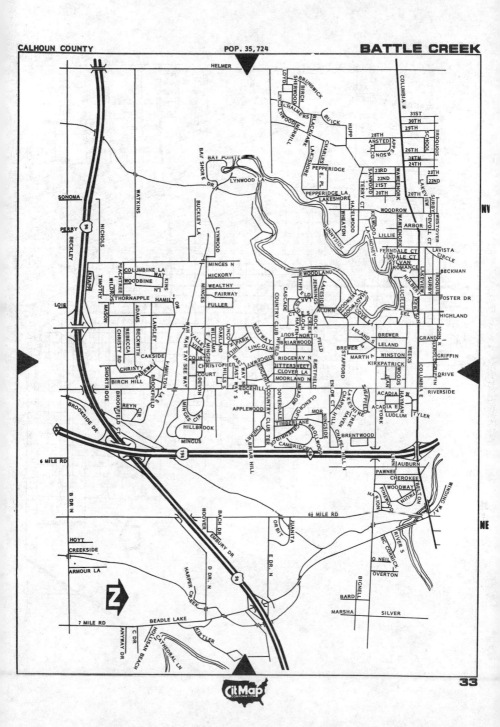

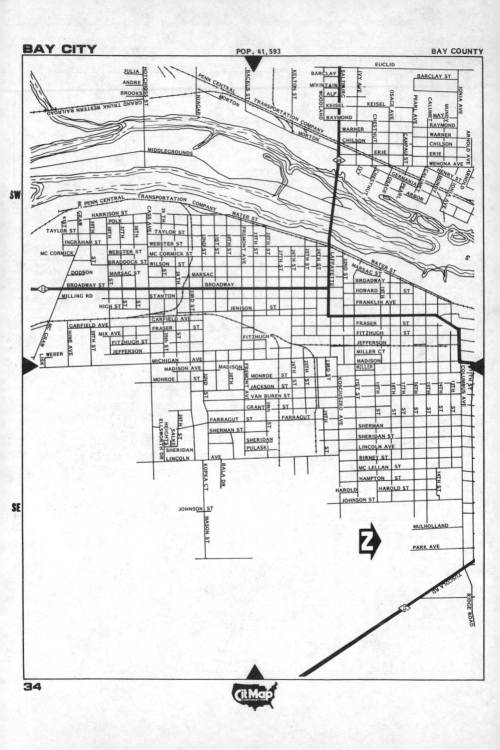

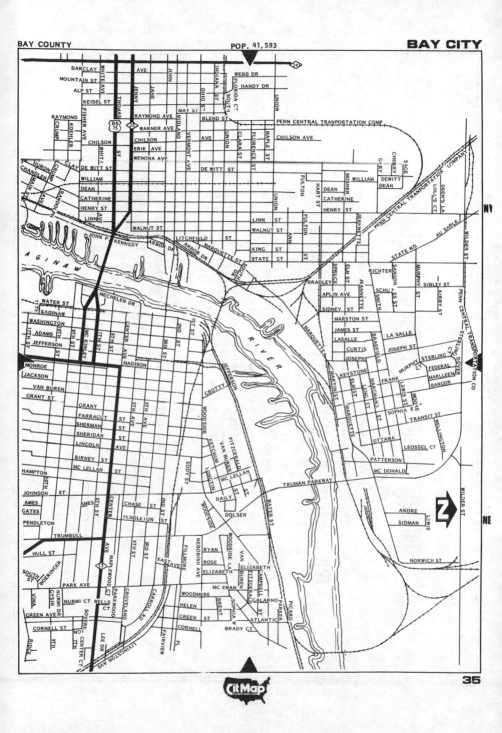

Street			Street			Street			Street		
ADAMS	34	SW	FREMONT	35	SE	MADISON	34	SW	SOVEREIGN DR	34	SE
ALP	34	SW	FULTON	34	NW	MAIN	34	SW	SPRUCE	34	NW
AMES	34	SE				MAPLE	34	NW	STANTON	35	SW
ANDRE	34	NE	GALARNO	34	NE	MAPLEWOOD CT	34	SW	STATE	34	NW
ANN	34	NW	GARFIELD AVE	35	SW	MARCHAND	34	NE	STERLING CT	34	NW
APLIN	34	NW	GARY	34	NW	MARLLEEN DR	34	NE	STERLING ST	34	NW
ARBOR	34	SW	GATES	34	SW	MARQUETTE	34	NW			
ARNOLD	35	NW	GERMANIA AVE	35	NW	MARSAC	34	SW	TAYLOR	35	SW
ATLANTIC	34	NE	GRANT	34	SE	MARSTON	34	NW	TRANSIT	34	NE
AU SABLE RD	34	NW	GREEN AVE	34	SE	MARTIN	34	NE	THOMAS	34	SW
			GROVELAND RD	34	SE	MASON ST	35	SE	TRUMAN PARKWAY	34	SE
BACKUS	35	SW	GYSIN CT	34	SE	MAY	34	SW	TRUMBULL	34	SE
BALA DRIVE	35	SE				MECHELEN DR	34	SW	TUSCOLA	35	NE
BANGOR	34	SW	HAMPTON	34	SE	MICHIGAN AVE	35	SE			
BARCLAY	34	SW	HANDY DR	34	SW	MIDLAND	34	SW	UNION	34	NW
BIRNEY	34	SE	HAROLD	35	NE	MIDDLEGROUNDS	35	SW			
BLEND	35	SW	HARRISON	35	SW	MILLER CT	35	NE	VAN BUREN	34	SW
BOEHRINGER CT	34	SE	HART	34	NW	MILLER	35	SE	VERMONT	34	SW
BRADDOCK	35	SW	HEIGHTS CT	35	SE	MILLING	35	SW	VINA CT	34	NW
BRADFIELD	34	NW	HELEN	34	NW	MIX	34	SE	WALNUT	34	NW
BRADLEY	34	NW	HENRY	34	NW	MONROE	34	SE	WARNER	34	SW
BRADY CT	34	SW	HIGH	35	SW	MOORE	34	NE	WASHINGTON AVE	34	SW
BRENT	34	SE	HINE	35	SW	MORTON	35	NW	WATER	34	NE
BROADWAY	35	NW	HOTCHKISS	35	SW	MOSHER	34	NW	WEBB DR	34	SW
BROOKS	35	SW	HOWARD	35	NW	MOUNTAIN	34	SW	WEBER CT	35	SW
			HULL	34	SE	MULHOLLAND	35	NE	WEBSTER	34	SW
CALUMET	35	NW	HURON AVE RD	34	NW	MUNDY AVE	35	NW	WELLINGTON	34	NE
CAMPBELL	34	NE				MURPHY CT	34	NW	WELLS CT	34	SW
CAMPAU	34	NW	INDIANA	34	SW	MURPHY	34	NW	WENONA AVE	34	SW
CARROLL RD	34	SE	INGRAHAM	35	NW				WHITE	34	NW
CASS AVE	34	SW	IONIA AVE	35	NW	NEBOBISH AVE	34	SW	WILDER RD	34	NW
CATHERINE	34	NW	IVY AVE	34	NW	NIAGARA	35	SW	WILLIAM	35	NW
CENTER CT	34	SE				NORWICH	34	NE	WILSON	35	SW
CENTER AVE	34	SE	JACKSON	34	SE	NURMI CT	34	SE	WOODLAND	35	NW
CHANDLER	34	NW	JAMES	34	NW	NURMI DR	34	SE	WOODMERE AVE	34	SE
CHASE	34	SE	JANE	34	SW				WOODSIDE	34	SE
CHERRY LA	34	NW	JEANETTE	34	NW	OHIO	34	SW	WOODSIDE LA	34	SE
CHESTNUT	35	NW	JEFFERSON	34	SW	OSAGE	35	NW	1ST	34	SW
CHILSON	34	SW	JENISON	35	SW	OTTAWA	34	NE	2ND	34	SW
CLARA	34	SW	JENNY	34	SW	PARK AVE	34	NE	3RD	34	SW
CLAY	34	SW	JOHN	34	SW	PARKER	34	SW	4TH	34	SE
COLUMBUS AVE	35	NE	JOHN F KENNEDY DR	34	SW	PARKWOOD CT	34	SE	5TH	34	SE
CORNELL	34	SE	JOHNSON	34	SW	PATTERSON	34	NE	6TH	34	SW
CROTTY AVE	34	SE	JOSEPH	34	NW	PEARL	35	NW	7TH	34	SW
CRUMP	34	SW	JULIA	35	SW	PENDLETON	34	NE	9TH	34	SW
CURTIS	34	NW				PICARD	34	NE	10TH	34	SW
			KELTON	35	NW	POLK	35	SW	11TH	35	NE
DAILY	34	SE	KETCHUM	34	NE	PULASKI	35	NE	13TH	35	NE
DEAN	34	NW	KEYSTONE	34	SE				14TH	35	NE
DEEN'S LA	34	NW	KEISEL ST	34	SW	RANDOLPH AVE	34	SW	15TH	35	NE
DE WITT	34	NW	KING	34	NW	RAYMOND	34	NW	16TH	35	NE
DODSON CT	35	SW	KIRBY	34	NW	RICHTER	34	NW	17TH	35	NE
DOLSEN	34	SE	KOEHLER	34	NE	RIDGE RD	34	SW	18TH	35	NE
DOVER LA	34	NE	KOSCIUSZKO AVE	35	NE	ROSE CT	34	SE	19TH	35	NE
EAST AVE	34	SE	KOPKA CT	35	NE	RYAN	34	SE	21ST	35	NE
EDDY	34	SE							22ND	35	NW
ELIZABETH	34	NE	LA SALLE	34	NW	SAGE	34	NW	23RD	35	NW
ELLSWORTH DR	35	SE	LAFAYETTE AVE	35	NW	SAGINAW	34	SW	24TH	35	NW
ELM	34	NW	LEE DR	34	NW	SALKE	34	SE	25TH	35	NW
ERIE	34	SW	LENG	34	NE	SALZBURG AVE	35	NW	26TH	35	NW
			LEWIS ST	34	NE	SANSON	34	NW	27TH	35	NW
FAIRVIEW AVE	34	SE	LINCOLN AVE	34	SW	SCHUTES	34	SE	28TH	35	NW
FARRAGUT	34	SE	LINN	34	NW	SHERIDAN	34	SE	29TH	35	NW
FEDERAL PL	34	NE	LISK DR	34	SE	SHERMAN	34	SE	30TH	35	SW
FILLMORE PL	34	SE	LITCHFIELD	34	NE	SIBLEY	34	NW	31ST	35	SW
FISHER AVE	34	SW	LIVINGSTON	34	SE	SIDMAN	34	NE	32ND	35	SW
FITZGERALD	34	SW	LEOSSEL	34	NE	SIDNEY	34	NW	33RD	35	SW
FITZHUGH	35	NE	LOLL'S CT	34	NE	SMITH	34	NW	34TH	35	SW
FLORENCE	34	NW	LONGTIN	34	SE	SOPHIA EAST	34	NE	35TH	35	SW
FLORIDA CT	35	NE				SOPHIA WEST	34	NE	36TH	35	SW
FRANK	34	NE	McCORMICK	35	SW	SOUTH DR	34	SW	37TH	35	SW
FRANKLIN	35	NW	McDONALD	34	NE	SOUTH ST	34	SE	38TH	35	SW
FRASER	35	NW	McEWAN	34	SW	SOUTH UNION	34	SW	39TH	35	SW
			McGRAW	35	SW				41ST	35	SW
			McKINLEY	34	SW						
			McLELLAN	34	SE						

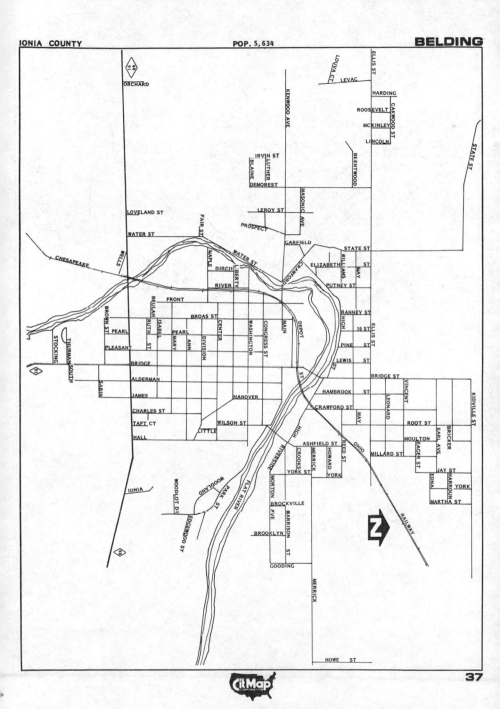

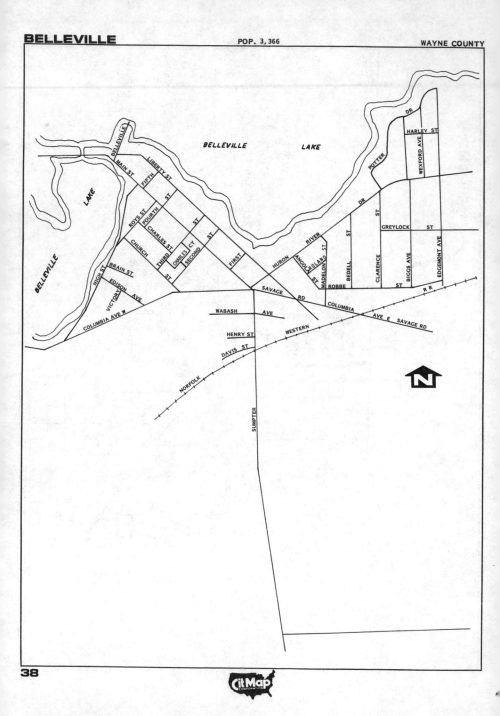

NOTES

BENTON HARBOR
ST. JOSEPH

STREET INDEX

BENTON HARBOR

ACORN	41	SW
ADAMS	39	NE
AGARD	42	NW
ALBERT	43	SE
ALGONQUIN E.	42	SE
ALGONQUIN W.	42	SW
ALLEN	42	NW
ALMA	42	SE
AMES	42	NW
ANN	41	SW
ANSLEY	41	SW
ANTHONY	41	SW
APPLE AVE	39	SE
ARBOR	41	SE
ARCHER	41	NW
BACON SCHOOL	42	SE
BAIRD	42	NW
BALDANZ	40	SE
BALDWIN	42	NW
BARBARA	40	SE
BEECHWOOD CIR	39	NE
BELLVIEW	39	SE
BEND	41	SE
BENJAMIN	41	SE
BENSON	40	NW
BENTON	40	SW
BERG	40	SE
BERNICE	41	NE
BERRION	42	NW
BERT	40	SE
BEVERIDGE	41	NW
BEVERLY CT	40	NE
BIRDIE	40	SE
BISHOP	42	NW
BLACKHAWK	41	NE
BLOSSOM LANE	41	NE
BLUFFWOOD	41	SE
BOTHAM	41	NW
BOUGHTON	39	SE
BOYNTON	42	NW
BRADFORD	41	NE
BLAIRCUFF	41	SW
BRENDA	41	SE
BRICE	40	SW
BRIDGEMAN	40	SE
BRITIAN AVE	39	SE
BROAD	39	SW
BROADWAY	42	NW
BROOK CT	41	NE
BROWN SCHOOL	41	SW
BROWNWAY	41	NE
BRUNN	41	NE
BRYAN	41	NE
BUENA VISTA	40	NW
BURDELL	41	SW
BURKETT	41	SW
BURTON	40	SW
BUSS	40	SW
BUTLER	40	SE
CAMBRIDGE	41	SW
CARLEY	41	SW
CARLTON	42	NW
CARRIE	41	SE
CARTLEY	42	NE
CATALPA	39	SW
CATHERMAN	40	SW
CAYUGA	41	NE
CELINA	41	SW
CHEROKEE	41	NE
CHESTNUT	40	SW
CHIMERA	41	NW
CHIPPEWA	41	NE
CHURCH	39	SW
CIRCLE DR	42	NW
CLARDELLE	41	SW
CLARK	42	NW
CLAY	42	NW
CLEMENS	41	SE
CLIFF	41	SW
CLINTON	40	SE
COLES	41	NE
COLFAX	39	SW
COLLEDGE	42	NW
COLLEGE	40	SW
COLLINS	40	NW
COLONIAL	41	NW
COLUMBIA	42	NW
COLUMBUS	42	NW
COMINGS	41	NW
COMMONWEALTH	41	NE
CONCORD	42	NE
CONKEY	40	SW
CONNELL CT	42	NW
CONNELL	42	SE
COOK	42	SE
CORA	42	SE
CORNELIA	42	SE
COUNCIL	42	NE
COURT	39	SW
CRESTVIEW	41	SW
CRIBBS	42	SW
CROSS	42	NW
CRYSTAL AVE	42	NE
CRYSTAL CT	42	NE
DALE	41	SW
DAMCO	40	NW
DELAWARE	42	NW
DELL	41	SE
DELSING	42	NW
DELTA	42	SE
DERFLA	42	SE
DEWEY	42	NW
DILLER	42	SW
DIVISION	42	NW
DIXIE	42	NW
DODA	42	NW
DONNA	41	NW
DOUGLAS	40	SW
DOVER LANE	41	SW
DOWNEY	41	SE
DOWNING	42	NW
DOZER	41	SW
DUVAR	40	SW
DUVERNE	41	NW
EAMEN	41	NE
EASTERN	41	NE
EASTLAND	40	SE
EDGECUMBE	40	SW
ELIZABETH	42	SW
ELLEN	42	SW
ELM	39	SW
ELM TERRACE	41	NE
ELVERN DR	41	NE
EMERSON	42	NE
EMERY	42	NW
EMPIRE	41	SW
ENDERS	40	NW
ESTHER	40	NE
ETTA	39	NE
EUCLID	42	NE
EVANS	42	SW
EVERGREEN	42	NW
FAIRLAWN	41	SE
FAIRPLAIN	41	SE
FAIRVIEW	41	SE
FELTON	40	SE
FERGUSON	42	NW
FIRST AVE	41	NW
FISK	41	NE
FLOWER	40	NW
FORRES	41	NW
FORREST	40	SW
FORT	39	NE
FRANK	41	SW
FREDERICK	40	SE
FRICKIE	41	NE
GAINES	42	SW
GARD	41	NW
GARDEN	41	SW
GARFIELD	39	SE
GARY	41	SE
GEORGE	41	SE
GERALD	41	NE
GESTNER	40	SE
GERTRUDE	40	SW
GLEN DR.	42	NW
GLENCOE DR	42	NE
GLENWOOD	40	SW
GOLF	39	NE
GOLFVIEW	41	NE
GRAHAM	39	SE
GRANADA	41	NW
GRAND	41	SW
GRANDEUR	41	SW
GRANDVIEW	41	NE
GRANT	41	SE
GREENLEY	41	NE
GROVE	42	NE
GUERNSEY	39	SE
HAGAR	41	NE
HALL	40	SW
HAMPTON	41	NE
HANLEY	41	NE
HANNAH CT	41	NE
HARLEM	42	NW
HARRISON AVE	41	NE
HARRYS	41	NE
HASTINGS	41	NE
HATCH	40	NE
HAWTHORNE	41	NE
HAZEL	39	NE
HELMER CT	41	NE
HENRY	40	NE
HERR	41	NW
HICKORY	41	SE
HICKORY LANE	39	NE
HIGHLAND	41	NW
HIGH	40	SW
HIGHLAND CT	40	SW
HIGH POINTE RD	41	NE
HIGMAM	39	NE
HILL	41	SW
HILL CREST	41	NW
HILLTOP	41	NW
HILLVIEW CT	41	NW
HOLLY	40	SE
HOOVER	41	NE
HOWARD	41	NW
HOYT	39	SW
HULL	40	SW
HUNTER	41	NE
HURD	42	NW
HUTCHINSON	41	NE
INDIANA	42	NW
INDUSTRIAL LANE	39	SE
INDUSTRIAL AVE	39	SE
INDUSTRIAL CT	39	SE
IRVING DR	40	SE
JAKWAY	41	SE
JAMES	42	SE
JAMESWAY	41	SE
JEAN DR	39	NE
JEAN ANN	41	NE
JEANKLOCK BLVD	39	NE
JEFFERSON CT	39	SE
JENNINGS	42	NW
JEWWIT	40	NW
JOHN	40	SW
JOHNSON	42	NE
JONES	39	SW
JOYCE	40	NW
KAY DR	40	NW
KAMBER	39	SW
KAREN CT	41	SW
KEAI	41	SW
KEDZIE	41	SW
KENSINGTON	39	NE
KERTH	41	SW
KESTER AVE	42	SE
KEVIN	41	NW
KIM	41	SW
KINGSLEY	41	NW
KIRBY	39	SE
KIRBY CIR	42	SE
KLINE	39	SE
KLOCK	39	SE
KROWLOW	41	NE
LAKE	39	SW
LAKESHORE	39	NE
LAKEVIEW	41	NW
LANDON	41	NW
LANE	41	SW
LANGLEY	41	NE
LA SALLE	41	NW
LASEIN	41	NE
LATTIMER	41	SE
LAUREL	40	NE
LAUSMAN	41	SE
LAVETTE	41	SE
LAWTON	39	NE
LEE	40	SE
LEROY	41	SW
LESTER	40	NE
LEWIS	41	SE
LILLAN	40	SE
LINDA LANE	41	NW
LINDEN	42	SW
LOCUST	41	SW
LOMAR	41	SW
LOMBARD	41	NE
LONESOME PINE TR	41	NE
LOOMIS	40	SW
LORA	41	NW
LORENZO	41	SW
LOUIS DR	40	NW
LOUIS CT	40	NW
LOVETTE	41	SE
LYNN	41	SW
LYNWOOD	41	NE
LYOLA	41	NE
MADELINE	40	NW
MADISON	41	NW
MAIDEN	41	NW
MAIN	39	SW
MAMER	40	SW
MANOR	41	NE
MARGARET	40	NW
MARILYNN	41	SW
MARION MILLER	41	SW
MARKET	39	SW
MARROL	41	SE
MARSH	39	SW
MARTIN LUTHER KING HWY	40	SW
MARVIN	41	SE
MAY	41	SE
MAYNARD	42	NW
MCALLISTER	42	NW
MCCORD	41	NE
MC GULGAN	40	SW
MC INTOSH	40	NE
MC LIN	41	NE
MEADE	41	NE
MEADOW	41	NE
MEADOW TERRACE	41	SE
MEADOWBROOK	42	NE
MELODY	41	NW
MENDEL	40	NW
MERRIMAC	42	NE
MIAMI	41	NE
MICHIGAN AVE	41	NW
MIDDLEBROOK	41	SW
MIDWAY	41	NE
MILLER	41	SE
MILTON	42	NW
MINERAL	40	SW
MOCASSIN	41	NE
MOHAWK	41	NE
MOHAWK MANLEY CT	41	NE
MONICA	41	NE
MONITOU	41	NE
MONROE	42	NW
MONTE	40	NW
MONTE CT	40	NW
MONTEREY	41	NE
MONTEZUMA	41	NE
MORE	41	NE
MORRISON	39	SW
MORTON	42	NW
MOUNTCURVE	41	NE
MURPHEY	41	NW
MYRTLE	41	NW
NAPIER AVE	41	NW
NASH	41	SW
NELSON	41	SW
NEWMAN TERRACE	42	NW
NICKERSON AVE	42	NW
NICKERSON CT	42	NW
NILES	41	SW
N. GLENDALE	42	NE
N. OTTAWA	41	NE
N. PIER	39	SW
NORTH SHORE DR	39	SW
NORTON	42	NW
NORWOOD	42	NW
OAK	39	SE
OAK GLEN	39	NE
OAKWOOD	41	SE
OAKWOOD CT	39	SE
ODEN	40	SW
OHIO	39	SE
OOD HICKORY	41	SW
OLIVE	39	SW
ONONDAGA	41	NE
ORCHARD	41	NE
ORLANDO CT	42	NW
ORTEGA	40	NW
OTTAWA	41	NE
OX CREEK	39	SE
PACK	40	SE
PADDOCK	41	SW
PALLADIUM	41	SE
PARK	39	SW
PARK DEN	41	SE
PARKER	41	NE
PARKWAY	41	SW
PARR	41	NE
PARSAL	42	SE
PASADENA	40	SW
PAVONE	40	SW
PAW PAW AVE	41	SE
PEACH	40	NW
PEARL	40	SW
PERESON	40	SE
PETRIE	41	NW
PIER	40	NE
PINE CT	41	SE
PIONEER	41	NW
PIPESTONE	41	SW
PIXLEY	41	NW
PLAZA DR	42	SW
POLFUS	42	SW
POLLARD	39	NE
PONTIAC	41	NE
PORT	39	SW
PRICE	41	SW
PROSPECT	39	SW
RACKCLIFFE	42	NW
RAVINA AVE	42	NW
RED ARROW HWY	40	SW
REDLINE	40	SE
REEDER	42	NE
REGGIE DR	42	NE
RICHARD	42	SW
RIDGEVIEW	41	SE
RIDGE WAY	39	NE
RIFORD	40	SW
RITKIN	40	SW
RIVER	42	SE
RIVERBOUND	42	SE
RIVERSIDE	40	SW
RIVERVIEW	39	SE
RIVERWOOD	41	SW
RIZZO CT	42	NW
ROBBINS	41	NE
ROCKY	39	NE
ROCKY GAP	39	NE
ROGER	41	SE
ROLAND	40	SE
RONCY	41	SE
ROYAL CREST	41	SE
ROYALTON	41	SE
RUTH	40	SE
ST. JOSEPH RIVER DRIVE	42	SE
SALEM	41	SE
SAMUEL	41	SE
SCHULTZ	40	SW
SEARLES	41	SW
SEELY	40	SW
SENECA	41	NE
SHERIDAN	41	SE
SHIP	39	SW
SHORE LANE	39	SW
SHOREHAM CT	39	NE
SLOPE	39	NE
SMALLAGE	40	SE
SMITH CT	39	SE
SODUS TOWNLINE	42	SE
SOMERLATION	42	SW
SORT	42	NW
S. GLENDALE	42	NW
SOUTHPORT	42	NW
SOUTH STATE	41	SW
SPENCER	41	SE
SPRING VALLEY	42	SE
STADIUM DR	42	NW
STAR	40	NW
STATE	39	SW
STEVENS	42	NW
STEWART	42	NW
STRATTON	42	NW
SUMMER	40	NW
SUNNYDALE	41	NW
SUNNYSIDE	40	NW
SUN PRAIRIE	41	SW
SUNSET	41	NE
SUNSET CT	41	NE
SUPERIOR	42	NW
SUSAN	41	SW
SUTHERLAND	41	NW
SWERT	40	SE
SYLVAN	39	NE
TANBARK	41	NE
TAUBE	40	NE
TAYLOR	40	NE
TECUMSEH	42	SE
TERRA	40	SE
TERRITORIAL	39	SE
THAYER	40	SE
THRESHER	40	SW
THOMAS	40	SW
TICORNIA	39	SW
TOWER DR	40	SE
TREBOR	41	SW
TRUMAN	39	SE
TUCKER	41	SE
UNION	42	NW
URBANDALE	42	SW
VALLEY LANE	41	SW
VALLEY VIEW	41	SW
VANBRUNT	41	NW
VENTOR	41	SW
VERNON	41	NW
VERONICA	41	NW
VILLA CT	40	NE
VINELAND	40	SW
VINEWOOD	40	SW
VINEYARD	40	SW
VIRGINIA	42	SW
VIRGINIA CT	39	SW
VISTA LAKE DR	40	SE
VISHT	40	SE
WABASH	40	SW
WADENA	41	SE
WAGNER	41	NE
WAHN	42	SW
WALLACE	41	NW
WALNUT	40	SW
WALTON AVE	42	SE
WARD	40	NE
WARREN	42	NW
WARWICK	41	NW
WASHINGTON	41	SW
WAUCEDA	41	NW
WAVERLY	42	NW
WAYNE	41	NE
WEDGEWOOD	41	SE
WELD	41	SW
WELLS AVE	40	SE
WESTERN AVE	41	NE
WHITNEY DR	42	NW
WHITTLESEY	41	NW
WILLA	41	SE
WILLIAMS	40	SE
WILLOW	41	SE
WILSON	41	SW
WINANS	40	SW
WINCHESTER	41	NW
WINDSOR	41	SW
WISCONSIN	41	NW
WISSING	41	SW
WOLCOTT	41	NE
WOOD AVE	40	NE
WOODLEY	42	SW
WOODWARD	40	SW
WYNDWICKE	42	SW
ZOSCHKE	42	NE
1st ST	39	SE
2nd ST	39	SE
3rd ST	39	SE
4th ST	39	SE
6th ST	39	SE
8th ST	39	SE
9th ST	39	SE
10th ST	39	SE

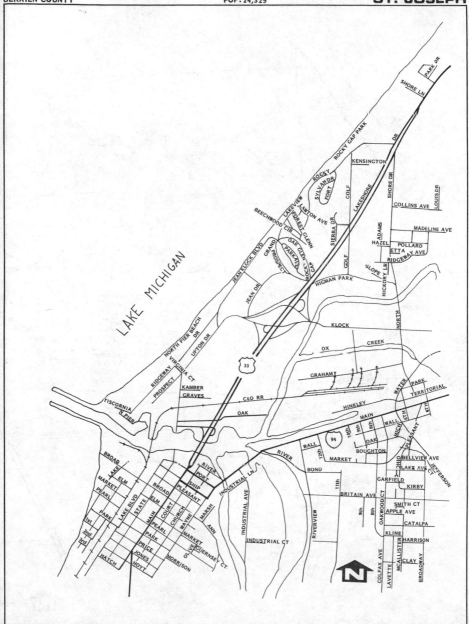

BENTON HARBOR
ST. JOSEPH

POP.24,329

BERRIEN COUNTY

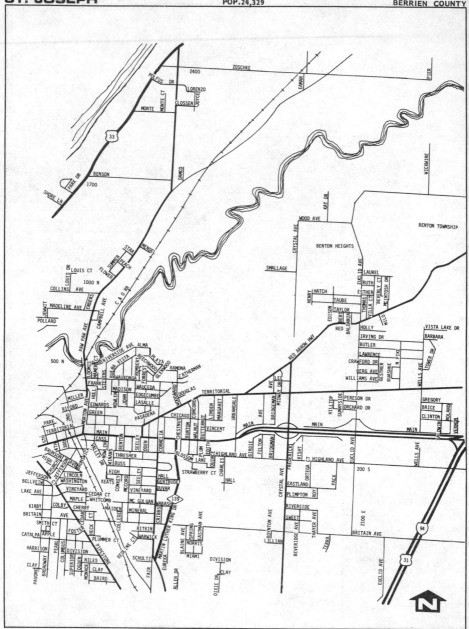

40

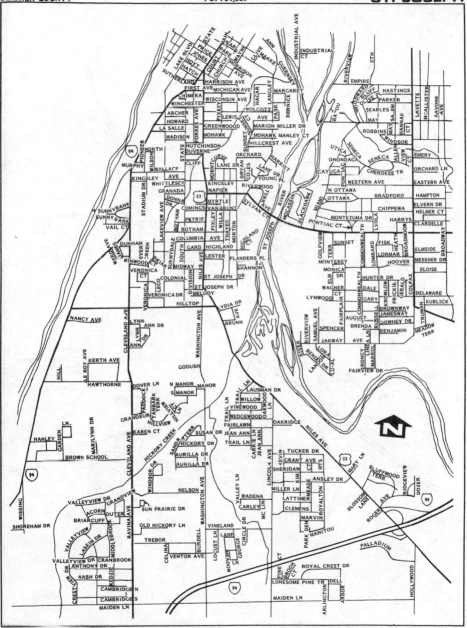

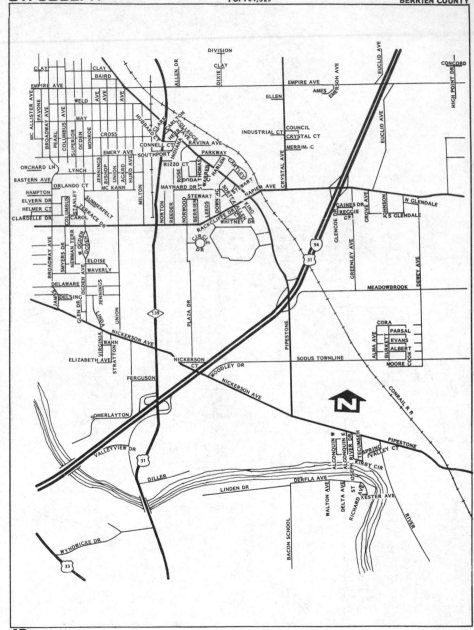

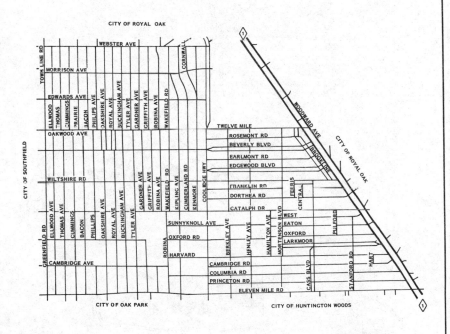

CITY OF ROYAL OAK

WEBSTER AVE

TOWN LINE RD

CORNMALL

MORRISON AVE

EDWARDS AVE

ELLWOOD
THOMAS
CUMMINGS
PRAIRIE
BACON
PHILLIPS AVE
OAKSHIRE AVE
ROYAL AVE
BUCKINGHAM AVE
TYLER AVE
GARDNER AVE
GRIFFITH AVE
ROBINA AVE
WAKEFIELD RD

OAKWOOD AVE

TWELVE MILE

ROSEMONT RD

BEVERLY BLVD

EARLMONT RD

EDGEWOOD BLVD

WOODWARD AVE

CITY OF ROYAL OAK

BROOKLINE

CITY OF SOUTHFIELD

WILTSHIRE RD

GARDNER AVE
GRIFFITH AVE
ROBINA AVE
WAKEFIELD RD
KIPLING AVE
CUMBERLAND RD
KENMORE
COOLIDGE HWY

FRANKLIN RD

DORTHEA RD

CATALPH DR

FERRIS

CENTRAL

GREENFIELD RD
ELLWOOD AVE
THOMAS AVE
CUMMINGS
BACON
PHILLIPS
OAKSHIRE AVE
ROYAL AVE
BUCKINGHAM AVE
TYLER AVE

SUNNYKNOLL AVE

BERKLEY AVE

HENLEY AVE

HAMILTON AVE

MORTENSON BLVD

WEST

EATON

OXFORD

LARKMOOR

PILFORD

OXFORD RD

ROBINA

HARVARD

CAMBRIDGE AVE

CAMBRIDGE RD

COLUMBIA RD

PRINCETON RD

ELEVEN MILE RD

CASS BLVD

STANFORD RD

HART

CITY OF OAK PARK   CITY OF HUNTINGTON WOODS

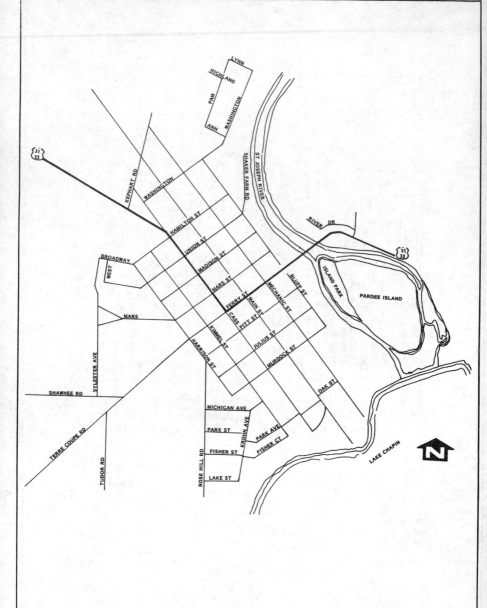

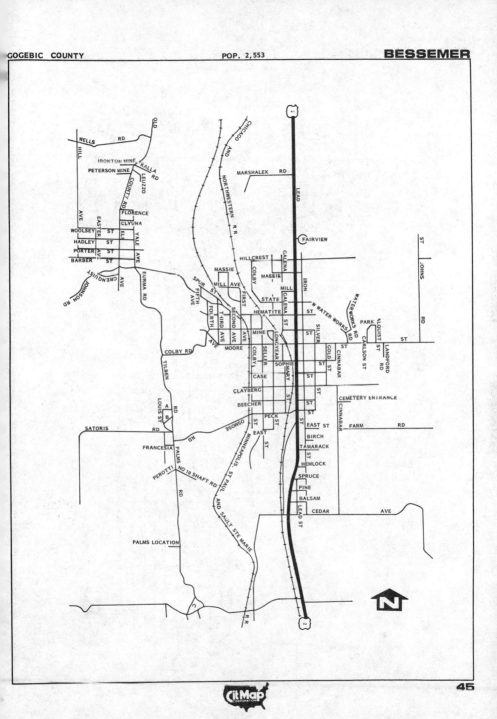

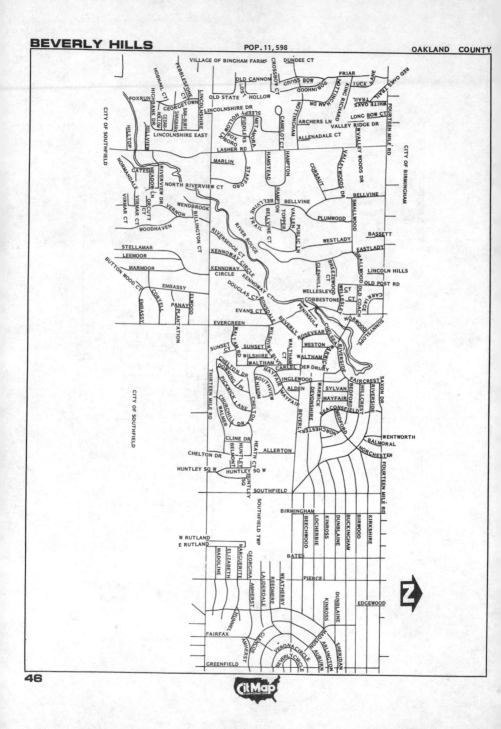

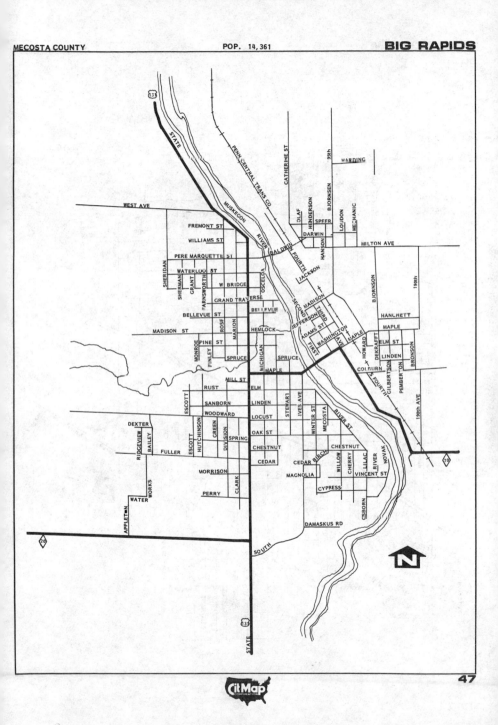

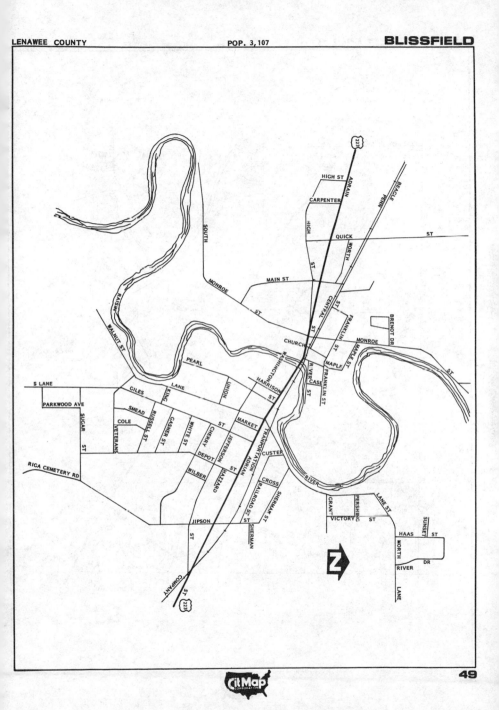

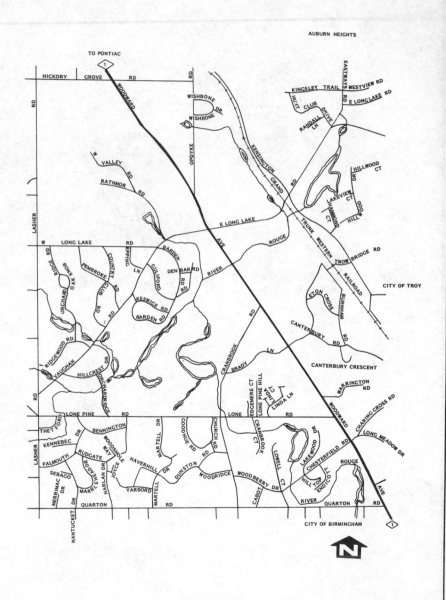

AUBURN HEIGHTS

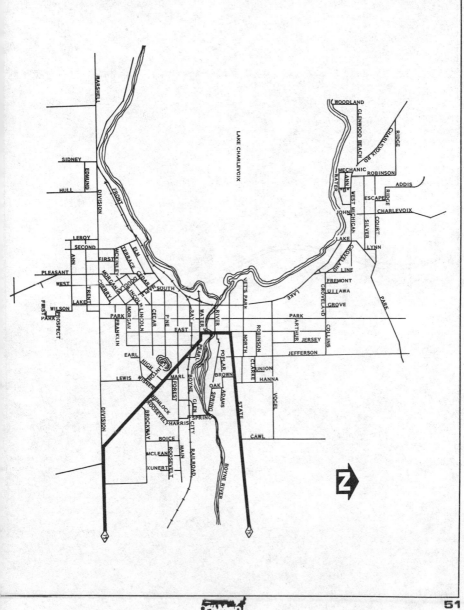

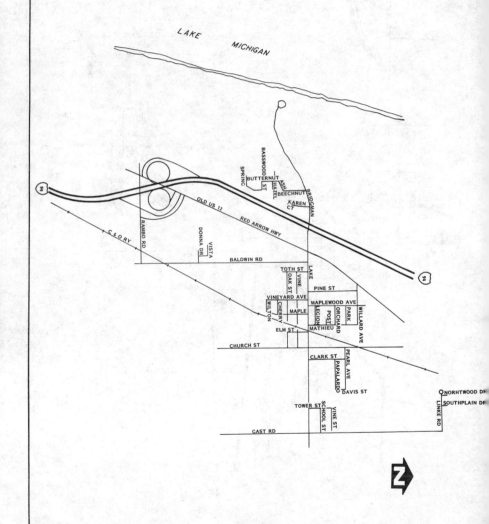

LAKE MICHIGAN

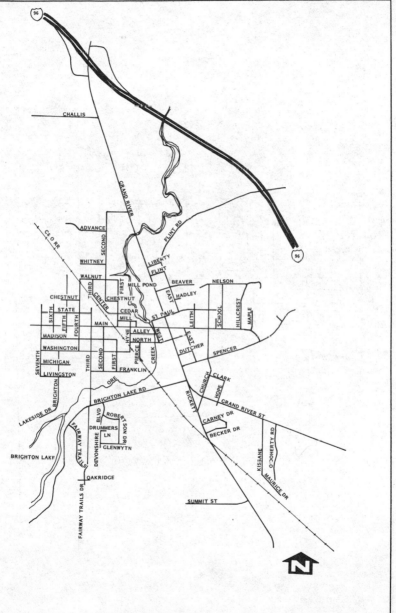

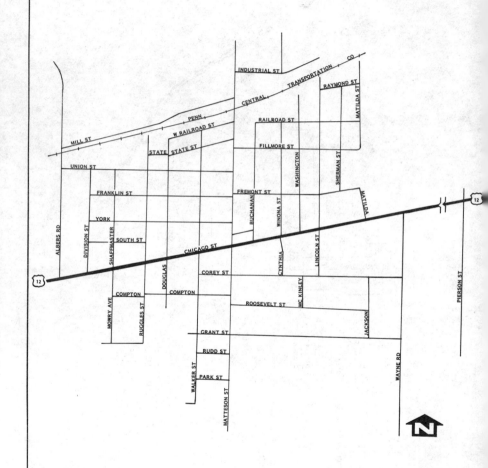

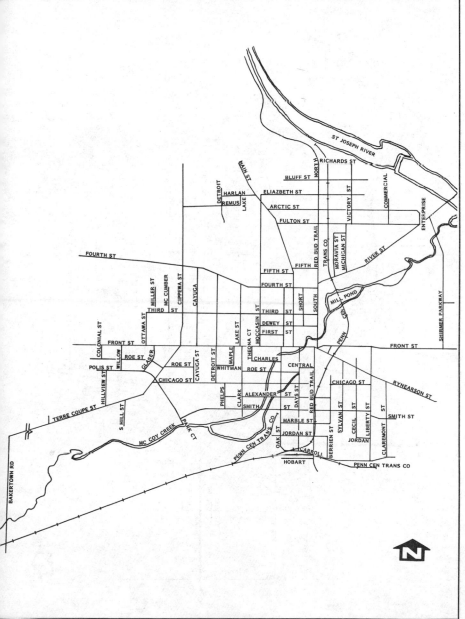

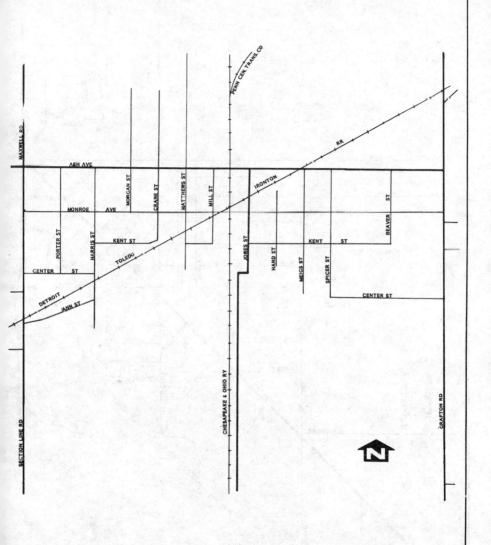

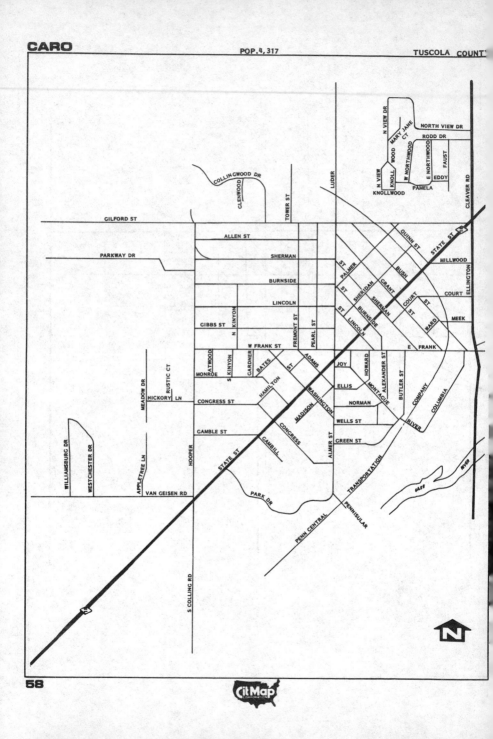

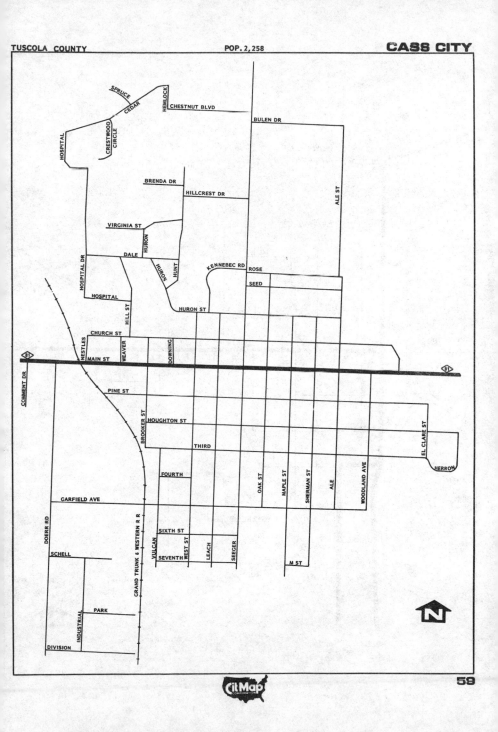

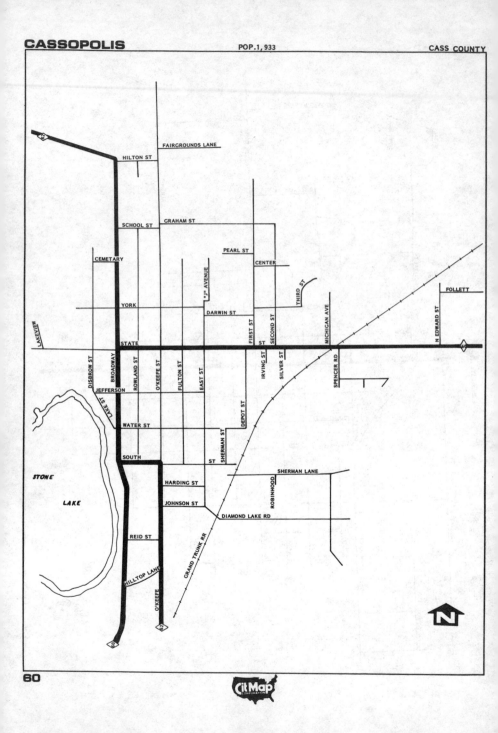

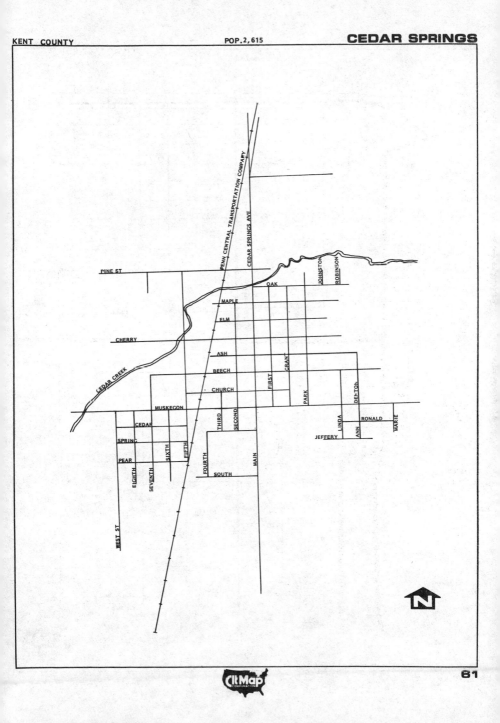

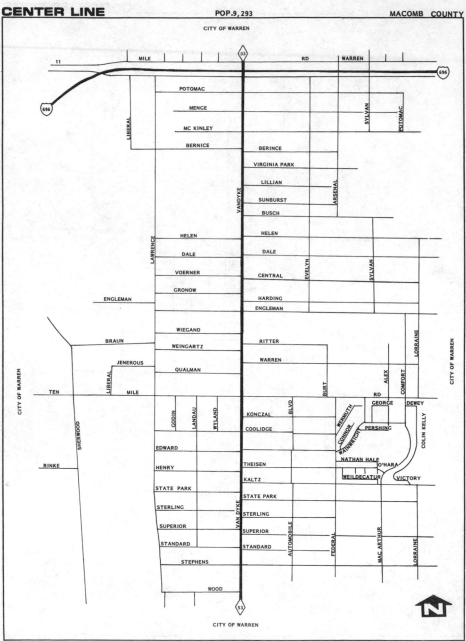

CITY OF WARREN

11 MILE RD WARREN

CITY OF WARREN

CITY OF WARREN

CITY OF WARREN

CHARLEVOIX

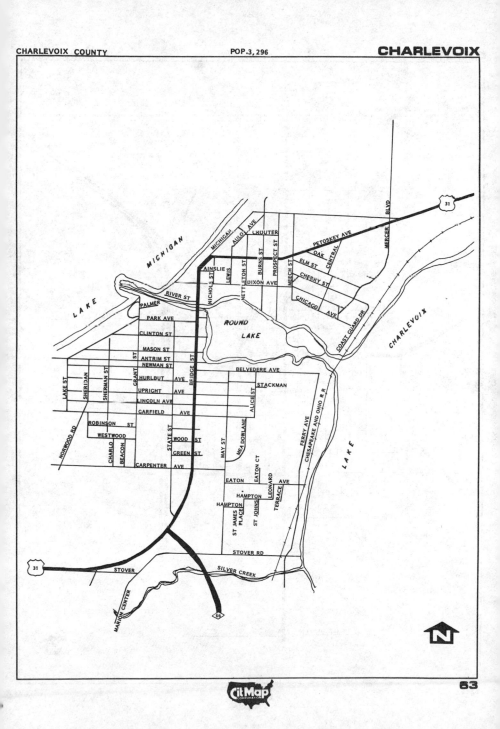

POP. 8,251

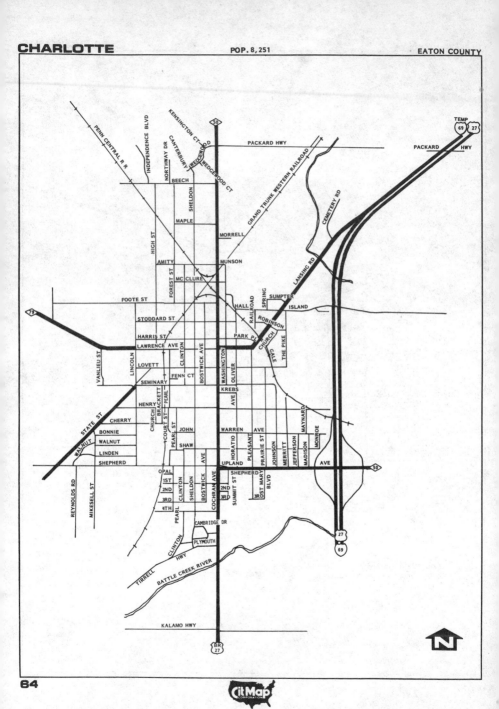

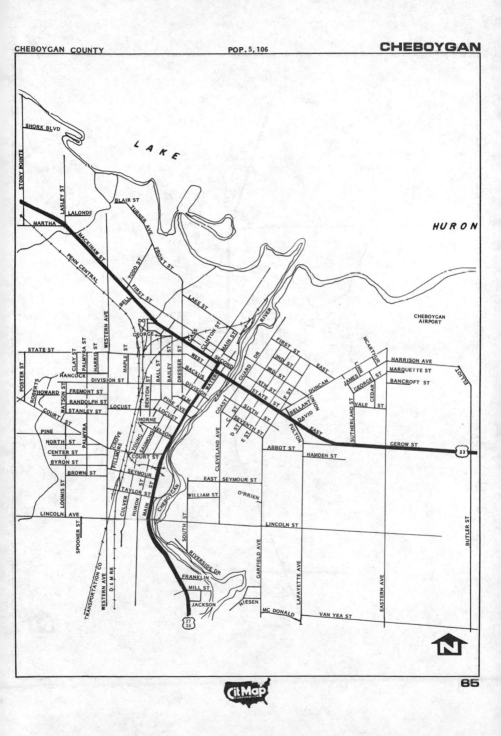

HICKORY CT
NUT
MAPLE CT
BUTTER
CHESTNUT
SYCAMORE

SIBLEY RD

OWEN
CT
HOWARD
ELM ST
DEWEY
MC KINLEY
ST
ST

RAILROAD ST
COMPANY

LETTS CREEK
BUCHANAN ST
RD

NORTH
BATES
ST
FILMORE
JACKSON
HARRISON
MADISON

MONROE
ST
TRANSPORTATION
ST

MIDDLE ST
PARK
JEFFERSON
ST

CHANDLER ST
SOUTH ST
ORCHARD
ADAMS

GARFIELD
CONGDON
SUMMIT
EAST
WASHINGTON

GRANT ST
LINCOLN
VAN BUREN ST
CLAREDALE

PENN CENTRAL
CLEVELAND

WILKINSON ST
PIERCE ST
FLANDERS
WENLEY

MAYWOOD
WOOD

DALE ST
TAYLOR
BOOK

MEADOWLANE
WELLINGTON
MAIN ST
FREER

LANE
ARTHUR
OLD US 12

MANCHESTER RD

94
94

CitMap
CORPORATION

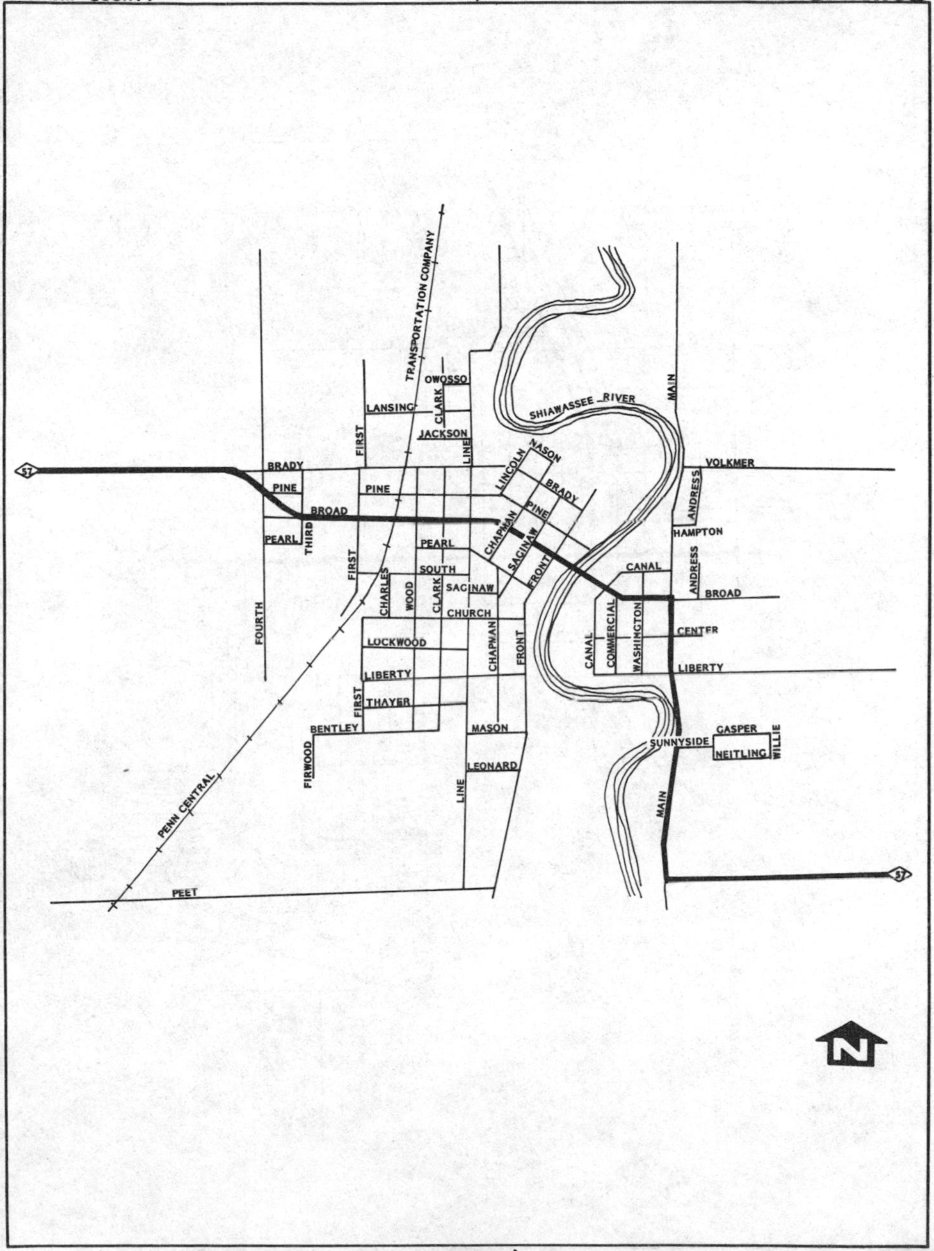
57
BRADY
PINE
BROAD
PEARL
THIRD
FOURTH
FIRST
LANSING
OWOSSO
CLARK
JACKSON
LINE
TRANSPORTATION COMPANY
PINE
PEARL
SOUTH
CHARLES
WOOD
CLARK
SAGINAW
CHURCH
LOCKWOOD
LIBERTY
FIRST
THAYER
BENTLEY
FIRWOOD
MASON
LEONARD
LINE
CHAPMAN
FRONT
LINCOLN
NASON
BRADY
PINE
CHAPMAN
SAGINAW
FRONT
SHIAWASSEE RIVER
MAIN
VOLKMER
ANDRESS
HAMPTON
CANAL
ANDRESS
BROAD
CANAL
COMMERCIAL
WASHINGTON
CENTER
LIBERTY
SUNNYSIDE
GASPER
NEITLING
WILLIE
MAIN
57
PENN CENTRAL
PEET
N

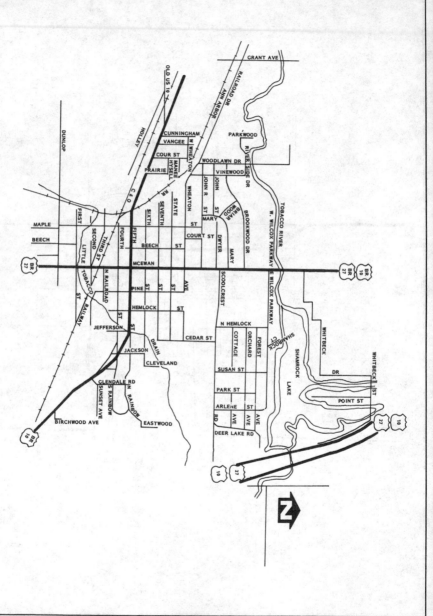

CROOK ROAD

CURTIS

BATCHAWANA

NAKOTA AVE

WEBIK AVE

CHOCOLAY AVE

SAMOSET AVE

14 MILE

BATCHEWANA

WEBIK

CHOCOLAY

ELMWOOD

LANGLEY

WEBIK

KENILWORTH PL.

ANDERSON

15 MILE RD

MASSOIT

MANITOU AVE

MANITOU

LANGLEY

WRIGHT

SCHOOL

DREON

GARGANTUA AVE

WEST AVE

MARIAS AVE

KINROSS AVE

SHENANDOAH BLVD

SELFRIDGE

BAKER

STEPHEN

SHENANDOAH

MARC

STEPHEN

MARIAS

BYWOOD RD

BYWOOD AVE

AVE

ELMSFORD

STEPHEN CT

BYWOOD

PARK

AVE

REDRUTH BLVD

NAHMA

CLAWSON

BROADACRE

JOHN

PHILLIPS

BAKER

HIGHLAND

ELMWOOD

OAKLEY

CUSTER AVE

CUSTER

AVE

CHIPPEWA

MASSOIT

TECUMSEH

NAKOTA

CHARLEVOIX

TACOMA

GERALD

COUNCIL AVE

WASHINGTON AVE

N. WASHINGTON

ELMSFORD DR

KNOLLWOOD BLVD

DRIVE

LEROY AVE

ST

CITY OF ROYAL OAK

ST

S MAIN ST

MADISON AVE

JEFFERSON AVE

RD

AVE

N

MAIN

AVE

AVE

AVE

CITY OF TROY

BAUMAN

GLADWIN

WALPER

ST

TACOMA ST

GARDNER

CHORIN

BOWERS ST

LINCOLN

FISHER CT

ROTH

BAKER

HENDRICKSON

ELMWOOD

RENSHAW AVE

FLORENCE AVE

PARE ST

AVE

HIGH ST

BELLEVUE AVE

BAUMAN AVE

DONALD AVE

ALLEN AVE

PARKLAND BLVD

GROVE AVE

GARDNER AVE

CLAWSON AVE

BOSHMA

LERNER

LERNER BLVD

ST

BOWERS AVE

GOODALE

GOODALE CT

BLVD

ROCHESTER ROAD

COOLIDGE RD

GRANT

HUDSON

WILSON

KEY WEST

GORDON CT

HUNTLEY AVE

ESSEX AVE

AVE

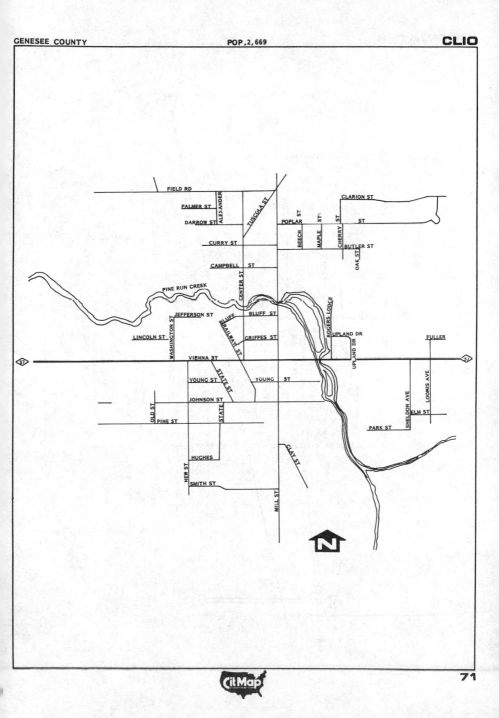

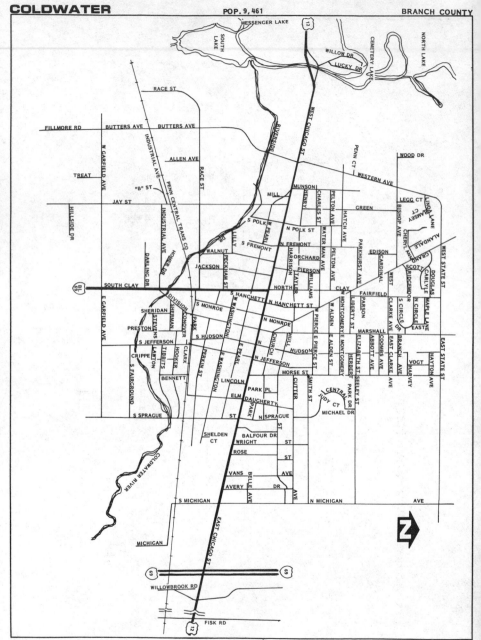

CitMap
CORPORATION

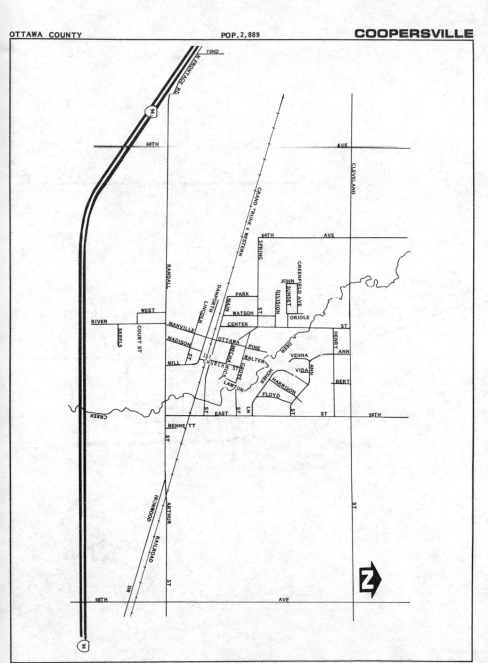

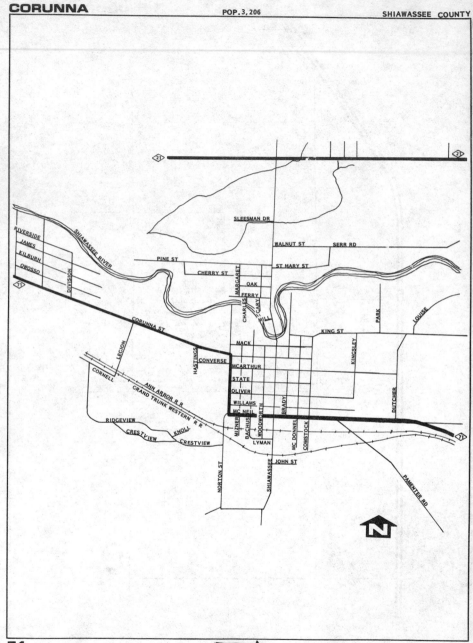

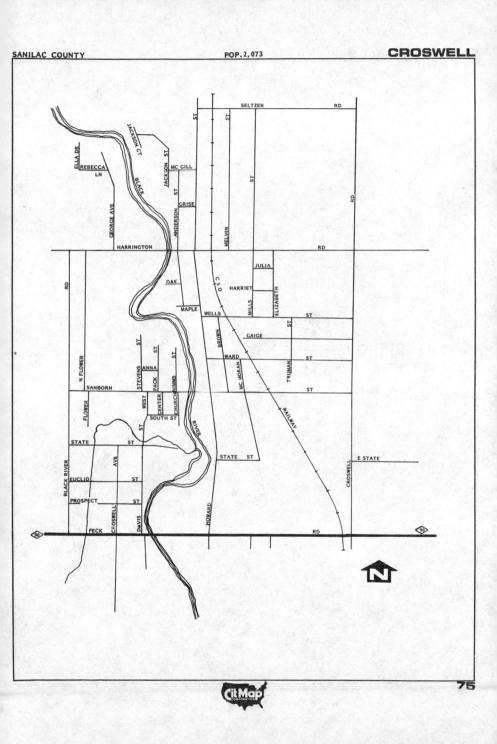

POP. 1,965

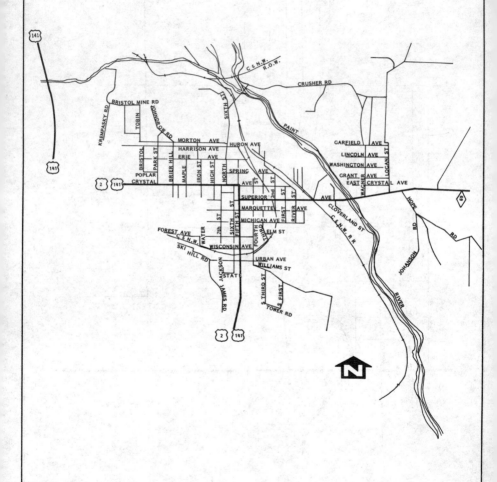

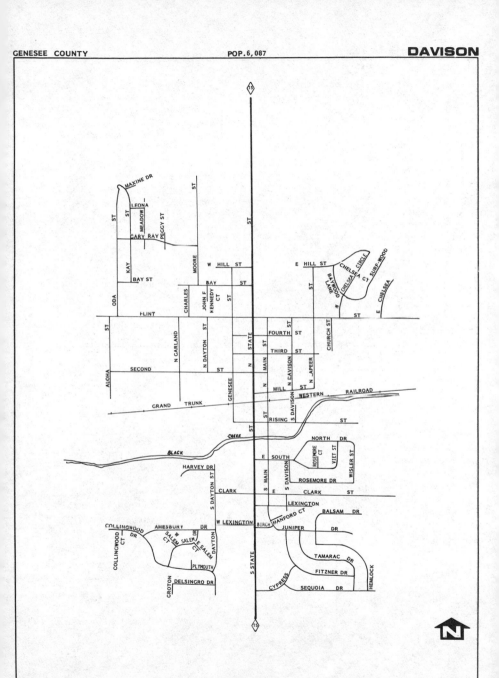

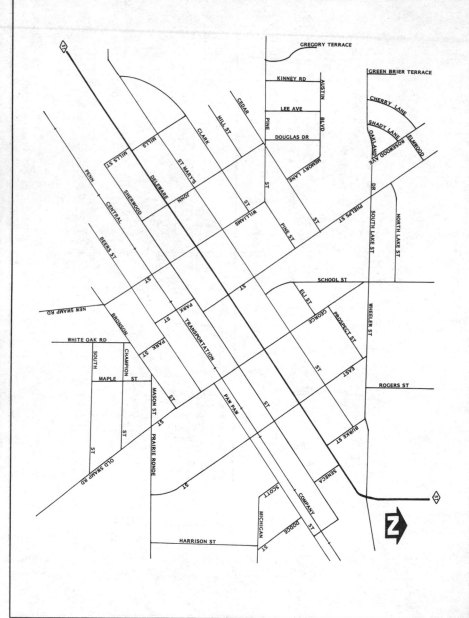

AARON	136	NW
ABBOT	145	NW
ABBOTT DETROIT	148	NW
ABBOTT LINC. PK	163	NW
ABBOTT R.ROUGE	156	SE
ABINGTON DET.	117	SE
ABINGTON D. BORN	145	SW
ABINGTON	131	NE
ACACIA	115	NE
ACACIA CT N	117	NW
ACACIA CT S	117	NW
ACADEMY	143	SW
ACKLEY DETROIT	122	SW
ACKLEY W.LAND	140	SW
ADAIR	136	SE
ADAMS D.BORN	145	SW
ADAMS AVE LIVONIA	112	NW
ADAMS CT WAYNE	150	NE
ADDISON	133	SW
ADELAIDE DETROIT	106	NW
ADELAIDE WY.DOT	171	NE
ADELE DETROIT	171	SE
ADMIRAL	151	NE
AFFELDT	128	SE
AFTON DETROIT	105	NW
AFTON RD S.GATE	162	SW
AGNES DETROIT	137	NW
AGNES ECORSE	156	SW
AGNES AVE S.GATE	162	SE
AIR COACH	151	NE
AIRLINE	160	SW
AIRPORT ROMULUS	159	NE
AKRON DETROIT	107	SW
AKRON W.LAND	140	SE
AKRON D.BORN	146	SW
ALABAMA	127	NE
ALAMEDA	105	NE
ALAMO	140	SE
ALANSON	140	SE
ALARD	163	NW
ALASKA DETROIT	133	NW
ALASKA W.LAND	134	SE
ALBANY	107	SE
ALBER	132	SW
ALBERT DETROIT	101	SE
ALBERT TAYLOR	169	NE
ALBERTA	140	SE
ALBERTUS PL	135	NE
ALBION	108	NE
ALBION WY. DOT	171	SE
ALCOMA	140	SE
ALCOY	109	NW
ALDEN DETROIT	105	SE
ALDRICH CT	98	SW
ALDRIN AVE	169	SE
ALEXANDER LIVONIA	114	NE
ALEXANDER RIVER ROUGE	156	SE
ALEXANDER ECORSE	164	NW
ALEXANDER DR. E	149	SE
ALEXANDER DR. N	150	SW
ALEXANDRINE DET.	135	SW
ALEXANDRINE DEARBORN	143	NW
ALEXANDRINE E. DETROIT	136	NW
ALEXIS	156	SW
ALFRED DETROIT	136	SW
ALFRED INKSTER	151	NE
ALFRED WY.DOT	164	NW
ALGER DETROIT	121	SW
ALGER PL GR. PT	125	SW
ALGER INKSTER	141	SE
ALGONAC	108	NE
ALGONQUIN W.LAND	124	SW
ALGONQUIN DETROIT	138	NW
ALICE HAMTRAMCK	121	SE
ALICE DEARBORN	153	NE
ALINE INKSTER	141	SE
ALINE GR. PT W	111	NW
ALKALI	163	SE
ALLARD GR. PT W	111	SW
ALLARD GR. PT E	111	SW
ALLEGAN LIVONIA	98	NW
ALLEN AVE LIVONIA	113	NE
ALLEN PL DETROIT	151	NW
ALLEN CT LIVONIA	113	NE
ALLEN MELVINDALE	154	SE
ALLEN ALLEN PK	162	NW
ALLENDALE	133	NE
ALLENTON	140	SE
ALLONBY	117	SE
ALOIS	112	SW
ALPER	127	NE
ALPINE LIVONIA	99	SW
ALPINE DETROIT	133	NW
ALL SAINTS	146	SE
ALPEER	163	NE
ALPENA HAMTRAMCK	121	NE
ALPENA W.LAND	140	SE
ALSTEAD	100	SE
ALTA	140	NW
ALTER RD	138	NE
ALTON R.FORD TWP	115	NE
ALVARO AVE	169	SW
ALVIN W.LAND	140	NW
ALVIN GARDEN CTY	141	NE
ALVIN CT GAR. CTY	141	NE
ALWAR	109	NE
ALWYNE	105	SE
AMAZON	146	NW
AMBOY	142	NW
AMERICAN	133	NW
AMERICAN RD	144	NE
AMES HWY	152	SE
AMHERST INKSTER	142	NW
AMHERST D.BORN	147	NW
AMHERST DETROIT	145	SW
AMHERST D.BRN HT	152	NE
AMITY	137	NW
AMRAD	107	NE
AMRHEIN	112	SW
AMSTERDAM	135	NW
AMY	150	NE
ANATOLE	111	SW
ANCHESTEN	102	SE
ANCHOR	156	NE
ANDERSON	147	SW
ANDOVER	108	NW
ANDOVER D.BORN	145	NW
ANDOVER D.BRN HT	152	NE
ANDOVER CT INKS.	151	NW
ANDREWS	162	SW
ANGELINE AVE	113	SW
ANGELINE CIR	112	SE
ANGELIQUE	162	NE
ANGLIN	107	SW
ANITA W.LAND	127	NE
ANITA GR. PT.	110	NE
ANNA DETROIT	121	SW
ANNA TAYLOR	160	SE
ANNABELLE	156	NW
ANNAPOLIS DET.	151	NE
ANNAPOLIS WAYNE	150	NW
ANN ARBOR LIVON.	126	NW
ANN ARBOR D.BRN	126	NE
ANN ARBOR TR	127	NE
ANNE D.BRN HTS.	154	NW
ANNE LINC. PK.	154	SE
ANNE ALLEN PK	155	SW
ANNETTE	172	SW
ANNIN	106	NW
ANNLAND	119	SW
ANNOTT	108	NE
ANNSBURY	123	NW
ANSELM	130	SW
ANSON	156	NE
ANTAGO	100	NE
ANSTELL	123	NW
ANTHONY D.BRN	132	SW
ANTHONY ROMULUS	167	NW
ANTIETAM	136	SW
ANTHOM	147	SW
ANTOINE	163	SE
ANTOINETTE	135	NW
ANTRIM	141	SW
ANTWERP	109	NW
APACHE	127	SW
APHAN	145	NW
APOLLO VILLA RD	169	SW
APPLE	146	NE
APPLE WAY	167	SE
APPLEGROVE	164	NW
APPLETON	102	SW
APPLEWOOD	163	NE
APPOLINE	104	NE
ARBOR ROMULUS	167	NW
ARCADIA	133	NE
ARCH	171	NE
ARCHDALE	103	SW
ARCHER	102	NW
ARCOLA DETROIT	122	NW
ARCOLA GAR. CTY	141	NE
ARDEN LIVONIA	100	SE
ARDEN PK. DETROIT	120	SE
ARDMORE DETROIT	104	NW
ARDMORE D.BORN	142	NW
ARENAC	141	SW
ARGUS	102	SW
ARGYLE D.BORN	132	SW
ARGYLE S.GATE	171	NW
ARGYLE DETROIT	105	NE
ARIZONA LIVONIA	127	NE
ARIZONA E. DET.	106	SW
ARKDALE	167	NE
ARLENE CT	149	SE
ARLINGTON DET.	107	SW
ARLINGTON INKS.	142	NW
ARLINGTON D.BORN	143	NW
ARLINGTON AL. PK.	155	SW
ARLINGTON LIN. PK	154	SE
ARMADA DETROIT	107	SW
ARMADA W. LAND	140	SE
ARMOUR	122	NE
ARMSTRONG AVE	169	SW
ARMY	147	SW
ARNDT	136	NW
ARNO	154	SE
ARNOLD REDFORD	115	NE
ARNOLD D.BRN HT	129	NE
ARNOLD DETROIT	146	NW
ARROWHEAD	127	SW
ARTESIAN	117	NW
ARTESIAN	131	NW
ARTHUR	131	SE
ARTHUR HARPER WD	111	NW
ARTHUR LIVONIA	126	NE
ARTHUR D.BORN	132	SW
ARTHUR W.LAND	127	SW
ASBURY PK	117	SE
ASA	133	NW
ASH DETROIT	135	SW
ASH WAYNE	140	SW
ASH INKSTER	151	NE
ASH WY.DOT	154	NW
ASHBY D.BORN	145	SW
ASHBY W.LAND	140	SE
ASHLAND	125	NE
ASHLEY D.BRN HTS	129	SW
ASHLEY DETROIT	111	SW
ASHURST DR	113	NW
ASHTON	131	NW
ASHTON RD	103	SW
ASTER	162	NE
ASTON	165	NW
ASTOR	122	NE
ATHENS	123	NW
ATKINSON	120	SW
ATLANTA	123	NW
ATLAS DETROIT	121	NW
ATLAS ROMULUS	150	SW
ATTILLA	164	NW
ATTWOOD DR	150	NW
ATWATER	148	NE
AUBREY REDFORD	115	NE
AUBREY TAYLOR	167	NW
AUBREY E TAYLOR	167	NW
AUBREY W TAYLOR	167	NW
AUBURN	131	NW
AUBURN DETROIT	156	SW
AUBURN INKSTER	142	NW
AUBURN D.BORN	142	NE
AUBURNDALE LIV.	113	NE
AUDETTE	153	NE
AUDITORIUM DR	148	NE
AUGUSTA	172	SW
AUIS	146	SE
AURORA	118	SE
AUSTIN DETROIT	148	NW
AUSTIN LINC. PK	163	NE
AUTO CLUB DR	144	NW
AUTRY	113	SW
AVALON H.LAND PK	120	NW
AVALON TAYLOR	152	SE
AVALON ROMULUS	150	NW
AVERHILL CT	138	NW
AVERY	134	NE
AVON WAYNE	150	NE
AVON CT GR.PT. W	128	SW
AVON CT W.LAND	111	NE
AVON RD DETROIT	103	SW
AVONDALE DETROIT	138	NE
AVONDALE D.BORN	141	SE
AZALIA PL	150	NE
AZTEC	127	SW
BACKUS AVE	171	NW
BACON	147	SW
BADELI	128	SE
BADGER	122	NW
BAGLEY	148	NW
BAILEY D.BORN	152	NE
BAILEY LINC. PK	162	NE
BAINBRIDGE AVE	100	NW
BAKER DETROIT	147	NW
BAKER TAYLOR	160	NW
BAKEWELL	127	SW
BALDWIN D.BORN	136	NE
BALDWIN DETROIT	122	SE
BALFOUR A. PK	162	SW
BALFOUR GR.PT.PK	138	NE
BALL	151	SW
BALLANTYNE RD GR. POINTE SH.	111	SE
BALLANTYNE E.	111	SE
BALLANTYNE W.	111	SE
BALMORAL LIVONIA	99	SE
BALMORAL AVE GARDEN CTY	127	SW
BALMORAL DETROIT	105	NE
BALSAM AVE	171	NW
BALTIMORE	135	NW
BALTREE CT	111	NW
BANBURY LIVONIA	99	NW
BANBURY RD LIV.	99	NW
BANCROFT	140	SE
BANGOR	134	SW
BANK	146	SE
BANKLE CT. N	129	SE
BANKLE CT S.	129	SE
BANNER	152	NE
BANNISTER	140	SE
BARAGA	161	NE
BARBARA DETROIT	115	NW
BARBARA LIVONIA	113	NW
BARBARA W.LAND	139	NW
BARBARA WAYNE	167	NE
BARBER WAYNE	150	NE
BARBER CT BROWNSTONE TWP	167	NE
BARBERRY AVE	163	SW
BARCHESTER	139	SW
BARCLAY D.BORN	145	NW
BARCLAY	145	NW
BARCLAY RD GR.PT	111	SW
BARKER	122	SE
BARKLEY	113	NE
BARKRIDGE CIR	139	NW
BARLOW	109	NW
BARLUM	133	SE
BARNUM	162	SE
BARR	119	SW
BARRETT	123	NW
BARRINGTON D.BRN	143	NE
BARRINGTON INKS.	141	SE
BARRINGTON GR. POINT PK	138	NE
BARRON	156	NE
BARRY ROMULUS	158	NW
BARRY WAYNE	123	SW
BARRY DETROIT	151	NW
BARTH	165	NW
BARTLETT AVE	123	NW
BARTON DETROIT	133	SW
BARTON GAR. CTY	141	NW
BASKE	160	NW
BASSETT LIVONIA	126	NW
BASSETT DETROIT	155	SE
BASSETT AVE LIV.	112	NW
BATAVIA W.LAND	140	SE
BATAVIA R.ROUGE	156	SE
BATES	148	NE
BAUBEE	146	NW
BAUMAN	106	NW
BAUMEY	163	SE
BAYHAN	152	NW
BAYLIS	105	SE
BAYSIDE	156	NW
BAYVIEW	140	NW
BEACH	164	NW
BEACON LIVONIA	113	SW
BEACON HILL	125	SE
BEACONSFIELD AVE	138	NE
BEALS	136	NE
BEAMAN	137	NW
BEANUM CT	150	SW
BEARD	146	NE
BEATRICE W.LAND	140	SE
BEATRICE ALLEN PK	154	SE
BEATRICE DETROIT	156	NW
BEATRICE LIVONIA	[illegible]	NW
BEAUBIEN	121	SW
BEAUCHAMP	151	SE
BEAUFAIT GR.PT	110	NE
BEAUFAIT DETROIT	122	SW
BEAUPRE AVE	125	NW
BEAVER	143	NW
BEAVERLAND	102	SW
BEAVERLAND W	102	SW
BECKER	162	NW
BEDFORD D.BORN	154	NW
BEDFORD DR WESTLAND	139	NE
BEDFORD DR SOUTHGATE	162	SE
BEDFORD LA GR.PT	124	NW
BEECH DETROIT	135	SW
BEECH D.BORN	143	SW
BEECH AVE INKSTER	151	NW
BEECH CT	129	NE
BEECHCREST	130	SE
BEECHDALE	152	NE
BEECHDALY	101	SW
BEECHER	147	NE
BEECHMONT	142	NE
BEECHNUT AVE	141	NE
BEECHTON	133	SE
BEECHTREE DR	144	NW
BEECHWOOD DET.	133	NE
BEECHWOOD RIVER ROUGE	156	SW
BEECHWOOD AVE	127	SE
BELAND	108	NE
BELANGER	125	NW
BELANGER PK RD	156	SE
BELDING	105	SW
BELFAST	133	NW
BELL	156	SW
BELLAIRE	162	NW
BELLCREEK	99	SE
BELLCREEK CT	99	SW
BELLE	146	NE
BELLEDALE	160	SW
BELLETERRE	133	NE
BELLEVUE	126	NW
BELMONT	121	NE
BELMONT D.BORN	143	NE
BELMONT ALLEN PK	162	NW
BELTON DETROIT	130	NW
BELTON GAR. CTY	141	NE
BELVIDERE	122	SE
BENDIX	149	NE
BENDON	140	SW
BENHAM	122	SW
BENITEAU	137	NE
BENNET	153	NW
BENNETT WY. DOT	164	SW
BENNETT AVE LIV.	98	SE
BENNETT CT	98	SE
BENSON	164	NW
BENSON DR	127	NE
BENTLER	116	SE
BENTLEY LIVONIA	114	NW
BENTLEY W.LAND	140	SE
BENZIE	140	SE
BERDEN	110	SE
BEREA	129	SW
BERESFORD AVE	120	NE
BERKSHIRE D.BORN	146	SW
BERKSHIRE AL. PK	154	SW
BERKSHIRE R.VIEW	170	SE
BERKSHIRE LA GR. POINTE	124	NW
BERKSHIRE RD GR. PARK	138	NE
BERN	130	NW
BERNARD	121	NW
BERNARD TAYLOR	161	NE
BERNS CT	111	SW
BERRES	121	NE
BERRY DETROIT	107	SW
BERRY W.LAND	139	SE
BERT LA INKSTER	141	NW
BERVILLE	140	SE
BERWICK LIVONIA	113	NE
BERWICK W.LAND	127	NE
BERWICK D.BORN	145	SW
BERWYN	115	NW
BESSEMORE	122	NE
BETHUNE E	121	SW
BETHUNE W	121	SW
BETRAM	127	NE
BETTY LA	141	NW
BEVERLY GR. POINT	125	SE
BEVERLY ALLEN PK	154	SW
BEVERLY CT DET.	133	NE
BEVERLY RD ROM.	151	SW
BEVERLY PLAZA	151	SW
BEWICK	122	SE
BIBBINS	157	SE
BICENTENNIAL	98	NE
BIDDLE DETROIT	134	SW
BIDDLE ROMULUS	158	NW
BIDDLE WAYNE	150	NW
BIDDLE AVE WY.DOT	164	SW
BILTMORE DETROI	103	SE
BILTMORE	142	NW
BINDER	107	SW
BINGHAM	145	NE
BINE	162	SE
BINRCH DETROIT	117	SE
BIRCH D.BORN	143	SE
BIRCH TAYLOR	153	SW
BIRCH ROMULUS	167	NE
BIRCH LA GR.PT.W	111	SE
BIRCHCREST D.BRN	105	NW
BIRCHCREST DR DETROIT	154	NE
BIDDLE WY.DOTTE	164	SW
BIRCHDALE	151	SE
BIRCHLAWN AVE	127	SW
BIRCHWOOD INKS.	141	NE
BIRRELL AVE	163	SW
BIRWOOD	104	NE
BISHOP RD	110	SW
BISMARK	121	SE
BISON	127	SW
BLISS	108	NW
BIVOUAC	147	NW
BLACKBURN	113	NE
BLACKFOOT	127	SW
BLACKMORE	108	NE
BLACKSTONE DET	102	NE
BLACKSTONE INKS.	142	SW
BLAINE	133	NE
BLAIR DETROIT	122	SE
BLAIR ALLEN PK	162	NW
BLAIR LA D.BORN	145	SW
BLAIRMOOR CT	111	NE
BLAKE	106	NW
BLANCHE	155	NE
BLAND	146	SW
BLATY	161	NW
BLESSER	132	SW
BLOCK AVE	127	SE
BLOOM	107	SE
BLOOMFIELD AVE	155	NE
BLOOMFIELD DR	98	SW
BLOOMFIELD RD	105	NW
BLOOMSBURY PL	136	SW
BLOSSOM LA	111	SW
BLOSSINGHAM	142	NE
BLOSSINGHAM CIR	142	NE
BLOWERS	132	NE
BLUEBIRD LA	150	NE
BLUEHILL	110	SE
BLUE SHIES DR	98	NW
BLYTHE	132	NW
BOBRICH DR	98	SE
BOCK RD	141	NE
BOEING	115	SW
BOHL	122	SE
BOLDT	142	SE
BOLLETTE AVE	163	SW
BONAIR	130	SW
BONANZA	151	NE
BONDE	164	NE
BONDIE ALLEN PK	162	NW
BONDIE WY.DOT	163	SE
BONITA	109	SE
BONNIE	127	SE
BONZANO	164	NW
BOONE	145	NW
BOOTH	139	SW
BORDEAU	119	SE
BORMAN	117	SW
BORTLE	136	NE
BOSTON	142	SE
BOSTON POST	113	SW
BOSTON BLVD E	120	SW
BOSTON BLVD W	120	SW
BOSTWICK	147	SW
BOTSFORD	121	NW
BOULDER	110	NW
BOURASSA	164	NW
BOURNEMOUTH	111	SW
BOWIE DR	162	SW
BOWLES	132	SE
BOXWOOD	133	NE
BRACE	131	NW
BRADBY DR	136	SW
BRADEN	133	NW
BRADFORD	108	NE
BRADLEY	137	NW
BRADY	101	NE
BRADY RD	159	NE
BRADY DR	143	NE
BRAILE	102	NE
BRAINARD	135	SW
BRAINARD	143	NE
BRAMELL	130	SW
BRAMFORD	108	NW
BRANCASTER RD	111	SW
BRANCH W.LAND	140	SE
BRANCH DETROIT	156	NW
BRANDON W.LAND	139	NW
BRANDON DETROIT	147	NW
BRANDT	169	NW
BRANDT AVE	141	NW
BRANDT RD	167	NW
BRANFORD	145	SW
BREAKFAST	115	NW

BRECKENRIDGE 134 SE
BREMEN 162 NW
BRENDIN CT 100 SW
BRENNAN 156 NE
BRENNER 161 NW
BRENTWOOD DET. 186 NW
BRENTWOOD LIV. 100 NE
BRENTWOOD INKST. 142 NW
BRENTWOOD D.BRN 143 NE
BRENTWOOD E 108 NW
BREST AVE 162 SE
BRETTON DR LIV. 99 NW
BRETTON DR DET. 103 SW
BREWSTER D.BORN 145 NW
BREWSTER ST 136 NW
BRIAN 168 NW
BRIAN DR 161 NW
BRIARCLIFF DR 111 NE
BRIARCLIFF RD 105 NE
BRIARWOOD PL 139 SE
BRIDGE 128 NW
BRIDGE AVE 99 NW
BRIDGE AVE 127 SE
BRIDGE RD 172 SW
BRIGGS 162 SE
BRIMSON 108 SW
BRINGARD 109 NE
BRINKER 107 NW
BRINKET 137 NW
BRINSON 171 SW
BRISTOL LIVONIA 98 SW
BRISTOL W.LAND 128 NE
BRISTOL DETROIT 99 SW
BRISTOW 121 NE
BRITAIN 105 SW
BROADMOOR 113 NE
BROADMOOR CT 99 SE
BROAD STONE 111 SE
BROADSTREET 133 NE
BROADWAY DETROIT 135 SE
BROADWAY ECORSE 164 SW
BROCK 109 SW
BROCK RD 139 NE
BROCKTON 121 NE
BRODY W.LAND 123 SE
BRODY ALLEN PK 123 SW
BROMBACK 121 NW
BROMLEY 156 NW
BROOK 141 SW
BROOKFIELD AVE
     LIVONIA 99 NE
BROOKFIELD PL
     WAYNE 139 SW
BROOKLAWN 130 SE
BROOKLINE R.VIEW 170 SE
BROOKLINE 145 SW
BROOKLYN 148 NE
BROOKS 138 SW
BROOKSIDE CT 153 NW
BROOKSIDE N. 153 NW
BROOKSIDE S. 153 NW
BROOKVIEW LIVONIA 98 SW
BROOKVIEW DR 98 SE
BROOKWAY 167 NW
BROOKWOOD LA 145 SW
BROUSEVILLE 163 SW
BROWN 134 NW
BROWN AVE
     GARDEN CITY 141 NW
BROWNLEE 156 NE
BRUCE 137 NW
BRUCE 151 SW
BRUCKNER 146 NE
BRUNSWICK 124 NE
BRUSH 106 SW
BRUSH CT WAYNE 142 SW
BRUSH ST WAYNE 142 SW
BRYAN 129 SW
BRYANSTON
     CRESCENT 136 SW
BRYAR 139 NW
BRYAR 145 NE
BRYDAN 119 SW
BRYDEN 133 NW
BRYS DR N. 111 NE
BRYS DR S. 111 NE
BRYSON 150 NW
BUCHANAN 151 NW
BUCKINGHAM LIV. 113 NW
BUCKINGHAM D.BRN 143 NW
BUCKINGHAM
     ALLEN PARK 162 SE
BUCKINGHAM
     LINCOLN PARK 163 NW
BUCKINGHAM
     SOUTHGATE 162 SW
BUCKINGHAM RD 124 NW
BUELOW CT 147 SW
BUENA VISTA AVE 118 SW
BUFFALO BLVD 121 NE
BUFFALO CT 197 SE
BULWER 146 NE
BURCHILL CT 122 NE
BURDENO 156 NE
BURGER 121 NW
BURGER 143 NW
BURGESS 102 NW
BURKE 167 NE
BURLEY 146 SW
BURLINGAME 120 NE
BURLWOOD DR 144 NW
BURNATTE 133 NW
BURNING TREE PL 167 SW

BURNLY 128 SW
BURNS 143 SW
BURNS S.GATE 163 SW
BURNS AVE INKS. 151 NW
BURNS DR DET. 99 SW
BURNSIDE 121 NW
BURR 152 SE
BURRELL 134 SE
BURROUGHS 135 NW
BURT CT 116 NE
BURT RD 102 NE
BURTON DETROIT 151 NW
BURTON ROMULUS 167 SW
BURTON CT LIVON. 99 SW
BURWELL 133 SW
BUSHEY 147 NW
BUTLER 121 NE
BUTLER RD 145 NE
BUTTERNUT DET. 135 SW
BUTWELL 125 NW
BYFIELD 140 NW
BYFIELD 145 SW
BYRD 154 NW
BYRON DETROIT 120 SW
BYRON R.ROUGE 156 NE
C ST 123 SW
CABACIER 148 NW
CABOT 133 SW
CADET 147 NW
CADIEUX RD 110 SE
CADILLAC WAYNE 150 NE
CADILLAC GAR.CITY 127 SE
CADILLAC BLVD
     DETROIT 122 SE
CADILLAC SQ. 148 NE
CADMUS 140 SW
CADY 140 SW
CAELY 121 NE
CAHALAN 146 SE
CAIRNEY 122 SE
CALDWELL 140 SW
CALEDONIA 140 SW
CALHOUN D.BORN 145 NE
CALHOUN W.LAND 140 SE
CALIFORNIA LIV. 127 NE
CALIFORNIA TAYL. 156 SW
CALIFORNIA
     HIGHLAND PK 120 NE
CALIFORNIA S.GATE170 SE
CALLENDER AVE 163 SW
CALUMET 140 SW
CALVERT 130 SW
CALVIN GR. PT 125 NW
CALVIN TAYLOR 156 SW
CALVIN LINC.PK 162 NE
CAMBRIA 140 SW
CAMBRIDGE DET. 102 NW
CAMBRIDGE 99 SE
CAMBRIDGE
     D.BORN HT 129 NE
CAMBRIDGE D.BORN 142 SE
CAMBRIDGE
     MELVINDALE 154 NE
CAMBRIDGE W.LAND 139 SW
CAMBRIDGE
     GARDEN CITY 127 SE
CAMBRIDGE 6.GATE 171 SW
CAMDEN 123 NW
CAMERON 106 NE
CAMERON S.GATE 162 SE
CAMERON GR. PT 125 SW
CAMILLE 123 SW
CAMPBELL DET. 133 SE
CAMPBELL D.BORN 146 NE
CAMPBELL R.ROUGE 156 SW
CAMPUS
     D.BORN HTS. 130 SE
CANAL 138 NW
CANDLER 130 SW
CANFIELD E 122 SE
CANFIELD W D.BRN 129 NE
CANFIELD W DET. 135 NW
CANTERBURY
     WESTLAND 127 SE
CANTERBURY
     DEARBORN 146 SW
CANTON 111 NW
CANTON 121 SW
CANYON DETROIT 110 SW
CANYON W.LAND 139 NW
CAPE COD 160 SW
CAPITOL DET. 113 SE
CAPITOL LINCOLN 163 NW
CAPRI TER 127 NE
CARBIDEX 162 SW
CARBON 156 NE
CARBONDALE 133 NW
CARDINAL LA 140 SW
CARDONI 106 NE
CARDWELL 141 NE
CARIBOU 127 SW
CARL DR 114 SW
CARLETON 145 NW
CARLIN 132 NW
CARLING 130 SE
CARLISLE 139 SE
CARLSON 139 SW
CARLSTON AVE 156 SW
CARLTON 141 SE
CARLYSLE 121 SW
CARLYSLE CT 154 NW
CARMAN 106 NW
CARMEL DETROIT 106 NW
CARMEL LA GR. PT 125 NE

CARNEGIE ST 166 SW
CAROL LIVONIA 100 SE
CAROL MELVINDALE 155 NW
CAROLEE 152 NE
CAROLINE GR. PT 125 NW
CAROLINE DETROIT 162 NW
CARPENTER 111 NE
CARRIE 108 SW
CARRIE 108 NW
CARROUSEL 128 SW
CARSON 146 NE
CARTER DETROIT 133 NW
CARTER 162 NW
CARTNER 146 NE
CARTRIDGE 147 SW
CARY 168 NE
CARY S 157 SW
CASCADE DETROIT 119 SE
CASCADE W.LAND 140 SW
CASCO 140 SW
CASEVILLE 140 SW
CASEGRAIN 147 SW
CASINO 110 SW
CASINO WAY 137 SW
CASMERE 121 NE
CASPER 143 SW
CASPIAN 140 SW
CASS DETROIT 148 NE
CASS DEARBORN 145 SW
CASS TAYLOR 161 NW
CASTLE DETROIT 165 NW
CASTLE D.BORN 132 SE
CASTLE BLVD 171 NW
CASTLETON 118 SW
CATALPA AVE 171 NW
CATHERINE 130 NE
CATHEDRAL 130 NE
CAVALRY 147 NW
CAVELL 114 SW
CAVOUR 114 NE
CECIL 133 SE
CECILE 127 NE
CEDAR HARPER WDS 110 NE
CEDAR CT 126 NW
CEDAR ST 171 NW
CEDAR WAY ROM. 167 SE
CEDAR GROVE 119 NW
CEDARHURST PL 106 SW
CEDARLAWN DET. 118 SE
CEDARLAWN DR 162 SW
CEDAR RIDGE CT 169 SW
CEDAR RIDGE DR 169 SW
CELESTINE 109 SE
CENTER INKSTER 151 NW
CENTER WAYNE 139 SE
CENTRAL PARK DR 142 NW
CENTERBROOK 111 NE
CENTERVILLE 140 SW
CENTRAL DETROIT 133 NW
CENTRAL ROMULUS 167 SW
CENTRAL WY. DOT 171 SE
CENTRAL GAR.CTY 128 SE
CENTRALIA 101 NW
CENTRE 135 SE
CENTURY DR 145 SW
CHADWICK 118 SW
CHALFONTE DET. 118 NW
CHALFONTE GR. PK 125 SW
CHALMERS 138 NW
CHAMBERLAIN DET 158 NW
CHAMBERLAIN
     WAYNE 166 SW
CHAMPAIGN 162 NE
CHAMPINE 111 SW
CHANDLER DETROIT 121 SW
CHANDLER LINC.PK 163 NW
CHANDLER PARK DR 124 NW
CHANNING 140 SW
CHAPEL 102 SW
CHAPIN 121 SE
CHAREST 106 NE
CHARLEMANGE 122 NE
CHARLES DETROIT 151 NW
CHARLES GR. PT 125 SW
CHARLES D.BORN 145 NW
CHARLES R.ROUGE 156 NE
CHARLES TAYLOR 153 SW
CHARLESTON 106 NW
CHARLEVOIX DET. 136 NW
CHARLEVOIX
     WESTLAND 140 SE
CHARLEVOIX GR. PT 124 SE
CHARLESWORTH CT 129 SW
CHARLESWORTH RD 142 NE
CHARLOTTE DET. 135 SW
CHARLOTTE ECORSE 156 SW
CHARTER 155 SW
CHARWOOD 102 NW
CHASE D.BORN 132 SW
CHASE RD ROMULUS 157 NW
CHATEAUFORT PL 136 SW
CHATFIELD 146 SE
CHATHAM DETROIT 130 NW
CHATHAM ALLN PK 162 NW
CHATHAM R.VIEW 170 SE
CHATSWORTH 124 NW
CHEBOYGAN 140 SE
CHELSEA REDFORD 115 NE
CHELSEA DET. 123 NW
CHELTENHAM 130 SW
CHENE 121 SE
CHENLOT 119 SE
CHERBONEAU PL 136 SW

CHERNICK 160 NE
CHEROKEE GAR.CTY 152 NE
CHEROKEE DR DET. 132 NW
CHERRY DETROIT 167 NE
CHERRY AVE 141 SE
CHERRY AVE ROM 167 NW
CHERRY AVE
     SOUTHGATE 171 NW
CHERRY LA 142 NW
CHERRY GROVE 164 NW
CHERRY HILL 143 SW
CHERRY HILL CT 143 SE
CHERRY HILL TR 141 NE
CHERRYLAWN DET. 104 NE
CHERRYLAWN
     SOUTHGATE 162 SW
CHERRY VALLEY DR 142 NE
CHESHIRE 139 SW
CHESPEAKE 115 SW
CHESQUIERE CT 111 SW
CHESTER DETROIT 110 SE
CHESTER GAR. CTY 127 SE
CHESTERFIELD DET.105 NW
CHESTERFIELD
     TAYLOR 152 SW
CHESTNUT WAYNE 168 NE
CHESTNUT D.BORN 154 NW
CHESTNUT R.ROUGE156 SE
CHESTNUT W.DOT 171 NW
CHESTNUT ST INK. 141 SE
CHEYENNE 104 NW
CHICAGO 142 SE
CHICAGO BLVD 120 SW
CHICAGO W. 127 NW
CHIEF 127 SW
CHIPMAN 147 NE
CHIPPEWA 101 NE
CHOPE PL 124 NW
CHOPIN 133 SW
CHOVIN 145 NW
CHRIST CHURCH LA 125 SE
CHRISTIANCY 147 NW
CHRISTINE GR.PT 125 NE
CHRISTINE W.LAND 127 SW
CHRISTINE D.BORN 154 NE
CHRISTOPHER 121 NE
CHURCH R.LAND PK 106 SW
CHURCH DETROIT 148 NW
CHURCH CT 110 NE
CHURCHILL 134 NW
CHURCHILL AVE 162 SE
CHURCHILL BLVD 170 NE
CICOTTE 125 SW
CICOTTE ALLEN PK 156 NE
CICOTTE LINC. PK 163 NW
CINCINNATI 151 SW
CINCINNATI AVE
     ROMULUS 150 SW
CINDY 127 NW
CIRCLE DR 127 NW
CITRIN DR 159 NW
CIVIC PL 132 NE
CIVIC CENTER DR 148 NE
CLAIR AVE 141 SW
CLAIREPOINTE 138 NW
CLAIRMOUNT 133 NE
CLAIRVIEW
     GR. PT SHORES 125 NW
CLAIRVIEW DET. 111 SE
CLAIRVIEW
     D.BORN HTS 129 NE
CLAIRVIEW CT E
     GR. PT WOODS 111 SW
CLARENCE AVE 155 NE
CLARENDOLL 133 NE
CLARION 122 NE
CLARITA AVE 98 NE
CLARK WAYNE 139 SE
CLARK WY.DOTTE 163 SW
CLARK R.VIEW 171 SW
CLARK AVE 147 SE
CLARK ST 149 NE
CLARKDALE 147 NE
CLAUDE 161 SE
CLAUDIA CT 127 NW
CLAY 121 SW
CLAYBURN 131 NE
CLAYTON DETROIT 146 NE
CLAYTON W.LAND 140 SW
CLEMENT CIR E 125 NE
CLEMENT CIR N 125 NE
CLEMENT CIR S 125 NE
CLEMENT CIR W 125 NE
CLEVELAND DETROIT 147 NE
CLEVELAND LIVON. 114 SE
CLEVELAND D.BORN143 NE
CLEVELAND WAYNE 167 NE
CLEVELAND LINC.PK163 NW
CLEVELAND ROM. 150 SW
CLIFF 108 SW
CLIFFORD DETROIT 135 SE
CLIFFORD WY.DOT 164 NW
CLIFTON 133 SE
CLINTON TAYLOR 156 SW
CLINTON WY.DOT 163 NE
CLINTON D.BORN 145 NW
CLINTON ST WAYNE 150 NW
CLIPPERT DETROIT 146 NE
CLIPPERT TAYLOR 169 SW
CLOUGH 108 SE
CLOVER DETROIT 154 NE
CLOVER D.BORN 145 NW
CLOVERDALE 119 NW
CLOVERLAWN DET.115 NW

CLOVERLAWN TYLR. 161 SW
CLOVERLAWN LIN.PK163 SW
CLOVERLY RD 125 NW
COACHWOOD CT 170 SE
COBALT 146 SE
COBB D.BORN 146 NW
COBB RD DETROIT 133 SE
COCHISE 127 SE
COCHRANE 170 NW
CODDING 112 SW
CODY 107 SW
COE 137 SW
COGSWELL RD 165 NW
COHL 163 SE
COLFAX 133 NE
COLFVIEW 122 SW
COLGATE 152 NE
COLLEGE 108 SE
COLLEGE DETROIT 139 NW
COLLEGE D.BORN 130 SE
COLLEGE W.LAND 139 NW
COLLEGE LINC. PK 154 SE
COLLEEN CT 142 NW
COLLINGHAM 109 NE
COLLINGWOOD 120 SW
COLLINS HAMTRACK 121 SW
COLLINS AVE ROM. 167 NW
COLLINS CT
     BR. TWP 169 SW
COLEMAN 131 SE
COLEMAN 155 NW
COLONIAL GR. PT W111 SW
COLONIAL
     DEARBORN HTS. 129 NE
COLONIAL INKSTER 141 SE
COLONIAL DETROIT 156 NW
COLONIAL CT GR.PT111 SW
COLONIAL CT AL.PK162 NW
COLONY TAYLOR 161 SW
COLONY LA D.BORN 143 NW
COLORADO LIVON. 127 NE
COLORADO AVE ROM166 SW
COLORADO AVE
     H.LAND PK 120 NE
COLSON 151 SW
COLTON 105 NE
COLUMBIA RED.TWP 115 SW
COLUMBIA W.LAND 139 SE
COLUMBIA D.BORN 143 SW
COLUMBIA E. DET. 135 SE
COLUMBUS DET. 134 NE
COLUMBUS WAYNE 150 NE
COLUMBUS ST
     WAYNE 150 SW
COLVIN 171 SW
COLWELL 162 NE
COMANCHE 127 SE
COMMERCE 127 SE
COMMERCE DR N 145 NW
COMMERCE DR S 145 NW
COMMERCIAL 147 SW
COMMONWEALTH 135 SE
COMMONWEALTH AVE
     SOUTHGATE 171 NW
COMMOR 121 NW
COMPASS 159 NW
COMSTOCK LIVON. 98 NE
COMSTOCK HAMTK. 121 NE
CONANT 106 NE
CONCORD LIVONIA 113 SW
CONCORD DETROIT 122 NW
CONGER 122 SW
CONGRESS 148 NE
CONGRESS E 136 SE
CONLEY 107 SE
CONNECTICUT AVE 126 NE
CONNER 138 NW
CONNER 108 SE
CONNORS LA 123 SE
CONOVER PL 165 SW
CONRAD 146 NE
CONSTANCE DET. 131 NW
CONSTANCE CT 108 NE
CONTINENTAL 138 NW
CONTINENTAL CIR 160 NW
CONTINENTAL DR 160 NW
CONTINENTAL PKWY144 NE
CONWAY W.LAND 127 NE
CONWAY DETROIT 155 NE
COOK DETROIT 133 NW
COOK S.GATE 170 SE
COOK RD 114 SE
COOKE 142 SE
COOLEY DETROIT 128 NW
COOLIDGE
     DEARBORN HTS.129 SW
COOLIDGE WAYNE 150 NE
COOLIDGE LINC.PK 163 SW
COOLIDGE HWY 156 SE
COOPER DETROIT 122 SE
COOPER TAYLOR 156 SW
COPE 123 SE
COPLAND 109 SW
COPLIN 124 SW
COR A R.ROUGE 156 SW
COR A WY.DOT 164 SW
CORA AVE 155 NW
CORAM 109 NW
CORBETT 123 NW
CORBIN DETROIT 155 SE
CORBIN AVE
     MELVINDALE 155 NE
CORDELL DETROIT 147 SE
CORDELL ROM.TWP 151 SE
CORDOVA 107 NE

CORE 126 SE
COREY PL 127 NE
CORKTREE CT 167 SE
CORMAN 155 SE
CORNELL 143 SW
CORNWALL 124 SW
CORONA DR 142 SW
CORTLAND AL. PK 154 SW
CORTLAND AVE HILL PARK 120 NW
COTTRILL 139 SE
COULBURN 109 NW
COULTER 133 SW
COUNCIL HAMTRAM 121 SE
COUNCIL LINC. PK 155 SE
COUNTRY LA 130 SE
COUNTRY CLUB CIRCLE 170 SW
COUNTRY CLUB CT R. VIEW 170 SW
COUNTRY CLUB CT LIVONIA 98 SE
COUNTRY CLUB DR CR. PT. FARM 110 NE
COUNTRY CLUB DR GR. PT FARM 125 NE
COUNTRY CLUB LA GR. PT. FARM 111 SE
COURVILLE 109 SE
COVENTRY DETR. 106 NW
COVENTRY LIVONIA 113 NW
COVENTRY W.LAND 128 NE
COVENTRY DR 162 SE
COVENTRY LA 111 NE
COVERT 108 NE
COVINGTON DET 105 SE
COVINGTON DR 139 SW
COWAN RD 127 SE
COYLE 118 SW
CRAFT 111 SE
CRAIG GR. PT WDS 111 SW
CRAIG DETROIT 121 SE
CRAIG ROM. TWP 157 SE
CRAIG AVE GARDEN CITY 127 SE
CRANBROOK DET. 104 NE
CRANBROOK R. VIEW 170 SE
CRANDELL 154 NE
CRANE 122 SE
CRANFORD D.BORN 142 NW
CRANFORD GR. PT 125 SW
CRANMORE 119 NW
CRANSHAW 119 SW
CRANSTON 113 NE
CRAWFORD DET. 147 SW
CRAWFORD AVE BROWNSTOWN TWP 167 SE
CRECENT CT 139 SW
CRESCENT INKSTER 142 SW
CRESCENT D. BORN 142 SE
CRESCENT AL. PK 162 NW
CRESCENT CT 142 SE
CRESCENT DR 116 NE
CRESCENT LA 111 SW
CRESSWELL 122 SE
CRESTMONT 130 SE
CRESTON 140 SE
CRESTVIEW 143 SW
CRESTWOOD 129 SW
CRIXDALE E 108 NW
CROCUSLAWN 132 NE
CROISSANT 154 NW
CROMWELL D. BORN 143 NW
CROMWELL DETROIT 148 NW
CRONIN 142 NW
CROSLEY 145 NW
CROSSMAN 157 NE
CROWLEY DETROIT 133 SE
CROWLEY ROMULUS 149 SE
CROWLEY TAYLOR 153 SW
CROWN W. LAND 139 NE
CROWN DETROIT 156 NW
CRUEBNER 108 NE
CRUSADE 110 NW
CRUSE 118 NW
CRUSSLEY 147 SW
CRYSLER AVE 162 SW
CRYSTAL CT 151 NE
CULLEY RD 168 NE
CULBER 154 NW
CUMMINGS 152 NW
CUNNINGHAM AVE 171 NW
CURRIE CT 112 SE
CURRIER 151 NE
CURT 122 SW
CURTIS DETROIT 98 SE
CURTIS DEARBORN 144 NE
CURWOOD 107 SW
CUTLER 137 NW
CUSHING 110 NW
CUTTRELL 147 SW
CUSTER 121 SW
CYMBAL 122 SW
CYNTHIA AVE 170 NE
CYPRESS DETROIT 146 NW
CYPRESS TAYLOR 153 SW
CYPRESS RD ROM. 151 SW
DACOSTA 143 NW
DAILEY 133 NE
DAILEY CT 133 NE
DAKOTA W.LAND 126 NE
DAKOTA E 106 SW
DALBY 101 NE
DALE D. BORN HTS. 130 NW
DALE ALLEN PARK 162 NW
DALE DEARBORN 146 SW
DALE DR W. LAND 115 NE
DALLAS 121 SW
DALRYMAPLE 119 SW
DALZELLE 148 NW
DAMMAN 110 NE
DAN 121 SE
DANBURY 106 NW
DANCY 151 NW
DANE 121 SE
DANFORTH 121 SE
DANIEL 152 NW
DANIELS DETROIT 133 SE
DANIELS TAYLOR 168 SW
DANVERS 145 SW
DANZIG 128 NW
DARCY 116 NW
DARDANELLA 98 NW
DARIN 168 NE
DARK AVE 170 NE
DARMOUTH DETROIT 154 NW
DARTMOUTH CT 139 NE
DARTMOUTH D.BORN 152 NE
DARTMOUTH DR 139 NE
DARWIN 108 SW
DARWIN 140 NW
DARSHER 154 SE
DAVENPORT 135 SW
DAVEY CT 128 SW
DAVID DETROIT 122 SE
DAVID TAYLOR 161 NW
DAVID ME. DALE 155 NW
DAVIS PL DETROIT 135 NE
DAVIS ST 163 SE
DAVISON 108 SW
DAVISON RED. TWP 115 SW
DAVISON AV H. LAND 107 SW
DAVISON AVE W DET. 118 SE
DAVISON FWY 120 NW
DAWES 132 NE
DAWSON AVE 128 SE
DAYTON DETROIT 131 SW
DAYTON DETROIT 133 SW
DAYTON W. LAND 140 SW
DEACON 156 NW
DEAN DETROIT 107 SW
DEAN WAYNE 168 NW
DEAN LA GR. PT 125 NW
DEARBORN WAYNE 150 NE
DEARBORN D. BORN 146 SE
DEARBORN DETROIT 156 NE
DEARBORN RD N. DEARBORN 144 SE
DEARBORN RD S. MELVINDALE 145 SW
DEARBORNDALE 153 NW
DEARING 107 SW
DEBORAH LIVONIA 126 NW
DEBORAH RED. TWP 127 NW
DEBRA CT 152 SW
DE BUEL 122 NW
DECATUR W. LAND 140 SW
DECATUR D. BORN 143 SW
DEE 171 NE
DEEPLANDS CT 111 SE
DEEPLANDS RD N. 111 SE
DEEPLANDS RD S. 111 SE
DEERFIELD W. LAND 140 SW
DEERFIELD D. BORN 142 NW
DEERING 100 NE
DEFER 137 NE
DEHNER 112 SW
DELAND 157 SE
DELANY 150 SE
DELAWARE RED. TWP 115 NW
DELAWARE LIVONIA 101 NW
DELAWARE DETROIT 120 SE
DELHAY 114 SW
DELISLE 156 NE
DELMAR 121 NW
DELTA DETROIT 107 SE
DELTA W. LAND 140 SE
DELTON 140 SW
DEMEAN 155 SE
DEMING 147 NW
DEMING PL 123 SE
DENBY 101 NW
DENICE 140 NE
DENMARK 146 SW
DENNE 100 SW
DENNIS 146 NE
DENNISON 133 SW
DENTON 121 SE
DENVER 125 NW
DENWOOD 142 NE
DENWOOD S 142 NE
DE PETRIS WAY 125 NE
DEQUINDRE 106 NW
DERBY 106 NW
DESMOND 147 NW
DESNER 107 SE
DESOTO DETROIT 119 NW
DE SOTO INKSTER 142 SW
DETROIT DETROIT 124 NE
DETROIT D.BORN 154 NW
DETROIT IND. EXPY 158 NW
DETROIT LINC. PK 162 NE
DEVERAUX 133 SE
DEVINE 123 NW
DEVOE 162 SE
DEVON DETROIT 109 SW
DEVON W. LAND 139 NW
DEVONSHIRE D. BRN. 143 NW
DEVONSHIRE AL.PK 154 SW
DEVONSHIRE R. VIEW 170 SE
DEVONSHIRE RD 124 NW
DEWEY REDFORD TWP 111 SW
DEWEY DETROIT 135 NW
DEXTER DETROIT 105 SE
DEXTER AVE ROM. 166 SW
DEY 156 NE
DIANE W. LAND 127 NE
DIANE ROMULUS 157 NE
DICKERSON 138 NW
DILLINGHAM DR 139 NW
DILLON RD 141 NW
DISTEL 146 SE
DIVERSEY 133 SW
DIVISION DETROIT 136 SW
DIVISION R. ROUGE 156 NE
DIVISION AV INKSTR 141 SW
DIX S 155 NE
DIX HWY DEARBORN 146 NE
DIXFORD 155 SW
DIXIE 115 NW
DOBEL 108 SW
DOBSON 140 NW
DODGE DETROIT 151 SW
DODGE ROMULUS 167 SW
DOLAN 153 SW
DOLORES 100 SE
DOLPHIN 130 SW
DOLPHIN CT 130 SW
DOLSON 116 SW
DOMINE 121 NE
DONALD LIVONIA 112 NW
DONALD RED. TWP 115 NE
DONALD DETROIT 136 SE
DONALD D. BORN 132 SW
DONALD CT 115 NE
DONALDSON 143 SE
DONCASTER AVE 169 SW
DONCASTER CT 169 SW
DONNA LIVONIA 99 NE
DONNA W. LAND 128 NW
DONNELLY GAR. CTY 141 NE
DONNELLY AVE BROWNSTOWN TWP 169 SW
DONNELLY CT 169 SW
DORA AVE 155 NE
DORAIS 113 NW
DORCHESTER 137 NW
DOREMUS 121 NE
DORIS LIVONIA 100 NW
DORIS REDFORD TWP 115 SE
DORIS AVE H. LAND 120 NW
DOROTHY DETROIT 121 NE
DORR 140 SE
DORSET AVE 167 NW
DORSET CT 162 SE
DORSEY 140 SE
DORTHERN 125 NW
DOUGLAS GAR. CTY 152 NW
DOUGLAS INKSTER 140 NW
DOVER RED. TWP 130 NW
DOVER DETROIT 133 NW
DOVER GAR. CTY 127 SE
DOVER D.BORN HTS 142 NW
DOVER DEARBORN 144 NE
DOVER DR W.LAND 127 NW
DOW 115 NW
DOWLING 126 NE
DOWLING CT 139 SE
DOWNING AVE 155 SE
DOXTATER 142 NW
DOYLE 108 SW
DOYLE PL W 111 SE
DRAGOON CT 147 NW
DRAGOON CT 147 NW
DRAKE 108 SW
DRAKE AVE S.GATE 162 SE
DRENNAN 156 SW
DRESDEN 108 SE
DRESDEN 109 SW
DREXEL DETROIT 138 NW
DREXEL D.BORN HT 146 SW
DRIFTON 109 SW
DRISCOLL 144 NE
DROUILLARD 163 SW
DRU 167 SW
DRYSDALL AVE 170 NW
DRYDEN 140 SW
DUANE 119 SE
DUBAY 108 SW
DUBOIS HAMTRAMCK 121 NW
DUBOIS DETROIT 136 SW
DUCHARME PL 136 SW
DUCHESS 110 SW
DUDLEY 169 SE
DUMAY AVE 170 NW
DUMBARTON 133 NE
DUNCAN DETROIT 156 NW
DUNCAN TAYLOR 153 NW
DUNCAN TAYLOR 168 NW
DUNDEE DETROIT 133 NE
DUNDEE R.VIEW 170 SE
DUNKIRK 156 NW
DUNN RD 121 SE
DUNNING AVE 142 SW
DUNSTON 162 SW
DUPAGE 169 NW
DUPLEX 163 SW
DU PONT 156 NE
DUPREY 110 NE
DURAND DETROIT 136 NE
DURAND INKSTER 151 NE
DURHAM 105 NW
DU ROSE 125 SE
DUXBURY 144 SE
DWYER 107 SE
DWIGHT DETROIT 129 SW
DWIGHT R.ROUGE 156 NE
DYAR HAMTRAMCK 121 NW
DYAR 125 SE
EAGLE DETROIT 133 NW
EAGLE DEARBORN 146 NW
EAGLE W.LAND 140 SW
EARL 149 NE
EARLS PL 134 SE
EASLEY 140 NE
EASON AVE 105 SW
EAST & WEST 163 NE
EASTBOURNE RD 111 SW
EASTBROOK 111 NE
EASTBURN 109 NW
EASTERN INKSTER 141 SE
EAST ELECTRIC 163 SE
EASTERN PL 134 NW
EASTHAM 100 SE
EASTLAND DR 110 NE
EASTLAND VIL. DR 110 NE
EASTLAWN DETROIT 138 NW
EASTLAWN WAYNE 150 NE
EAST MAPLE 151 NE
EASTPORT 140 SW
EASTWIND LA 167 SE
EASTWOOD 108 SE
EASTWOOD 110 NW
EASTWOOD DR 141 SE
EATON 156 SW
ECKLES RD 112 NW
ECORSE 151 SE
EDCLIFF CT 164 NW
EDDON AVE 155 NE
EDEN 153 NW
EDGEFIELD 110 SE
EDGEMERE 125 SE
EDGEMONT 125 SW
EDGEMORE 109 NE
EDGETON 100 SW
EDGERTON W. LAND 140 SW
EDGERTON D. BORN 144 SE
EDGEVALE 106 SW
EDGEWOOD DETROIT 154 NW
EDGEWOOD LIVONIA 99 SW
EDINBOROUGH 142 SE
EDINBOROUGH RD 102 SW
EDINGTON RD 113 NW
EDISON DETROIT 119 SE
EDISON D. BORN 143 SE
EDISON AVE S. GATE 163 SE
EDITH 130 SW
EDLIE 137 NE
EDMORE 110 NW
EDMUND WAYNE 166 SW
EDMUND PL DET 135 SE
EDMUNDTON DR 111 NE
EDNA 143 SE
EDSEL INKSTER 142 SW
EDSEL DEARBORN 155 SE
EDSEL FORD FWY 134 NE
EDSHIRE 111 SE
EDWARD H. LAND PK 106 SW
EDWARD DEARBORN 143 NW
EDWARD INKSTER 141 NW
EDWARD N. HINES DR LIVONIA 127 NW
EDWARD N. HINES DR DEARBORN HTS 130 SE
EDWIN DETROIT 121 NE
EDWIN WESTLAND 139 SW
EDWIN S. DR 156 NE
8 MILE RD E. 109 NW
8 MILE RD W. 104 NW
8TH DETROIT 148 NW
8TH ST ECORSE 163 NE
8TH ST MELVINDALE 155 NW
8TH ST WYANDOTTE 171 NW
18TH ST DETROIT 148 NW
18TH ST ECORSE 156 SW
18TH ST WYANDOTTE 163 SE
EILEEN 115 SW
ELAINE W. LAND 140 SW
ELAINE TAYLOR 161 NE
ELAINE S. GATE 162 SE
ELBA REDFORD TWP 115 NW
ELBA PL DETROIT 136 NW
ELBRIDGE 140 SW
ELBRIDGE 121 NE
ELDON 108 SW
ELDON 122 NW
ELDRED 147 NW
ELDRIDGE 121 NE
ELEANOR 130 SW
ELECTRIC DETROIT 155 SE
ELECTRIC R. VIEW 171 SE
ELECTRIC E W-DOT 171 NE
11TH DETROIT 148 NW
11TH ST ECORSE 156 SW
11TH ST WYANDOTTE 163 SE
ELFORD CT 111 SE
ELGIN 108 SW
ELIAS 140 NE
ELIJAH McCOY DR 134 NW
ELIM CT 125 SE
ELIOT 135 NE
ELISA 139 NE
ELIZA 164 NW
ELIZABETH GR. PT. 138 SW
ELIZABETH DEARBORN HTS. 130 SW
ELIZABETH DETROIT 135 SW
ELIZABEHT WAYNE 140 SW
ELIZABETH R. ROUGE 156 SW
ELIZABETH AVE MELVINDALE 155 NW
ELIZABETH N D. BRN 143 NW
ELKHART 110 NW
ELKTON 140 SW
ELLAIR PL 125 SW
ELLEN LIVONIA 99 SW
ELLEN DETROIT 120 NW
ELLERY 121 NE
ELLERY PL 122 SW
ELLIOT 156 SW
ELLIS DETROIT 132 NE
ELLSWORTH 140 SW
ELLWARD 167 NE
ELM DETROIT 135 SW
ELM DEARBORN 143 SE
ELM WAYNE 167 NW
ELM HARPER WOODS 110 NE
ELM R. ROUGE 156 SE
ELM TAYLOR 161 NW
ELM ROMULUS 167 NE
ELM AVE INKSTER 141 SE
ELM ST WYANDOTTE 171 NE
ELM CIRCLE DR 142 SW
ELMDALE DETROIT 123 NW
ELMDALE D. BRON 143 SE
ELMER 133 SW
ELM GROVE DR 127 NE
ELMHURST AVE 120 NW
ELMIRA 113 SE
ELMO 108 SE
ELMSLEIGH LA 125 SW
ELMVIEW 157 SE
ELMWOOD DETROIT 122 SW
ELMWOOD D. BORN 143 SW
ELON 129 SE
ELON CT 129 SE
ELSA DETROIT 123 SW
ELSA GROSSE ILE 172 SW
ELSIE 113 NE
ELSINORE 115 NW
ELSMERE 146 SE
ELTON 156 SW
ELWOOD 149 NW
EMANON 132 SE
EMELINE 107 SE
EMERSON DETROIT 138 NW
EMERSON INKSTER 141 NE
EMERSON W. LAND 140 SW
EMERY DETROIT 106 NW
EMERY 108 NW
EMERY D.BORN HTS 130 SW
EMILENE 156 SW
EMILY 108 SW
EMILY 155 SW
EMILY CT 127 SE
EMIT RD 169 SW
EMOGENE 155 SW
EMORY CT W. 111 SW
EMORY CT E 111 SW
EMMETT 162 SW
EMMONS DETROIT 123 SW
EMMONS BLVD W-DOT 163 NE
EMMONS CT W-DOT 164 NW
EMPIRE 162 SW
EMDICOTT 135 NW
ENFIELD 144 NE
ENGLE 137 NE
ENGLESIDE 108 SE
ENGLEWOOD DET. 120 NE
ENGLEWOOD AL. PK 162 NW
ENSLEY 140 SW
ENTERPRISE DR MELVINDALE 154 SE
ENTERPRISE DR WESTLAND 139 NE
EPWORTH 133 NE
ERBIE 122 NW
ERIE 147 SW
ERLE 106 SW
ERNEST 99 SW
ERSKINE 136 NW
ERWIN 140 SW
ESPER 132 NE
ESSEX DETROIT 138 NE
ESSEX D. BORN 146 SW
ESSEX ROMULUS 158 NW
ESSEX TAYLOR 161 NE
ESTHER 151 NE
ETHEL DETROIT 156 NW
ETHEL LINC. PK 163 NE
ETON 152 NE
EUCLID WAYNE 150 NE
EUCLID LINC. PK 154 SE
EUCLID E. DETROIT 121 SE
EUCLID W 120 SE
EUGENE DETROIT 123 SW
EUGENE D. BORN 145 NE
EUREKA DETROIT 107 SE
EUREKA AVE W-DOT 171 NE
EUREKA RD ROMULUS 106 NE
EVANGELINE 129 NE
EVANS DETROIT 146 SE
EVANS WAYNE 150 NE
EVANSTON 110 SW
EVELYN 99 SW
EVERGREEN RD 102 NE
EVERTS 110 SW
EWALD CIR 119 SW
EWERS 146 NE
EWING 158 SW
EXECUTIVE PLAZA DR 144 NE
EXETER 106 NW
EXILIA 169 NE
FABER 121 NE

STREET INDEX

Street	#	Dir
FAIR CT	111	NW
FAIR ACRES DR	125	NE
FAIRBAIRN	142	SW
FAIRCHILD W. LAND	139	SE
FAIRCHILD DETROIT	156	NW
FAIRCREST	109	NE
FAIRFAX LIVONIA	99	NW
FAIRFAX GR. PT PK	124	SE
FAIRFAX TAYLOR	161	NE
FAIRFIELD GAR. CRY	127	NE
FAIRFIELD LIVONIA	113	NE
FAIRFIELD DETROIT	105	NE
FAIRFORD RD	111	SE
FAIRGROVE	170	NW
FAIRHOLME	111	NE
FAIRLANE LIVONIA	99	NW
FAIRLANE W.LAND	140	NW
FAIRLANE DR	144	NW
FAIRMOUNT DETROIT	109	NE
FAIRMOUNT D.BORN	142	SE
FAIRMOUNT CT DEARBORN	142	SE
FAIRPORT	109	NW
FAIRVIEW DETROIT	123	ST
FAIRVIEW DEARBORN HTS.	130	SE
FAIRWAY LIVONIA	98	NE
FAIRWAY DEARBORN HTS.	130	SE
FAIRWAY CT D.BRN	142	SE
FAIRWAY DR D.BRN	142	SE
FAIRWAY DR DET.	105	SE
FAIRWAY LA	111	NE
FAIRWOOD D.BRN	142	NW
FAIRWOOD DR WESTLAND	129	SW
FALCON HAMTRK.	121	NE
FALCON D.BORN	146	SE
FARGO	99	NE
FARLEY	129	NE
FARMBROOK	110	SE
FAIRMOUNT RIVER ROUGE	156	SW
FARMER	135	SE
FARMINGTON	99	NW
FARNHAM	99	NW
FARNSWORTH	122	SW
FARNUM W.LAND	172	SE
FARNUM AVE INKS.	151	NW
FARR	122	SW
FARRAGUT	140	SW
FARRAND AVE	120	NE
FAUST	131	NW
FAYETTE	106	NW
FEDERAL	147	NW
FELCH	122	SE
FELICE	164	SW
FELLRATH	152	NE
FENELON	107	SE
FENKELL	116	NE
FENMORE	103	SW
FENTON	129	NE
FENWICK	146	NW
FERDINAND	147	NW
FERGUSON	117	NE
FERN	146	SE
FERNDALE	157	SE
FERNEY	146	SW
FERNHILL	106	NW
FERNWOOD DETROIT	158	SW
FERNWOOD AVE INK.	141	NW
FERRIS H.LAND PK	106	SW
FERRIS DETROIT	163	NE
FERRIS LINC. PK	163	NE
FERRY	122	SW
FERRY E	135	NW
FERRY W	135	NW
FIELD	122	SW
FIELDING	130	NE
5TH DETROIT	122	SW
5TH WAYNE	150	NW
5TH TAYLOR	152	SW
5TH ECORSE	156	SW
15TH DETROIT	148	NW
15TH ECORSE	156	SW
15TH WYANDOTTE	163	SE
51ST	146	NE
52ND	146	NE
FIGUEROA	129	SW
FILBERT DETROIT	109	NE
FILBERT W.LAND	140	NE
FILER	140	NE
FILMORE LIVONIA	99	NW
FILMORE WAYNE	150	NE
FILMORE TAYLOR	160	NE
FILMORE RD ROM.	157	NE
FINDLAY	108	SE
FINLEY	122	SE
FIRESTONE	145	NW
1ST DETROIT	164	NW
1ST WAYNE	150	NW
1ST TAYLOR	152	SW
1ST WYANDOTTE	172	NW
FIRWOOD	133	NE
FISCHER	122	SE
FISHER AVE	155	NE
FISHER FWY	147	SW
FISHER RD	125	NW
FISKE	137	NW
FITZGERALD	98	NE
FITZPATRICK	131	NW
FITZPATRICK CT	131	NW
FIVE POINTS	102	SE
FLAMINGO LIVONIA	100	NW
FLAMINGO W.LAND	128	NW
FLANDERS DETROIT	109	SE
FLANDERS AVE SOUTHGATE	163	NE
FLEETWOOD	110	NE
FLEMING DETROIT	106	NE
FLEMING D.BRN HTS	121	NW
FLETCHER DETROIT	107	NW
FLETCHER WAYNE	149	NE
FLORA WAYNE	139	SE
FLORA DETROIT	156	NW
FLORA AVE MELVINDALE	155	NE
FLORAL	100	NE
FLORANE	139	SE
FLORENCE DETROIT	103	SE
FLORENCE GAR.CTY	141	SE
FLORENCE INKSTER	101	SE
FLORENCE R.ROUGE	156	SW
FLORIAN	121	SW
FLORIA LIVONIA	127	NE
FLORIDA DETROIT	133	SW
FLOYD	123	SE
FLOWER CT	135	NE
FLYNN	140	SE
FOCH	100	SE
FOLEY	118	SW
FONVILLE CT	99	NW
FONVILLE DR	99	NW
FORD DETROIT	127	SW
FORD AVE W.DOT	163	SE
FORD BLVD LIN.PK	162	SE
FORD RD D.BORN	145	NW
FORD ST	133	SE
FORDALE	155	NE
FORDCROFT RD	111	SE
FORDHAM	109	NE
FORD LINE RD	162	SE
FORDSON RED. TWP	115	SW
FORDSON DETROIT	155	NE
FORDSON S D.BRN	143	NW
FORDSON CT	143	SW
FORDSON HWY	129	NE
FORDYCE	121	SW
FOREST W.LAND	127	SW
FOREST R.ROUGE	156	SW
FOREST LINC. PK	163	NW
FOREST WY.DOT	171	NE
FOREST AVE SOUTHGATE	170	NW
FOREST AVE WAYNE	150	NE
FOREST E DET.	135	NW
FOREST E DET.	135	NW
FOREST W DET.	135	NW
FOREST LA	135	NW
FORESTDALE AVE	167	NE
FOREST HILLS	130	SE
FORESTLAWN	108	SW
FORMAN	156	NE
FORRER	117	SW
FORT DEARBORN	143	NW
FORT E DETROIT	136	SE
FORT S DETROIT	135	SW
FORT W DETROIT	148	NE
FORTUNE	146	SE
FOSTER	122	SW
FOSTER	151	SW
FOUNTAIN	127	NW
FOURNIER	109	SW
14TH DETROIT	148	NW
14TH ST ECORSE	156	SW
14TH ST WY.DOTTE	163	SE
4TH TAYLOR	152	SW
4TH ST WY.DOTTE	150	NW
FOX REDFORD TWP	101	NW
FOX ALLEN PK.	162	SE
FOX AVE INKSTER	151	NW
FOXCROFT	130	SE
FOXGLEN DR	170	SW
FRAN CT	127	SW
FRANCAVILLA DR	99	SE
FRANCES	142	SW
FRANCIS DEARBORN	143	SE
FRANCIS AVE MELVINDALE	155	SW
FRANKFORT	124	NE
FRANKFORT	123	NE
FRANKLIN D.BORN	142	SE
FRANKLIN INKSTER	142	NE
FRANKLIN WAYNE	150	NE
FRANKLIN CT	109	SE
FRANSWORTH	136	NW
FRAZIER R.ROUGE	156	SW
FREDA DEARBORN	132	NE
FREDA INKSTER	142	NW
FREDERICK	135	NW
FREDERICK	152	NW
FREELAND	104	NW
FREEMAN	127	NW
FREER	146	NE
FREMONT LIVONIA	100	NW
FREMONT PL DET.	135	NW
FRENCH RD	108	SE
FRENCH RD	123	SW
FREUD	138	NW
FRIEDA CT	168	NW
FRONTEMAC	122	SW
FRUMAN CT	128	SW
FRUMAN CT E	128	SW
FULLERTON	118	SW
FULTON	146	SE
FERGUSON	117	NE
FURGERSON AVE	155	NW
GABLE DETROIT	133	SW
GABLE DR LIVONIA	99	NW
GABRIEL AVE	157	SE
GABRIEL RICHARD	143	NE
GAGE DETROIT	134	NE
GAGE TAYLOR	152	SE
GAHONA	144	SW
GAINES	117	SW
GAINSBOROUGH INKSTER	141	SE
GAINSBOROUGH RD DETROIT	103	SW
GALE	156	NW
GALLAGHER	107	SW
GARDEN LIVONIA	114	NE
GARDEN DETROIT	126	NE
GARDEN D.BORN	143	SW
GARDEN AVE	128	SE
GARDEN AVE GARDEN CITY	141	NE
GARDENDALE RD	105	NW
GARDNER	99	SE
GARFIELD REDFORD TWP.	101	NE
GARFIELD R.VIEW	171	SW
GARFIELD DETROIT	155	SW
GARFIELD WAYNE	150	NE
GARFIELD LINC. PK	163	NE
GARFIELD WY.DOT	164	SW
GARFIELD PL DET.	135	NE
GARLAND	123	SW
GARLAND	137	NW
GARNET	122	SE
GARNER	149	NW
GARRISON D.BORN	143	NW
GARRISON LA SOUTHGATE	170	NE
GARVETT	128	NE
GARVIN	107	SE
GARY DETROIT	106	NW
GARY	124	SW
GARY TAYLOR	152	SW
GARY ROMULUS	158	NW
GARY LA LIVONIA	99	NW
GATES	156	SE
GATESHEAD	111	SW
GAVEL	118	NE
GAY	112	NW
GAYLORD DETROIT	107	SE
GAYLORD RD. TWP	115	NW
GAYLORD LIVONIA	99	NW
GREAT LAKE	156	SE
GENESSE	156	SE
GENESEE	120	SE
GENEVA H.LAND PK	105	SE
GENEVA D.BORN	143	SW
GENNESSE	140	SE
GEORGE D.BORN HT	129	SW
GEORGE INKSTER	141	NW
GEORGELAND	119	SW
GEORGIA DETROIT	151	NE
GEORGIA LIVONIA	127	NE
GEORGIA	122	SE
GEORGIA BRN. TWP	169	SE
GEORGIA R.VIEW	170	SE
GERALD H.LAND PK	120	NE
GERALD WAYNE	150	NE
GERALDINE	128	NW
GERISCH	146	SE
GERONIMO	127	SW
GERTRUDE INKSTER	141	NE
GERTRUDE WAYNE	150	NE
GIBSON	135	SW
GIESE	108	SW
GILBERT	133	SE
GILBO	108	SW
GILCHRIST DETROIT	103	NE
GILCHRIST W.LAND	139	SW
GILL RD	99	NW
GILLETT	121	SW
GILMAN LIVONIA	100	NE
GILMAN GAR. CTY	141	NE
GILROY	156	NW
GIRARDIN	122	SW
GIRARDIN	108	NW
GITA AVE	114	NE
GITA CT	114	NE
GITRE	114	NE
GLADSTONE	134	NW
GLADWIN DETROIT	123	SE
GLADWIN TAYLOR	169	NE
GLADWIN WAYNE	140	SE
GLADYS	133	SE
GLASTER	133	NE
GLASTONBURY	127	SE
GLASTONBURY RD	117	NE
GLEASOM	155	SE
GLEN	141	SE
GLEN ARBOR	111	NE
GLENCO	122	SE
GLENDALE AVE	119	SE
GLENFIELD	109	SE
GLENGARY	129	NE
GLENHURST	102	NW
GLENIS	133	SE
GLENIS	160	NW
GLENMEADOW CT	139	SW
GLENMORE	101	NW
GLEN CT	146	SE
GLENN PL	120	NE
GLENWOOD	109	NE
GLENWOOD	139	SW
GLENWOOD	156	SW
GLENWOOD AVE	141	SE
GLINNAN	146	SE
GLOBE	126	SE
GLOBE	139	SE
GLORIA	150	NE
GLOUCESTER	139	NW
GLOUCESTER DR	105	NE
GLYNN CT	125	SW
GODDARD	107	SW
GODDARD CT	160	SW
GODDARD RD	162	SW
GODDARD RD	163	NE
GODDARD RD	121	NW
GOETHE	137	NW
GOETHE AVE	125	SW
GOETHE AVE	123	SE
GOFF	100	NE
GOLDEN BLVD	149	SE
GOLDENGATE W.	106	NW
GOLDEN RIDGE	167	SE
GOLDSMITH	147	NW
GOLFCREST CT	143	NE
GOLFCREST DR	143	NE
GOLFVIEW	98	NE
GOLFVIEW	130	SE
GOLFVIEW	129	NW
GOODELL	164	NW
GOODELL	100	NE
GOODSON	121	NE
GOODWIN	121	SW
GORDON	123	SW
GOUGH AVE	155	NW
GOULD	132	SW
GOULD	147	SW
GOVIN	146	SE
GRACE	122	SE
GRACE	149	NW
GRACELAND	142	SE
GRAHAM	116	NW
GRAHAM	133	SW
GRAHAM	156	SW
GRAND AVE	120	NW
GRAND BLVD E.	122	SW
GRAND BLVD E.	136	NE
GRAND BLVD W.	147	SE
GRANDE DR	167	SE
GRAND HAVEN	121	NW
GRANDMONT	117	SE
GRANDMONT	122	NE
GRANDMONT	131	NE
GRANDON AVE	127	NW
GRAND RIVER AVE	117	NE
GRAND TRAVERSE	140	SW
GRANDVIEW	141	NW
GRANDVIEW CT	101	NE
GRANDVILLE	117	NW
GRANDY	121	SE
GRANGE RD	170	SW
GRANGER	122	SE
GRANT	107	SW
GRANTLAND	112	SW
GRATIOT	109	NE
GRAVES	122	SE
GRAVIER	124	NE
GRAY	133	SW
GRAY	123	SE
GRAYFIELD	102	SW
GRAYLING	121	SE
GRAYTON	125	SW
GRAYTONA	113	SW
GREAT LAKE	155	SE
GREGOIRE	137	NW
GREELEY	106	NE
GREEN	147	SW
GREEN CT	111	NE
GREEN CT	163	NW
GREEN LA	114	NE
GREENBUSH	139	SE
GREENBUSH CT	117	SW
GREENDALE	106	SW
GREENFIELD CT	99	SE
GREENFIELD RD	155	NE
GREENLAND CT	99	SE
GREENLAWN	105	NW
GREEN LAWN	160	NE
GREENSBURO	110	SW
GREENSPAN	147	NW
GREENVIEW	131	NW
GREENVIEW AVE	167	NE
GREENWAY	133	NE
GREENWOOD	124	NE
GREENWOOD	139	NW
GREENWOOD CIR	139	NW
GREGORY	143	SE
GREGORY	162	NE
GREINER	109	SW
GRENNADA	114	NW
GRENNADA AVE	113	NE
GREY	162	NW
GREYDALE	102	NW
GREYFRIARS	155	SW
GRIFFIN	121	SE
GRIFFIN CT	99	SW
GRIGGS	118	NE
GRIMM	100	NE
GRINDLE PARK	143	SW
GRINNELL	122	NW
GRISWOLD	148	NE
GRIXDALE E.	106	SE
GRIXDALE W.	106	SE
GROESBECK HWY	108	NE
GROSCHNER	161	NW
GROSSE POINTE BLVD	125	NE
GROSSE POINTE CT	109	SW
GROTTO CT	109	SW
GROVE	177	NE
GROVE AVE	105	NE
GROVELAND AVE	167	SE
GROVER	109	SW
GROVER AVE	157	SE
GRUSSEL	147	NW
GUIDOT	153	SW
GUILFORD	124	NE
GULLEY PL	142	NE
GULLEY RD	142	SE
GUNSTON	108	SE
GUGIN	136	CW
GUTHRIE	122	NW
GUTHRIE	117	NE
HACKETT	117	NE
HAFELI	122	SW
HAGGARTY	132	SE
HAGUE	121	SW
HAIG	160	NW
HAIGH	143	SW
HALDANE DR	98	NE
HALE	136	NW
HALE	171	SW
HALECREEK AVE	167	NW
HALL	123	NW
HALL	151	NW
HALL PL	125	NE
HALLECK	121	NW
HALLER	114	NE
HALLY	128	NW
HALTINER AVE	158	SE
HAMANN	155	NW
HAMBLETON	113	SW
HAMBURG	109	NW
HAMILTON	143	SW
HAMILTON	121	SW
HAMILTON	155	SW
HAMILTON	150	NE
HAMILTON AVE	155	SW
HAMILTON CT	125	NE
HAMILTON RD	105	SE
HAMLET	107	NE
HAMLIN CT	125	NE
HAMMER	98	SE
HAMMOND	133	SE
HAMPDEN	168	NW
HAMPSHIRE	99	NW
HAMPSHIRE	123	NE
HAMPSHIRE	127	SE
HAMPSHIRE	143	NE
HAMPSHIRE CT	99	SE
HAMPTON	124	SW
HAMPTON CT	98	SE
HAMPTON CT E.	127	SW
HAMPTON CT W.	127	SW
HAMPTON RD	111	NE
HANCOCK E	136	NW
HANCOCK W	135	NW
HANCOCK DR	169	NE
HANDY	125	SE
HANFORD AVE	154	SE
HANLEY	121	NE
HANLEY	154	SE
HANLON	140	NW
HANLON	127	NW
HANNA	106	NE
HANNA AVE	155	NE
HANNAN RD	126	NW
HANOVER	152	NE
HANOVER	154	SE
HANSON	133	SE
HARBAUGH	141	SW
HARBOR	138	NE
HARBOR CT	125	NE
HARCOURT AVE	154	SE
HARDING	138	NE
HARDING	150	NE
HARDING	153	NE
HARDING	123	SW
HARDY	99	NE
HARLOW	103	SW
HARLOW AVE	154	SE
HARMON	162	NW
HARMON	140	NE
HARMON CT	127	SW
HARNED	125	NE
HARNOR CT	120	SE
HAROLD	154	SE
HARPER	110	SE
HARPER AVE	121	SE
HARRELL	123	NW
HARRIET	142	NW
HARRIET	155	NE
HARRINGTON	147	SW
HARRIS ST	156	NE
HARRISON	100	SE
HARRISON	114	NW
HARRISON	155	SE
HARRISON	154	SE
HARRISON AVE	141	NE
HARRISON BLVD	163	NE
HARRISON RD	135	SW
HARROUN	150	NW
HARROUN CT	150	NW
HART	137	NE
HART	123	SE
HARTEL	114	SE
HARTEL	128	NE
HARTFORD	134	NW
HARTWELL	142	SE
HARWELL	145	NE
HARWELL	152	SE
HARTWICK	121	SW
HARTWICK	162	NE
HARVARD	105	NE
HARVARD	143	SW
HARVARD RD	110	SW
HARVEY	127	SW
HARVEY	147	SE

Street		Street		Street		Street		Street		Street	
HASKELL	160 NE	HILL	105 SE	HUNTINGTON	128 NW	JOANNE	126 NE	KEPPEN	154 SE
HASKELL AVE	157 NE	HILL	142 NW	HUNTINGTON	170 SE	JOBIN AVE	171 NW	KERBY CT	125 NE
HASS	130 SW	HILL	156 NW	HUNTINGTON RD	103 SW	JOE	142 NW	KERBY RD	125 NW
HASSE	107 SE	HILL N.	140 SE	HUNTLEIGH	128 SW	JOHANNA	116 NE	KERCHEVAL	137 NE
	SE	HILL S.	140 SE	HUNTLEY AVE	169 SW	HOHNATHON	145 NE	KERR AVE	163 SW
HASTINGS	135 NW	HILL WAY	167 NW	HUNTLEY CT	169 SW	JOHN C. LODGE FWY	104 NW	KERSTYN DR	168 NW
HATHAWAY	127 NW	HILLBROOK AVE	99 NE	HURLBUT	122 SE	JOHN C. LODGE SERVICE DR	135 SW	KESSLER	102 SW
HATHON	122 SW	HILLCREST	125 NE	HURON	169 NE	JOHN DALY RD	152 NW	KEWADIN CT	141 SE
HAVANA	106 NW	HILLCREST DR	142 SE	HURON	153 NE	JOHN HAUK RD	141 NE	KEWEENAW	140 SE
HAVENLOCH	142 NW	HILLCREST DR	139 SW	HURON RIVER DR	157 SW	JOHN HIY RD	133 SW	KEYES W.	161 SW
HAVERHILL	109 SE	HILLGER	137 NE	HUSSAR	147 NW	JOHN KRONK	146 NW	KILBOURNE	133 SW
HAWTHORNE RD	111 NW	HILLS DR W.	147 NW	HYACINTIIE	156 SW	JOHN MONTEITH	143 NE	KIM	154 SE
HAWTHORNE	106 NE	HILLSBRIAR DR	167 SE	HYDE	122 SW	JOHN R	106 NW	KIMBERLY	170 NE
HAWTHORNE	141 NE	HILLSDALE	171 SE	HYDE PK	151 SE	JOHN R	139 SE	KIMBERLY CT	133 NE
HAWTHORNE	121 NW	HILLSIDE	129 SW	HYDE PK DR	167 SE	JOHNSON	147 NE	KIMLAND CT	129 NW
HAWTHORNE	127 SE	HILLVIEW	118 NW	HYMAN	139 SW	JOLIET PL	136 SW	KINCAID AVE	155 NE
HAWTHORNE PK	127 SE	HILLVIEW DR	128 SE	IDA LA E.	111 SW	JONAS	162 NE	KING	136 SW
HAWTHORNE RD	111 NW	HILLSBORO	133 NE	IDA LA W.	111 SW	JONATHON	132 SW	KING	121 SW
HAYES	151 NW	HINBARK	139 SE	IDAHO	105 SE	JONES	157 SE	KING	154 SW
HAYES	123 NE	HINDLE	121 NW	IDAHO	127 NE	JOSEPH	162 NE	KING RICHARD	110 SW
HAYES	152 SE	HINTON	171 SE	ILIAD	116 NW	JOSEPH	162 NE	KINGS CT E.	111 SW
HAZEL	152 NW	HIPP	161 NE	ILIENE	104 NE	JOS. CAMPAU	107 SW	KINGS CT W.	111 SW
HAZEL	160 NW	HIPP	169 NE	I ILLINOIS	127 NE	JOS. CAMPAU	136 NW	KINGSBURY	112 NW
HAZEL	134 SW	HIVELEY AVE	141 NW	ILLINOIS	136 NW	JOSEPHINE	121 SW	KINGS HWY	163 NE
HAZEL	162 SE	HIX	98 NW	IMPERIAL HWY	101 NE	JOSEPHINE	141 SE	KINGSBURY	142 NE
HAZEL	163 SE	HIX RD	139 NW	INA	143 NW	JOSEPHINE	150 NW	KINGSBURY CT	112 NW
HAZEL CT	150 SW	HIXFORD	139 NW	INDIAN	101 NW	JOSEPHINE	155 SE	KINGSLEY	121 SW
HAZEL ST	150 SW	HIZMET DR	100 SE	INDIAN CIR	150 SW	JOSEPHINE	164 NW	KINGSLEY	132 SE
HAZEL RIDGE	109 SE	HOBART	164 NW	INDIANA	127 NE	JOSHUA DOORE RD	169 NE	KINGSLEY RD	170 NW
HAZELTON	130 NW	HOGARTH	134 NW	INDIANA	118 SE	JOSLYN AVE	105 SE	KINGSTON	154 NW
HAZELWOOD	133 NE	HOLBORN	122 SW	INDIANDALE	120 NW	JOY RD	127 NW	KINGSTON CT	126 SW
HAZELWOOD	141 NW	HOLBROOK	121 NE	INDUSTRIAL	146 SW	JUDITH	139 SE	KINGSTON RD	105 NW
HAZLETT	133 SE	HOLCOMB	122 SE	INDUSTRIAL	166 NE	JUDITH AVE	168 NE	KINGSVILLE	110 NW
HEALY	107 SE	HOLDEN	132 NW	INDUSTRIAL DR E.	151 NW	JUDY	127 NE	KINGSWOOD	104 NW
HEARST AVE	150 SW	HOLFORD	156 SW	INDUSTRIAL DR N.	151 NW	JULIAN	133 NW	KINGSWOOD	102 NW
HEATHER LA	111 NE	HOLIDAY RD	111 SW	INDUSTRIAL DR S.	151 NW	JULIE	158 NW	KINGSWOOD AVE	145 SW
HEATHER PL	150 NE	HOLLAND	152 SW	INDUSTRIAL RD	113 SE	JULIUS	135 SE	KINGSWOOD CT	139 SW
HECK PL	136 NW	HOLLANDER	143 NW	INFANTRY	147 NW	JUNCTION	133 SE	KINLOCH AVE	101 NW
HECLA	134 NE	HOLLY	146 NW	INGLIS	146 NW	JUNE	140 NE	KINMORE	142 NE
HEDGE	121 NE	HOLLY	147 SW	INGRAM	99 NE	JUSTINE	107 SE	KINMORE CT	142 NE
HEES	127 NW	HOLLYWOOD	106 NW	INGRAM	127 NE	JUSTINE	143 NE	KINYON DR	162 NW
HEIDELBERG	136 NW	HOLLYWOOD	148 SW	INKSTER RD	169 SE	KAIER	146 SE	KIPKE	115 NW
HEIDT	166 SW	HOLLYWOOD	151 SW	INSELRUME	137 SW	KAIER	155 SE	KIPLING	134 NE
HEINTZ	122	HOLMES	121 NW	INTERVALE	118 NW	KALAMAZOO	140 SE	KIPLING	167 NW
HEINZE	143 NW	HOLMES	133 SW	INVERNESS	105 SE	KALASKA	101 NW	KIRBY	150 NE
HELEN	122 NW	HOLMUR	105 SW	IOSCO	140 SE	KALINE	135 SW	KIRBY E.	122 SW
HELEN	141 SE	HOMEDALE	133 SW	IOSCO	140 SE	KALSH	107 NW	KIRBY W.	105 NW
HELEN	148 NE	HOMER	146 SE	IOWA	127 NE	KANDT	142 SW	KIRKWOOD	133 SE
HELEN	162 SE	HOMEFIELD	152 SE	IRENE AVE	151 NE	KANE N.	116 NW	KIRKWOOD	133 SW
HELEN AVE	170 SE	HOMEPLACE	142 SE	IRIS	138 NE	KANTER	125 SW	KITCH	162 SW
HELEN AVE	111 NW	HOMESTEAD	161 SE	IRMA	149 SE	KARBON	154 NW	KITCHENER	138 NW
HELEN CT	168 NW	HOMESTEAD AVE	155 NW	IRON	136 SE	KAREN	128 NW	KLEBBA	161 SE
HELENA	166 SW	HOMESTEAD PL	135 NE	IRONSIDE	133 SE	KAREN	114 SE	KLEIN	121 SE
HEMINGWAY	115 SW	HOMORAN	164 NW	IRONSTONE LA	167 SE	KAREN	158 NW	KLEINOW	156 SW
HEMLOCK	133 SW	HOOKER	134 NE	IRONTON	156 SE	KARIN DR	102 SW	KLENK	138 NE
HEMLOCK	132 SW	HOOVER	162 NE	IRONWOOD	133 NE	KARL	102 SW	KLINGER	107 SW
HENDERSON	133 SW	HOOVER	150 NE	IROQUOIS	122 SE	KARL AVE	170 NE	KLINK AVE	151 NW
HENDRICKS	136 SW	HOPE	115 NW	IROQUOIS	127 SE	KARLE	139 NE	KNIGHT AVE	101 SE
HENDRICKSON DR	129 SW	HOPKINS	152 NE	IRVING	145 NE	KATHERINE	169 SE	KNODELL	122 NE
HENDRIE	122 SW	HORACE JACKSON AVE	150 SW	IRVING	161 NW	KATHRYN AVE	141 NE	KNOLL	139 NE
HENDRIE LA	125 NE	HORATIO	165 NW	IRVING DR	99 NW	KAUFMAN	153 NW	KNOLL WAY	167 NW
HENLEY PL	156 NE	HORGER	132 SW	IRVINGTON	106 NW	KAY	133 NE	KNOLLWOOD DR	145 SW
HENN	132 SW	HORGER	158 SE	IRVINGTON	115 SW	KEAL	102 SW	KNOLSON	125 SW
HENNEPIN	172 SW	HORTON	112 SW	ISABELLE	151 NE	KEAN	143 SW	KNOX	156 SW
HENNEPIN AVE	141 NE	HORTON	121 SW	ISHAM	122 NE	KEATING	106 NW	KNURLWOODE DR	171 SW
HENRY	113 NW	HOSMER	137 NW	ISLAND LA	125 SW	KEELER	118 NW	KOESTER	171 SW
HENRY	156 NE	HOUGHTON	112 NW	IVANHOE	115 NW	KEELSON DR	148 SW	KOLB	137 NW
HENRY	130 NW	HOUGHTON	98 SW	IVANHOE	133 NE	KEIBLER	117 SE	KOLB	162 SW
HENRY	151 NE	HOUSING	155 SW	JACKSON	170 NW	KEITH	129 NW	KONKEL	147 NW
HENRY	135 SW	HOUSTON	154 NW	JACKSON	162 SW	KELLER	156 NE	KOPERNICK	147 NW
HENRY AVE	155 NW	HOWARD	125 NE	JACKSON AVE	111 NW	KELL CT	168 NE	KORTE	144 NE
HENRY CT	141 NE	HOWARD	148 NE	JACOB	121 NE	KELLOGG	122 SE	KORTE AVE	138 NE
HENRY RUFF RD	100 SW	HOWARD	147 NW	JACQUELYNE	114 NW	KELLOGG PL	135 NE	KOTHS	162 NV
HERBERT	139 NE	HOWARD	155 SW	JAHN	98 NW	KELLY RD	110 NW	KRAFT PL	169 SE
HERBERT	126 SE	HOWARD	163 NW	HAMES	156 NE	KELSEY	172 SW	KRAMER	132 NE
HERBERT	119 SW	HOWE	143 SW	JAMES	164 SW	KEMPA	108 NW	KRAUSE	171 SW
HEREFORD	124 NE	HOWE	150 NW	JAMES AVE	127 SE	KEMPA	151 SW	KRAUTER	127 NE
HERITAGE CT	130 SE	HOWE CT	143 SW	JAMES AVE	163 SW	KENDAL	132 SW	KRESGE	122 NE
HERKMER	156 NE	HOWELL	115 NW	JAMES COUZENS	104 NW	KENDALL	116 NW	KRESS	102 SE
HERMAN AVE	157 NE	HOWELL	133 NE	JAMESON	137 NW	KENDALL AVE	120 NW	KRISTIN LA	170 SW
HERMOSE AVE	167 SE	HOY	114 NW	JAMESTOWN	146 NE	KENDALL CT	118 NW	KUBIS	128 SE
HERN	123 NW	HOYT	99 NE	JAMISON	113 NE	KENILWORTH	120 SE	KULICK	147 NE
HEROUX ST	157 SE	HUBBARD	113 SW	JAN	129 NW	KENILWORTH	132 SW	KURTSELL	141 SE
HERRICK	106 NW	HUBBARD	143 SW	JANE	109 SW	KENMORE DR	111 NE	LABADIE	164 SW
HERSHEY	147 SW	HUBBARD	163 NW	JANE	154 SE	KENNEBEC	108 SE	LA BELLE AVE	120 NW
HESSE	147 SW	HUBBARD AVE	127 NE	JANEY	152 NE	KENNEBEC	162 SE	LA BELLE CIR	111 SW
HESSEL	102 NW	HUBBARD CT	140 NE	JANICE	162 SE	KENNEBEC AVE	118 SE	LABLANCE	
HEWITT	121 NE	HUBBARD DR	161 NW	JANICE CT	101 NW	KENNEDY	127 NW	LACLEDE	163 NE
HEYDEN CT	16 SE	HUBBELL	114 SW	JARVIS	112 SW	KENNEDY	129 SW	LACROSSE	127 NW
HEYER	112 NW	HUBBELL	118 SW	JASPER	162 SE	KENNEDY DR J F	126 SE	LADYWOOD	98 SW
HEYER	149 SW	HUBBELL	143 NW	JASON	116 NW	KENNEDY PL	120 NE	LAFAYETTE	115 NE
HEYWOOD ST	149 SW	HUBER	121 NE	JAY	98 NE	KENNEYT	105 NW	LAFAYETTE	142 NE
HIBBARD	137 NW	HUBERT	162 NE	JEAN	168 SE	KENNETH	129 NW	LAFAYETTE	146 SE
HIGH	163 SW	HUBERT	167 SE	JEAN CT N.	139 SW	KENNEY	122 NW	LAFAYETTE B .VD	146 SF
HICKORY	98 NW	HUCK	141 SE	JEAN CT S.	139 SW	KENOSHAW	143 NW	LAFONTAINE	111 SV
HICKORY	109 NW	HUDSON	134 NE	JEANINE	100 SW	KENSINGTON	160 NE	LAHSER RD	102 NW
HICKORY	142 SE	HUDSON	143 SW	JEFFERSON	143 SW	KENSINGTON	162 SE	LAING	130 SW
HICKORY	135 SW	HUDSON	159 NW	JEFFERSON CT	136 SE	KENSINGTON RD	108 SE	LAKE CT	125 SW
HICKORY LA	139 NE	HUDSON	103 NE	JEFFERSON E.	124 SW	KENT	123 NE	LAKECREST LA	125 SW
HICKORY HOLLOW DR	150 NE	HUFF	98 SW	JEFFERSON W.	156 SW	KENT	165 NW	LAKELAND AVE	125 SW
HIDDEN LA	114 NW	HUFF	126 SW	JEFFERY	141 SW	KENT CT	162 SE	LAKEPOINTE AVE	138 NE
HIGBIE PL N.	111 SE	HUFF	112 NW	JEFFRIES FWY	115 SW	KENTFIELD	108 SE	LAKESIDE CT	125 SW
HIGBIE PL S.	111 SE	HUGH	100 NW	JEFFRIES FWY	112 SW	KENTFORD	117 NW	LAKESIDE DR	111 SE
HIGH ST	146 NE	HUGHES	119 NE	JENNIE	146 NE	KENTUCKY	104 NE	LAKE SHORE LA	111 SE
HIGHLAND	143 NW	HUGHES TER	134 NE	JENNIFER	129 NW	KENTUCKY	118 SE	LAKEVIEW	123 NE
HIGHLAND	163 SW	HULL	106 NE	JENNIFER CT	129 NW	KENWOOD	129 NW	LAKEVIEW	112 SW
HIGHLAND	162 NW	HUMBOLD	112 NW	JENNINGS	118 SW	KENWOOD	159 NW	LAKEVIEW CT	138 NE
HIGHLAND S.	143 NW	HUMPHREY	119 SE	JEROME	107 SW	KENWOOD	151 NW	LAKEVIEW	144 NE
HIGHLAND AVE	120 NW	HUMPHREY AVE	162 SW	JEROME	123 SW	KENWOOD CT	125 NE	LAKEVIEW CT	124 NW
HIGHVIEW	142 NE	HUNT	157 SE	JEROME	145 NW	KEOUGH	169 SE	LAKEWOOD	125 SW
HILDALE E.	107 NE	HUNT ST	149 NE	JEWELL	98 NE			LAMAR	100 SW
HILDALE E.	107 NW	HUNT CLUB	126 NW	JOAN	170 SE			LAMBERT	122 SW
HILDALE E.	108 NW	HUNTER AVE	127 SW	JOAN AVE	150 SW				
HILDEBRANDT RD	159 NE	HUNTINGTON	110 NW	JOAN CT	109 NW				
				JOANN	109 NW				

Street	No.	Dir.
LAMBIE PL	147	NE
LAMONT	148	NE
LAMONT	107	NE
LAMOTHE	134	NE
LAMOYNE	113	NW
LAMPHERE	102	SW
LANARK	110	SE
LANCASHIRE CT	99	SW
LANCASHIRE DR	127	SE
LANCASHIRE RD	103	SW
LANCASHIRE RD	99	SW
LANCASTER	110	NE
LANCASTER	114	NE
LANCASTER CT	112	NW
LANCE	168	SW
LANCO	132	NE
LANE	146	SE
LANEWOOD	128	NE
LANG	155	NE
LANMAN	134	SW
LANNETTE	109	SE
LANNOO	111	SW
LANSDOWNE	110	NW
LANSDOWNE DR	139	NE
LANSING	147	NW
LANSON	145	NW
LANTZ E.	107	NE
LAPEER	140	SE
LAPHAM CT	98	SW
LAPHAM DR	98	SW
LAPOINTE	169	NE
LAPPIN	109	NW
LARCHMONT	133	NE
LARCHMONT DR	139	NE
LARCHWOOD	106	NW
LARK	122	SW
LARKDALE	167	NE
LARKINS	133	SE
LARKSPUR LA	167	NE
LARME	154	SW
LARNED	148	NE
LASALLE	119	NE
LASALLE E.	134	NW
LASALLE W.	134	NW
LASALLE CT	119	NE
LASALLE GARDENS N.	134	NE
LASALLE GARDENS S.	134	NW
LATHERS	141	NE
LAUDER	104	NW
LAUDERDALE	147	SE
LAURA	123	SW
LAURA	149	NE
LAUREL	127	NW
LAUREL AVE	99	NW
LAUREL PARK DR. N.	98	SW
LAUREL PARK DR S.	98	SW
LAUREN	168	NW
LAURENCE	162	NE
LAURENWOOD DR	139	SW
LAW	143	NW
LAWLEY	107	SW
LAWN	142	NW
LAWNDALE	133	SW
LAWRENCE	139	NW
LAWRENCE	143	NW
LAWRENCE	126	NE
LAWRENCE	98	SW
LAWRENCE	139	NW
LAWRENCE CT	139	SE
LAWRENCE CT	139	NW
LAWRENCE DR	142	NW
LAWTON	105	SE
LEACH	137	NW
LEADER	168	NE
LEANDER	122	NW
LEAR CT	128	SE
LEBLANC	163	SW
LEBLANC	164	NW
LE BLANC	156	SW
LE BLANC	155	SE
LEDGECLIFF	128	SW
LEDYARD	135	SW
LEE	171	NE
LEE	111	NE
LEE PL	120	SW
LEE GATE	122	NE
LEELAWAU	140	SE
LEEWIN	101	NE
LEGRAND	122	SW
LEHIGH	152	NE
LEHMAN	122	SW
LEIB	136	SE
LEICESTER CT	120	SE
LEIDICH	123	NW
LEIGH	156	NE
LEITH	141	SE
LEJEUNE	163	NE
LELAND	143	SW
LELAND	135	NW
LEMAY	137	NE
LENAWEE	140	SE
LENNANE	101	NE
LENNON	111	NW
LENOIR	156	SW
LENOIR	162	SE
LENORE	101	NE
LENORE AVE	155	NW
LENOX	138	NW
LEO	161	SE
LEON	113	SW
LEONA	141	NE
LEONA	115	NE
LEONARD	156	NW
LEONARD	145	NE
LERNOULT	122	SE
LEROY	132	NE
LEROY	156	NE
LEROY	167	NW
LEROY AVE	171	NW
LEROY AVE	169	SE
LESLIE	111	SW
LESLIE	160	NW
LESLIE	140	SW
LESLIE	120	NW
LISLIE	161	SW
LESSING	137	NW
LESURE	118	SW
LEVAN	98	NE
LEVERETTE PL	148	NW
LEVERNE	115	SW
LEWERENZ	147	SW
LEWIS	127	SW
LEWISTON RD	125	NW
LEXINGTON	101	NW
LEXINGTON	115	NW
LEXINGTON PKWY	141	SW
LEXINGTON RD	111	SW
LIBERAL	109	NE
LIBERTY	162	NE
LIBERTY	121	SE
LIBERTY	151	NW
LIBERTY	128	NW
LIBRARY	135	SE
LICHFIELD RD	105	NE
LIDDESDALE	115	NW
LIDDICOT	139	SE
LIEBOLD	156	NW
LILA LA	142	NW
LILAC PL	156	SW
LILLBRIDGE	137	NE
LINCOLN	163	SE
LINCOLN	135	SW
LINCOLN	163	NE
LINCOLN	153	NW
LINCOLN	150	NE
LINCOLN AVE	120	NW
LINCOLN RD	156	SW
LINCOLNSHIRE DR	105	NE
LINDA	114	NW
LINDBERGH	163	SE
LINDEN	156	SW
LINDEN	154	NE
LINDENWOOD DR	145	SW
LINDSAY	103	SE
LINDSDALE	133	NE
LINNHURST	137	SE
LINSDALE	133	NE
LINVILLE	139	NE
LINVILLE	156	NW
LINWOOD	134	NW
LIONEL	126	NE
LIPTON	133	NE
LISA	158	NW
LISBON	147	NW
LITHGLOW	145	NW
LITTLEFIELD BLVD	104	NW
LITTLE STONE	111	SW
LIVERNOIS	105	NW
LIVERPOOL	112	NE
LIVINGSTON	161	SW
LIVONIA CT N.	114	NW
LIVONIA CT S.	114	NW
LLOYD	143	SW
LOCH LOMOND	142	SE
LOCHDALE	129	NE
LOCHMOOR BLVD	110	NE
LOCKWOOD	137	NE
LOCKWOOD	161	NE
LODEWYCK	110	SW
LODGE	137	NW
LODGE LA	143	NW
LOGAN	137	NE
LOG CABIN	105	SE
LOG CABIN RD	141	NW
LOIS	145	NE
LOITER WAY	137	SW
LOLA	147	NW
LOLA DR	101	SW
LOMBARD TR	134	SE
LONDON	105	SW
LONDON	104	NW
LONE OAK DR	144	NW
LONE PINE DR	127	SE
LONG	100	NE
LONG BLVD	143	NE
LONGACRE	117	SE
LONGFELLOW	120	SW
LONGMEADOW	145	SW
LONGSDORF	171	SW
LONGTIN AVE	163	NE
LONGVIEW	130	SW
LONGWOOD E.	106	SW
LONGWOOD W.	106	SW
LONGWORTH	98	SW
LONGYEAR	122	SW
LONNIE	127	NE
LONS	115	NE
LORAINE	133	SW
LORAINE	151	SE
LORAINE	135	SW
LORAINE	167	SE
LORAINE	134	SE
LORATO	135	SW
LORENZ	150	SE
LORETTO	109	SW
LORI	171	NE
LORI	152	SW
LORMAN	137	NW
LORMAN	159	NE
LORNE	153	SE
LORUSS	139	NW
LORUSS CT	139	NW
LOTHROP	134	NW
LOTHROP	125	NW
LOUIS	129	NE
LOUIS	137	NW
LOUIS	156	SW
LOUISE	127	NE
LOUISE	100	NW
LOUISE	162	NW
LOUISE AVE	105	SE
LOUISANA	106	NW
LOUISANA	127	NE
LOVELAND	99	NE
LOVETT	134	SW
LOVETT CT	151	NW
LOWDELL	155	NE
LOWELL	105	NE
LOWER ROUGE PKWY DR	142	SW
LOWREY	146	SW
LOZIER	124	SW
LUANA	154	SW
LUCE	107	SE
LUCE	140	SE
LUCERNE	105	NE
LUCERNE	115	NW
LUCERNE	142	SW
LUCERNE DR	162	SW
LUCKY	121	SE
LUCY	162	NW
LUDDEN	136	NW
LUDINGTON	171	SE
LUDINGTON	141	SE
LUMLEY	133	SW
LUMPKIN	106	NE
LUMPKIN	121	NW
LUTHER	156	NW
LYCASTE	137	SE
LYDIA	140	SE
LYFORD	122	NW
LYMAN PL	121	SW
LYNCH RD	122	NW
LYNDON	113	NE
LYNDON BLVD	115	NW
LYNN	121	NW
LYNN	158	NW
LYNX	127	NE
LYON	156	NE
LYONS	114	NE
LYSANDER	134	SE
LYTLE	141	NW
MABEL AVE	120	NW
MACARTHUR	101	NW
MAC CRARY	109	SE
MACK AVE	126	NE
MACKAY	107	SW
MACKENZIE	133	NW
MACKENZIE	127	NE
MACKENZIE CT	128	NE
MACKINAC	133	NE
MACINTYRE	102	NW
MACOMB	136	SW
MACON	122	NE
MADDELEIN	109	NE
MADDEN	160	NW
MADDEN CT	160	NE
MADEIRA	106	SE
MADISON	125	NW
MADISON	143	NW
MADISON	153	NW
MADISON	150	NE
MADRID	163	NE
MAES	139	NW
MAGNOLIA	134	SW
MAGNOLIA	141	SE
MAIDEN	123	NW
MAIN ST	150	NW
MAINE	127	NE
MAISON	111	SW
MAJESTIC	127	SW
MAJESTIC	133	SW
MAJOR	155	NE
MALCOLM	123	NW
MALCOLM	123	NW
MALCOLM AVE	106	SE
MALLINA	111	SW
MALLORY	98	SW
MALTA	116	NW
MALVERN	122	SW
MALVERN	128	SE
MALVINA	162	NE
MANCHESTER	128	NE
MANCHESTER AVE	106	SE
MANCHESTER BLVD	111	SW
MANDALAY	133	NW
MANDALE	146	SE
MANDERSON	105	SE
MANHATTAN	162	NE
MANILA	122	SE
MANISTEE	140	SE
MANISTIQUE	138	NE
MANNING	109	NW
MANNING CT	141	NE
MANOR	104	NE
MANOR	162	NW
MANOR AVE	125	NW
MANOR DR	162	SE
MANOR PARK DR	127	SE
MANSFIELD	132	SE
MANSFIELD	103	SE
MANSFIELD	128	SW
MANSON	147	NE
MANSUR	135	NW
MANUFACTURERS DR.	139	NE
MAPLE	113	SW
MAPLE	156	SE
MAPLE	145	NE
MAPLE	167	NW
MAPLE AVE	155	NE
MAPLE LA	155	NE
MAPLE St	171	NE
MAPLELAWN	162	SW
MAPLELAWN	160	SE
MAPLE RIDGE	109	SE
MAPLETON RD	125	NE
MAPLEVIEW	109	NW
MAPLEWOOD	133	NE
MAPLEWOOD	100	NE
MAPLEWOOD AVE	127	NE
MAQUADE	119	SE
MAR-ANN	141	NE
MARANTETTE	148	NW
MARBUD	109	NE
MARC	158	NW
MARCELLO DR	127	SE
MARCO DR	127	SE
MARCONI	167	SE
MARCUS	121	NE
MARDEN	149	NE
MARENE	102	SW
MARFORD	121	NW
MARGARET	157	NE
MARGARET	155	NE
MARGARET	153	NW
MARGARET W.	106	SW
MARGARETA	103	NE
MARGARETA	98	NW
MARIAN CT	111	NE
MARIE	156	SW
MARIE	146	NW
MARIE	112	NW
MARIE AVE	139	NW
MARIETTA	137	NW
MARIGOLD PL	150	NW
MARILYN	150	NW
MARIO ANN CT	157	SE
MARION	155	SE
MARION	162	NE
MARION	143	NE
MARION	115	NE
MARION-CRESCENT	129	NE
MARION INDUSTRIAL HWY	156	SE
MARISE	126	NE
MARJORIE	122	NW
MARK	170	NE
MARK	100	SW
MARK LA	102	SE
MARKESE	162	NE
MARKET	112	SE
MARKET	170	SW
MARKEY	140	SW
MARK TWAIN	104	NW
MARLBORO	147	NW
MARLBOROUGH	138	NE
MARLBOROUGH	162	NW
MARLER	121	SW
MARLOWE	104	NW
MARNE	110	SE
MARQUETTE	139	NW
MARQUETTE	137	NE
MARQUETTE AVE	106	SE
MARRY	122	SE
MARSEILLES	110	SE
MARSH	137	NE
MARSHA	171	NW
MARSHA	98	SW
MARSHALL	155	NE
MARSHALL	133	NE
MARSHALL	171	SE
MARSTON	121	SW
MARTEL AVE	145	SW
MARTHA N.	143	NW
MARTHA S.	143	NW
MARTIN	146	NE
MARTIN	139	SW
MARTIN	113	NE
MARTIN AVE	113	NE
MARTINDALE	133	NE
MARVIN	145	NE
MARX	106	NE
MARY	154	SW
MARY AVE	157	NE
MARYLAND	124	NW
MARYLAND	127	NE
MASON	140	SE
MASON	146	SE
MASON	116	NW
MASON	162	NE
MASON CT	112	NW
MASSACHUSETTS AVE	120	NE
MATHER	133	SW
MATTHEWS	136	SE
MATTHEWS	171	SW
MAUMEE	125	SW
MAXINE	150	NE
MAY	122	NE
MAY	143	SE
MAY	154	SW
MAYBURN	129	SW
MAYBURY GRAND	134	NW
MAYFAIR	161	SE
MAYFAIR	153	SE
MAYFIELD	109	SE
MAYFIELD AVE	99	NE
MAYFLOWER	163	NE
MAYLAWN	163	NE
MAYVILLE DR	100	SW
MAYWOOD	122	SW
MAYWOOD BLVD	170	NW
MC BRIDE	157	NE
MC BRIDE PL	118	SW
MC CANN AVE	162	SE
MC CLELLAN	122	SE
MC CORMICK	110	NW
MC DONALD	152	NW
MC DONALD	151	NE
MC DOUGALL	107	SW
MC GRAW	133	SW
MC GREGOR	147	NW
MC GUIRE	152	SW
MC KINLEY	153	NW
MC KINLEY	171	SE
MC KINLEY	163	NE
MC KINLEY PL	125	NW
MC KINNEY	100	SW
MC KINSTRY	147	SE
MC KITRICK AVE	155	NW
MC LAIN	162	NE
MC LEAN AVE	107	SW
MC MILLAN	147	NW
MC MILLAN	143	NW
MC MILLAN	125	NW
MCNAMARA DR	99	SW
MCNICHOLS RD E.	106	SE
MCNICHOLS RD W.	106	SW
MC PHERSON	121	NW
MEAD	145	NW
MEAD S	145	NW
MEADLAWN	130	SW
MEADOW AVE	167	NE
MEADOW CIR	151	NW
MERRIMAN	166	SE
MICHELLE	158	NW
MICHELLE CT	141	NW
MICHELLE CT	152	SW
MICHIGAN	162	SE
MICHIGAN AVE	141	SW
MICHIGAN AVE E.	149	NE
MICHIGAN AVE W.	150	NW
MIDDLE	132	NE
MIDDLE BELT RD	147	NE
MIDDLEBORO AVE	113	NE
MIDDLEBURY	144	SE
MIDDLEBURY N.	145	SW
MIDDLEBURY W.	145	SW
MIDDLEPOINTE	132	NE
MIDDLESEX	132	SW
MIDDLESEX BLVD	138	NE
MIDFIELD	117	NE
MIDLAND AVE	106	SW
MIDWAY	130	SW
MIDWAY	162	NE
MIDWAY	147	NW
MIDWAY N.	162	NW
MIDWAY S.	162	NW
MILBANK	108	NW
MILBOURN	128	NW
MILBURN	100	NW
MILDRED	150	NE
MILDRED N.	143	NW
MILES	122	SW
MILES AVE	162	SE
MILFORD	133	SE
MILI	162	NE
MILITARY	143	SE
MILITARY	147	NW
MILITARY	133	NE
MILITARY N.	143	NW
MILITARY S.	143	SE
MILITARY CIR	130	SW
MILL ST	163	NE
MILLARD	161	NE
MILLER	164	SW
MILLER	121	NE
MILLER	168	NE
MILLER RD	145	NE
MILLS	152	SE
MILNER	122	NE
MILWAUKEE	121	SW
MINERVA	139	SE
MINERVA	110	SE
MINDEN	109	SW
MINNEAPOLIS	124	NE
MINNESOTA	106	SW
MINNIE	162	NE
MINOCK	115	NW
MINOCK CIR	115	NW
MINT	146	SE
MINTON	126	NW
MINTON CT	127	NW
MINTON CT	126	NW
MIRABEAU PL	125	NE
MIRIAM	157	NE
MISSAUKEE	140	SE
MISSOURI	134	NE
MITCHELL	107	SW
MOCCASIN	127	SW
MOFFAT	122	SE
MOGUL	109	SE
MOHAWK	134	SW
MOHAWK	127	SW
MOHAWK	142	NE
MOHICAN	127	SW
MOLENA	162	NE
MOLINO	171	NE
MONARCH	109	NE
MONEART	107	SW

MONICA	105	NW	NAVARRE PL	136	SW	OAKDALE AVE	163	SW	PALLISTER	134	NE	PERRY PL	163	SE
MONMOUTH AVE	139	NW	NAVIN DR	99	NW	OAKFIELD	103	SE	PALMER	144	NE	PERSHING	100	SE
MONNIC CT	135	NE	NAVY	146	SE	OAKFIELD AVE	106	SE	PALMER RD	141	SE	PERSHING	146	SE
MONROE	136	SE	NEAL	122	SE	OAKLAND CTG	142	SE	PALMER E.	121	SE	PERSHING	139	SE
MONROE	164	NW	NEBRASKA	127	NE	OAKLAND DR	142	SW	PALMER AVE	155	NE	PERTH AVE	113	NE
MONROE	143	SE	NECKEL	132	SW	OAKLAWN	162	SW	PALMERSTON DR	156	SW	PETERBORO	135	SW
MONTANA W.	106	SE	NEFF RD	110	SE	OAKLEY	100	SE	PALMETTO	122	NW	PETER HUNT	122	NE
MONTANA CT	127	NE	NEGAUNEE	101	NW	OAKLEY	107	NE	PALMS	147	NE	PETERS	155	SE
MONTCALM W.	140	SE	NEGAUNEE	171	SE	OAKMAN	132	NE	PAMCO	113	SE	PETOSKEY	105	SW
MONTCALM W.	135	SE	NEIBEL	121	NW	OAKMAN CT	119	NE	PAMELA	168	NE			
MONTCLAIR	137	NE	NEIMAN	156	SW	OAKMAN BLVD	119	SW	PAMELA CT	139	NE	PFENT	109	NW
MONTEREY	170	NW	NELSON	168	SW	OAK POINTE DR	139	SW	PANAM	151	NE	PHELPS	122	SW
MONTE VISTA	109	NE	NELSON	118	SW	OAKRIDGE	130	SW	PANAMA	133	SW	PHELPS AVE	171	NW
MONTGOMERY	134	NW	NETHERWOOD AVE	163	SW	OAK TREE LA	167	NE	PARDEE	143	NW	PHILADELPHIA E.	121	SW
MONTICELLO	142	NW	NETT	122	NW	OAKVIEW	141	NE	PARDEE CT	153	NE	PHILADELPHIA W.	120	SE
MONTIE RD	103	SE	NEVADA	127	NE	OAKVIEW	139	NW	PARDO AVE	141	NE	PHILIP	138	NW
MONTLIEU	108	SW	NEVADA E.	106	SE	OAKWAY DR	137	SE	PARENT	139	NE	PHILLIPS	98	NW
MONTMORENCY	140	SE	NEVADA W.	106	SW	OAKWAY RD	137	SE	PARIS	154	SE	PHILOMENE	163	NW
MONTROSE	103	NE	NEVEUX	124	NE	OAKWOOD	139	NE	PARK	135	SE	PHIPPS	142	SW
MONTVILLE	120	NW	NEVILLE AVE	157	SW	OAKWOOD BLVD	154	NE	PARK	142	SW	PHYLLIS	107	SE
MOON	110	SE	NEW ST	164	NW	OAKWOOD	154	NW	PARK	162	NE	PHYLLIS		
MOORE	151	NE							PARK	113	SE	PHYLLIS	161	SW
MOORE	168	NW	NEWARD	148	SE	UAKWOOD AVE	140	SE	PARK	172	SW	PICHE	111	SW
MOORE CIR	151	NE	NEWBERN	107	SW	OCEANA	140	SE	PARK			PICADILLY RD	105	NW
			NEWBERRY	147	NW	OCEANA	162	NW	PARK N.	157	SE	PICKFORD AVE	90	SE
MOORE CT	151	NE	NEWBERRY PL	125	NW	O'CONNOR	155	SW	PARK S.	157	SE	PICKWICK CIR	161	NE
MOORE PL	134	NW	NEWBERRY ST	150	NW	O'CONNOR	163	NE	PARK AVE	98	SE	PICNIC WAY	137	SW
MOORE ST	149	NE	NEWBURGH RD	139	SE	OGDEN	115	NE	PARK AVE	109	SW	PIEDMONT	131	NW
MORAN	107	SW	NEWCASTLE	152	SE	OGDEN	133	SW	PARK DR	109	SW	PIERCE	136	NW
MORANG	110	NW	NEW CASTLE	111	SW	OGDEN AVE	149	NW	PARK LA	112	NE	PIERCE	151	NW
MORGAN	122	NW	NEWHALL	122	NW	OGEMAW	140	SE	PARK LA	172	SW	PIERCE AVE	141	NE
MORGAN DR	157	NE	NEWMAN	143	SE	OHIO	104	NE	PARK LA	127	SE	PIERCE CT	141	NW
MORLEY	126	SW	NEWPORT	124	SW	OHIO	133	NW	PARK PL	148	NE	PIERSON	102	NE
MORLEY	143	SE	NEWPORT	158	NW	OKLAHOMA	121	NW	PARK PL	150	SW	PIERSON CT N.	116	SE
MORLEY	161	SW	NEWTON	121	SE	OLA	151	SE	PARK ST	150	NW	PIERSON CT S.	116	SE
MORLEY CT	143	SE	NEW YORK	142	SW	OLD BROOK LA	125	NE	PARK TERR	111	NW	PILGRIM	101	SE
MORLEY DR	142	NW	NEW YORK	162	NE	OLD COLONY	130	SE	PARK CREST DR	111	NW	PINE	35	SW
MORLOCK	98	NE	NEW YORK	124	NE	OLD GODDARD RD	163	SW	PARKDALE AVE	112	SE	PINE	54	NW
MORNING GLORY PL	150	NE	NIAGARA	150	NE	OLDHAM	152	SE	PARKDALE CT	113	SW	PINE	169	NW
MORNING SIDE	146	SW	NICHOLS	150	NW	OLD HOMESTEAD	154	NW	PARKDALE TER	133	SE	PINE	156	SE
MORNINGSIDE DR	111	NE	NICOLET PL	136	SW	OLD MILL PL	119	SE	PARKER	99	NE	PINE	71	NE
MORNINGSTAR	98	NW	NIGHTINGALE	142	NE	OLDTOWN	110	SE	PARKER	177	SE	PINE CT	125	SE
MOROSS	132	NW	NIEMI	167	SW	OLD TOWN	170	SE	PARKER	143	SW	PINE ST	151	NW
MOROSS CT	132	NW	19TH ST	155	SE	OLGA	123	NW	PARKGROVE	109	SE	PINECREST DR	154	SW
MOROSS PL	125	NE	19TH ST	163	SE	OLIVE	157	SE	PARKGROVE DR	127	SW	PINEHURST	104	SE
MOROSS RD	110	NW	9TH ST	171	NE	OLIVER	121	NE	PARKHURST	112	NW	PINEHURST CT	113	NW
MORRELL	147	NE	9TH ST	163	NE	OLIVET	146	SE	PARKHURST PL	106	SW	PINETREE	113	SE
MORRIS	154	SE	NIVER	162	NW	OLMSTEAD	103	NW	PARKINSON	146	NE	PINEWOOD	109	NW
MORRIS	150	NW	NIXON AVE	169	SE	OLSON	128	NW	PARKLAND AVE	130	SW	PINEWOOD	122	EE
MORROW	121	SW	NOBLE	115	NE	OLYMPIA	101	NE	PARKLAND BLVD	127	SE	PINGREE	163	SW
MORROW AVE	156	SW	NOBLE	135	SW	OMAHA	155	SW	PARKLANE DR	112	NE	PIPER	151	NE
MORROW CIR	132	NE	NULA	98	NW	OMAHA BEACH DR	143	SE	PARKRIDGE DR	170	SW	PIQUETTE	135	SW
MORROW CIR S.	132	SE	NORBORNE	101	NW	OMAR	146	SE	PARKSIDE	105	NE	PITKIN	122	SW
MORROW	132	SE	NORBORNE CT N.	129	SW	OMARA	111	SE	PARKSIDE	154	NE	PITT	146	NE
MORSE	133	SE	NORBORNE CT S.	129	SW	OMIRA	106	SE	PARKVIEW	138	NW	PITT	164	NW
MOSELLE PL	125	NW	NORCROSS	123	NW	ONAWAY CTG	151	NE	PARKVIEW DR	139	SW	PITTSBURG	133	SE
MOSS AVE	106	SW	NORENE	139	SW	ONTARIO	124	NE	PARKVILLE	100	NE	PLAIN WAY	167	NW
MORTENVIEW	169	NE	NORFOLK AVE	100	SW	ONTONAGON	140	SE	PARKWAY W.	155	SW	PLAINFIELD	104	SE
MORTON	142	NW	NORFOLK CT	104	NW	OPAL	125	NW	PARKWAY	171	SW	PLAINVIEW	102	NE
MORTON	133	SE	NORMA AVE	139	NW	OPAL DR	145	NW	PARKWAY DR	111	NE	PLAINVIEW CT	112	NE
MOTOR BOAT LN	137	NW	NORMAN	101	NW	OPORTO AVE	100	SW	PARKWOOD	144	NW	PLATT	136	NW
MOUND	107	SE	NORMAN	155	NW	ORANGE AVE	171	NW	PARKWOOD AVE	141	SE	PLAZA S.	169	NW
MOUNTAIN WAY	107	NE	NORMAN	126	SW	ORANGE ST	171	NE	PARSONS	135	SW	PLAZA DR	155	NE
MT. ELLIOTT	107	SE	NORMANDALE	145	NW	ORANGELAWN	113	SE	PASADENA	120	NW	PLEASANT	155	NE
MOUNT VERNON	142	NW	NORMANDY	145	SW	ORCHARD	104	NW	PATRICIA	135	SW	PLEASANT AVE	113	NE
MT OLIVET	108	SW	NORMILE	132	NE	ORCHARD	156	SE	PATRICIA	156	NW	PLEASANT RIDGE E.	129	SW
MT VERNON	121	SW	NORRICE	140	SE	ORCHARD	171	NW	PATTERSON CRI	142	NW	PLEASANT RIDGE W.	129	SW
MT VERNON DR	160	SW	NORTH	105	SW	ORCHARD	168	NE	PATTON	100	NE	PLUM	98	NW
MOYES	133	SE	NORTH DR	145	NE	ORCHARD	167	NE	PATTON	130	NE	PLUM AVE	142	SW
MUELLER	161	NW	NORTHFIELD	133	NE	ORCHARD DR	139	SE	PATTON	122	NW	PLUM ST	171	NW
MUIR RD	125	NE	NORTHFIELD AVE	99	SE	ORCHARD LA	142	SE	PAUL	151	NW	PLUMER	145	SW
MUIRLAND	105	SE	NORTHGATE	140	SE	OREGON	133	NE	PAUL	161	SE	PLYMOUTH RD	113	SW
MULBERRY	171	NE	NORTHGATE	98	SE	OREGON	125	SE	PAULA	122	NW	POINCIANA	101	NW
MULBERRY	134	SE	N. HAMPTON	156	NW	OREGON	139	SE	PAULINA	172	NW	POINTER	66	NW
MULBERRY AVE	162	SE	NORTHAMPTON AVE	136	SW	ORIOLE	168	NE	PAWNEE	101	SW	POLAND	121	NW
MULFORD PL	120	NE	NORTHAMPTON CT	154	NW	ORION	108	SW	PAXTON CT	151	NE	POLK	153	NE
MULKEY	146	SW	NORTHLAND	151	NE	ORLEANS	134	SW	PAYNE	151	NE	POLK	156	SW
MULLANE	146	SE	NORTHLAND DR	98	NE	ORMOND	156	NW	PAYNE CT	145	NW	POLLICE	145	SE
MUNGEY	125	NW	NORTHLAWN	105	NW	ORR	151	SW	PAYTON	110	SW	POLLYANNA CT	99	NW
MUNGER	98	SW	NORTH MAPLE	151	NE	OSAGE	154	SW	PEACH AVE	171	NW	POLLANNA DR	99	NW
MUNGER CT	98	SE	NORTHMORE	142	NW	OSBORN	145	NE	PEACH TREE	111	SE	POMONA	101	SW
MUNICH	122	NW	NORTHWAY CT	162	NE	OSBORNE PL	145	NE	PEAR TREE LA	111	NE	POMONA	125	NW
MUNSON	152	SE	NORTHWAY NE	162	NE	OSCODA	140	SW	PEARL	146	NE	POND WAY	167	NE
MURAT	122	NW	NORTHWAY NE	162	NE	OSISKETA	125	SW	PEARL AVE	162	SE	PONTCHARTRAIN		
MURRAY	161	NW	NORTHWESTERN	134	SW	OSMUS	99	NE	PEASE	122	NW	BLVD	105	SE
MURRAY	143	NW	NORTHWOOD	141	SE	OTIS	146	NW	PEDIMONT	122	NW	PONTIAC	137	NW
MURRAY	122	SE	NORTHWOOD DR	144	NW	OTSEGO	133	NE	PEERLESS	110	NE	PONTIAC	132	SW
MURRY HILL	103	SE	NORTON CT	111	SW	OTTAWA	140	SE	PELHAM	164	NW	POPLAR	134	SE
MURWOOD	102	NW	NORVELL	122	SE	OTTERSUN CT	113	SW	PELHAM	162	NW	POPLAR	140	SW
MUSKEGON	100	SE	NORWALK	121	SW	OTTO	133	NW	PELKEY	109	SW	POPLAR	171	NE
MUSKET	147	SW	NORWAY	156	NW	OUTER DR	104	NE	PELOUZE	133	SE	POPLAR AVE	162	SE
MUSKOKA	125	NE	NORWICH RD	99	SW	OUTER DR	103	SE	PEMBERTON RD	138	NE	PORATH	145	NE
MYLER	152	SE	NORWOOD	107	NW	OUTER DR	154	NE	PEMBRIDGE PL	136	SW	PORATH CT	145	NE
MYRON	150	NW	NORWOOD	142	NE	OUTER DR E.	107	NW	PEMBROKE DR	98	NE	PORTAGE	121	NW
MYRON	163	NW	NOTRE DAME	152	NE	OUTER DR E.	109	SE	PENN	152	NW	PORTER	148	NW
MYRON DR	99	SW	NOTRE DAME	125	NW	OUTER DR E.	124	NW	PENN CT	98	SW	PORTER	147	NW
MYRTLE	143	NW	NOTRE DAME CT	152	NE	OUTER DR E.	122	NE	PENN DR	98	SW	PORTER	147	SE
MYRTLE	152	NE	NOTTINGHAM DR	125	NW	OUTER DR E.	123	NW	PENNIE	152	NE	PORTER	155	SW
MYRTLE	156	NE	NOTTINGHAM RD	110	SW	OUTER DR S.	155	SW	PENNINGTON DR	122	NW	PORTER AVE	163	NW
MYRTLE	135	SW	NOVARA	109	NE	OUTER DR W.	155	SE	PENNSYLVANIA	166	SW	PORTLAND	139	SW
NAGLE	122	SW	NOWAK	133	SE	OVEN PL	159	NE	PENNSYLVANIA	155	SE	PORT	138	NW
NANCY	120	NE	NOWLIN	125	NW	OWEN	121	SW	PENROD	117	NW	POWELL	156	NW
NANCY	127	NW	NUERNBERG	108	SW	OXBOW	128	NW	PENROSE	146	NW	POWERS	154	NW
NANCY	107	SW	NYE	114	NW	OXFORD	142	SW	PEORIA	109	SE	PRADO CT	42	SW
NANCY	140	NW	NYE CT	114	NW	OXFORD	171	NE	PEPPER	163	NE	PRAIRIE	105	NW
NANKIN BLVD	127	NW	NYMAN	149	NW	OXFORD CT	162	SE	PERBIN	128	NW	PRENTIS	135	NW
NANKIN CT	126	NE	OAK	114	NE	OXFORD DR N.	111	SE	PERE AVE	126	NW	PRESCOTT	121	NE
NANKIN LAKE DR	126	NE	OAK	100	SE	OXFORD DR S.	111	SE	PERKINS	133	SE	PRESCOTT	138	SE
NARDIN	119	SE	OAK	143	NW	OXFORD RD	111	NW	PERRIN	128	NW	PRESSLER	122	SW
NASH	143	NW	OAK	156	SE	OXLEY	103	NE	PERE AVE	126	NW	PREST	103	SE
NASHUA	137	SW	OAK E.	126	SW	OZCA	157	SE	PERKINS	133	SE	PRESTON	136	NW
NASHVILLE	109	SW	OAK	153	SW	PACET CT	111	SE	PERRIN	128	NW	PRESTON PL	111	SW
NATHALINE	115	SW	OAK ST	171	SW	PACIFIC	133	NE	PERRIN	156	SE	PRESTWICK S.	111	SW
NATIONAL	135	SW	OAKBROOK AVE	167	NW	PACKARD	108	NW	PERRIN DR E.	128	NE	PREVOST	103	SE
NAUMANN	107	SW	OAKDALE	98	SE	PADERESKI	100	SE	PERRIN DR W.	128	NE	PRIMROSE PL	139	NW
NAVAHOE	138	NW	OAKDALE	147	NE	PAGE	147	NE	PERRY	135	SW	PRINCE HALL DR	136	SW
NAVARRE	137	SW	OAKDALE	146	SE	PAGEL	163	NE	PERRY	157	SE	PRINCESS	142	SW

DETROIT — STREET INDEX

Street	No.	Quad
PRINCETON	105	SW
PRINCETON	142	SW
PRISCILLA LA	113	SW
PRIVATE	171	NW
PRIVATE RD	115	SE
PRIVATE RD	170	NW
PRIVATE FLANDERS	170	NW
PROCTOR	133	SW
PROGRESS	162	NE
PROMENADE	109	SE
PROMENADE	162	NW
PROSPECT	156	SE
PROSPECT	145	NW
PROVENCAL RD	111	SE
PRYOR	137	NW
PULASKI	121	NW
PULFORD	136	NW
PULLMAN AVE	163	SW
PURITAN	100	SW
PURLING BROOK	100	NW
PUTMAN	135	NW
QUAKERTOWN LA	98	SW
QUANDT	162	NW
QUARRY RD	171	SW
QUEEN	109	SE
QUEENSTON	105	NE
QUINCY	105	SW
QUINN	108	NW
RACHO RD	169	NE
RACHO SCHOOL DR	169	NE
RACINE	109	SW
RACKHAM	161	NE
RADCLIFFE	127	SW
RADCLEFFE	133	SW
RADEMACHER	147	SW
RADFORD	133	NE
RADNOR	110	SE
RADNOR CIR	125	SE
RADOM	121	NE
RAE CT	127	NE
RAHN	110	SW
RAILROAD AVE S.	155	NE
RAINBOW	144	SE
RALEIGH	112	SE
RALEIGH SQ	162	SW
RALPH	140	NW
RALSTON	106	NW
RAMBLEWOOD	113	NW
RAMEY	129	SE
RAMSAY	151	NE
RAN	161	SW
RANCOON	133	NW
RANDALL	147	NE
RANDOLPH RD	139	NW
RANDY	128	NW
RANKIN	147	SW
RANSPACH	147	NW
RATHBONE	125	SW
RATHBONE	146	SE
RAUPP AVE	155	SW
RAVENSWOOD	133	NE
RAVENWOOD BLVD	139	NE
RAVENWOOD DR	139	NE
RAVINE	100	SW
RAY	171	SW
RAY	162	NW
RAYBURN	98	SE
RAYMER	140	SE
RAYMOND	111	SW
RAYMOND	122	NE
RAYMOND CT	154	NW
RAYNOR	135	SE
REAUME	172	SW
REAUME PKWY	170	NE
REBECCA CIR	126	NE
REDFERN	102	SW
REDMAN	127	SW
REDMOND	110	NW
REDWOOD LA	167	NW
REECK RD	162	SW
REED AVE	155	NW
REEDER	147	SE
REGENE	140	SW
REGENT	171	NE
REGINA	163	NW
REGINALD	143	NW
REGIS	112	SW
REGULAR	147	SW
REID	147	SW
REINVALOT	172	SW
REISENER	156	NE
REMINGTON E.	106	NE
RENAUD RD	111	SW
RENAUD RD N.	111	NW
RENAUD RD S.	111	NW
RENEE AVE	102	NE
RENFREW RD	105	NE
RENO	109	NW
RENO	164	NW
RENO	171	SW
RENSELLOR	100	NE
RENVILLE	133	SW
RENWICK DR	98	NE
REO	124	SE
REO CT	98	SW
REO DR	98	SW
REUTER	145	NE
REVA	118	SW
REVERE	107	SW
REX	110	NW
REX	142	NE
REXWOOD	100	SW
REYNOLDS	107	SW
REYNOLDS	141	SE
RHODE ISLAND	120	NE
RIAD	110	NW
RIALTO AVE	155	SE
RICH	134	SW
RICHARD	151	NE
RICHARDSON	129	SW
RICHARDSON	157	SE
RICHARDSON	122	NW
RICHFIELD	98	SW
RICHLAND	127	NW
RICHMOND	162	SE
RICHMOND	142	NE
RICHTER	156	SE
RICHTER	123	SW
RICHTON AVE	120	NW
RICKHAM CT N.	139	SW
RICKHAM CT S.	139	SW
RICKIE	127	NW
RIDGE	140	SW
RIDGE	156	SW
RIDGE RD	125	NE
RIDGEBROOK PATH	111	NE
RIDGEMONT	142	NE
RIDGEMONT	125	NE
RIDGEMONT CT	142	NE
RIDGEWAY	129	NE
RIDGEWOOD	133	NE
RIEDEN	146	NE
RIES	155	SE
RIGA	114	NE
RIOPELLE	106	NE
RISDON	147	NE
RITA	128	NW
RITZ	127	NE
RIVARD	136	SW
RIVARD AVE	125	NW
RIVER CT	163	NE
RIVER LA	143	NW
RIVER RD	111	NE
RIVERBANK	163	SE
RIVERBANK N.	164	SW
RIVERBANK S.	163	SE
RIVERBANK RD	162	SE
RIVERBRIDGE DR	167	SE
RIVERDALE	142	SE
RIVERDALE E.	102	SW
RIVEROAK DR	102	SW
RIVER OAKS N.	111	NW
RIVER OAKS	142	SW
RIVER PARK	130	SW
RIVER PARK DR N.	142	SW
RIVER PARK DR S.	142	SW
RIVER PARK DR W.	142	SW
RIVERSIDE	130	SW
RIVERSIDE DR	99	SW
RIVERSIDE DR	138	SW
RIVERSIDE DR	163	SE
RIVERVIEW	130	NW
RIVERVIEW	116	SW
RIVER VIEW	141	SE
RIVIERA	133	NE
ROBERT	122	NE
ROBERT	161	NW
ROBERT AVE	155	NW
ROBERTSON	145	NW
ROBIN	142	NE
ROBIN	168	NE
ROBINDALE	142	NE
ROBINSON	152	NW
ROBINSON	154	SW
ROBINWOOD E.	106	NW
ROBINWOOD W.	106	NW
ROBINWOOD CT	172	SW
ROBSON	104	SW
ROBY	135	SW
ROCHELLE	142	NW
ROCHELLE	109	SE
ROCHESTER	119	SE
ROCKCASTLE	110	SE
ROCKFORD	142	NE
ROCKFORD	143	SW
ROCKDALE	130	SE
ROCKLAND	115	NW
ROCKLAND CT	129	SW
ROCKWOOD	121	NE
ROCKWOOD	156	SW
ROEMER	145	NW
ROGELL DR	159	NW
ROGER	135	SW
ROGERS	147	NW
ROGGE	108	NW
ROHNS	122	SE
ROLAND	122	NW
ROLANDALE	111	SW
ROLF	139	NE
ROLFS PL	136	NE
ROMAINE	157	NE
ROMEYN	147	NW
ROMULUS	157	NE
RONALD	157	NE
RONDA	162	SE
RONDO	109	NW
ROOSEVELT	147	NE
ROOSEVELT	141	SE
ROOSEVELT	154	SE
ROOSEVELT AVE	111	SW
ROOSEVELT PL	125	SW
ROSALIE	144	NE
ROSA PARKS BLVD	105	SW
ROSCOMMON	110	NE
ROSE	110	NE
ROSE	163	NW
ROSE	162	NE
ROSE AVE	155	SE
ROSE DR	160	NW
ROSEBURY	123	NW
ROSEDALE	121	NW
ROSEDALE	162	NE
ROSEDALE AVE	163	SW
ROSELAND	113	SE
ROSELAWN	105	NW
ROSELAWN	127	NE
ROSELLA	161	NE
ROSEMARY	109	SE
ROSEMARY	142	NW
ROSEMARY	123	NW
ROSEMONT	103	SW
ROSETTA	130	SW
ROSEVERE N.	143	NW
ROSEWOOD	162	SW
ROSEWOOD	141	SE
ROSEWOOD	157	SE
ROSEWOOD	161	SW
ROSLYN	127	NW
ROSLYN	154	NE
ROSLYN PL	105	NE
ROSLYN RD	105	NE
ROSLYN RD	111	NW
ROSS	112	NW
ROSS	152	NE
ROSS AVE	152	NE
ROSS CT	115	NE
ROSS DR	115	NE
ROSSINI	109	NE
ROSSITER	110	NW
ROSSLYN AVE	141	NW
ROTUNDA DR	145	NE
ROUGE CIR	130	SE
ROUGE CT	130	SE
ROUGE RD	155	SE
ROUGE RIVER DR	129	NW
ROUGEWAY	100	SE
ROULO	146	NW
ROWAN	147	SW
ROWE	108	NE
ROWE	141	SW
ROWLEY	107	SE
ROXBURY	110	SW
ROXFORD	142	NE
ROY	133	SW
ROYAL GRAND	115	NE
ROYALT	108	NW
ROYCROFT	113	NE
ROYCROFT AVE	113	NE
RUBY	145	NW
RUDGATE	162	SW
RUEDISALE CT	136	NE
RUGG	122	NW
RULOFF	156	SE
RUNYON	108	SE
RUPERT	107	SE
RUSH AVE	127	SE
RUSHMORE	168	NW
RUSKIN	147	NE
RUSSELL	127	NE
RUSSELL	106	NW
RUSSELL	124	NE
RUSSELL	155	SW
RUSSELL	163	NE
RUSTIC	141	SW
RUSTY	160	NE
RUTH	121	NE
RUTH	155	SW
RUTH	162	SE
RUTHERFORD	103	SE
RUTLAND	117	SE
RYAN	161	SW
RYANWOOD DR	170	SW
RYLAND	101	SW
SABELLE	107	SW
SADDLE LA	111	SE
SAGINAW	122	SW
SAGINAW	140	SE
SAINT	147	SW
ST AGNES CT	135	NE
ST ALOYSIUS ST	157	SW
ST ANTOINE	121	SW
ST AUBIN	106	NE
ST AUBIN PL	121	SW
ST CLAIR	137	NE
ST CLAIR AVE	125	NW
ST CYRIL	122	SW
ST DAVID	143	NE
ST HEDWIG	147	NW
ST IGNACE	171	SE
ST JAMES	146	NW
ST JEAN	137	NE
ST JOE	139	SW
ST JOHN	155	NE
ST JOHNS	162	SE
ST JOSEPH	132	SE
ST LAWRENCE	122	SW
ST LOUIS	157	SW
ST MARON PL	136	SW
ST MARTINS AVE	98	NW
ST MARYS	157	NE
ST MICHAEL	141	SE
ST PAUL	135	SW
ST PAUL	137	NW
ST PATRICK	122	NE
ST STEPHENS	103	SE
ST THOMAS	122	SW
SALEM	129	NE
SALEM LA	129	NE
SALINA	146	SW
SALLAN	121	NE
SALLIOTTE	155	SE
SALLY CT	152	SW
SALTER	141	SE
SAMPSON	148	NW
SAMUEL	151	NW
SANDBURG	167	NW
SANDERS	156	NW
SANDRA	142	NW
SANDRA	127	NE
SANFORD	108	SE
SANFORD	127	NE
SANGER	133	SW
SANILAC	110	NE
SAN JOSE	115	NW
SAN JUAN	105	NW
SANSBURN	140	SW
SANTA ANITA	114	NE
SANTA BARBARA	143	NW
SANTA CLARA	104	SE
SANTA MARIA	101	SW
SANTA ROSA DR	105	SW
SARASOTA	115	NE
SARASOTA CT	129	NE
SARATOGA	109	NE
SARENA	133	SW
SARGENT	150	SW
SARSFIELD	147	NE
SARVIS	147	NW
SAUER	108	SE
SAULINO	146	NW
SAVANNAH W.	143	NW
SAVERY	119	SE
SAVOIE BLVD	100	SE
SAVOY	147	NE
SAWYER	143	NW
SAXON	133	SW
SCARSDALE	103	SW
SCHAEFFER HWY	104	NW
SCHALLER	128	SW
SCHEFFER PL	122	SW
SCHILLER	137	NW
SCHLAFF	145	NW
SCHLEY	139	SE
SCHOENHER	109	NW
SCHOMBERG	161	NW
SCHOOL	140	NW
SCHOOLCRAFT	113	SE
SCHRADER	120	NW
SCHUPER	124	NW
SCHULTZ	162	NE
SCHULTZ	157	SE
SCHUMAN	127	SE
SCONE	113	NE
SCOTT	136	NW
SCOTT	142	SE
SCOTT CT	172	NW
SCOTT DR	168	NW
SCOTT ST	139	SW
SCOTTEN	147	NW
SCOTTSDALE CIR	126	NW
SCOVEL PL	134	NW
SCRIPPS	138	NE
SCRIPPS	125	SE
SEARS	152	SW
SEARS AVE	114	SW
SEATTLE	167	NE
SEAVITT	162	SW
SEAWAY FWY	162	SW
2ND BLVD	124	SE
2ND	152	SW
2ND AVE	120	NW
2ND ST	164	NW
2ND ST	172	NW
SECOR PL	135	NE
SEEBALDT	133	NE
SELDEN	135	SW
SELFRIDGE	147	NE
SELKIRK	122	SW
SELMA	139	SE
SELTZER	128	NE
SELWYN RD	171	NW
SEMINOLE	101	NW
SEMINOLE	121	NW
SENATOR	146	SE
SENECA	115	NW
SENECA	122	SW
SEQUOIA	127	SW
SERVICE RD	146	SE
7 MILE RD	98	NW
7 MILE RD E.	117	NW
7TH ST	156	SW
7TH	171	NE
17TH	148	NW
17TH ST	163	SE
SEVERN N.	111	SW
SEWARD	120	SE
SEXTON	130	SW
SEYBURN	122	SE
SEYMOUR	145	NW
SEYMOUR	145	NW
SHACKET	128	NW
SHADDICK	133	SW
SHADOW	142	NW
SHADOWLAWN	129	SW
SHADOW NOOK	137	SE
SHADY LA CT	147	NE
SHADY HOLLOW DR	143	NE
SHADY SIDW	126	SE
SHAFTSBURY RD	103	SW
SHAKESPERE	110	NW
SHANNON	161	NW
SHARI	129	NE
SHARON	141	SW
SHARON	133	SW
SHARON	133	SW
SHARON DR	126	SE
SHAWASSEE	140	SE
SHAWNEE	127	SW
SHEAHAN	142	NW
SHEFFIELD	140	SW
SHEFFIELD RD	105	NW
SHELBOURNE CT	125	NW
SHELBOURNE RD	111	SW
SHELBY	148	NE
SHELLYE CT	127	NW
SHENANDOAH	170	SE
SHENANDOAH RIVER DR	126	NE
SHERBOURNE	142	NW
SHERBOURNE	154	NE
SHERBOURNE RD	104	NE
SHERIDAN	122	SW
SHERIDAN	143	SW
SHERIDAN	141	NE
SHERMAN	102	NW
SHERWOOD	112	NW
SHERWOOD	98	SE
SHERWOOD	154	NE
SHERWOOD CT	98	SW
SHERY LA	162	SE
SHIAWASSEE RD	140	SE
SHIELDS	107	SW
SHIPHERD	136	NE
SHIPHERD CT	137	SW
SHIRLEY	118	SW
SHIRLEY	142	NW
SHOEMAKER	122	NE
SHOOK	157	NE
SHORE	131	SW
SHOREHAM	111	SE
SHORT	139	SE
SHOTKA RD	141	NE
SHREWSBURY DR	99	NE
SHREWSBURY	115	NW
SIBLEY	167	SW
SIDNEY AVE	158	SW
SIEBERT	122	NE
SIEBERT AVE	168	NW
SIEGEL	123	SE
SIL DR	160	NW
SILVERY LA	147	NW
SILBERY LA N.	162	NW
SILVIO DR	127	SE
SIMMS	108	SE
SIMS	150	NW
SIMS	142	NW
SIOUX	115	SW
SIRE	146	SE
SIRRON	115	SW
6TH ST	163	NE
6 MILE RD	99	NE
6TH ST	164	NE
6TH ST	171	NE
16TH	148	NW
16TH ST	156	SW
16TH ST	163	SE
SLEEPY HOLLOW	127	NW
SLOAN	146	SE
SLOAN	153	SW
SLOAN DR	115	SW
SLOAN	121	NW
SMART	133	SW
S.M.E. DR	143	NE
SMITH	121	SW
SMITH	154	NW
SMITH	159	NW
SMITH	171	SW
SMITH	157	NE
SNOW	154	SW
SNOW CT	154	NW
SNOWDEN	118	NE
SNOWDEN CT	154	NW
SOBIESKI	121	NE
SOBIESKI	107	SE
SOLVAY	146	SE
SOMERSET	110	SW
SOMERSET AVE	141	NE
SOMERSET DR	142	NW
SOHHEIL CT	171	SE
SOPHIA ST	139	SE
SORRENTO	104	NE
SOUTH	146	SE
SOUTHAMPTON	154	NE
SOUTHAMPTON AVE	98	SW
SOUTHAMPTON CT	99	SW
SOUTHAMPTON	125	NW
SOUTHFIELD FWY	117	SW
SOUTHFIELD RD	163	NE
SOUTHLAND E.	168	NW
SOUTHLAND W.	168	NW
SOUTH MAPLE	171	SW
SOUTHWESTERN	115	NW
SPAIN	167	NW
SPAIN CT	167	NW
SPARLING	107	SW
SPARTA	135	SW
SPAULDING CT	135	SW
SPINOZA DR	159	NW
SPOKANE	133	NE
SPRAGUE	135	SW
SPRING ARBOR DR	141	SW
SPRINGER	139	SW
SPRINGFIELD	123	SW
SPRING GARDEN	109	SW
SPRINGHILL	152	NE
SPRINGHILL AVE	167	NE
SPRINGLE	123	SE
SPRING VALLEY	127	NW
SPRINGWELLS	133	SW
SPRINGWELLS BLVD	109	SW
SPROAT	135	SW
SPRUCE	135	SW

STREET INDEX
DETROIT

SPRUCE 152 NE
SPRUCE 163 SE
SPRUCE 167 NE
SPRUCE AVE 171 NW
STACEY AVE 168 NW
STACEY CT 98 SW
STACEY DR 98 SW
STACEY 127 SW
STAHELIN 103 SW
STAIR 146 NE
STAMFORD DR 99 NW
STAMWICH BLVD 100 SW
STANDISH 113 SW
STANDISH 147 NE
STANDISH 127 SW
STANFORD 134 SW
STANFORD 152 NE
STANHOPE AVE 111 SW
STANLEY 134 NE
STANLEY AVE 155 SW
STANMOOR W. 100 SE
STANSBURY 101 NW
STANTO 134 NE
STANTON 125 NE
STANWOOD CT 151 NE
STARK 147 NW
STARK RD 113 NW
STATE 154 SW
STATE 135 SE
STATE FAIR E. 109 NE
STATE FAIR W. 106 NW
STATE FAIR 108 NW
STATLER 160 NE
STAWELL 133 NW
STEADMAN 145 NW
STEARNS 119 SW
STECKER 146 NW
STEEL 104 NW
STEEMER 116 SW
STEGER CT 105 SW
STEGNER 116 SW
STEINER 121 SE
STEINHAUER 141 NW
STELLWAGEN 150 NW
STENDER 106 SE
STEPHANIE 157 NE
STEPHEN 128 NW
STEPHENS 143 SW
STEPHENS RD 125 NW
STERLING 143 NW
STERLING 157 NE
STERLING 162 NE
STERRITT 122 NE
STEVENS 106 SW
STEVENS 161 NE
STEWART 163 NE
STEWART 158 NW
STIEBER 140 SW
STIMSON 135 SW
STOCKTON 107 SW
STOCKWELL 109 SE
STOEPEL 105 NW
STOEPELS PL 135 NE
STOKER 156 NW
STOLL 161 SW
STOLLMAN 142 NW
STONE 146 SE
STONEHOUSE 98 SW
STONEHURST 111 SE
STONER 156 SE
STOTTER 108 NW
STOUT 102 SE
STRASBURG 109 SW
STRATFORD RD
DETROIT 105 NE
STRATFORD
RIVERVIEW 170 SE
STRARFORD PL
GR. POINTE 125 SW
STRATHCONA DR 105 NE
STRATHMOOR 104 NW
STRATMANN 110 NW
STRATTON 146 NE
STREAM WAY 167 NW
STROH DR 135 SE
STRONG 122 SW
STUART 136 NE
STUART LA 145 SW
STUDENT 115 NW
STUDIO 153 SW
STURGIS 108 NE
STURTEVANT AVE 120 NW
SUBURBAN 164 SW
SULLIVAN 164 SW
SUMMER 101 NE
SUMNER 146 NW
SUMMERS 113 NE
SUMMERS CT 112 NW
SUMMERSIDE 114 NE
SUMMIT 147 SE
SUMMIT AVE 156 SW
SUNBURY 100 NE
SUNCREST 130 SW
SUNDERLAND RD 103 SW
SUNNINGDALE 142 NW
SUNNINGDALE DR 111 NW
SUNNYDALE 100 SE
SUNNYDALE AVE 98 SW
SUNSET 107 SW
SUNSET 100 NW
SUNSET DR 114 NW
SUNSET LA 125 SE
SUPERIOR 165 NW
SUPERIOR 156 SW
SUPERIOR AVE 170 NW
SUPERIOR BLVD 171 NW
SUPERIOR ST 171 NE
SURREY 99 SW
SURREY HEIGHTS 139 NW
SUSAN 170 SE
SUSAN CT 141 NW
SUSAN DR 160 NW
SUSANNA 98 NW
SUSSEX 112 NE
SUSSEX 103 SE
SUSSEX 143 NW
SUTTON 139 SW
SUZANNE 108 NW
SWANSON 150 NE
SWAIN 147 SE
SWATHMORE CT
CENTER 98 SW
SWATHMORE CT N. 98 SW
SWATHMORE CT S. 98 SW
SYBLEY ST 167 SE
SYCAMORE 135 SW
SYCAMORE ST 111 NE
SYLBERT CT 115 SE
SYLBERT DR N. 115 SE
SYLBERT DR S. 115 SE
SYLVAN 134 SW
SYLVAN 143 NW
SYLVESTER 136 NW
SYLVESTER 161 NW
SYLVIA 152 NW
SYLVIA 142 SW
SYRACUSE 143 SW
SYRACUSE 107 SE
TACOMA 109 NE
TAFT WAYNE 167 NW
TAFT ROMULUS 151 SW
TALBOT 121 NE
TAMI CIR 141 NW
TANGLEWOOD DR 137 SE
TAPPAN 122 NW
TARNOW 133 SW
TATE 129 NE
TAWAS TR 127 SW
TAYLOR DETROIT 120 SW
TAYLOR WAYNE 150 NE
TEACO 123 SE
TEAK LA 170 NW
TECUMSEH
REDFORD TWP 115 SW
TECUMSEH ECORSE 156 SE
TEGGE CT 151 NW
TELEGRAPH RD
DEARBORN HTS 101 NE
TELEGRAPH RD S
DEARBORN 143 NW
TEMPLE 135 SW
TENNANT 142 NW
TENNESSEE 138 NW
TENNY 143 SE
TENNYSON AVE 120 NE
10TH DETROIT 148 NW
10TH ST ECORSE 156 SW
10TH ST WY. DOT 163 SE
TEPPERT 108 NE
TERMINAL 137 NE
TERNES DETROIT 145 NW
TERNES DEARBORN 146 NW
TERREL 129 SW
TERRELL 108 NW
TERRENCE 100 SE
TERRI 127 NE
TERRY DETROIT 118 SW
TERRY ROMULUS 158 NW
TEXAS DEARBORN 154 NW
TEXAS CT LIVONIA 127 NE
THADDEUS BLVD 156 NE
THAMES 139 SE
THATCHER 102 SE
THAYER 133 SW
THEISEN 132 SE
THEODORE 135 NE
THERESA 139 NE
THE STRAND 137 SE
THINBARK CT 139 SE
3 MILE DR 124 NW
3RD DETROIT 106 SW
3RD WAYNE 150 NW
3RD TAYLOR 152 SW
3RD ST ECORSE 164 NW
30TH 134 SW
35TH 134 SW
31ST 134 SW
32ND 134 SW
33RD 134 SW
THOLE CT 105 SW
THOMAS ALLEN PK 162 NE
THOMAS TAYLOR 161 SW
THOMAS INKSTER 151 NW
THOMPSON CT 136 NW
THOMSON 120 NW
THORNCROFT CT 139 SW
THORNHILL PL 136 SW
THORNTON 118 SW
THORN TREE 111 SE
THOROFARE 172 SW
THORPE 128 NE
TILLMAN DETROIT 134 SW
TILLMAN D.BORN 143 SE
TIMBER RIDGE DR 144 NW
TIMBER TRAIL DR 142 NW
TIMES SQ. 135 SE
TIREMAN 133 NE
TIPTON 151 NE
TOBIN DR 142 SW
TOBINE RD 157 NE
TOD 140 SE
TOLEDO DETROIT 155 SW
TOLEDO RD
SOUTHGATE 163 SW
TOLES LA 111 NE
TOMAHAWK 127 SW
TONNANCOUR PL 125 SE
TONQUISH 127 SW
TORONTO 156 NW
TORREY CT DET. 134 SW
TORREY RD
GR. PT.WOODS 111 SE
TOURAINE RD 125 NW
TOURNIER 117 NW
TOWN LA 130 SE
TOWN CENTER DR 144 NW
TOWNSEND DET. 122 SW
TOWNSEND CT
BROWNSTOWN TWP 169 SW
TOWNSLEY 170 SE
TRACEY 104 NW
TRACTOR D.BORN 140 NW
TRACTOR DET. 156 NW
TRAFALGAR TYLR. 153 SW
TRAFALGAR
WESTLAND 140 NE
TRAIL RIDGE CT 169 SW
TRAIL RIDGE DR 169 SW
TRAVER 148 NW
TRAVERSE 122 NE
TRAVIS 170 SE
TRAYNOR 170 SE
TREADWAY PL 137 NW
TREADWELL 139 SE
TRENTON DETROIT 133 SW
TRENTON RD
SOUTHGATE 171 NW
TRENTON TER
DEARBORN 143 SW
TREVOR PL 136 SW
TRINITY 102 NE
TROESTER 109 SE
TROJAN 102 NW
TROLLY IND. DR 152 SW
TROMBLY 121 SE
TROMBLEY 124 SE
TROMLEY 141 NE
TROWBRIDGE DET. 121 NE
TROWBRIDGE
DEARBORN 147 SW
TROY 152 SE
TRUMBULL
HIGHLAND PK 120 NW
TRUMBULL DET. 135 SW
TULANE 153 NW
TULLER 119 NW
TUMEY 108 SW
TURBO 151 NE
TURNER DETROIT 119 NW
TURNER DETROIT 135 NE
TUSCANY CT 112 NW
TUSCOLA DET. 135 SW
TUSCOLA W.LAND 140 SE
TUXEDO D.BORN 146 SW
TUXEDO
HIGHLAND PARK 120 NW
12TH ECORSE 156 SW
12TH ST WY.DOT 163 SE
20TH DETROIT 147 NE
20TH ST WY.DOT 163 SW
28TH 134 SW
25TH 147 NE
21ST DETROIT 147 NE
21ST ST WY.DOT 163 SW
24TH 147 NE
29TH 134 SW
22ND DETROIT 147 NE
22ND WY.DOT 163 SW
23RD DETROIT 134 SE
23RD WY.DOTTE 163 SW
TYLER DETROIT 118 SW
TYLER WAYNE 150 NE
TYLER AVE
H.LAND PARK 120 NW
TYLER RD
ROMULUS 157 NW
TYNDALL 150 SW
TYRONE 110 SE
ULSTER 102 SW
UNDERWOOD 133 NE
UNION DETROIT 152 NE
UNION ECORSE 156 SW
UNION CT S.GATE 171 SW
UNIVERSAL 154 NW
UNIVERSITY
D.BORN HTS. 130 SE
UNIVERSITY
WESTLAND 140 NW
UNIVERSITY
LINC. PK 154 SE
UNIVERSITY
MELVINDALE 155 SW
UNIVERSITY 125 NW
UNIVERSITY PL
GR. POINTE 110 SE
UNIVERSITY PK DR 98 SW
UPLAND 139 SE
UTHES 147 NW
UTAH 127 NE
UTICA 119 SW
VACRI LA 99 SW
VALADE 171 SW
VALLEY
D.BORN HTS 130 SE
VALLEYVIEW
RIVERVIEW 170 SE
VALLEY VIEW
WESTLAND 127 NE
VALLEY VIEW DR
DEARBORN 144 NW
VAN CT 133 SE
VAN RD 98 NE
VAN ALSTYNE
BOULEVARD 172 NW
VAN ANTWERP 110 NE
VAN BORN CT 152 NE
VAN BORN RD 152 NE
VAN BUREN
D.BORN HTS 132 NW
VAN BUREN DET. 133 NW
VAN COURT 113 SE
VANCOUVER 133 NE
VANDERBUILT 146 SE
VAN DYKE 108 NW
VAN DYKE 122 NW
VAN DYKE PL 137 SE
VANLAWN 140 NW
VAN PETTEN ST 157 SW
VANSULL 140 NW
VARGO 98 SE
VARJO 108 SW
VARNEY 122 SW
VASSAR DETROIT 100 NW
VASSAR WY.DOT 171 SE
VAUGHAN 102 NE
VENDOME 125 NE
VENICE DETROIT 123 NW
VENICE D.BORN 144 SW
VENNESS AVE 171 NW
VENOY RD 158 NE
VENTURA CT 99 SW
VERI AVE 98 NE
VERMONT LIVONIA 127 NE
VERMONT DETROIT 148 NW
VERNE 102 SW
VERNIER CIR 111 NE
VERNIER RD 110 NE
VERNON 142 NE
VERNON AVE 169 SW
VERNOR HWY E 124 SE
VERNOR HWY E 137 NW
VERNOR HWY W. 147 NE
VERONA 109 NE
VERONICA 112 SE
VERONICA AVE 171 NW
VICKSBURG 134 NW
VICKSBURG 151 NE
VICTOR 120 NE
VICTORIA 107 SW
VICTORIA 155 SE
VICTORIA 102 NW
VICTORIA ST 156 NE
VIERTEL CT 136 NW
VIGO 133 SE
VILLAGE 171 SW
VILLAGE RD 144 SW
VINCENNES 125 NE
VINCENT 121 NE
VINCENT 142 NW
VINCENT 139 SW
VINEWOOD 147 SE
VINEWOOD 150 SW
VINEWOOD 147 SE
VINEWOOD 150 SW
VINEWOOD AVE 171 NE
VINING 158 NE
VINTON 122 NE
VIOLETLAWN 132 NE
VIRGIL 102 SW
VIRGINIA 111 NE
VIRGINIA 127 NE
VIRGINIA 171 NE
VIRGINIA 169 SW
VIRGINIA PK 120 SE
VISGER CT 156 SW
VISGER RD 155 SE
VISTA 137 SW
VIVIAN 152 NE
VOIGHT 171 SW
VOIGHT 172 SW
VOLTE 118 SW
VOSS 156 NE
VOTROBECK CT 102 NE
VOTROBECK DR 102 NE
VREELAND 171 SW
VULCAN 121 SW
WABASH 148 NW
WABASH 105 SW
WABASH 157 SW
WABASH AVE N. 155 NE
WABASH AVE S. 155 NE
WADE 124 NW
WADE 165 NW
WADSWORTH 113 SW
WADSWORTH 118 SW
WAGER 119 SE
WAGNER 133 SE
WAHRMAN AVE 157 SE
WAGNER CT 143 SE
WAKENDEN 101 NW
WAKEFIELD RD 105 NW
WALBRIDGE 122 SW
WALDEN 122 NW
WALDO 146 NE
WALKER 136 SE
WALKER ST 149 NE
WALL ST 127 SE
WALL ST 155 SW
WALLACE 122 SW
WALLACE 140 SW
WALLICK PL 135 NE
WALLINGFORD 124 NE
WALNUT 151 NE
WALNUT 154 NW
WALNUT 168 NW
WALNUT 156 SW
WALNUT 165 NW
WALNUT 171 NE
WALTON 139 SE
WALTON 133 SE
WALTER AVE 170 SW
WALTHAM 109 NW
WALWIT 145 NW
WANAMAKER 116 NW
WANDA 106 SE
WARD 104 NW
WARD 152 SE
WARD AVE 162 SE
WARING 155 SE
WARING 156 NW
WARNER 123 SW
WARNER CT 111 NW
WARNER RD 125 SE
WARREN 127 SW
WARREN E. 124 NW
WARREN W. 133 SW
WARREN CT 135 NE
WARREN RD 126 SW
WARRINGTON 129 SW
WARRINGTON DR 105 NW
WARSAW 135 NE
WARWICK 154 SE
WARWICK ST 155 SW
WASHBURN 104 NE
WASHINGTON
LIVONIA 127 NE
WASHINGTON
DEARBORN 143 SW
WASHINGTON
INKSTER 152 NE
WASHINGTON
WAYNE 158 NW
WASHINGTON
LINCOLN PARK 163 NE
WASTENAW 110 NW
WATERBURY DR 170 SW
WATERLOO 125 NW
WATERLOO 136 NE
WATERMAN 147 SW
WATKO 107 SW
WATSON PL 135 SE
WATSONIA 143 NW
WATT 151 NW
WAVENEY 124 NW
WAVERLEY
DEARBORN HTS 143 NW
WAVERLY S.
DEARBORN 143 NW
WAVERLY AVE
HIGHLAND PARK 119 NE
WAVERLY DR
SOUTHGATE 170 NW
WAVERLY LA 125 SE
WAYBURN 110 SW
WAYLAND 151 NE
WAYNE 113 SW
WAYNE RD 158 NW
WAYNECORSE 149 SE
WAYNESBORO 150 NE
WAYSIDE DR 139 NE
WAYSIDE PL 137 SW
WEAVER 117 SW
WEBB 120 NW
WEBSTER 111 SW
WEBSTER
WESTLAND 127 SW
WEBSTER
ECORSE 164 NW
WEDDEL 170 SW
WEIR 146 NW
WEITHHOFF 142 SW
WEITZEL CT 122 SW
WELCH 146 SW
WELLESLEY 145 NW
WELLESLEY DR
DETROIT 105 NE
WELLSLEY DR
INKSTER 141 SW
WELLINGTON
DETROIT 121 SW
WELLINGTON
DEARBORN 143 NW
WELLINGTON
INKSTER 152 NW
WELLINGTON AVE
TAYLOR 152 NW
WELLINGTON PL 125 SW
WELTON 119 SW
WENDELL 146 NE
WENDY R.VIEW 171 SW
WENDY LA
GR. PT. WOODS 111 NE
WENTWORTH 100 SW
WESLEY AVE 162 SE
WESSON 133 SE
WEST ST 111 NE
WESTBROOK 116 NE
WESTBROOK 102 SE
WESTBROOK DR 98 SE
WESTCHESTER RD 138 NE
WESTCIRCLE 143 NW
WESCOTT AVE
W.LAND 139 NW
WESCOTT CT
SOUTHGATE 170 NW
WESTCOTT DR
S.GATE 170 NW
WEST END 146 SE

Street	No.	Dir.
WESTERN	146	NW
WESTERN AVE	141	SW
WEST ELECTRIC	163	SE
WESTFIELD DETROIT	133	NW
WESTFIELD ECORSE	164	NW
WESTGATE	115	NW
WESTLAKE	152	NE
WESTLAND	127	SW
WESTLAND D.BORN	144	NE
WESTLAND CT	127	SW
WESTLAND EST WESTLAND	127	SW
WESTLANE	143	NE
WESTLANE CT	143	NE
WESTLAWN	146	SW
WEST MAPLE	151	NE
WESTMINSTER	121	SW
WESTMINSTER	170	NW
WESTMORE AVE	99	NE
WESTOVER	132	NE
WEST PARKWAY	102	SW
WESTPHAL	142	NW
WESTPHALIA	109	NW
WEST POINT DETROIT	169	NW
WEST POINT DEARBORN	143	NE
WESTSCHOOL	161	NE
WESTVALE	165	NW
WESTWICKE DR	150	NE
WESTWIND	125	NE
WESTWOOD DETROIT	117	SW
WESTWOOD CIR WESTLAND	126	NW
WESTWOOD CT ROMULUS	167	SE
WETHERBY	133	NW
WEXFORD	107	SW
WEXFORD	127	SW
WEYHER LIVONIA	100	NE
WEYHER DETROIT	123	NE
WHALEN	121	NW
WHEELER	133	SW
WHEELOCK	146	SE
WHITBY GAR. CTY	128	SW
WHITBY CT LIVON.	99	NW
WHITBY RD LIVON.	99	NW
WHITCOMB DET.	103	SE
WHITCOMB DR GR. PT. FARMS	125	SW
WHITE	163	NE
WHITEFIELD	133	NE
WHITEFIELD CT	142	NE
WHITEHALL	128	NE
WHITEHEAD	133	SE
WHITEHILL	110	SW
WHITEHORN AVE	157	SE
WHITEWOOD	133	SW
WHITING	121	SE
WHITINGTON	146	SW
WHITLOCK	133	SW
WHITMORE DET.	106	SW
WHITMORE D.BORN	143	NE
WHITNEY DETROIT	134	NW
WHITNEY WAYNE	139	SW
WHITTAKER	146	SE
WHITTIER D.BORN	142	SE
WHITTIER RD GR. POINTE PK	109	SE
WICK RD	157	NW
WICKHAM	159	NW
WICKS LA	111	NE
WIGHT	136	SE
WILBUR REDFORD TWP	115	NE
WILCOX DETROIT	131	SW
WILDBRANCH DR	144	NW
WILDEMERE	105	NW
WILDOFX CT	167	SE
WILDWOOD DETROIT	106	NW
WILDWOOD DEARBORN	143	NE
WILDWOOD AVE	127	SW
WILDWOOD DR	111	NW
WILFRED	109	SE
WILKE	148	SE
WILKIE	152	SE
WILKENS	136	SW
WILLARD	122	SE
WILLETTE	133	SE
WILLIAM TAYLOR	169	NE
WILLIAM CT E.	111	SE
WILLIAM CT W.	111	SE
WILLIAMS LIVON.	98	NE
WILLIAMS GR. PT FARMS	125	NW
WILLIAMS DET.	111	SW
WILLIAMS INKSTER	151	NE
WILLIAMS CT LIV.	98	NE
WILLIAMS ST WAYNE	149	NE
WILLIAMSBURG D.BORN HTS	145	SW
WILLIAMSBURG RIVERVIEW	170	SE
WILLIAMSBURG CT HARPER WOODS	110	NE
WILLIAMSBURG CT RIVERVIEW	170	SE
WILLIAMSON	132	SW
WILLIAMSON CT	132	SW
WILLIS E.	136	NW
WILLIS W.	135	SW
WILLOW COVE	154	NE
WILLOW E.	154	NE
WILLOW W.	154	NE
WILLOW CT ROMULUS	167	SE
WILLOW LA W.LAND	139	NW
WILLOW LA GR. PT FARMS	111	SE
WILLOWAY	143	NE
WILLOW TREE	167	NE
WILMER	126	SE
WILSHIRE DET.	109	SE
WILSHIRE LIVONIA	126	NE
WILSHIRE PKWY W.LAND	139	SE
WILSON DEARBORN	143	NW
WILSON LINC. PARK	163	NE
WILSON WAYNE	150	NE
WILSON CT BRN. TWP	169	SW
WINCHESTER W.LAND	127	SE
WINCHESTER DEARBORN	142	SE
WINCHESTER LINC. PK	163	NW
WINCHESTER E. DETROIT	106	NW
WINDER	135	SE
WINDHAM	148	NE
WINDMERE AVE	162	SE
WINDMERE CIR	170	SE
WINDMILL POINT DR	138	NE
WINDSOR DETROIT	125	NW
WINDSOR AVE WESTLAND	127	SE
WINFIELD DET.	122	NW
WING PL	147	NE
WININFRED	150	NE
WINKLEMAN	121	SE
WINONA W.LAND	127	SE
WINONA D.BORN	142	SE
WINONA ALLEN PK	154	SW
WINONA AVE HIGHLAND PK	120	NE
WINSLOW ST	150	NW
WINSTON	101	NE
WINTER DETROIT	135	NE
WINTER CT GARDEN CITY	141	NW
WINTHROP	103	SE
WINTHROP PL GR. PT FARMS	125	NE
WINWOOD AVE	169	SE
WINWOOD CT	169	SE
WISCASSET	145	SW
WISCONSIN	127	NE
WISCONSIN	118	SE
WITHERELL	135	SE
WITT	146	SE
WOHLFEIL	160	NE
WOLFF	147	NE
WOOD LIVONIA	98	SE
WOOD DETROIT	122	NE
WOOD AVE MELVINDALE	155	NW
WOODBINE DEARBORN HTS	101	NE
WOODBINE INKSTER	142	SW
WOODBOURNE	141	SW
WOODBRIDGE	136	SW
WOODBROOK DR	140	SE
WOODBURY DEARBORN	144	SE
WOODCREST DR HARPER WOODS	110	NW
WOODCREST DR DEARBORN	143	NE
WOODCROFT	142	SE
WOODHALL	110	SE
WOODINGHAM	150	NE
WOODINGHAM DR	105	NW
WOODLAND DETROIT	121	NW
WOODLAND INKS.	141	SW
WOODLAND DEARBORN	145	SW
WOODLAND DR HARPER WOODS	110	NE
WOODLAND PL GR. POINTE	125	SW
WOODLAWN DET.	122	NW
WOODLAWN TAYLOR	160	NE
WOODMERE	146	NE
WOODMONT HARPER WOODS	110	NE
WOODMONT DET.	167	NE
WOODMONT CT ROMULUS	167	NE
WOODMONT CT WAYNE	139	SW
WOODMONT PL DETROIT	131	NE
WOODRING	99	NE
WOODRING CT	99	SE
WOODROW REDFORD TWP	101	NW
WOODROW DETROIT	133	SE
WOODROW WILSON	120	NW
WOODS CIR DET.	136	SW
WOODSFIELD	141	NE
WOODSHIRE	129	SW
WOODSIDE DET.	154	NW
WOODSIDE ROMULUS TWP	151	SE
WOODSIDE DR DEARBORN	144	GW
WOODSIDE DR HARPER WOODS	110	NE
WOODSIDE DR BELLE ISLE	137	SE
WOODSTOCK	105	NE
WOODSTON	105	NE
WOODVIEW LA	144	NW
WOODWARD ECORSE	164	NW
WOODWARD AVE DETROIT	135	NW
WOODWARD ST WAYNE	149	NE
WOODWORTH REDFORD	115	NW
WOODWORTH DEARBORN	145	NW
WOODWORTH CIR DEARBORN HTS	129	NW
WORCESTER PL	106	SW
WORCHESTER DR	139	NW
YACAMA	106	NW
YALE	127	SW
YALE DETROIT	113	NW
YALE INKSTER	142	SW
YATES	122	SE
YELLOWSTONE	119	SE
YEMANS	121	NE
YINGER	132	SW
YONKA	107	SW
YORK DETROIT	135	NW
YORK INKSTER	152	NE
YORK N. D.BORN	143	NW
YORK S.	143	NW
YORKDALE	127	SE
YORKDALE CT	127	SE
YORKSHIRE AVE S.GATE	162	SE
YORKSHIRE CT RIVERVIEW	170	SE
YORKSHIRE DR LIVONIA	99	NE
YORKSHIRE DR RIVERVIEW	170	SE
YORKSHIRE RD GR. PT PARK	110	SW
YORKTOWN	111	NE
YORKVILLE	115	NE
YOSEMITE	119	NE
YOST N. CT	162	NE
YOST S.	162	NE
YOUNG DETROIT	109	SE
YOUNG LA GR. PT.WOODS	111	NE
YUMA	107	SW
ZENDER	136	NW
ZEIGLER	154	NW
ZELLMER AVE	167	NE
ZIEGLER	162	SW
ZINOW	121	NW
ZORN	140	SW

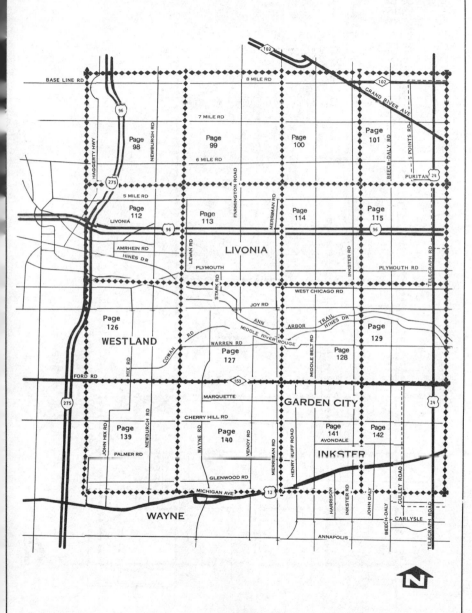

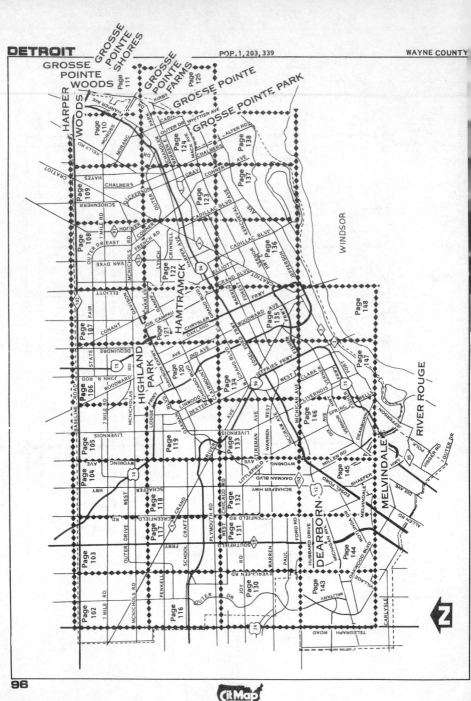

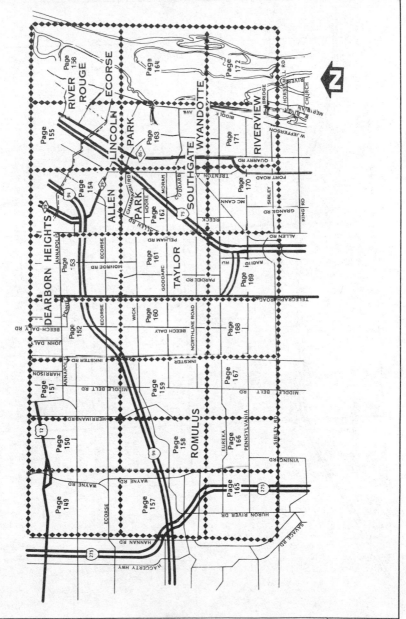

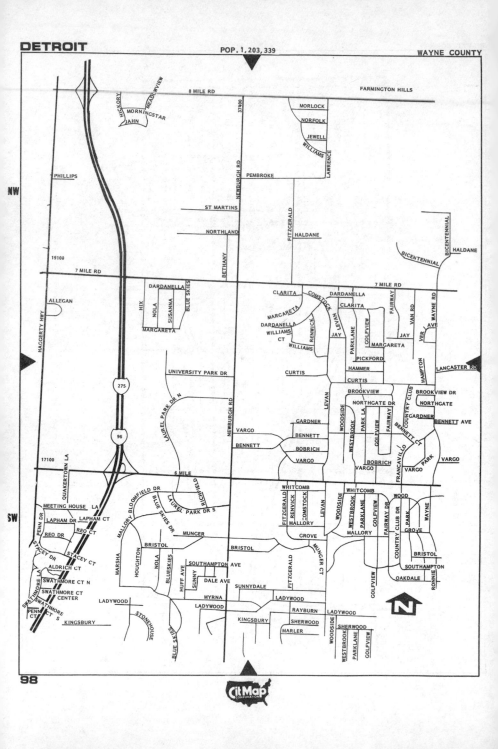

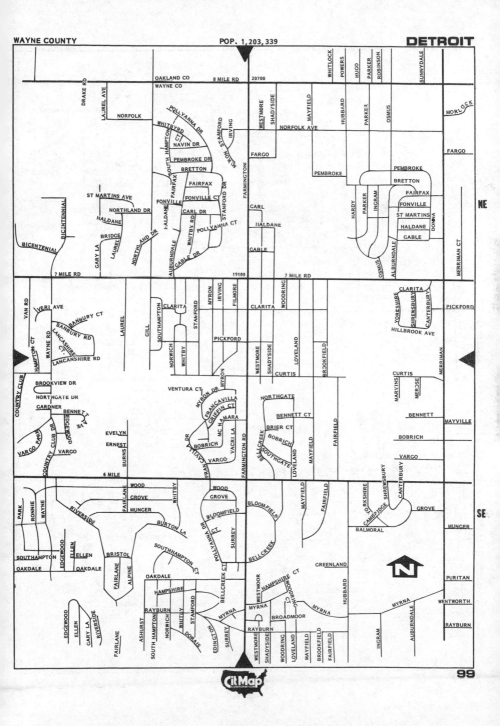

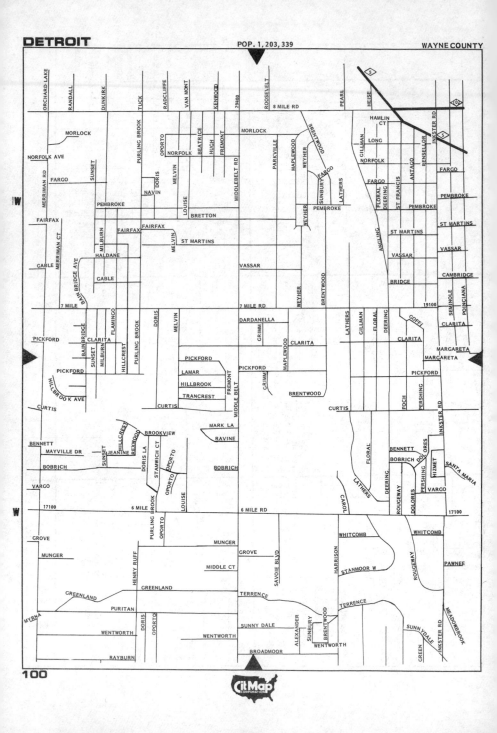

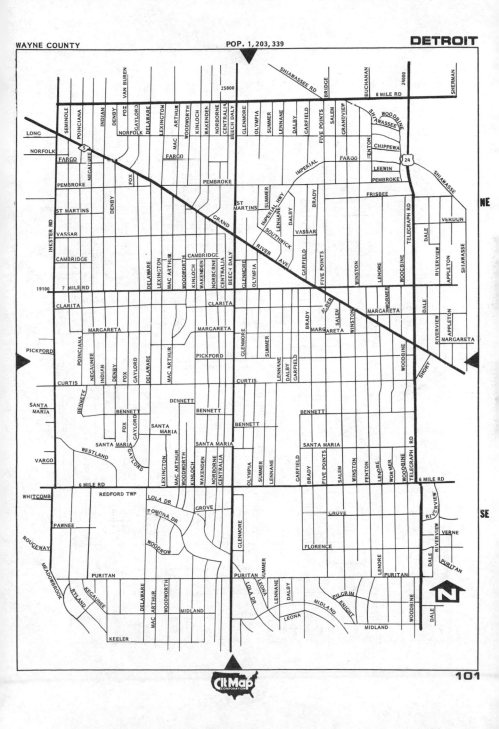

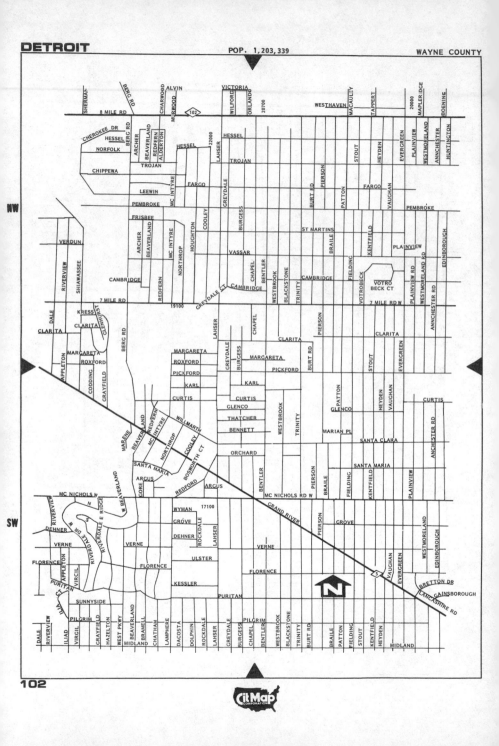

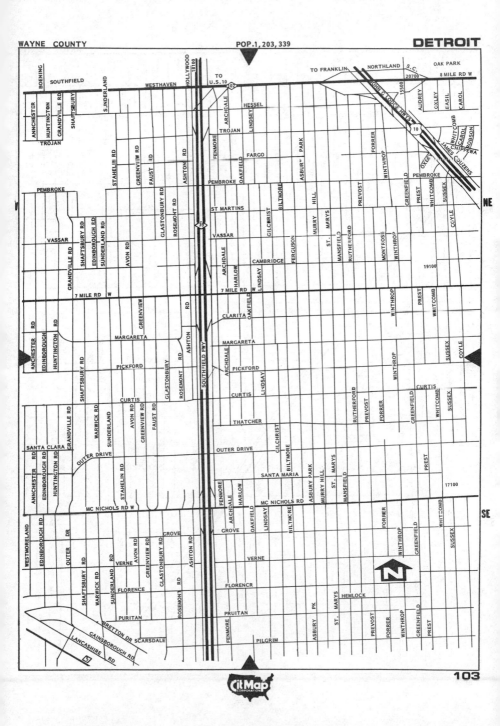

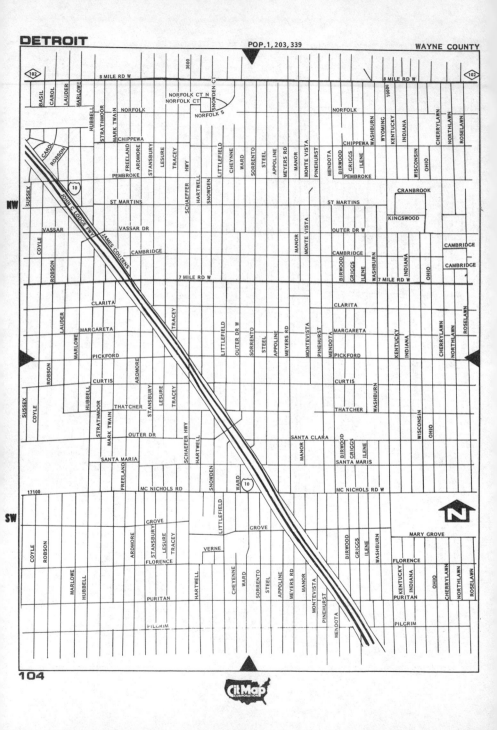

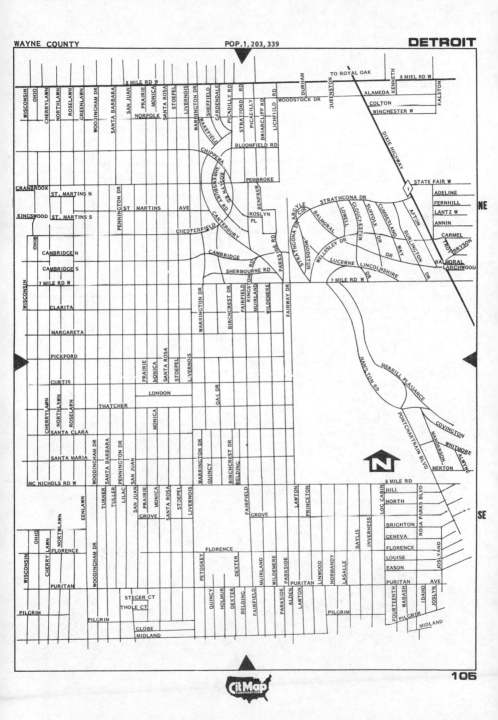

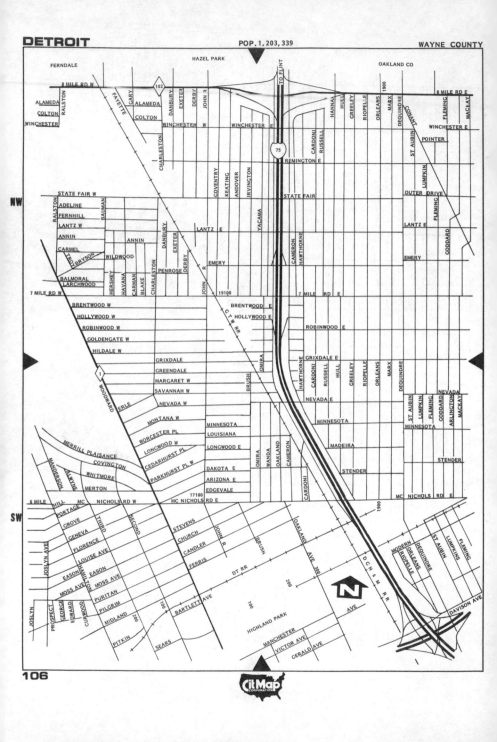

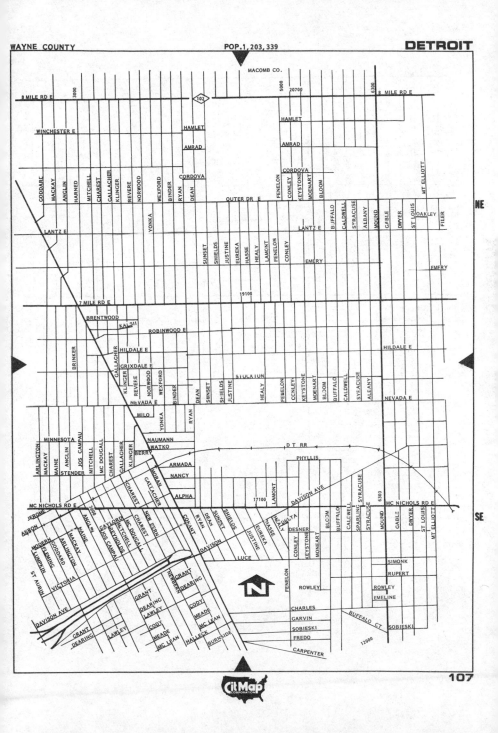

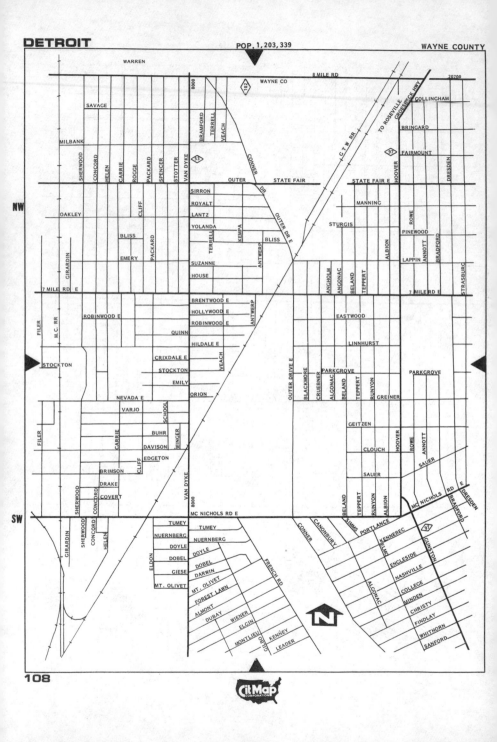

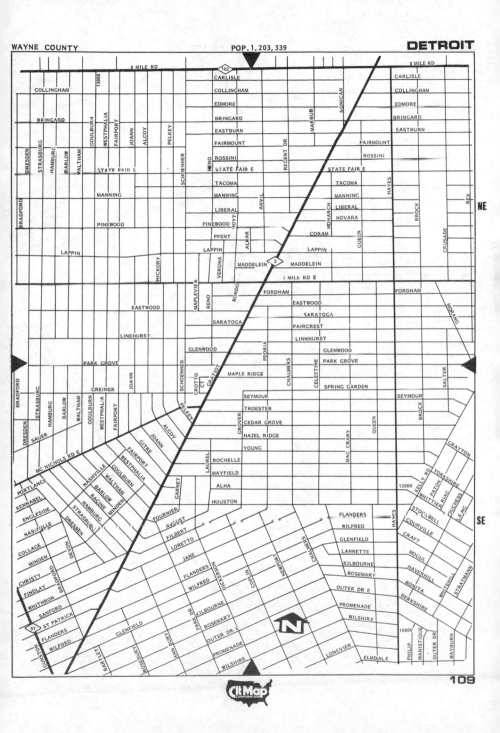

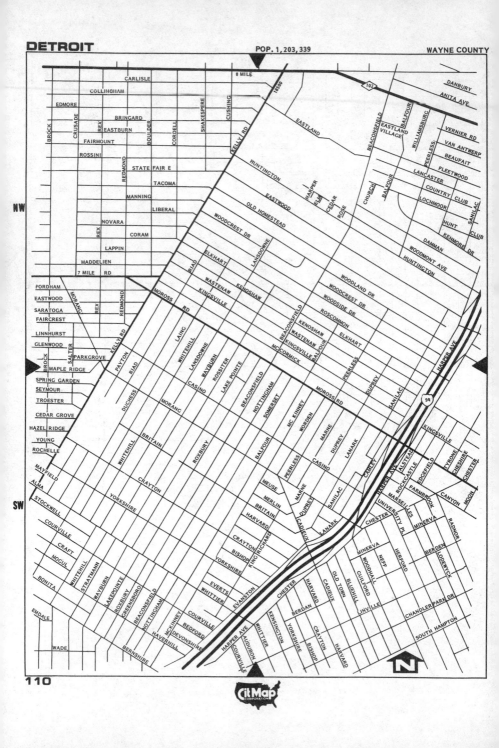

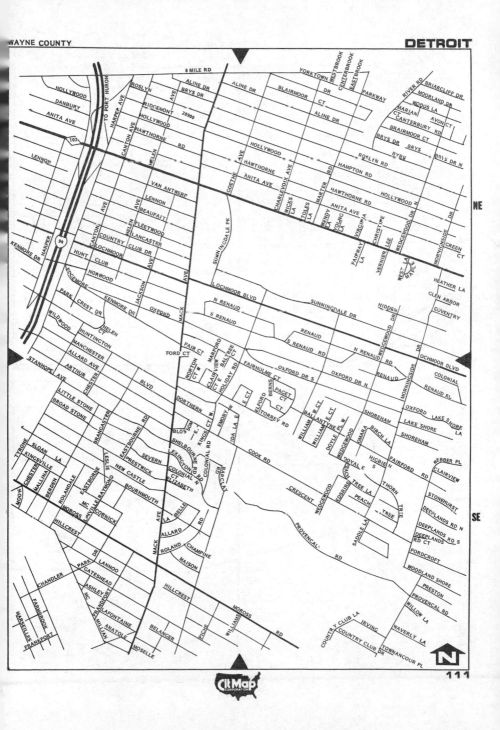

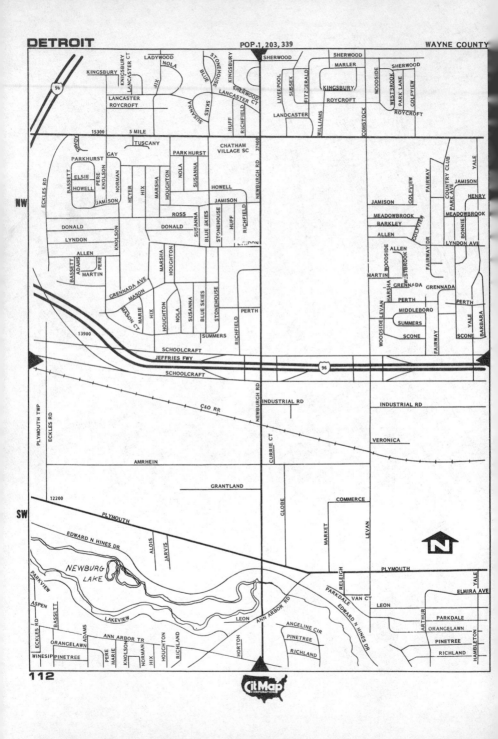

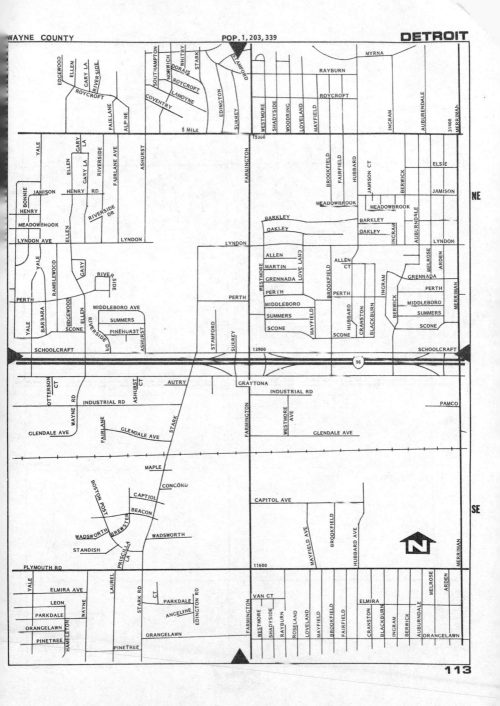

NE

SE

N

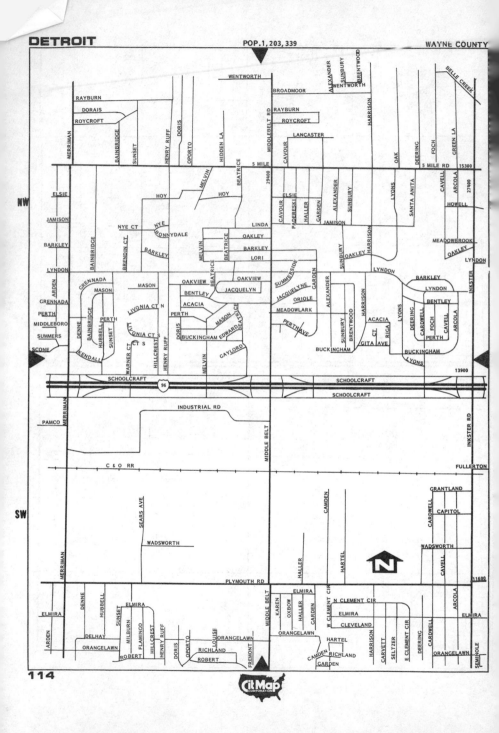

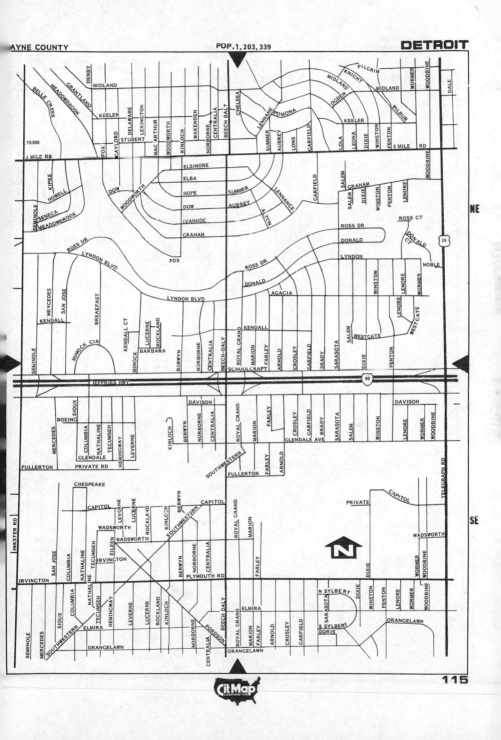

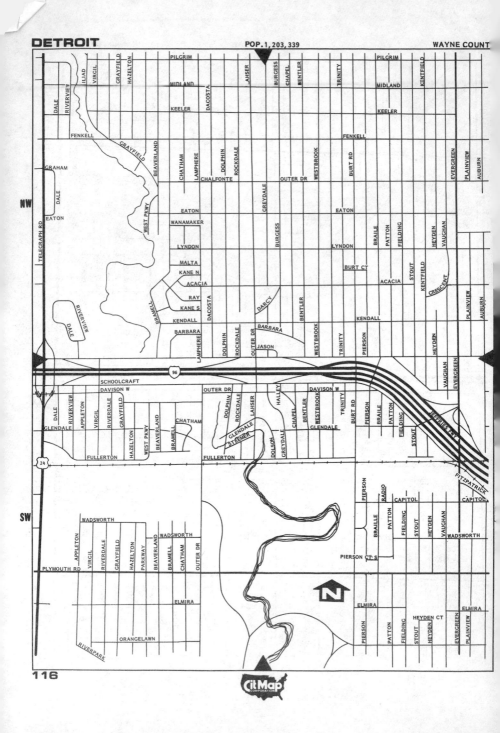

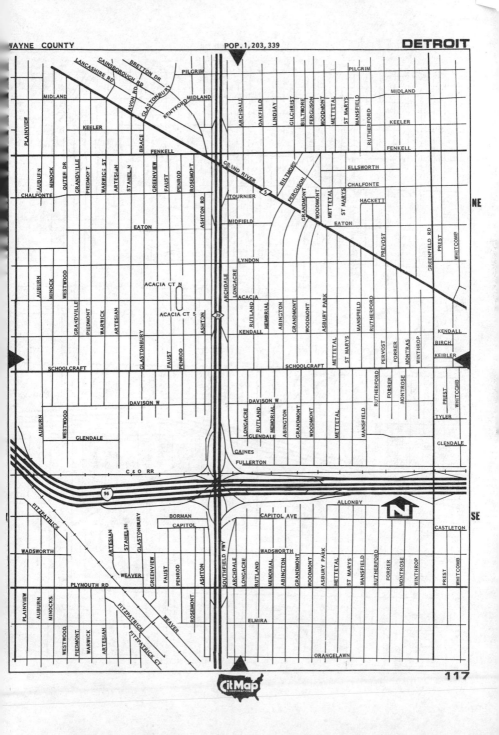

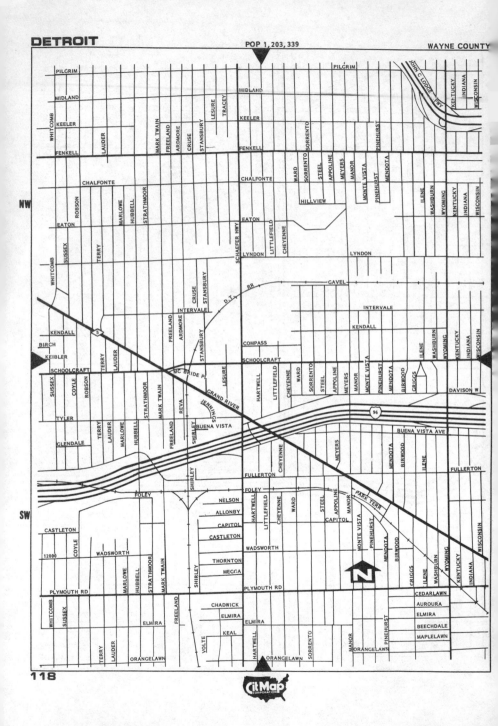

NW

SW

CitMap
INCORPORATED

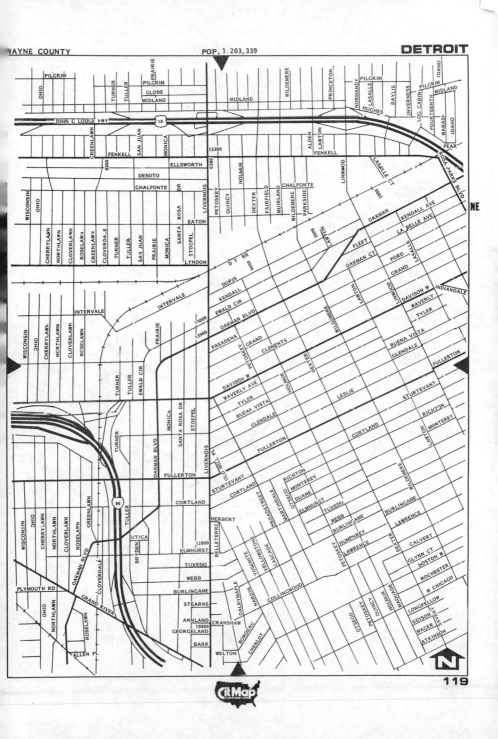

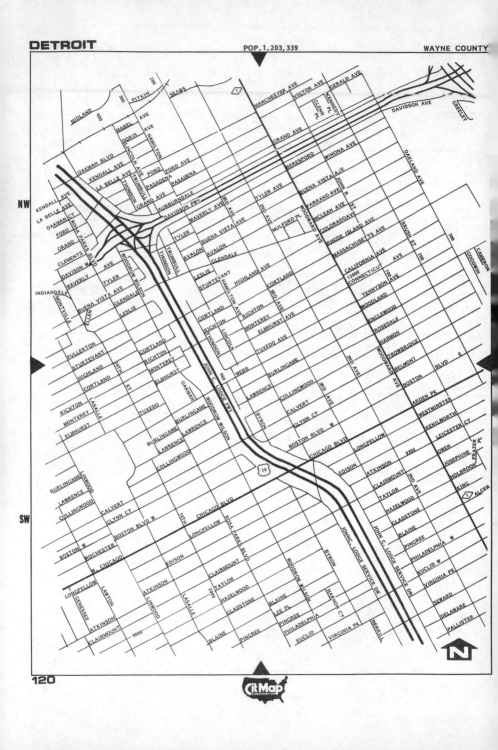

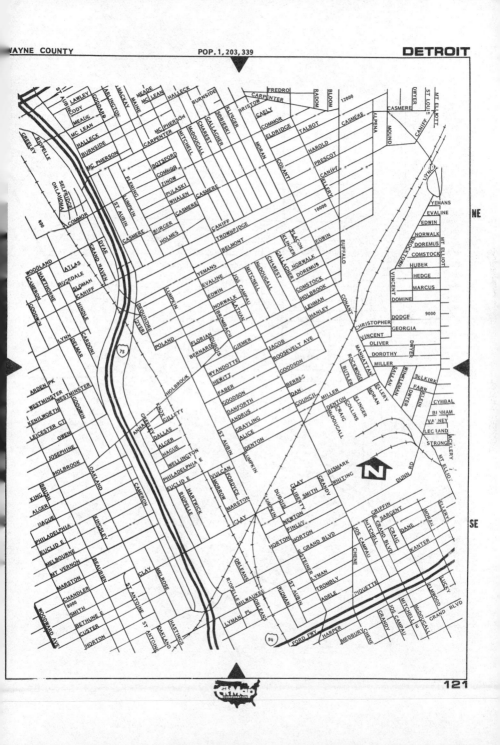

NE

SE

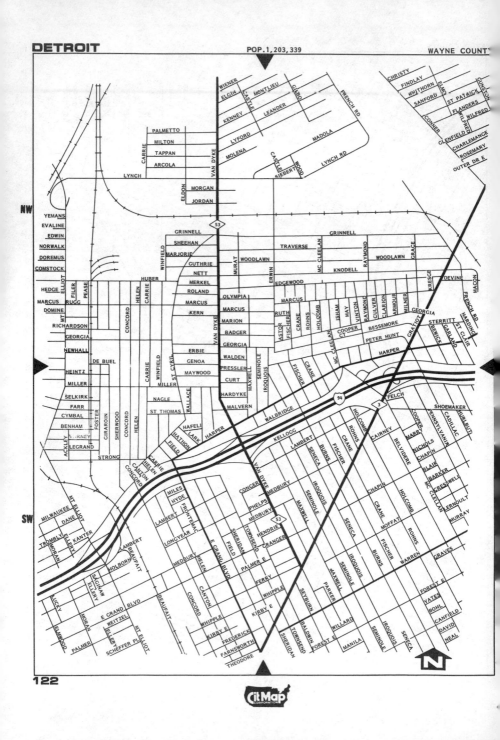

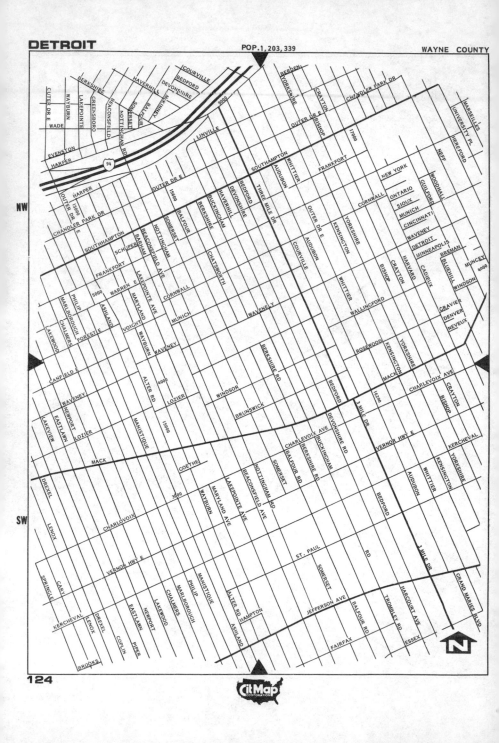

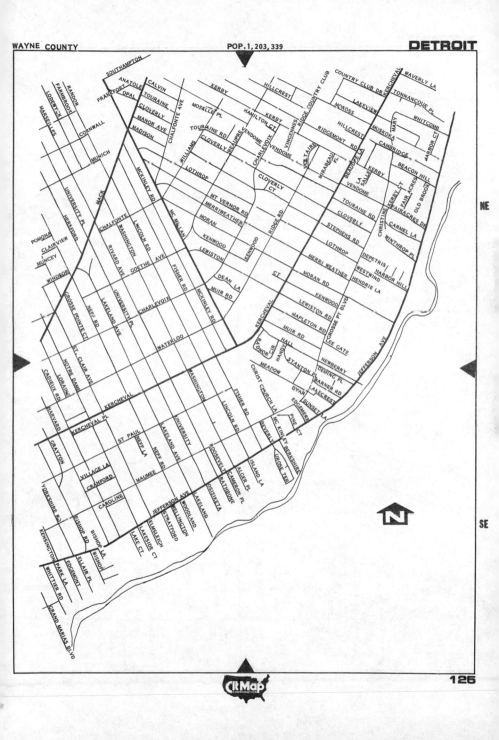

NE

SE

N

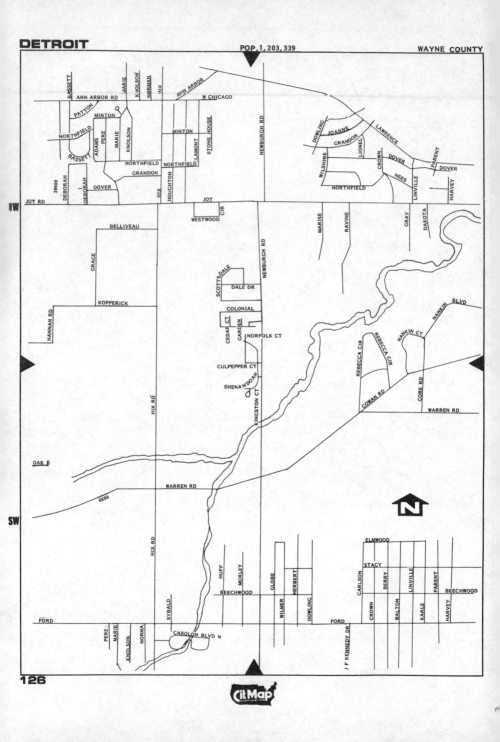

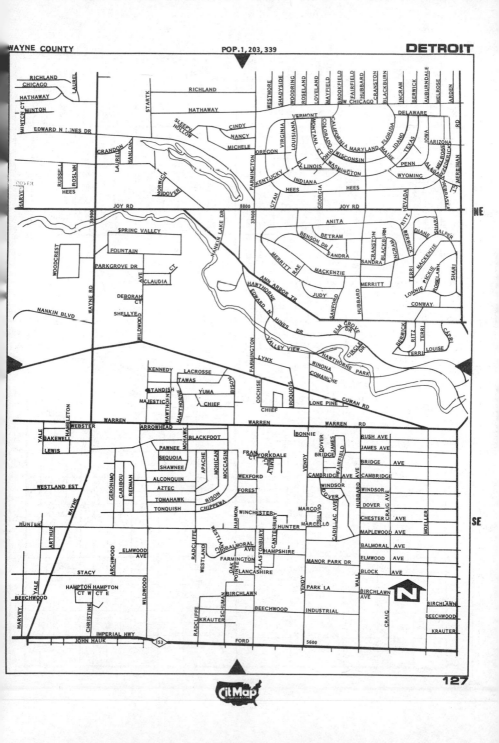

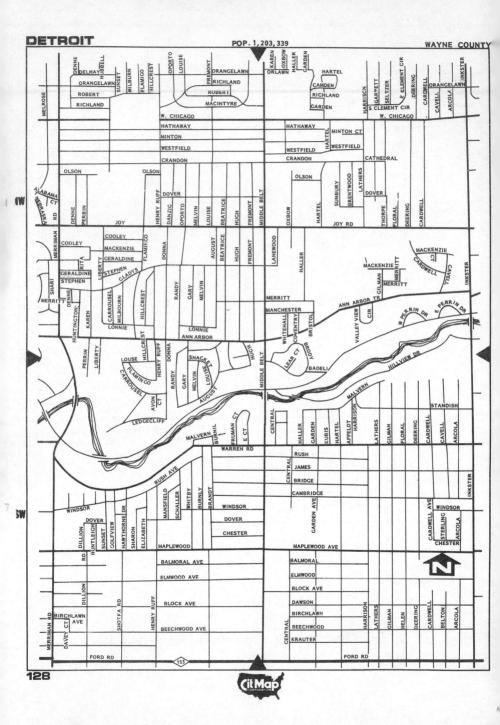

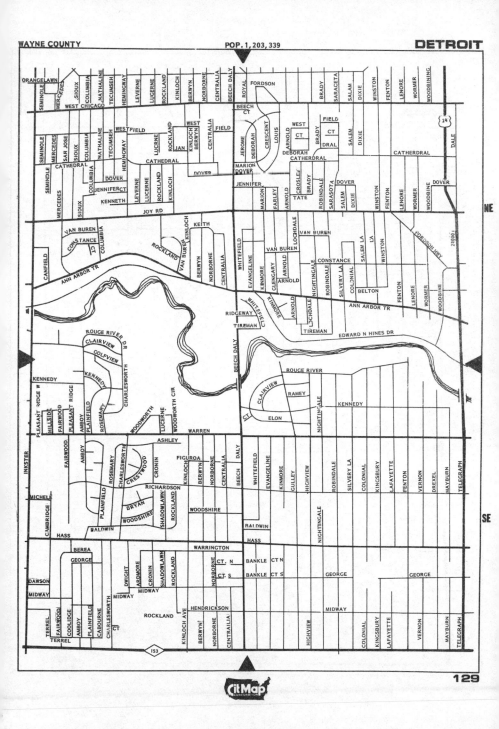

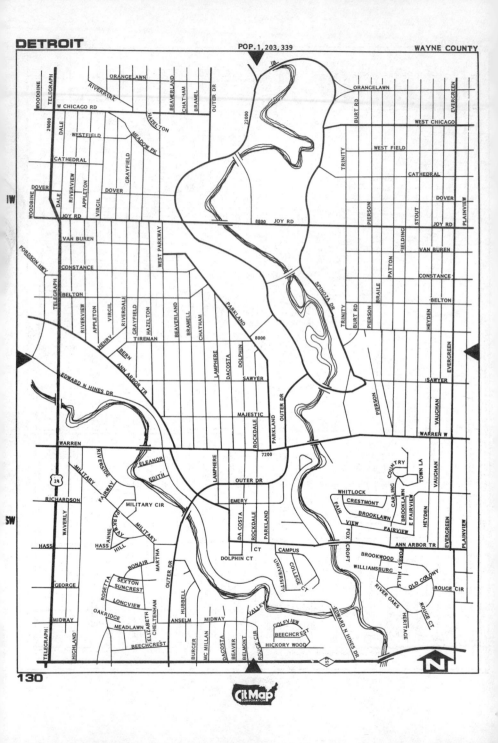

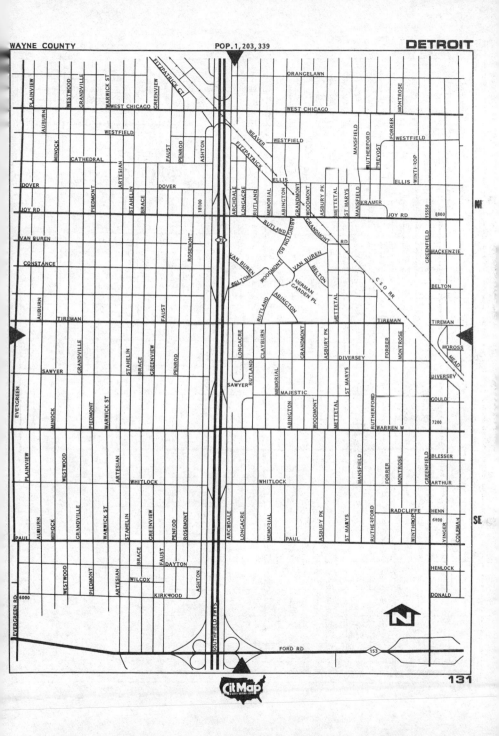

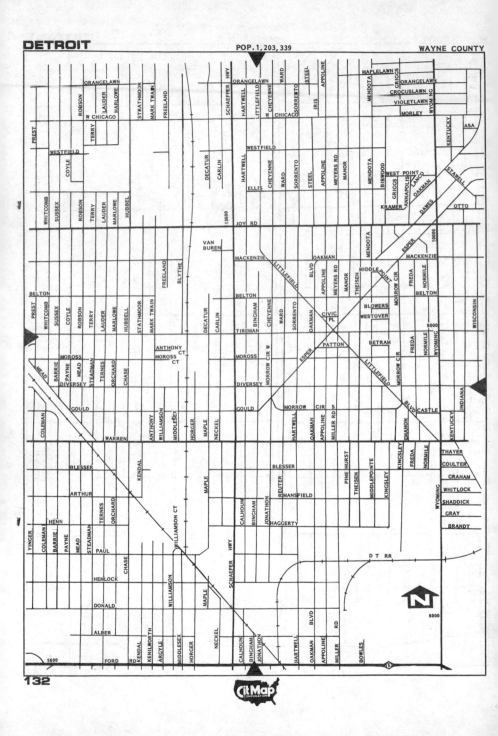

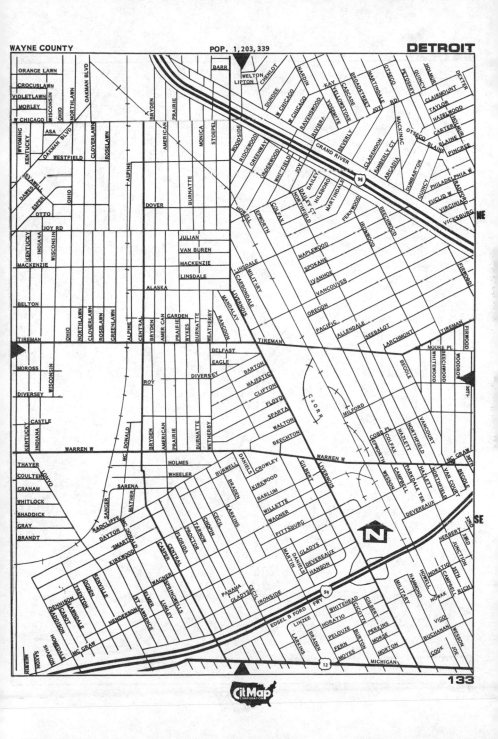

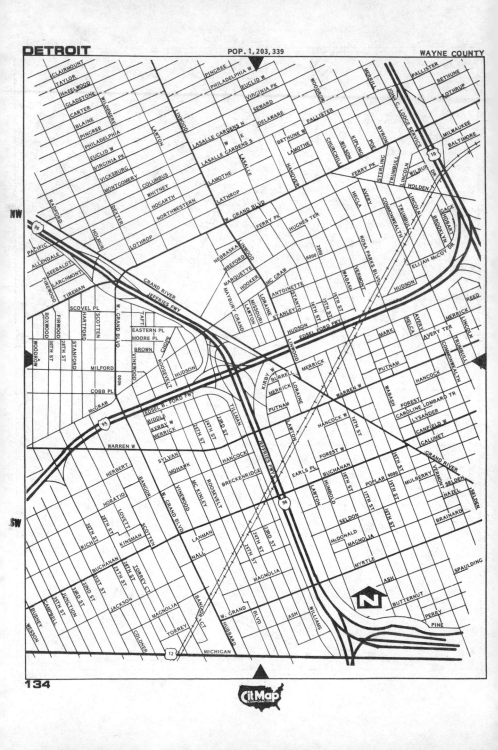

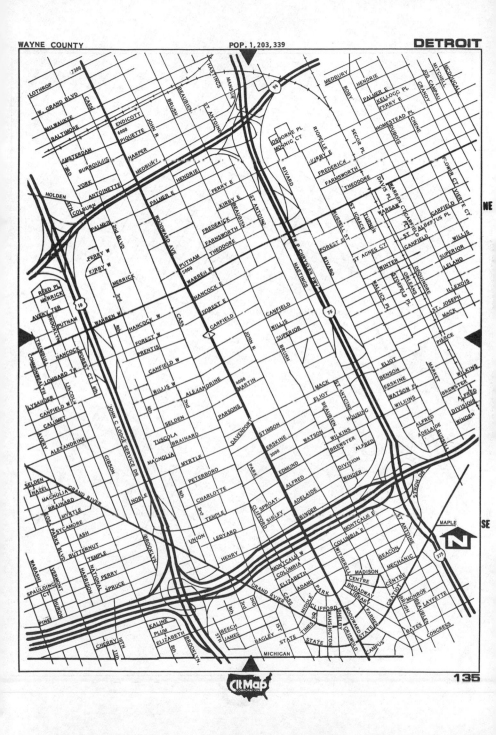

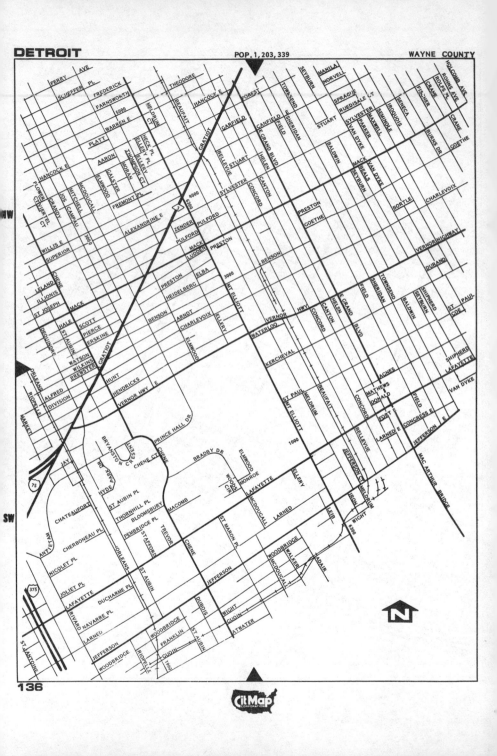

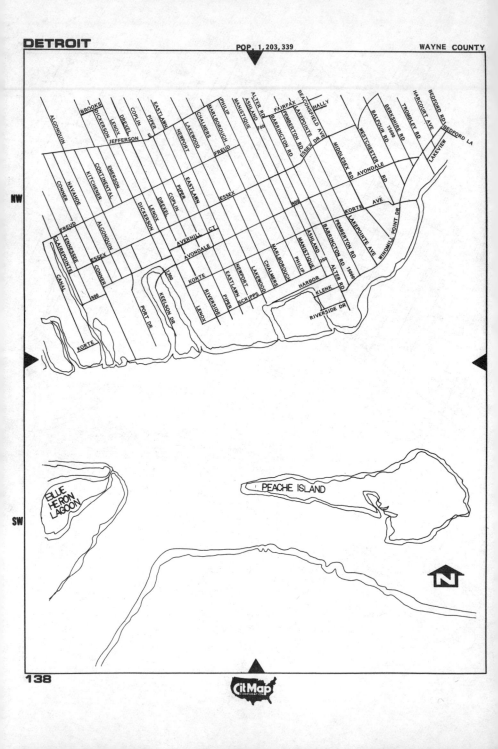

PEACHE ISLAND

BLUE HERON LAGOON

CitMap
CORPORATION

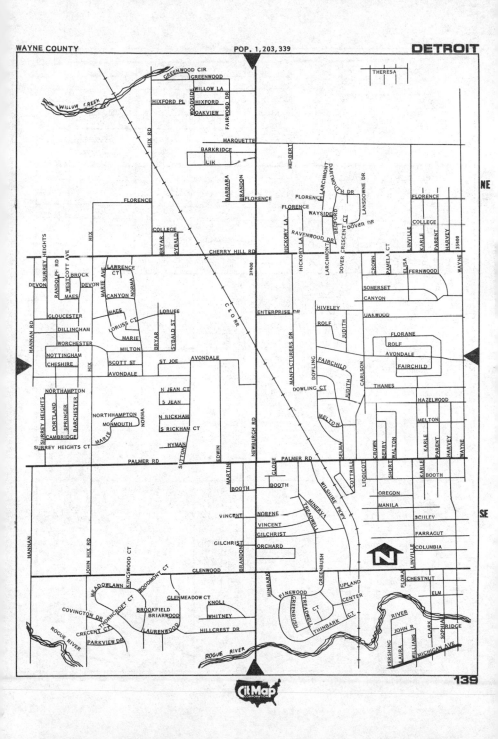

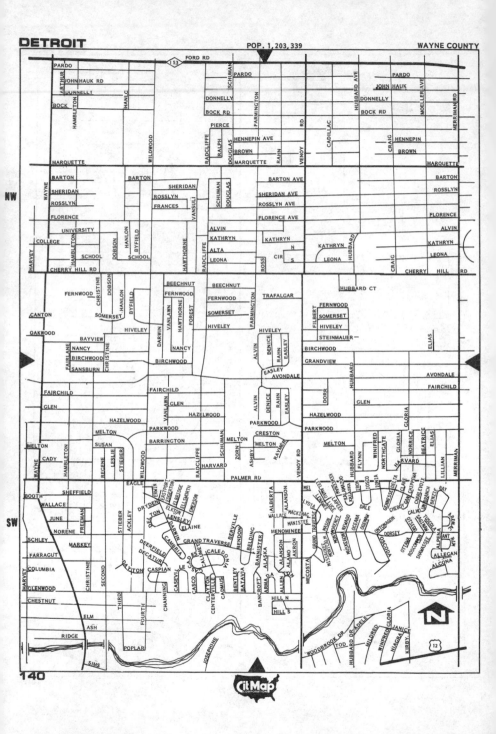

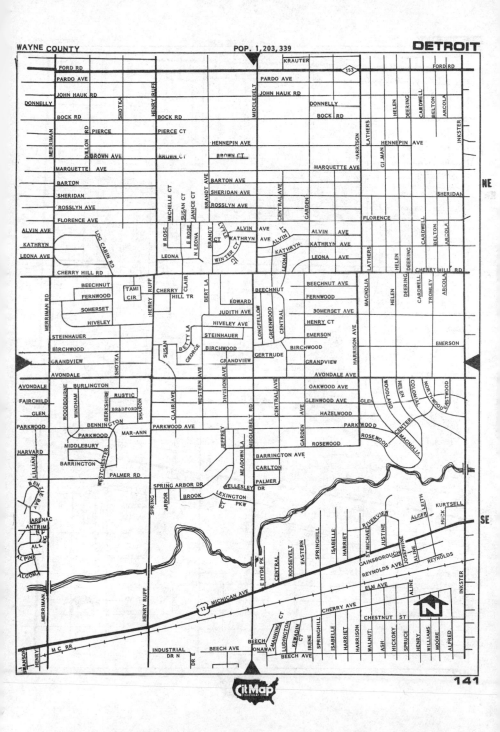

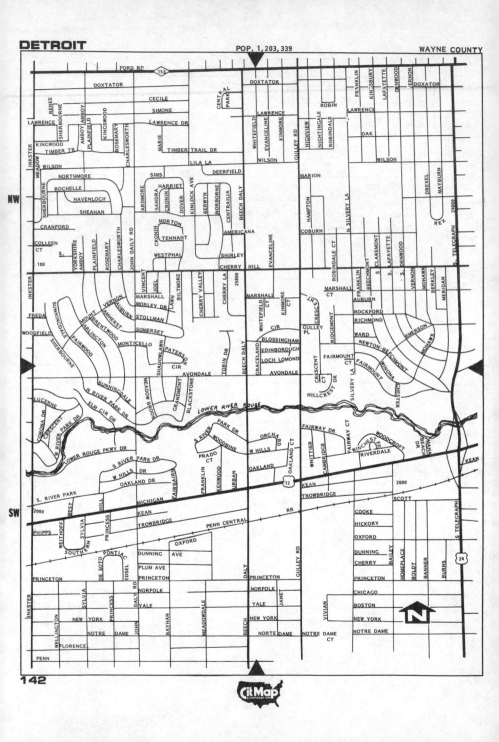

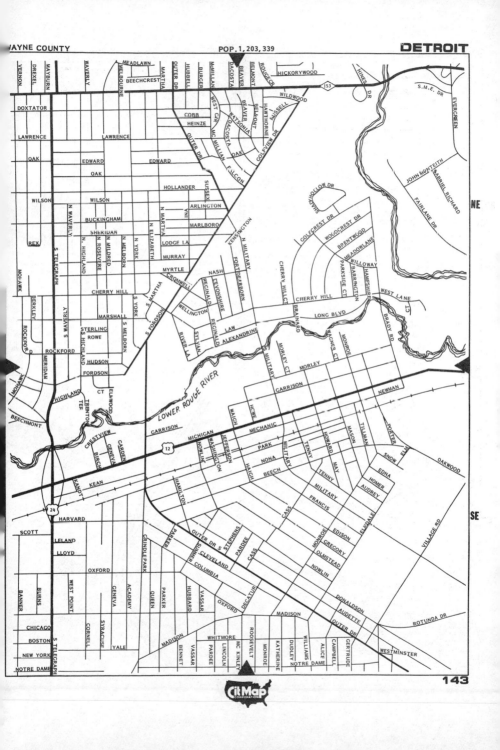

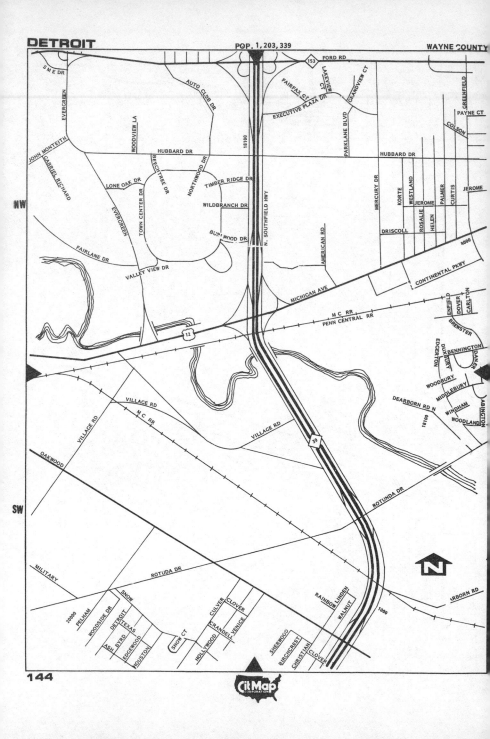

POP. 1,203,339

FORD RD
153

S M E DR

EVERGREEN

AUTO CLUB DR

FAIRFAX CT
LAKEVIEW CT
GRANDVIEW CT

EXECUTIVE PLAZA DR

PARKLANE BLVD

GREENFIELD

PAYNE CT

COLSON

WOODVIEW LA

HUBBARD DR

18100

HUBBARD DR

JOHN MONTEITH

GABRIEL RICHARD

BEECHTREE DR

NORTHWOOD DR

TIMBER RIDGE DR

WILDBRANCH DR

MERCURY DR

KORTE
WESTLAND
JEROME
ROSALIE
HELEN
PALMER
CURTIS

JEROME

NW

LONE OAK DR

TOWN CENTER DR

EVERGREEN

BURLWOOD DR

N. SOUTHFIELD HWY

DRISCOLL

FAIRLANE DR

VALLEY VIEW DR

AMERICAN RD

CONTINENTAL PKWY

3000

MICHIGAN AVE

M C RR
PENN CENTRAL RR

12

ENFIELD
DOVER
CARLTON

BREWSTER

EDGERTON
DUXBURY
BENNINGTON

ABINGTON

WOODBURY

VILLAGE RD

MIDDLEBURY

VILLAGE RD

M C RR

DEARBORN RD N

WINDHAM

18100

WOODLAND

VILLAGE RD

VILLAGE RD

29

OAKWOOD

ROTUNDA DR

SW

N

MILITARY

ROTUDA DR

SNOW

RAINBOW
LINDEN
WALNUT

20000

PELHAM

WOODSIDE DR

DETROIT
TEXAS

BYRD

CULVER
CLOVER

SNOW CT

CRANDELL
VENICE

SHERWOOD

SEARBORN RD

1000

ASH

EDGEWOOD

HOUSTON

HOLLYWOOD

BIRCHCREST
CHRISTIAN
CLOVER

CitMap
CORPORATION

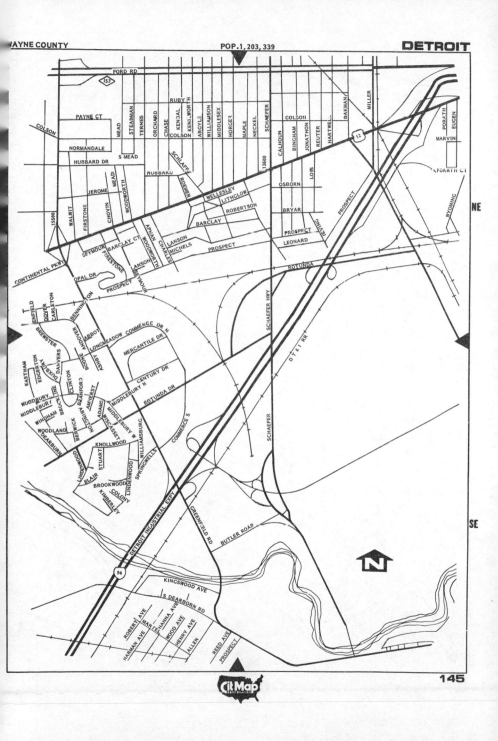

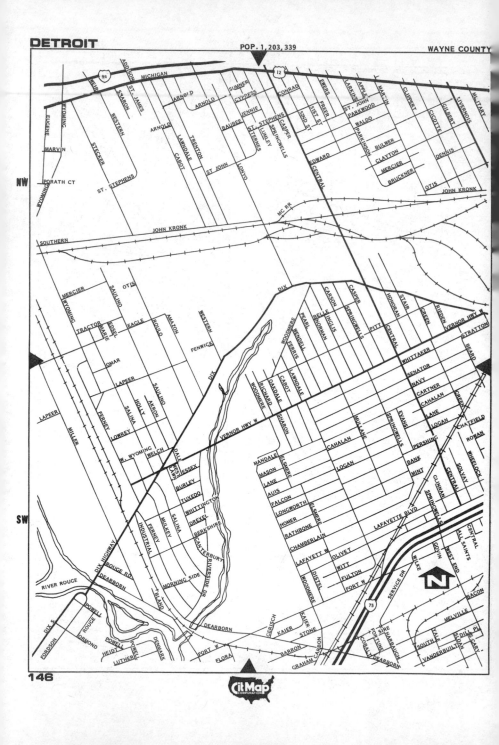

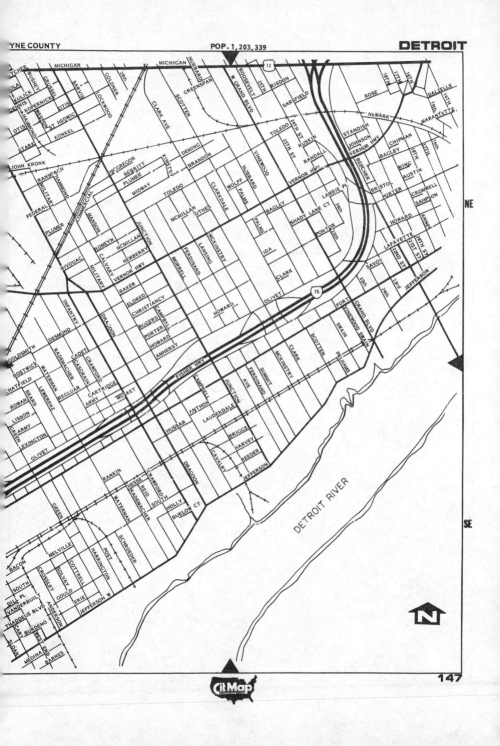

DETROIT RIVER

N

NE

SE

CitMap
CORPORATION

DETROIT RIVER

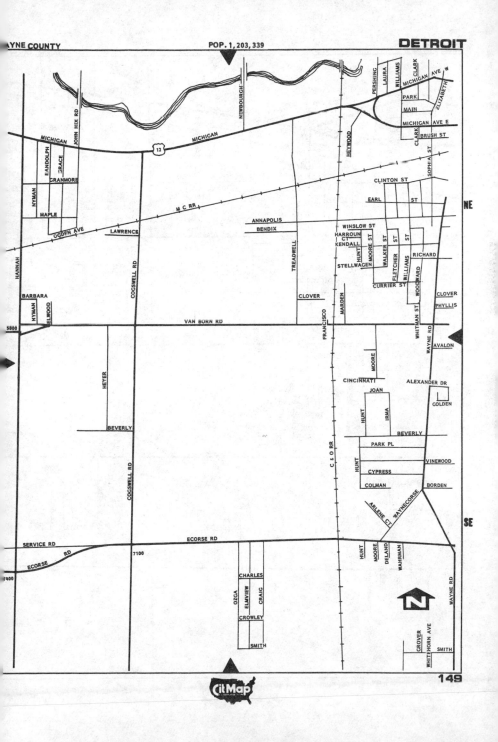

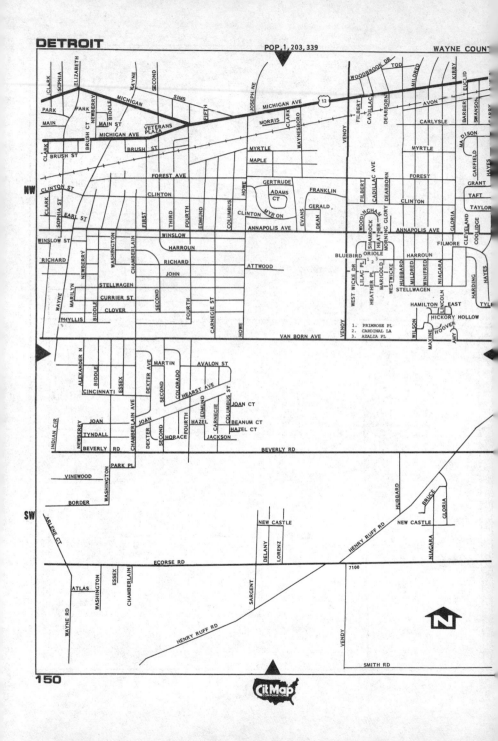

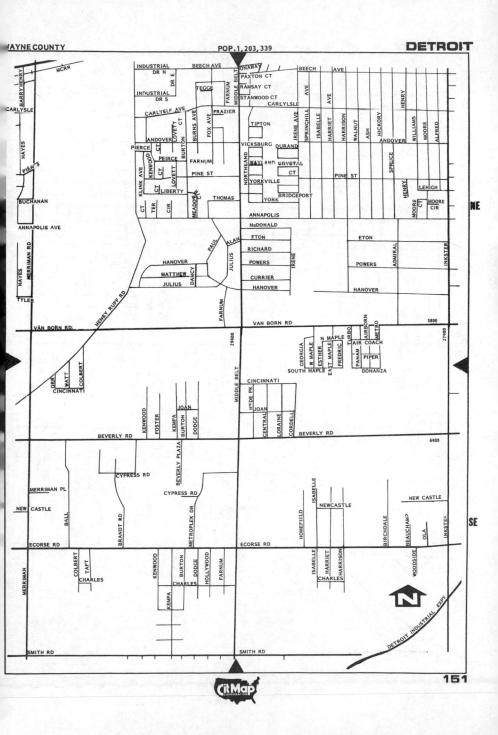

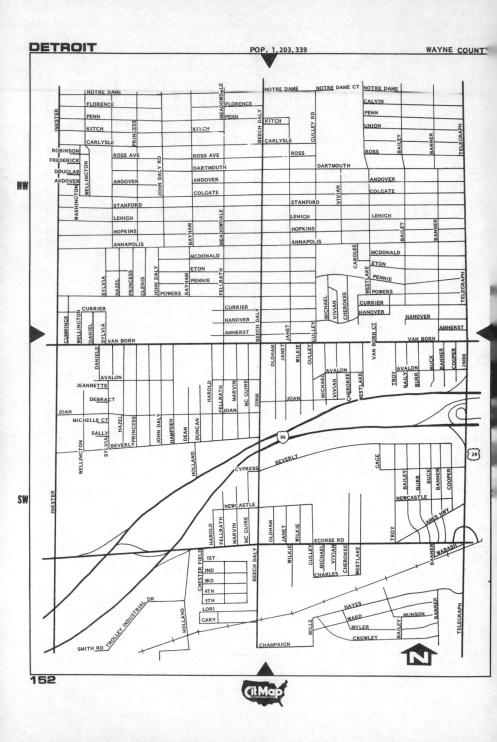

NW

SW

CitMap
CORPORATIONS

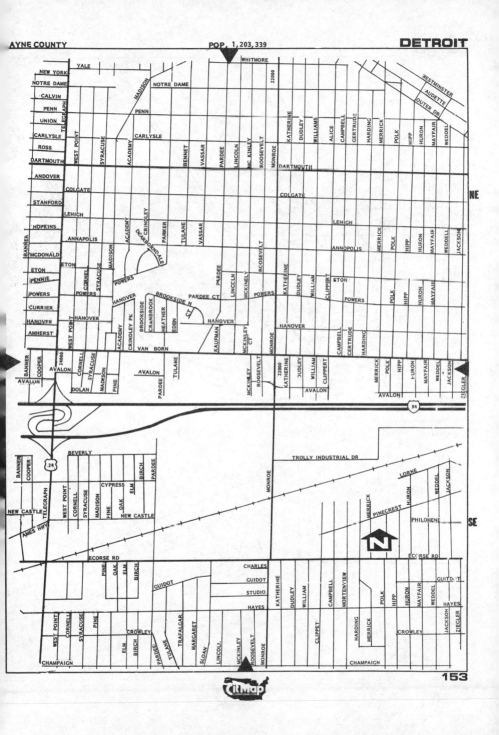

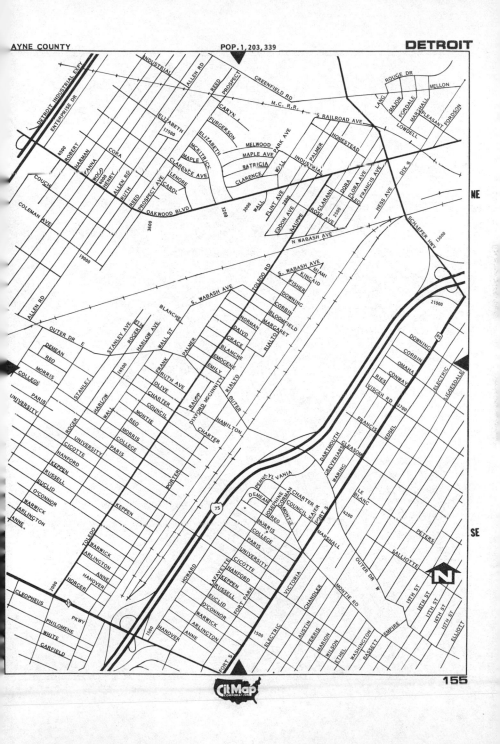

POP. 1,203,339

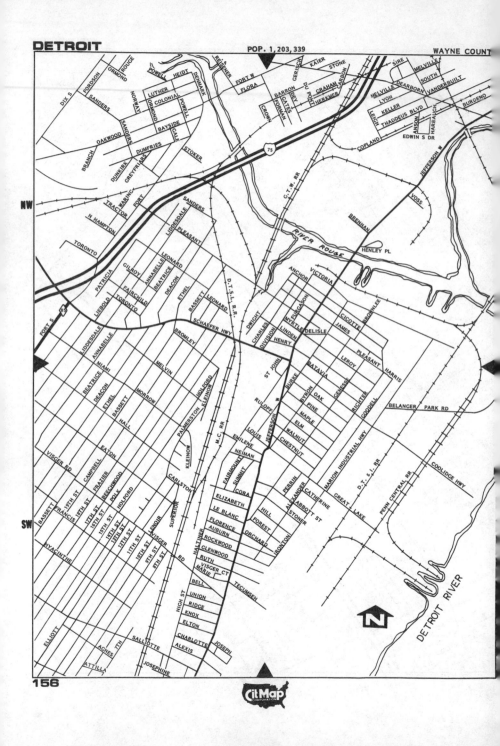

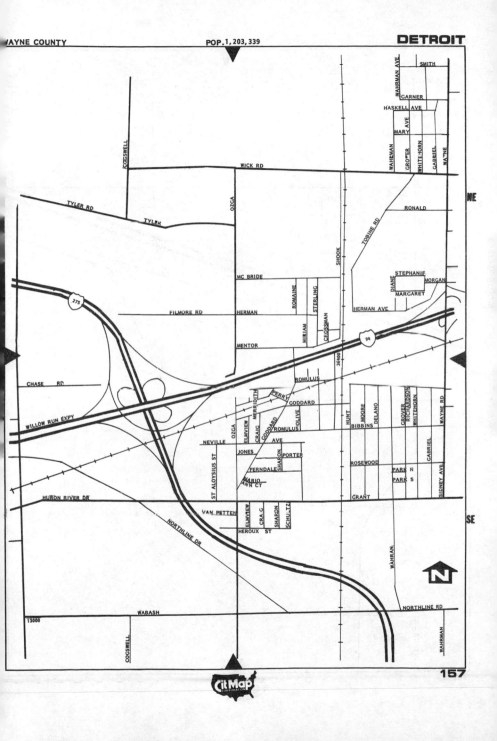

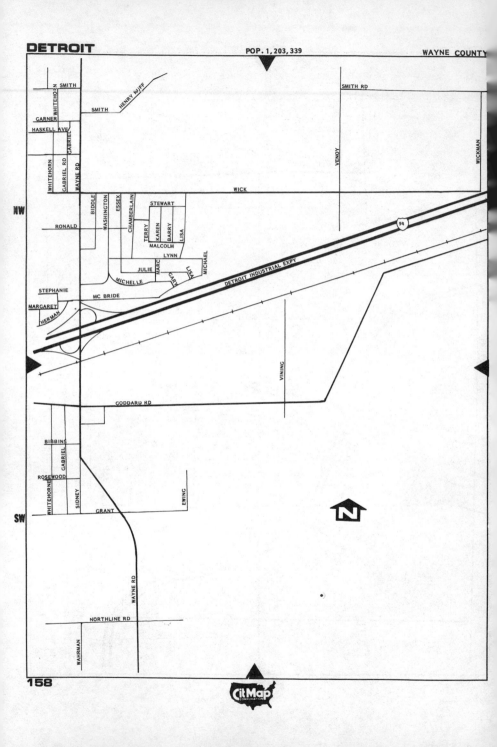

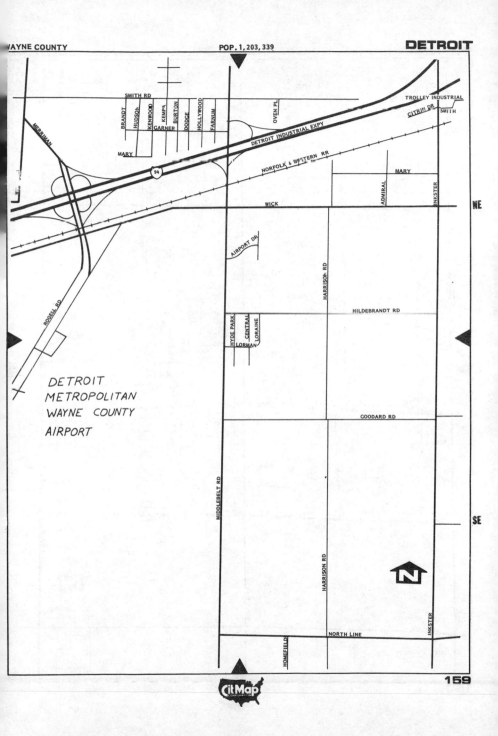

SMITH RD

BRANDT
HUDSON
KENWOOD
KEMPA
GARNER
BURTON
DODGE
HOLLYWOOD
FARNUM

OVEN PL

TROLLEY INDUSTRIAL

CITKIN DR

SMITH

MERRIMAN

MARY

DETROIT INDUSTRIAL EXPY

94

NORFOLK & WESTERN RR

MARY

ADMIRAL

INKSTER

WICK

NE

AIRPORT DR

HARRISON RD

HILDEBRANDT RD

ROGELL RD

HYDE PARK
LORMAN
CENTRAL
LORAINE

DETROIT
METROPOLITAN
WAYNE COUNTY
AIRPORT

GOODARD RD

MIDDLEBELT RD

SE

HARRISON RD

N

INKSTER

HOMEFIELD

NORTH LINE

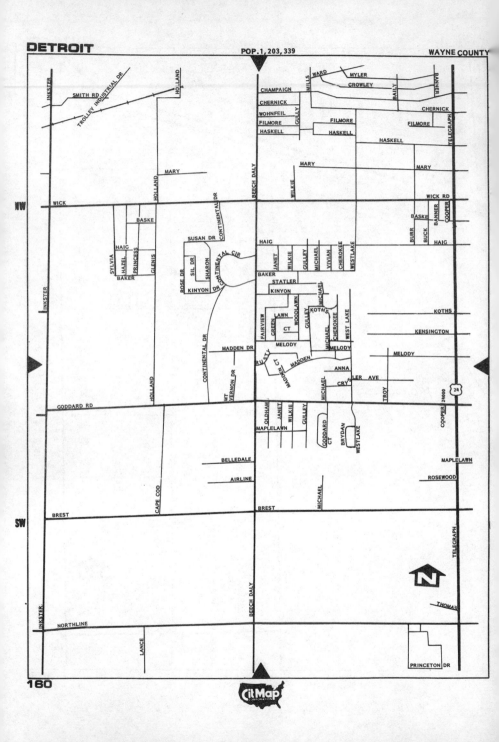

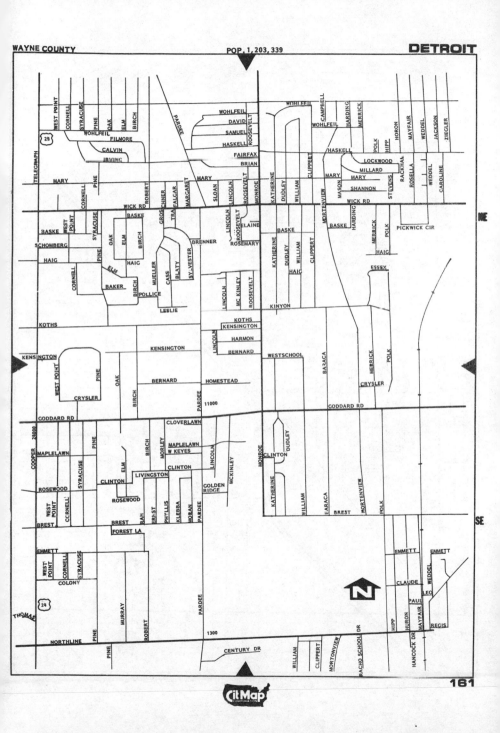

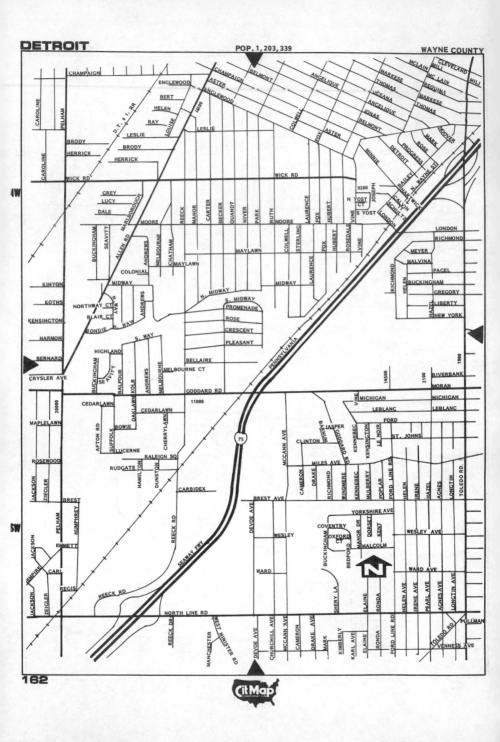

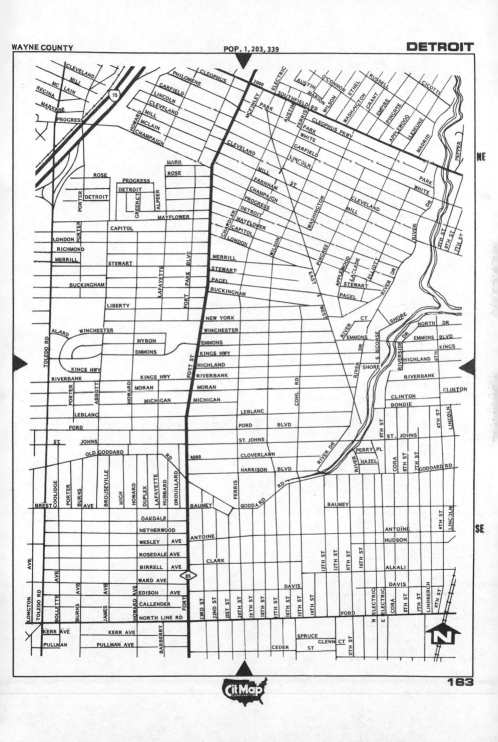

NE

SE

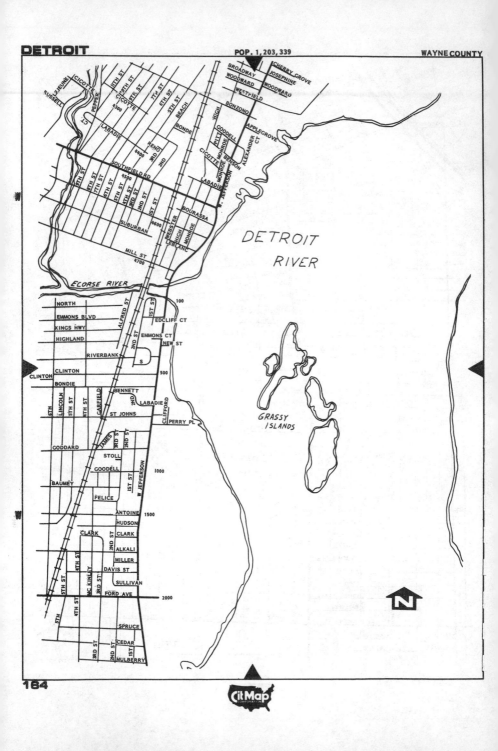

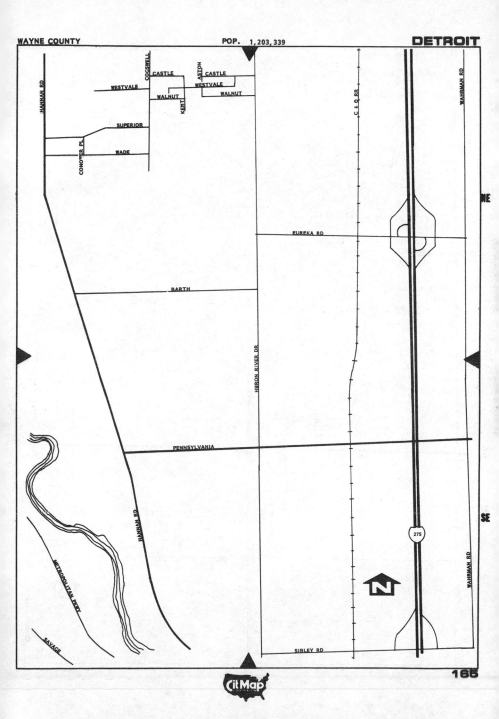

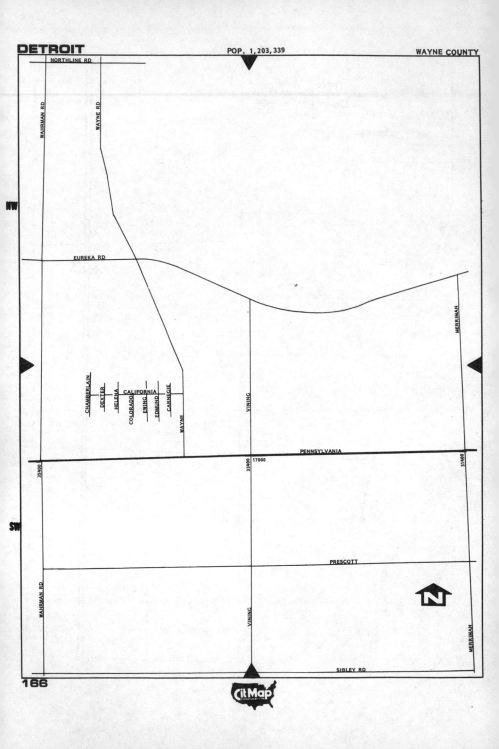

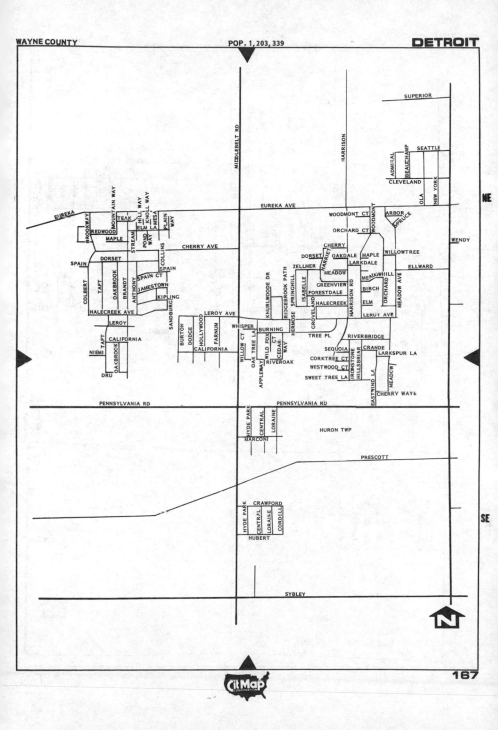

SUPERIOR

SEATTLE

ADMIRAL BEAUCHAMP

CLEVELAND NEW YORK

OLA

NE

WENDY

EUREKA AVE

WOODMONT CT

ARBOR

SPRUCE

ORCHARD CT WOODMONT

CHERRY AVE

WILLOWTREE

CHERRY

DORSET HARRIET OAKDALE MAPLE

ELLWARD

LARKDALE

MEADOW

MEADOWHILL

ZELLMER

GREENVIEW

BIRCH

FORESTDALE

ELM

HALECREEK

LEROY AVE

GROVELAND

TREE PL

RIVERBRIDGE

SEQUOIA GRANDE

CORKTREE CT LARKSPUR LA

WESTWOOD CT

SWEET TREE LA

CHERRY WAYE

EUREKA

MOUNTAIN WAY

HILL WAY KNOLL WAY

ELM LA MESA

STREAM

PLAIN WAY

REDWOOD TEAK

BROOKWAY

MAPLE POND WAY

SPAIN DORSET COLLINS

SPAIN SPAIN CT

COLBERT

TAFT OAKBROOK BRANDT ANTHONY

JAMESTOWN

KIPLING

HALECREEK AVE

SANDBURG

LEROY

TAFT CALIFORNIA

NIEMI OAKBROOK

DRU

BURTON DODGE HOLLYWOOD FARNUM

CALIFORNIA

LEROY AVE

WHISPER

WILLOW CT

OAK TREE LA

APPLEWAY WILD FOX

BURNING CEDAR CT

RIVEROAK

KNURLWOODE DR

RIDGEBROOK PATH

SPRINGHILL

ISABELLE

HERMOSE

HARRISON RD

ORCHARD MEADOW AVE

LEROY AVE

IRONSTONE

HILLSBRIAR

EASTWIND LA

MEADOW

PENNSYLVANIA RD PENNSYLVANIA RD

HYDE PARK

CENTRAL

LORAINE

MARCONI

HURON TWP

PRESCOTT

SE

HYDE PARK CRAWFORD

CENTRAL LORAINE CORDELL

HUBERT

SYBLEY

N

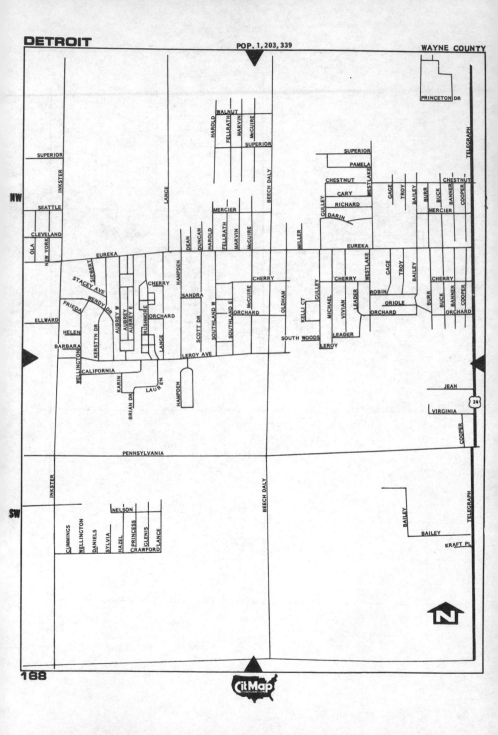

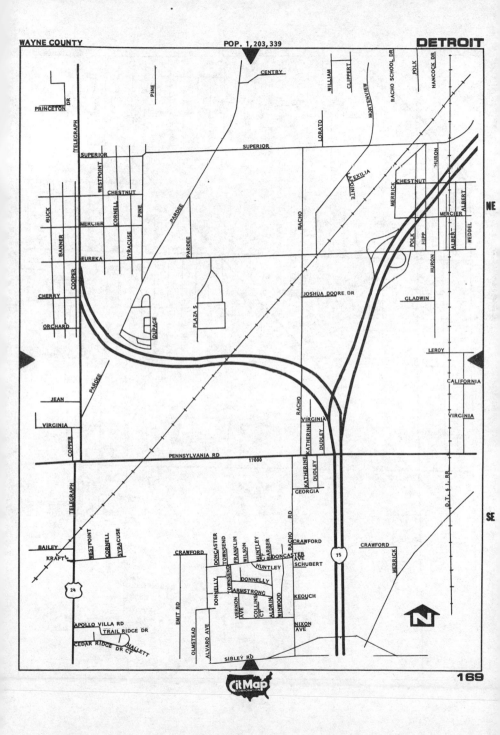

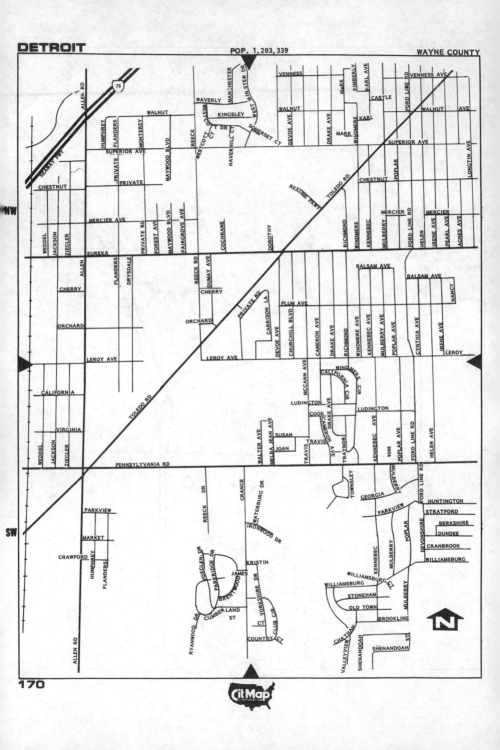

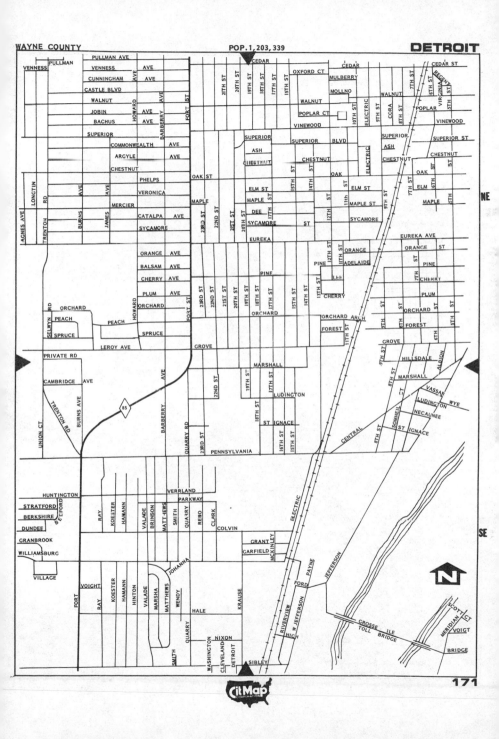

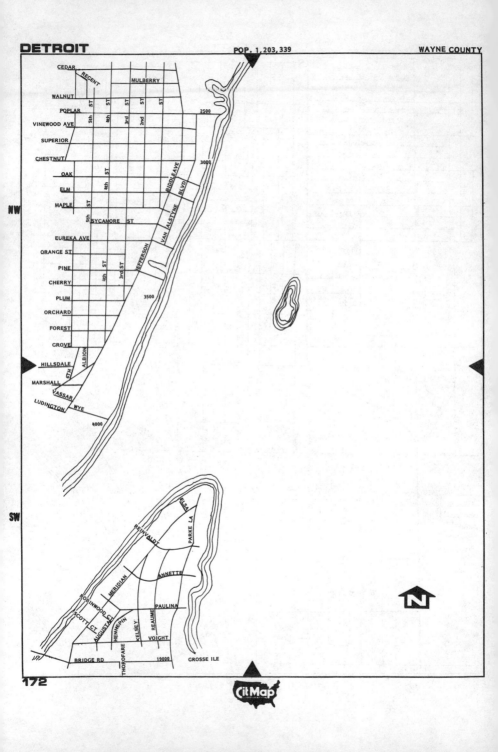

NW

SW

CEDAR
REGENT ST
MULBERRY
WALNUT
POPLAR
5th ST
4th ST
3rd ST
2nd ST
ST
2500
VINEWOOD AVE
SUPERIOR
CHESTNUT
3000
OAK
4th ST
ELM
5th ST
BIDDLEAVE BLVD
MAPLE
5th SYCAMORE ST
VAN ALSTYNE
JEFFERSON
EUREKA AVE
ORANGE ST
PINE
4th ST
3rd ST
CHERRY
PLUM
3500
ORCHARD
FOREST
GROVE
ALBION
HILLSDALE
5TH
MARSHALL
VASSAR
LUDINGTON   WYE
4000

REYNALD
REINVALD
PARKE LA
MERIDIAN
ANNETTE
ROBINWOOD CT
PAULINA
SCOTT CT
AUGUSTA
HENNEPIN
KELSEY
REAUME
VOIGHT
BRIDGE RD
THOROFARE
19000
GROSSE ILE

N

CitMap

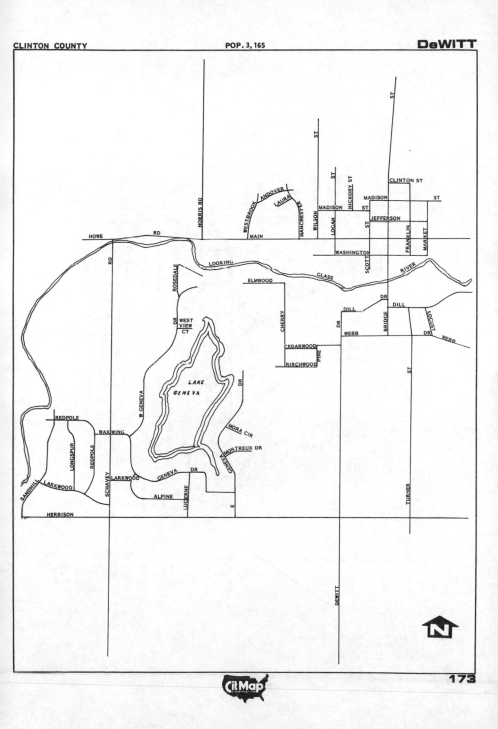

POP. 6,307

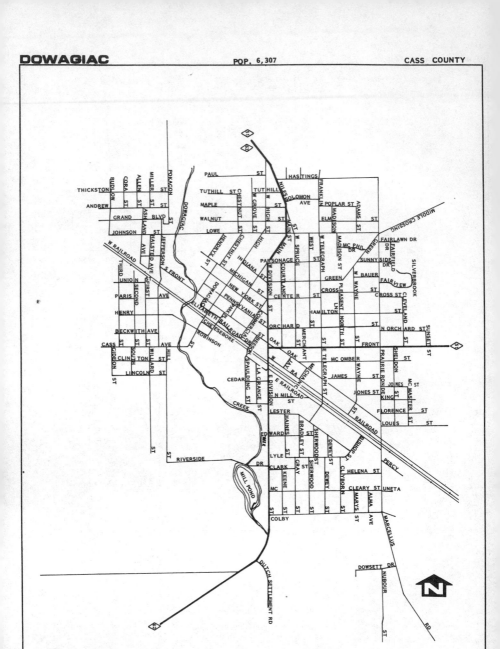

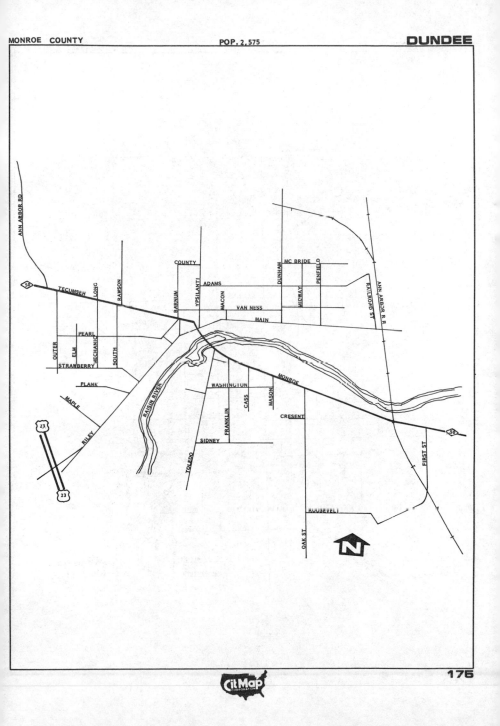

POP. 4, 238

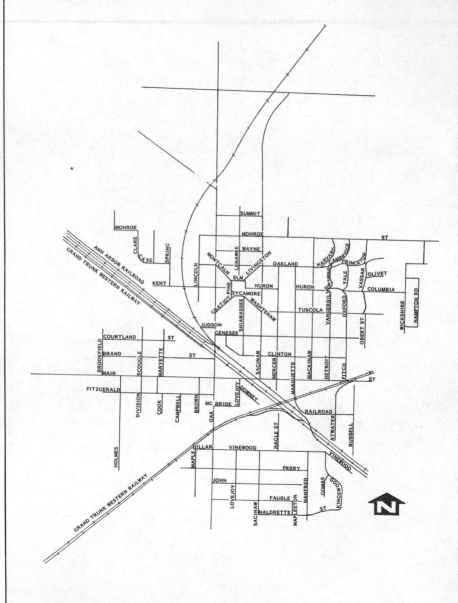

CITY OF WARREN

CITY OF DETROIT

CITY OF HARPER WOODS

CITY OF ST CLAIR SHORES

CITY OF ROSEVILLE

BEECHWOOD
JULIANA
EGO
JACOB
LYDIA
AGNES
COLLINSON
VERONICA
LINCOLN
TOEPPER
FIRWOOD
OAKWOOD
BIRCHWOOD
HAYES
ELMWOOD
MAPLEWOOD
CRESCENTWOOD
CRESTWOOD
CHESTNUT
ASH
GRATIOT
GROVE
NEILS
COVENS
OAK
ETHLYN
NEILS
CHARLES R.
BEECHWOOD
FIRWOOD
OAKWOOD
HAYES
LINWOOD
STEPHENS
HAYES
VALLEY
LAETHAM
CHESTERFIELD
BROCK
STRICKER
EIGHT MILE
EGO
JULIANA
SPRENGER
COLLINSON
VERONICA
JEAN
LINCOLN
CRUSADE
UNIVERSAL
REDMOND
VIRGINIA
LINWOOD
DALE
GROVE
NINE MILE RD.
S PARK
CHARLES R.
N PARK
CAMDEN
DEERFIELD
HENRIETTA
EVERGREEN
SEMRAU
DALE
GROVE
FLOWER
FERN
ROSEBUD
PHLOX
WILSON
FOREST
BELL
HAUSS
CHESTERFIELD
VIRGINIA
NEVADA
BOULDER
BOULDER
PLEASANT
TOEPPER
MELROSE
SHAKESPEARE
LISCOMB
HOFER
MELROSE
NORTON
ALSORA
EVERGREEN
NICOLAI
SEMRAU
GOMER
GRATIOT
MANCHESTER
DODGE
TEN MILE RD.
PIPER
REIN
CUSHING
DONALD
RAUSCH
DAVID
LAMBRECHT
TUSCANY
GASCONY
BRITTANY
NORMANDY
SCHROEDER
WILMOT
STRICKER
JULIANA
EGO
SPRENGER
COLLINSON
VERONICA
LINCOLN
ASH
OAK
SAXONY
PIPER
REIN
CUSHING
DONALD
RAUSCH
DAVID
SAXONY
LAMBRECHT
TUSCANY
BRITTANY
NORMANDY
SCHROEDER
SHAKESPEARE
MELROSE
SHAKESPEARE
REIN
WILMOT
LEXINGTON
SHAKESPEARE
MAY
BELL
CUSHING
DWIGHT
ADLAI
SAXONY
LAMBRECHT
TUSCANY
BRITTANY
SCHROEDER
LEXINGTON
ROSALIND
TEPPERT
WILSON
FOREST
STEPHENS DR.
HAUSS
WILMOT
WARRINGTON
EMILE
JULIANA
EGO
ROSALIND
COLLINSON
RAVEN
VERONICA
EASTLAND
CT.
FAIRLANE
CT.
KELLY
TOEPPER
MOTT
PROSPER
ASH
OAK
LISTER
CURTAIN
ROSETTA
EMPIRE
HOLLAND
ALMOND
ROSALIND
LEXINGTON
ROSALIND
TEPPERT
ROXANA
ALMOND
COURTLAND
KELLY
NORTON
SEMRAU
WARRINGTON
FOREST
COURTLAND
CT.
MICHAEL
ROXANA
ALMOND
COURTLAND
KELLY
FOREST
HAUSS
WARRINGTON
EIGHT MILE RD.
KELLY
BEACONSFIELD
LISTERSIDE
MORNINGSIDE
ROSETTA
RAVEN
PETERSBURG
MARINO
HOLLAND
MOTT
PETERSBURG
MARINE
RAVEN
JOHNSTON
HOLBROOK
NORTON
DIJON
BISCAYNE
ELSMERE
SPINDLER
SEMRAU
PETERSBURG
MARINE
RAVEN
BEACONSFIELD
MABREY
RIDGECROFT
WILLOWBY
GREENBRIER
BECK
HAUSS

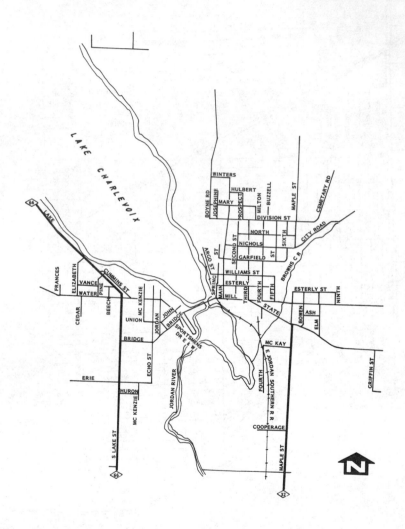

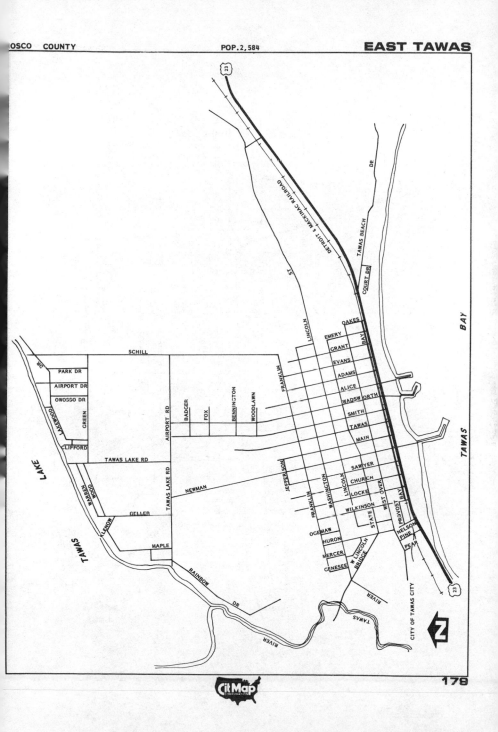

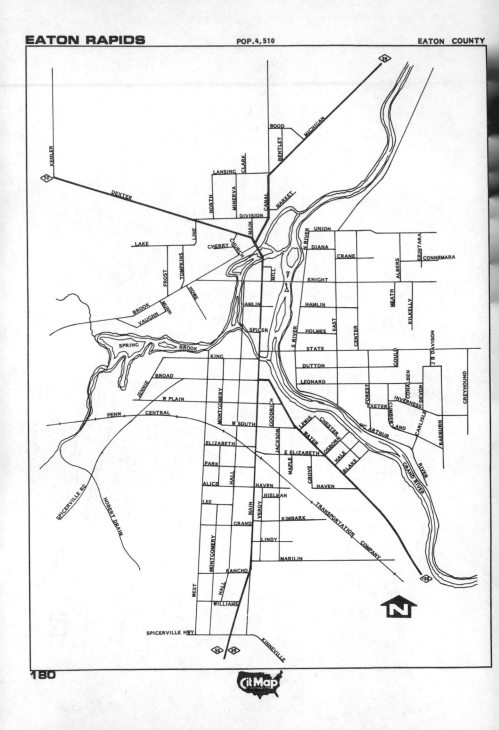

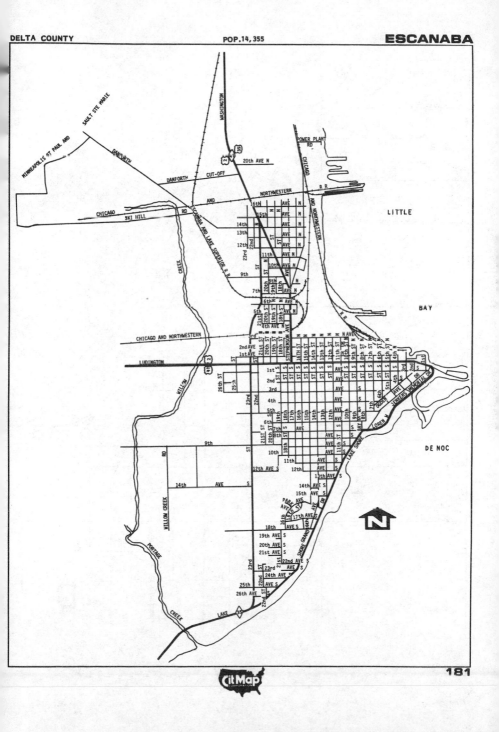

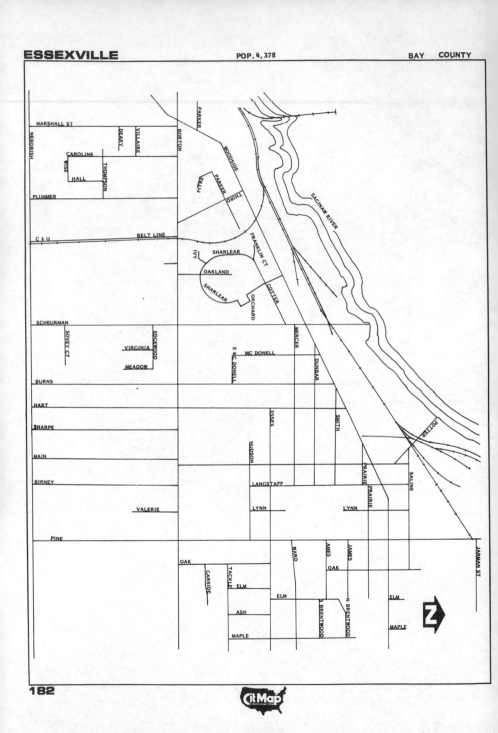

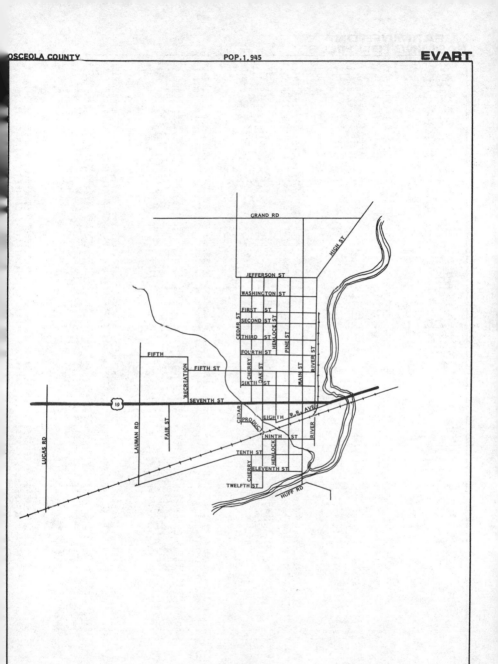

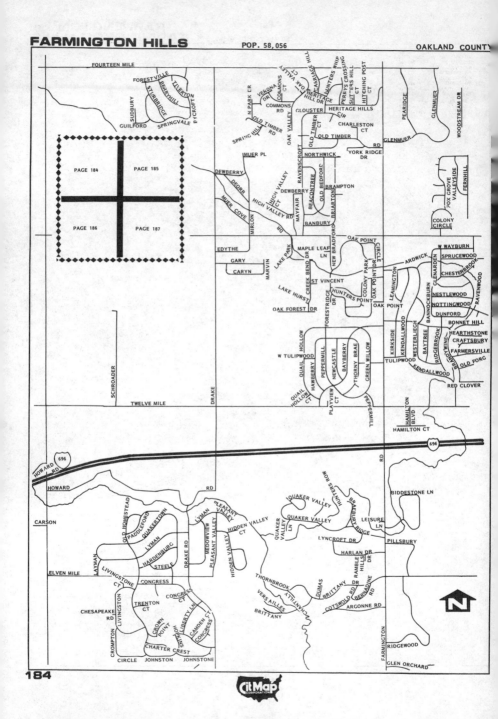

PAGE 184	PAGE 185
PAGE 186	PAGE 187

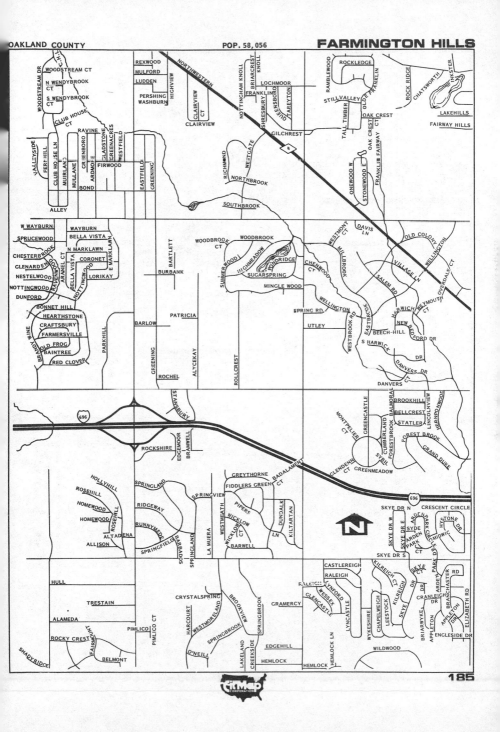

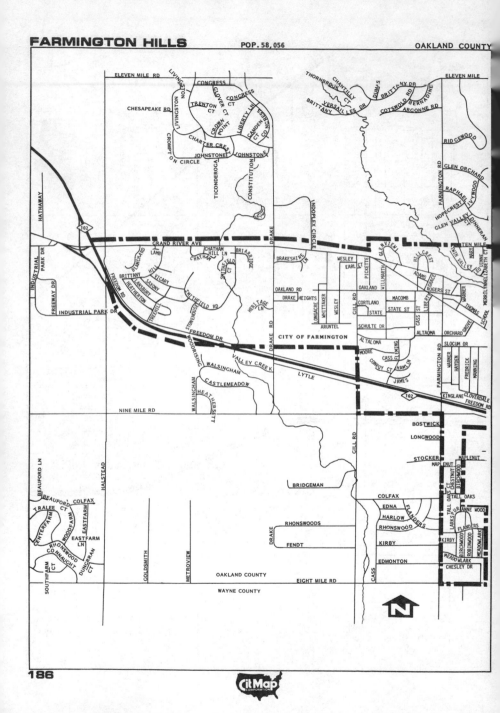

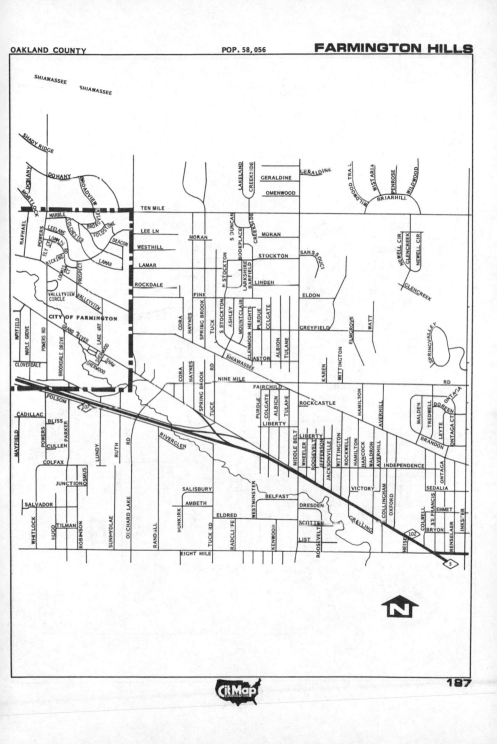

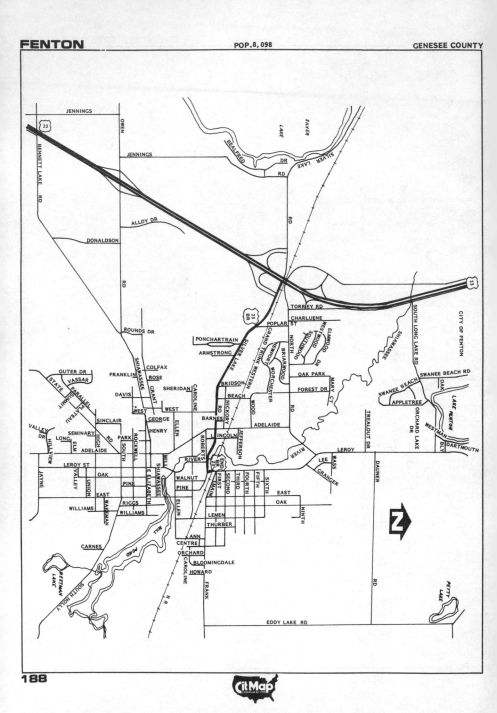

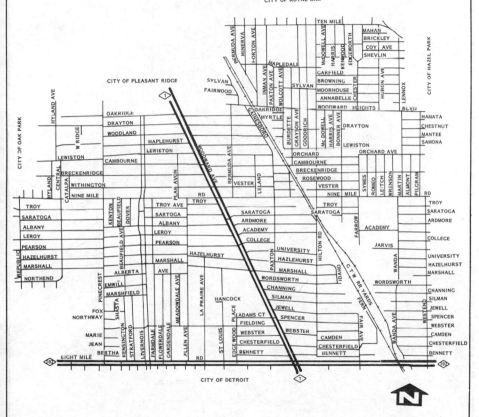

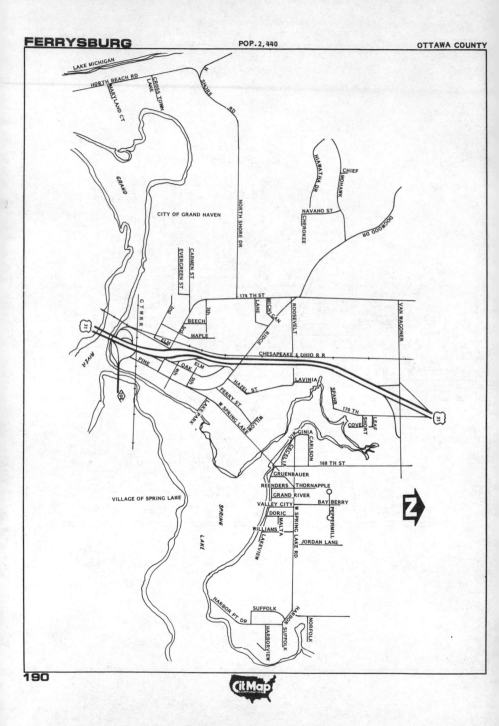

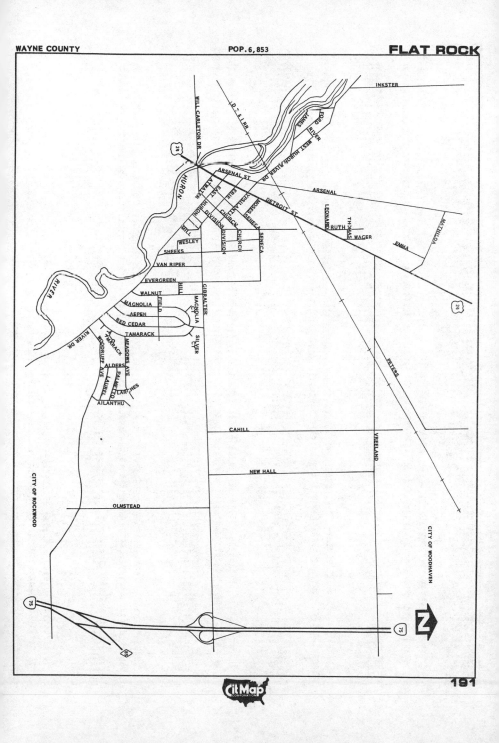

Street	No.	Dir.
ACQUE	206	SW
ADAIR	203	SW
ADAMS	202	SW
ADDISON	202	SE
ADKINS CT	204	SE
AFAF	199	SW
AGREE	202	SE
AIRPORT	211	SW
AITKEN	208	SW
ALA	210	SW
ALABAMA	203	SW
ALBERT	207	NE
ALBERTA	210	SW
ALCONA	210	SW
ALCOTT	205	SW
ALDON LA	304	SW
ALEXANDER	202	SW
ALGONQUIN	213	NE
ALLEN	212	NE
ALLENDALE PL	206	SE
ALLISON DR	198	SE
ALMA AVE	199	SW
ALPENA	214	NW
ALPHA WAY	203	NE
ALTOONA	206	NE
ALVORD	212	NE
AMBASSADOR E	202	NW
AMOS	203	SE
AMY	209	SE
AMY-JO	199	NW
ANDREW	202	NE
ANN ARBOR	207	SE
ANN DR	207	SE
APACHE DR	209	NE
ARAPAHO DR	209	NE
ARDEN	207	SE
ARENDAL DR	203	NE
ARIZONA AVE	203	SW
ARLENE	206	SW
ARLINGTON	208	NE
ARMSTRONG	198	NE
ARROW	213	NE
ARROWHEAD DR	209	NE
ARTHUR	214	NW
ASHLAWN DR	212	NE
ASHWOOD	201	SW
ASPEN CT	212	SW
ASSOCIATES DR	213	NW
ASYLUM	207	SE
ATCHEZ DR	199	SW
ATHERTON	214	NW
ATHERTON TERR	214	NW
ATWOOD	207	SE
AUBREY	202	NE
AUDREY	210	SW
AUGUSTA	202	SW
AUSTIN AVE	199	SW
AUSTIN PL	207	NE
AVALON DR	211	SW
AVENUE A	202	SE
AVENUE B	207	NE
AVENUE C	207	NE
AVERILL	204	SW
AVIS DR	210	SW
AVON	207	NE
AXFORD	207	SE
BAGLEY	206	SE
BAGWELL	208	SE
BAKER	202	SW
BALDWIN BLVD	202	NW
BALFOUR CT	212	NW
BALLARD DR	198	NE
BALLENGER HWY	206	NE
BALTIMORE BLVD	202	NW
BALTWOOD	206	NW
BANBURY PL	198	SW
BANGS	207	NW
BARBER	198	SE
BARCEY CT	213	SE
BARCH	199	NW
BARKS	208	SE
BARLOW	207	SE
BARNES	213	SW
BARNEY	206	SE
BARRIE	212	NE
BARRINGTON	209	NW
BARTH	201	SW
BARTLETT PL	207	SW
BARTON	208	SW
BARTON DR	208	SW
BASIL LA	201	SW
BASSETT PL	201	SE
BATES	198	NE
BAYBERRY	212	NW
BEACH	207	NE
BEACON	201	SW
BEACON HILL	205	NW
BEAVER	206	SW
BEAVERIDGE	211	NW
BECKER	207	SW
BEDE	213	NW
BEECHER	206	NW
BEECHWOOD	203	SE
BEGOLE	201	SW
BEL AIR DR	212	SW
BELLE AVE	203	SW
BELLINGHAM	215	SW
BELL TREE	198	SE
BELLVIEW	200	SW
BELMONT	208	SW
BELSAY	215	NW
BELVIDERE	213	NW
BEN HOGAN	204	NE
BENMARKS PL	204	NW
BENNETT	214	NE
BENNETT CT	203	SW
BENNETT DR	203	SW
BENSON	208	NW
BENT	201	NE
BENTLEY	310	NE
BERENT	214	SW
BERGEN	212	SE
BERGER DR	201	NE
BERKLEY	206	NE
BERKSHIRE DR	209	SW
BERMUDA	199	NW
BERMUDA LA	199	NW
BERNEDA DR	204	NE
BERRYWOOD	212	NW
BERYL	201	NW
BETA LA	203	NE
BETTY LA	211	SE
BEVERLY BLVD	201	SW
BICENTENNIAL	198	NW
BIRECK	207	NW
BILLINGS	202	NE
BILSKY	214	NW
BINGHAM	209	NW
BIRCICREST	201	NE
BIRCHDALE CT	206	NE
BIRCH LANE	198	SW
BISHOP	202	NW
BLACK	202	NE
BLACKBERRY LA	212	NW
BLACKINGTON	201	SW
BLACKTHORN DR	204	SE
BLADES	208	SW
BLAIR	206	NE
BLANCH	210	SE
BLANCHARD	208	SW
BLOOR	212	NE
BLUEBERRY	212	NE
BLUE BIRD LA	205	NE
BLUE LAKE DR	204	NE
BLUFF	207	NW
BOATFIELD	212	SE
BOBBY JONES DR	204	NE
BOB WHITE DR	205	NE
BOGARDOS	208	SW
BOLAN	201	NE
BONBRIGHT	202	SE
BOSTON	207	SW
BOULEVARD DR W	203	NW
BOYNE	212	SE
BRABBS	210	SE
BRABYN	206	SW
BRADLEY	206	SE
BRADY	213	SW
BRAMBLEWOOD	209	SE
BRANCH	203	NE
BRAND CT	207	SW
BRANDON	211	NE
BRAY	200	NE
BRENT	209	NW
BRENTWOOD	206	NW
BREWSTER	209	NW
BRIAN	205	SE
BRIAR HILL	211	NE
BRIAR LANE	204	SE
BRIARWOOD	212	NW
BRIGGS	210	SE
BRIGHTON	210	NE
BRIMFIELD	209	NW
BRISTOL	215	SW
BRISTOLWOOD	212	SW
BROAD	208	NW
BROAD CT	208	SW
BROADWAY	203	SW
BROOK	207	SE
BROOKGATE DR	212	SW
BROOKHOLLOW	206	NE
BROOKSIDE	208	NE
BROOKWOOD	205	SW
BROWN	206	SW
BROWNELL BLVD	201	SW
BROWNING	213	NW
BRUCE	207	SE
BRUNSWICK	212	NE
BRUSH	207	NE
BRYAN	207	NE
BRYANT	211	SE
BRYNMAWR PL	204	SE
BUCKEYE CT	207	NE
BUCKINGHAM	214	NW
BUICK	202	NE
BUNDY AVE	199	SW
BUNKER HILL	205	NW
BURGESS	201	SE
BURKE	213	SW
BURLINGTON	209	NW
BURNELL	206	NW
BURNS	203	SE
BURR BLVD	208	SW
BURROUGHS	214	NW
BURTON	208	NW
BUTLER	203	NW
BYERS	214	NW
CADET	208	NW
CADILLAC	207	NW
CADWELL CT	203	NE
CAERLON	211	SW
CALDWELL	207	NW
CALUMET	208	NW
CALVIN DR	210	SW
CAMBORNE	198	SW
CAMBRIDGE	207	SW
CAMDEN	212	NE
CAMELIA	199	SW
CAMELOT	211	SE
CAMPBELL	212	NE
CAMPUS DR	207	NW
CANNIFF	201	NE
CANTERBURY	201	NE
CATERBURY LA	201	NE
CAPTAINE LA	213	SW
CARD DR	214	SW
CARDIFF BLVD	199	NE
CARLSON DR	210	SE
CARLTON	202	NE
CARMAN	212	SE
CARMANWOOD	212	NW
CARMANWOOD DR	212	SW
CARNATION CT	204	NE
CAROLINE	204	SW
CARPENTER	198	SE
CARR	203	NE
CARRIE	204	SE
CARTIER	206	NE
CARTON	202	SE
CASHIN	204	SE
CASS AVE	198	SW
CASSIUS	202	SW
CASTLE LA	201	NE
CASTO	210	SW
CATALINA	212	NE
CECIL DR	200	SW
CEDAR	199	SW
CENTER	214	NW
CENTER RD	200	NN
CENTERWOOD	204	SW
CERDAN DR	213	SW
CHALMERS	208	NE
CHANDLER	208	NE
CHARLES AVE	199	SE
CHARTER OAK	212	SW
CHARWOOD	199	NW
CHASE	207	SW
CHATEAU DR	198	SW
CHATFIELD	206	NE
CHATHAM	198	SE
CHELAN	208	SW
CHELSEA CIR	207	SW
CHEROKEE	213	NE
CHERRY	207	NE
CHERRYLAWN	201	NE
CHERRYLAWN DR	215	NE
CHERRY TREE	212	SW
CHERRYWOOD DR	209	SE
CHERYL DR	204	SW
CHESTNUT	199	SW
CHEVROLET	206	NE
CHEYENNE	213	NE
CHICAGO	201	NE
CHICAGO BLVD	211	NE
CHICORY DR	214	SE
CHIPPEWA	202	SE
CHRISTNER	214	NW
CHRISTOPHER	207	SW
CHRYSLER	199	NE
CHURCH	207	NE
CHURCHILL	203	SE
CIRCLE DR	213	NE
CIRCLE LA	205	SE
CLAIRMONT	206	SW
CLAIRWOOD DR	206	NW
CLANCY	206	SE
CLARA	206	SE
CLARENDON	206	NE
CLARICE	214	NW
CLARK	207	NE
CLAUDE	311	NW
CLAYWARD DR	204	SE
CLEMENT	201	SW
CLEO CT	198	SE
CLEVELAND	208	NW
CLIFFORD	207	NE
CLINTON	212	NE
CLIO	198	SE
CLOVERDALE PL	206	NE
CLOVERLAWN DR	201	NW
CLOVIS AVE	199	NE
CLUBOK DR	198	NE
CLYDE	202	NE
COGGINS	203	NE
COIN	214	NW
COLBY	201	SE
COLCHESTER	211	NE
COLDWATER RD	198	NW
COLE	207	NE
COLERIDGE	213	NW
COLFAX	207	NE
COLLADAY	208	NE
COLLEGE	199	SW
COLLINGWOOD	213	NW
COLON	203	SE
COLONIAL	198	SE
COLORADO AVE	203	SW
COLUMBINE	213	NW
COMANCHE	213	NE
COMER	204	NE
COMMERCE	208	NE
COMMONW'TH	208	NE
COMSTOCK	201	SE
CONCORD	205	NW
CONCORD PASS	205	NW
CONNECTICUT	215	SW
CONNELL	213	NE
CONROY	205	NW
COOK	205	NW
COOPER AVE	201	NE
COPEMAN	203	SW
COPEMAN BLVD	203	NW
CORAL	204	SW
CORALENE	198	SW
CORNELIA	207	NE
CORNELL AVE	199	SW
CORNELL AVE N	199	SW
CORNELL AVE S	199	SW
CORY	212	NW
COTTAGE GROVE	207	NW
COUNTRY LANE	213	NE
COUNTRYSIDE DR	205	SE
COURT	209	NW
COURTSEY	204	SW
COVENTRY	206	SE
COVERT	202	NW
CRABTREE LA	210	SE
CRAIG DR	204	SW
CRAIGHTON CT	213	NW
CRAMPTON CIR	204	NE
CRANBROOK CIR	212	NW
CRANWOOD CT	199	SW
CRANWOOD DR	199	SW
CRAPO	208	NW
CRAWFORD	212	NE
CREEKWOOD TR	210	NW
CRESCETN	207	SW
CRESTBROOK LA	212	NW
CRESTLINE CIR	205	SW
CRESTLINE DR	205	SW
CRESTMOOR DR	210	NW
CRESTWOOD DR	206	SE
CRISSMAN	202	NE
CROCKER	208	NW
CROMWELL	208	NW
CRONK	208	NW
CROOKED LA	211	NE
CROSBY	205	SW
CROSS	207	SE
CROWN POINT	205	NW
CUMBERLAND	208	NW
CUMMINGS	206	SW
CURRY	204	SW
CUSTER	213	NW
CUTHBERTSON	213	NW
CUTLER	208	SW
CYPRESS	199	NW
DAKOTA	203	SW
DALE	204	SW
DALLAS	215	SE
DAMON	202	SW
DANA LA	198	SE
DANIEL	200	SW
DARCEY LA	204	SW
DARLENE	215	NW
DARLING	206	SW
DARON PL	199	NW
DARTMOUTH	201	SE
DARYLL DR	199	SW
DAVENPORT CT	212	SE
DAVENPORT DR	212	SE
DAVID	211	SE
DAVID BERGER	209	NW
DAVISON RD	208	NE
DAY	215	SW
DAYTON	201	SW
DAYTON PL	201	SW
DEARBORN	213	NE
DECAMP	212	NE
DEFREEST	201	NE
DELANEY	204	NW
DELAWARE AVE	203	SW
DELIA	202	SE
DELL	214	NW
DELMAR	201	SE
DELTA	203	SW
DENHILL	215	NE
DENIES	210	SW
DETROIT	199	NW
DEVONSHIRE	206	SE
DEWEY	202	SW
DEXEL DR	209	SE
DEXTER	203	SE
DIANE DR	201	SW
DICKINSON	207	SW
DONALDSON BLVD	206	NE
DONNELLY	202	SW
DONOVAN	213	NE
DORAN	201	NW
DOROTHY	209	NW
DORTCH DR	214	NE
DOT AVE	205	SW
DOUGHERTY PL	206	SW
DOUGLAS AVE	203	SE
DOUGLAS-JOEL	198	NE
DOWAGIAC AVE	199	NE
DOWDALL	204	NW
DOWNEY	204	SW
DOWNEY AVE	199	SW
DREXEL	203	SW
DREXEL AVE	203	SW
DRUMMOND	206	NE
DUBLIN	214	SW
DUDLEY	213	SE
DUKETTE	207	SW
DUNKIRK	199	NE
DUPONT	199	NW
DURAND	201	SW
DURHAM	199	NE
DWIGHT	207	SW
DYECREST	204	NE
EARLMOOR	209	NW
EAST	200	NW
E. BOULEVARD	203	NE
E. COURT	210	NW
EASTDALE DR	205	NW
E. FORR	204	NE
EASTGATE	215	SW
EASTHAMPTON	209	SW
EASTLAWN	201	SE
E. LEWIS	208	NW
EASTMONT	200	SW
EASTMORELAND	210	NE
E. VERNON	208	NE
EASTWOOD	201	SW
ECKINGER	204	NE
ECKLEY	209	SW
EDDINGTON	213	NW
EDDY	208	NW
EDGEMONT	206	NE
EDGEWOOD	207	NW
EDITH	212	NE
EDMUND	202	NE
EDWARDS AVE	202	NW
EDWIN	202	NW
EGLESTON	204	SE
EIGHT	207	SE
EIGHTH AVE	207	NW
ELBERON	206	NE
ELDON	199	NW
ELDORADO DR	206	NW
ELDRED	198	SW
ELDRIDGE	202	NW
ELEGAST	211	SW
ELENORA DR	206	NW
ELEVENTH AVE	207	NE
ELIZABETH	207	NE
ELIZABETH CT	207	NE
ELLIS PARK DR	214	SE
ELMRIDGE	200	SW
ELMWOOD	201	SW
ELODIE	306	NW
ELSIE	210	SE
EMERSON	201	SW
EMIL	206	SW
ENERGY DR	200	SW
ENGLEWOOD DR	214	SE
EPSILON TRAIL	203	NE
ERHARDT DR	198	NW
ERIE	202	SW
ERSKE	222	SW
ESTA DR	204	NE
ESTHER	202	SW
ETHEL	206	NE
EUCLID	207	NW
EUGENE	215	NE
EUSTON	212	NE
EVELYN	208	SW
EVERGREEN	209	SW
EVERGREEN PKWY	209	SW
EXECUTIVE PLAZA	212	NW
FAIRBANKS	208	SW
FAIRFAX	202	NE
FAIRFIELD	204	SE
FAIRHAVEN	199	NW
FAIR LA	207	SE
FAIR LANE	205	SE
FAIROAKS DR	212	SE
FAIR WAY CT	205	SW
FAIRWOOD DR	212	SE
FARAH	198	SW
FARLEY	209	SW
FARMCREST	204	SE
FARMHILL	199	NW
FARNUM	205	SW
FARNUM	206	SE
FATHER	207	NE
FENMORE	201	NE
FENTON	212	SE
FENTONLAWN DR	212	SE
FENWICK CIR	209	NW
FERN	208	SW
FERNDALE	206	NE
FERRIS	208	SE
FIELDING	206	SE
FIFTH	207	NW
FINCH LA	205	NE
FINNEY CT	207	NE
FIRST	207	NE
FLAMINGO DR	199	NW
FLEMING	201	NE
FLINT ASPHALT	214	SW
FLINT PARK BLVD	202	NW
FLORAL PARK	208	NW
FLORINE AVE	198	NE
FLOWERDAY DR	199	NE
FLUSHING	206	NW
FOREST	201	SE
FOREST HILL	206	NW
FOSS AVE	199	SW
FOSTER	202	NE
FOURTH	207	NE
FOURTH AVE	207	NE
FOURTEENTH ST	208	SW
FOX	207	NE
FOXBORO LA	206	SW
FOX CIR	208	SW
FOXCROFT CIR	209	SW
FOXCROFT LA	209	SW
FRANCES	202	SW
FRANK	206	NE
FRANKLIN	208	NW
FRASER	206	SE
FREEDOM LA	205	NW
FREEMAN	212	NE
FREMONT	206	NE
FRIEL	213	SW
FULSOM	210	NW
FULTON	199	SE
FUREY	213	SW
GAINEY	206	SE
GAMMA LA	203	NE

CitMap
CORPORATION

Street	No	Dir	Street	No	Dir	Street	No	Dir	Street	No	Dir
GARDEN CT	202	NW	HOLTSLANDER AVE	199	SE	KNICKERBOCKER	199	SW	MARK	201	SW	NEOME	207	NW
GARDEN DR	199	NW	HOME AVE	198	SW	KNIGHT	206	SE	MARKHAM	212	NE	NERREDIA	211	NW
GARDEN DR S	199	NW	HOMESTEAD	213	NE	KNOLLRIDGE LA	212	SW	MARLONE	208	SE	NEUBERT	212	NE
GARDENVIEW	207	NE	HOOVER	206	SW	KNOTTINGHAM DR	211	SW	MARMION	209	NW	NEWALL	202	SE
GARLAND	207	NE	HORTON	203	NW	KOSTA	213	SE	MARQUETTE	206	SE	NEWCOMBE	209	NW
GEHRING	205	SW	HOSLER	209	SW	KRA-NUR DR	210	NE	MARSHALL	203	SE	NEW YORK AVE	203	SW
GENA AVE	201	SE	HOURAN	206	NW	KURTZ AVE	199	NE	MARTHA	210	SW	NIAGARA	207	NW
GENESEE	201	SE	HOUSER	204	NW	LAFAYETTE	208	NE	MARTHAROSE CT	198	SW	NIGHTINGALE DR	205	NE
GENESSEE AVE	199	SW	HOWARD	208	SW	LAKEFOREST	201	NE	MARVIN	202	SE	NINTH AVE	207	NW
GENESERET	208	NW	HOWE	214	NE	LAKESIDE	200	SW	MARY	207	NE	NOLEN DR	206	NE
GENEVIEVE	210	NE	HOYLE	204	NW	LAKEVIEW	213	NW	MARYLAND AVE	203	SW	NORBERT	206	NE
GEORGE	199	NE	HUBBARD	206	SE	LAKEWOOD	208	SE	MASON	207	NE	NORTH	199	SE
GERARD	212	SW	HUCKLEBERRY	212	NW	LANDON	201	SE	MASSACHUSETTS	203	SW	N. AIRPARK	211	SW
GERARD CT	212	SW	HUGGINS	204	SW	LANNING DR	204	SE	MATHEWSON	207	NW	N. KEARSLEY	204	NW
GIBSON	206	SE	HUGH	210	NW	LAPORT AVE	199	NE	MAUVIE	208	NW	N. PARK	200	NW
GILBERT	206	NW	HUGHES	206	SE	LAPEER	209	SE	MAXINE	208	NW	N. SYCAMORE	205	SW
GILLESPIE	202	SE	HULL	212	SE	LARCHMONT	206	SE	MAXSON	206	NW	N. TERM	204	NW
GILMARTIN	208	SE	HUMBOLDT	201	SE	LARKIN	213	SE	MAYBELLE DR	214	NW	NORTHWOOD	201	SW
GLADE	204	SW	HUMPHREY	199	NW	LARK LA	205	NE	MAYBURY	208	SW	NORTON	212	SW
GLADWIN	207	NW	HUNTER	201	NW	LASALLE	110	NE	MAYOR ST	210	NW	NORWOOD DR	209	SW
GLEN AVE	202	NW	HUNTINGTON	212	SW	LASK	206	NW	MAYWOOD	201	SE	NOTTINGHAM DR	209	SW
GLENBROOK CIR	207	NE	HURLEY	202	SE	LAUREL	213	NE	MAYWOOD DR	201	NE	OAK	207	SE
GLENCARRY	213	NE	HURON	212	NE	LAUREL OAK CT	212	NW	MC ALPINE DR	199	NW	OAK-BROOK CIR	212	NW
GLENDALE	214	NE	HURST DR	206	NW	LAUREL OAK DR	212	NW	MC ARAS	207	NW	OAKLEY	213	NW
GLENWOOD	207	SW	IDA	207	SW	LAURENE	201	NE	MC CLELLAN	201	SE	OAKRIDGE DR	211	SE
GLOUCESTER	209	SW	ILLINOIS	208	NW	LAVELLE	201	SW	MC CLURE AVE	203	SE	OAKWOOD	207	NE
GOLD	208	NE	INA	202	NE	LAVENDER	206	NE	MC CLURE AVE	203	SE	O'BRIEN	198	NE
GOLFSIDE	206	NE	INDEPENDENCE	205	NE	LAWNDALE	201	SE	MC COLLEM	201	SE	O'CONNOR	201	NW
GOLFVIEW DR	205	SE	INDIANA	208	NW	LAWNWOOD CT	212	SE	MC COLLEM	201	SE	ODETTE	202	SW
GOODRICH	208	SW	INDIAN BOW	213	NE	LAWNWOOD LA	212	SE	MC CREERY	207	SE	O'HEREN	213	NW
GOREY	209	NW	INDUSTRIAL	199	SE	LAYMAN DR	204	NW	MC EWEN	210	SW	OKLAHOMA	203	SW
GORTON CT	207	NW	INDUSTRIAL AVE	202	SE	LAYTON BLVD	203	NE	MC INTOSH	207	NW	OLD CARRIAGE	212	SW
GRACELAWN AVE	201	NW	INDLESIDE	212	NE	LE BEAU	199	NW	MC KEIGHAN	214	NW	OLD CARRIAGE CT	212	SW
GRADY CT	200	SE	INLAND	200	SW	LEE	209	NW	MC KINLEY	214	NW	OLD COLONY	212	SW
GRAM	213	SW	IRENE	206	SE	LEERDA	201	NE	MC KINLEY BLVD	213	NE	OLEANDER	199	NW
GRAND BLVD	199	SW	IRON	214	SW	LEITH	202	SE	MC LEAN	212	SE	OLIVE	203	SW
GRAND TRAVERSE	212	NE	IRVING CT	212	NE	LELAND	212	NE	MC PHAIL	208	SE	OLIVER ST	213	NW
GRANDY	208	NW	ISLAND	213	NE	LENNIE	214	NW	MC QUEEN	206	SE	ORANGE BLOSSOM	198	SE
GRANT	202	NE	IVA	210	NW	LENNOX	207	SE	MEADE	208	NE	ORANGE LA	198	SE
GRANVILLE	212	SW	IVAN CT	212	NE	LESLIE CT	207	NE	MEADOWBROOK	204	NE	ORCHARD CT	206	NC
GRATIOT	206	SE	IVANHOE	209	NW	LESLIE DR	201	NE	MEADOWCROFT DR	214	NE	OREGON AVE	203	NW
GRAY	202	SW	IVES	209	NE	LESTER	206	SE	MEIDA	206	SW	OREN	202	SE
GREEN	202	SW	JACKSON	201	SE	LETA	211	SW	MEISNER	203	SE	ORGOULD	207	NW
GREENBRIAR LA	212	NW	JACQUE	206	SW	LEVERN	205	SE	MELODY LANE	204	SE	ORIOLE	205	NE
GREENBROOK LA	201	NE	JAMES	213	SW	LEWIS	199	NW	MENDELL BERGER	198	NW	ORKNEY DR	211	SW
GREENLAWN	201	NE	JAMES P.	207	NE	LEWIS BLVD	203	SW	MENLO	208	SW	ORR	203	SE
GREENLY	213	NW	JAMESTOWN CT	212	SW	LEWIS RD	203	NW	MENOMINEE	213	NE	ORVILLE	208	SW
GREEN TREE DR	212	SW	JAMIESON	207	SW	LEXINGTON	207	SE	MENTON	213	NE	OSCEOLA	202	NE
GREENVIEW DR	205	SE	JANE AVE	203	SW	LIBERTY	207	SE	MERCURY	210	SE	OSSINGTON	212	SE
GREENWAY	201	SW	JANET HIGGINS	201	SW	LILA	204	SE	MERIT DR	204	NE	O'TOOLE LA	199	NW
GREENWOOD CT	206	NW	JANICE DR	198	SE	LILLIAN DR	198	SE	MERLE	210	SW	OTSEGO	210	SW
GRIGGS	201	NE	JANNEAN CT	200	SW	LINCOLN	212	NE	MERLIN	211	SW	OTTAWA	210	SW
GRISWOLD DR	198	NW	JARVIS	207	SE	LINCOLN DR	207	SW	MERRILL	207	NE	OTTO	212	SE
GROVELAND	203	NW	JASMINE	208	SW	LINDA	204	SE	MIAMI LA	201	NE	OVERHILL DR	211	NE
HAAS DR	214	NE	JEAN	207	NW	LINNAEUS	207	SE	MICHAEL CT	207	SE	OWEN	204	NE
HALL	201	SE	JEFFERSON	209	NW	LINSEY BLVD	209	SW	MICHAEL DR	207	SE	OXFORD LA	211	NE
HAMILTON	202	SW	JENNINGS	201	NW	LINTON	213	SW	MICHIGAN	203	SW	OXLEY DR	198	SE
HAMMERBERG	212	NW	JEWELL	200	SW	LINWOOD	208	SW	MIDDLECROFT	205	SE	PACKARD	210	NE
HAMMOND	206	SE	JOAL LA	204	SW	LIPPINCOTT BLVD	209	SE	MIDDLESEX	200	SW	PADDINGTON	212	NW
HAMPDEN	211	NE	JOHNSON	206	SW	LIVINGSTON DR	213	NW	MIDDLETON	206	SE	PADUCAH	206	NE
HAMPSHIRE	198	SW	JOLIET	207	NW	LLOYD	201	SE	MIDWAY CIR	208	SE	PAGE	207	NE
HAMPSTEAD DR	203	NE	JOLSON	213	SE	LOBDELL	207	NW	MILANO	215	NE	PALADIN DR	212	NE
HARCOTT	212	SE	JOSE	206	NW	LOCKHEAD	214	NW	MILBOURNE	198	SW	PALMER	209	NW
HARMON	202	SE	JOSEPH	200	SE	LODER CT	214	NW	MILDRED	202	SE	PALMETTO	199	NW
HARMONY DR	204	SE	JOSEPHINE	202	SW	LODGE	206	SW	MILLBROOK DR	207	NE	PARK	208	SW
HAROLD	213	NW	JOY	206	NW	LOMBARDY	205	NE	MILLER	211	NE	PARLBELT DR	198	SE
HARRISON	207	NE	JOYCE	213	NE	LOMITA	202	NE	MILLIKEN	201	SE	PARKFOREST #3	201	SW
HARRY	200	SW	JOYNER	208	SE	LONG	214	SE	MILLIKEN CT	200	SE	PARKFRONT	201	SW
HARTIGAN	199	NW	JUDD	212	SE	LONGWAY	208	NW	MILLS ACRE	205	NW	PARKHURST	201	SE
HARVARD	199	NW	JUDITH ANN	198	SW	LONGFELLOW	202	NW	MILTON DR	213	NW	PARKLAND	202	SE
HARVARD AVE	199	NW	JUDY CT	200	SW	LORADO AVE	199	SW	MINERVA DR	201	NW	PARKSIDE DR	211	NE
HARWINE	201	NW	JULIAH AVE	199	SW	LORAINE	209	NW	MINNESOTA	208	NW	PARKTON	201	NW
HARWOOD DR	199	NW	KAGEY CT	207	NV	LOUISA	207	NE	MINNIE	206	SE	PARKWAY AVE	201	NW
HASSELBRING	207	SW	KANSAS	208	NW	LOWDEN LA	206	SE	MISSOURI	208	NW	PARKWAY CT	212	SE
HASTINGS	208	NW	KAREN DR	198	SE	LOWELL BLVD	213	NW	MITCHELL	204	NW	PARKWOOD	212	SE
HATHAWAY DR	200	SW	KATHLEEN	207	SE	LUDWIG	213	NE	MITSON BLVD	206	NW	PARTRIDGE	207	SE
HATHERLY	206	NW	KATY	199	NW	LYLE	210	NE	MOCKINGBIRD LA	205	NE	PASADENA	202	SW
HAWTHORNE DR	211	NW	KEARS	208	NW	LYMAN	203	SW	MOHAWK	213	NE	PATERSON	202	SW
HAZEL	214	SW	KEARSLEY	208	NE	LYNBROOK	212	NW	MOLLWOOD	204	NE	PATRICK	209	NW
HAZELTON	207	SW	KEATS	213	NW	LYNCH	208	NW	MONROE	207	SE	PAWNEE DR	205	NW
HECTOR	208	SE	KEENE DR	204	SW	LYNDON AVE	201	NW	MONTANA AVE	203	SW	PAYNE	207	NE
HEDGETHORN CT	204	SE	KELLAR AVE	198	NE	LYNN	204	SW	MONTCALM	215	SW	PEACH TREE DR	199	NW
HEDGETHORN CIR	204	SE	KELLY LA	201	NE	LYNNE AVE	205	NW	MONTCLAIR	208	NW	PEACHWOOD DR	212	SW
HEILMAN	213	SW	KELSO	208	NE	LYON	207	NE	MONTERAY	206	SE	PEARL	210	SE
HELBER	201	SW	KENDALL	210	SW	LYNTON	212	NW	MONTIETH	207	NW	PEER ST	212	SE
HEMPHILL	214	NW	KENDALL DR	210	SE	MABEL AVE	203	SW	MONTROSE	201	NW	PEMBERTON	200	SE
HENDERSON	207	NE	KENNELWORTH	208	SW	MAC AVE	199	NW	MOORE	201	NW	PENBROOK	212	NW
HENRY	203	SE	KENNETH	213	NE	MAC DONALD	214	NW	MORNINGSIDE DR	209	NE	PENCOMBE PL	206	SE
HERRICK	206	SE	KENOVA DR	205	NE	MACKIN	201	NE	MORRIS	213	SE	PENCELLY	213	NW
HIBISCUS	199	NW	KENSINGTON	208	NW	MACOMBER	208	NE	MORRISH	209	SW	PENNSYLVANIA	208	NW
HIDDEN OAKS CT	212	SW	KENT	209	SW	MADELON CT	205	NW	MORRIS HILLS	199	NE	PENOYER	207	NE
HIGHFIELD	212	SE	KENT DR	208	SE	MADISON	213	NW	PKWY			PENWOOD	199	NW
HIGHLAND	207	NW	KENTUCKY	208	NW	MAGNOLIA	199	NW	MORRISON	213	SW	PERRY	207	NW
HIGHWOOD	198	SW	KENTWOOD	212	NW	MAIN	200	NW	MOTT AVE	201	NW	PERRY CT	207	SE
HILL	199	NW	KENWOOD	207	SW	MAINES	201	NE	MOULTON DR	212	SW	PETRIE	207	NE
HILLCREST	213	NE	KERMIT	201	NE	MAJOR	212	NW	MOUNTAIN	208	NE	PETTIBONE	212	SE
HILLCREST BLVD	214	NW	KETTERING	210	NE	MALLERY	201	SW	MT. ELLIOT	206	SE	PERAGA PL	213	NE
HILLCREST CIRCLE	204	NE	KETZLER DR	211	NW	MANDEVILLE	212	SE	MULBERRY	212	NW	PHEASANT	205	NE
HILLCREST CIR N	204	NE	KEVIN-DAVID	198	NE	MANITOU	213	NE	MUNSON	209	SE	PHILADELPHIA	203	SW
HILLCREST CIR S	204	NE	KEYES	202	SW	MANN	206	SE	MURPHY	201	SW	PHILLIP	212	SE
HILLCROFT DR	200	SE	KILLARNEY PARK	214	SW	MANN HALL	206	SE	MURPHY DR	201	SW	PHILLIPS	212	SE
HILLS	208	NE	KILLIAN COURT	198	NE	MANN HALL	206	SE	MURRAY HILL	199	NW	PICKARD	213	NW
HILLTON LA	198	SW	KIMBALL	208	SW	MANNING	208	NE	MYRTLE	201	NE	PICKFORD	203	SE
HILLVIEW	198	SW	KIMBERLY WOODS	198	SW	MANOR	214	SW	MYRTON	213	SW	PICKWICK PL	212	SW
HITCHCOCK	203	NW	KING	207	NE	MANOR DR	204	SW	NASH DR	205	NW	PIERCE	208	NE
HOBSON AVE	201	NW	KINGS LA	212	SE	MANSFIELD	206	SE	NASSER	198	NE	PIERSON	202	NW
HODGENS PKWY	215	SW	KINGSWOOD DR	212	SW	MAPLE	211	SE	NATALIE DR	213	SW	PIERSON PL	208	NW
HOFF	213	SE	KIRK	207	NW	MAPLELAWN DR	215	SW	NATHAN	203	SE	PINEHURST	212	NW
HOGARTH	206	SE	KIRKWOOD	201	SE	MARENGO	202	NW	NEBRASKA	208	NW	PINGREE	209	SW
HOLBROOK AVE	198	NE	KISSNER	198	SE	MARGATE CIR	202	NE	NEDRA	201	NE	PIPER AVE	202	SE
HOLIDAY DR	211	SE	KLEIN	199	NE	MARIA	212	SW	NEEBISH	213	NE	PIPE CT	207	NE
HOLLY	204	SW	KNAPMAN	203	SE	MARILYN	204	NE	NEFF	199	NW	PITKIN	209	NW
HOLMAN	207	NE	KNAPP	204	NE	MARION BLVD	201	NE	NELSON	208	NW	PLAINFIELD AVE	203	NW
			KNAPP DR	206	SE	MARJA	201	NE	NELSON CT	215	SW	POE	213	NW

Street	No.	Dir	Street	No.	Dir	Street	No.	Dir	Street	No.	Dir
POLLY	200	SW	SAVOY	213	SE	THAYER	207	SW	WICKFIELD DR	212	SE
PONTIAC	207	NW	SAXON	214	NW	THETA PASS	203	NE	WILLARD CT	207	NE
POPLAR	208	NE	SAYRE CT	200	NW	THETFORD	200	SW	WILLENA DR	199	NW
POTTER	204	SE	SCHAF DR	200	NW	THIRD	207	NE	WILLIAMS	207	NE
PRATT	215	SE	SCHAFER DR	210	NW	THIRTEENTH ST	208	SW	WILLIAMSBURG	212	SW
PREMIER	200	SW	SCHUMACHER	212	SE	THISTLEWOOD DR	204	SE	WILLIAMSON	212	SE
PRESTON	201	SW	SCHUYLER DR	205	SF	THOM	203	SE	WILLIS	209	SW
PRESTWOOD	208	SW	SCOTT	205	SE	THOMAS	206	NE	WILL-JO LA	211	SE
PRINCETON AVE	199	SW	SCOTTWOOD	214	SW	THOMPSON	208	NW	WILLOW	208	NW
PRINGLE	213	SE	SECOND AVE	207	NW	THORNAPPLE	204	SE	WILLOW BROOK	212	NW
PROCTOR	201	SE	SEMINOLE	207	NW	THORNDALE DR	204	SE	WILLOWDALE DR	205	SE
PROPER	213	SW	SENECA	201	SE	THORNFIELD LA	206	SW	WILLOW WOOD	212	SW
PROSPECT	206	NE	SENTINEL RIDGE	206	SW	THORNTON	201	SE	WILLS	202	NW
PROVIDENCE	209	SW	SEVENTH	207	SE	THORNTREE DR	204	SE	WILMAR	204	NE
PULASKI	202	NW	SEVENTH AVE	207	NW	THRUSHFIELD	212	SW	WILSHIRE	198	SW
QUINLAN DR	213	SE	SEYMOUR	208	SE	TIFFIN	206	NE	WILTON PL	203	NE
RABB	207	SE	SHADYCROFT DR	214	NE	TILDEN	202	SE	WINANS	208	SW
RABLEE	211	NE	SHAMROCK LA	201	NE	TILLIE	208	SW	WINDEMERE	208	NE
RACE	202	SW	SHANNON	214	SW	TILLINGHAST	208	SW	WINDLAND DR	201	NW
RADCLIFFE	207	SW	SHAW	213	NE	TIMBERLANE DR	212	NW	WINDRUSH	203	NE
RALPH	209	NW	SHAWNEE	213	NE	TIMBERVIEW	206	SW	WINDSOR	212	NW
RALSTON	208	SW	SHELDON LA	211	SE	TIPPERARY LA	205	NW	WINDY WOOD DR	198	SW
RAMSAY BLVD	207	SW	SHELLY	213	NW	TIPTREE PATH	203	NE	WINIFRED	203	SE
RANDY CT	201	NE	SHRFF	208	NE	TITAN DR	199	NW	WINONA	201	SE
RANGELEY	209	NW	SHERMAN AVE	201	NW	TOBIAS	208	SW	WINSFORD BYWAY	202	NE
RANKIN	201	SE	SHERRY DR	204	SW	TOBY-BETH	198	NE	WINTERS DR	204	NE
RASCH CT	207	SE	SHERWOOD DR	206	SE	TOMMY ARMOUR	204	NE	WINTHROP BLVD	202	NW
RASKOB	206	NE	SHILLELAGH DR	205	NE	TORONTO	207	SE	WISCONSIN	208	NW
RASPBERRY	212	NW	SHORE DR	206	NE	TORRANCE	203	SE	WISNER	201	NE
RAY	207	NW	SHUBERT	213	SW	TORREY	211	SE	WITHERBEE	202	SW
RAYMOND	210	SW	SIMCA DR	212	SW	TOURAINE	200	SE	WOLCOTT	206	NE
RAYWOOD	201	SW	SIMCOE	212	NE	TOWER	208	NE	WOOD	207	NW
READY	213	SW	SITKA	215	SW	TRANSUE	210	SE	WOODBINE	202	NW
RED	213	NW	SIXTH	207	SE	TREMONT AVE	199	SW	WOODBOURNE DR	212	SE
RED BIRD LA	205	NE	SIXTH AVE	207	NW	TROTWOOD LA	212	SE	WOODBRIAR DR	212	SW
REID	207	SW	SKANDER	198	SW	TROUT DR	208	SE	WOODBRIDGE	206	NE
REMELL	208	SE	SLOAN	212	NE	TRUMBULL AVE	201	SE	WOODCLIFF	198	SW
REMINGTON	212	NE	SLOAN HGTS	206	NE	TUCKER	207	NE	WOODCROFT	207	SW
RENAULT DR	212	SW	SMITHWICK CIR	209	SW	TUSCOLA	208	NE	WOODHALL	201	NE
RETHA CT	198	SW	SOMERSET LA	209	NW	TUXEDO	212	NE	WOODHAVEN	198	SW
REX AVE	199	SE	SONNY	201	SE	TWELFTH	207	SE	WOODLAND	210	SE
REYNOLDS	206	SW	SOUTH	200	NW	TWILIGHT DR	203	SE	WOOD LANE	209	SW
RHEA	204	SW	S. AIRPOARK	211	SW	TYRONE	206	NE	WOODLAWN	208	NE
RICE	204	SW	SOUTH DR	207	SW	UNION	207	NE	WOODLIN	198	SE
RICHFIELD	204	SW	SOUTHGATE DR	212	SW	UTAH	203	SE	WOODMOOR DR	210	NE
RICHFIELD RD	205	SE	S. KEARSLEY	204	NW	UTLEY	211	NW	WOODROW	203	SE
RIDGE	204	SW	S. KEARSLEY DR	204	NW	VALENCIA	210	NE	WOODSIDE	208	NW
RIDGECLIFFE DR	206	SW	SOUTHLAWN	213	NE	VALLEY	209	SW	WOODSIDE DR	208	SW
RIDGECREST	200	SE	S. SYCAMORE	201	SW	VALLEY LA	204	NW	WOODSLEA	208	SW
RIDGECREST CT	200	SE	SOUTHWOOD	213	SW	VALLEY LANE DR	210	SW	WOODSTEAD	204	SW
RIDGELAWN	208	SW	SPARTAN	213	SE	VALORIE LA	198	SE	WORCHESTER	209	SW
RIDGELAWN AVE	208	SW	SPENCER	202	SE	VAN BUREN	206	SE	WRIGHT	207	NE
RIDGEVIEW CT	200	SE	SPRINGER	206	NW	VAN BUSKIRK	207	SW	WROXTON DR	206	NW
RIDGEVIEW DR	200	SE	SPRINGFIELD	209	SE	VAN CAMPEN	212	SW	WYOMING AVE	203	SW
RIDGEWAY AVE	201	NW	SPRING VALLEY	201	NW	VANLUE	207	SE	YALE	199	SW
RIEGLE	204	SW	SQUIRE LA	205	NW	VANSLYCK	212	SW	YEAGER DR	214	SW
RINN	210	SE	STADIUM DR	207	NE	VANWAGONER	202	SW	YORK AVE	199	SW
RISEDORPH	204	SW	STAFFORD	199	SE	VARTY	209	NW	YORKSHIRE	200	SW
RIVERBEND	206	NW	STANDFORD	206	NW	VASSAR	215	NE	YOUNG	208	NW
RIVER BIRCH	206	NW	STANLEY	208	SW	VELDON	201	SW	ZIMMERMAN	206	SW
RIVER DALE	206	NW	STARKWEATHER	208	NW	VERDUN	199	NW	ZUNI DR	209	NE
RIVER FOREST DR	206	NW	STATLER DR	205	SW	VERMILYA	212	NE			
RIVER HILL DR	206	NW	STEDRON AVE	201	NE	VERNON	212	NE			
RIVERIDGE CT	200	SE	STEEPLECHASE	206	SW	VICTORIA	212	NE			
RIVER OAKS DR	206	SW	STEM LA	198	NE	VILLAGE DR	212	SW			
RIVER POINT DR	206	NW	STEPHENS	212	SW	VINELAND CT	215	NE			
RIVERSIDE DR	203	SW	STERLING	201	SE	VIRGINIA	199	NE			
RIVER VALLEY DR	206	NW	STEVENS	207	NE	VOXBURG	207	SW			
RIVIERA	212	NW	STEVENSON	206	NE	WABASH	201	SE			
ROANOKE	201	SW	STEVER	203	SW	WAGER	202	NE			
ROAT	209	SE	STEWART	202	NW	WAGNER	215	SE			
ROBBIE LA	199	SE	STIFFLER	199	NW	WALDMAN	212	NW			
ROBERTA	210	SE	STOCKBRIDGE	205	SW	WALLACE ST	208	SW			
ROBERTS	202	NE	STOCKDALE	210	NE	WALLER	210	SW			
ROBERTS DR	207	NE	STOCKER	206	SE	WALTER	201	SE			
ROBIN	202	SW	STOCKTON	207	SE	WALTON	206	SW			
ROBINDALE DR	214	NE	STONE	207	NW	WAREHOUSE DR	213	SE			
ROCHDLAE DRIVE	198	SW	STONECREEK	207	NE	WARNER	208	SW			
ROCKCREEL	212	NW	STONY POINT	205	NW	WARREN	202	SE			
ROCKFORD	206	NE	STONY RIDGE	212	SW	WARRINGTON	201	NE			
ROOME CT	208	NE	STUMP	204	NW	WARWICK DR	209	SW			
RONALD	212	NE	SUBURBAN CT	202	NW	WASHINGTON	208	NW			
RONNIE	212	SW	SUE-ANN LA	211	SW	WASHTENAW	201	SW			
ROOSEVELT	208	NW	SUGAR WOOD CT	206	NW	WATCH HILL DR	212	SW			
ROOT	207	NE	SUMMIT	199	SW	WATER	207	NE			
ROSCOMMON	210	SW	SUNDAY	206	SW	WATSON	204	NE			
ROSE ANNA	200	SE	SUNDERLAND PL	212	SE	WAY	209	NE			
ROSEDALE	202	NE	SUNNYDALE	210	SW	WAYNE	208	SE			
ROSELAND	203	SE	SUNNYMEAD	214	NE	WEAVER	203	SE			
ROSELAWN DR	201	NE	SUNNYSIDE	208	SW	WEBSTER	200	SE			
ROSEMARY	208	SE	SUNRIDGE DR	205	SW	WEILMAN	206	SW			
ROSENFIELD	198	NE	SUNSET DR	206	SW	WELCH BLVD	201	SE			
ROSETHORN CIR	204	SE	SURREY LA	210	SE	WELCOME DR	204	SW			
RUSSELL AVE	199	SW	SUSAN	201	NE	WELLER	208	SW			
RUSSET CT	198	SE	SUSSEX	201	NE	WELLINGTON	207	SE			
RUTH AVE	199	SW	SUTTON	206	NE	WELLS	212	SW			
RYAN	206	SW	SWALLOW DR	206	NE	WESLEY	202	SW			
SAGINAW	207	NE	SAYZE	206	SW	WESTCHESTER DR	212	SE			
ST. CLAIR	207	NW	SYCAMORE CIR	205	SW	WESTCOMBE	206	SE			
ST. JOHN	200	SW	SYLVAN	207	SE	WESTERN	203	NE			
ST. MARTINS CIR	212	SE	TACKEN	205	SW	WESTMONT	212	SW			
ST. MARTINS DR	212	SE	TACOMA	207	SE	WESTMORELAND	202	NW			
SALISBURY	206	SE	TAFT	208	NW	WESTON	204	SE			
SALISHAN CIR	204	SW	TALLEY DR	206	NW	WESTOVER	205	SE			
SALLY CT	198	SE	TALL OAKS	206	SW	W. VERNON	208	NE			
SAM SNEAD DR	204	NE	TAYLOR	202	SW	WESTWOOD PKWY	211	NE			
SANDALWOOD DR	209	SE	TEBO	209	SW	WHISPERING OAK	212	SW			
SANDPIPER DR	205	NE	TEMPLE	199	NE	WHITE	202	SW			
SANDY LA	210	SE	TENNYSON	213	NW	WHITINGHAM DR	209	SW			
SAN JUAN	206	NW	TENTH AVE	207	NW	WHITMAN	213	NW			
SANTA BARBARA	201	NE	TERM	214	NW	WHITNEY	208	SW			
SANTA CLARA CT	206	NW	TERRACE	213	NE	WHITTEMORE	212	SE			
SANTA CRUZ	206	NW	TERRY AVE	199	NE	WHITTIER	204	SW			
SARA ROSE	198	NE	THACKERAY	202	NW	WHITTLESEY	205	SW			
SARATOGA DR	205	NE				WICKFIELD CIR	212	SE			

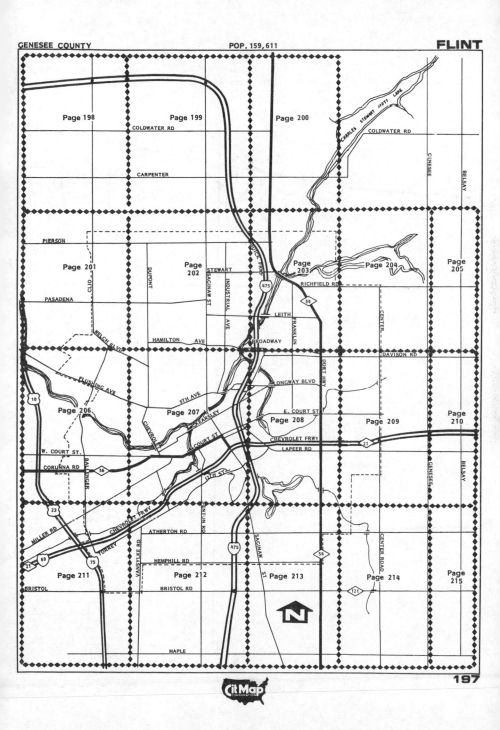

Page 198
Page 199
Page 200

COLDWATER RD
CHARLES STEWART MOTT LAKE
COLDWATER RD

GENESEE
BELSAY

CARPENTER

PIERSON

Page 201
Page 202
STEWART
Page 203
Page 204
Page 205

BUICK FRWY
DUPONT
SAGINAW ST
INDUSTRIAL AVE
475
RICHFIELD RD
CENTER

PASADENA
54

LEITH
FRANKLIN

WELCH BLVD
HAMILTON AVE
BROADWAY

DAVISON RD

FLUSHING AVE
10
5TH AVE
LONGWAY BLVD
DORT HWY

Page 206
Page 207
CHEVROLET
KEARSLEY
E. COURT ST
Page 208
Page 209
Page 210

W. COURT ST.
COURT ST.
CHEVROLET FRWY
21

CORUNNA RD
BALLINGER
56
LAPEER RD

12TH ST.

23
CHEVROLET FRWY
FENTON RD

MILLER RD
TORREY
ATHERTON RD

69
75
VANSYLKE RD
475
SAGINAW ST
54

27
HEMPHILL RD

Page 211
Page 212
Page 213
Page 214
Page 215
BRISTOL
BRISTOL RD
121

MAPLE

N

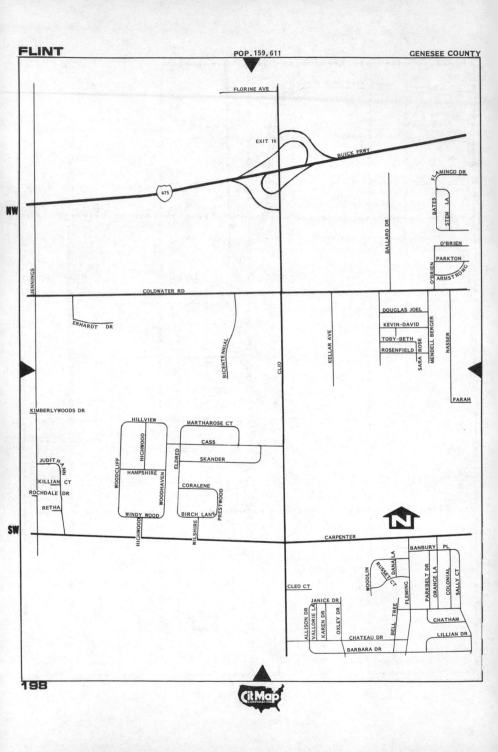

NW

SW

FLORINE AVE

EXIT 16

BUICK FRWY

475

FLAMINGO DR

BATES

STEM LA

O'BRIEN

PARKTON

O'BRIEN

ARMSTRONG

BALLARD DR

JENNINGS

COLDWATER RD

ERHARDT DR

BICENTENNIAL

CLIO

KELLAR AVE

DOUGLAS JOEL

KEVIN-DAVID

TOBY-BETH

ROSENFIELD

SARA ROSE

MENDELL BERGER

NASSER

FARAH

KIMBERLYWOODS DR

HILLVIEW

MARTHAROSE CT

HIGHWOOD

CASS

WOODCLIFF

ELDRED

SKANDER

JUDITH ANN

HAMPSHIRE

KILLIAN CT

CORALENE

ROCHDALE DR

PRESTWOOD

RETHA

WINDY WOOD

BIRCH LANE

HIGHWOOD

WOODHAVEN

WILSHIRE

CARPENTER

N

BANBURY

PL

WOODLIN

RUSSET CT

DANALA

PARKBELT DR

ORANGE LA

COLONIAL

SALLY CT

CLEO CT

JANICE DR

FLEMING

ALLISON DR

VALLORIE LA

KAREN DR

OXLEY DR

BELL TREE

CHATHAM

CHATEAU DR

LILLIAN DR

BARBARA DR

CitMap
CORPORATION

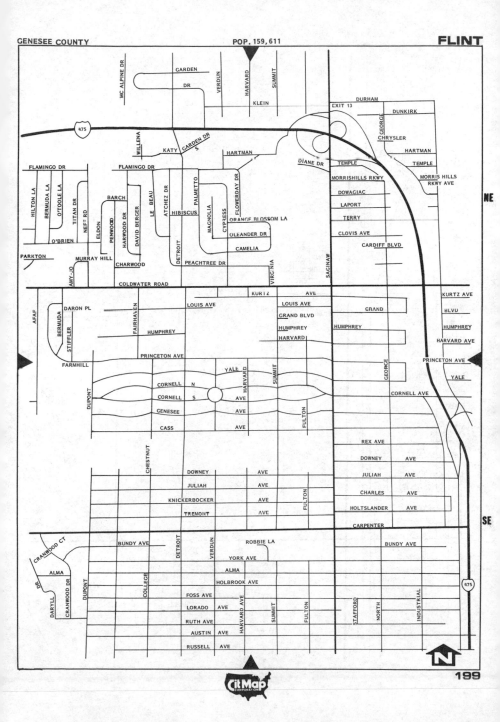

NE

SE

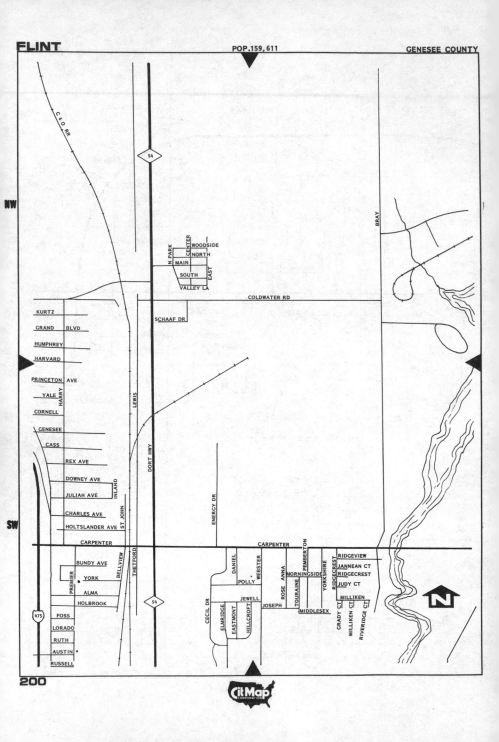

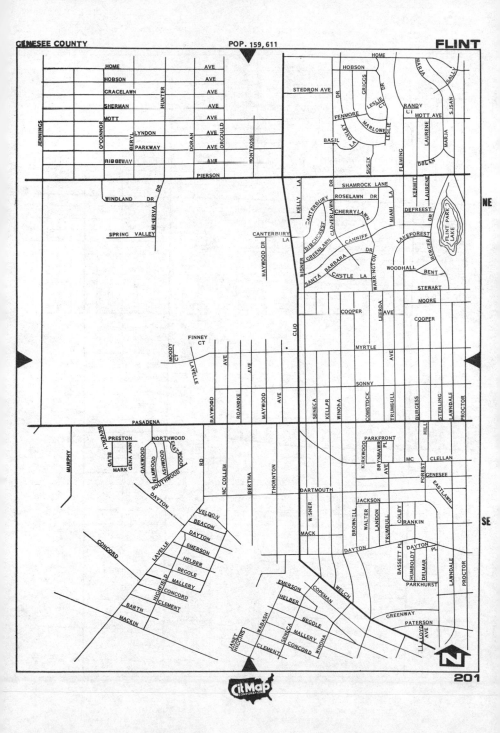

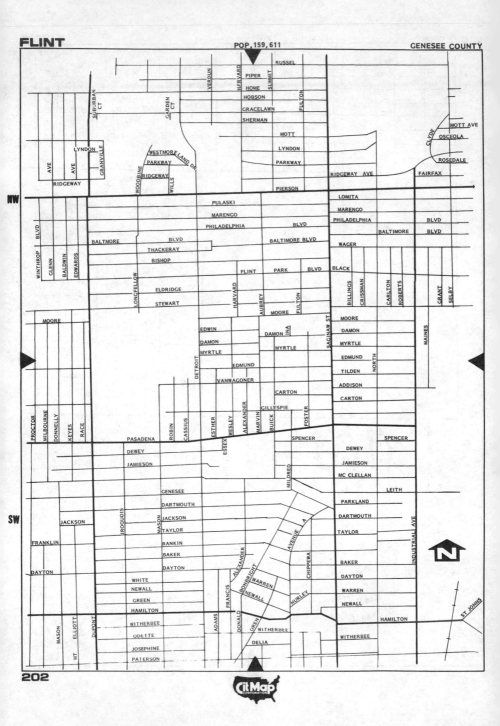

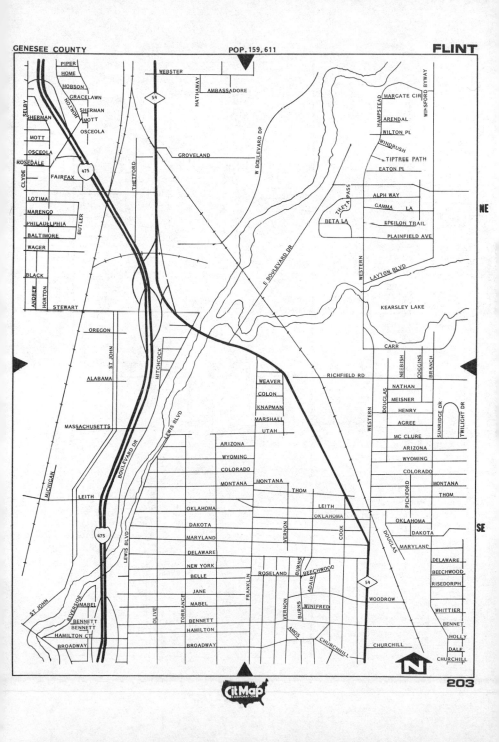

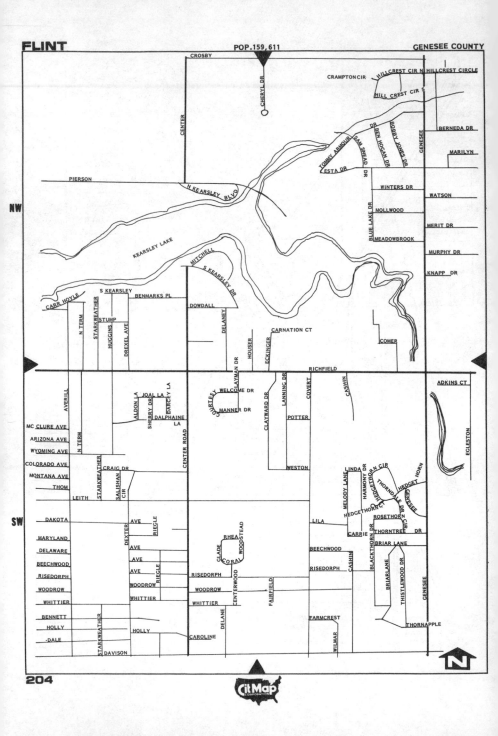

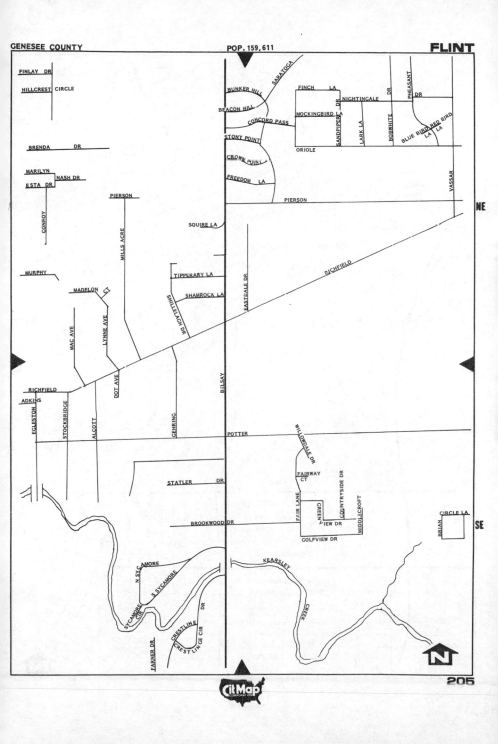

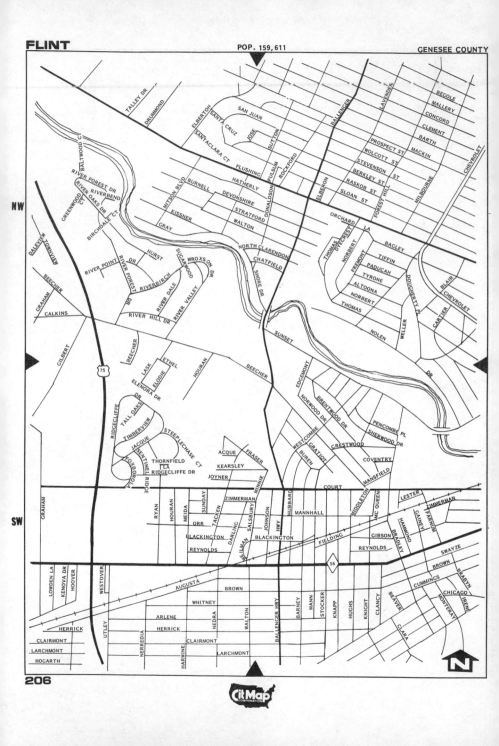

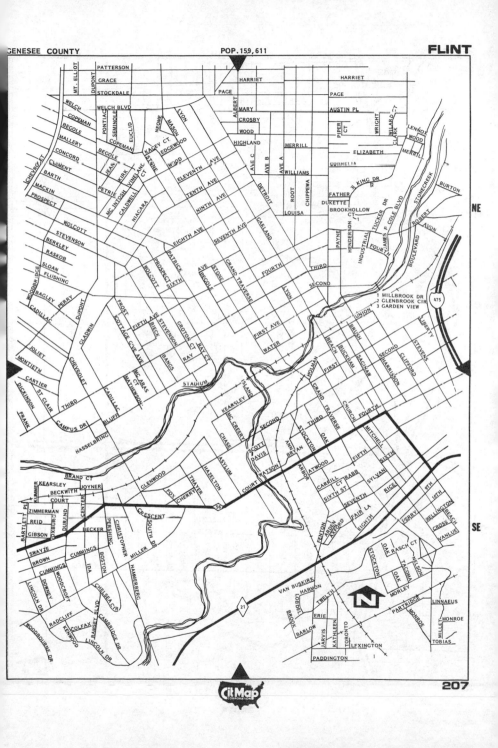

POP.159,611

NE

SE

1 MILLBROOK DR
2 GLENBROOK CIR
3 GARDEN VIEW

475

N

CitMap
CORPORATION

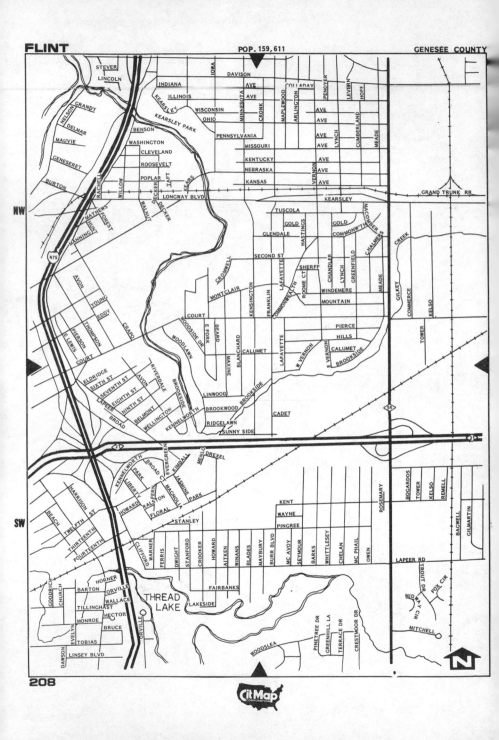

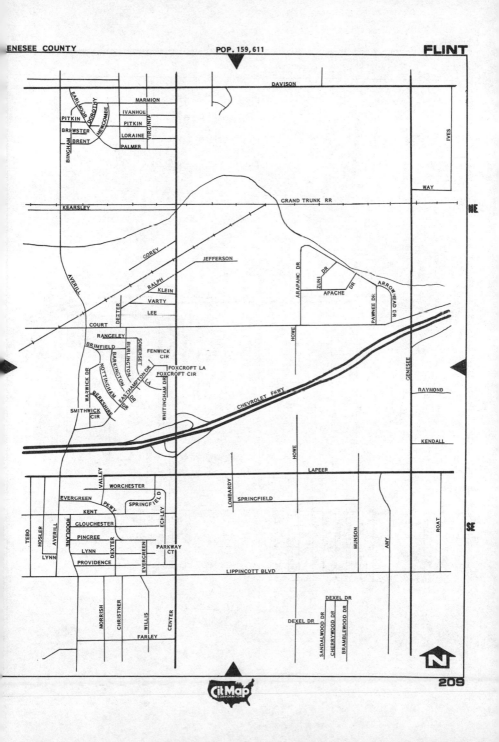

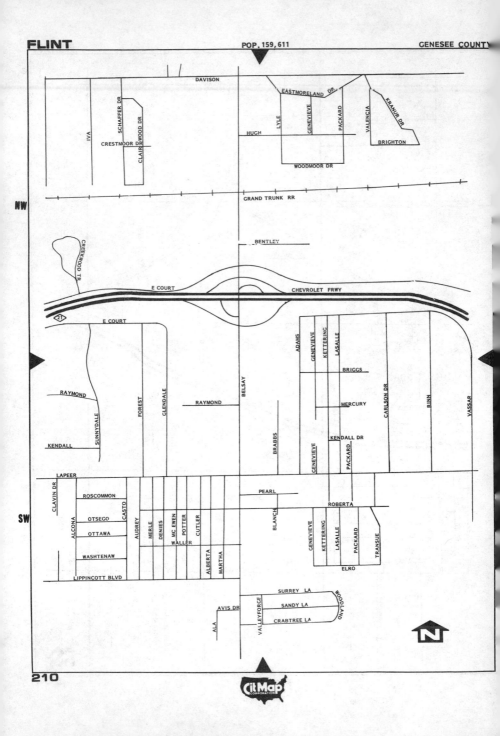

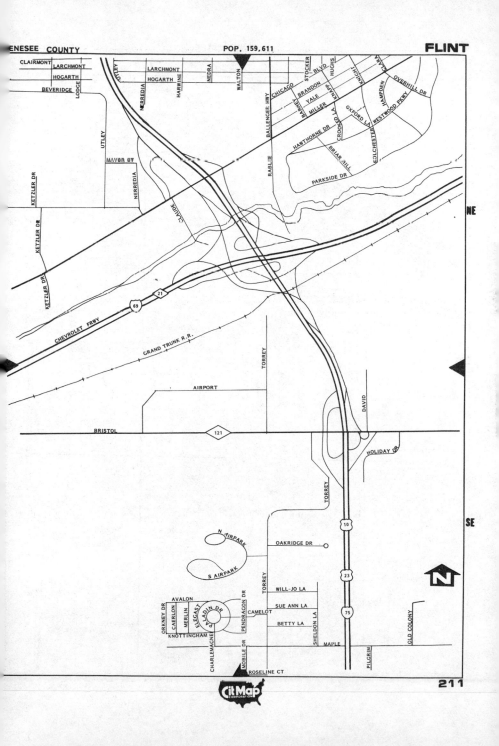

POP. 159,611

CLAIRMONT LARCHMONT
HOGARTH
BEVERIDGE

LARCHMONT
HOGARTH

NEDRA

WALTON

STOCKER

HUGHS

OVERHILL DR

LODGE

UTLEY

NERREDIA

HARWINE

BALLENGER HWY

CHICAGO

BRANDON

YALE

MILLER

BARNEY

KNAPP

WESTWOOD PKWY

HAMPDEN

OXFORD LA

CROOKED LA

EDLCHESTER

KETZLER DR

MAYOR ST

UTLEY

NERREDIA

CLAUDE

HAWTHORNE DR

BRIAR HILL

RABLIE

PARKSIDE DR

KETZLER DR

KETZLER DR

KETZLER DR

NE

21

69

CHEVROLET FRWY

GRAND TRUNK R.R.

TORREY

AIRPORT

DAVID

BRISTOL

121

HOLIDAY DR

TORREY

10

SE

N AIRPARK

OAKRIDGE DR

S AIRPARK

TORREY

23

N

WILL-JO LA

ORKNEY DR

AVALON

CAERLON

MERLIN

ELEGAST

PALADIN DR

PENDRAGON DR

SUE ANN LA

CAMELOT

BETTY LA

SHELDON LA

75

OLD COLONY

KNOTTINGHAM

CHARLEMAGNE

MOBILE DR

MAPLE

PILGRIM

ROSELINE CT

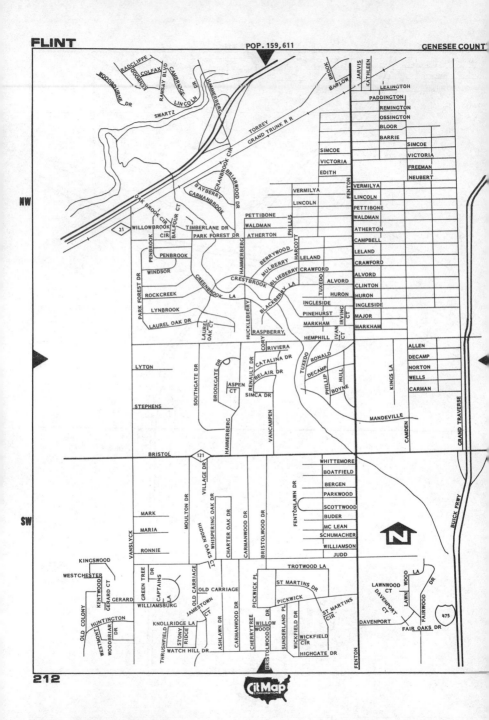

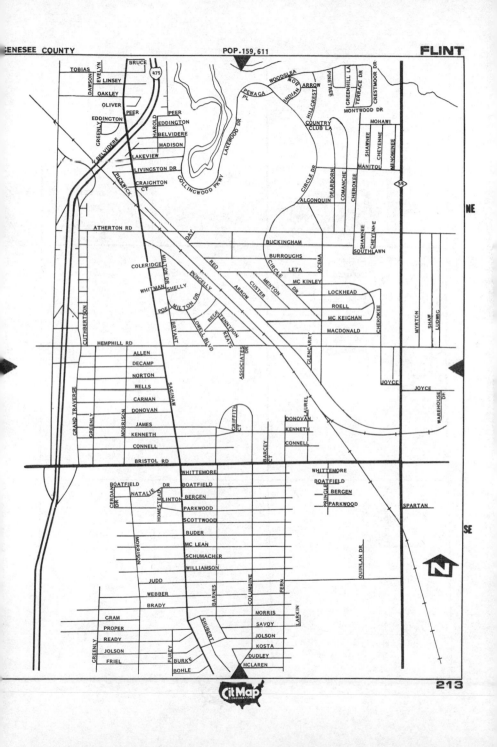

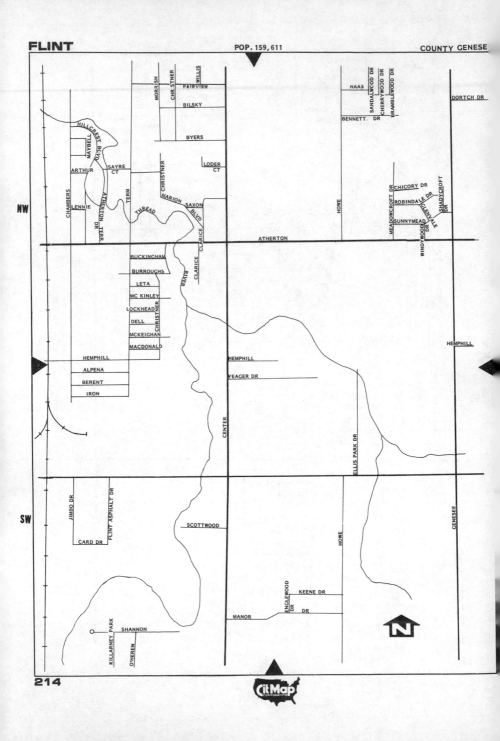

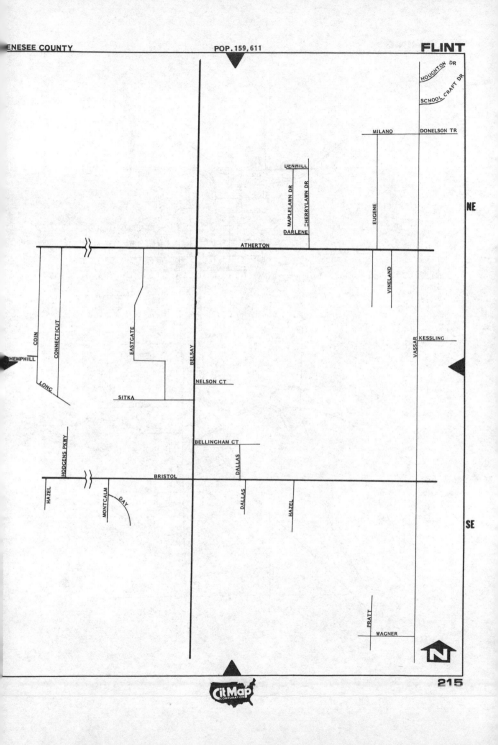

HOUGHTON DR

SCHOOL CRAFT DR

MILANO   DONELSON TR

NE

DENHILL

MAPLELAWN DR   CHERRYLAWN DR

EUGENE

DARLENE

ATHERTON

VINELAND

COIN   CONNECTICUT

EASTGATE

BELSAY

VASSAR   KESSLING

HEMPHILL

LONG

NELSON CT

SITKA

HODGENS PKWY

BELLINGHAM CT

DALLAS

BRISTOL

HAZEL

MONTCALM   DAY

DALLAS

HAZEL

SE

PRATT

WAGNER

N

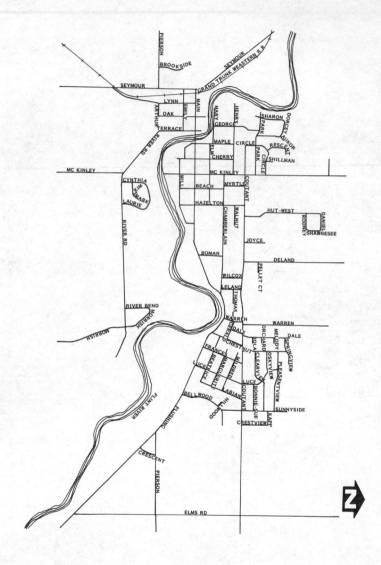

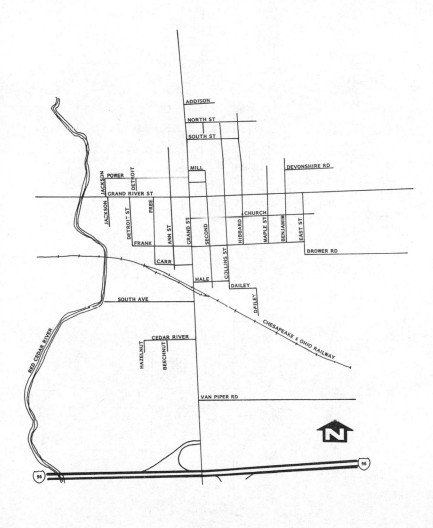

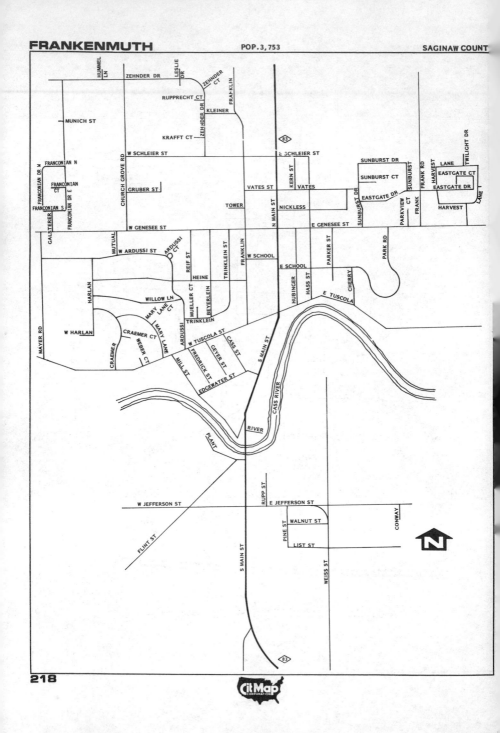

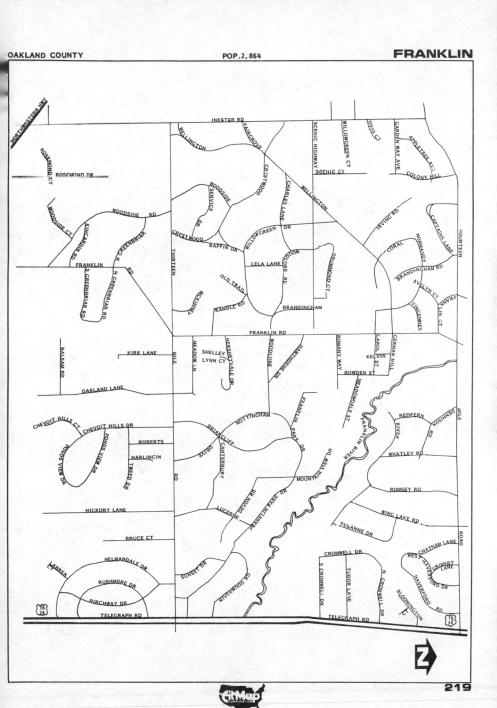

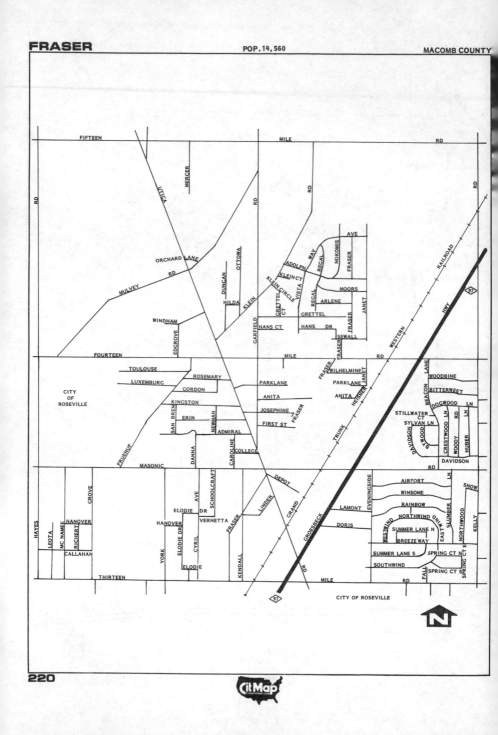

FIFTEEN MILE RD

MERCER

UTICA

ORCHARD LANE

RD

MULVEY

DUNCAN

OTTOWA

KLEIN

HILDA

WINDHAM

EDGROVE

GARFIELD

HANS CT

RD

AVE

NOKOMIS

FRASER

REGAL

WAY

ADOLPH

KLEIN CT

KLEIN CIRCLE

VISTA

GRETTEL CT

MOORS

REGAL

ARLENE

GRETTEL

HANS DR

FRASER

SEWALL

JANET

RAILROAD

HWY

97

FOURTEEN MILE RD

TOULOUSE

LUXEMBURG

ROSEMARY

GORDON

KINGSTON

ERIN

SAN BREN

NEWMAN

ADMIRAL

DANNA

CAROLINE

COLLEGE

PARKLANE

ANITA

JOSEPHINE

FIRST ST

FRASER

FRASER

WILHELMINE

PARKLANE

ANITA

HESTER

JANET

WESTERN

RD

TRUNK

LANE

BEACON

WOODBINE

BITTERWEET

DOGWOOD

LN

STILLWATER CT

SYLVAN LN

DAVIDSON

BY-WOOD

RD

CRESTWOOD LN

WOODY

LN

HUBER

CITY OF ROSEVILLE

PRUEHUF

MASONIC RD

DAVIDSON RD

HAYES

LEOTA

MC NAMEE

RICHERT

HANOVER

GROVE

CALLAHAN

YORK

HANOVER

ELODIE DR

CYRIL

ELODIE

ELODIE AVE

VERNETTA

SCHOOLCRAFT DR

FRASER

LINDEN

KENDALL

DEPOT

GRAND

GROESBECK

RD

DN

EVENINGSIDE

AIRPORT

WINSOME

RAINBOW

LAMONT

DORIS

WESTWIND

NORTHWIND

SUMMER LANE N

BREEZE WAY

SUMMER LANE S

SOUTHWIND

ONIW

EAST

SLUMBER

NORTHWOOD

SPRING CT N

SPRING CT S

FALL

SNOW

KELLY

SPRING CT E

THIRTEEN MILE RD

97

CITY OF ROSEVILLE

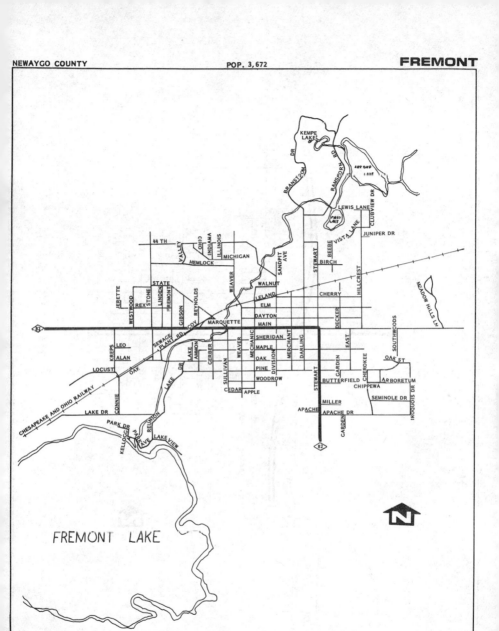

FREMONT LAKE

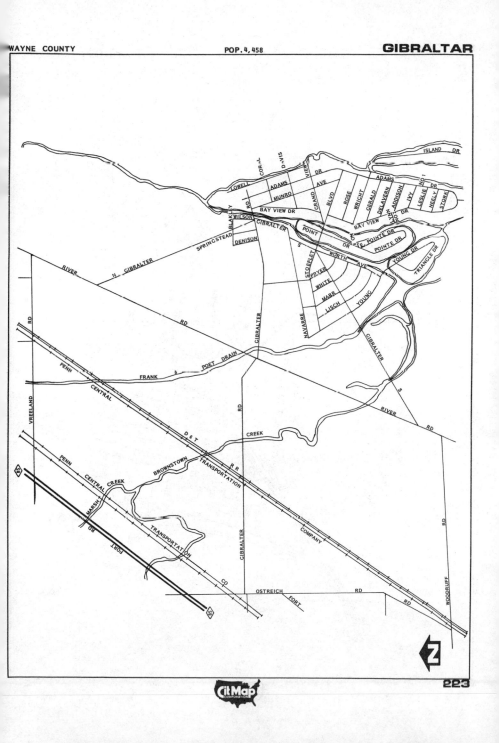

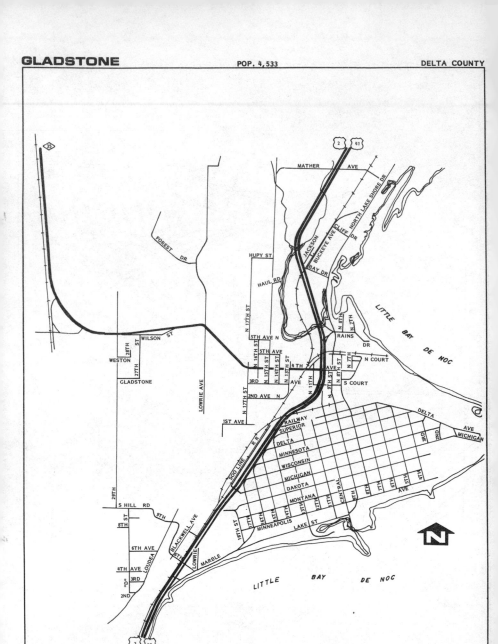

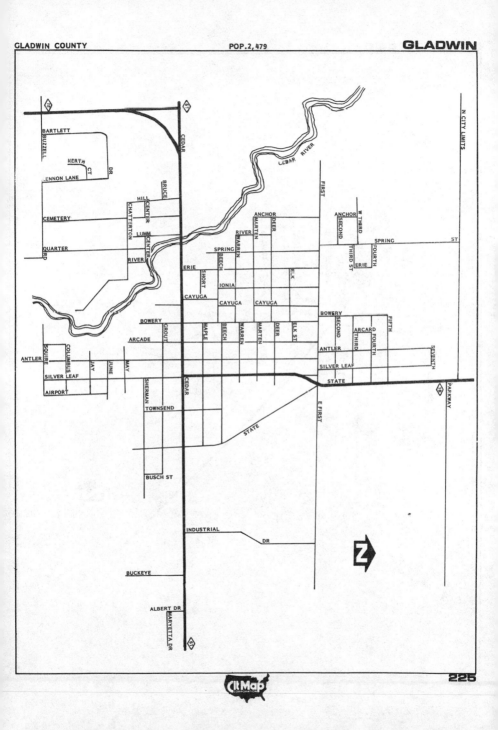

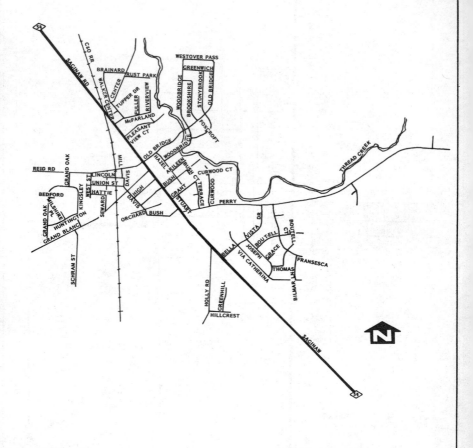

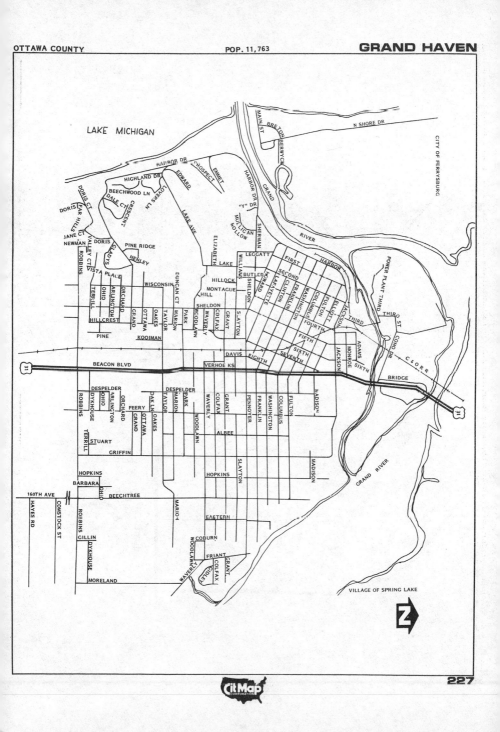

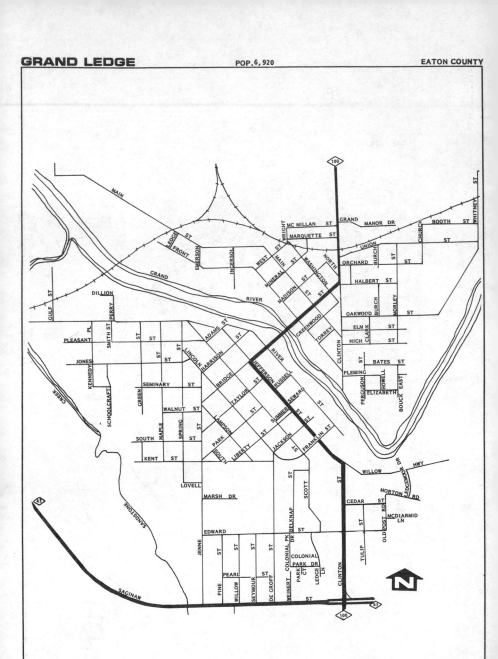

Street	Page	Dir
A ST	249	SW
AARON	253	NE
ABBIE LA	260	NE
ABBINGTON DR	256	NE
ABEL ST	253	SE
ABERDEEN ST	245	NE
ABIGAIL ST	257	NW
ABINGTON DR	240	NW
ABIGADOR TRAIL	240	NW
ACADEMY DR	251	NW
ACTON RD	243	SE
ADA DR	252	SE
ADAIR	241	SW
ADAMS ST	250	SW
AIRE ST	239	NW
AIRVIEW	256	SW
AIR WAY ST	241	NW
AIDS ST	260	NE
ALABAMA AVE	249	SE
ALBANY ST	249	SE
ALBERS ST	248	SW
ALBERT DR	251	SW
ALBERTA	245	NE
ALDER DR	254	SW
ALDRICH AVE	260	NW
ALEDA AVE	261	NW
ALEWA DR	248	NW
ALEXANDER RD	250	SE
ALEXANDER ST	250	SW
ALFRED AVE	250	NW
ALGER ST	257	NW
ALGANSEE DR	241	SW
ALGONAC DR	243	SE
ALGONQUIN CT	241	SW
ALICIA AVE	242	NW
ALLEN ST	249	SW
ALLERTON AVE	250	SE
ALLISON AVE	242	SE
ALLYSON AVE	261	NE
ALMONT	256	NW
ALPENHORN AVE	239	SE
ALPINE AVE	239	NW
ALPINE CHURCH	239	SE
ALPINE HILLS ST	244	NW
ALTA PL	251	NE
ALTA VISTA AVE	251	NW
ALTO AVE	250	SW
AMBER AVE E	261	SW
AMBER AVE W	261	SW
AMBER DR N	261	SW
AMBER DR S	261	SW
AMBERLY DR	256	SE
AMBERLY CT	256	SE
AMERICAN	261	NW
AMES ST	245	SW
ANCIENT DR	259	NW
ANDERSON DR	251	SW
ANDERSON PL	244	SW
ANDOVER CT	259	NE
ANDOVER LA	257	NW
ANDOVER RD	261	SW
ANDOVER ST	259	NE
ANDREW ST	261	NW
ANGIE AVE	244	NE
ANITA	253	NE
ANN ST	244	NW
ANNCHESTER DR	257	NW
ANNETTE	240	NW
ANNIE AVE	243	SE
ANNSBURY CT	259	NE
ANTISDEL PL	250	NW
ANTOINE ST	249	SE
APACHE CT	253	SE
APPLE CT	242	SW
APPLE RD	248	NE
APPLE BLOSSOM	242	SW
APPLEBROOK CT	242	SW
APPLE HOLLOW CT	242	SW
APPLE JACK AVE	242	SW
APPLELEAF CT	246	NE
APPLELEAF DR	246	NE
APPLE RIDGE CT	242	SW
APPLETON CT	246	NE
APPLETON DR	246	NE
APPLEVIEW CT	262	SW
APPLEVIEW DR	246	NE
APPLEWOOD DR	262	NW
ARAPAHO DR	253	SE
ARBOR LA	245	SW
ARBOR ST	245	SW
ARDEN ST	254	SW
ARDMORE ST	257	NW
ARGENTINA DR	242	NW
ARGO DR	252	SE
ARGUS DR	257	NW
ARIANNA ST	244	SW
ARIEBILL CT	254	SW
ARIEBILL ST	254	SW
ARLINGTON DR	251	NE
ARLINGTON PL	249	NE
ARLINGTON ST	245	NE
ARTHUR AVE	250	NE
ARTIS DR	258	NW
ARUNDEL DR	257	NW
ARY CT	249	SE
ASBURY RD	257	NW
ASH AVE	261	NE
ASHER LA	245	SW
ASHLAND AVE	245	SW
ASHTON RD	261	SW
ASHVILLE DR	246	NW
ASPEN CT	254	SW
ASSUMPTION AVE	240	NW
ASTER PL	246	NE
ATHLONE AVE	247	NE
ATLANTIC ST	244	SW
ATLAS AVE	250	SW
ATWOOD ST	239	NW
AUBURN AVE	240	NE
AUBURN AVE	250	NE
AUBURN AVE	245	NE
AUDOBON CT	241	SW
AUDLEY DR	241	NE
AUSTERLITZ	241	NE
AU SALLE DR	241	SW
AVALON TERR	250	NW
AVERILL AVE	260	SE
AVON	241	SW
AVONDALE RD	257	NW
AYLESWORTH	252	SE
B ST	249	SE
BAGLEY AVE	251	SW
BAILEY PARK DR	240	SW
BAKER PARK DR	256	SW
BALDWIN ST	250	NW
BALDWIN ST	261	SW
BALL AVE	245	NW
BALLARD ST	256	NW
BALL PARK BLVD	248	NE
BALSAM AVE	241	SW
BALTIMORE DR	251	NW
BANBURY AVE	246	SW
BARAGA ST	250	NW
BARBARA ST	244	NW
BARBER TERR	243	SW
BARBARRY DR	254	SW
BARCLAY AVE	249	NW
BARFIELD DR	257	NW
BARKER AVE	249	NW
BARKWAY DR	260	SE
BARKWOOD CT	247	NE
BARNARD ST	251	SW
BARNETT PL	245	SW
BARNETT ST	244	SE
BARNUM ST	260	NW
BARON	239	SW
BARRETT AVE	253	NE
BARTH AVE	250	SW
BARTLETT ST	249	NE
BATAVIA PL	250	NW
BATCHAWANA ST	257	NW
BATES ST	250	SW
BATTLEBORE	262	SW
BAXTER ST	250	SW
BAYBERRY DR	239	SE
BAYNTON AVE	256	SW
BAYVIEW	259	NW
BAYWOOD DR	246	NW
BEACON ST	249	SE
BEAUMONT DR	243	SE
BEAUREGARD AVE	239	NW
BECK ST	250	SE
BECKWITH AVE	245	SW
BECKWITH LA	246	SW
BEECH ST	234	SE
BEECHTON	246	NE
BEECHWOOD DR	251	SW
BEECHWOOD ST	245	NE
BEGOLE ST	247	
BEKINSHIRE DR	239	NW
BEKIUS CT	249	SE
BELFAST	256	NW
BELKNAP AVE	245	NW
BELL AVE	241	SW
BELLCLAIRE AVE	253	SE
BELLECLADE DR	257	NE
BELLEWOOD DR	261	SW
BELLEWOOD CT	261	SW
BELMAR DR	256	SE
BELMONT	243	SW
BELVEDERE DR	251	SW
BEMIS ST	257	NW
BENJAMIN AVE	240	SE
BENNING AVE	242	SE
BENSON AVE	250	NW
BENTBROOK DR	262	SW
BERKEY AVE	256	NW
BERKLEY DR	256	SE
BERKSHIRE DR	256	SE
BERLIN PL	245	SW
BERWYCK RD	257	NW
BERWYN	254	NE
BETTY ST	239	SE
BEULAH	256	NW
BEVERLY	254	NE
BIDDEFORD CT	239	NW
BIDDEFORD DR	239	NW
BIG SPRING DR N	253	SE
BIG SPRING DR S	253	SE
BILLANTAU ST	256	NW
BILLMAR ST	253	SW
BINGHAM CT	239	NE
BIRCH	256	NE
BIRCH DR	249	SE
BIRCHCREST DR	248	NE
BIRCHVIEW CT	254	NW
BIRD AVE	246	NE
BISHOP AVE	252	SE
BISSEL	261	NW
BLACKFOOT CT	253	SE
BLACKFOOT DR	253	SE
BLACK HAWK	253	SE
BLACKSTONE	256	NW
BLAINE AVE	245	SW
BLANCHARD CT	254	NW
BLANCHARD ST	254	NW
BLANFORD AVE	254	NW
BLIVEN PL	249	SE
BLOSSOM ST	256	SE
BLUE ASH ST	261	NW
BLUEBERRY DR	243	SE
BLUEBIRD	254	SW
BLUEGRASS DR	259	NE
BLUEHILL DR	241	NW
BLUE WATER	254	NW
BLUFF DR	241	NW
BLUMRICH ST	249	SW
BLYMIER	249	NW
BLYTHE CT	243	SE
BLYTHE DR	243	SE
BOITWOOD DR	244	SE
BONANZA DR	241	NE
BONA VISTA DR	248	NE
BOND AVE	249	NE
BONITA DR	256	SE
BONNELL AVE	251	SE
BONNEVILLE CT	241	NE
BONNEVILLE DR	241	NE
BONNIE AVE	261	NE
BONNIE AVE	258	NE
BOONE CT	254	SE
BORGLUM AVE	245	NW
BOSTON ST	250	SW
BOSTWICK AVE	249	NE
BOTSFORD AVE	245	NW
BOULEVARD	254	NE
BOWDOIN ST	245	NW
BOWDOIN PINES DR	239	NW
BOWEN BLVD	261	NE
BOWEN AVE	261	NE
BOWNE ST	244	NE
BOYU AVE	241	HW
BOYES AVE	246	NW
BRADFORD ST	245	SW
BRADFORD ST	246	SE
BRADY ST	239	SE
BRAEBURN ST	252	NE
BRAMALEA DR	261	SE
BRANDON	243	SE
BRANDYWINE	239	NE
BRECKEN RIDGE	241	NE
BREENS CT	249	SE
BREGG ST	241	NW
BREMER ST	253	SW
BRENDA	253	NE
BRENNER ST	245	SW
BRENTON DR	256	SE
BRENTWOOD DR	257	NW
BRETON AVE	257	SE
BRETON CT N	262	NW
BRETON LA	257	NW
BRETON RD	257	NE
BRETON IND. PK	257	SE
BRIAN DR	260	NW
BRIAR LA	261	NW
BRIAR BANK PL	241	NE
BRIARCLIFF DR	245	NE
BRIAR HILLS DR	245	NE
BRAIRWOOD AVE	253	SE
BRIDGE ST	248	NW
BRIDLE CREEK CT	261	SW
BRIDLE CREEK ST	261	SW
BRIGGS BLVD	240	SW
BRIGHTON DR	251	SW
BRINDAL CREEK ST	262	NW
BRINKS ST	257	NE
BRISAM ST	247	NE
BRISTOL AVE	243	SE
BRISTOLWOOD DR	243	NE
BRITTON CT	257	NE
BROADMOOR AVE	257	SE
BROADVIEW	256	NW
BROADWAY AV NW	244	NW
BROADWAY AVE	253	SW
BROCKWOOD DR	241	NE
BROMLEY DR	257	SW
BROOK	253	SE
BROOKCROSS DR	261	SE
BROOKFIELD AVE	245	NW
BROOKGATE CT	239	NE
BROOKGATE DR	239	NE
BROOKLANE AVE	245	NE
BROOKMARK ST	261	SE
BROOKRIDGE CT	261	SE
BROOKRIDGE DR	261	SE
BROOKSHIRE CT	256	SW
BROOKSHIRE DR	256	SW
BROOKSIDE DR	253	SE
BROOKVIEW DR	245	SE
BROOKWOOD CT	261	NE
BROOKWOOD DR	261	NE
BROWN	256	NW
BROWNWOOD AVE	243	SE
BURCE CT	253	SE
BRUCE DR	253	SE
BRUCE ST	245	NE
BRUNSINK DR	251	NW
BUCHANAN AVE	249	SE
BUCK CREEK DR	254	SW
BUCK CREEK CT	254	SW
BUCKLEY ST	249	NE
BUDDY ST	261	NE
BUNNY SIDE	239	SW
BURCHARD ST	251	SW
BURGIS AVE	261	NE
BURKE AVE	245	SE
BURLINGAME AVE	259	NE
BURNINGTREE DR	257	NW
BURNSIDE ST	256	SW
BURRITT ST	257	NE
BURR OAK ST	244	SE
BURRWOOD ST	252	SE
BURTON ST	257	NE
BURTON ST	253	NE
BUTLER AVE	250	SW
BUTTERWORTH DR	247	SE
BUTTERWORTH ST	249	NW
BYERLY AVE	252	SE
BYERS	245	NW
BYRON ST	250	NW
BYRON CTR. AVE	259	SW
CADILLAC DR	250	SE
CADWELL AVE	249	NW
CALEDONIA ST	244	SE
CALGARY ST	285	NE
CALGARY ST	259	NW
CALIFORNIA ST	259	NW
CALIAN AVE	242	NE
CALKINS AVE	250	NW
CALVARY AVE	244	SW
CALVERT AVE	242	NE
CALVIN	250	NW
CAMBRIDGE BLVD	250	SE
CAMBRIDGE DR	250	SE
BAMBHI		NE
CAMELOT CT	258	NW
CAMELOT DR	258	NW
CAMILLE DR	258	NW
CAMPBELL	250	NW
CAMPUS DR	257	NE
CAMPUS PK	262	SW
CANAL AVE	253	NW
CANRIGHT ST	240	SW
CANTON ST	249	NW
CANYON DR	248	NE
CANYONSIDE DR	241	SW
CAPEN ST	250	NW
CAPILANO DR	257	NW
CARAVAN LN. AVE	261	SW
CARD	241	SW
CARDINAL DR	243	NE
CARGIL ST	243	NE
CARLA	253	NE
CARLTON AVE	240	SW
CARLTON AVE	245	NW
CARLLON PK	253	SE
CARMAN AVE	244	SE
CARMAL AVE	253	SE
CAROL AVE	260	NW
CAROLINE AVE	260	NW
CARPENTER AVE	243	SW
CARRIAGE HILL DR	261	SE
CARRICK AVE	261	NW
CARRIER ST	244	SE
CARRIER CREEK BLVD	250	SW
CARROLL AVE	250	NW
CASCADE RD	251	SE
CASCADE W. PKWY	252	SE
CASIMER	250	SW
CASPIAN AVE	259	NW
CASS AVE	250	SW
CASTLE DR	252	NW
CASTLE BLUFF CT	257	SW
CATHERINE PL	250	NW
CAULFIELD AVE	249	SW
CAVANAGH ST	261	SE
CAYUGA ST	248	NE
CEDAR ST	245	SW
CEDAR CREEK	245	SW
CEDAR CREST DR	241	SW
CEDAR HILL DR	241	SW
CEDAR RDIGE DR	241	SW
CENTENNIAL AVE	248	NE
CENTENNIAL CT	248	NE
CENTER AVE	254	NE
CENTRAL AVE	250	SW
CENTURY DR	249	SE
CHALET LA	259	NW
CHAMBERLAIN AVE	257	NW
CHAMBERLAIN CT	257	NW
CHAMPION AVE	261	NW
CHANDY CT	241	NE
CHANDY DR	241	NE
CHANUTE AVE	253	SW
CHAPEL	254	SW
CHAPMAN CT	250	SW
CHARLES AVE	250	SW
CHARLOTTE AVE	243	SW
CHARRING CROSS AVE	257	NE
CHASSELL ST	259	NW
CHASSERAL ST	239	SW
CHATEAU ST	239	SW
CHATEAU ST	239	SW
CHATHAM ST	249	NW
CHELSEA RD	246	NW
CHENEY AVE	240	SW
CHEROKEE DR	253	SE
CHERRY DR	250	NW
CHERRY ST	245	NE
CHERRY HILL	246	SW
CHERRYWOOD CT	243	SW
CHERRYWOOD LA	243	SW
CHERYL AVE	261	SE
CHESANING DR	257	NW
CHESANING DR S	257	NW
CHESAPEAKE DR	246	SW
CHESAPEAKE DR	246	SW
CHESHIRE DR	245	SW
CHESTER ST	250	SW
CHESTERFIELD BLVD	247	NW
CHESTNUT AVE	253	SW
CHESTNUT ST	253	SW
CHEVY CHASE	253	SE
CHEYENNE DR	253	SE
CHICAGO DR	249	SW
CHICKASAW CT	253	SE
CHILDS AVE	239	SW
CHIPPEWA DR E	250	SE
CHIPPEWA DR W	250	SE
CHIPWOOD LA	248	NE
CHOCTAW DR	253	SE
CHRIS LA	239	NW
CHRISTIE AVE	261	SW
CHUBB AVE	249	NW
CHURCH AVE	253	NE
CHURCH PL	249	SE
CIRCLE SHORE DR	262	NW
CISNE AVE	260	NE
CLANCY AVE	249	NE
CLAREMONT PL	250	NW
CLARION AVE	254	NE
CLARK ST	239	SE
CLAUDIA AVE	261	SW
CLAY AVE	260	NE
CLAYSTONE ST	257	NE
CLAYTON AVE	247	NW
CLEARBROOK ST	256	SE
CLELLANDON CT		
CLEVELAND AVE	249	SW
CLIFFORD AVE	252	SE
CLIFTON PL	250	NW
CLINTON AVE	247	NW
CLOVEN AVE	254	NE
CLOVER CT	249	NE
CLOVER DR	243	SE
CLOVER CREST DR	243	NE
CLOVERDALE AVE	242	SW
CLOVERLY CT	243	NE
CLOVERLY DR	243	NE
CLYDE PARK AVE	260	SW
CLYDON AVE	254	NW
COACH LA	257	SE
CODY CT	249	SE
COGSWELL ST	244	NW
COIT AVE	240	NE
COIT RD	249	SW
COLBY AVE	260	NW
COLDBROOK ST	244	SE
COLE AVE	245	SW
COLFAX ST	244	SE
COLGATE AVE	254	SW
COLLEGE AVE	245	SW
COLLINDALE AVE	243	SW
COLLINGWOOD AVE	256	NW
COLLINS AVE	256	NW
COLONIAL AVE	240	SW
COLORADO	250	SE
COLRAIN ST	256	NW
COLUMBIA AVE	245	SW
COLUMBUS ST	240	SW
COMANCHE CT	253	SE
COMMERCE AVE	249	NE
COMMON WAY	258	NE
COMMONS AVE	249	SE
COMSTOCK BLVD	245	NW
CONCHISE	253	SE
CONCORD	239	SW
CONCORD AVE	257	NW
CONGER ST	245	NW
CONGRESS PL	250	NW
CONKLIN CT	240	SE
CONLON AVE	251	SW
CONLON DR	257	NW
CONRAD ST	244	SW
COOLIDGE	250	NW
COOPER AVE	250	SW
CORA ST	244	SW
CORAL VALLEY DR	258	NE
CORAL VALLEY DR	258	NE
CORDELIA ST	249	SW
CORINNE ST	249	SE
CORNELIA AVE	244	NW
CORNELIUS	256	NE
CORNWALL AVE	249	SE
CORONADO ST	251	NE
COTSWOLD LA	251	NE
COTTAGE GROVE	249	SE
COTTAGE ROW AV	240	SW
COUNTRY LA	258	NW
COUNTRY CLUB DRIVE	243	SW
COUNTRY CLUB DR	243	SW
COUNTRYSIDE DR	241	NW
COUNTRYWOOD DR	262	SW
COUNTRYWOOD DR	262	SW
COURTNEY CT	244	SW
COURTNEY ST	244	SW
COVELL AVE	243	SE
COVINGTON RD	257	NW
CRABAPPLE CT	242	SW
CRAHEN AVE	252	NW
CRANBROOK DR	246	SW
CRARY ST	250	SW
CREE CT	241	SE
CREEK DR	239	NE
CREEKBLUFF PL	243	NW
CREEKRIDGE DR	262	NW
CREEKSIDE DR	261	NE
CREEKVIEW DR	261	NE
CREELY CT	242	NW
CRESCENT DR	242	NE
CRESCENT ST	249	SW
CREST HILL DR	241	NW
CRESTLINE CT	259	NE
CRESTMOOR CT	262	SW
CRESTMOOR DR	262	SW
CRESTON PLAZA	244	NE
CRESTWOOD DR	248	NE
CRIPPEN AVE	260	SE
CRISFIELD DR	241	NE
CROFTON ST	249	SW
CROMWELL AVE	250	SW

GRAND RAPIDS

STREET INDEX

CROOKED PINE CT	259	SW
CROOKED PINE DR	259	SW
CROOKED TREE AV	259	NW
CROSBY ST	244	SW
CROSWELL	251	SW
CROWN ST	260	NE
CRYSTAL ST	253	NE
CUMMINGS AVE	242	SW
CUNNISON AVE	249	SW
CURTIS DR	260	NW
CURTIS ST	245	SW
CURVE ST	249	SW
CURVEBROOK ST	261	SW
CURWOOD AVE	261	NE
CUSICK PL	244	SE
CUSTER PL	250	NW
CUTTER PKWY	252	SE
CYPRESS	254	SE
DADE ST	241	SW
DAKOTA	239	SE
DALE CT	245	SE
DALE ST	244	SE
DALLAS AVE	250	SW
DALTON AVE	254	NE
DANA DR	256	SW
DANA ST	239	SE
DANBURY DR	257	NW
DANIEL ST	260	NE
DANUBE LA	241	NW
DANVERS CT	258	SE
DANVERS DR	258	SE
DARBY AVE	251	SW
DARTMOUTH ST	244	SW
DAVIS AVE	244	SW
DAWES CT	261	NE
DAWSON AVE	245	NE
DAY AVE	244	NW
DAYLOR DR	241	SW
DAYTON ST	249	NW
DEAN ST	244	SE
DEAN LAKE AVE	246	NW
DEBAAR DR	260	SE
DE BOER ST	249	SW
DECKER PL	249	NW
DECKER PL	249	NE
DEEPWOOD CT	259	NE
DEEPWOOD DR	259	NE
DE LAAT AVE	254	NE
DELANGE ST	257	NW
DELAWARE ST	250	SW
DELI CT	246	NE
DELI DR	246	NE
DELONEY AVE	249	NW
DELRAY AVE	252	SE
DELWOOD AVE	254	NE
DEMING	256	NW
DEN HERTOG	254	SE
DENNIS AVE	250	NW
DERBY DR	243	SE
DERBYSHIRE	256	SE
DEVON DR	251	NE
DEVONSHIRE DR	243	NE
DEVONWOOD CT N	241	NE
DEVONWOOD CT S	241	NE
DEVONWOOD DR	241	NE
DEWBERRY DR	246	SW
DEWEY AVE	249	NE
DE WITT ST	241	NE
DEXTER PL	249	NE
DIAMOND AVE	243	NW
DIAMOND PL	250	NW
DIANE ST	261	NW
DICK AVE	243	SE
DICKINSON ST	249	SW
DIVISION AVE	239	SE
DIVISION AVE	249	NE
DIXIE AVE	254	NW
DODGE ST	239	NW
DOLBEE AVE	250	SW
DOLPHIN	260	NW
DON ST	260	NE
DONAHUE	254	NE
DONALD PL	250	NW
DONNA	253	NE
DONOVAN CT	250	NW
DOORNBOS AVE	254	NE
DORCHESTER AVE	249	SW
DOREMUS PL	249	SE
DORIS ST	245	NW
DORMAY	254	NW
DOROTHY ST	244	SW
DORRIE AVE	250	NW
DORROLL ST	245	NE
DOUGLAS ST	249	NW
DOVER PL	244	SW
DOWNING ST	252	SW
DRAKE ST	247	NE
DREXEL CT	245	SE
DREXEL DR	245	SE
DRUMMOND BLVD	262	NW
DUBLINE AVE	242	NE
DUCHESS AVE	251	SE
DUCOMA DR	243	SW
DUDLEY AVE	250	NW
DUIKER AVE	245	NW
DUNHAM ST	250	SW
DUNLAP ST	243	SE
DUNNINGAN AVE	246	NE
DURANT ST	251	SW
DURHAM AVE	239	NE
DU SHAME ST	243	SE
DUTCHESS CT	242	SW
DWIGHT AVE	250	NW
DYKEMA CT	250	SW
EAGLE ST	244	NW
EARLDON AVE	250	NW
EARLE AVE	253	NE
EAST DR	258	SW
EAST PL	250	NW
E BELTLINE AVE	246	SE
E. BELTLINE CT	241	SE
EAST BOURN DR	251	NE
EASTBROOK ST	256	SE
E. COLLIER AVE	258	NW
EASTERN AVE	240	SW
EASTERN PL	245	NW
EAST FOREST DR	252	SE
EASTGATE ST	251	SW
EASTHILL DR	240	NW
EASTLAKE CT	240	NW
EASTLAKE DR	252	SE
EASTLAWN RD	251	SW
E. MALL DR	258	NE
EASTMONT DR	252	SE
EASTMOOR AVE	252	NW
E. NORWALK DR	256	SE
EAST POINT CT	241	NW
EASTRIDGE DR	251	NE
EASTRIDGE CT	251	NE
EASTVIEW CT	251	NE
EAST PARIS	252	SW
EASTWOOD AVE	251	SW
EASY ST	259	NW
ECKLUND ST	245	NE
EDGEHILL DR	251	SE
EDEN ST	259	NW
EDENBORO ST	242	SE
EDGELAWN DR	261	SW
EDGEMERE DR	251	SW
EDGEMONT DR	259	NE
EDGEWATER DR	241	SW
EDGEWOOD AVE NE	245	N
EDGEWOOD AVE SE	245	NW
EDGEWOOD ST	253	SE
EDINBURGH DR	252	SW
EDISON AVE	243	SE
EDISON PARK AVE	248	NE
EDITH AVE	245	SE
EDMONTON ST	259	NW
EDMONTON ST	245	NE
EDMUND AVE	245	SW
EDNA	256	NW
EDSEL ST	261	NW
EDWARD AVE	250	SE
EDWIN ST	244	SE
EFFIE PL	245	NW
EFFINGHAM DR	261	SE
EIGHTH ST	243	SE
EKHART ST	245	SE
ELBON ST	254	NE
EL CAMINO DR	243	SW
ELCENTRO BLVD	251	NW
ELDEE DR	260	SE
ELDEA CT	249	SE
ELDERWOOD CT	243	NE
ELDERWOOD DR	243	NE
ELDON	241	SW
ELEORADO DR	251	SW
ELEANOR ST	245	NW
ELEVENTH ST	244	SW
ELIZABETH ST	244	SE
ELLA AVE	253	NE
ELLEN AVE	249	SW
ELLIOTT ST	257	NW
ELLORA CT	261	SW
ELLORA DR	261	SW
ELLSMERE ST	245	NE
ELLSWORTH AVE	249	NE
ELMBROOK AVE	254	NW
ELMDALE ST	239	SE
ELMER DR	246	NW
ELMGROVE CT	244	SW
ELMHURST AVE	251	SW
ELMRIDGE DR	243	NW
ELMWOOD DR	251	SW
ELWELL ST	260	NE
ELWOOD AVE	251	NE
ELWOOD AVE	251	SW
EMBRO DR	262	NW
EMERALD AVE	245	NW
EMERALD LAKE DR	246	NW
EMERSON AVE	244	NW
EMILY AVE	245	NE
EMPEROR ST	249	NW
ENGLE ST	248	SE
ENGLESIDE	258	NW
ENGLEWOOD DR	257	NW
ENTERPRISE ST	262	NW
EOLA ST	256	NW
ESCOTT AVE	244	SW
ESSEX AVE	240	SW
ESTELL DR	251	SW
ETHELWIN AVE	241	NW
ETON ST	249	SW
EUCLID	249	SE
EUREKA AVE	250	SW
EVANGELINE ST	250	NW
EVANS ST	250	NW
EVANSDALE ST	242	NW
EVELYN ST	245	NE
EVENTIDE DR N	246	SW
EVENTIDE S	246	SW
EVERGLADE DR	256	NW
EVERGREEN ST	250	SW
EVERNIA AVE	256	NW
EVERT ST	242	SE
EWING AVE	250	SW
EXETER RD	257	NW
FAIR ST	249	SE
FAIRBANKS ST	249	NE
FAIRCREST AVE	247	NW
FAIRFIELD AVE	243	SW
FAIRLANE DR	245	SW
FAIRLANES AVE	253	SW
FAIRMEADOW DR	253	SW
FAIRMEADOW DR N	253	SW
FAIRMOUNT ST	251	NW
FAIRPOINT CT	253	SW
FAIRVIEW AVE	249	NE
FAIRVEIW ST GRANDVILLE	253	SW
FAIRWAY DR WALKER	247	NE
FAIRWOOD CT	253	SW
FAITH CT	253	NE
FAITH ST	253	NE
FALLINGBROOK	261	SE
FARNHAM ST	260	NE
FAWNWOOD CT	262	NW
FAWNWOOD DR	262	SW
FAY AVE	242	SE
FAYETTE AVE	253	SW
FEDERAL AVE	254	NE
FENMORE DR	241	SW
FENNESSY ST	247	NW
FENWICK ST	242	SE
FENWOOD ST	247	SW
FERN AVE	245	SW
FERNANADO ST	240	SW
FERN CREEK LA	260	SW
FERNDALE AVE	247	NW
FERNHILL DR	248	NE
FERNRIDGE	252	SE
FERNWOOD DR	251	NE
FERRIS ST	243	NE
FERRY ST NW G.R.	249	NE
FERRY ST G-VILLE	253	NW
FESCUE DR	260	SE
FIFTH ST	249	NE
FIFTHIETH ST	259	NE
FIFTY-FIFTH ST	269	SE
FIFTY-FIRST ST	260	NE
FIFTY-FOURTH	260	SE
FIFTY-NINTH	261	SE
FIFTY-SECOND ST	259	SW
FIFTY-SIXTH	259	SW
FILKINS DR	239	SW
FINK AVE	239	SE
FINNEY AVE	249	NE
FINSBURY LA	243	SE
FIRESIDE DR	261	SW
FIRST	249	NW
FISK ST	250	SW
FITCH PL	250	NW
FITZHUGH AVE	250	NW
FITZHUGH AVE	240	SE
5 MILE RD	241	SE
FLAMINGO AVE	260	NW
FLAT ST	250	NW
FLEETWOOD DR	247	SW
FLETCHER DR	251	NW
FLINTE CT	249	SE
FLORA ST	249	NW
FLORAL DR	251	SW
FLORALVIEW DR	239	NW
FLORENCE CT	245	SW
FLORIDA AVE	260	NE
FLOYD ST	254	SE
FORD AVE	245	SW
FORDSON AVE	244	NW
FOREST CREEKD R	258	SW
FOREST GROVE AV	254	NW
FOREST HILL AVE	252	NE
FOREST PARK CT	259	NE
FOREST RIDGE	241	NW
FORESTVIEW	241	NW
FORREST AVE	245	SW
FORRESTER ST	256	NE
FORTIETH ST	253	SW
FORTY-EIGHTH ST	261	NW
FORTY-FOURTH ST	260	NE
FORTY-SECOND ST	253	SW
FORTY-SEVENTH	260	NW
FORTY-THIRD ST	259	NW
FOSTER AVE	245	NW
FOSTER CT	245	NW
FOUNTAIN ST	249	NE
4 MILE ROAD	239	SE
4 MILE ROAD	240	SW
FOURTH ST	249	NE
FOX ST	249	SE
FOXBORO CT	243	NW
FOXCROFT AVE	239	NE
FOX RIDGE DR	246	NW
FOX RUN RD	259	NW
FRANCO ST	254	NE
FRANK ST	244	SE
FRANKLIN G-VILLE	253	NE
FRANKLIN GRAND RAPIDS	249	SE
FRANSMAN PL	249	NW
FREDERICK AVE GRAND RAPIDS	244	NW
FREDERICK DR E. GRAND RAPIDS	251	SW
FREEMAN AVE	249	SW
FREETON DR	260	SE
FREMONT AVE	244	SW
FREYLING PL	250	NW
FRONT AVE	244	SE
FRONTAGE RD WYO.	250	NW
FRONTAGE RD G.R.	248	SE
FRONTIER ST	259	NE
FRONTIER CT	259	SE
FRUIT ST	250	NW
FRUITLAND AVE	244	NW
FRUITWOOD CT	248	NE
FRUITWOOD DR	248	NE
FULLER AVE	239	SE
FULLER CT	261	NE
FULLERTON CT	240	SW
FULTON ST	247	NE
FULTONWOOD DR	251	NW
GARDEN TOWN DR	254	NE
GABLE ST	254	SE
GAGE ST	239	SW
GARDEN ST	249	SE
GARFIELD AVE	244	NW
GARFILED CT	244	NW
GARLAND ST	262	NE
GARRET DR	246	NW
GATEWOOD DR	261	SE
GAY AVE	250	NW
GAYNOR AVE	244	NW
GELOCK AVE	249	NW
GENESSEE ST	250	NE
GENEVA AVE	250	SW
GENTIAN CT	261	SE
GENTIAN DR	261	SE
GEORGETOWN DR	256	NE
GERALD AVE	245	NW
GERALD R FORD FREEWAY	246	SW
GERDA ST	261	NE
GEZON AVE	244	SE
GHILDA PL	250	NW
GIBSON ST	250	SW
GIDDINGS AVE	250	SE
GILBERT ST	250	SW
GILL AVE	244	SE
GILLETTE ST	250	NW
GILMOUR ST	251	SW
GILNERS CT	249	SW
GILPIN ST	244	NE
GLADIOLA AVE	254	SE
GLADSTONE AVE	250	NE
GLENAIRE DR	244	NW
GLENBROOK AVE	254	NW
GLENBROOK DR	261	SE
GLENCAIRIN DR	243	NW
GLENCREEK AVE	253	SW
GLENDALE ST	251	NW
GLENECHO	257	NW
GLENGARY CT	257	NW
GLENHAVEN AVE	248	NE
GLENMOOR CT	262	SW
GLENMOOR DR	262	SW
GLENN DR	251	NE
GLENOAK DR	239	SE
GLENVALLEY DR	244	NW
GLENVIEW DR	242	NW
GLENWOOD AVE	250	SE
GLOBE ST	251	SE
GLOUCESTER ST	246	SW
GODFREY AVE	249	SW
GODWIN	256	NW
GOLD AVE	249	NW
GOLDEN ST	254	SE
GOLDSBORO PL	250	NW
GOLFRIDGE DR	257	NW
GOODMAN AVE	254	SW
GOODRICH ST	249	NE
GORDON ST	253	SE
GORHAM DR	257	NW
GRACELAND ST	244	NE
GRACEWOOD DR	252	NE
GRAHAM RD	248	NE
GRAHAM ST	249	SE
GRANADA CT	242	SE
GRANADA DR	242	SE
GRAND AVE	250	NW
GRAND BLVD	245	SE
GRAND ST G-VILLE	253	SE
GRAND CHATEAU	261	NW
GRAND RIVER DR	241	NE
GRANDVILLE AVE	249	SE
GRANT ST	249	SE
GRANT ST	243	SE
GRANTWOOD AVE	261	NW
GRAPE AVE	241	SW
GRATIOT ST	243	SE
GREEN ST	249	SE
GREENACRES DR	261	NW
GREEN APPLE DR	242	SW
GREENBRIER CT	252	NW
GREENBRIER DR	252	NW
GREENBORO	261	SW
GREENFIELD AVE	254	NW
GREENINGS AVE	246	NE
GREENLEAF CT	256	SE
GREEN OAK LA	261	NW
GREENRIDGE DR	239	SE
GREENTREE DR	257	NW
GREENVALE DR	259	NE
GREENVALLEY DR	239	SE
GREEN VIEW	257	NE
GREENVIEW DR	259	NE
GREENWICH RD	251	NE
GRENADA DR	257	NE
GRENADIER CT	259	NE
GRENDIER DR	259	NE
GRETTEL AVE	239	NW
GRIDLEY AVE	242	SE
GRIGGS ST	256	NW
GRISWOLD ST	256	NW
GROENINK ST	244	NW
GROOTERS ST	256	SE
GROSS DR	248	NE
GROVE CT	244	SE
GROVE PL	244	SE
GROVE ST	244	SE
GROVE BLUFF CT	257	NW
GROVE BLUFF DR	257	NW
GROVELAND AVE	254	SE
GUILD ST	[illegible]	NE
GULLIVER	239	NW
HACHMUTH DR	239	SW
HACKLEY	241	NE
HADDEN AVE	250	SW
HAGEN DR	256	SW
HAGUE AVE	254	NE
HAIFLEY ST	249	SE
HAINES ST	243	SE
HALENA ST	245	NW
HALIFAX AVE	259	NW
HALL ST G.R.	249	SW
HALL ST WALKER	247	SW
HAMILTON AVE	244	SE
HAMPSHIRE ST	257	NE
HAMPTON AVE	250	NE
HAMPTON CT KENTWOOD	258	NW
HAMPTON DOWNS	257	SE
HAMSTEAD DR	243	SE
HANCHETT AVE	243	SE
HANCOCK ST	250	SW
HANOVER ST	245	SW
HANSEL ST	239	NW
HANSEN AVE	250	NW
HARDING ST	243	NE
HANNA LAKE DR	262	SE
HARDWICK ST	261	SW
HARDWOOD AVE	253	NE
HARLAN AVE	250	NW
HARP ST	261	NW
HARTFORD AVE	247	NE
HARTLEY ST	244	NW
HARVEST AVE	253	SE
HARVEY ST	250	NW
HASTINGS ST	250	NW
HATHAWAY DR	251	NE
HATTUS AVE	239	SE
HAUGHEY AVE	260	NE
HAVANA AVE	249	SW
HAVANA AVE	260	NW
HAVERHILL DR	262	SW
HAYDEN ST	249	SW
HAZELWOOD AVE	254	SE
HAZEN ST	256	NW
HEATH DR	257	NW
HEATHCLIFFE DR	257	NW
HEATHER LA	252	NW
HEATHER ST	251	SW
HEATHERFIELD DR	246	SW
HEIDE AVE	239	NE
HELEN	254	NE
HELMLONDE AVE	243	NW
HEMLOCK ST	249	NW
HENRY AVE	250i	SW
HENRY ST G-VILLE	253	SE
HERMAN AVE	260	NW
HERMITAGE ST	250	NW
HERRICK AVE	245	SE
HERSMAN ST	252	NE
HESTER PL	249	NE
HEYBOER AVE	249	NW
HIAWATHA RD	250	SE
HICKORY AVE	256	SE
HIDDEN LAKE LA	251	NE
HIDDEN VALLEY	261	SE
HIGGINS AVE	253	SE
HIGH ST	249	SW
HIGHBLUFF DR	246	SW
HIGHLANDER DR	252	NW
HILL AVE	243	SE
HILLBURN AVE	243	SW
HILLCREST AVE	243	SE
HILLMOUNT ST	243	SE
HILLSIDE DR	244	NW
HILLVIEW AVE	250	NE
HILLWOOD CT	261	NE
HIMES ST	256	SW
HOAG AVE	241	SE
HOBART ST	256	NW
HODENPYL RD	251	NW
HOEHN ST	243	SW
HOGADONE AVE	249	NW
HOGAN	249	SW
HOLBORN DR	243	SE
HOLLAND AVE	250	NW
HOLLIDAY DR	259	NE
HOLLIS DR	245	NE
HOLLISTER AVE	250	NW
HOLLY ST	260	NE
HOLLY PARK AVE	261	NW
HOLLYWOOD ST	245	NE
HOLTMAN CT	241	SW
HOLTMAN DR	241	SW
HOLYOKE DR	256	SE
HOME AVE	245	NW
HOME ST	249	SE
HOMEWOOD ST	254	SE
HONEYBROOK	254	SW
HONEYWOOD	254	SW
HOOVER ST	245	SW
HOPE ST	250	NE
HOPEDALE DR	262	NW
HOPSON ST	245	SW
HORTON AVE	255	NE
HOUSEMAN AVE	245	NW
HOVEY ST	249	NW
HOWARD ST	250	SW
HOWLAND ST	244	SE
HOYLE AVE	244	NW
HOYT ST	256	NW

HUBAL	254	SE
HUBBARD ST	250	SW
HUBERT ST	245	SW
HUFFORD AVE	244	NW
HUGHART ST	249	SE
HUMBOLT ST	250	SW
HUNSBERGER AVE	241	SW
HUNTERS RIDGE	262	NW
HUNTINGTON DR	250	NE
HURD ST	251	NE
HUTCHINSON AVE	252	SW
HYDE PARK AVE	260	NE
HYLANE AVE	246	NW
HYNES AVE	249	SE
IDA AVE	243	SE
IDEMA DR	251	SE
ILLINOIS AVE	261	NW
IMOGENE AVE	239	SE
IMPERIAL DR	242	SW
INDIAN DR	241	NE
INDIANA AVE	249	NW
INDIAN TRAIL	131	SW
INDIAN MOUNDS DRIVE	248	SW
INDIAN RIDGE DR	246	NW
INDIAN SPRINGS	253	SW
INGERSOLL ST	259	NW
INLET PL	250	NW
INNES ST	250	NW
INNWOOD DR	256	NW
INTERURBAN AVE	260	SE
INVERNESS RD	257	NW
IONIA AVE	249	NE
IOWA	254	SE
IPSWICH DR	239	SW
IRA AVE	243	SE
IRIS PL	250	NW
IRONWOOD DR	261	SW
IRONWOOD LA	261	NW
IROQUOIS DR	250	SE
IRVING ST	250	NW
ISABELLA CT	250	SW
ISLANDVIEW AVE	241	NW
ITHACA ST	254	NW
IVANHOE AVE	251	NE
IVANREST AVE	253	SE
IVES AVE	249	NW
IVY DR	241	SW
IVY LA WYOMING	261	SW
JACK ALAN ST	253	SW
JACKSON ST	249	NW
JAGLIN DR	240	SE
JAMES AVE	250	SW
JAMESTOWN CT	262	SW
JAMESTOWN DR	262	SW
JANE ST	239	NW
JANES AVE	244	NE
JASMINE AVE	241	SE
JAYDALE ST	242	NE
JEAN ST	260	NE
JEFFERSON AVE	249	NE
JEFFERSON DR	256	NW
JEFFERY CT	261	SE
JEFFERY DR	261	SE
JENISON ST GRANDVILLE	253	SW
JENNETTE AVE	244	SW
JENNIFER ST	261	NW
JENNINGS ST	256	NE
JESSE ST	245	NW
JESSICA ST	261	NW
JOAN AVE	244	NE
JOHN ST	249	NW
JOHNATHAN CT WALKER	242	SW
JOHNATHAN CT GR	246	NE
JAHANTHAN DR	246	NE
JOHN BALL PK DR	249	NW
JOHN "C" CT	261	NE
JOHNSON ST	242	NW
JOHNSTON ST	256	NW
JOLIETTE AVE	259	NW
JONES ST	244	NW
JONFIELD AVE	261	NW
JONQUIL ST	260	SE
JOSLIN ST	256	NW
JUANITA DR	261	SW
JUDD AVE	249	SW
JU-LE-ON DR	247	SW
JULIA ST	245	NW
JULIVAN AVE	261	NW
JUNEBERRY	256	SE
JUNIOR RD	242	NW
JUNIPER AVE	245	SE
JUPITER AVE	241	SW
JUSTIN AVE	242	SE
KALAMAZOO AVE	250	SW
KAREL JEAN CT	259	NW
KAREN AVE	260	NE
KATE DR	251	SE
KATHERINE DR	244	NE
KATHLEEN ST	256	SW
KATRINA DR	261	SW
KEARNY DR	241	SW
KEEWEENAW DR	241	SW
KELEKENT AVE	261	SW
KELLOGG ST	250	NW
KELLOGG WOODS DRIVE	260	SE
KELSEY ST	245	NE
KENAN AVE	244	SW
KENEBERRY	251	SW
KENDALL ST	256	SE
KENDALWOOD CT	245	NW
KENDALWOOD ST	240	SW
KEN-O-PAR ST	261	NE
KENESAW DR	251	SW
KENMOOR AVE	252	NW
KENNILWORTH DR	252	SW
KENOSHA DR	256	NW
KENOWA AVE	242	NW
KENSBORO AVE	245	NE
KENSINGTON AVE	249	SW
KENT BLVD	251	NW
KENTFIELD ST	254	SW
KENT HILLS RD	245	SW
KENTLAND CT	256	SW
KENTRIDGE DR	256	SE
KENTUCKY AVE	256	NW
KENT VIEW DR E	245	SW
KENT VIEW DR N	245	SW
KENT VIEW DR W	245	SW
KENTWOOD AVE GRANDVILLE	253	NE
KENTWOOD DR G.R	245	SW
KENWOOD ST	245	NW
KERWIN ST	243	SE
KEWADIN	245	SW
KEYHILL AVE	258	NW
KIMBALL AVE	261	NE
KING CT	249	NE
KINGBRIDGE TERR	259	NW
KINGSBURY ST	239	SW
KINGS ROW CT	242	SW
KINGSTON DR	256	SE
KINGSWOOD DR	251	NE
KINNEY AVE	242	SW
KINNROWE	242	NE
KIOWA CT	262	SE
KIRK CT E	252	SE
KIRK CT W	252	SE
KIRK DR	252	SE
KIRKSHIRE DR	256	SE
KITTERY DR	239	NE
KLEYLA DR	260	SE
KLOET ST	243	NE
KNAPP CT	245	NE
KNAPP ST	245	NE
KNICKERBOCKER CT	259	NE
KNICKERBOCKER ST	259	NE
KNOB HILL DR	241	NW
KNOLLVIEW CT GR. RAPIDS	257	NE
KNOLLVIEW WYOMING	259	NW
KNOX ST	241	NE
KONKLE DR	241	NW
KOSCIUSZKO ST	250	NW
KRAKOW PL	249	NW
KREFT ST	241	SW
KREISER ST	250	SE
KROPE ST	261	NW
KRUPPYVILLA DR	251	NW
KUSTERER AVE	242	SE
LA BELLE ST	249	SE
LACROSS ST	254	SE
LAFAYETTE AVE	245	NW
LAGRANGE CT	258	NW
LAGRAVE AVE	249	SE
LAKE DR	250	NW
LAKE EASTBROOK	257	NE
LAKE FOREST ST	240	SE
LAKE GROVE AVE	251	SW
LAKE MICHIGAN DR	248	NE
LAKESIDE DR	251	NW
LAKEVIEW DR	251	NE
LAKEVIEW LA	240	SE
LAMAR DR	254	SE
LAMBERTON CT	240	SE
LAMBERTON ST	240	SE
LAMBERT CT	249	NE
LAMBERTON LAKE DR	240	SE
LAMDALE CT	258	NW
LAMONT AVE	243	NW
LAMOREAUX DR	239	SE
LAMPLIGHT LA	258	NE
LANCASHIRE CT	256	SE
LANCASHIRE ST	256	SE
LANCASTER AVE	243	SW
LANCO CT	243	SE
LANCO ST	243	SE
LANE AVE	249	NW
LANE DR	245	SW
LANGDON AVE	250	NW
LANGLEY ST	256	SE
LANKAMP ST	244	NE
LANSING ST	251	SW
LANTANA	262	NE
LANTERN CT	239	NE
LANTERN DR	239	NE
LARAME AVE	239	SE
LARCHMONT DR	259	NE
LARKLANE ST	261	NE
LARKWOOD DR	262	NW
LARUE ST	253	NE
LASALLE AVE	247	NW
LAUDERDALE AVE	251	NE
LAUGHLIN DR	242	SE
LAURA AVE	239	SE
LAUREL AVE	251	SW
LAUREL ST	249	SW
LAVILLE AVE	248	SE
LAWRENCE ST	244	NE
LEE ST	249	SW
LEELANAU	241	SW
LEFFINGWELL AVE	246	SE
LEISURE DR	258	NW
LEISURE SOUTH DR	261	SW
LEITH ST	243	SE
LELAND AVE	239	SE
LEMANS CT	258	SW
LENAWEE RD	256	NE
LENORA AVE	243	SE
LENORA ST	248	NE
LENORA TER	248	NE
LEROY ST	260	NE
LESTER AVE	241	SW
LETELLIER ST	249	NW
LEWISON AVE	243	NE
LEXINGTON AVE	249	NE
LEYDEN AVE	249	NW
LIBERTY ST	249	NW
LIBRARY ST	249	NE
LILA ST	253	SW
LILAC CT	250	NW
LILLIAN ST	250	NE
LINACRE AVE	247	NE
LINCOLN AVE	244	NW
LINCOLN AVE	242	NW
LINCOLN LAWNS DR	247	NE
LINDEN AVE	250	SW
LINDENWOOD	268	NE
LINWOOD	256	NE
LISTER CT	244	SE
LITTLEFIELD DR	251	NW
LIVINGSTON AVE	249	NE
LLEWLLYN CT	254	SW
LOCH LOMOND AVE	251	NE
LOCKE AVE	253	SE
LOCKHART DR	243	SE
LOCKHAVEN ST	252	NW
LOCKMERE DR	261	SE
LOCKRIDGE DR	245	SW
LOCKWOOD ST	250	NW
LOCUST AVE	250	SE
LOFTWOOD DR	261	SE
LOGAN ST	249	SE
LOMBARD ST	253	NE
LONDON ST	249	SW
LONDONDERRY DR	261	SE
LONGMEADOW ST	243	NW
LONGVIEW	241	NW
LONSDLAE DR	250	NE
LOOKOUT ST	244	SW
LORALEE	256	SE
LORI LA	240	SE
LORETTA DR	246	NW
LOTUS AVE	256	NE
LOUIS ST	249	NE
LOUISE ST	256	NE
LOUISIANNA AVE	260	NE
LOUSMA DR	256	SW
LOVERS LA	240	NW
LOVETT AVE	251	SW
LOWELL AVE	250	SE
LOWEMONT CT	243	NE
LOWRY CT	262	NE
LUCAS DR	253	SW
LUCAYA CT	253	SW
LUCE ST	253	SW
LUDLOW DR	252	SW
LURAY AVE	248	NE
LUTHER ST	260	SE
LUTON AVE	250	NW
LUXEMBURG ST	252	SE
LUXFORD AVE	239	SE
LYDIA ST	245	SW
LYLES ST	261	NW
LYNCH ST	249	SW
LYNNELANE ST	248	NE
LYON ST	249	NE
MABEL ST	239	SE
MACDONALD ST	243	SE
MACK AVE	250	NW
MACKINAW RD	250	SE
MACOMB AVE	248	NW
MACRACE	253	SE
MADERIA AVE	247	SW
MADISON AVE	250	SW
MAETHY ST	256	NW
MAGNOLIA AVE	260	NE
MAIN ST	253	SW
MAJESTIC ST	261	SW
MAJORS PL	249	SE
MALL DR	257	NE
MALLORY AVE	254	SE
MALTA ST	250	NW
MANDERLY	241	SW
MANHATTAN LA	251	SE
MANHATTAN RD	251	SE
MANITOBA CT	241	SW
MANITOU DR	241	SE
MANKATO	253	SW
MANNING AVE	242	NW
MANORWOOD DR	261	SE
MANTLE ST	254	SE
MANWARING PL	249	SW
MANZANA CT	247	NE
MAPLE ST G.R.	249	NE
MAPLE ST G VILLE	249	SE
MAPLE CREEK AVE	262	NW
MAPLEGROVE DR	243	SE
MAPLEHILL AVE	252	NE
MAPLE HOLLOW ST	261	NE
MAPLELAWN ST	256	SW
MAPLELEAF TERR	246	SW
MAPLEROW AVE	242	SE
MAPLEVALLEY ST	257	SW
MAPLEVIEW DR	240	NW
MAPLEVIEW ST	261	NE
MAPLEWOOD RD	251	NE
MARCELLA AVE	249	NW
MARDELL PL	249	NW
MARGARTE	256	NE
MARIDELL AVE	243	SE
MARIETTA ST	245	SW
MARIGOLD	252	SE
MARILYN ST	259	NW
MARINE ST	248	NW
MARION AVE	249	NW
MARIS ST	250	NW
MARK ST	240	SE
MARKET	249	NE
MARKWOOD LA	248	NE
MARLBORO ST	242	SE
MARLENE ST	239	NW
MARLIN	260	NW
MARLIN AVE	242	SE
MARLOWE DR	261	NW
MARSHALL AVE	261	NW
MARSHALL AVE	250	SW
MARTIN AVE	256	NW
MARTINDALE AVE	249	SW
MARWOOD CT	261	NE
MARWOOD DR	261	NE
MARY AVE	251	SE
MARYANN ST	242	NE
MARYLAND AVE	246	NW
MARYWOOD DR	245	NW
MASON ST	244	SE
MATHEWS CT	244	SE
MATILDA ST	245	SW
MAUDE AVE	245	SW
MAUMEE DR	256	NE
MAXWELL AVE	251	SW
MAYAKA CT	253	SW
MAYAPPLE DR	242	SW
MAYBELLE ST	245	SW
MAYBERRY ST	256	SE
MAYFAIR DR	250	NE
MAYFIELD AVE	240	SW
MAYHEWWOOD ST	256	NW
MAYNARD AVE	247	NE
MCCARTY ST	244	NW
MCCLOW	253	SW
MCCONNELL ST	249	NE
MCCOY DR	251	SE
MCCRELLIS AVE	239	SE
MCINTOSH AVE	246	NE
MCINTOSH CT	242	SW
MCINTYRE CT	253	SW
MCKINLEY CT	250	NE
MCREYNOLDS AVE	244	SW
MEADE DR	254	SE
MEADOWBROOK AVE	254	SW
MEADOWBROOK ST	257	NW
MEADOWLANE DR	261	NE
MEADOWVALE DR	251	NW
MEADOW WAY	257	NE
MEELICAL	252	SW
MELEANA DR	259	NW
MELBOURNE ST	244	NE
MELITA AVE	245	NW
MELROSE DR	257	NW
MELVIN	254	NE
MENOMINEE DR	264	NE
MERCER DR	251	NW
MERRIFIELD ST	256	NW
MERRILL AVE	249	SW
MERRITT ST	256	NW
MERYTON AVE	239	NE
METZRY CT	241	NE
METZGAR DR	239	NW
MEURS CT	254	NE
MEYER AVE	254	NE
MIAMI AVE	254	NW
MICHAEL AVE	260	NW
MECHELL DR	240	SW
MICHIGAN PL	250	NW
MICHIGAN ST	249	NE
MICK AVE	261	SW
MICK DR	261	SW
MIDDLEBORO DR	251	NW
MIDDLEBORO LA	251	NW
MIDLAND DR	251	NW
MIDVALE	246	SW
MILAN AVE	260	NW
MILDRED AVE	256	NW
MILDRED AVE	261	SW
MILFORD ST	243	SE
MILL ST	253	SW
MILLA AVE	239	SE
MILLBANK ST	256	SE
MILLBROOK ST	256	SE
MILLCREEK AVE	239	SE
MILLER AVE	244	NW
MILLER PARKWAY	260	SE
MILTON ST	250	NE
MILWAUKEE AVE	249	NW
MINNIE AVE	254	SE
MISSAUKEE	253	SW
MISSION ST	242	SE
MODEL CT	258	SE
MOERLAND CT	243	NW
MOERLAND DR	243	NW
MOFFET RD	239	NW
MOHAVE CT	253	SW
MOHAVE DR	253	SW
MOHAWK AVE	253	SE
MOHLER ST	242	NW
MOHRHARDT ST	249	NE
MONIQUE DR	245	NW
MONROE AVE	244	NE
MONROE AVE	245	NW
MONTCLAIR AVE	243	NE
MONTEBELLO ST	261	NW
MONTE CARLO DR	258	SW
MONTE CARLO CT	258	SW
MONTE CELLO DR	248	NE
MONTEREY DR	250	SE
MONTREAL ST	259	NW
MONTREAT CT	246	NW
MONTREAT DR	246	NW
MONTROSE ST	244	NE
MORE ST	250	NW
MOREWOOD CT	256	SE
MOREWOOD DR	256	SE
MORGAN ST	244	SW
MORLEY AVE	245	NE
MORNINGSIDE DR	251	NE
MORNINGSIDE DR	262	NE
MORRIS AVE	250	SW
MORRISSEY	240	SW
MT VERNON AVE	249	NE
MULBERRY AVE	241	NW
MULFORD DR	256	NE
MULLINS AVE	242	NE
MULLINS CT	242	NE
MURPHY ST	238	NW
MURRAY ST	260	NE
MUSKEGON AVE	244	SW
MUSTANG CT	241	NE
NANCY ST	260	SE
NARDIN ST	253	NE
NARROW COVE	258	NW
NASON ST	244	NW
NATIONAL AVE	249	NW
NATURE TRAIL DR	257	SW
NAGEL AVE	249	NW
NAGOLD ST	249	NW
NAHAHO ST	253	SE
NAYLOR ST	249	SW
NEEDHAM CT	244	NW
NEGAUNEE DR	257	NW
NELAND AVE	250	SW
NELSON AVE	256	NE
NETHERFIELD ST	239	NE
NEVADA ST	256	NE
NEW AVE	249	SE
NEWARK AVE	256	NE
NEWBERG AVE	248	NE
NEWBERRY ST	244	SE
NEWCASTLE	261	NE
NEWCASTLE	256	SE
NEWHOUSE AVE	247	NE
NEWPORT ST	254	NE
NEWTON AVE	250	NW
NIAGARA AVE	250	SW
NINTH ST	244	SW
NIPAWIN CT	241	SW
NIPIGON DR	241	SW
NIPPON DR	241	SW
NIXON	242	SE
NOBLE ST	250	SW
NOLAN AVE	242	SE
NORA ST	261	SW
NORDBERG AVE	244	SW
NORFOLK RD	257	NW
NORMAN AVE	251	NW
NORMAN DR	256	SE
NORTH AVE	250	NW
NORTHBORO CT	241	SW
NORTH DR	258	SW
N. DORROLL ST	245	SE
NORTHERN DR	258	NE
NORTHFIELD DR	245	SW
NORTHGATE DR	241	SW
N. HAMPTON DR	246	SW
NORTH KENT MALL AVENUE	241	SW
NORTHLAND DR	241	NE
NORTH LAKE DR	240	SE
NORTHLAWN ST	245	NE
N. NORWAY ST	258	NW
NORTH OTTILLIA	256	NW
NORTH PARK ST	240	SW
NORTHRIDGE DR	241	NW
NORTHRUP AVE	243	SW
NORTHSHIRE	251	SE
NORTHVALE DR	241	SW
NORTHVIEW AVE	241	NW
NORTHVIEW CT	241	NW
NORTHVILLE	241	NW
NORTHWAY DR	242	SE
NORTHWOOD ST	245	NW
NORTON CT	245	SW
NORWOOD AVE	250	SE
NOTTINGHAM RD	251	NE
NURSERY AVE	254	SW
OAK BURN AVE	252	SE
OAKCREST ST	254	SE
OAKDALE ST	250	SW
OAKES ST	249	NE
OAKES ST G-VILLE	253	NE
OAKFIELD AVE	256	NE
OAK FOREST CT	258	NW
OAK FOREST DR	258	NW
OAK GROVE ST	243	SW
OAKHILL ST	250	SW
OAK HOLLOW DR	251	NE
OAKHURST AVE	243	SW
OAK INDUSTRIAL DRIVE	251	NW
OAKLAND AVE	249	SE
OAKLAND DR	254	SW
OAKLAWN ST	245	NE
OAKLEIGH AVE	243	NW
OAKLEY PL	250	NW
OAK PARK DR	256	SE
OAKRIDGE AVE	239	SE
OAK VALLEY AVE	254	SE
OAKRIDGE AVE	239	SE
OAK VALLEY AVE	254	SE

OAKVIEW 259 NW
OAKWOOD AVE 245 NW
OAKWOOD DR 251 SW
O'BRIEN 247 NE
OBSERVATORY AV 258 NW
OGDEN AVE 251 SW
OHMANN AVE 248 NW
O'KEEFE PL 249 NW
OKEMOS DR 250 SE
OLDENBURG CT 246 NE
OLDE POINTE DR 241 SW
OLDE RIDGE DR 241 SW
OLD FARM DR 242 SW
OLD GATE RD 243 SE
OLD ORCHARD DR 239 SE
OLD TOWN RD 256 SE
OLD VALLEY CT 262 SE
OLIVE AVE 249 NW
OLIVET ST 253 NE
OLIVIA ST 248 SW
OLYMPIA ST 249 SW
OMAHA DR 253 SE
OMAHA ST 253 SW
OMEMA AVE 257 NW
ONAWAY 252 NE
ONEKAMA DR 257 NE
ONTARIO AVE 245 NE
ONTONAGON AVE 257 NW
ORCHARD AVE 251 SW
ORCHARD HILL 250 NW
ORCHARD LANE 242 NW
OREGON AVE 254 NW
ORIOLE AVE 260 NW
ORIOLE CT 260 NW
ORLANDO AVE 252 SE
ORVILLE ST 256 NE
OSCEOLA AVE 244 SW
OSCODA DR 241 SW
OSGOOD PL 249 SE
OSWALD ST 245 NW
OSWEGO ST 248 NE
OTSEGO ST 257 NW
OTTAWA AVE 249 NE
OTTILIA ST 256 NW
OVERBROOK LA 256 NW
OXFORD RD 257 NW
OXFORD ST 249 SW
PACKARD AVE 250 NW
PADDOCK ST 250 NW
PAGE ST 244 SW
PALMER ST 245 SE
PALMER ST 244 SE
PALMER PARK DR 260 NW
PAMELA AVE 261 NW
PANNELL ST 243 NE
PARADE DR 244 NE
PARCHMENT DR 252 SW
PARIS AVE 240 SW
PARK ST 244 NW
PARKDALE AVE 254 SE
PARKHURST AVE 243 SE
PARKLAND AVE 244 SW
PARK LANE DR N. 244 SW
PARKLANE DR S. 244 NE
PARKRIDGE DR 257 NW
PARKSIDE AVE 247 NW
PARKVIEW ST
  WYOMING 259 NW
PARKWAY DR 240 NW
PARKWOOD ST 257 SE
PARKWOOD ST 241 NW
PARMELEE AVE 243 SW
PARMELEE CT 243 SW
PASADENA DR 245 NW
PAT AVE 244 SW
PATRICIA CT 259 NW
PATTERSON AVE 252 NW
PATTON AVE 243 SE
PAUL N ST 256 NW
PAWNEE DR 243 SW
PAXTON AVE 241 NW
PEARL ST 249 NE
PEBBLE BEACH DR 252 NW
PECK ST 253 NE
PEMBERLEY AVE 239 NE
PEMBROKE DR 261 SE
PEMBROKE ST 261 NW
PEMBROKE ST 261 NE
PENN AVE 245 SW
PENNY AVE 261 NW
PENWOOD CT 261 SE
PERKINS AVE
  GRAND RAPIDS 246 SW
PEPRY AVE 254 NW
PERSHING DR 244 NW
PETTIBONE AVE 249 NW
PHEASANT AVE 261 SE
PHEASANT RUN DR 257 SW
PHILADELPHIA 250 SE
PHILLIPS AVE 249 NE
PHILPOT 257 NE
PICKETT ST 260 NW
PICKFORD 256 SE
PICKWICK AVE 240 SW
PIERCE PL 250 NW
PIKE ST 249 NE
PINCKNEY CT 239 NW
PINDELL AVE 240 NW
PINE AVE NE
  GRAND RAPIDS 244 SW
PINE AVE
  GRANDVILLE 253 SW
PINE FOREST DR 241 SE
PINE LA
  WYOMING 260 NE
PINEBELL CT 261 NE

PINEBLUFF DR 261 SW
PINEBROOK AVE 261 SW
PINE CREEK 254 SW
PINECREST AVW 251 SW
PINECROFT LA 259 NE
PINE DALE DR 254 SW
PINEHURST AVW 260 NE
PINE ISLAND DR 245 NW
PINEKNOLL CT 261 NE
PINEKNOLL DR 261 SW
PINENEEDLES CT 261 SW
PINESBORO DR 246 NW
PINETREE AVE 261 SE
PINE VALLEY
  CREEK 247 SE
PINEVIEW ST 253 SW
PINEWAY DR 253 SW
PINNACLE CT 259 NE
PINNACLE DR 259 NE
PINNACLE DR E. 259 NE
PIONEER CLUB RD 251 NE
PIPPIN DR 242 SW
PLAINFIELD AVE 244 SW
PLAS ST 254 SW
PLASTER CT 259 NW
PLASTICO AVE 249 SW
PLATEAU DR 259 NE
PLAZA DR 257 NE
PLEASANT
  GRAND RAPIDS 249 SE
PLEASANT
  ALPINE TWP 239 SE
PLEASANTCREEK
  AVE 240 NW
PLEASANT GROVE
  TER 241 SE
PLEASANT RIDGE ST 251 NE
PLUM ST 253 NE
PLUTE DR 253 SE
PLYMOUTH AVE 245 NE
PLYMOUTH AVE 250 NE
PLYMOUTH TERR 250 NE
POHENS AVE 248 NW
POHENS CT 244 NW
PJINSETTIA AVE 256 SE
POINT 251 SW
POINT-OF-WOODS 257 SW
POKOGON RD 256 NE
PONCA CT 253 SW
PONCA DR 253 SW
PONTIAC RD 250 SE
POPLE LA 260 NE
PORTER ST 254 NW
PORTER HILLS DR 251 NE
PORTLAND AVE 245 NE
PORTSHELDON ST 213 SW
PORTSMOUTH PL 250 NW
POTTER AVE 261 NW
POWERS AVE
  GRAND RAPIDS 249 NW
POWERS AVE
  WALKER 244 NW
POWERS CT
  WALKER 244 NW
PRAIRIE PKWY 254 SW
PRAIRIE ST 253 SW
PRAIRIEVILLE DR 260 NW
PRESTON AVE 241 NW
PRESTON RIDGE 243 NW
PRIMROSE AVE 261 NW
PRINCE ST 250 SW
PRINCE ALBERT
  ST 261 NW
PRINCETON BLVD 251 SW
PRIVATE DR
  GRAND RAPIDS 243 SE
PONDEROSA DR 254 SW
PROSPECT AVE 245 NW
PUEBLO CT 253 SW
PUGLISE DR 252 NE
PURCHASE DR 240 SW
PURE ST 240 SW
PUTNAM ST
QUARRY AVE 244 NE
QUEBEC AVE 259 NW
QUEEN AVE 244 SE
QUEENSBURY DR 261 SE
QUETZAL CT 241 NW
QUEENS WOOD 241 NE
RACE ST 250 NW
RADCLIFF AVE 257 NE
RADCLIFFE DR 257 NE
RAEBORO 261 SE
RALEIGH AVE 258 SE
RALPH AVE 256 NW
RAMBLEWOOD AVE 262 SW
RAMBLEWOOD CT 262 SW
RAMONA ST 250 SW
RAMSOM AVE 249 NE
RAND ST 241 SW
RAMSWOOD CT 241 NE
RAMSWOOD DR 241 NE
RANDALL AVE 242 NW
RANDOLPH AVE 249 SE
RANCH DR 254 SW
RANGER HILLS DR 252 SE
RATHBONE ST 248 SE
RAVANNA ST 256 SE
RAVINE DR 248 NE
RAVENSWOOD DR 253 SW
RAYBROOK AVE 257 NE
RAYMOND PL 250 NW
READAPPLE CT 242 SW
REDWING CT 253 SW
REDWING DR 253 SW
REDWOOD DR 261 NW
REDWOOD LA 261 NW

REED ST 250 SE
REEDS LAKE BLVD 251 NW
REEDS LAKE N ARM 251 NW
REEDS LAKE S ARM 251 NW
REGENT ST 260 SE
REGINA ST
  GRAND RAPIDS 245 NE
REGINA ST
  WYOMING 259 NW
REHOBOTH ST 245 NE
REMEMBRANCE RD 242 NW
REMICO ST 254 SW
RENA ST 249 SW
RENNSLAER ST 244 SW
RESTMOR ST 253 SW
REVERE ST 240 SW
REXFORD DR 253 SW
REYNARD ST 256 SW
RHODES AVE 260 NE
RICHARD TERR 250 NE
RICHARDS
  GRAND RAPIDS 251 SW
RICHARDSON 241 NE
RICHMOND ST 242 NE
RICHWOOD DR 256 SE
RICKMAN AVE 240 SE
RIDGE AVE 241 NW
RIDGEBROOK DR 261 SE
RIDGEBROOK DR 261 SE
RIDGECROFT AVE 257 NE
RIDGECROFT DR 257 NE
RIDGEFIELD DR 257 NE
RIDGEFIELD ST 246 NE
RIDGELAND CT 259 NE
RIDGELINE DR 241 NW
RIDGEMOOR AVE 257 NE
RIDGEPARK DR 257 NE
RIDGEVIEW ST 256 SE
RIDGEWAY ST 245 NE
RIDGEWOOD AVE
  E. GRAND RAPIDS 256 SE
RIDGEWOOD ST 261 NW
RIEMEN CT 261 NE
RIEMEN DR 261 NE
RIFLE RANGE RD 240 NE
RINQUETTE PL 249 SE
RIPLEY ST 241 NE
RITZEMA ST 249 SW
RIVER BANK 244 SW
RIVER BEND DR 247 SW
RIVERCREST ST 244 NE
RIVERDALE 241 NW
RIVERSIDE DR 244 NE
RIVER ST 253 SW
RIVER POINT 241 NE
RIVERVIEW AVE 244 NW
RIVIERA ST 258 SW
RIVIERA DR 248 SW
ROANOKE DR 246 SW
ROBERT AVE 239 SE
ROVERTSON ST 242 NW
ROBEY PL 250 NW
ROBINSON RD 250 NE
ROVINWOOD AVE 251 NW
ROCKBLUFF CT 241 NW
ROCKHILL CT 241 NW
ROCKHILL DR 241 NW
ROCK RIVER 241 NW
ROCKWOOD 254 NW
ROCKY MOUNTAIN 261 NW
RODNEY CIR 245 NW
ROGER ST 244 NW
ROGER B. CHAFFEE
  MEMORIAL BLVD 256 SW
ROLLING HILLS DR 257 NW
ROLLINGVIEW AVE 259 NW
ROMENCE ST 251 NW
RONDO ST 261 SW
RONDO ST 261 SW
ROSALIE AVE 256 NE
ROSE PKWY 256 NE
ROSEBURY AVE 256 SW
ROSELL AVE 256 NW
ROSEMARY ST 256 NW
ROSEMONT AVE 257 NE
ROSEWOOD AVE 256 NW
ROSEWOOD DR
  E. GRAND RAPIDS 250 SE
ROSEWOOD DR
  E. GRAND RAPIDS 250 SE
ROSEWORHT ST 261 SW
ROSS CT 261 SW
ROSSMAN AVE 256 NW
ROTHBURY CT 246 NE
ROTHBURY DR 246 SW
ROTHWOOD
  CONCOURSE 261 SW
ROWE AVE 245 NW
ROWLAND AVE
  GRAND RAPIDS 257 NE
ROWLAND AVE
  KENTWOOD 258 NW
ROY AVE 241 NE
ROYAL ELM DR 240 NW
ROYAL OAK ST 252 SW
ROYS AVE 254 SW
RUBY AVE 256 NE
RUDGATE DR 254 SW
RUDY ST 240 SW
RUMFORD DR 239 SW
RUMSEY ST 261 SW
RUNIDO CT 261 SW
RUNIDO DR 261 SW
RURAH AVE 256 SW
RUSCHE 239 NE
RUSSET DR 246 SE
RUSSETT CT 242 SW

RUSSVIEW CT 241 SE
RUSSVIEW DR 241 SE
RUSSWOOD ST 245 NW
RUSTIS AVE 253 SW
RUSTY DR 256 SW
RYAN AVE 242 SE
RYPENS DR 242 SE
SACINAN RD 256 NE
ST. ANDREWS 252 SW
ST. ANDREWS CT 252 SW
ST. ANDREWS DR 252 SW
ST. CLAIR AVE 257 NW
ST. IVEN ST 240 SW
ST. LAWRENCE AVE 241 NW
SALADIN ST 258 NW
SALEM AVE 249 SE
SALERNO DR 249 SW
SANDALWOOD CT 241 NW
SANDPIPER 258 NW
SANDRA 243 NE
SANDY CT
  KENTWOOD 261 SW
SANDY DR
  GRAND RAPIDS 240 SE
SANDY ST
  KENTWOOD 261 SW
SANDY SHORE DR 262 NW
SANFORD AVE 253 NE
SANGRA AVE 251 SW
SAN JOSE DR 251 SW
SAN JUAN DR 251 SW
SAN LUCIA DR 251 SW
SAN LU RAE DR 251 SW
SANTA BARBARA DR 250 SE
SANTA CRUZ DR 251 SW
SANTA MONICA DR 251 SW
SARASOTA AVE 251 SW
SARNIA ST 249 SW
SAUK TR E 257 NW
SAUK TR N 257 NW
SAUK TR S 257 NW
SAUNDERS ST 247 SE
SAWYER CT 247 SE
SAXONY N 257
SCENICVIEW 241 SW
SCHIMPERLE DR 241 SW
SCHOOL ST 239 SE
SCHOOLCRAFT ST 250 NW
SCOTT AVE 249 NW
SCRIBNER AVE 244 SE
SECOND ST 249 NW
SEMINOLE RD 250 SE
SENIOR RD 242 NW
SENORA AVE 256 SW
SENTINAL ST 259 NE
SENTRY 257 NE
SERVICE DR ST-DALE 242 NE
SERVICE DR
  GRAND RAPIDS 247 NW
SERVICE DR
  GRAND RAPIDS 247 NW
SEVENTH ST 242 SE
SEWARD AVE 244 SE
SEYMOUR AVE 243 SE
SHADOWLANE DR 246 NW
SHADOWLAWN CT 246 NW
SHADY PINE LA 258 NE
SHAFFER AVE 257 SE
SHAMROCK ST 249 SW
SHANAHAN ST 243 SW
SHANGRAI-LA DR 256 NE
SHANNAN DR 243 NW
SHARON AVE 254 NE
SHARON CT 254 NE
SHARP DR 243 NE
SHAMMUT CT 243 SW
SHAWNEE DR 257 NW
SHEFFIELD 249 SW
SHELBY ST 249 SW
SHELDON AVE 249 NE
SHENANDOAH DR 248 NW
SHERIDAN AVE 249 SE
SHERI LYNN DR 257 SW
SHERIN DR 240 SE
SHERMAN ST 250 SW
SHERRY ST 259 NW
SHERWOOD AVE 253 NE
SHIAWASSEE DR E. 257 SW
SHIAWASSEE DR N. 257 NW
SHIRLEY ST 254 SW
SHIWASSE DR 256 NE
SHOPPING CTR. RD 251 SW
SHOREHAM PL 242 SW
SHORE HAVEN DR 252 NW
SHORT ST 245 NW
SHOSHONE DR 253 SE
SHOTTERY DR 251 NE
SIBLEY CT 248 NE
SIBLEY ST 248 NE
SIERRA AVE
  KENTWOOD 258 NW
SIERRA DR
  KENTWOOD 258 NW
SIGSBEE ST 250 SW
SILBER AVE 256 NE
SILVER CREEK AVE 250 SE
SILVERLEAF ST 261 SW
SIMMONS AVE 245 SE
SIMPSON CT 248 NE
SINCEL DR 239 SW
SINCLAIR AVE 245 NW
SIX MILE RD 239 NE
SIXTH ST 243 SE
SKORY AVE 256 SW
SKYLINE DR 248 NW
SLIGH BLVD 243 NW
SLOBEY ST 261 NW

SLUYTER ST 260 NE
SMITH CT 249 SE
SNOW APPLE DR 245 SW
SOCORRO DR 251 NE
SOMERSET DR 251 NW
SOUTH ST 253 SE
SOUTHAMPTON 253 SW
S. DORKALL ST 245 NE
S. EDGEWOOD 257 NE
SOUTHGLOW CT 261 NW
SOUTHLAND AVE 257 SW
S. NORWALK DR 256 SE
S. NORWAY ST 258 NW
S. OTTILLIA ST 256 NW
S. SERVICE DR 249 SW
SOUTHSHIRE 253 SE
SPARKS DR 258 NW
SPARTAN AVE 261 NE
SPARTAN IND. DR 259 NW
SPAULDING AVE 252 NE
SPENCER ST 245 SW
SPRING AVE 245 NE
SPRINGBROOK DR 239 SE
SPRINGBROOK
  PKWY 239 NE
SPRINGFIELD ST 239 NE
SPRING HILL ST 259 NW
SPRINGWOOD CT 261 SE
SPRINGWOOD DR 261 SW
SPRUCE HALLOW
  DR 241 SE
SPRUCE LA
  WYOMING 256 NW
SPRUCEWOOD DR 243 SW
STAFFORD AVE 260 NE
STAHL DR 258 NW
STANDALE PLAZA 247 NE
STANDARD AVE 248 NE
STANDISH AVE 240 SW
STANFORD DR 262 NW
STANLEY TERR 250 NW
STANWOOD DR 242 SE
STARK AVE 242 SE
STARR ST 258 NE
STAUFFER AVE 262 NW
STEELE AVE 249 SW
STEHOUWER ST 243 NE
STERLING AVE 244 SW
STERNER ST 248 NW
STEVENS ST 249 SE
STILESGATE CT 256 SE
STILESGATE ST 256 SE
STOCKING AVE NW 244 SW
STODDARD AVE 245 SW
STOLPE ST 249 SW
STONE ST 249 SW
STONEBRIDGE DR 259 NW
STONE HILLS ST 243 SE
STONY CREEK AVE 239 NE
STORMZAND DR 250 NE
STORRS ST 253 SE
STORY 250 NW
STOWELL 239 SE
STRAIGHT AVE 249 NE
STRATFORD CT
  E. GRAND RAPIDS 251 SW
STRATMOOR PL 251 SW
STROBEL AVE 243 SE
STUART AVE 261 NE
STUYVESANT AVE 260 NW
SUBURBAN SHORES 241 SW
SUDBURY ST 259 NW
SU-LEW AVE 247 SW
SUMMER AVE 249 NE
SUNLIN'CT 244 SE
SUNNYBROOK AVE 251 NW
SUNNY CREEK CT 241 NE
SUNNYCREEK ST 261 NE
SUCCVVIEW 253 SW
SUNSET AVE 247 NE
SUNSET HILLS AVE 242 SE
SUNVIEW CT 253 SE
SUNVJEW DR 253 NW
SUMMITVIEW CT 241 SE
SUMMITVIEW DR 241 SE
SUPERIOR ST 253 SE
SURREY PL 281 SE
SUTTER CT 241 SW
SWANK DR 258 SW
SWANSEA DR 257 NE
SWEET ST 244 SE
SWEET BRIAR CT 241 SE
SWENSBERG AVE 255 NE
SWIONTEK PL 249 NW
SYCAMORE ST 254 SW
STLVAN AVE 250 SE
STLVIA ST 244 SW
SYRACUSE AVE 239 NW
SYSCO CT 258 SE
TABOR RD 239 NW
TAFT AVE
  WYOMING 254 SE
TAFT CT
  GRAND RAPIDS 249 NE
TAMARACK AVE 244 NW
TAMPA ST 261 SE
TAOS AVE 252 NE
TAPLIN ST 253 SE
TARPON 254 SW
TAYLOR AVE 244 SE
TEKONSHA RD 257 NW
TEMPLE ST 250 SW
TENBY CT 246 SW
TENHAAF CT 249 SE
TENTH ST 242 SE

TENWAY DR 257 NW
TERMINAL ST 249 SW
TERRACE WALK
  AVE 240 SW
TERRY CT 262 NE
TERRY DR 262 NE
TEXAS ST 243 NE
THELMA AVE 256 NW
THIRD ST 249 NW
THIRTIETH ST 254 SW
30th ST
  GRANDVILLE 253 SE
THIRTY-EIGHTH ST 253 SW
THIRTY-FIFTH ST 254 SE
THIRTY-FIRST ST 254 SW
THIRTY-FOURTH
  ST 254 SE
THIRTY-NINTH ST 254 SE
THIRTY-SECOND
  ST 254 SE
THIRTY-SEVENTH 258 SE
THIRTY-SIXTH ST 253 SW
THIRTY-THIRD ST 254 SW
THOMAS ST 250 SW
THOREAU CT 241 SW
THORNAPPLE CT 244 SW
THORNDYKE AVE 260 NW
THORNWOOD ST 254 NE
THREE MILE RD 242 NW
THREE MILE RD 245 NW
THUNDERBIRD AVE 253 SW
TIMBER LA 254 SW
TIMBERLANE LA 245 NE
TIMBERVIEW CT 241 NW
TIMBERVIEW DR 240 NE
TIMBERWOOD DR 262 NW
TIMMINS ST 262 NW
TIMOTHY DR 256 SW
TIOGA DR 254 SW
TODD 240 NW
TOLFORD AVE 249 NW
TOMAHAWK DR 253 SE
TOMAHAWK TURN 241 SE
TOREN ST 250 SW
TORONTO AVE 259 NW
TOWNER AVE 249 NW
TOWNER CT 249 NW
TOWNSEND AVE 240 SW
TRAIL ST 243 SW
TRAILMOBILE TR 260 SE
TRAILS END 258 NE
TRAIL VIEW DR 241 NE
TRAVELO ST 261 NW
TRAVIS ST 244 SE
TREASURE ST 259 NE
TREMONT BLVD 258 NE
TRENTON ST 259 NW
TRENTWOOD 259 NW
TRIANN 261 NW
TRINIDAD AVE 242 SE
TROJAN DR 259 NW
TROWBRIDGE ST 259 SW
TRUXTON DR 245 SW
TUELL ST 243 SW
TULIP ST 259 SW
TULLER AVE 243 NE
TURNER AVE 244 SE
TURTLE BEND 259 NW
TUTTLE AVE 250 NW
TWELFTH ST 244 SW
TWENTY-EIGHTH ST 253 NE
29th ST 253 NE
TWENTY-NINTH ST 252 NE
TWENTY-SEVENTH 254 NW
TWENTY-SIXTH ST 253 NE
TYLER CT 249 NE
TYLER ST 253 SW
UMATILLA ST 250 SW
UNDERHILL AVE 249 SW
UNDERWOOD AVE 250 NW
INION AVE 245 NW
UPLANDS DR 251 NE
UPTON ST 251 NE
URBAN AVE 260 NE
VALENTINE ST 241 SW
VALLEY AVE
  GRAND RAPIDS 249 NW
VALLEY AVE
  WALKER 244 NW
VALLEY CREST DR 247 SW
VALLEY FORGE DR 248 NE
VALLEY LANE CT 262 SW
VALLEY LANE DR 262 SW
VALLEYRDIGE AVE 259 NW
VALLEYVIEW ST 259 NW
VALLEYWOOD DR 257 NE
VAN ALLEN ST 259 NW
VAN AUKEN ST 256 SE
VANBUREN AVE 244 SW
VANCOUVER AVE 259 NW
VANDENBERG PL 250 SW
VANDERVEEN CT 259 NE
VANDINE PL 250 SW
VAN ESS AVE 243 SW
VAN HAAFTEN PL 250 SW
VAN PORTFLIET DR 242 SE
VAN RAALTE DR 250 SW
VASSAR ST 257 NW
VERMONT AVE 253 SW
VERMONT CT 253 SW
VERNON ST 250 NW
VERNOR AVE 241 NE
VERTA DR 241 NE
VESTA LA 257 NW
VETERANS MEM. DR 248 SW
VETO ST 249 NW

VIADUCT ST 253 NE
VICTOR AVE 251 SW
VICTORIA AVE 252 NW
VICTORY CT 249 NE
VICTORY CT 249 NE
VICTORY PL 249 SE
VIEW POND DR 261 NE
VILAS AVE 249 SE
VILLAGE DR 256 NE
VILLA MONTEE DR 258 SW
VILLAGE RIDGE 258 SW
VINDALE ST 260 NE
VINE ST 253 NE
VINECROFT ST 243 NE
VINELAND AVE 256 NE
VINELAND PL 250 NW
VINEYARD AVE 241 SW
VIRGINIA ST SE 250 NW
VISSER PL 250 NW
VOORHEIS AVE 244 NW
URIES ST 210 SW
WABASH CT 241 NW
WABASH DR 241 NW
WAKEFIELD AVE 240 NW
WAKEFIELD CT 240 NW
WALBRIDGE ST 244 SE
WALDON WOODS DR 254 SW
WALDORF ST 243 NE
WALDRON ST 254 NE
WALKENT DR 243 SE
WALKER AVE 243 NE
WALKER PL 243 SE
WALLACE AVE 253 NE
WALLACE CT 253 NE
WALLEN AVE 249 SE
WALLINGFORD AVE 239 NE
WALMA AVE 262 NE
WALNUT ST 245 SW
WALNUT HILLS DR 257 SW
WALSH ST 256 NW
WALTHAM AVE 252 NW
WALTON AVE 260 NE
WALWOOD DR 246 SW
WALWOOD TERR 246 SW
WANDA AVE 241 NW
WANDERCREST ST 261 NW
WARREN AVE 250 NW
WARRINGTON ST 247 NW
WARWICK RD 257 NF
WASHINGTON AVE
  GRANDVILLE 253 NW
WASHINGTON ST
  GR. RAPIDS 249 NE
WASHTENAW DR 240 SW
WATERBURY DR 261 SE
WATERBURY PL 261 SE
WATERCREST 254 NW
WATERFORD DR 240 SW
WATERGATE DR 254 SW
WATERLOO ST 259 NW
WATKINS ST 250 SW
WATSON ST 249 NW
WAUSAUKEE DR 241 SE
WAYBURN 253 SE
WAYBURY ST 242 SW
WAYSIDE DR 258 NE
WEALTHY ST 250 NW
WEBB AVE 242 SE
WEBBER AVE 243 SE
WEBSTER 244 SW
WEDGEWOOD CT
  GRANDVILLE 253 SW
WEDGEWOOD CT
  WYOMING 254 SW
WEDGEWOOD DR
  WYOMING 254 SW
WELLERWOOD ST 245 NW
WELLINGTON AVE 250 NW
WELLS ST 240 SW
WEMBLEY CT 259 NE
WENDAN DR 251 NE
WENDLER AVE 249 SW
WENDOVER RD 248 NE
WENTWORTH AVE 254 SW
WERNER AVE 242 SE
WEST AVE
  WYOMING 254 NE
WEST DR K-WOOD 245 SW
WESTBORO DR 251 NW
WESTBROOK DR 243 NW
WESTCHESTER DR 252 SW
W. COLLIER AVE 249 NE
WEST ELM ST 248 SE
WESTEND AVE 243 SE
WESTERN 240 NW
WESTFIELD DR 239 NE
WESTGATE AVE 239 NE
WEST GRAND BLVD 242 SW
WESTLAKE DR 241 NW
WESTMONT DR 248 NW
WESTMOOR DR 243 SE
WESTNEDGE AVE 249 NE
W. NORWALK 256 SE
WESTON ST 249 NE
WEST RIVER DR 239 NW
WESTSHIRE DR 239 NW
WEST VIEW AVE 243 SW
WESTWAY DR 247 NE
WESTWOOD DR 240 SE
WEYMOUTH DR 256 SE
WHALEN CT 249 NW
WHARF CIR 258 NW
WHIPPERILL CT 257 NW
WHISPERINGBROOK
  DRIVE 257 SW

WHISPERINGBROOK
  COURT 257 SW
WHISPERING LANE
  DRIVE 241 SE
WHISPERING WAY 258 NW
WHITE AVE G.R. 244 SW
WHITE ST G-VILLE 243 NE
WHITE HILLS AVE 252 NW
WHITFIELD RD 257 NW
WHITING ST 248 SE
WHITMORE AVE 242 SE
WHITNEY CT 245 NW
WIDDICOMB AVE 244 SW
WIELAND PL 244 SE
WILBERT AVE 244 SW
WILCOX PARK DR 250 NE
WILDRIDGE CT 246 NW
WILDRIDGE DR 246 NW
WILES 254 SW
WILES CT 254 SW
WILFRED G VILLE 243 SW
WILFRED AVE G.R. 246 NW
WILKSHIRE AVE SW 260 NE
WILL AVE 244 SE
WILLARD AVE 256 NW
WILLIAMS ST 249 NE
WILLIAMSON AVE 240 SW
WILLIS AVE 253 SE
WILLOW CT G.R. 249 NE
WILLOW DR N. PK 240 SW
WILLOW CREEK DR 254 SW
WILLOW SHORE DR 262 NW
WILMINGTON AVE 239 SE
WILMONT ST 261 SE
WILNELLA DR 256 NE
WILSHIRE DR 251 SW
WILSON AVE 242 SW
WINCHELL ST 256 NW
WINCHESTER PL 249 NE
WINDOVER DR 256 NW
WINDSOR 250 NW
WINDVIEW AVE 259 NW
WINDY WOOD ST 262 NE
WINESAP DR
  WALKER 242 SW
WINFIELD AVE 254 NW
WING AVE 262 SE
WINGATE DR 257 SE
WINGED FOOT DR 252 NF
WINICK ST 250 SE
WINIER AVE 249 NE
WINNIPEG AVE 259 NW
WINONA AVE 248 NE
WINSLOW ST 243 NE
WINSTON WAY 245 NE
WITHVIEW AVE 246 SW
WOLFBORO DR 262 SW
WOLF RIVER DR 242 SW
WOLVERINE ST 240 NW
WOOD 251 SW
WOODCLIFF AVE
  GR. RAPIDS 251 SE
WOODCLIFF LA GR 257 NE
WOODCREST DR 258 NE
WOODFIELD CT 241 NE
WOODHILL CT 255 NC
WOODLAKE CT 259 NW
WOODLAKE ST 259 NW
WOODLAND AVE 243 SW
WOODLAWN AVE
  E. GR. RAPIDS 250 SW
WOODLAWN ST G.R 257 NW
WOODMONT ST 243 NE
WOODPATH DR 243 SW
WOODRIDGE ST NE 245 NW
WOODROW AVE 243 SE
WOODSBORO CT 246 NW
WOODSBORO DR 246 NW
WOODSIDE DR 250 NE
WOODSTOCK AVE 256 SW
WOODWARD AVE
  WYOMING 256 NE
WOODWARD LA EGR 250 NE
WOOLSEY DR 249 SW
WOOSTER AVE 257 NW
WORCESTER DR 246 SW
WORDEN ST 250 SW
WORRIDGE 250 NW
WRENWOOD ST 254 NE
WRIGHT ST 245 NW
WRIGHT WIND DR 258 NE
WYANDOTTE DR 241 SW
WYOMING AVE 254 SW
"X" AVE 242 NE
YELLOWSTONE DR 253 SE
YORK DR 257 NW
YORKSHIRE ST 256 SE
YORKTON AVE 259 NW
YOUELL AVE 259 NW
ZEELAND CT 250 NW
ZENO ST 249 SE

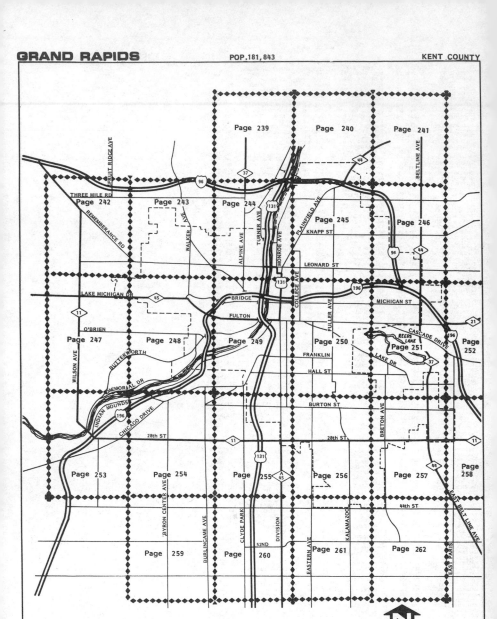

Page 239

Page 240

Page 241

FRUIT RIDGE AVE

BELTLINE AVE

48

37

96

THREE MILE RD

Page 242

Page 243

Page 244

131

PLAINFIELD AVE

Page 245

Page 246

REMEMBERANCE RD

WALKER AVE

ALPINE AVE

TURNER AVE

MONROE AVE

KNAPP ST

96

44

LEONARD ST

COLLEGE AVE

131

LAKE MICHIGAN DR

45

BRIDGE

196

FULLER AVE

MICHIGAN ST

21

11

O'BRIEN

FULTON

CASCADE DRIVE

196

REEDS LAKE

Page 247

Page 248

Page 249

Page 250

Page 251

Page 252

WILSON AVE

BUTTERWORTH

FRANKLIN

LAKE DR

37

HALL ST

MEMORIAL DR

INDIAN MOUNDS

196

BURTON ST

BRETON AVE

CHICAGO DRIVE

28th ST

11

28th ST

11

131

44

Page 253

Page 254

Page 255

85

Page 256

Page 257

Page 258

BYRON CENTER AVE

BURLINGAME AVE

CLYDE PARK

DIVISION

44th ST

EAST BELT LINE AVE

52ND

Page 259

Page 260

EASTERN AVE

KALAMAZOO

Page 261

Page 262

EAST PARIS

N

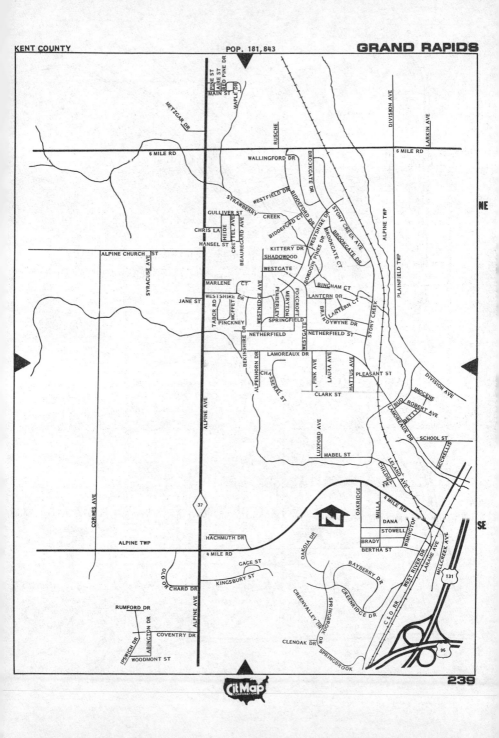

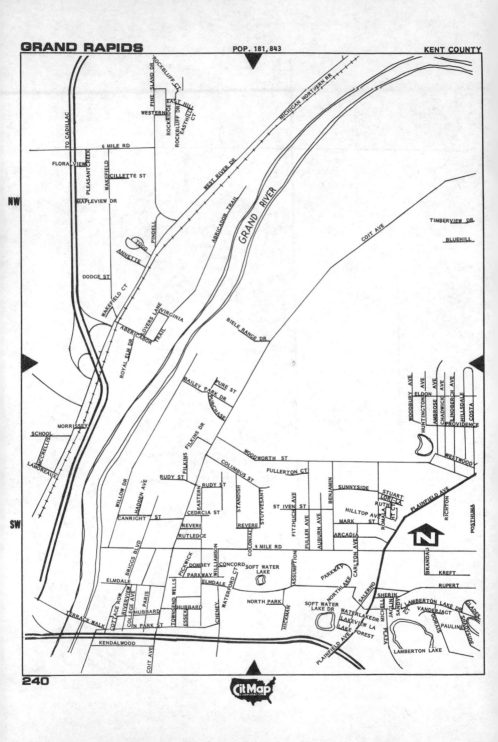

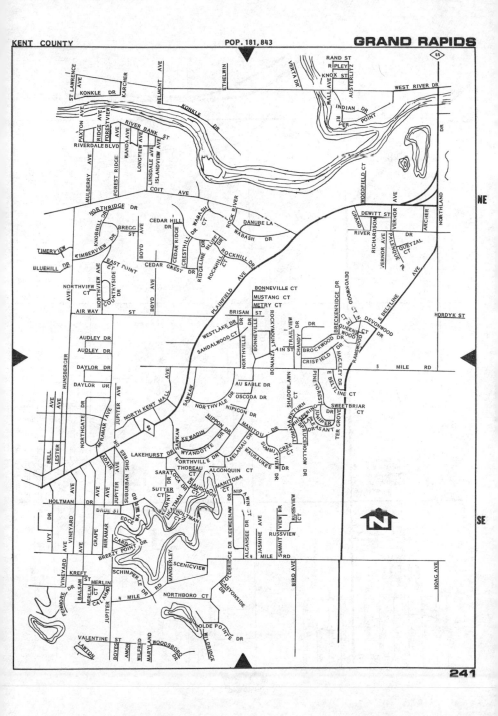

NE

SE

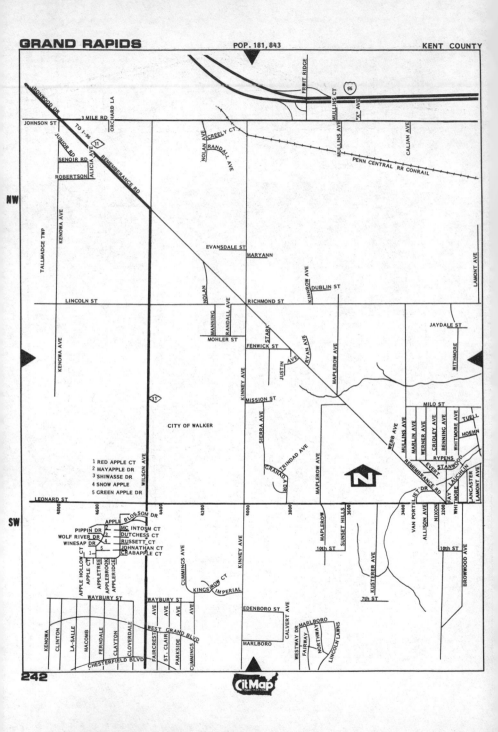

IRONWOOD DR

JOHNSON ST
3 MILE RD
ORCHARD LA
FRUIT RIDGE
96
MULLINS CT
"X" AVE

TO I-96
JUNIOR RD
SENOIR RD
ROBERTSON
ALICIA AVE
REMEMBRANCE RD

NOLAN AVE
RANDALL AVE
CREELY CT
CALJAN AVE
MULLINS AVE
PENN CENTRAL RR CONRAIL

NW

KENOWA AVE
TALLMADGE TWP
KENOWA AVE

EVANSDALE ST
MARYANN
LAMONT AVE

NOLAN
KINNROW AVE
DUBLIN ST
LINCOLN ST
RICHMOND ST
MANNING
RANDALL AVE
MOHLER ST
FENWICK ST
STARK
JUSTIN AVE
RYAN AVE
JAYDALE ST
WITHMORE

KINNEY AVE
MISSION ST
SIERRA AVE
MAPLEROW AVE
MILO ST
MULLINS AVE
MARLIN AVE
WERNER AVE
CRIDLEY AVE
BENNING AVE
WHITMORE AVE
TUELL
HOEHN

CITY OF WALKER

WILSON AVE

TRINIDAD AVE
GRANAD
HOLLY
MAPLEROW AVE
WEBB AVE
REMEMBRANCE RD
RYPENS
EVERT
STANWOOD
LAUGHLIN
LANCASTER
LAMONT AVE

1 RED APPLE CT
2 MAYAPPLE DR
3 SHIWASSE DR
4 SNOW APPLE
5 GREEN APPLE DR

LEONARD ST
4800
4600
4400
4200
4000
3800
MAPLEROW
SUNSET HILLS
3600
3400
VAN PORTELLE DR
ALLISON AVE
NIXON
FAY
WHITMORE
3200

SW

APPLE BLOSSOM DR
MC INTOSH CT
PIPPIN DR
DUTCHESS CT
WOLF RIVER DR
RUSSETT CT
WINESAP DR
JOHNATHAN CT
CRABAPPLE CT
APPLE HOLLOW CT
APPLE CT
APPLETREE
APPLEBROOK
APPLERIDGE

CUMMINGS AVE
KINNEY AVE
10th ST
10th ST
BROWWOOD AVE
KUSTERER AVE
7th ST

WAYBURY ST
WAYBURY ST
KINGS ROW CT
IMPERIAL

EDENBORO ST
CALVERT AVE
WESTWAY DR
FAIRWAY DR
MARLBORO
NORTHWAY
LINCOLN LAWNS

KENOWA
CLINTON
LA-SALLE
MACOMB
FERNDALE
CLAYTON
CLOVERDALE
FAIRCREST AVE
ST. CLAIR AVE
PARKSIDE AVE
CUMMINGS AVE
WEST GRAND BLVD
CHESTERFIELD BLVD
MARLBORO

CitMap

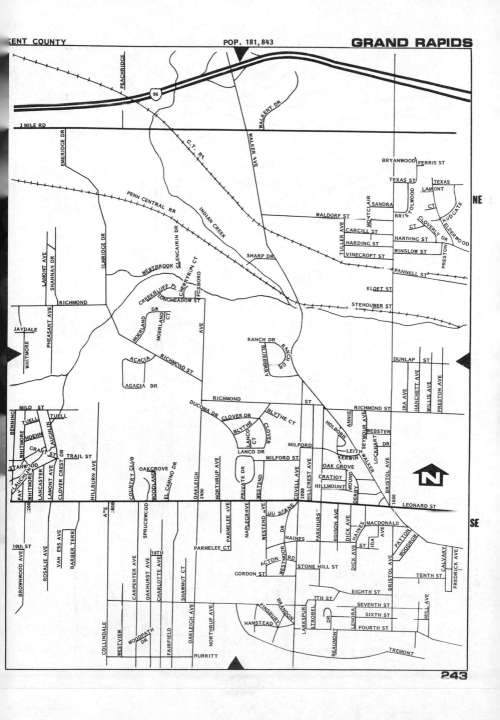

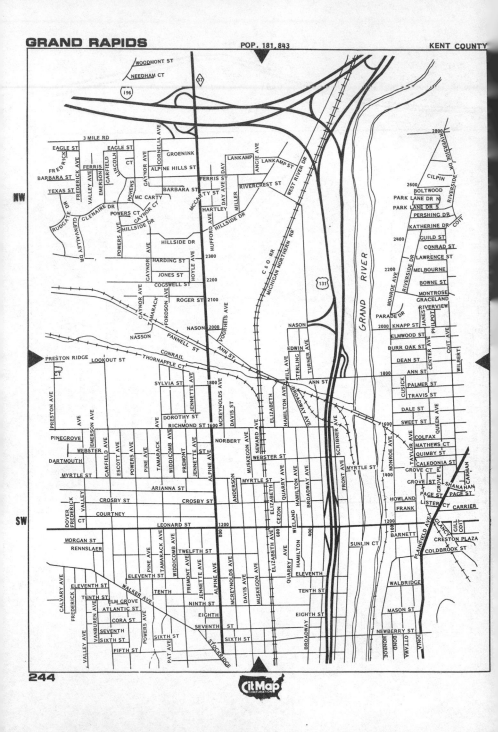

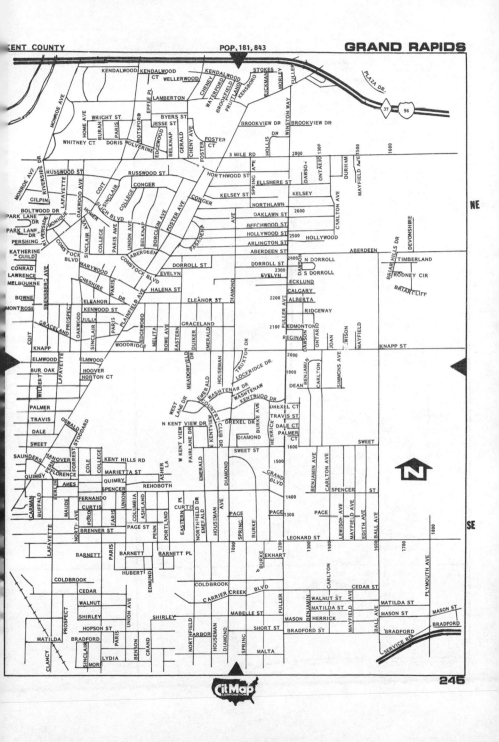

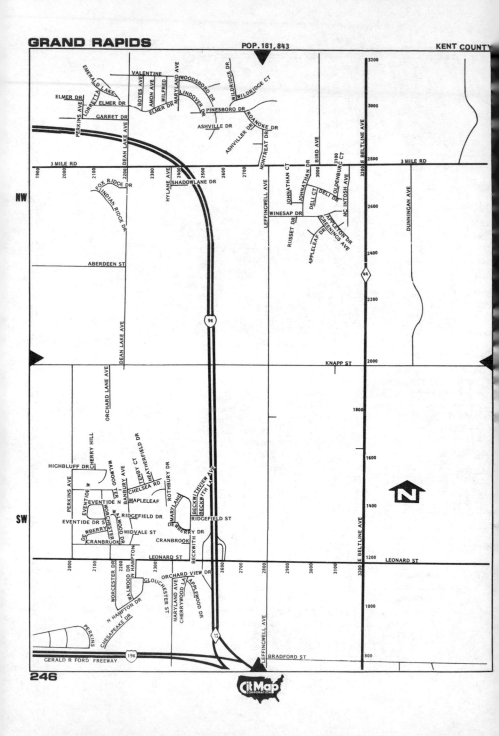

NW

SW

N

3 MILE RD

3 MILE RD

KNAPP ST

LEONARD ST

LEONARD ST

BRADFORD ST

CitMap
CORPORATION

GERALD R FORD FREEWAY

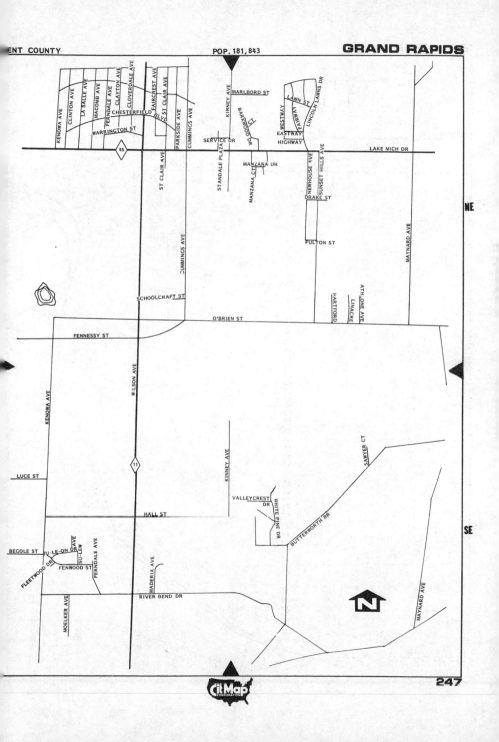

POP. 181,843

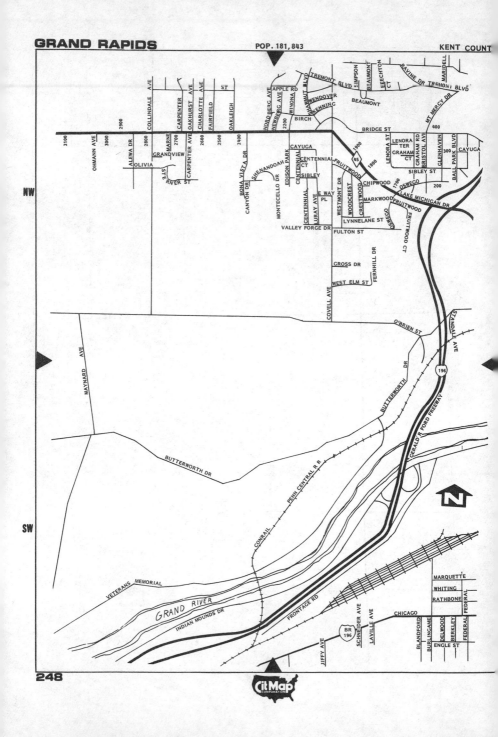

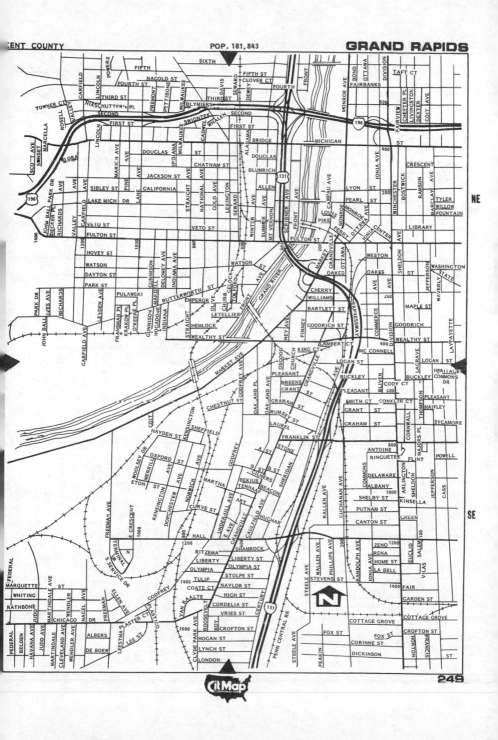

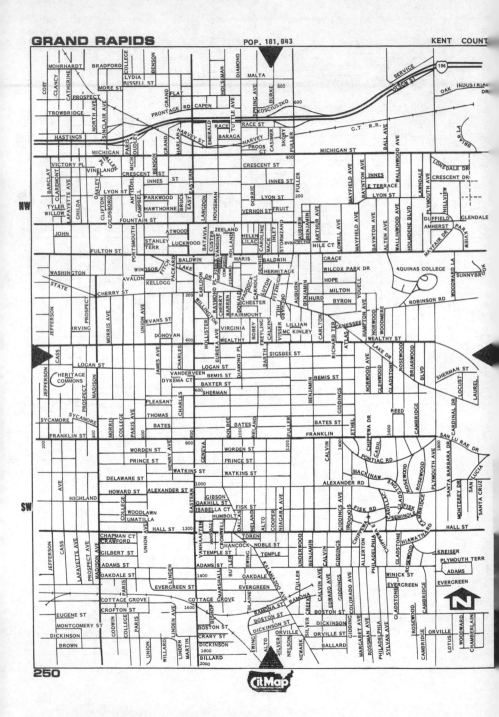

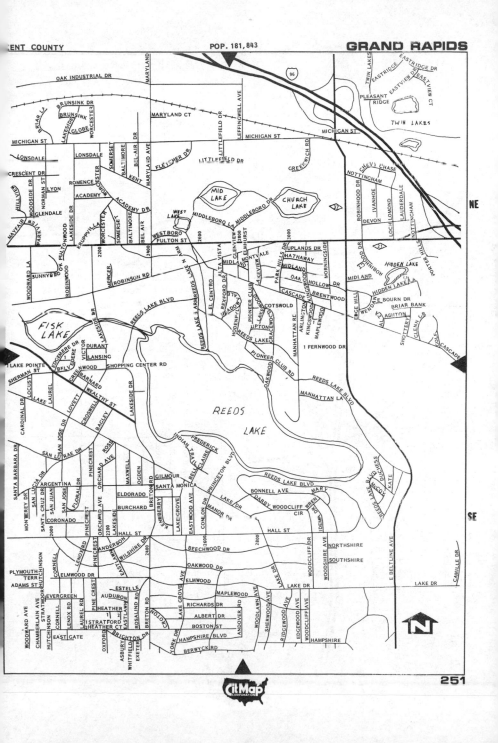

NE

SE

N

NW

SW

MICHIGAN ST

CRAMEN AVE

TAOS AVE

PUGLIESE DR

CALBRAITH AVE

CLEARVIEW AVE

WHITE HILLS AVE

4000

4400

4800

5200

100

FOREST HILL AVE

HEATHER LANE

GREENBRIER CT

GREENBRIER

SHORE HAVEN DR

PRIVATE DR

LOCKHAVEN

BAYWOOD

PEBBLE BEACH

EASTMOOR AVE

HERSMAN ST

WINGED FOOT DR

BRAEBURN ST

ORLANDO

CARNOUSTIE AVE

BAYWOOD DR

ST ANDREWS

SEMONTS

ARROWHEAD AVE

PRESTWICK

GREENBRIER

96

CASCADE

RD CASCADE WEST PKWY

800

G.T.

RR

5200

SPAULDING AVE

ADA DR

PARCHMENT DR

FOREST HILL

DELRAY AVE

KIRK DR

ORLANDO

PATTERSON

SARASOTA

ARGO DR

CLIFFORD AVE

BYERLY AVE

CASCADE AVE

MAPLEHILL AVE

WESTCHESTER

WALTHAM

KENMOOR

LUDLOW

KENNILWORTH

BALFOUR

FARNSWORTH

CASTLE

EDINBURGH

DOWNING

MEDICAL PARK DR

MEDICAL PARK

CUTTER PKWY

AYLESWORTH

LUXEMBURG

EAST PARIS AVE

1000

1200

HIDDEN TARN

MARIGOLD

EASTMONT

KIRK DR

BURRWOOD

HALL

OAK BURN

ST

KIRK CT W

KIRK CT E

CASCADE RD

1200

FERNRIDGE

RANGER HILLS DR

CAMILLE DR

1400

1600

FOREST HILL

EAST FOREST

N

CLOVERLEAF DR

BLUEGRASS DR

SPAULDING

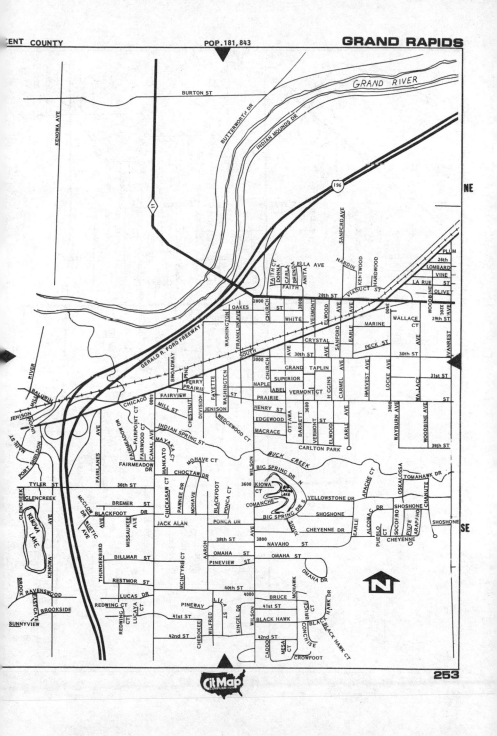

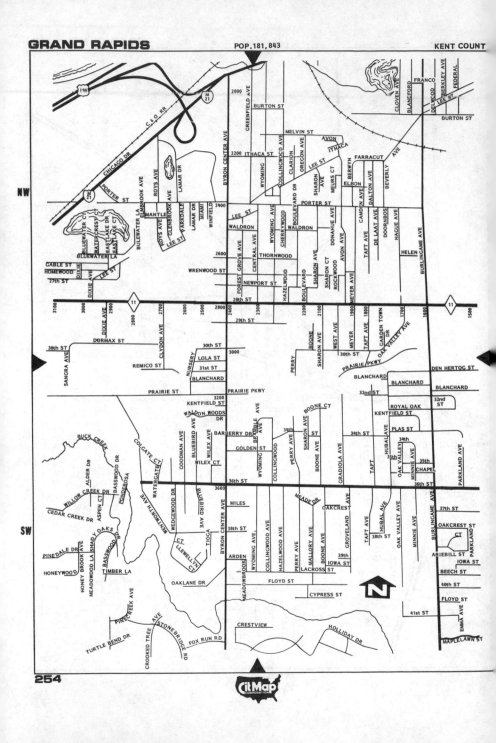

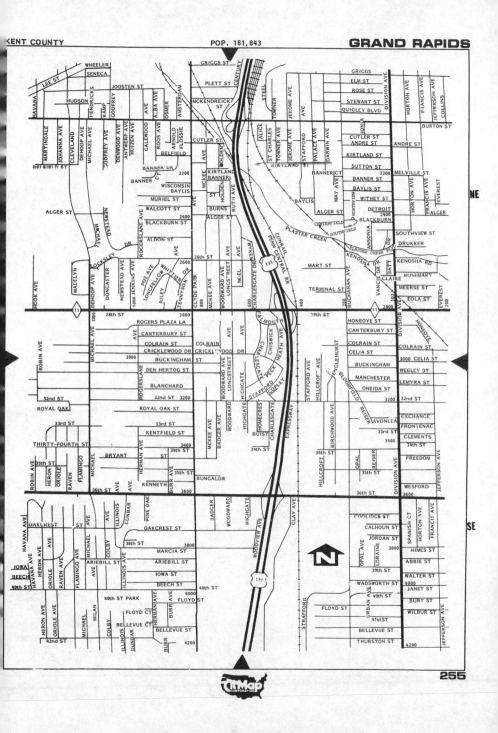

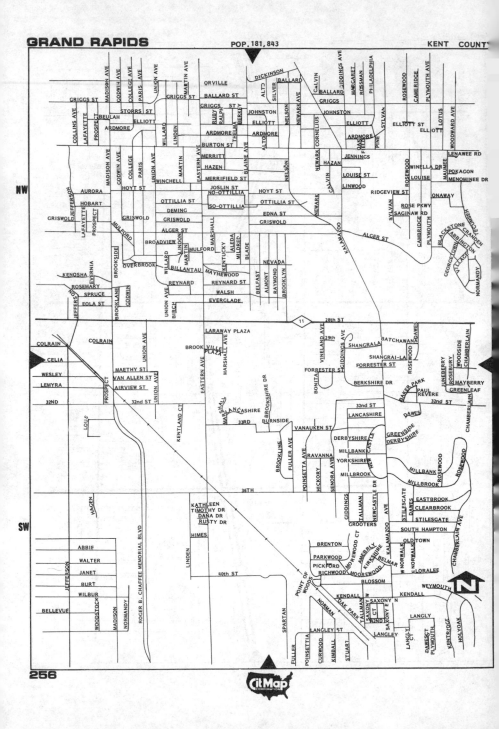

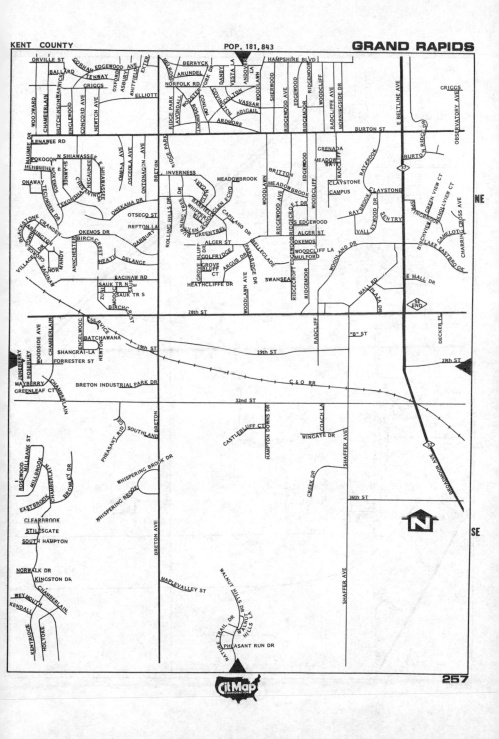

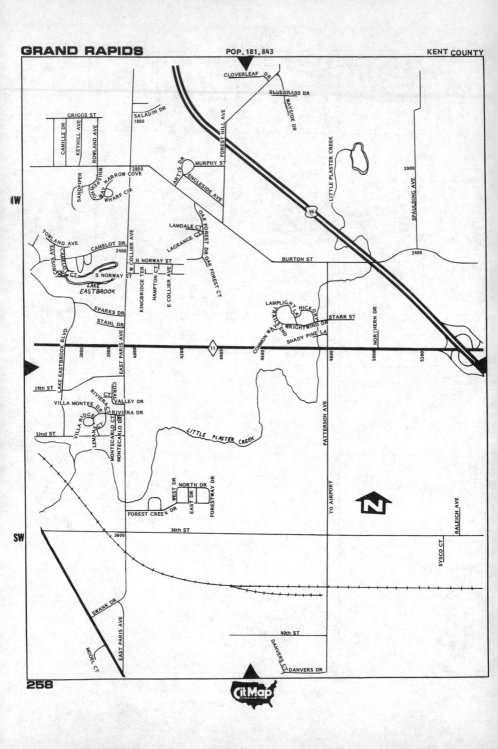

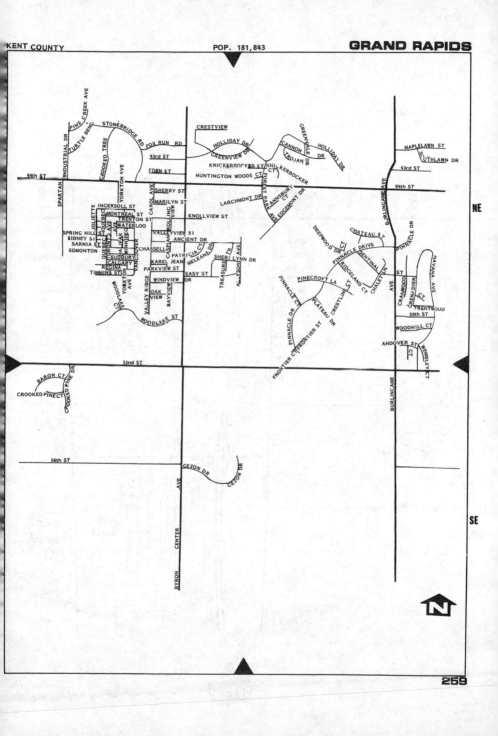

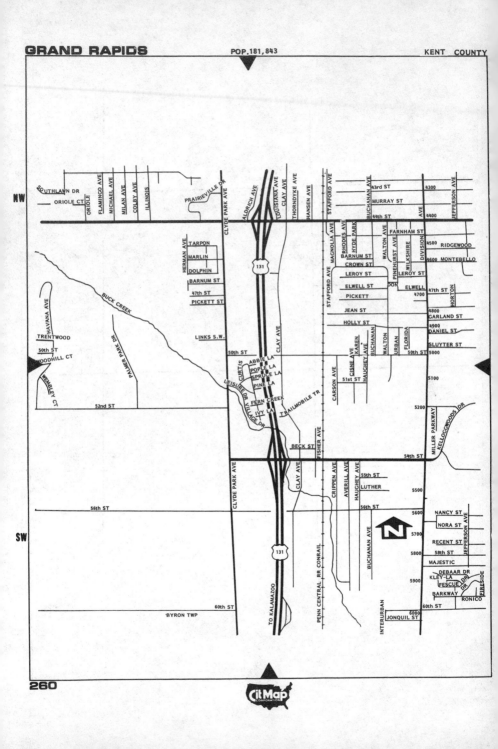

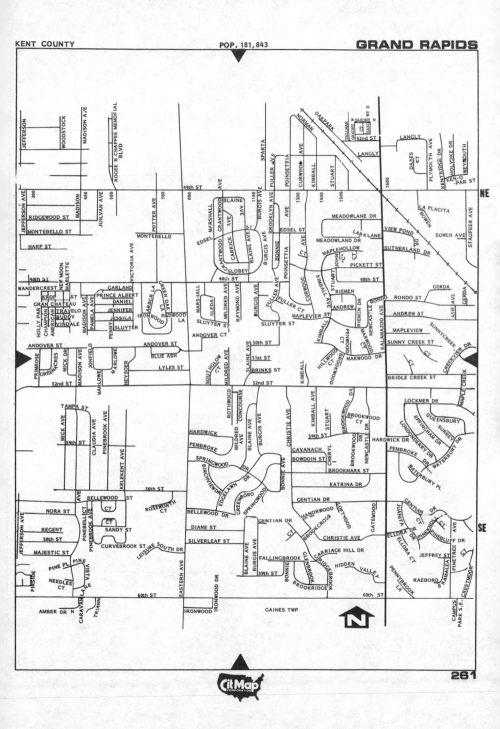

NE

SE

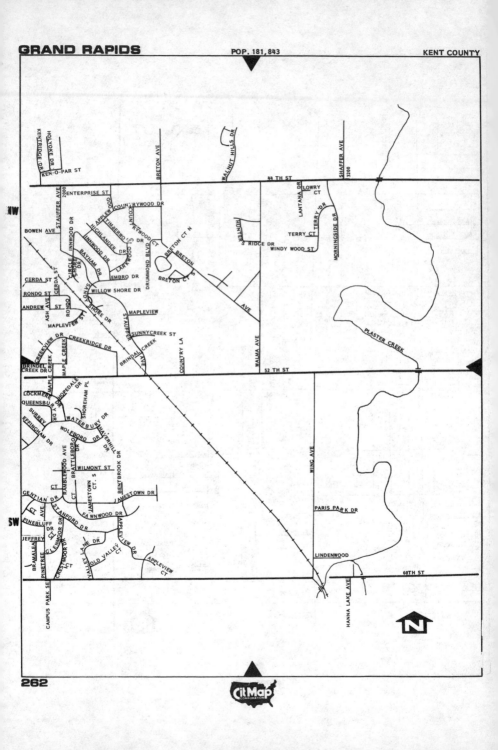

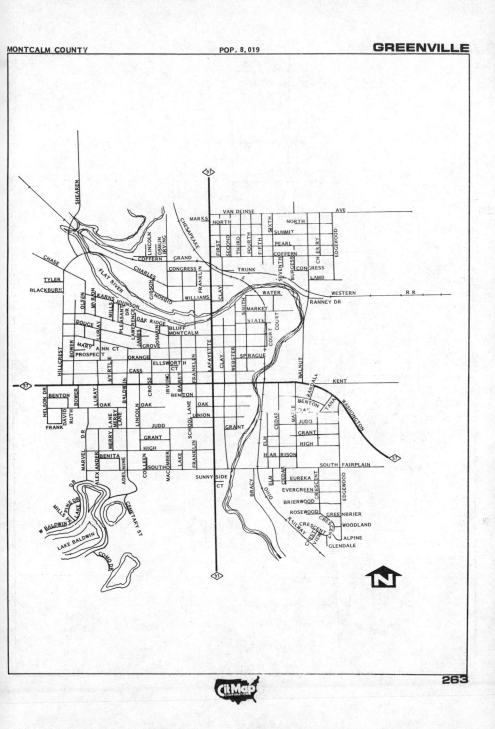

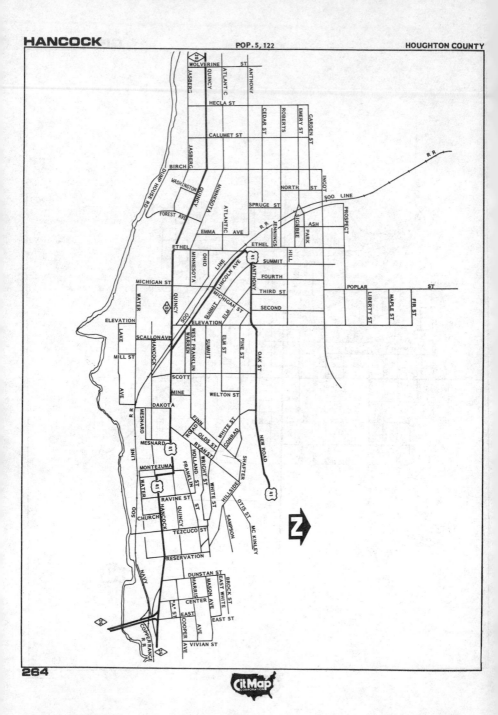

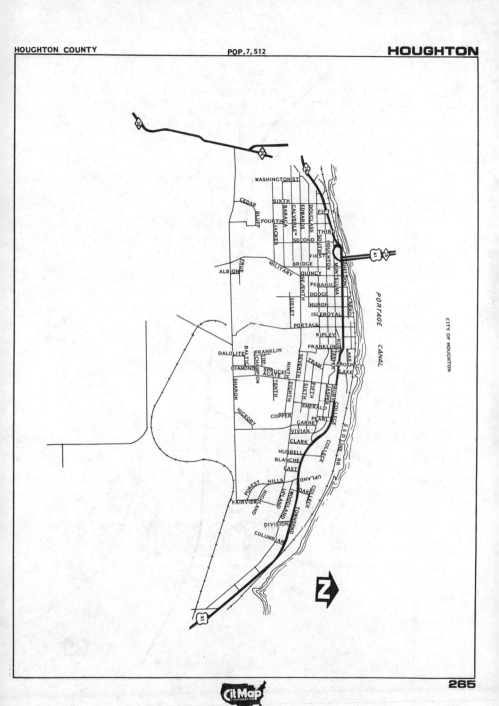

CITY OF HOUGHTON

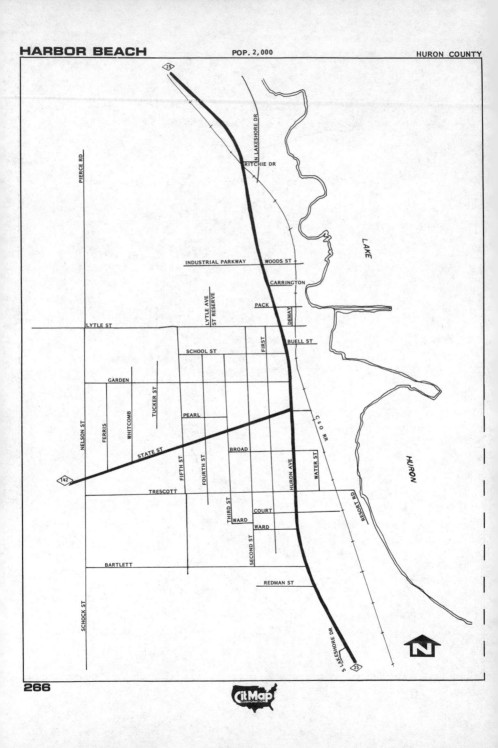

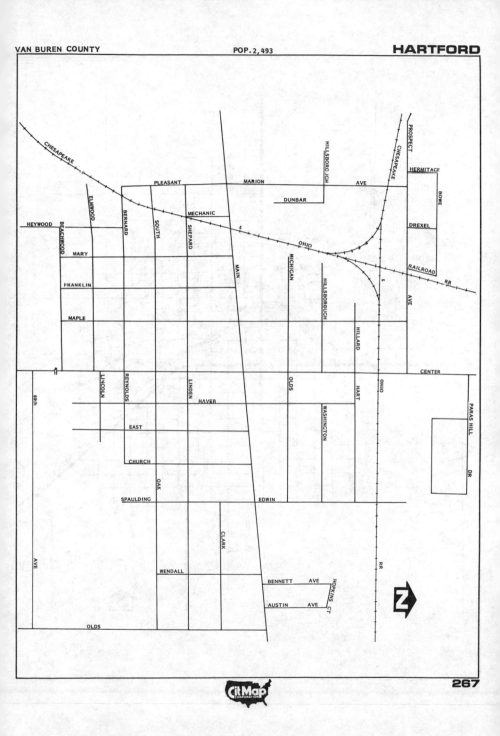

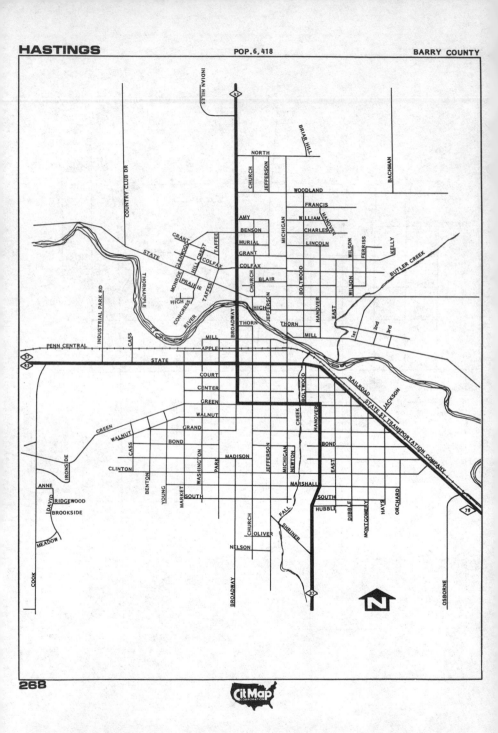

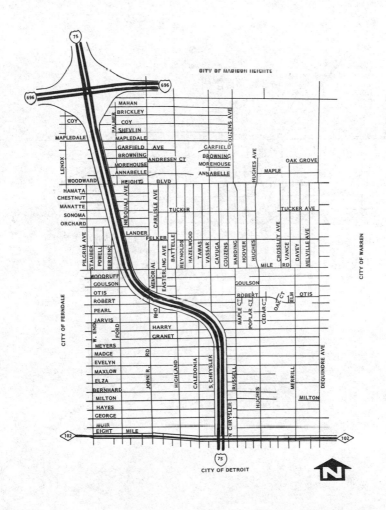

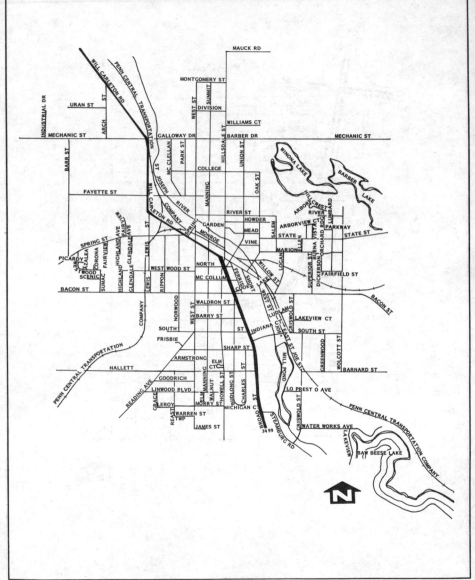

NOTES

ALDEN	272	SE
ALLEN RD	272	NW
APPLE	271	SW
ARDMORE	272	SW
ASTERR	272	SW
AZALEA	272	NW
BAY	272	NW
BAYVIEW	272	NW
BEACH DR	272	NW
BERISCH	272	NW
BIRCHWOOD	271	NE
BLACK BASS	272	SW
BLUEBELL	272	SW
BRECADO	272	SW
BROOK	271	NE
BROOKFIELD	272	SW
BROOKSIDE	271	SW
CALVIN	271	NE
CAMBRIDGE	271	NE
CENTRAL	271	SW
CHEROKEE	271	SW
CHERRY	272	NE
CLEVELAND	272	NE
CLOVER	271	NE
COLLEGE	271	SW
COLONIAL	272	SE
COLUMBIA	271	NW
CONCORD	272	SW
COOLRIDGE	271	NE
COUNTRY CLUB RD	271	SE
CRESENT	272	SE
CRESTVIEW	272	SW
CYPRESS	271	NE
DARTMOUTH	271	NE
DIEKMA	272	NE
DYKEMA	271	NW
EAST END	272	NW
EAST GATE	272	SW
ELM	272	NW
ELMDALE CT	272	NE
EUNA VISTA CT	271	NE
FAIRBANKS	271	NW
FAIRHILL	272	SE
FLORAL	272	NW
FRANKLIN	272	NW
GARRETSON	271	NW
GLENDALE	271	NE
GOLDEN ROD	272	SW
GRAAFSCHAP	272	SW
GRANDRIDGE CT	272	SW
GRANDVIEW	271	NE
GROVE	272	NW
HARRIGON	272	NE
HARVARD	271	NE
HAZEL	271	SW
HEATHERWOOD	272	SW
HIAWATHA	272	NW
HIGHLAND	271	NW
HOMESTEAD	271	NE
HOOVER	271	NE
HOPE	271	NE
JANICE	272	SW
KENWOOD	272	SE
KIRKVIEW	272	SE
KNOLLCREST	272	SW
KOLLEN PARK DR	272	NE
LAKE	272	NW
LAKEVIEW DR	272	NW
LARKWOOD DR	272	SW
LAWNDALE	272	NE
LEGION	271	NE
LEGION CT	271	NE
LEXINGTON	271	NE
LINCOLN	271	SW
LOCUST	272	NW
LUGERS	272	NW
LYNDEN	271	NE
MAPLE	272	NE
PARLENE	272	SW
MARRYLANE	272	SW
MEADOW	272	SE
MEADOWBROOK	272	SW
MIDWAY	272	NW
MOHAWK	272	NW
MORNING SIDE	271	SE
MYRTLE	272	SW
NEW CASTLE	272	SW
OLD ORCHARD	272	SW
OLD ORCHARD RD	272	SW
ORLANDO	271	NE
OTTAWA	272	SE
PAW PAW DR	271	NE
PINE	271	NE
PIONEER	272	SE
PLASMAN	272	NE
PLASMAN	272	SE
PROSPECT	271	SW
RAYMARKET RD	271	NE
REED	271	NW
RIVER	272	NE
RUTH	272	SW
SHOSHONE	272	NW
SORRENTO CT	271	NE
SORRENTO DR	271	NE
SOUTH SHORE	272	NW
SOUTHGATE	272	SW
SPRUCE	271	NW
SPRUCE CT	271	NW
STANDISH	272	SE
STATE ST	272	NE
SUNRISE DR	271	NE
THOMAS	272	NE
TIMBERWOOD	271	NE
VAURAALTE	272	NE
WALNUT	271	NW
WASHINGTON BLVD	272	NE
WAVERLY	271	SE
WELLINGTON	271	NE
WEST END	272	NW
WILDWOOD	272	SE
WINDCREST	271	SE
WOODBRIDGE	271	NE
ZOME CT	272	SE
1st ST	271	NW
10th ST	272	NE
11th ST	272	NE
119th ST	271	NE
12th ST	272	NE
13th ST	272	NE
14th ST	272	NE
15th ST	272	NE
16th ST	272	NE
17th ST	272	NE
18th ST	272	NE
19th ST	272	NE
2nd ST	271	NW
20th ST	272	NE
21st ST	272	NE
22nd ST	272	NE
23rd ST	272	NE
24th ST	272	NE
25th ST	272	NE
26th ST	272	NE
27th ST	272	SE
28th ST	272	SE
29th ST	272	SE
3rd ST	271	NW
30th ST	272	SE
31st ST	272	SE
32nd ST	272	SW
33rd ST	272	SE
34th ST	272	SE
35th ST	272	SE
36th ST	272	SE
37th ST	272	SE
38th ST	272	SE
39th ST	272	SE
4th ST	271	NW
40th ST	272	SE
5th ST	271	NW
54th ST	271	SE
6th ST	272	NE
7th ST	272	NE
8th ST	272	NE
9th ST	272	NE

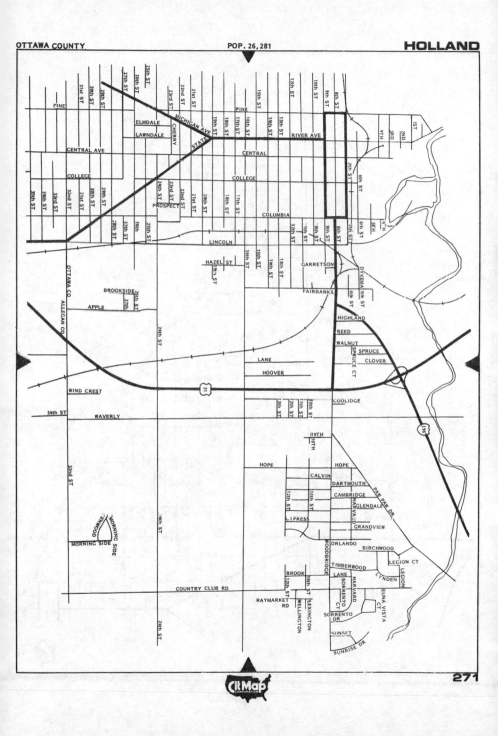

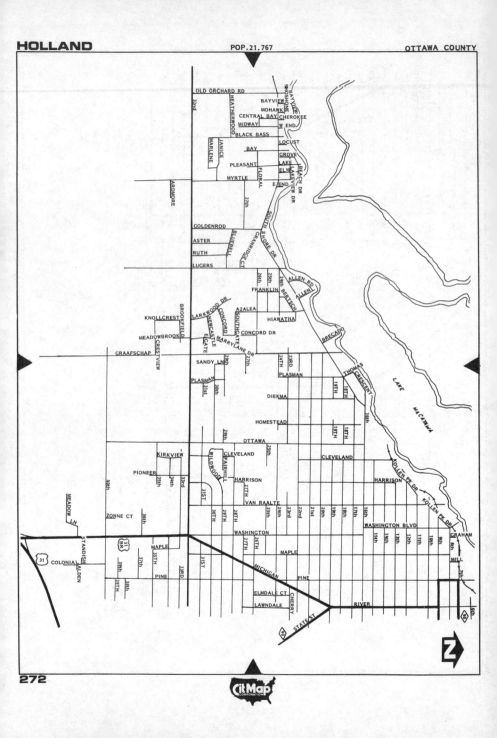

QUICK

MUD LAKE

GRANGE
ODESSA
SUNSET
LUMBERT
MAR ON DR
WINFRED
EMMA
JANICE
HOWARD
MARY ANN DR
DELPHINE
BEVINS
HARTNER DR
RICHARD DR
HARTNER
BEVIN DR
AIRPORT
LAKE

HALL RD

OAKWOOD
HOLLY BUSH DR
HOLLY BUSH CT
BUSH LAKE
ASH
LAKEVIEW
SEMINOLE
ROSETTE
CLOUD
THOMAS
ASH

RICE LAKE

C.L.Q. RR
SAGINAW
SHERWOOD
NORTH
SECOND
MICHIGAN
EMILY
FRONT
OAKLAND ST
FIRST ST
BROAD ST
ELM
SIMONSON LAKE
MAPLE ST
CLARENCE ST
PARK AVE
CORBIN
EAST RD

MORRISON ST
SHIAWASEE RIVER
GTW RAILROAD
MARTHA
JONES
CHURCH
SHERMAN
LEGRAND
JOHN
WASHINGTON
GRANT
BAIRD ST
COLLEGE
CENTER
FULTON
E. BAIRD ST

FRANKLIN ST
LENNY
LOCKE
HADLEY ST
COGSHALL
HASTINGS
FERN
WICK
HARDEN ST
EAST RD

ROSE ST
MILLPOND
ROSE

N

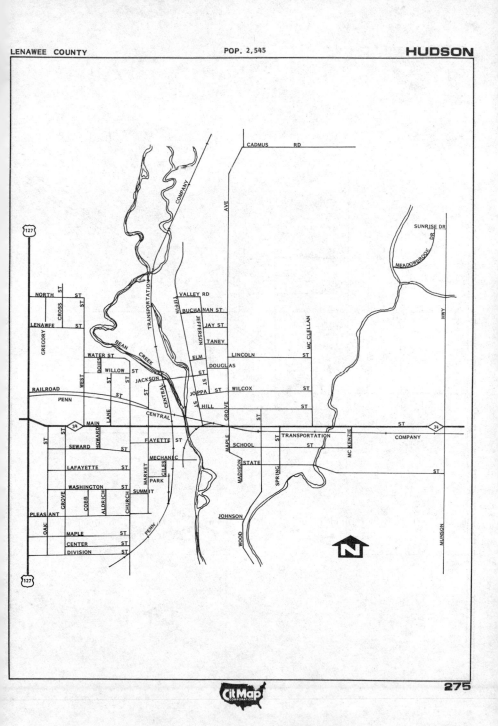

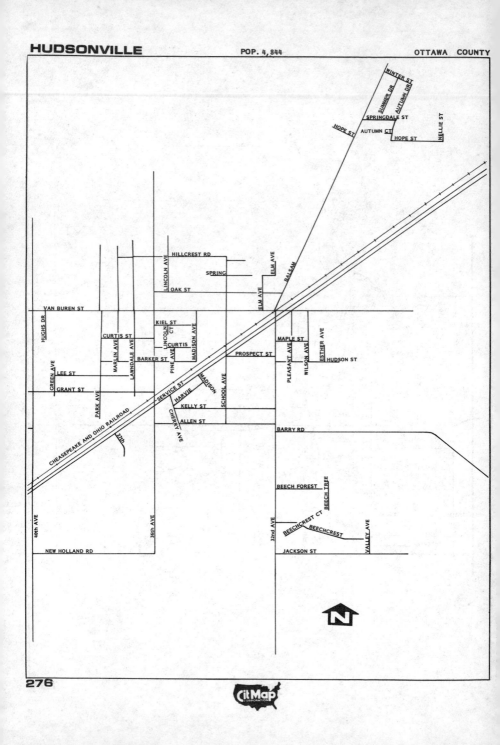

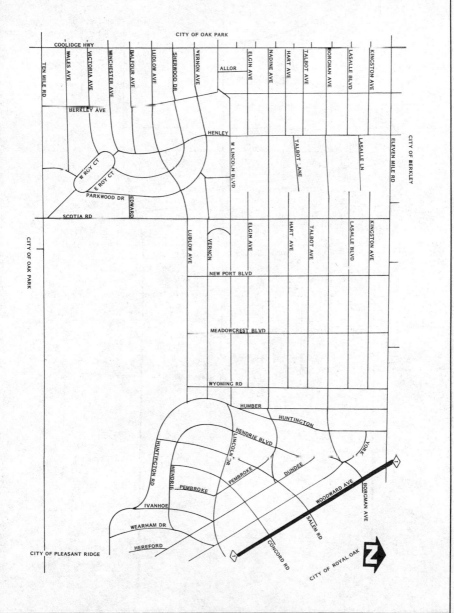

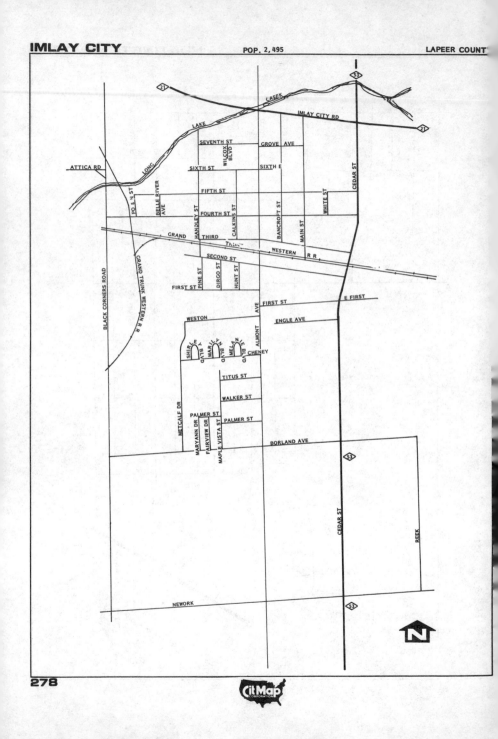

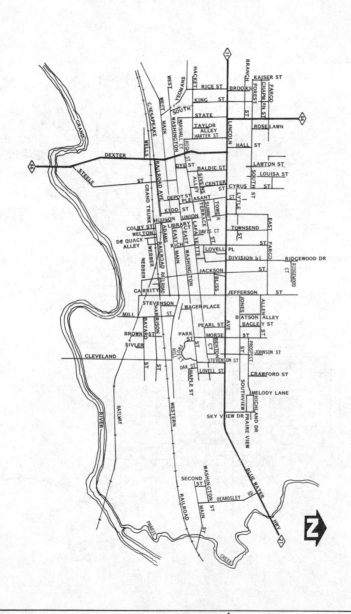

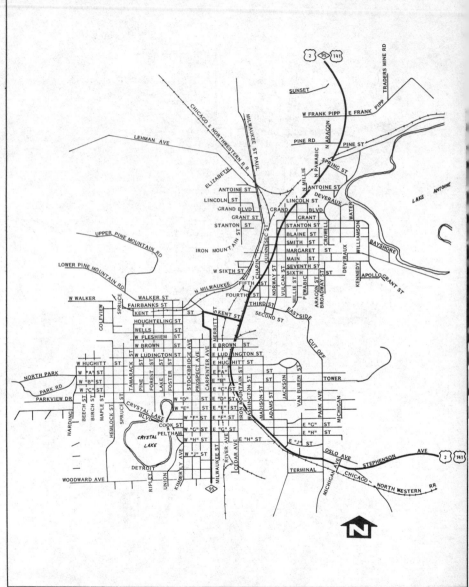

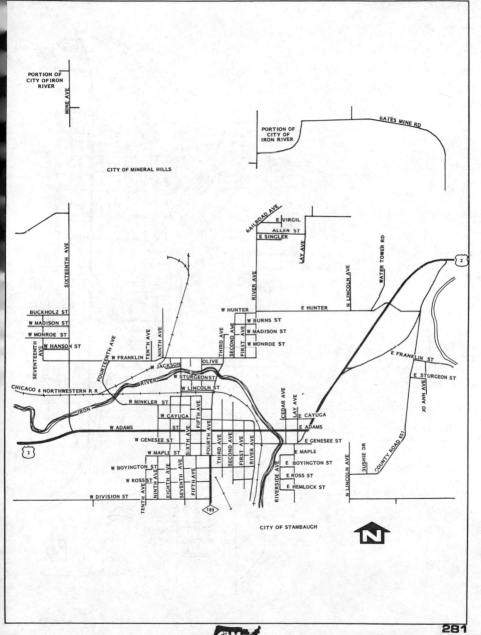

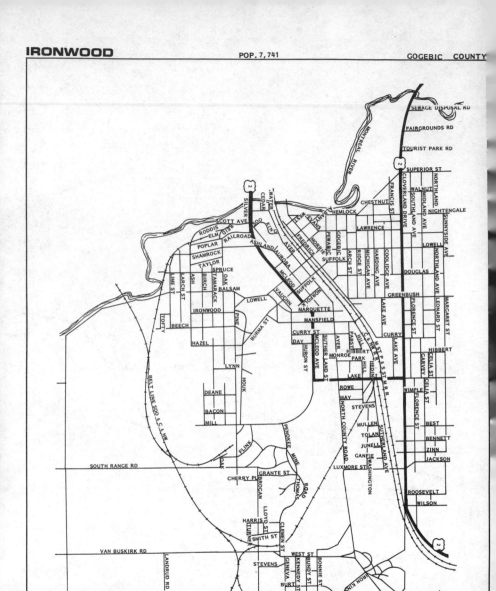

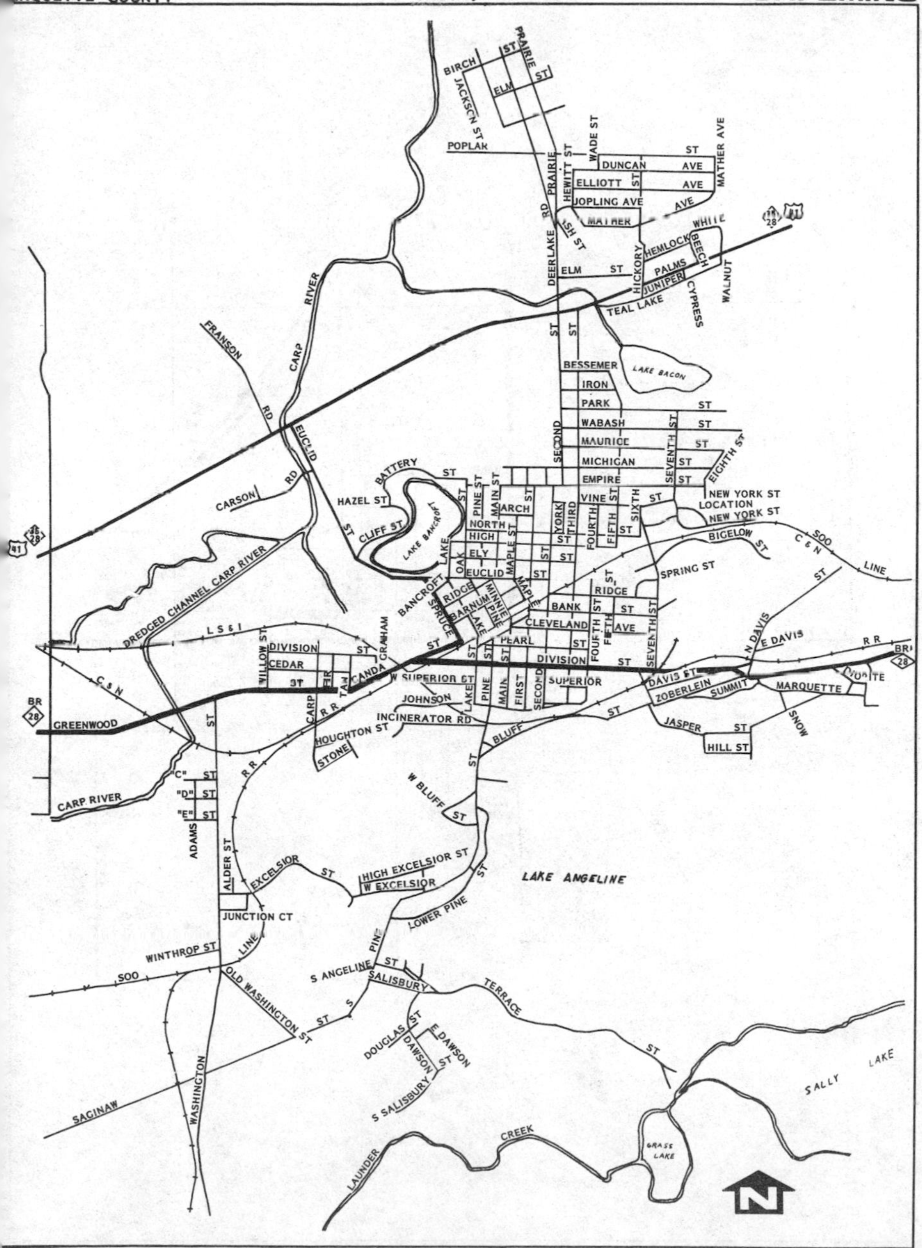
PRAIRIE
BIRCH
ST
ST
ELM
JACKSON ST
POPLAR
WADE ST
MATHER AVE
DUNCAN AVE
ELLIOTT AVE
HEWITT ST
JOPLING AVE
MATHER AVE
WHITE
DEER LAKE RD
PRAIRIE
ASH ST
HEMLOCK
BEECH
HICKORY
PALMS
JUNIPER
ELM ST
TEAL LAKE
CYPRESS
WALNUT
28
41
FRANSON RD
CARP RIVER
LAKE BACON
BESSEMER
IRON
PARK ST
WABASH ST
MAURICE ST
MICHIGAN ST
EMPIRE ST
SECOND ST
SEVENTH ST
EIGHTH ST
EUCLID
CARSON RD
BATTERY ST
HAZEL ST
CLIFF ST
LAKE BANCROFT
PINE ST
MAIN ST
ARCH
NORTH
HIGH
ELY
EUCLID
YORK
THIRD
FOURTH
FIFTH
SIXTH
VINE ST
NEW YORK ST
LOCATION
NEW YORK ST
BIGELOW ST
SOO
C & N
LINE
DREDGED CHANNEL CARP RIVER
OAK
LAKE
MAPLE ST
BANCROFT
RIDGE
BARNUM
MINNIE
PINE
SPRUCE
LAKE
SPRING ST
RIDGE ST
BANK ST
CLEVELAND AVE
PEARL
DIVISION ST
SUPERIOR
FOURTH ST
FIFTH ST
SEVENTH ST
N DAVIS
E DAVIS
R R
BR 28
DAVIS ST
ZOBERLEIN
SUMMIT
MARQUETTE
DIORITE
SNOW
JASPER ST
HILL ST
LS & I
WILLOW ST
DIVISION ST
CEDAR
ST
GRAHAM
CANDA
W SUPERIOR CT
FIR
TAM
CARP
R R
JOHNSON
INCINERATOR RD
LAKE
PINE
MAIN
FIRST
SECOND
BLUFF ST
HOUGHTON ST
STONE
C & N
BR 28
GREENWOOD
ST
"C" ST
"D" ST
"E" ST
CARP RIVER
ADAMS
R R
W BLUFF ST
ALDER ST
EXCELSIOR ST
HIGH EXCELSIOR ST
W EXCELSIOR
LAKE ANGELINE
ST
JUNCTION CT
LOWER PINE
WINTHROP ST
LINE
SOO
PINE
S ANGELINE ST
SALISBURY
TERRACE ST
OLD WASHINGTON ST
ST S
DOUGLAS ST
E DAWSON
DAWSON ST
S SALISBURY
WASHINGTON
SAGINAW
SALLY LAKE
GRASS LAKE
LAUNDER CREEK
N

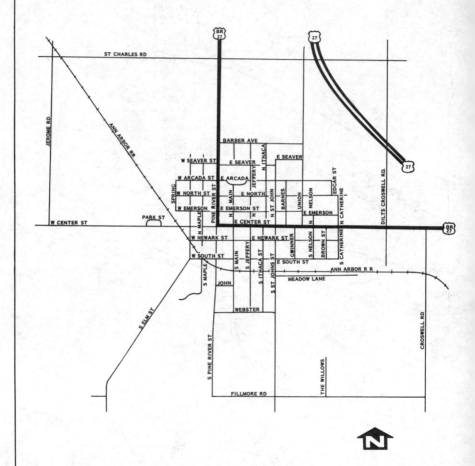

STREET INDEX
JACKSON

ABBINGTON 288 NW
ACACIA BLVD 291 NW
ACKERSON LAKE 292 SE
ACKERSON LK DR 292 SE
ACRES DR 291 NW
ADA 289 SW
ADAMS 288 SW
ADDISON 291 NE
AGNES 290 NE
AIRLINE DR SE 288 SE
AIRPORT 287 NE
ALBERT 288 SW
ALDRIGHT DR 290 NE
ALCONQUIN 291 SE
ALDER ST 287 SE
ALDRICH DR 288 NW
ALISON 292 NE
ALLEN 288 SE
ALMARK 288 SE
ALMO TERR 292 NW
ALPINE LA 288 SE
ALSTON DR 290 NE
AMBLESIDE 291 NW
AMHERST 291 NE
AMOS 289 SW
AMUR 288 SE
ANDREW AVE 288 NW
ANGLING 292 NW
ANN 289 SW
ANN ARBOR RD 289 SE
ANNETTA AVE 291 SE
APPLE 288 NE
APPLE LANE 292 NE
ARBOR HILL 290 NW
ARCUS S. 291 NW
ARCUS W. 291 NW
ARGYLE 287 SE
ARLENE 291 NE
ARMENSKO LA 290 NW
ARMORY CT 288 SW
ARNOLD 288 SW
ASHTON 287 SE
AUDUBON AVE 291 NW
AURORA DR 291 NW
AUSTIN AVW 288 SW
AUSTSCOTT DR 291 SW
AVONDALE 291 NE
BACKUS 288 SW
BACON 287 SW
BADGLEY 291 SW
BAGG 291 SE
BAGLEY AVE 292 NW
BAILEY 287 NW
BAKER 289 NW
BALDWIN AVE 289 SE
BALOMARL DR 290 NW
BARNES 287 SE
BARRETT AVE 287 SE
BARRETT LA 287 NE
BATES 289 SW
BAXTER 289 SW
BEACON 287 SE
BEECH 288 SE
BEECHER 289 SW
BELDEN 287 SE
BELL AVE 291 NE
BELLEVUE 287 SE
BENDER 289 SW
BENNETT 288 SW
BERKLEY 287 SE
BERKSHIRE BLVD 290 SE
BERRY 291 SE
BEST 289 SE
BEVERLY PARK PL 291 NW
BIDDLE 288 SE
BILEDA CT 288 NE
BIRCHWOOD 287 SE
BIRD 291 SE
BIRDSELL 291 NE
BITTERSWEET BLVD 290 NE
BLACKMAN 288 SW
BLACKSTONE 288 NE
BLAIRMOOR 291 SW
BLAKE 289 NW
BLAKELY AVE 289 SW
BLOOMFIELD BLVD 291 NW
BLUE LA 290 NE
BLUESTONE 291 SW
BLUE SPRUCE 291 SW
BOARDMAN 288 NW
BOLAND 298 NE
BONNIE 292 SW
BOW 291 NE
BOWEN 288 SW
BRABERN 288 NW
BRENTWOOD 287 SE
BRIAR 291 NW
BRIDGE 288 SE
BRIGGS CT 287 NE
BRIGHTON 291 NW
BRISCOE 289 SW
BRISCOE PL 289 SW
BROADCREST 291 NW
BROADMORE S 291 SW
BROADMORE W 291 SW
BROOKLEY 288 NE
BROOKLYN 292 NW
BROOKSIDE BLVD 290 SE
BROOKSIDE DR 291 SW
BROWN 288 SW
BROWNING AVE 288 SW
BRYANT AVE 288 SW
BUNTING 290 NW
BURR 288 SE
BUSH 288 SW
BUTTERNUT TRAIL 290 NE
CALHOUN 288 SW
CAMBRIDGE AVE 291 NW
CAMLES CT 290 SE
CAMPBELL DR 288 NW
CANSON 288 SW
CANTABURY LA 290 SE
CARLTON 287 SE
CAROLYN 291 NW
CARR 288 SW
CARROLL AVE 288 SW
CARSON 289 SW
CASCADE CT 291 NW
CASCADE DR 291 NW
CASS AVE 291 SE
CATALINA AVE 290 NW
CATALPA DR 292 NE
CATHERINE 287 SE
CENTER 288 SW
CHANTER 288 NE
CHAPIN 288 SE
CHARLENE 292 SW
CHARLES 291 NE
CHARLOTTE 289 SW
CHEROKEE 291 SE
CHEROKEE LANE 289 SW
CHERRY 289 NW
CHERRYWOOD DR 287 SE
CHESHIRE 288 NW
CHSNING 288 SW
CHESTER 289 SW
CHESTNUT 288 SW
CHIPPEWA 289 SW
CHITTOCK AVE 288 SE
CHLEBUS 292 NW
CHRISTOPHER 287 SE
CHRISTY AVE 288 SW
CLARA 292 NW
CLARK 288 NW
CLARKWAY 289 SE
CLEVELAND 288 SW
CLIFF 291 NW
CLINTON 288 NW
COBB 290 NE
COLFAX 291 NW
COLUMBUS 288 SE
COMMERCE 292 NE
COMMONS BLVD 207 SE
COMMONWEALTH 288 NW
COMPTON 289 SE
COMSTOCK 291 SE
CONCORD 287 SE
CONCORD SQ 291 NW
CONDAD 287 SE
CONGER DR 287 SE
CONNABLE 287 NE
COOLEY PL 288 SE
COOLIDGE 291 NW
COOPER 288 NE
CORTLAND 288 SW
COUNTRY MANOR 290 SW
COUNTY FARM 287 NW
COVE 291 SE
CRAIG 287 NE
CREGLOW DR 291 NW
CRESCENT 291 NW
CREST 291 SE
CREST AVE 292 NW
CRESTBROOK 292 SW
CRESTBROOK CIR 292 SW
CRESTWOOD LANE 290 NE
CROSS 288 NW
CULVER 289 SE
CUMMINGS 287 SW
CURTIS AVE 289 SE
CURVE ST 288 NE
CYPRESS LA 288 SE
DALE 291 NW
DALTON 289 NE
DAMON 291 NE
DARTMOOR LA 290 SE
DARMOUTH DR 291 NE
DAWN 291 NW
DEERFIELD DR 287 SE
DEER RIDGE 290 SE
DELHEM BLVD 288 NW
DE MAY CT 287 SE
DENECOURT 291 SE
DENTON 287 NW
DEPUY AVE 288 SE
DETROIT 289 SE
DETTMAN 291 NW
DEVONSHIRE 288 NW
DEWEY AVE 288 NW
DEYO 288 SE
DEYO ALLEY 288 SE
DIANELEE DR 290 NW
DIBBLE 290 SE
DONEY 288 NW
DORMAY 291 SE
DORN 291 NE
DORSET DR 287 SE
DORVIN DR 290 NW
DOUGLAS 291 NW
DOUGLAS CT 291 NW
DOVER 288 SW
DRAPPER 291 SE
DRESDEN DR 290 NE
DUGUID 291 SE
DURAND 288 SW
DWIGHT 289 SW
EAST AVE 288 SW
E. BARDSTONE 291 SW
EASTFIELD 292 SW
EASTLANE 291 NW
E. MARDEE 291 SW
E. WALMONT 291 NW
ECHO BEACH DR 291 SE
EDGEWOOD 288 SW
EDGEWOOD DR 291 SE
EDWARD 288 SW
EDWIN DR 288 NE
EGGLESTON 291 NE
EIGHTEENTH 288 SW
ELAINE 292 SW
ELDERBERRY DR 288 NW
ELGIN 288 SE
ELIZABETH 288 SE
ELKTON DR 292 SE
ELLERY AVE 288 SW
ELM AVE 289 NW
ELM HURST LA 290 NW
ELMWOOD AVE 288 SW
EMELIA 292 NW
EMMA 292 NW
EMMETT 291 SW
EMORY ST 288 SW
ENGLEWOOD 290 SE
ENTERPRISE 292 NW
ENTERPRISE CIR 292 NW
ERIE 288 NW
ESSEX LA 291 NW
EUCLID AVE 291 NE
EUGENE AVE 291 SE
EVANSTON DR 287 SE
EVELYNE 287 SE
EVERGLADE 291 NE
EVERHARD 288 SE
EXECUTIVE DR 292 NW
FACTORY 292 NE
FAIRFAX 289 SE
FAIRVIEW AVE 289 SE
FAIRVIEW DR 291 NE
FAIRWAY DR 290 NW
FAIRYLAND AVE 289 SE
FAYETTE CT 291 SW
FELDMAN 292 NE
FELTERS 292 NE
FERN AVE 288 SW
FERGUSON RD 291 SW
FERNWOOD AVE 287 SE
FIFTH 288 SW
FIRST 288 SW
FISHER 291 SW
FLANSBURG 292 NE
FLEETWOOD LA 287 SW
FLEMING AVE 289 SW
FLORAL 289 SW
FLORENCE 289 SW
FLOYD AVE 291 SE
FOOTE 288 SW
FORBES 289 SW
FORD AVE 289 SE
FOREST 287 SE
FOREST CT 291 SE
FOREST LAKE DR 290 SE
FOURTH 288 SW
FRANCIS ST 291 NE
FRANLIN 287 SE
FRANKS DR 287 SE
FREY 288 SE
FROST 288 NE
FULFORD 287 SE
GALE 291 NE
GANSON 289 SW
GANTON DR 290 SE
GARFIELD 291 NW
GARY PAUL LA 291 SE
GAY AVE 292 NW
GEMILL 290 NE
GEORGE 288 SE
GERALD AVE 291 SE
GETTYSBURG 291 NW
GIBSON PL 288 SE
GILBERT 288 SE
GILMAN PL 291 NE
GILROY 291 NW
GLASGOW 287 NW
GLEN 291 NW
GLENDALE 291 NE
GLENNGARRY 290 NE
GLENWOOD AVE 288 SW
GOLF AVE 291 SE
GOLF CLUB BLVD 287 SE
GORHAM 289 SW
GRACEL 288 NE
GRANADA 287 NE
GRANT AVE 291 SE
GREENTREE 291 SE
GREENWOOD 288 SE
GREGORY 289 SW
GREGORY PL 289 SW
GRINNELL 288 SW
GRISWOLD 287 NW
GROVEDALE 291 NW
GYPSY LANE 289 NE
HACKETT 289 SE
HAGUE AVE 291 SE
HALL AVE 289 SE
HALLETT 288 SW
HALSTEAD BLVD 290 NE
HAMBURG 288 SE
HAMILTON 288 SW
HAMLIN 288 SE
HAMPTON DR 291 NW
HAPPY VALLEY 290 SE
HARBEN 291 NE
HARDING 291 NW
HARRIS 288 SE
HARSHBARGER 292 NE
HORTON 290 SE
HARWICH LA 290 NE
HATHAWAY LA 292 SE
HATT DR 289 SE
HAWKINS 288 NE
HAYES 287 SE
HAZELWOOD 291 SE
HEATHER LA 287 NE
HEARTHSTONE 291 SE
HELENA AVE 289 SE
HENRIETTA 287 SW
HENRY 287 SE
HERBERT J AVE 291 NW
HERKIMER DR 291 NW
HEYSER 288 NW
HIBBARD 290 SW
HICKORY LA 288 NW
HIGBY 291 SW
HIGH 291 NW
HIGHLAND AVE 288 NW
HILL 290 SW
HILLCREST BLVD 291 SE
HILLVIEW DR 291 NE
HINCKLEY BLVD 288 SE
HOBART 291 SW
HOLLIS 288 NE
HOLLYWOOD 287 SW
HOMEWILD 290 SE
HORSESHOE PASS 290 SE
HOWARD 287 SE
HOWELL 288 NE
HOYER 292 NE
HUDSON 291 SE
HUNTINGTON DR 290 SE
HURON ST 288 NE
INDUSTRIAL AVE 292 NW
INGHAM 288 SE
IRENE 289 NW
IROQUOIS 291 SE
IRVING 288 SE
JACKSON 288 SE
JACQUELINE 289 SW
JAMAICA DR 290 NE
JAMES A MCDIVITT 287 SW
JAMES R 288 SW
JASPER 290 NW
JAY 288 SW
JEFFERSON 288 SW
JEFFREY CT 291 NW
JERICHO 291 NW
JOAN 291 NE
JOHN 288 NE
JOHNSON 288 SW
JONQUIL CT 288 SE
JOY AVE 288 SW
JUDY 290 NW
JUDY LANE 289 NW
JULIA 292 NW
JULIAN 291 SE
JUSTIN AVE 291 SE
KATHMAR DR 291 SW
KATHMAR DR N. 291 SW
KATHMAR DR W. 291 SW
KAY DR 291 SE
KENILWORTH 290 SE
KENMAR DR 292 SE
KENNEDY 288 SW
KENNETH 287 SE
KENSINGTON DR 291 NW
KENT 291 NE
KENWOOD CT 289 SW
KEY ST 289 SW
KIBBY 290 NW
KIMBERLY DR 287 SE
KINTS CT 288 NW
KIRKWOOD 287 SE
KNOLLWOOD 289 SW
LAFAYETTE 291 NW
LAKE 288 SE
LAKE SHORE 291 SE
LAKESIDE 291 SE
LAKEVIEW TERR 291 SE
LAMOINE 289 SE
LANCASHIRE DR 290 SE
LANCASTER 288 SW
LANSING AVE 288 NW
LARKSPUN CT 291 NE
LARRY DR 291 NW
LARSON 288 SW
LAUREL CT 291 NE
LAUREL LA 291 NE
LAWRENCE 287 SE
LEAH 292 NE
LEEWILLA DR 290 NE
LELAND DR 290 NE
LEO 287 SE
LEONARD 288 NW
LEORA LANE 287 SW
LEROY 288 SW
LEVANT 291 NW
LEWIS 291 NE
LIBERTY 288 SE
LINCOLN 288 SW
LINDEN AVE 291 NW
LINWOOD 291 NE
LOCHMOOR BLVD 291 SW
LOCHMOOR CT 291 SW
LOCKWOOD 289 SW
LOCUST 291 SW
LOESSER AVE 291 NW
LONGFELLOW AVE 288 SW
LOOKOUT CIR 290 SE
LOOMIS 288 SW
LOREN RD 290 NE
LORRAINE 287 SE
LOSEY AVE 292 NW
LOUIS GLICK HWY 288 SE
LOWE 290 SE
LOWELL AVE 288 SW
LUCERINE DR 290 NW
LUCILLE 291 NE
LUETTA AVE 292 NE
LUMLEY AVE 289 SE
LYNNBROOK DR 287 NE
LYNN DR 288 NW
MAC ARTHUR 289 SE
MADISON 288 SW
MAGUIRE 289 SW
MAIDSTONE 291 NW
MAIN 287 SE
MALTBY 288 SE
MALVERN 291 SW
MANSION 291 NE
MANTLE 289 SW
MAPLE 290 NE
MAPLE DALE 290 SE
MAPLE WOOD 291 NW
MARIE CT 287 NE
MARILYN CT 292 NE
MARION AVE 287 SE
MARKET 292 NW
MARKS DR 287 NE
MARSHALL 288 NE
MARTHA 288 NE
MASON 288 SE
MATHEWS 289 SW
MATT ST 289 SW
MAUNTA LA 291 SW
MAURICE AVE 291 SE
MAX 287 SE
MAYBROOK 291 SW
MAYFIELD DR 287 SE
MAYNARD AVE 288 SW
MC BRIDE 288 SW
MC CAIN 290 NW
MC CUEN 291 SE
MC DEVITT AVE 291 SE
MC GILL 289 NW
MC GILLIVARY 289 SW
MC GRAW AVE 292 NE
MC KAY 288 SW
MC KINLEY 288 SW
MEADOW HGTS 291 SE
MEADOW LA 291 NE
MECHANIC 288 SE
MERIDAN 292 SW
MERRIMAN 288 SE
METZMONT DR 291 SW
MEYERS AVE 291 SE
MICHAEL DR 288 NW
MICHIGAN AVE 287 SW
MICOR DR 292 NW
MIDBERRY 291 SW
MIDDAY 291 NW
MIDWAY DR 292 NE
MILES DR 292 SW
MILWAUKEE 288 SE
MONA 288 NW
MITCHELL 288 SE
MOHAWK 290 SE
MONROE 288 SW
MONTGOMERY 288 SW
MONTROSE 292 NE
MORNINGSTAR DR 291 NW
MORRELL 287 SE
MORRILL 288 SW
MORRIS ST 288 NW
MOUND AVE 291 NW
MUNITH 289 NE
MURDOCK CT 287 NE
MURPHY 288 NW
MYERS CT 292 NE
MYRLICE CT 291 SE
MYRTLE 288 NE
NAOMI 290 NE
NAPOLLEON 291 NE
NECKER 288 SE
NEWELL AVE 288 NW
NEWTON 288 NE
NINETEENTH 288 SW
NORFOLK 288 SW
NORTH 288 SE
N. BARDSTONE 291 SW
NORTHCREST LA 288 SW
NORHTFIELD DR 292 SW
NORTHLANDS AVE 288 NW
N. STARR 288 SE
NORHTWOOD LA 288 SW
NORWOOD 291 NE
OAK 288 SE
OAKDALE AVE 291 NW
OAK GROVE 290 NE
OAK GROVE AVE 287 SE
OAKHILL AVE 288 SW
OAKLAND 292 SW
OAK RIDGE DR 291 NW
OAKWOOD 291 NW
O'BRIEN 287 SW
O'LEARY 289 NW
ORANGE 289 SW
ORCHARD 288 SE
ORCHARD CT 292 NE
ORNE 292 NW
OSAGE 289 SW
OTSEGO 288 SE
OUTER DR 288 NW
OVERHILL 291 NE
OXFORD 288 SW
PACE AVE 289 SW
PAGE AVE 288 SE
PALMER 291 NE
PARK 291 NW

JACKSON

PARK AVE	288 SE	
PARK DR	291 NE	
PARK DR A.	291 SE	
PARKER	289 SW	
PARKSIDE BLVD	290 SE	
PARKVIEW	290 NW	
PARKWAY	291 NW	
PARNALL	288 NW	
PATTIE	288 SW	
PAWNEE	291 SE	
PEACH	289 SW	
PEARL	288 SE	
PERLMAN	288 SE	
PERRINE	288 SE	
PERSHING AVE	287 SE	
PHILLIPS	291 SE	
PHILLIPS CT	288 NE	
PIERCE	291 NE	
PIGEON	291 NE	
PINEHURST DR	290 SE	
PINE RIDGE DR	290 NE	
PIONEER DR	290 NW	
PITTMAN	288 SW	
PLEASANT	289 SW	
PLEASANT RUN MEADOWS	287 NE	
PLYMOUTH	288 SE	
POLLO	289 SW	
POOLE	288 NW	
PORTER	288 NE	
POPS CT	288 NW	
PRAIRIE	291 NE	
PRICE	288 NE	
PRINGLE	289 SW	
PRIVATE DR	291 SE	
PROBERT	291 SW	
PRODUCTION	292 SW	
PROSPECT	291 NW	
PRUDY DR	290 SE	
QUARRY	288 SE	
RANCH BLVD	291 NW	
RANDOLPH	291 NW	
RAVENWOOD	290 SE	
REDBUD CT	287 NE	
REDWOOD LA	291 NE	
RENFREW BLVD	290 NW	
RENFREW DR	290 NW	
REYNOLDS	290 NW	
RHODES	288 SE	
RIDGE	291 SE	
RIDGEWAY	291 NE	
RIDGEWOOD	289 SE	
RIMROCK TRAIL	290 NE	
RIVER	288 NE	
RIVES JUNCTION	287 NE	
ROBERTS	289 SW	
ROBINSON	287 SW	
ROCK	288 SW	
ROCKEFELLER DR	291 SE	
ROCKWELL	287 SE	
RODMAN DR	291 SE	
RONALD	289 SE	
ROOSEVELT	291 NW	
ROSEDALE	291 NW	
ROSEHILL	288 NE	
ROTHWELL	289 SW	
ROTUNDA DR	291 NW	
ROWAN	291 NW	
ROWENA	288 NE	
ROYAL DR	288 NW	
RUSSELL	289 SW	
RUTH	292 NW	
RUTLEDGE	287 SE	
SAGAMORE	291 SE	
SAINE DR	288 NE	
SAINES MANOR DR	288 NW	
ST ANTHONY DR	290 NE	
ST ANTHONY DR N.	290 NE	
ST ANTHONY DR S.	290 NE	
ST BARNARD DR	289 NW	
ST CLAIR AVE	288 NW	
ST DAVID DR	289 NW	
ST JOHN	288 NE	
ST LUKE DR	289 NW	
ST MARK DR	289 NW	
ST MATHEW DR	289 NW	
SALEM WAY	290 NE	
SAMARITAN DR	291 NW	
SANDSTONE	290 NW	
SARADAN DR	287 NE	
SARAH	291 SE	
SAVOY	287 SE	
SCHELLING DR	292 NW	
SECOND	288 NE	
SECOND CT	288 SW	
SEMINOLE PL	289 SW	
SENECA DR	289 SW	
SEQUOIA	287 SW	
SERVICE	290 NW	
SEVENOAKS	291 NW	
SEVENTEENTH	288 SW	
SEVENTH	288 SW	
SEYMOUR	289 NW	
SEYMOUR AVE	289 NW	
SHADY RIDGE DR	290 SE	
SHARDALE DR	292 SE	
SHARON DR	291 SE	
SHEFIELD DR	290 SE	
SHERIDAN	289 SW	
SHERWOOD DR	290 NW	
SHERWOOD LAKE DR	288 NW	
SHIRLEY DR	288 NW	
SHOEMAKER	291 SW	
SHORT	291 NE	
SHOWERMAN	289 NW	
SIOUX	291 SE	
SIXTH	291 NW	
SMALLEY	291 NW	
SMILEY WAY	290 NE	
SNOW DRIFT PASS	290 SW	
SOUTH	290 NE	
SOUTHFIELD DR E.	292 SE	
SOUTHFIELD DR W.	292 SW	
S. MARDEE	291 SW	
SOUTH ST E.	292 NE	
SOUTHWAY	291 NW	
SOUTHWIND	290 NW	
SPARKS	288 NW	
SPENCER	287 NE	
SPRING	288 SE	
SPRING ARBOR	290 NW	
SPRINGCREST BLVD	290 NE	
SPRINGCREST DR	287 SE	
SPRINGPORT	287 NW	
SQUIRES MANOR	290 SE	
STANFORD LA	291 NE	
STANLEY	291 NE	
STATEN DR	291 SE	
STATE	288 SW	
STATE W.	292 NE	
STEVENS	291 NE	
STONEWALL	291 NW	
STRATHMORE LANE	291 NW	
STREATOR	289 SW	
SULGRAVE AVE	291 NW	
SUMMIT	291 NE	
SUMMIT AVE	288 SE	
SUMMIT PL	291 NE	
SUNBURST DR	291 NW	
SUN CIR	291 NW	
SUNNYHEART AVE	289 NE	
SUNRISE CT	292 NE	
SUNSET	288 NW	
SUTTON	289 SE	
SWEET AVE	288 SE	
SYCAMORE	289 SE	
TAMARACK TR	290 SW	
TAMIE WAY	290 NE	
TANNER	288 NE	
TAYLOR	288 SW	
TEFFT AVE	287 SE	
TENEYCK	288 SE	
THE PARKWAY	290 NW	
THIRD	288 NE	
THOMAS CT	288 SW	
THOMAS DR	288 SW	
THOMPSON	288 SW	
THORNTREE BLVD	290 NE	
THORNWOOD	290 NW	
THORPE DR	290 SE	
THORREZ	287 SW	
TIMBERCREST TR	290 SE	
TIMBERLANE DR	290 NE	
TOMLINSON	289 SW	
TORO	287 SW	
TRACEY DR	291 NW	
TRAIL	288 SW	
TRICIA DR	290 NW	
TRINITY LA	290 NW	
TRUMBLE	291 SE	
TULSA DR	290 NE	
TWENTIETH	288 SW	
TWENTY-FIRST	288 SW	
TWENTY-FOURTH	288 SW	
TWENTY-SECOND	288 SW	
TWENTY-THIRD	288 SW	
TWLIGHT	290 NE	
TYSON	289 SW	
UNION	288 SW	
UPLAND	291 NW	
VALOR DR	288 SE	
VANDERCOOK	291 SE	
VANDERLYN	289 SE	
VANDOORN	288 SE	
VARDEN DR	288 SW	
VERA CRUZ	291 SE	
VERNON	288 SW	
VINE	287 SE	
VINING AVE	292 NW	
VIRGINIA	288 SW	
VOY ST	287 SW	
VROOMAN	290 SW	
WAKEMAN	288 NE	
WALCOTT	291 NE	
WALKER	288 SW	
WALL	291 NE	
WALMONT	291 SW	
WALMONT W.	291 SW	
WALMONT S.	291 SW	
WALMONT N.	291 SW	
WALNUT	290 SE	
WARREN AVE	290 NE	
WARWICK	290 SE	
WARWICK CT	288 SE	
WASHINTON AVE	287 SW	
WATER	288 SE	
WATERLOO AVE	288 SW	
WATTS	289 SW	
WAYNE	288 SW	
WEBB	288 SW	
WEBSTER	288 SW	
WEDGEFIELD S. BLVD	191 SW	
WELLS	288 SE	
WELLSLEY DR	290 NW	
WELLWORTH AVE	292 NW	
WENDELL LA	290 SE	
WEST AVE	288 SW	
WESTCHESTER BLVD	287 SE	
WEST CONCOURSE	291 NW	
WESTFIELD DR	290 NE	
WESTLEY	288 SE	
WESTLANE	291 NW	
W. MARDEE	291 SW	
WESTMINSTER	288 SW	
WEST MORRELL	287 SE	
WESTWOOD BLVD	290 NE	
WHITLOCK	289 SW	
WHITNEY	288 SE	
WILDWOOD AVE	287 SE	
WILDWOOD CT	287 SE	
WILDWOOD LA	291 NW	
WILKINS	288 SE	
WILLIAMS	290 NE	
WILLIAMS LAKE DR	291 SW	
WILLIAMSON	288 SW	
WILLOW	289 SW	
WILSON	288 SE	
WINDEMERE DR	287 NE	
WINIFRED	288 SW	
WINONA PL	291 NW	
WINSTON DR	291 NW	
WINTERS CT	288 SE	
WINTHROP	288 SW	
WISNER	288 NW	
WOODBINE BLVD	290 NE	
WOODBRIDGE	291 NE	
WOODFIELD	291 NW	
WOODLAND	290 NE	
WOODLAND AVE	287 SW	
WOODLANE	291 SE	
WOODLAWN AVE	291 NW	
WOODRUFF PL	288 SW	
WOODSUM	291 NE	
WOODWARD	288 SW	
WOODWAY	291 NW	
WOODWORTH	288 NW	
WOODVILLE	287 SW	
WREN	291 NE	
WRIGHT	291 NE	
WRIGHT CT	291 NE	
YOUNG	289 NE	
Z YCMUNT LAND DR	292 NE	

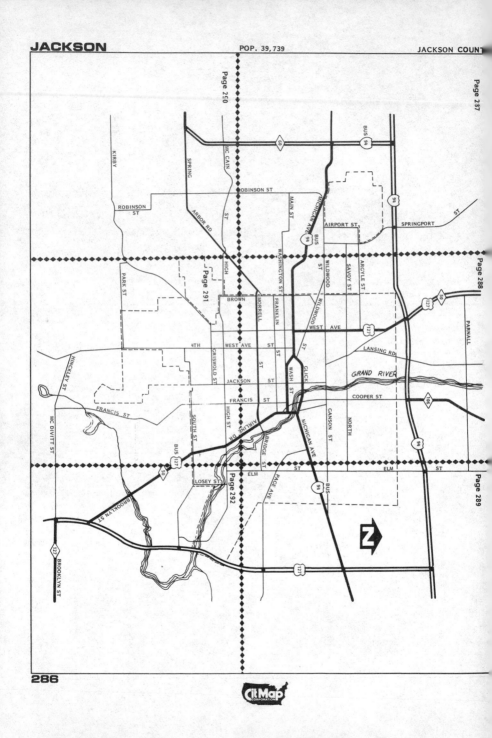

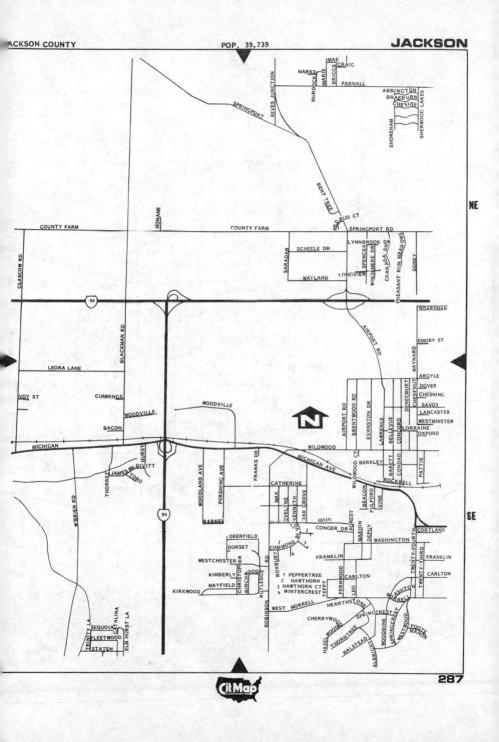

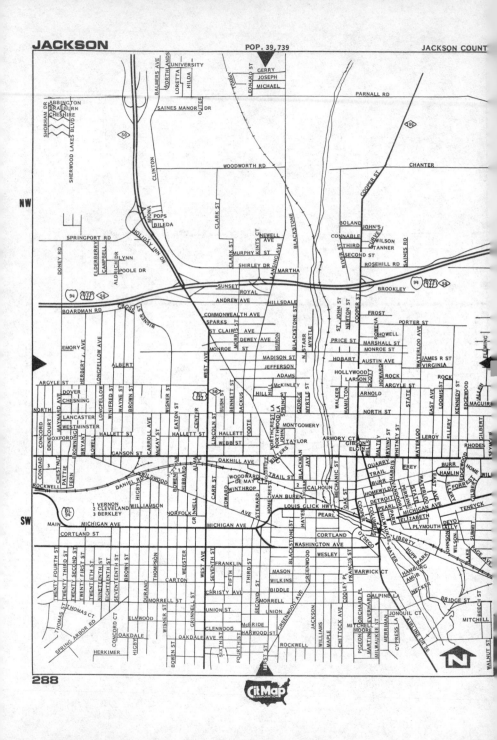

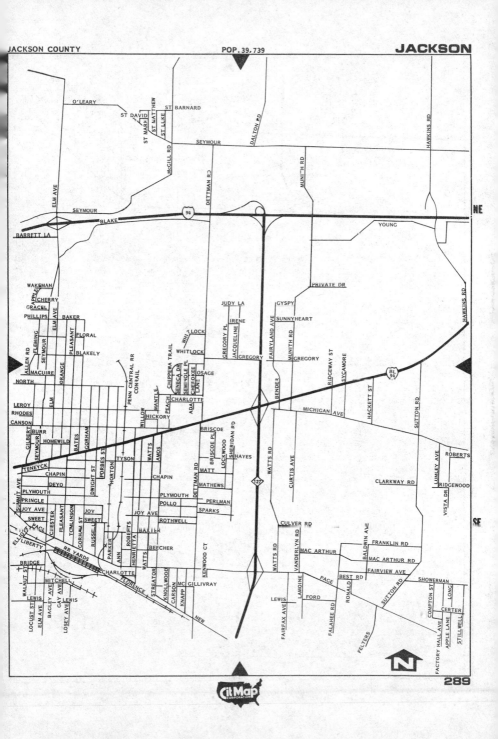

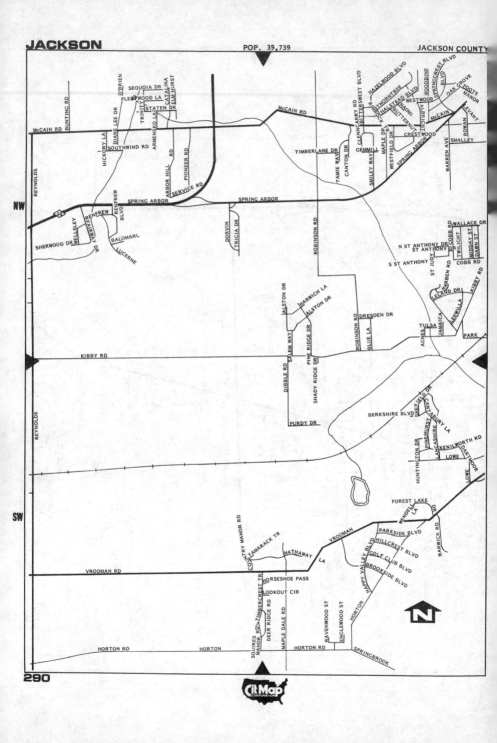

JACKSON

POP. 39,739

JACKSON COUNTY

290

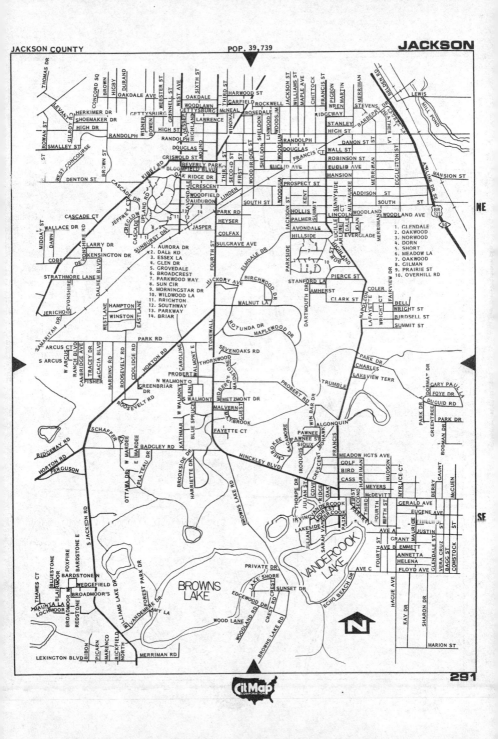

1. AURORA DR
2. DALE RD
3. ESSEX LA
4. GLEN DR
5. GROVEDALE
6. BROADCREST
7. PARKWOOD WAY
8. SUN CIR
9. MORNINGSTAR DR
10. WILDWOOD LA
11. BRIGHTON
12. SOUTHWAY
13. PARKWAY
14. BRIAR

1. GLENDALE
2. OAKWOOD
3. NORWOOD
4. DORN
5. SHORT
6. MEADOW LA
7. OAKWOOD
8. GILMAN
9. PRAIRIE DR
10. OVERHILL RD

BROWNS LAKE

VANDERCOOK LAKE

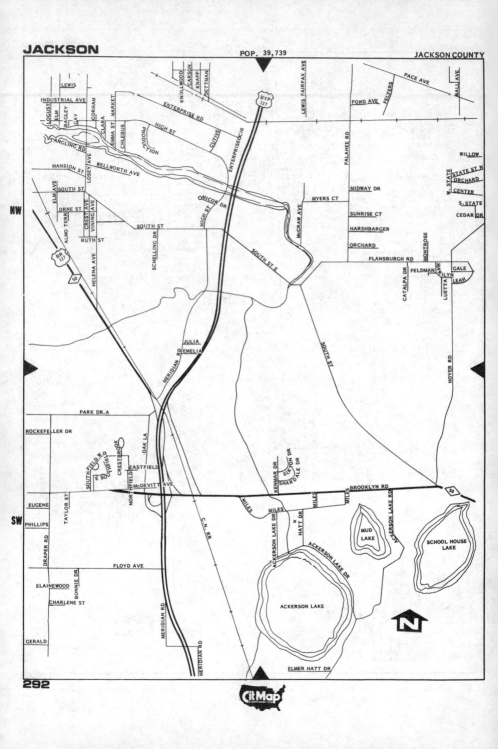

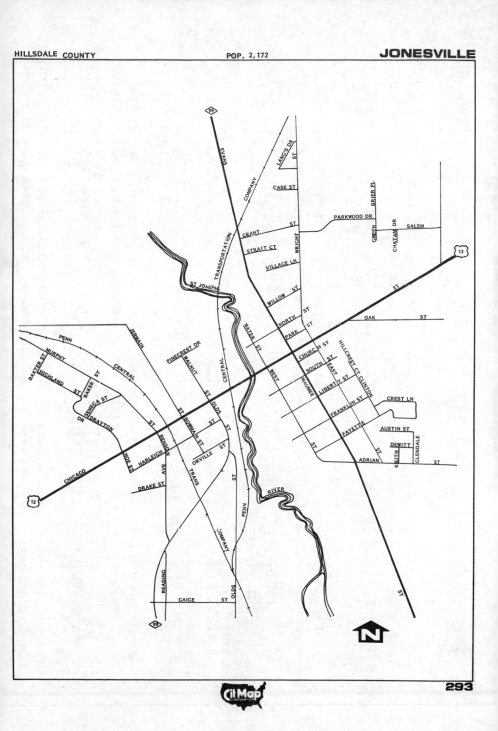

ABBEY ST 303 NE
ABBOT AVE 304 NE
ABBOTT CT 304 NE
ABERDEEN DR 301 NE
ACADEMY ST 302 SW
ACORN LA 301 NE
ADA ST 299 NW
ADAMS ST 301 SE
ADELAIDE ST 302 NE
ADIOS DR 301 NE
ADKINS CT 305 SE
ADMIRAL AVE 305 NW
AIRPORT RD 302 SE
ALAMO AVE 298 SW
ALBANY ST 302 SW
ALBATROSS 304 NW
ALBERT AVE 300 SW
ALCOTT AVE 302 NW
ALCOTT PL 302 NE
ALDEN PL 302 NE
ALDERSGATE 302 NE
ALEXANDER ST 299 SE
ALFA CT 305 NE
ALGER ST 302 NW
ALGONQUIN ST 304 SE
ALICE ST 305 NW
ALIDOR ST 304 NW
ALLARDOWNE ST 302 SW
ALLEN BLVD 304 SW
ALLEN ST 299 NW
ALLENDALE ST 303 NW
ALPINE ST 300 NW
ALTA VISTA AVE 305 NW
ALTEN ST 304 NW
ALTHEA ST 298 SE
ALVAN 303 SW
AMBERLY ST 304 NE
AMES DR 305 SE
AMHERST AVE 301 SE
AMOS ST 302 SW
AMPERSEE AVE 299 SW
AMSTERDAM ST 299 SW
AMVET MEMORIAL PKWY 303 NW
AMY DR 305 SW
ANDORA AVE 298 SW
ANDREA LA 304 SE
ANDREWS ST 303 SW
ANDY AVE 302 SW
ANGLING RD 301 SW
ANN ST 300 NW
ANTHONY ST 304 NW
APPLE ST 305 SW
APPLECROFT AVE 305 SE
APPLEWOOD ST 304 NE
ARBOR ST 299 SW
ARBORCREST 305 SW
ARBUTUS TR 304 NE
ARCADIA RD 301 NE
ARCHWOOD ST 304 SE
ARGYLE AVE 301 NW
ARLINGTON ST 298 SE
ARROW 305 NW
ARTHUR AVE 300 SW
ASBURY AVE 305 SW
ASH ST 302 SW
ASHLEY DR 305 NW
ASHTON AVE 300 NW
ASPEN DR 298 NW
ATHOL CT 305 SW
ATTLEE 298 SE
AUBURN LA 303 SW
AUDITORIUM DR 301 NE
AUDUBON DR 301 NE
AUSTIN CT 305 SE
AUSTIN DR 305 SE
AUSTIN ST 302 NW
AUSTRIAN PINE WAY 304 NE
AUTUMN ST 306 NW
AVON ST 305 NW
AVONDALE CIRCLE 300 SW
AVONDALE DR 300 SW
AXTELL ST 302 SW
AZALEA ST 302 SW
AZUBA AVE 303 NW
BACH 303 NW
BACON AVE 304 SE
BAKER DR 304 SE
BALA CYNWYD CT 301 SE
BALCH ST 301 SE
BALDWIN RD 299 NW
BALFOUR DR 304 NE
BALKEMA ST 303 NW
BALMORAL ST 306 SE
BANBURY RD 304 NE
BANK ST 302 SE
BARBER AVE 302 SE
BARBERRY AVE 305 SW
BARCLAY DR 299 SE
BARD AVE 300 NW
BARNARD AVE 304 SE
BARNEY RD 298 SE
BARRINGTON DR 305 SE
BARRINGTON DR 301 NW
BAYWOOD DR 304 NE
BEACON ST 299 SE
BEALWOOD AVE 305 SE
BEAUVOIS ST 305 SE
BECKLEY DR 301 NW
BEDFORD ST 303 SW
BEECH AVE 302 SW
BEECHMOUNT AVI 305
BEEKMAN CT 302 NW
BEETHOVEN AVE 304 SW

BELFORD ST 302 NE
BELARD ST 306 NW
BELLAIRE AVE 304 NE
BELLEVUE PL 302 NW
BELMONT ST 302 NW
BENDER RD 302 SE
BENEDICT ST 300 SE
BENJAMIN AVE 301 NE
BENNETT ST 302 NE
BENTON AVE 301 SE
BERKLEY ST 298 NW
BERKSHIRE DR 301 NE
BERMUDA ST 306 NW
BERRY ST 300 SE
BERWICK AVE 306 NW
BESSIE ST 299 SW
BEVERLY ST 299 SW
BEVERTON ST 298 NW
BILLY CT 301 NW
BIRCH AVE 299 NE
BIRCH LA 299 NW
BIRCHTON AVE 302 SW
BIRCHWOOD DR 304 NW
BISCAYNE AVE 306 NW
BISHOP AVE 306 NW
BITTERSWEET ST 305 NW
BIXBY RD 299 SE
BLACKBERRY LA 301 SW
BLAIR ST 302 SW
BLAKESLEE ST 299 SW
BLANCHE AVE 302 SW
BLINDMANS COVE 301 NW
BLOOMFIELD AVE 302 SE
BLUEBIRD 304 NE
BLUEGRASS ST 304 NW
BOARDMAN ST 303 NW
BOBOLINK LANE 301 NE
BOBOLOU AVE 303 SW
BOB-WHITE AVE 304 SW
BOEKELOO ST 302 SW
BOERMAN AVE 304 NE
BONNER CT 300 SW
BOND DR 305 NW
BONTE DR 303 SW
BORGESS DR 300 SW
BOSKER AVE 299 SW
BOSTON AVE 305 NW
BOSWELL LA 301 NW
BOYLAN ST 299 NE
BRACKETT AVE 299 NE
BRADFORD ST 305 NW
BRAEMAR LA 298 SE
BRAHMS 304 SW
BRANCH AVE 306 SW
BRANDYWINE RD 301 SE
BRATCHER ST 305 NW
BRAVO CT 305 SW
BRENDA LA 300 NW
BRENDA LA E 300 NW
BRENDA LA W 300 NW
BRENNERTON DR 302 SE
BRENT AVE 305 NW
BRENTWOOD AVE 302 NW
BRETTON DR 298 SE
BRIAR PL 300 NW
BRIARCREST DR 305 SE
BRIARHILL DR 304 NW
BRIARWOOD DR 300 NW
BRIDGE ST 299 SE
BRIGHAM ST 304 NE
BROADWAY 301 NE
BRONSON AVE 302 NW
BRONSON BLVD 302 SW
BRONX AVE 300 SW
BROOK DR 300 NW
BROOKCREST DR 305 SW
BROOKFIELD ST 303 NW
BROOKHAVEN DR 301 SE
BROOKLYN BLVD 301 SE
BROOKMONT 300 NW
BROOKMOOR LA 305 SW
BROOKSIDE CT 302 NW
BROOKVIEW ST 303 NW
BROOKWOOD DR 305 SW
BROWN AVE 305 SW
BROWNELL PL 302 NE
BROWNELL ST 298 SE
BROWNIE'S CT 303 SW
BRUCE DR 301 NE
BRUNING ST 305 NE
BRYANT ST 304 SW
BRYN MAWR DR 304 NW
BUCHANAN AVE 302 SW
BUCKHORN ST 304 NW
BUCKOUT AVE 301 NW
BUENA VISTA 302 NE
BURDICK PL 302 NE
BURDICK ST 299 SE
BURKE CT 305 SE
BURKE ST 302 SE
BURKWOOD DR 304 NW
BURNHAM DR 302 SE
BURNHAM ST 306 SE
BURNING TREE RD 304 NW
BURRELL AVE 299 SW
BUR OAK CT 302 SW
BUR OAK ST 302 SW
BURROWS RD 302 NW
BURRWOOD AVE 305 NW
BURT DR 299 NE
BUSH ST 299 SW
BUSHOUSE CT 304 NW
BUTLER CT 299 SW
BUTTERNUT LA 299 NW
BYE ST 305 SE

BYRD DR 302 SE
BYRON ST 303 NW
CABOT ST 303 SW
CADILLAC ST 299 SW
CALHOUN ST 298 SE
CALICO AVE 305 SW
CALIFORNIA AVE 301 NE
CAMARY LA 303 SW
CAMBRIDGE DR 302 SE
CAMBRIDGE TERR 302 SE
CAMEO AVE 305 NW
CAMERON ST 302 NE
CAMPBELL AVE 302 SE
CANTERBURY AVE 298 SW
CANTON ST 300 NW
CAPRI ST 306 NW
CARDINAL DR 301 NW
CARLETIN AVE 302 NW
CARLSBROOK LA 304 NE
CARLYLE DR 301 NE
CARMEL ST 302 NW
CAROLEE ST 302 SW
CARR ST 302 NE
CARRAGE PL 302 SW
CARRIE 302 NW
CARTER ST 300 SE
CASKILL 303 NE
CASPER ST 300 SW
CASS ST 303 NE
CASTLE ST 300 SW
CASTLEAIRE 305 NW
CASTLEWOOD 305 NW
CASTLETON LA 301 NW
CATHERINE ST 302 NW
CAVES CT 299 SW
CEDAR CT 302 NW
CEDAR ST 302 NW
CEDARBROOK DR 300 SE
CEDARCREST AVE 304 SW
CEDARVIEW DR 304 SW
CELERY ST 303 NE
CENTER ST 299 SW
CENTERIDGE RD 301 NE
CENTRAL AVE 305 NW
CENTRAL PL 302 NE
CENTRE AVE 304 SW
CENTURY AVE 301 NE
CHALFONTE AVE 302 SW
CHAMBERLAIN ST 302 SW
CHAMBRAY ST 305 NW
CHANDLER AVE 299 NE
CHAPARRAL ST 298 SW
CHAPEL ST 304 SW
CHARING CROSS 299 SE
CHARLES AVE 305 SE
CHARLES ST 305 SE
CHARLIE CT 305 NE
CHARLOTTE AVE 298 SE
CHARTER AVE 304 SE
CHARWOOD 305 SE
CHATEAU 305 SE
CHATHAM CIR 303 SW
CHELSEA LANE 305 SE
CHEMICAL DR 306 NW
CHENE DR 302 SE
CHEROKEE ST 298 SE
CHERRY ST 302 NW
CHERRY HILL ST 298 SE
CHERRYVIEW DR 304 SE
CHERRYWOOD ST 304 NE
CHESHIRE ST 306 NW
CHESTNUT ST 299 SW
CHESTWOOD 300 NW
CHEVY CHASE RD 301 NE
CHICAGO AVE 300 SW
CHICKADEE DR 304 NW
CHILSOM TR 301 NW
CHIPPEWA ST 304 SW
CHOPIN AVE 304 SW
CHRISTINA CT 302 NE
CHRYSLER ST 302 NW
CHUBB AVE 303 NE
CHURCH ST 299 SW
CHURCH ST 299 SW
CIATO 300 NW
CIMARRON ST 299 SE
CIRCLE ST 302 NE
CIRCLEWOOD DR N 301 SW
CIRCLEWOOD DR S 302 SW
CIRCLEWOOD DR W 302 SW
CITADEL ST 301 SE
CLARA 302 NW
CLAREMOUNT 304 NW
CLARENCE DR 305 SE
CLARENCE ST 301 NE
CLARK AVE 300 SW
CLAXTON ST 302 SW
CLAY ST 299 SW
CLAYMOOR DR 301 NW
CLEARVIEW ST 302 SE
CLIFFWOOD AVE 305 SE
CLIMAX AVE 298 SE
CLINTON ST 302 SW
CLOVER ST 302 NW
CLOYSTER CT 302 NW
COACH LITE 304 NE
COBB AVE 299 NW
COBBLESTONE LA 302 SW
CODDINGTON LA 301 NW
COLBY AVE 299 NE
COLCHESTER AVE 300 NW
COLGROVE AVE 300 SW
COLLETTE ST 302 SE
COLLINGWOOD DR 299 SW
COLLINS CT 302 NE

COLLINS ST 302 NE
COLONIAL AVE 305 NW
COLONIAL TR 301 NW
COLONY WOODS DR 304 SW
COMMERCE LA 299 NE
COMMONWEALTH PL 298 SE
COMSTOCK AVE 303 NE
CONANT ST 299 SW
CONCORD ST 301 NE
CONCORD PLACE 301 NE
CONDOR CT 304 NE
CONNECTICUT DR 305 NW
CONRAD ST 303 NE
COOLEY DR 304 NE
COOLEY ST 299 SW
COOLIDGE AVE 298 SE
COOPER AVE 300 SW
COOPERAGE CT 304 SE
COPELAND AVE 303 NE

CORK ST 302 SW
CORLOT ST 300 NW
CORNELL ST 305 NW
CONSTANCE CT 305 SE
CONSTANCE RD 305 SE
COTTAGE AVE 302 NE
COTTONDALE AVE 305 NW
COULTER AVE 305 NW
COVENTRY AVE 298 NW
COVINGTON RD 303 SW
COX'S DR 306 SW
COY AVE 302 NE
CRAFT AVE 300 SW
CRANBROOK AVE 298 SE
CRANE AVE 302 NW
CRANSTON ST 306 NW
CRAPO RD 298 NW
CRAWFORD ST 302 NW
CREEK ST 299 SW
CRESCENT DR 302 NE
CRESTON AVE 302 NW
CRESTVIEW AVE 298 SE
CRICKET LA 301 SW
CRICKLEWOOD CT 304 SE
CRIMSON LA 301 NW
CROCKETT AVE 305 SW
CROMWELL 305 NW
CROSS ST 300 SE
CROSSFIELD AVE 303 NW
CROSSTOWN PKWY 302 NW
CROSSWIND DR 301 NE
CROWN ST 298 SE
CROYDEN AVE 298 NW
CRUMPS RD 303 SW
CRYSTAL LA 301 SW
CUMBERLAND 298 SW
CURRY CT 305 NE
CURTIS AVE 305 SW
CYPRESS ST 304 NW
DAKOTA AVE 305 NW
DALE ST 302 SW
DANDALE ST 305 SW
DANIEL ST 300 SW
DARBY LA 298 SW
DARLING ST 300 NW
DARMO ST 302 SW
DARTMOUTH ST 298 SE
DARWOOD AVE 299 SE
DARYL CT 304 NE
DATE ST 305 NW
DAVCLIFF ST 304 NE
DAVENTRY AVE 304 NE
DAVIS CT 302 NW
DAVIS ST 302 NW
DAWES AVE 300 SE
DAWNLEE AVE 307 NW
DAYTON AVE 300 SE
DEADWOOD DR E 303 SW
DEADWOOD DR N 303 SW
DEADWOOD DR S 303 SW
DEADWOOD DR W 303 SW
DEARBORN AVE 300 SW
DEBBIE LA 301 NW

DEERFIELD ST 304 NE
DEERLAND ST 298 NE
DEHAAN DR 302 SW
DELAWARE CT 3?? NW
DELL AVE 300 SW
DELL ST 305 NW
DELLWOOD ST 305 NW
DELOOFS ALLEY 299 NW
DELRAY ST 299 SW
DELTA CT 305 NW
DEN ADEL CT 302 NW
DEN BLEYKER PL 302 NE
DENNER ST 299 SW
DENNIS CT 299 SW
DENWAY CIR 302 NW
DEN WAY DR 302 NW
DERHAMMER AVE 302 SW
DEVELOPMENT RD 306 SW
DEVON AVE 299 SW
DEVON ST 305 NW
DEVONSHIRE AVE 298 SW
DEWBERRY ST 304 SE
DEWEY AVE 302 NE
DEXTER AVE 300 NW
DICKENS CT 304 SW
DICKIE DR 301 NW
DINGLEY RD 302 NW
DIVISION ST 302 NE
DIXIE AVE 302 NW
DIXIE CT 302 NW

DIXIE DR 305 SE
DOBBIN DR 301 NW
DOCSA ST 300 SW
DOGWOOD DR 305 SW
DOLPHIN ST 305 SW
DONCREST DR 298 SE
DONNEGAL AVE 301 NE
DONNINGTON TERR 298 NW
DONOVAN DR 303 SW
DORCHESTER DR 303 SW
DORI DR 301 SW
DORMITORY RD N 301 NE
DORMITORY RD S 301 NE
DORRELL CT 300 SW
DORSET ST 305 NW
DOUGLAS AVE 299 SW
DOUGLAS CT 299 SW
DOUGLAS DR 299 NE
DOVE CT 304 NE
DOVER RD 301 NE
DOWNING ST 304 NW
DRAKE RD 298 SW
DREXEL PL 299 NW
DRIFTWOOD AVE 301 NW
DRURY LANE 305 SE
DUBLIN AVE 301 NW
DUCHESS DR 302 SW
DUFFIELD CT 302 NW
DUKE ST 305 SW
DUKESHIRE AVE 298 SW
DUNHILL TERR 298 SW
DUNKLEY ST 299 SW
DUPONT AVE 303 SW
DUTTON PL 302 NW
DUTTON ST 302 NW
DUXBURY ST 301 NE
DWIGHT AVE 299 SE
DWILLARD DR 300 SW
EAGLE CT 304 NE
EAGLE RIDGE DR 300 NE
EARL ST 299 SW
EAST DR 304 SW
E CAMPUS DR 302 NW
E CENTER CT 305 SE
EASTERN AVE 301 NE
EASTLAND AVE 300 SW
E LONG LAKE DR 306 SE
E MAIN ST 299 SE
E MELODY AVE 305 SW
EAST SHORE DR 305 SW
E WOODFIELD AVE 303 NE
EASY ST 303 SW
ECHO CT 305 NW
ECKNER DR 302 NW
EDDIES LA 302 NW
EDGAR ST 302 NE
EDGECLIFF LA 301 NE
ENGEL CT 305 SW
EDGEMOOR AVE 302 NW
EDGERIDGE CIRCLE 302 NW
EDGEWATER 306 NW
EDGEWATER DR 301 NE
EDINBURG DR 301 NE
EDINGTON AVE 304 NE
EDISON ST 299 NW
EDMONDS ST 301 SW
EDNA BLVD 300 SW
EDWIN AVE 299 SW
EDWIN ST 306 SW
EGLESTON AVE 302 NE
ELAINE AVE 300 SE
ELDER ST 300 SE
ELDRED ST 302 NW
ELEANOR ST 299 SW
ELECTRA ST 300 SE
11TH ST 302 NE
ELGIN ST 302 NE
ELIZABETH ST 299 SW
ELKERTON AVE 300 SW
ELLA MARIE DR 298 SE
ELLENDALE ST 301 NW
ELM ST 299 SW
ELMHURST AVE 299 NE
ELMVIEW DR 299 NE
ELMWOOD CT 299 SW
ELMWOOD ST 299 SW
EL RANCHO DR 305 NE
ELSMERE ST 299 NE
EMBURY RD 301 NW
EMERALD DR 303 SW
EMERSON ST 302 NW
EMILY DR 305 SW
ENGLEMAN AVE 299 SW
ENOLA AVE 300 SW
ENTERPRISE DR 300 NE
ERMINE ST 303 NE
ESPANOLA AVE 299 NE
EUNICE AVE 299 NE
EVANS ST 302 SW
EVANSTON 302 NW
EVANSTON CT 302 NW
EVENTIDE AVE 301 SW
EVERGREEN DR 301 SW
EVERGREEN ST 304 SE
EVERHARD ST 299 SE
EWING AVE 304 SE
F AVE 298 SW
F AVE 304 NE
FACTORY ST 303 NW
FAIR ST 302 NE
FAIRBANKS AVE 300 SE
FAIRFAX AVE 302 SW
FAIRFIELD AVE 300 SW
FAIRFIELD RD 301 SW
FAIRLANE AVE 305 SE

Street	Pg	Dir
FAIR OAKS DR	301	NE
FAIRVIEW AVE	302	SW
FALCON CT	304	NE
FARGO AVE	299	SE
FARMERS AVE	302	NE
FARMINGTON AVE	304	SW
FARNHAM AVE	306	NW
FARRELL AVE	301	NW
FEDERAL CT	302	NE
FELLOWS AVE	302	NW
FENIMORE AVE	300	SW
FENWICK PL	302	NW
FERDON RD	301	NE
FERMENTATION RD	305	NE
FERNDALE AVE	298	SE
FERNDALE AVE	302	SE
FERRIS CT	299	SW
FERRIS ST	303	NE
FESCUE ST	304	NE
FG AVE	303	NE
FIELD AVE	303	NW
FIESTA LA	301	NW
FINEVIEW AVE	299	NW
FIR AVE	298	SW
FIRESIDE AVE	306	SW
FIRST ST	303	SE
FIRST ST	305	SE
FISHER ST	302	NE
FLAMINGO AVE	305	NW
FLEETWOOD DR	301	SE
FLETCHER AVE	298	SE
FLORAL DR	302	SW
FLORENCE ST	299	SE
FLORIDA	306	SW
FLOWER ST	302	NE
FOLEY ST	302	SE
FOREST DR	305	SE
FOREST GLEN	302	NW
FOREST HARBOR DR	300	SW
FORREST ST	302	NW
FOSTER AVE	303	NW
14TH ST	298	NE
FOURTH ST	302	NE
FOXCROFT DR	304	NW
FOX HOLLOW	304	SE
FOXTROT CT	305	NW
FRANCIE AVE	300	SW
FRANCIS CT	302	NE
FRANCIS ST	303	NE
FRANK ST	299	SW
FRANKLIN ST	302	NE
FRANKLIN ST	303	NW
FRATERNITY VILLAGE DR	301	NE
FREDERIC LA	303	NW
FREDERICK AVE	301	NW
FREDERICK DR	305	SE
FREDERICK ST	303	NE
FRIENDLY AVE	305	NW
FRONTIER ST	304	NW
FULFORD ST	302	NE
FULTON ST	302	NE
FUCLIO	301	NE
G AVE	298	NE
GABARDINE AVE	304	NW
GAR LA	301	NE
GARDEN LANE	305	NW
GARDEN RD	302	SE
GARDEN ST	302	NE
GARFIELD AVE	302	SW
GARLAND AVE	302	SW
GAYL AVE	300	SW
GAYWOOD ST	303	SW
GEMBRIT CIR	303	SW
GENESSEE RD	301	NW
GEORGE ST	299	NW
GEORGIA AVE	305	NW
GERNAAT CT	305	NE
GERTRUDE DR	300	SW
GIBSON ST	301	NE
GILKISON AVE	298	SE
GINGHAM AVE	305	SW
GLADYS CT	302	NW
GLADYS ST	305	NW
GLEN CT	299	NW
GLENDALE BLVD	299	NE
GLENDALOCK ST	300	NE
GLENGARRY AVE	298	NW
GLENGUILE ST	299	NE
GLENHARBOR DR	304	NW
GLENHAVEN AVE	300	NW
GLENN CT	304	SE
GLENNCOVE	302	SE
GLENROSE TERR	302	SE
GLENWOOD DR	301	NE
GOLDSWORTH DR	303	SW
GOLFVIEW	303	SW
GOODRICH RD	299	NW
GORHAM LANE	298	SW
GRACE RD	298	SE
GRAEFIELD CT	304	SE
GRAHAM ST	304	NE
GRANADA LA	301	NE
GRANDMARIAS AVE	300	NE
GRAND PRAIRIE RD	298	SE
GRAND PRE AVE	298	SE
GRAND TRAVERSE L	304	NW
GRANDVIEW AVE	302	NW
GRANT CT	302	SE
GRANT ST	302	SE
GRASSMERE	304	NE
GRAY ST	306	SW
GREENACRE DR	298	SW
GREENBRIAR DR	301	SE
GREENFIELD SHORES	306	SE
GREEN FOREST DR	305	NW
GREENHILL ST	301	SE
GREENLAND AVE	298	NE
GREENLAWN AVE	301	NE
GREENLEAF BLVD	305	SW
GREENLEAF CIR	301	SE
GREENSPIRE DR	304	SE
GREENVIEW AVE	301	NE
GREENWAY TERR	298	SW
GREENWICH PL	299	SW
GREENWOOD AVE	301	NE
GREGG CT	305	NW
GROSSE POINTE ST	302	SE
GROUSE CT	304	NE
GROVE ST	306	SW
GROVE ST	306	SW
GROVELAND AVE	299	NE
GULL RD	133	SE
GULLWYND DR	300	NE
GWYNEDD DR	302	SW
H AVE	298	SW
HAMELINK DR	302	SE
HAMILTON RD	299	NE
HAMLIN	303	SW
HAMLOCK	304	NE
HAMMOND AVE	299	SW
HAMPTON ST	304	NE
HAMPTON LAKE DR	304	SW
HAMPTON OAKS DR	305	SW
HANDEL ST	304	NE
HANOVER	303	SW
HARDING AVE	299	SW
HARDWICK AVE	305	NW
HARKINS CT	299	SW
HARLEY AVE	304	NW
HARRIGAN CT	302	NE
HARRISON CT	299	SW
HARRISON ST	299	SE
HARVARD ST	302	SE
HARVEY AVE	298	SE
HARWAY AVE	303	NE
HASKELL ST	298	SE
HAVENBROOK ST	298	NE
HAVERHILL AVE	306	NW
HAVERMAN CT	302	NW
HAWK DR	301	NW
HAWLEY ST	299	SW
HAWLEY CT	299	SW
HAYES ST	306	SW
HAYMAC DR	300	NW
HAYS DR N	300	NE
HAYS DR S	300	NE
HAYS PARK AVE	302	NE
HAZARD AVE	299	SE
HAZEL AVE	301	SE
HEALY ST	302	SE
HEATH AVE	303	NW
HEATHER LANE	303	NW
HEATHERDOWNS LA	304	NW
HEAVERLY DR	304	NE
HEAVERLY DR E	304	NE
HEAVERLY DR W	304	NE
HEILMAN CT	304	NW
HELEN AVE	302	NW
HENDERSON CT	299	SE
HENDERSON DR	305	NW
HENLEY AVE	304	NE
HENNING ST	304	NE
HENRIETTA ST	302	NE
HENRY CT	299	SW
HENRY ST	303	NE
HENSCHEL RD	298	NW
HENSHAW ST	299	NW
HENSON AVE	300	NW
HERBERT ST	299	NW
HERCULES AVE	299	NE
HIBBARD AVE	302	NE
HICKORY CT	302	SE
HICKORY PT	304	SE
HICKORY PT DR	304	SE
HICKORYVIEW DR	304	SE
HICK'S COR	303	NE
HIGGENS AVE	303	NE
HIGH RD	302	NW
HIGH ST	304	NE
HIGHFIELD DR	301	NW
HIGHGATE RD	298	NW
HIGHLAND AVE	299	SE
HIGHLAND DR	305	NE
HIGHLAND HILLS	299	SW
HILBERT ST	299	SE
HILL ST	300	SE
HILL'AN'BROOK DR	300	SE
HILLANDALE DR E	302	SW
HILLANDALE DR N	302	SW
HILLCREST AVE	302	NW
HILLSBORO CIR	304	NE
HILLSDALE AVE	298	SE
HILLSHIRE DR	301	NE
HILLSIDE PL	302	NE
HILLSIGHT ST	302	NW
HINSDELL PL	299	SW
HITCHING POST RD	304	SW
H J AVE	300	SE
HOEK ALLEY	302	NE
HOFFMAN ST	302	SW
HOL-HI DRIVE	302	SW
HOLIDAY LA	301	SE
HOLIDAY INN TER	301	NW
HOLLY AVE	304	NE
HOMECREST AVE	302	NE
HOMESTEAD LA	304	NW
HOOVER ST	301	SE
HOPKINS ST	299	SW
HORACE AVE	299	SE
HOTOP AVE	299	SE
HOUSTON PL	302	NW
HOUSTON RD	299	NE
HOWARD ST	301	NE
HOWLAND AVE	302	SE
HOWLANDBURG RD	299	NE
HUDSON ST	302	NW
HUGH CT	299	SW
HUGHES ST	302	SW
HULL ST	305	NE
HUMMINGBIRD CT	304	NE
HUMPHREY ST	300	SW
HUNTERS RIDGE DR	300	SW
HUNTINGTON AVE	300	SW
HURON AVE	298	SE
HUTCHINSON ST	302	SW
IBIS CT	304	NE
IBA ST	300	NW
IDAHO AVE	305	NW
IMPERIAL ST	302	SW
INDIANA ST	302	SE
INDIAN RD	302	SE
INDUSTRIAL DR	306	NW
INGLESIDE TER	299	NW
INKSTER AVE°	303	NE
IVERNESS LA	300	SW
IOWA AVE	304	NW
IROQUOIS TRAIL	209	SE
ISABELLE ST	304	NE
ISLAND AVE	298	NE
IVANHOE	302	SE
IVYWOOD CT	305	NW
JACAMAR CT	304	NE
JACILLE AVE	304	NE
JACK CT	301	NW
JACKSON CT	302	NE
JACKSON ST	302	NE
JACOBS CT	305	SE
JAMES ST	302	NE
JAMES WAY PORTAGE	305	SW
JASON CT	305	NW
JAWS ST	302	NE
JAY DR	301	NW
JEFFERSON AVE	299	SW
JEFFERSON PL	299	SW
JEFFERSON CT	299	SW
JENKS BLVD	298	SE
JENNINGS DR	300	NE
JENNISON AVE	298	SE
JERRY LA	304	NW
JILL AVE	300	SE
JODY LA	301	NW
JOHN ST K-ZOO	302	NW
JOHN ST PORTAGE	305	SE
JOHN ST CT	302	NE
JONATHON DR	305	SE
JOSEPHINE ST	303	NE
JOY AVE	304	SE
JUDGE AVE	299	SW
JULIE DR	304	NE
JUNCTION AVE	300	SW
JUNEDALE DR	298	SE
KALAMAZOO AVE	299	SW
KALANCO ST	302	NE
KALARAMA AVE	304	NE
KATIE CT	304	SE
KATYDID LA	301	SE
KAYLIN CT	305	NW
KEENAY CIR	302	SE
KELVERE AVE	305	NW
KENBROOKE AVE	301	SE
KENDALL AVE	298	SE
KENNILWORTH AVE	305	NE
KENSINGTON DR	301	SE
KENWOOD ST	298	SE
KEYES DR	299	NE
KEYSTONE ST	305	NW
KILGORE RD	302	SW
KILGORE SERVICE	302	SE
KIMAY	304	NE
KINCAID ST	304	NE
KING EDWARDS CT	303	SW
KING HIGHWAY	302	NE
KINGSBURY DR	305	NE
KINGSTON AVE KALAMAZOO	302	NE
KINGSTON DR	305	SE
KIRBY'S CIR	305	SE
KIRKWOOD DR	304	NE
KIWI CT	304	NE
KL AVE	301	NW
KNIGHT ST	302	SE
KNOLLWOOD AVE	301	NE
KNOX ST	301	SE
KONKLE ST	303	SE
KOOK AVE	302	NE
KOOK CT	302	NE
KROM AVE	299	SE
KROMDYKE LA PORTAGE	305	
KROMDYKE CT KALAMAZOO	302	NE
LA CROSS ST	298	SE
L AVE	303	NE
LAFAYETTE AVE	301	NE
LAKE ST PORTAGE	305	SW
LAKE ST K-ZOO	302	NE
LAKE ST, TWP	306	SW
LAKE ST COMSTOCK	303	NW
LAKE FOREST DR	301	SE
LAKE HILL DR	301	SE
LAKESIDE DR	302	SW
LAKE TERRACE DR	301	NE
LAKEVIEW AVE K-ZOO TWP	300	SW
LAKEVIEW DR PORT.	305	SE
LAKEWAY AVE	302	SE
LAKEWOOD DR K-ZOO TWP	300	SW
LAKEWOOD DR PORTAGE	305	SE
LAMA RD	302	SW
LAMAR DR	305	NW
LAMONT AVE	303	NW
LAMPLIGHTER LA	301	NW
LAMPLITE ST	304	NE
LANCASTER DR	304	NE
LAND B LAND DR	300	SE
LANDSDOWNE DR	302	SW
LANDS-END DR	298	NE
LANE BLVD	302	NE
LANFAIR AVE	299	NW
LANSING AVE	301	NE
LANTERN LA	299	SW
LARCH AVE	303	NE
LAREDO ST	299	SE
LARK DR	301	NE
LARKEN CT	300	SW
LARKSPUR AVE	298	SE
LARRY LA	301	NE
LaRUE ST	305	SE
LA SALLE ST	305	SE
LAUDEPDALE DR	298	SE
LAURA ST	302	NW
LAURELHILLS ST	298	NE
LAW AVE	301	NW
LAWRENCE ST	299	SW
LAWN CT	305	NW
LAY BLVD	302	SW
LEAWOOD ST	304	NE
LEEBARTON PL	302	NW
LEENHOUTS ST	303	NE
LEIGH AVE	300	SE
LEIGHTON CT	300	SW
LENOX AVE	305	NW
LEON AVE	306	SE
LEONA AVE	302	SE
LESLIE ST	300	NE
LESTER RD	303	NW
LEWSINDA AVE	304	NW
LEXINGTON AVE	303	SW
LEXINGTON CIR	303	SW
LIBERTY ST	302	SW
LIBRARY LA	305	SW
LILAC LA	301	NW
LILLIAN CT	302	NW
LINCOLN AVE	303	NW
LINCOLNSHIRE BLVD	303	SW
LINDA LA COOPER TWP	300	NW
LINDA ST PORTAGE	306	SW
LINDENWOOD ST	300	NW
LINK LA	299	NE
LINNEMAN AVE	305	NE
LINTON CT	302	NE
LINWOOD DR	302	NW
LISZT ST	304	SW
LITEOLIER ST	304	NE
LITTLE DR	301	NE
LLOY ST	304	SE
LOCKMOOR CT	298	SE
LOCUST PL	302	NW
LOCUST ST	302	NW
LOGAN AVE	301	SE
LOIS AVE	300	SW
LOMOND DR	301	NE
LONDONDERRY AVE	298	SW
LONG RD	302	NW
LONG LAKE DR	306	SW
LONGMEADOW	304	NE
LONGVIEW CT	305	SW
LONGVIEW ST	305	NW
LONSDALE	299	NW
LOOKOUT LA	303	SW
LORAC ST	305	SE
LOTTIE AVE	299	NE
LOUISA AVE	303	NW
LOVEBIRD CT	304	NE
LOVELL ST	302	NW
LOVERS LANE	302	SW
LOW RD	302	NW
LOWDEN ST	301	SE
LUCAS CT	299	SW
LUCERNE AVE	300	SW
LUCY ST	302	SW
LUDGATE LANE	301	NE
LUELLA CT	302	NE
LUELLA ST	302	NE
LULU ST	299	SW
LUM AVE	300	SW
LUM ST	302	SW
LYNN AVE	302	NE
LYNNHILL ST	301	SW
LYONS AVE	302	NE
M AVE	303	SE
MABLE ST	299	SW
MAGNOLIA CIR KALAMAZOO	301	SE
MAGNOLIA ST COMSTOCK TWP	300	SW
MAHONEY ST	306	SW
MAIDEN ALNE	299	NE
MAIN CT	302	NW
MAIN ST	299	SW
MALL DR	305	NW
MALLARD CIR	304	NE
MALTBY RD	298	SW
MANANA ST	300	NW
MANCHESTER RD	303	SW
MANDALAY DR	301	NE
MANHATTAN ST	305	NW
MANOR ST	298	SE
MANSFIELD AVE PORTAGE	304	NE
MANUFACTURING RD	306	NW
MAPLE AVE K-ZOO TWP	300	NW
MAPLE CT K-ZOO	302	NW
MAPLE ST K-ZOO	299	NE
MAPLE LT PARCHMT	202	NW
MAPLE HILL DR	298	SW
MAPLEVIEW AVE	304	SW
MAPLEWOOD DR	302	SW
MARCH ST	302	NE
MARFIELD AVE	305	NW
MARGARET AVE	302	NE
MARIGOLD AVE	305	NE
MARINE CT	303	NE
MARK ST	301	NW
MARKET ST	303	NE
MARLANE AVE	298	SE
MARLOW ST	303	NE
MARSHA ST	304	NW
MARTIN ST	299	SW
MARYWOOD ST	298	SE
MASON ST	299	SW
MASTENBROOK DR	306	NW
MAYFAIR ST	303	SE
MAYFIELD ST	305	SW
MAYNARD AVE	305	NE
MAYWOOD AVE	302	NE
McCAMLEY DR	305	SE
McCORMICK ST	303	NW
McCOURTIE ST	302	NW
McELROY ST	302	NE
McKINLEY ST	299	NE
McLISH CT	305	SE
MEAD ST	300	NW
MEADOW RD	301	NE
MEADOWBROOK LANE	301	SE
MEADOWCROFT AVE	298	NE
MEADOWLARK AVE	301	SE
MEADOWLARK LANE	302	SW
MEADOWOOD CT	300	NE
MEADOWVIEW AVE	300	NE
MEIN CT	298	SE
MELCREST ST	298	SE
MELROSE AVE	303	NW
MEMORY LANE	302	SE
MEREDITH DR	306	NW
MERRIE LA	302	NW
MERRILL ST	302	NW
MERRIMAC DR	301	NY
MERRY BROOK DR	301	NE
MERRYVIEW DR	302	NE
METZGER ST	302	SE
MEYERS ST	300	SW
MIAMI AVE	300	SW
MICHAEL AVE	300	NW
MICHIGAN AVE	299	SW
MICHIKAL	299	SW
MIDDLEBURY DR	301	NE
MIDFIELD RD	302	SW
MIDVALE TERRACE	304	NE
MIDWAY ST	299	NW
MILES AVE	301	SE
MILES PL	301	NW
MILHAM RD	303	SW
MILLS ST	299	SE
MILLARD CT	303	SW
MILLCORK ST	303	SW
MILLER RD	302	NE
MILLVIEW AVE	302	NW
MILLWOOD AVE	302	SE
MINOR AVE	302	NW
MINUTE MAN CIR	301	NW
MISSOURI AVE	305	NW
MITCHELL PL	299	SW
ML AVE	305	NW
MN AVE	305	NE
MOCKINGBIRD DR	301	NE
MOFFETT ST	304	NE
MOHAWK ST	298	SE
MOLHOEKS PL	302	SW
MOLINE ST	301	SE
MONARCH ST	302	SE
MONROE AVE	303	SW
MONTAGUE DR	302	NW
MONTEREY CIRCLE	299	SW
MONTE VISTA ST	305	SW
MONTICELLO AVE	305	NW
MONTROSE AVE	302	NW
MOONLITE AVE	301	NE
MOORE DR	301	NE
MOORSBRIDGE DR	306	SW
MORAINE TR	301	NE
MORELAND ST	302	NW
MORGAN ST	302	SE
MORNINGSIDE DR	302	NE
MOSEL ST	299	NE
MOUNT CT	302	NW
MOUNT ROYAL DR	301	NW
MOZART ST	304	NW
MT. OLIVET RD	300	NW

KALAMAZOO

STREET INDEX

MT. VERNON AVE	305	SW
MULHERN AVE	300	SW
MYRTLE ST	299	SE
N AVE	301	SW
NACY CT	304	SW
NANCY LA	301	NW
NAUMI ST	305	NE
NASSAU ST	300	SW
NAZARETH RD	300	NW
NEAL AVE	300	SE
NELLBERT ST	303	SW
NELSON AVE	298	SE
NEUMAIER CT	302	NE
NEVADA AVE	305	NW
NEWALL PL	302	NW
NEWELLS LANE	304	SE
NEW HAMPSHIRE	305	NW
NEWHOUSE ST	305	SW
NEWLAND PL	302	NE
NEWPORT RD	305	NE
NEWTON CT	302	NW
NICHOLS RD	298	NE
NOLA ST	299	SW
NORA ST	303	NW
NORFOLK CIR	304	NW
NORMAL CT	302	NW
NORMANDY AVE	300	NE
NORTH ST	298	SE
N. AMARILLO ST	300	NW
NORTHAMPTON RD	298	SW
N. CONCOURSE	305	NE
NORTH HILLS CT E	299	NW
NORTH HILLS CT W	299	NW
NORTH HILLS DR	299	SW
NORTHVIEW DR	298	NE
NORTON DR	302	NE
NORWAY AVE	299	SW
NOTTINGHAM AVE	301	NW
NOUGGLES ST	306	SW
O AVE	306	NW
OAK CT	302	NW
OAK ST	302	NW
OAK ST PORTAGE	305	SW
OAKCREEK AVE	300	NW
OAK GROVE AVE	299	NE
OAKHAVEN DR	304	SE
OAK HILL DR	304	SW
OAKHURST AVE	302	SW
OAKLAND DR	301	SE
OAKRIDGE LA	301	SE
OAK RIDGE RD	299	NW
OAKSIDE ST	305	SE
OAKVIEW DR	305	SW
OBSERVATION AVE	300	NW
OGDEN AVE	299	SE
OHIO AVE	305	NW
OLD CENTRE AVE	304	SE
OLD COLONY RD	302	SW
OLD FIELD PL	301	SW
OLD FIELD TR	301	SW
OLD KILGORE RD	302	SW
OLIVE ST	302	NE
OLIVER ST	302	NW
OLMSTEAD RD	302	NW
OLNEY ST	298	SE
ON AVE	304	NW
ONADAGA AVE	300	NW
OONAH PL	300	SW
ORAN AVE	300	SE
ORANOCO ST	300	NE
ORBECK AVE	300	SE
ORCHARD AVE	299	SE
ORCHARD DR	305	SE
ORCHARD PL	299	SW
ORCHARD HILL AVE	304	SW
OREGON AVE	305	NW
ORIENT AVE	299	NE
ORIOLE	300	NW
ORGANDY ST	305	SE
ORMADA DR	300	NE
OSBORNE ST	302	NW
OSHTEMO RD	301	NW
OSTRANDER ST	302	NE
OTTAWA AVE	298	SW
OUTER DR	305	NW
OUTLOOK ST	302	NW
P AVE	306	NE
PACKARD ST	303	NE
PADDINGTON ST	303	SW
PALM ST	305	NW
PALMER AVE	302	NE
PAMPAS LA	301	NE
PARCHGLEN PL	299	NE
PARCHMOUNT	299	NE
PARCOM ST	303	NE
PAR 4 CIRCLE	302	SW
PAR-4 RD	302	SW
PARK AVE	299	NE
PARK DR	299	NE
PARK PL	302	NW
PARK ST	299	SW
PARKDALE	299	NE
PARKER AVE	300	SE
PARKLAND TER	305	SW
PARKVIEW AVE	301	SW
PARKWAY DR	301	NW
PARKWOOD AVE	302	NW
PARKWYN DR	301	NE
PARSONS ST	299	SE
PASADENA ST	302	NE
PASMA AVE	305	SE
PATERSON ST	299	SW
PATERSON CT	299	SW
PATLAND DR	298	NE
PATRICIA ST	300	SE
PATTI CIR	300	NW
PATWOOD CT	299	SW
PAUL CT	305	SE
PEACHTREE ST	305	NW
PEARL CT	302	NW
PEARL ST	302	NW
PECAN AVE	305	NW
PEEKSTOK RD	302	SE
PEELER ST	320	NW
PEMBROOK ST	302	SW
PENNWAY ST	303	SW
PEPPERELL CT	304	SE
PERCY AVE	300	SE
PERRY ST	305	SW
PESOS	301	NE
PFITZER AVE	304	NE
PHAINT ST	304	SW
PHILLIPS ST	302	NE
PHILLIPS ST	303	NW
PHEOBE ST	304	SW
PHORNCROFT AVE	302	SW
PICCADILLY RD	298	SW
PICKARD ST	303	NW
PICKERING ST	304	SE
PICO ST	300	NW
PIERCE AVE	302	SW
PILLAR ST	303	NE
PINE ST	302	NE
PINE TER	301	NW
PINEGLADE DR	304	NW
PINE GROVE LA	301	NE
PINEHURST BLVD	298	SE
PINE KNOLL AVE	300	NW
PINE RIDGE RD	301	NE
PINE SHADOW DR	301	NE
PINE TREE TER	304	NE
PINEWOOD CIR	304	SE
PINGREE ST	303	NW
PINTO RD	300	NW
PIONEER ST	302	NW
PITCHER ST	299	SE
PITTSFORD DR	306	NW
PLAINFIELD AVE	300	NE
PLATEAU STREET	302	SW
PLEASANT AVE	302	SW
PLEASANT DR	305	SE
PLEASANT HOME CT	302	SW
PLEASANTVIEW DR	304	NW
PLOVER DR	304	SW
PLUMTREE AVE	305	SE
PLYMOUTH LANE	302	NW
POINT O'WOODS CIR	304	SE
POINT O'WOODS DR	304	SE
POLARIS AVE	300	NW
POMEROY ST	302	SE
POMPANO AVE	306	SW
PONCHO PL	301	NE
POND DR E	301	NE
POND DR W	301	NE
PONTIAC AVE	298	SW
POPLAR PL	302	NE
PORTAGE CT	320	NE
PORTAGE RD	305	NE
PORTAGE ST	302	NE
PORTAGE INDUSTRIAL DR	305	SW
POTOMAC AVE	303	SE
POTTER AVE	301	NW
PRATT'S RD	301	SW
PRESTWICK DR	303	NW
PRESTWICK LA	303	NW
PRIMROSE ST	304	SW
PRIVATE DR	299	SE
PRIVATE DR	298	SW
PRIVATE DR	299	NW
PRIVATE RD	303	NW
PROCTOR AVE	303	NE
PROSPECT PL	299	SW
PROSPECT ST	299	SW
PROSPERITY DR	305	SE
PROUTY ST	299	SW
Q AVE	304	SW
QR AVE	306	SE
QUAIL ST	305	NW
QUAKER AVE	301	SE
QUARTERLINE DR	305	SE
QUINCY AVE	304	SE
R AVE	306	SE
RABORN CT	301	SW
RACE ST	302	NE
RADCLIFFE AVE	304	NE
RAINBOW AVE	305	NW
RAMBLING RD	301	NE
RAMONA AVE	305	NE
RAMSGATE	304	NW
RANDOM RD	300	NW
RANGE STREET	300	NW
RANKIN AVE	301	NE
RANNEY ST	302	NW
RANSOM ST	299	SW
RAPP AVE	305	SE
RAVINE RD	298	NW
RAVINIA ST	302	NE
RAY ST	299	SE
RECEIVING DR	306	NW
RECENT	299	SE
RECREATION DR	301	NE
RED COAT LA	301	NW
RED MAPLE LA	299	NW
REDMOND AVE	302	SE
REDSTOCK AVE	304	NE
REDWOOD AVE	301	NE
REDWOOD LA	299	NW
REED CT	302	NE
REED AVE	302	NE
REESE CT	302	NW
REGAY ST	303	SW
REGINA AVE	305	NW
REMINE ST	302	NW
REVERE LA	301	NW
REX AVE	303	NE
REYCRAFT DR	302	SE
RICHARD AVE	302	NE
RICHARDSON ST	299	SE
RICHLAND AVE	298	SE
RICHMOND CT	301	NW
RIDGE RD	302	NW
RIDGEBROOK DR	302	SW
RIDGEFIELD RD	304	NE
RIDGEVIEW CIR	301	NE
RIDGEVIEW DR	301	NE
RIDGEWOOD ST	302	SW
RIO RD	301	NE
RIPLEY	303	NE
RITSEMA CT	299	SW
RIVER ST	299	SE
RIVER ST	303	NE
RIVERSIDE DR	303	NW
RIVERVIEW DR	298	NE
RIVINGTON ST	302	SW
ROANOKE ST	304	NE
ROBERT LANE	299	NE
ROBIN LA	302	SW
ROBIN HOOD DR	304	NE
ROBINSWOOD ST	304	NE
ROCKFORD ST	305	NW
ROCKINGHAM AVE	299	SE
ROCK LEDGE	299	SW
ROCKWELL CT	299	SE
ROCKWOOD DR	298	NW
ROCKY RD	300	NW
ROGER ST	305	SW
ROLLING HILLS AVE	299	NW
ROLLING HILLS AVE	304	SW
ROLLING RIDGE AVE	300	NW
ROLLRIDGE AVE	300	NW
ROMENCE RD	304	NW
ROOSEVELT AVE	299	NE
ROSE CT	302	NW
ROSE PK	302	NW
ROSE PL	302	NW
ROSE ST	299	SW
ROSEDALE AVE	299	NE
ROSELAND AVE	302	NE
ROSEVIEW DR	304	SE
ROSEWOOD AVE	304	NE
ROSKQM CT	302	NE
ROTHBURY ST	304	NE
ROY AVE	303	NW
ROYAL OAK AVE	305	SW
ROYCE AVE	302	SE
ROXBURY LA	301	SE
RS AVE	306	SE
RUGBY ST	301	SE
RUNNYMEDE DR	298	NE
RUSRIDGE AVE	298	SE
RUSSELL ST	302	NE
RUSSETT DR	301	NE
RUTH ST	305	NW
RUTHIN RD	301	SE
RYSKAMP CT	302	SW
RYSTOCK ST	303	NE
S AVE	306	SE
SABIN ST	298	SE
SAGE ST	298	SW
SAGEBRUSH ST	298	SW
SAIDLA RD	303	NW
ST ALBANS WAY	300	SW
ST ANTIONE AVE	301	NE
ST JOE AVE	303	NW
ST JOHN'S PL	302	NW
ST JOSEPH ST	302	NW
ST MARY'S ST	302	SE
SALEM LA	305	NW
SALLY'S CT	299	SW
SANDRA DR	300	NW
SANDY COVE DR	300	SE
SANDY RIDGE	305	SW
SANTOS ST	298	SE
SARATOGA AVE	300	NE
SAVANNAH AVE	300	NW
SAXONIA LA	300	NW
SCHIPPERS LANE	300	SW
SCHOLTEN CT	302	NE
SCHOOL ST	303	NE
SCHURING RD	304	NE
SCHUSTER AVE	303	NW
SCHUUR AVE	304	SW
SCOTS PINE WAY	304	SW
SEAMERS ST	300	SW
SECOND DR	305	SE
SECOND ST	302	NE
SEEMORE AVE	300	SE
SEMINOLE ST	298	SW
SENECA LA	301	NW
SENNE ST	303	SE
SEQUOIA ST	298	SW
SERVICE LA	299	NE
SEVILLE AVE	299	SE
SHADE TREE TERR	304	NE
SHADY LANE	305	SE
SHAFFER RD	299	SE
SHAKESPEARE AVE	303	NW
SHANGRI-LA DR	300	NW
SHANNON CT	300	SW
SHARON ST	299	NE
SHASTA DR	299	SE
SHAVER RD	305	SW
SHAW LA E	301	NE
SHAW LA W	301	NE
SHEFFIELD DR	301	NE
SHELDON CT	302	NE
SHELDON ST	302	NE
SHERIDAN DR	302	SE
SHERRY DR	305	NW
SHERWOOD AVE	299	SE
SHERWOOD DR	304	NE
SHIELDS ST	300	SE
SHIPPING DR	306	NW
SHIRLEY CT	304	SE
SHIRLEY DR	303	NE
SHOPPERS LA	299	NE
SHORBURY	304	NE
SHOREHAM ST	304	NE
SHORT RD	302	NW
SHUMAN ST	304	SW
SHUMWAY AVE	305	SE
SILVER HILLS AVE	300	NW
SIMMONS ST	300	NW
SIMPSON ST	299	SW
16TH ST	299	NW
SKINNER PL	302	NE
SKIRROW PL	302	NW
SKYLER DR	301	SE
SKYLINE	298	SW
SKYRIDGE AVE	301	NW
SLATER DR	300	NW
SLEEPER ST	303	NE
SMILEY DR	306	SE
SMITH CT	302	NE
SOLOMON	306	SE
SOLVEL ST	300	NW
SOMMERSET ST	303	SW
SONG BIRD LA	301	SW
SONORA ST	299	SE
SOUTH DR	306	SW
SOUTH ST	299	SE
SOUTH BRANCH ST	302	NE
S CONCOURSE	305	NE
SOUTHERN AVE	302	NE
SOUTHFIELD ST	305	SE
SOUTHLAND AVE	305	NW
S LONG LAKE DR	306	SE
SOUTH SHORE DR	305	SW
SOUTH SPRUCE DR	302	NW
SOUTHWORTH TER	299	SE
SPAFFORD DR	302	SW
SPANISH RD	299	NE
SPARROW AVE	300	NW
SPARTAN DR	299	NE
SPRAGUE AVE	302	NW
SPRING CT	302	NE
SPRING ST	302	NE
SPRINGFIELD ST	302	NW
SPRINGHILL DR	302	NW
SPRINGMONT AVE	301	SE
SPRINKLE RD	300	NE
SPRUCE DR	302	NW
SPRUCE BROOK RD	300	SE
SQUIRE HEATH LA	304	SW
STADIUM RD	301	NW
STAMFORD AVE	300	SW
STANDISH ST	302	SW
STAPLES AVE	299	SW
STAPLES CT	299	SW
STARBROOK ST	304	NE
STARLITE AVE	301	SW
STASSEN AVE	299	NW
STATE ST	302	NE
STEARNS AVE	302	NW
STEENARD RD	299	NE
STEGER AVE	300	SE
STETSON CT	302	NW
STEVENS AVE	301	SE
STEWART DR	303	NW
STOCKBRIDGE AVE	302	NE
STOLK DR	298	SW
STONE ST	302	NW
STONEBRIDGE CT	304	SE
STONEBROOKE AVE	298	SW
STONECROFT	304	SE
STONEGATE RD	298	NE
STONEHENGE DR	302	SW
STONEY BROOK RD	304	NW
STRATFORD DR	304	NW
STRATTON RD	300	NW
STUART AVE	299	SW
STURBRIDGE DR	300	NE
STURGEON BAY AVE	304	NE
SUFFOLK AVE	304	NE
SUGARLOAF AVE	304	SW
SULLIVAN ST	303	NE
SUMMER ST	299	SW
SUMMERDALE AVE	299	NE
SUMMERFIELD ST	300	NW
SUMMIT AVE	299	SW
SUNBURST DR	304	NW
SUNFIELD ST	300	NW
SUNNOCK AVE	302	SE
SUNBRIGHT	305	NW
SUNNYBROOK DR	301	SE
SUNNYCREST DR	300	SE
SUNNYDALE AVE	298	SW
SUNNYSIDE DR	300	SW
SUNSET DR	302	SW
SUNSET LANE	302	NW
SUN VALLEY DR	301	SE
SUNVIEW AVE	302	SW
SUPERIOR AVE	302	NE
SURPRISE AVE	303	NW
SURRY ST	305	NW
SUSAN AVE	300	SE
SUSSEX CT	305	NW
SUTHERLAND AVE	301	NE
SWALLOW AVE	304	SW
SWAN ST	304	SW
SWETISH DR	299	NW
SWIFT DR	301	NW
SYCAMORE LA	301	NE
SYDELLE AVE	298	SE
SYLVAN	306	SW
TAFT ST	299	NW
TALBOT CT	300	SW
TALIESIN DR	301	SE
TAMARIX AVE	302	SW
TAMFIELD AVE	304	NE
TAMPA ST	300	SW
TAMRACK ST	298	SW
TAMSIN AVE	301	SE
TAMWORTH ST	301	SE
TANDA	300	NW
TANGLEWOOD DR	305	SW
TATTERSALL RD	304	NE
TAYLOR ST	302	NE
TEAKWOOD	305	SW
TERRACE CT	302	NE
TEXAS DR	304	NW
TEXEL DR	300	SW
THAWER	300	NW
THIRD ST	302	SE
THOMAS CT	305	NW
THOMAS ST	299	NE
THOMPSON CT	299	SW
THORNHILL AVE	298	NE
THRASHER CT	304	SW
THRASHER LA	304	SW
THRUSHWOOD AVE	305	SE
TIBET AVE	300	NW
TIFFANY AVE	306	SW
TIFFIN ST	306	NW
TIMBERCOVE DR	304	SW
TIMBERCREEK CT	305	SW
TIMBERLANE DR	301	SE
TIPPERARY RD	301	NE
TOBEY DR	306	SE
TODD LA	301	NW
TOMS PL	301	NW
TOZAR CT	304	SE
TRACTION CT	303	NW
TRAILS END	302	NE
TRANQUIL ST	305	SE
TRAVIS RD	299	NE
TRAY LA	301	NW
TREEHAVEN DR	301	NE
TREMONT ST	302	NW
TRIMBLE AVE	300	SW
TROTWOOD ST	304	NE
TRUMAN ST	299	NW
TUDOR CIR	305	NW
TURWILL LANE	298	SW
12TH ST	301	SE
12TH ST N	298	NW
20TH ST	299	NE
25TH ST	300	NE
21ST ST	299	NE
24TH ST	300	NW
24TH ST	306	SE
26TH ST	300	NE
TWILIGHT AVE	300	NE
TWIN TER	303	SW
UNDERWOOD LA	303	SW
UNIFAB CT	302	SE
UNION ST	299	SW
UNIVERSITY AVE	302	NW
UPJOHN DR	302	NE
UPJOHN RD	305	NE
UPLAND DR	300	SW
UPPER DARBY	305	NE
UTAH AVE	305	NW
UTILITY RD	306	NW
VALE AVE	299	NE
VALENCIA LA	301	NW
VALE VIEW DR	298	SE
VALK BLVD	303	SW
VALLEY CIR N	303	SW
VALLEY CIR S	303	SW
VALLEY CIR W	303	SW
VALLEYWOOD CT	304	SE
VALLEYWOOD LA	304	SE
VAN BOCHOVE CT	302	NE
VANDE GIESSEN RD	301	NE
VANDERBILT AVE	304	SW
VANDER SALM CT	302	NW
VAN HOESEN BLVD	305	NW
VANRICK DR	303	SW
VAN VRANKEN CT	302	NW
VAN ZEE ST	302	NE
VASSAR DR	302	SE
VAUCELLES ST	305	SE
VELVET AVE	305	SW
VERDRIES CT	299	SW
VERLEEN ST	300	SE
VERNON CT	302	NE
VERNON ST	302	NE
VERONICA ST	304	NE
VICTOR ST	303	NW
VICTORIA CT	305	NE
VILLA DR	305	NW
VILLAGE CT	302	NW

Street	Page	Dir
VILLAGE ST	302	NW
VINCENT	301	SE
VINE PL	302	NW
VINE ST	302	NW
VIRGINIA AVE	299	SE
VISTA	301	NE
WAITE AVE	301	NE
WALBRIDGE ST	299	SE
WALCOTT ST	304	SE
WALDEN CT	300	SW
WALDO AVE	298	SW
WALDORF ST	299	NW
WALL ST	302	NW
WALLACE AVE	300	SW
WALNUT CT	302	NW
WALNUT ST	305	SW
WALNUTTREE TERR	302	SW
WARBLER DR	304	SW
WARREN PL	298	SE
WARUF AVE	306	SE
WARWICK ST	305	NW
WASHBURN AVE	300	SW
WASHINGTON AVE	302	NE
WASHINGTON CT	302	NE
WATER ST	299	SW
WATTERWORTH DR	301	NE
WATTLES PL	299	SE
WAVERLY DR	300	SW
WAVERLY ST	298	SE
WAYLEE	305	SW
WAYSIDE RD	300	SW
WEALTHY AVE	298	SE
WEAVER AVE	301	NE
WEAVER CIR	301	NE
WEAVER DR	305	SW
WEDGEWOOD DR	301	SE
WELBURY ST	304	NE
WELLINGTON RD	301	SE
WELLS PL	302	NE
WELLS ST	306	SW
WENDY LA	304	SE
WEST RD	305	NE
WESTBROOK ST	301	NE
WESTBURY LA	298	SW
W CENTER CT	306	SW
WESTCHESTER LANE	302	NW
WESTCHESTER ST	304	NE
WESTCOVE DR	304	NE
WEST END DR	305	SW
WESTERN AVE	301	NE
WESTFALL AVE	301	NE
WESTFIELD	304	NW
W LONG LAKE DR	306	SE
W MELODY AVE	305	SW
WESTMORELAND AVE	301	NE
WESTNEDGE AVE	299	NW
WETSHIRE ST	304	NE
WESTVIEW ST	301	NW
WESTWOOD DR	298	SE
WHEATON AVE	302	NW
WHEELER AVE	303	SW
WHIPPOORWILL DR	304	SW
WHISPERING BROOK CIR	305	SW
WHISTLER DR	304	SW
WHITBY AVE	304	NE
WHITCOMB ST	302	SW
WHITEGATE LA	301	NW
WHITEOAK DR	304	SE
WHITE OAK DR	302	SW
WHITES RD	301	SE
WHITMORE ST	300	NW
WHITTIER DR	303	SW
WILBUR ST	301	NE
WILDWOOD PL	302	NW
WILLARD CT	299	SW
WILLARD ST	299	SW
WILLETTE AVE	300	SE
WILLIAM ST	299	SW
WILLIS AVE	303	NW
WILLOUGHBY DR	305	NE
WILLOW BLVD	303	NW
WILLOW LA	299	NW
WILLOW RD	301	SE
WILLOW BROOK DR	300	SE
WILMETTE ST	298	SE
WILRAD CT	302	NW
WILSHIRE BLVD	302	NW
WILSON AVE	299	NE
WINCHELL AVE	301	NW
WINDEMERE ST	305	NW
WINDING BROOK DR	300	SE
WINDING WAY	298	NW
WINDSOR LANE	305	NW
WINDYRIDGE DR	302	SW
WINKFIELD AVE	304	NE
WINSFORD CT	304	SE
WINSTEAD ST	302	NE
WINTER FOREST DR	305	NW
WINTERS DR	302	SE
WINTRHOP AVE	306	NW
WINTON AVE	302	SE
WISTERIA STREET	302	SW
WITTERS CT	304	SW
WITWER CT	302	NE
WOLVERINE AVE	300	NW
WOOD ST	301	SE
WOODBURY AVE	299	SW
WOODCLIFF DR	301	SE
WOODCREST ST	305	SW
WOODDALE BLVD	306	SW
WOODEDGE	306	SW
WOODHAVEN DR	301	SE
WOODHEATH AVE	302	SW
WOODLAND AVE	304	NE
WOODLAWN AVE	301	NE
WOODLAWN DR	305	SW
WOODLURE DR	299	NW
WOODMERE LA	300	NE
WOODMONT DR	302	SE
WOODROW DR	300	SW
WOODS END	302	SW
WOODSTONE DR	301	SE
WOODVIEW DR	305	SW
WOODLAND AVE	299	SW
WORDEN ST	303	NE
WREN ST	300	NW
WRENWOOD ST	304	NE
WRIGHT S	303	NE
WYMAN RD	298	NW
WYNN RD	303	NE
YEW AVE	298	SW
YUCCA AVE	298	SW
ZUIDEMA CT	302	SE
ZYLMAN AVE	306	SW

NOTES

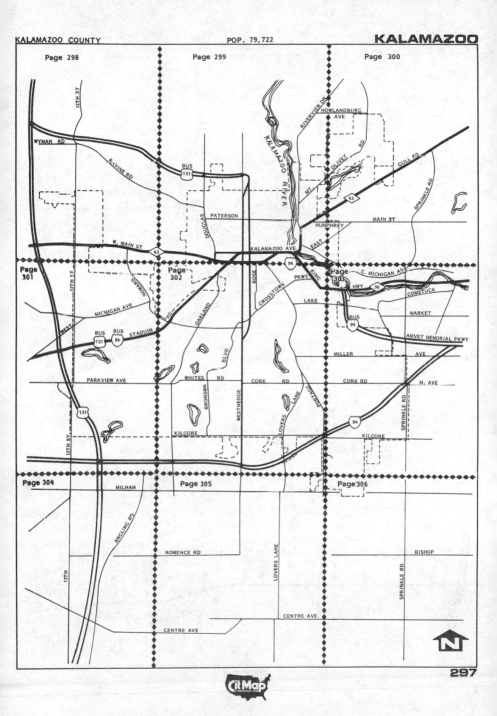

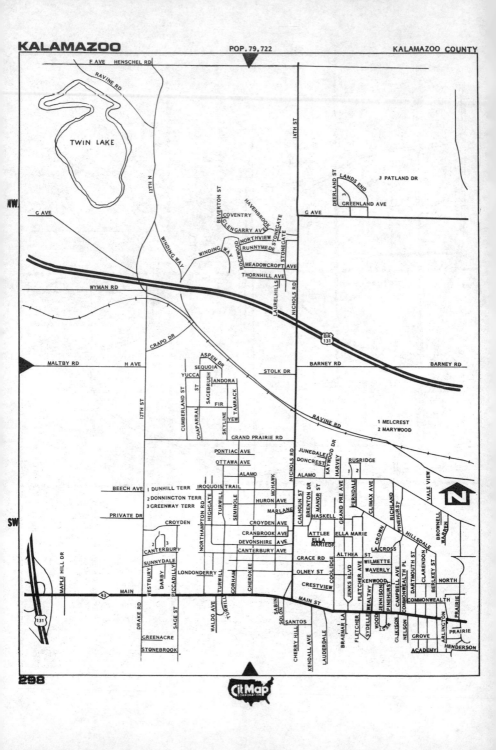

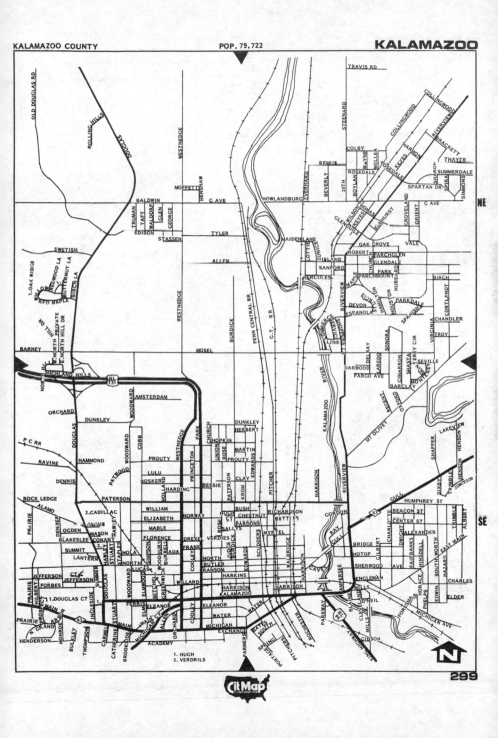

1. HUGH
2. VERDRILS

1. OAK RIDGE
2. CADILLAC
1. DOUGLAS CT

NE

SE

N

CitMap
CORPORATION

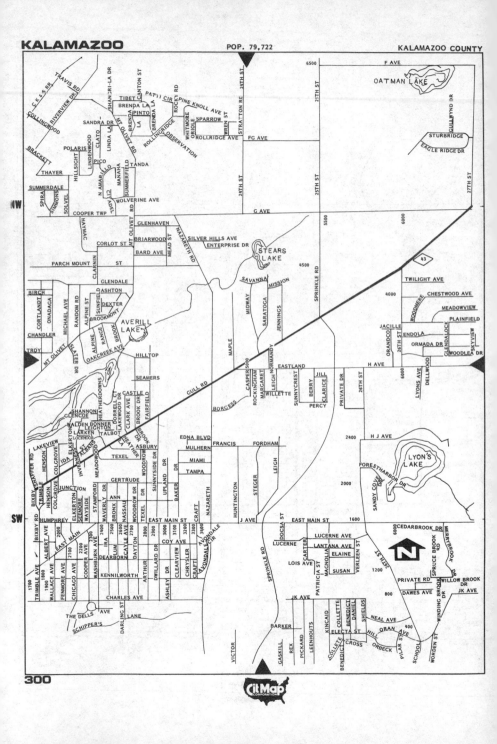

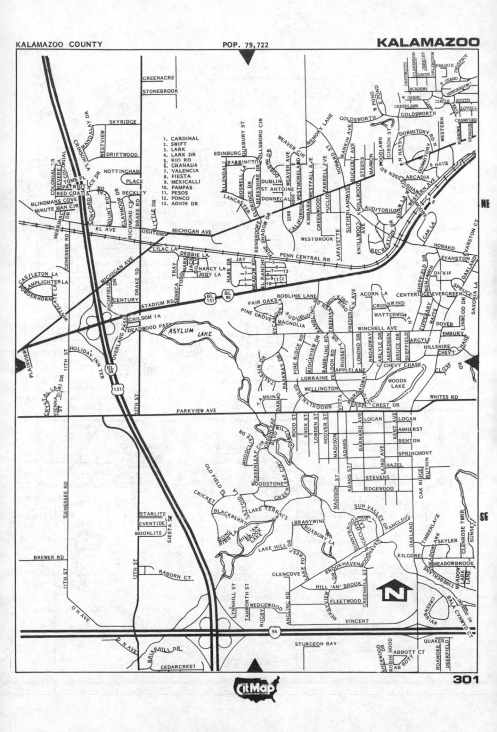

1. CARDINAL
2. SWIFT
3. LARK
4. LARK DR
5. RIO RD
6. GRANADA
7. VALENCIA
8. FIESTA
9. MEXICALLI
10. PAMPAS
11. PESOS
12. PONCO
13. ADIOS DR

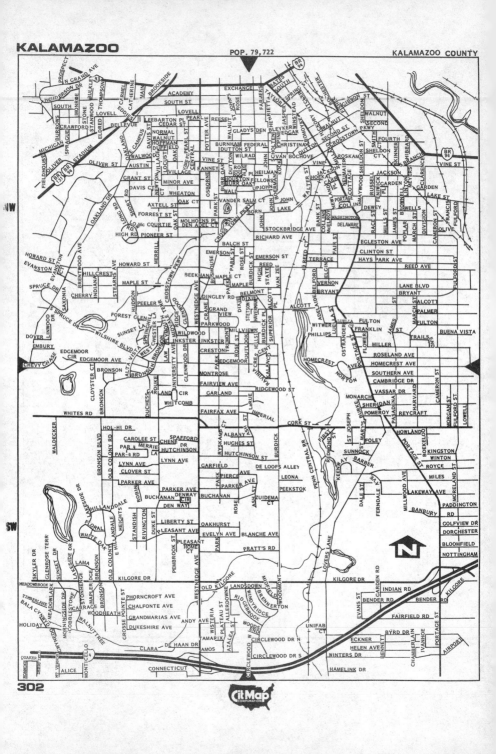

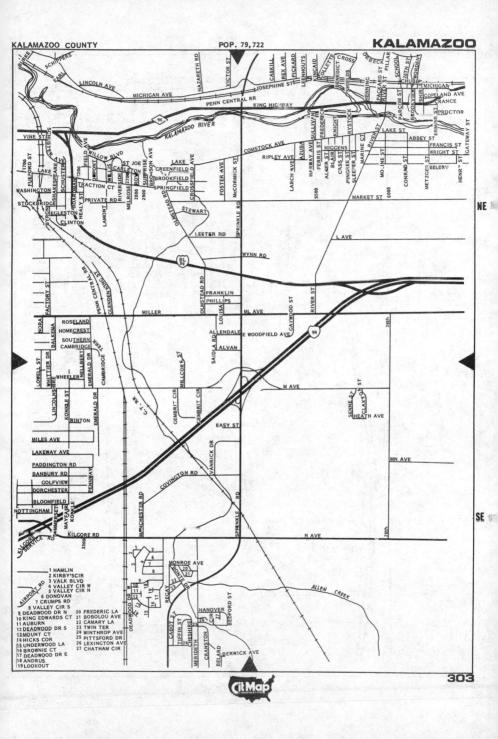

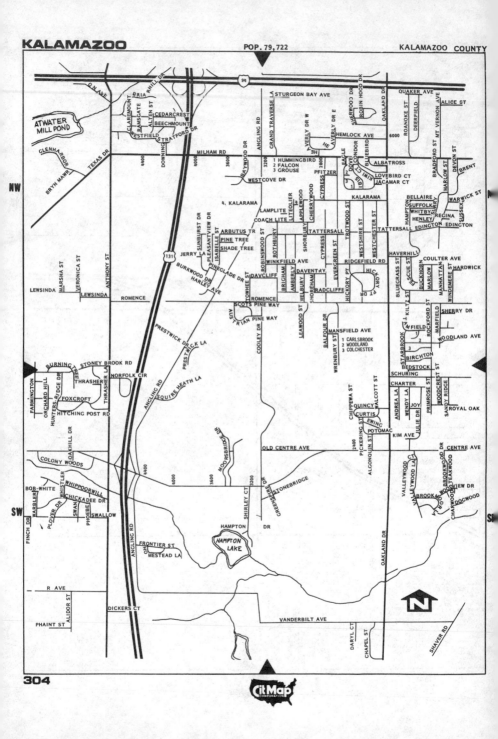

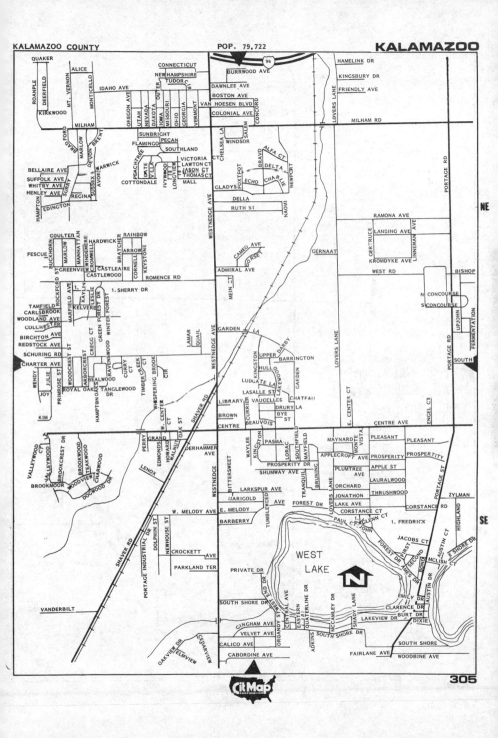

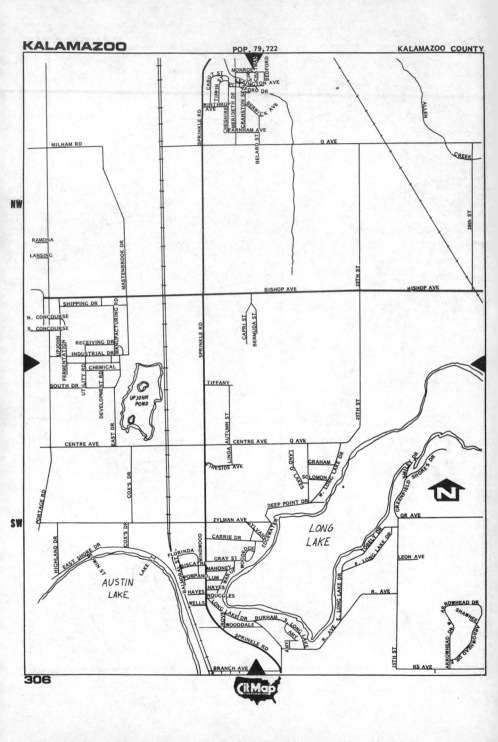

NW

SW

CitMap
CORPORATION

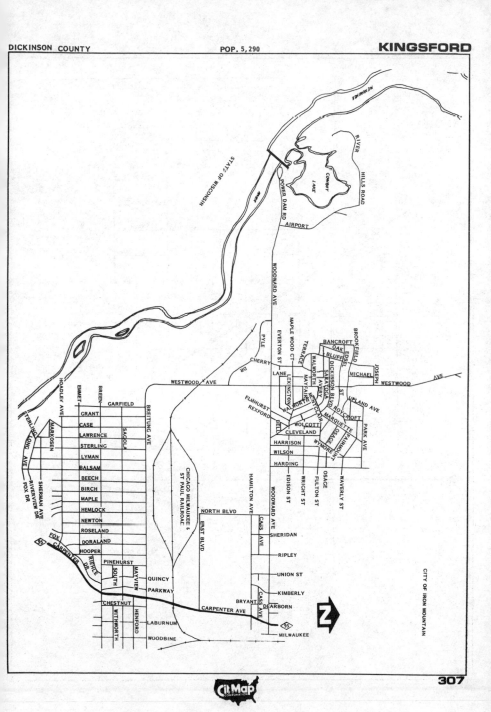

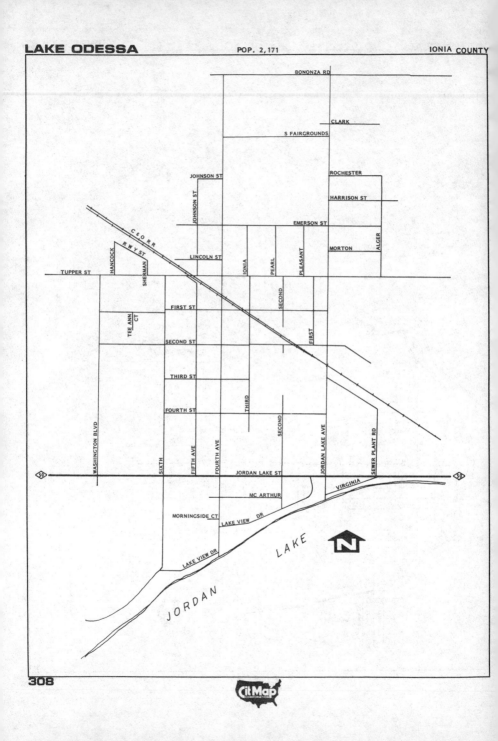

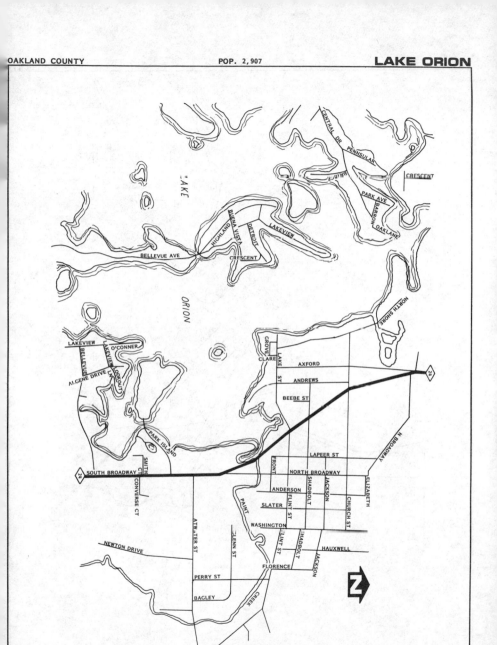

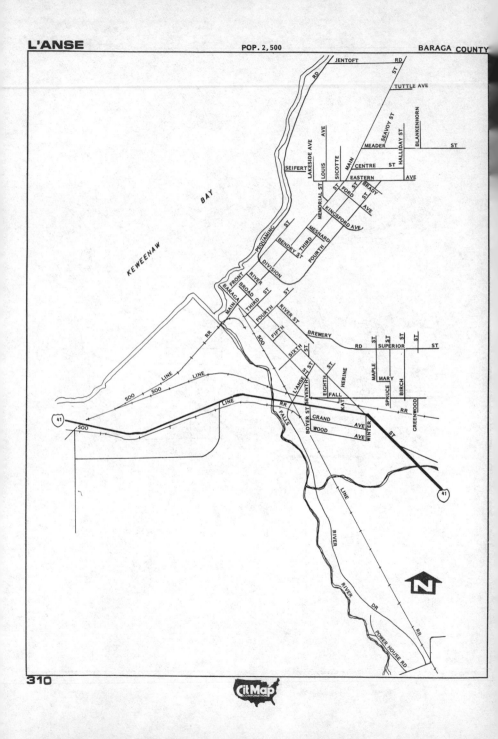

STREET INDEX LANSING

ABBEY CT	321	NE
ABINGTON	321	SE
ACKER LA	328	NW
ADA ST	323	SW
ADAMS ST	317	SW
ADDISON RD	315	SE
AFTON PL	316	SW
AIRPORT RD	315	NE
ALAN LA	315	SW
ALDEN DR	322	SW
ALDRICH DR	328	NE
ALFRED AVE	316	NW
ALGER ST	321	NW
ALLEGAN ST	321	NE
ALLEN ST	322	NE
ALLISON	328	NW
ALPHA ST	322	SW
ALPINE DR	327	NW
ALSAND CIR	316	NW
ALSDORF ST	321	SE
AMBERINA DR	315	SW
AMELIA LA	320	SE
AMERICAN RD	328	SW
AMHERST RD	316	NW
AMWOOD DR	328	SW
ANACAPRI DR	320	NW
ANDERSON ST	322	NW
ANDREA DR	316	NW
ANDREW AVE	316	NW
ANDREW JACKSON DR	328	SW
ANDRUS AVE	316	SW
ANNAPOLIS DR	328	SW
ANNETTA RD	327	SW
ANSON ST	327	NW
APPLE RIDGE	320	NW
APPLETON	328	NW
APPLE TREE LA	315	SE
APPLEWOOD DR	315	SE
APOLLO DR	316	NW
ARAGON DR	316	SW
ARCADIA DR	316	NW
ARDEN RD	315	SE
ARLENE DR	320	NE
ARLINGTON DR	320	NW
ARLINGTON RD	316	SW
ARMSTRONG RD LAN.	328	NW
ARMSTRONG DELTA	315	SW
ARTISAN DR	322	SE
ASH ST	317	SW
ASHLEY DR	327	SE
ASTOR AVE	321	SE
ATLAS AVE	321	SE
ATTWOOD DR	327	NE
AURELIUS RD	322	NE
AURORA DR	322	SE
AUTUMN LA	317	SE
AVALON ST	321	SW
AVERILL DR	321	SW
AVON ST	322	SW
BAKER ST	327	SE
BAILEY ST	323	NE
BALFOUR DR	327	SE
BALLARD ST	317	SW
BALZER ST	327	NE
BAMBI'S PATH	328	SW
BANCROFT AVE	321	NE
BANCHART ST	317	SW
BANK ST	322	SW
BARBARA DR	320	NE
BARCLAY	327	NW
BARDAVILLE ST	316	NW
BARNARD ST	322	NW
BARON BLVD	326	SW
BARNES AVE	321	NW
BARR AVE	328	NW
BARRITT ST	317	SE
BARSTOW RD	316	SW
BARTLETT ST	321	NE
BARTON DR	315	SE
BASCOM CIR	317	SE
BASSETT AVE	316	SE
BATES ST	317	SW
BATTENFIELD RD	328	NW
BAYOU PL	329	SW
BAYVIEW DR	326	NE
BAYWOOD BLVD	315	NE
BEACON HILL DR	316	SW
BEAL AVE	323	NW
BEARCREEK DR	315	SW
BEAUJARDIN DR	328	NE
BEAVER ST	317	SW
BEDFORD	321	SW
BEECH ST	322	NW
BEECHFIELD DR	328	SW
BEECH RIDGE DR	329	SW
BEECHWOOD	327	NE
BEE JAY DR	317	NW
BEL-AIR LA	327	NE
BELAIRE	321	SW
BELL ST	317	SW
BELLE CHASSE BLVD	329	NW
BELMAR	318	SW
BELMONT	321	SW
BENJAMIN DR	317	SW
BENNETT RD	317	NW
BENNINGTON DR.	320	NW
BENSCH ST	322	NE
BENTBROOK CIR	315	SW
BENTON BLVD	316	NW
BENTON ST	328	SW
BENTWOOD RD	315	SE
BERKLEY DR	321	SE
BERKSHIRE	321	SW
BERGMAN AVE	322	SW
BERNARD	327	NW
BERRY AVE	321	SE
BERRY RIDGE DR	329	SW
BERRYWOOD PL	315	SE
BERTEN ST	321	SE
BERWICK	327	NW
BERYL ST	328	SE
BETH LA	317	NW
BETTY CT	321	NW
BEULAH ST	322	NW
BILLMAR DR	323	SW
BILTMORE ST	316	NE
BIRCH ST	321	NE
BIRCHWOOD WAY	315	SW
BISHOP RD	326	SW
BITTERSWEET LA	320	SE
BLACK CT	317	SW
BLACKBERRY LA	315	SE
BLAIR ST	321	NE
BLAKE AVE	317	SE
BLANCHE AVE	320	NE
BLIESENER ST	327	SW
BLUEBELL DR	327	NE
BLUERIVER DR	326	NE
BLUFF ST	316	NE
BOETTCHER CT	328	NE
BOGART ST	327	NE
BOHNEY ST	322	SW
BOLLEY DR	317	SE
BOLLMAN DR	315	SW
BONAIR RD	316	SW
BORDEN CT	322	NW
BORN TR	328	SE
BOSTON BLVD	321	SE
BOXWOOD LA	315	SE
BOYTON DR	316	SW
BRAD ST	327	SE
BRADFORD LA	315	SW
BRADLEY AVE	321	SE
BRAE BURN DR	327	SW
BRANAN	321	SE
BRANDYWINE PL	317	NE
BRETTON RD	315	SE
BRIARFIELD DR	327	NE
S BRIARFIELD DR	330	NE
BRIARHILL DR	315	SW
BRIARWOOD DR	316	SW
BRIDGEPORT DR	326	SE
BRISBANE DR	321	SW
BRISTOL ST	327	NE
BRITTEN AVE	321	SE
BROADMOOR DR E.	315	NE
BROADMOOR DR W.	315	NE
BROOK RD DEWITT TWP	317	NW
BROOK ST LANSING	316	SE
BROOKDALE ST	328	SW
BRUCE AVE	321	NW
BRYNFORD AVE	321	NW
BUFFALO ST	321	NE
BURCHFIELD ST	322	SW
BURGUNDY BLVD	326	SW
BURNEWAY DR	327	NW
BURTON ST	317	NW
BURTRAW DR	320	SE
BUSH GARDENS LA	329	SW
BUTLER BLVD N.	321	NE
BUTLER BLVD S.	321	NE
BYRNES RD	316	SW
BYRON CIR	317	SE
CABOT ST	327	NW
CADILLAC AVE	321	SW
CADY CT	317	SW
CALHOUN	314	NE
CALL ST	317	SW
CALLIHAN CT	328	NE
CALSON DR	327	SE
CALVARY CIR	328	NW
CALVIN DR	327	NW
CAMBREY DR	316	SW
CAMBRIDGE RD	321	SW
CAMBRIDGE RD N.	321	SW
CAMBRIDGE RD S.	321	SW
CAMELOT DR	317	NE
CAMEO	328	SW
CAMERON	316	NE
CAMP ST	317	SW
CANARSIE DR	322	SW
CANTERBURY PL	321	SE
CANTON DR	320	NE
CANYON TR	315	SE
CAPITAL CITY BOULEVARD	316	NW
CAPITOL AVE N.	317	SW
CAPITOL AVE S.	322	NW
CARDIFF	320	SW
CARDINAL LA	315	SW
CAREY ST	321	NE
CAROL	321	SW
CARRIAGE HILL	315	NE
CARRIER ST	316	NE
CARVEL CT	327	NE
CASE ST	317	SW
CATALPA DR	327	NW
CATHERINE ST	321	NW
CATHERINE ST S.	321	SW
CATTAIL CORNER DRIVE	328	SE
CAVANAUGH RD	327	NE
CAWOOD ST	316	SE
CEDAR BROOK AVE	322	SW
CEDAR CT	327	NW
CEDAR ST N.	317	SW
CEDAR ST S.	322	SW
CEDAR ST (HOLT)	317	NW
CEDAR VIEW LA	328	SE
CENTENNIAL COURTYARD	328	SW
CENTER CT	317	SW
CENTER ST (HOLT)	317	SW
CENTER ST	323	NW
CENTRAL CIR	328	NW
CENTRAL CIR DR	320	SW
CHADBURNE DR	326	NE
CHANDLER RD	318	NE
CHANTICLEER TR	320	NW
CHARLES ST S.	322	NE
CHATEAU WAY	329	SW
CHATHAM RD	321	SE
CHELSEA AVE	321	NE
CHERBOURG DR	320	NW
CHERRY ST	322	NW
CHERRYLAND DR	328	NW
CHESAPEAKE DR	327	SW
CHESHIRE DR	326	SW
CHESLEY DR	320	NE
CHESLEY ST	320	NE
CHESTER RD	317	NE
CHESTNUT ST N.	321	NE
CHESTNUT ST S.	321	NE
CHICAGO AVE	316	SE
CHIEHO DR	315	SW
CHILSON AVE	317	NW
CHRIS J. DR	315	SW
CHRISTIANCY ST	322	SW
CHRISTIANSEN RD	327	NE
CHRISTINE DR	321	SW
CHRISTOPHER ST	316	SE
CHURCH CT	316	SE
CHURCHILL	327	NW
CINDY AVE	315	SW
CLAIBORNE DR	320	NE
CLARE ST	321	NE
CLAREMORE DR	328	SE
CLARK RD	315	SE
CLARK ST	317	SE
CLAYBORN RD	327	NW
CLAYTON ST	316	SE
CLEAR ST	322	NW
CLEARVIEW AVE	315	SE
CLEMENS AVE N.	322	NE
CLEMENS AVE S.	322	NE
CLEMENT RD	321	NW
CLEO ST	316	SE
CLEVELAND ST	317	SE
CLIFFORD ST	322	NE
CLIFTON AVE	322	SW
CLIMAX ST	322	NW
CLINTON ST	317	SW
CLINTON RD	315	NW
CLIPPERT ST N.	323	NW
CLIPPERT ST S.	323	NW
CLOVERLAND	328	NW
CLYDE ST	316	SE
CLYDESDALE RD	315	NE
COACH LIGHT COMMON	327	SW
COGSWELL DR	316	SW
COLCHESTER RD	316	SW
COLEMAN AVE	321	SE
COLEMAN RD	317	NW
COLEMAN RD E.	318	NW
COLLEGE RD	323	NE
COLLINS RD	328	NW
COLONIAL	322	SW
COLVIN CT	322	SW
COMFORT AVE	316	SE
COMMERCE AVE	328	NE
COMMONWEALTH AVE	317	SW
COMMUNITY ST	317	SW
CONCORD RD	321	SE
CONGRESS ST	317	SE
CONNERS AVE	327	NW
CONRAD AVE	328	SW
CONTINENTAL DR	321	SW
COOKIE	317	NW
COOLEY DR	321	SW
COOLIDGE AVE	316	SE
COOLIDGE RD	328	NE
COOPER AVE	321	SE
COPSY CORNER DR	328	SE
CORBETT ST	321	SE
CORNELIA DR	316	SW
CORNWALL DR	326	SW
COTTAGE AVE	322	NW
[illegible] CT	328	SW
COURT A	317	SW
COVINGTON	317	SE
COX BLVD	328	NW
CRANBERRY CT	320	NE
CRANBROOK AVE	316	NW
CREOLE WAY	329	SW
CREST ST	328	NW
CRESTON AVE	316	NW
CREYTS RD	315	SW
CROCUS AVE	327	NE
CROSS CT	322	NW
CROSS ST	316	SE
CULVER AVE	316	SE
CUMBERLAND RD	316	SW
CURRY LA	328	SW
CURTIS ST	316	SW
CUSTER AVE	322	NE
CYNWOOD ST	316	SE
CYPRESS ST	316	SE
DADSON DR	327	SE
DAFT ST	327	SE
DAHILIA DR	327	NE
DAKIN ST	322	NE
DALE AVE	317	NW
DALEFORD AVE	314	SE
DANA	317	NW
DANBURY CROSSROAD	327	SW
DARBY DR	316	SW
DARIEN DR	317	SE
DARRON DR	320	NE
DAVID LA	329	SW
DAVID ST	317	SW
DAVIDSON TR	322	SW
DAVIS AVE	321	SE
DAVIS HWY	326	NW
DEANNA DR	320	NE
DEERFIELD AVE	321	NW
DEERFIELD AVE S.	311	SW
DELAWARE DR	327	SW
DELBROOK AVE	327	NE
DELEVAN AVE	321	SE
DELL RD	328	SE
DELLEN ST	328	SW
DELRIDGE DR	329	SW
DELRAY DR	327	NE
DELTA ST	316	NW
DELTA RIVER RD	315	NW
DENALI DR	327	NE
DENNIS ST	327	NW
DENVER ST	322	SW
DEPOT ST	322	NW
DESANDER DR	317	NW
DETROIT ST N.	322	NE
DETROIT ST S.	322	NE
DEVONSHIRE AVE	322	SW
DEVONSHIRE DR	328	NW
DEWITT RD	316	NE
DEXTER DR N.	322	SW
DEXTER DR S.	322	SW
DIBBLE BLVD	320	NE
DIEHM RD	316	SE
DIER ST	328	NE
DILLINGHAM AVE	316	SW
DINSMORE DR	321	NE
DIVISION ST	320	SW
DOC STONG'S RD	328	SE
DODGE RIVER DR	317	SW
DONALD AVE LAN.	316	NW
DONALD DEWITT	328	NW
DONEGAL DR	326	SW
DONORA ST	322	SW
DONSON DR	327	SE
DORCHESTER CIR	327	NW
DORCHESTER WAY	320	NW
DORIS ST	327	NE
DORENE DR	320	NE
DORNELL AVE	327	NE
DORNET DR	320	NE
DORRANCE PL	322	NW
DOUGLAS AVE	317	SW
DOVELLE	316	SW
DOVER PL	321	SE
DOWNER AVE	317	SE
DOWNEY ST	316	NE
DREXEL RD	321	NW
DRURY LANE	317	SW
DRYER FARM RD	316	SW
DUMFRIES CIR	326	NE
DUNBAR DR	316	SW
DUNCKEL RD	329	NW
DUNLAP ST	321	SE
DUPRE AVE	326	SW
DURANT ST	316	SE
DURWELL DR	327	SE
DUVERNAY DR	328	NE
DWIGHT ST	317	SW
EARL LA	316	SW
EAST ST	317	NW
EAST ST N.	317	SW
E. ALDEN SQUARE	322	SW
EASTCIRCLE DR	320	NE
EASTFIELD RD	316	SW
E. GALWAY CIR	326	SW
EASTLAWN DR	328	NE
EAST THELMA DR	320	SE
EATON CT	327	NE
EATON RD	322	SW
EDDIE DR	315	SW
EDGEBROOK DR	316	SE
EDGEMONT BLVD	316	SW
EDGEWOOD BLVD	327	SE
EDGEWOOD CT	316	SE
EDGEWOOD RD	327	SE
EDISON AVE	322	SW
EDMORE ST	[illegible]	SE
EDMUND	315	SE
EDWARD ST	321	SE
EDWIN	321	SW
EIGHTH AVE	317	SW
EIGHTH ST N.	322	NW
EIGHTH ST S.	322	NW
ELIZABETH RD	315	SE
ELIZABETH ST	322	NE
ELLEN AVE	322	SW
ELLENDALE DR	328	SW
ELM ST E.	322	NW
ELM ST W.	322	NW
ELMIRA ST	317	NW
ELMORE RD	322	SW
ELMSHAVEN DR	320	NE
ELMWOOD DR	315	SE
ELVIN CT	322	NE
EMERALD	318	SW
EMERSON ST	316	SE
EMILY AVE	328	NW
ENGLEWOOD CT	316	SE
ENTERPRISE DR	328	NE
ERIE ST	322	NW
ESKES ST	317	NW
EUCLID PL	322	NW
EUREKA ST	322	NW
EVERETT LANE	322	SW
EVERETT ST	321	NE
EVERETT-DALE AVE	328	NW
EXECUTIVE DR	328	SW
FACTORY ST	317	SW
FAIRFAX RD	321	SW
FAIRFIELD AVE	317	NW
FAIRVIEW AVE N.	317	SE
FAIRVIEW AVE S.	322	NE
FAIRWAY LA	318	SW
FAITH CIR	328	NW
FARMSTEAD LANE	320	NW
FARRAND AVE	317	SW
FARR OUT PL	328	SE
FAUNA AVE	321	SW
FAYETTE ST	322	SW
FELT ST	316	NE
FELTON RD	315	NE
FENTON ST	327	NE
FERGUSON ST	322	NE
FERLEY ST	327	NE
FERN HILL CT	317	SW
FERNWOOD AVE	322	NE
FERROL CT	[illegible]	NW
FIDELITY RD	322	SW
FIELDCREST DR	315	SE
FIELDING DR	327	NW
FILLEY ST	316	SE
FIRESIDE DR	322	SW
FISHER DR	327	SE
FITTING AVE	316	SW
FLETCHER ST	321	SE
FLORENCE ST	317	NW
FONTAINE TRAIL	329	SW
FORBES ST	321	NE
FOREST AVE	322	SW
FOREST RD	322	SW
FOREST GLEN	316	SE
FOSTER AVE N.	322	NE
FOSTER ST	317	SE
FOXPOINTE	327	SW
FRANCIS AVE N.	322	NE
FRANCIS AVE S.	322	NE
FRANETTE RD	316	NW
FRANK ST	327	SW
FRANK 'N DOT CT	320	NW
FRANKLYNN DR	320	NW
FRED ST	328	NW
FREDRICK AVE	316	NE
FRIENDSHIP CIR	323	NW
FULTON PL	321	NE
GAGE ST	316	NE
GAIL LA	317	NW
GARDEN ST	322	SW
GARDENIA AVE	328	SW
GAREY CT	317	SW
GARFIELD AVE DELTA	315	SW
GARFIELD ST LANS.	322	SW
GARLAND ST	317	NW
GARY AVE	317	SW
GATEWOOD DR	320	NW
GATSBY CT	316	SW
GAY LANE	317	SE
GEERT CT	322	SE
GENESSEE DR N.	321	NE
GENESSEE DR S.	321	NE
GENESSEE ST E.	322	NW
GENESSEE ST W.	321	NW
GEORGE ST	321	SE
GEORGIA AVE	328	SW
GERALDINE DR	320	NE
GIBSON	327	NW
GIER ST E.	317	SW
GIER ST W.	316	SE
GILBERT CT	321	NE
GILFORD CIR	326	SE
GINGER SNAP LA	321	SW
GLADYS DR	320	NE
GLASGOW DR	321	SW
GLENBROOK	327	NW
GLENCOE WAY	316	SW
GLENDALE AVE	322	SW
GLENEDEN DR	316	SW
GLENN ST	316	SE
GLENROSE AVE	316	SE
GLENWOOD AVE	322	SW
GOODRICH ST	321	SE
GORDON AVE	321	SE
GOULD RD	316	SW
GRAHAM AVE	328	SW
GRAND AVE N.	322	NW
GRAND AVE S.	322	NW
GRAND CT	317	SW
GRANDELL AVE	316	NW
GRAND RIVER AVE N	315	NW
GRAND RIVER AVE E	317	SW
GRAND RIVER AVE W	316	SE
GRANDWOODS DR	315	SE
GRANGER DR	328	NW
GRANITE DR	320	NW
GRANT ST	322	SW
GRAPE ARBOR LA	315	SE
GRAY ST	321	NW
GREEN ST	317	SE
GREENBELT DR	317	NW
GREENBRIAR RD	315	SE
GREENCROFT RD	322	SW
GREENLAWN AVE	322	SW
GREEN MEADOWS DR	320	NW
GREENOAK AVE	316	NE
GREENWOOD ST LAN.	316	SE
GREENWOOD DEWITT	317	NW
GRENOBLE DR	320	NW
GRENVILLE LA	326	SE
GRISWOLD RD	317	NW
GROESBECK AVE	317	SE
GROESBECK BLVD	317	SE
GROVE RD	315	NE
GROVENBURG RD	327	SW
GUENTHER	320	SE

CitMap CORPORATION

LANSING

Street	Pg	Dir
GULL RD	320	NE
HAAC CT	322	NW
HAAC RD	327	SE
HACO DR	322	NW
HAGAN ST	316	SW
HALIFAX DR	327	NE
HALL ST	317	SW
HALLOWAY LA	328	NW
HAMELON ST	322	SW
HAMILTON AVE	322	SW
HAMMOND ST	321	SW
HAMPDEN DR	321	SW
HAMPSHIRE CIR	321	SW
HAMPSHIRE RD	321	SW
HANDY CT	317	SW
HANDY ST	317	SW
HANNAH ST	317	SW
HANOVER	320	SW
HAPEMAN ST	316	SE
HARDING AVE	328	SE
HARDING AVE	322	SW
HARLEY ST	322	NW
HAROLD ST	322	SW
HARPER'S WAY	328	SW
HARRIET AVE	320	NW
HARRIS ST	317	SW
HARRISON CT	315	SW
HART RD	326	NE
HARTFORD RD	326	NE
HARTON ST	322	NE
HARVEST LA	320	NW
HARWICK	316	SW
HASTING ST	320	NW
HATHAWAY ST	321	NW
HAVERHILL DR	327	NE
HAYFORD AVE N.	317	SE
HAZE ST	321	NW
HAZEL ST	317	NW
HAZEL ST E.	318	SE
HAZEL ST W.	322	SW
HAZELWOOD DR	328	SW
HEALD PL	322	NW
HEATHER LA	321	NW
HEATHGATE DR	326	NE
HEIGHTS AVE	317	NE
HEIN AVE	327	SE
HELEN ST	322	NW
HELMAN BLVD	328	SE
HEMLOCK PL	321	SE
HEPFER	327	NW
HERRICK DR	321	SE
HESS AVE	321	SE
HERBERT ST	322	NW
HICKORY ST LANS.	322	NW
HICKORY DEWITT	322	NE
HICKS CT	317	NW
HIGH ST	317	SW
HIGH ST E	317	SW
HIGH ST N	317	SW
HILL ST	322	NW
HILLBORN LA	321	NW
HILLCREST ST	327	SE
HILLGATE WAY	321	SW
HILLIARD RD	327	NE
HILLSDALE ST E.	322	SW
HILLSDALE ST W.	321	SW
HILLTOP DR	315	SW
HI-MOUNT CIR	317	NW
HODGE AVE	318	SW
HOLIDAY DR	321	SE
HOLLAND AVE	327	SW
HOLLY CT	321	SW
HOLLY WAY	321	SW
HOLLYWOOD ST	316	SE
HOLMES RD	316	SE
HOLMES ST N.	322	NE
HOLMES ST S.	322	NE
HOMER ST	316	SW
HOMEWOOD AVE	322	NW
HONEYSUCKLE LA	320	NW
HOOVER ST	320	NE
HOPKINS AVE	317	SE
HORACE RD	317	SE
HORSTMEYER RD	327	NW
HORTON AVE	317	SE
HOSMER ST N.	322	NE
HOSMER ST N.	322	NE
HOWARD AVE N.	322	NE
HOWARD AVE S.	322	NE
HOWE ST	316	SW
HOYT AVE	322	SW
HUGHES RD	327	NW
HULL CT	316	SW
HUNGERFORD ST	321	NW
HUNT ST	317	SW
HUNTER BLVD	320	NW
HUNTER'S RIDGE DR	328	NW
HUNTER RIDGEWOOD	328	NW
HURON	321	NE
HYLAND ST	316	SW
HYLEWOOD AVE	322	SW
ILLINOIS AVE	317	SE
IMPERIAL	317	SE
INDEPENDENCE LA	330	SW
INDIANA AVE	317	SW
NDUSTRIAL PKWY	322	NW
NGERSOL RD	315	NW
NCHAM ST	321	NW
ONIA ST E.	322	NW
ONIA ST W.	321	SW
NNER CT	321	SW
NVERARY	321	NW
NVERNESS AVE	321	NW
RENE CT	328	SE
RIS AVE	320	NW
IRVINGTON AVE	328	NW
IRVINGTON AVE E.	328	NE
ISBELL ST	322	NW
ISLAND	322	SW
IVAN DR	322	NW
JACKSON ST	317	SW
JAMES ST	317	SW
JANES WAY	321	SW
JASON CT	322	NW
JENISON AVE N.	316	SW
JENISON AVE S.	321	SW
JEROME ST	322	SW
JERREE ST	317	SW
JERRY RD	316	NE
JESSOP AVE	328	NW
JEWEL AVE	322	SW
JOHN ST	317	SW
JOHNSON AVE	317	SW
JOLLY RD	326	NE
JOLLY CEDAR CT	328	SE
JONES ST	322	SW
JONES LAKE ST	321	SE
JONI'S CIR	316	NW
JOSEPHINE ST	322	SW
JOSHUA ST	328	SW
JULIA ST	322	SW
JULIAN AVE	320	NW
JULIE DR	317	SW
JUNIPER	327	NE
JUNE ST	317	SE
JUSAMERE AVE	328	SW
JUSTICE ST	328	SE
KALAMAZOO PLAZA	322	NW
KALAMAZOO ST E.	322	NE
KALAMAZOO ST W.	321	SW
KAPLAN ST	316	SW
KAREN	327	NW
KAREN LEE DR	320	NW
KATE ST	318	SE
KAYNORTH RD	322	SW
KEEGAN CT	321	NW
KEENEY CT	322	NW
KELLYBROOK LA	328	SW
KELSEY AVE	328	SE
KENBROOK RD	327	NW
KENDALWOOD DR	317	NW
KENDON DR	326	NW
KENILWORTH DR	317	NE
KENNEDY DR	328	NW
KENTFIELD DR	328	NE
KENWAY DR	321	NW
KENWICK	322	SW
KERRY ST	316	SE
KESSLER	326	NW
KEYSTONE AVE	327	NE
KIEPPE'S CT	322	NE
KILBERRY RD	320	SE
KILBORN ST	316	SE
KILLARNEY CT	325	SE
KIMBERLY	321	NE
KING AVE	316	SE
KINGDON AVE	327	SE
KINGSLEY CT	320	SE
KIPLING BLVD	321	SW
KIRBY DR	320	NE
KIRKWOOD ST	317	SE
KNOLL CIRCLE	315	SW
KNOLLWOOD AVE	316	SW
KUERBITZ DR	316	NE
KURT DR	327	NW
KYES RD	322	SW
LABELLE RD	327	SE
LAFAYETTE AVE	316	SE
LAFAYETTE ST	316	NW
LAFAYETTE LA	326	NW
LAHOMA ST	321	SW
LAKE LANSING RD	317	NE
LAKEVIEW	316	SE
LAMA CIR	328	NW
LAMONT ST	316	SW
LAMOREAUX LA	329	SW
LANCELOT ST	317	NE
LANSDOWN DR	326	SW
LANSING AVE	316	SE
LAPEER ST	321	NE
LARCH	317	NW
LARCH ST S.	322	NW
LARNED ST	317	SW
LAROCQUE CIR	321	NW
LARRABEE DR	328	NW
LASALLE BLVD	322	NE
LASALLE GARDENS	322	NE
LATHAM ST	317	NE
LATHROP ST	322	NE
LAUDERHILL CIR	326	NE
LAURIE	327	NW
LAWDOR RD	321	SW
LAWLER CT	328	SE
LEAWOOD DR	322	SW
LE GRAND DR	327	NE
LEITRAM ST	321	NE
LELAND PL	321	NE
LEMROCK CT	316	SE
LENAWEE ST E.	322	NW
LENAWEE ST W.	321	NE
LENORE AVE	321	SW
LENTZ CT	321	NW
LEON ST	316	SW
LEONARD CT	321	SE
LERNER WAY	328	NW
LESHER PL	322	NW
LESLIE ST	322	NW
LIBBIE ST	320	SE
LIBERTY ST	317	NW
LIMERICK CIR	316	NE
LINCOLN AVE	322	SW
LINCOLN CT	315	SW
LINDBERGH DR	322	SW
LINDEN GROVE AVE	322	NW
LINDY DR	315	SW
LINVAL ST	322	SW
LINWOOD CIR	317	SW
LINWOOD ST	316	SW
LITTLE	322	NE
LOA ST	321	SE
LOCHMOOR ST	327	NW
LOCKBRIDGE DR	321	SE
LOCUST LA	320	NW
LODER CIR	328	NW
LOGAN ST	327	NW
LOGAN ST N.	321	NW
LOGAN ACCESS	321	SW
LONDAL CIR	328	SE
LONDAL CT	328	SE
LONDON DR	322	NE
LONG BLVD	328	SW
LONGMEADOW RD	327	NW
LORAINE ST	321	SE
LORETTA ST	328	SE
LOTIPAC PL	315	SW
LOUIS ST	321	SW
LOUISA ST	328	SW
LOWCROFT ST	322	SW
LOWELL RD	315	SW
LUCIE	327	NW
LUJER DR	328	NW
LUWANNA DR	328	NE
LYMAN DR	317	SW
LYNCOTT	328	NW
LYONS AVE	322	SW
MACDONALD ST E.	322	NE
MACDOUGAL CIR	326	NW
MACON AVE	316	SW
MADISON ST W.	316	SW
MAGNOLIA AVE N.	317	SE
MAGNOLIA AVE S.	322	SE
MAHLON ST	321	SE
MAIN ST E.	322	NE
MAIN ST W.	322	NE
MAISONETTE DR	328	SE
MAJESTIC	317	NW
MALIBU DR	321	SW
MALL DR E.	315	SW
MALL DR W.	315	SW
MALONEY ST	321	SE
MALPASO	328	NE
MANCHESTER ST	317	SW
MANDELL ST	328	SE
MANLEY DR	322	NE
MANOR DR	321	SE
MAPLE ST E.	317	NE
MAPLE ST W.	316	SE
MAPLEHILL AVE	328	NE
MAPLEWOOD AVE	320	NW
MARCIA DR	321	SE
MARCUS ST	320	NW
MARCY AVE	326	SE
MARGUERITE AVE	316	SE
MARILYN PLAZA	321	SW
MARION AVE	321	SE
MARION ST	327	SE
MARK AVE	317	NW
MARKLEY	322	SW
MARK TWAIN DR	317	SW
MARLAND DR	321	SE
MARLENE'S CT	328	SW
MAR-MOOR DR	321	SE
MARQUETTE ST	316	SE
MARSCOT DR	328	SE
MARSHALL ST	322	NE
MARTIN ST	321	SE
MARY AVE	317	NE
MARY ST	317	NE
MARYLAND AVE	317	SE
MARYS WAY	328	NW
MARYWOOD AVE	327	SE
MASON ST	327	NE
MASSACHUSETTS AVE	317	SW
MAX AVE	321	SE
MAY ST	321	SE
MAYBEL ST	327	NW
MAYCROFT RD	315	NW
MAYFIELD DR	317	NW
McARTHUR	316	SW
McCOURT ST	328	NW
McCULLOUGH ST	322	NE
McGARRY ST	328	SW
McINTYRE CT	322	SW
McKIM AVE	322	SW
McKINLEY ST	317	NE
McPHERSON AVE	322	NE
MEADOWCROFT DR	317	NW
MEADOWLANE DR	316	SW
MEADOWLAWN ST	317	NW
MEADOWLEDGE DR	320	NW
MEADOWVIEW LA	320	NW
MEAFORD ST	321	NE
MECHANIC ST	317	SE
MEESE DR	327	SE
MEL AVE	318	SW
MELODY LA	321	NE
MELVIN	316	SE
MEMORY LA	329	SW
MEMPHIS ST	321	NE
MERCANTILE WAY	316	SE
MERRILL ST	321	SE
MERSEY LA	321	NE
MICHELLE CIR	316	SE
MICHIGAN AVE E.	322	NW
MICHIGAN AVE E.	322	NW
MIDDLE ST	317	NW
MIDVALE AVE	322	SW
MIDWOOD ST	327	NW
MIFFLIN AVE	322	SW
MILDRED ST	316	NW
MILL ST	322	NE
MILLER RD	322	SW
MILLETT HWY	320	NW
MILLOAK AVE	328	SW
MILLSBOROUGH CIR E.	313	3W
MILLSBOROUGH CIR W.	315	SW
MILL STONE ST	328	SE
MILL STREAM LA	328	SW
MILL WHEEL DR	328	SE
MILLWOOD	315	NW
MINT RD	316	NE
MIRIAM ST	328	SE
MITCHELL AVE	316	SW
MOFFITT ST	327	NW
MONROE ST	317	NW
MONTEGO DR	327	NW
MONTEVIDEO DR	327	NW
MONTICELLO DR	327	NW
MOONLIGHT LA	322	SW
MOORES RIVER DR	321	SW
MORGAN ST	322	NE
MORNINGSIDE	316	SW
MORRIS AVE	315	SW
MOSELY AVE	317	SW
MOSHER ST	322	NE
MOTOR AVE	322	SW
MT HOPE AVE	322	SW
MT HOPE AVE W.	320	SW
MUNSON ST	322	NE
MUREL DR	326	NW
MUSKEGON AVE	316	NW
NANCY ST	339	SW
NARRAGANSET DR	322	SE
NETTIE AVE	317	NW
NEWARK AVE	327	NW
NEWKIRK DR	326	NW
NEWPORT DR	316	NW
NEWTON ST	316	SW
NINTH AVE	317	NW
NIPP AVE	321	NW
NOEL AVE	326	NW
NONETTE DR	327	NW
NORBURN WAY	339	SE
NORMAN ST	322	NW
NORTH ST E	317	SW
NORTH ST W	317	SW
NORTHAMPTON WAY	317	NW
N. DALE RD	316	NW
NORTHLANE DR	320	NW
NORTHRUP ST	330	NE
NORTHWARD DR	317	NW
NORTHWEST AVE	316	NW
NORWICH RD	322	SW
NORWICK ST	320	NE
NORWOOD RD	316	SW
NOTTINGHAM RD	321	SW
NOVIS AVE	317	NW
NUGGET DR	320	NW
OAK ST	317	SW
OAKBROOK DR	329	SW
OAKCLIFT	316	SW
OAKCREST DR	320	NE
OAK KNOLL DR	328	NW
OAKLAND AVE	316	SW
OBAN RD	321	SW
OHIO AVE	317	SE
OLD CASTLE CIR	326	NE
OLD ERIN WAY	320	NW
OLD GRAND RIVER AVE	315	SW
OLD MILL LA	315	SW
OLD RIVER TR	321	SW
OLDS AVE	316	SW
ONTARIO ST	322	NE
ORA ST	322	NW
ORCHARD ST	317	SW
ORCHARD GLEN AVE	328	SW
ORLEANS WAY	329	SW
ORMOND AVE	317	SE
OSBAND AVE	321	SE
OSBORN RD	321	NW
OTTAWA ST E.	322	NW
OTTAWA ST W.	321	NE
OTTO ST	322	NE
OVERLEA DR	316	SW
OWEN CT	316	SW
OWEN ST	316	SW
OXFORD RD	321	SW
PACIFIC ST	322	NE
PACIFIC PKWY	322	SW
PACKARD AVE	321	SW
PALISADE DR	321	SW
PALMER ST	321	NW
PAMELA	322	NE
PATRICIA ST	327	NE
PARIS AVE	322	NE
PARISAN DR	328	SE
PARK AVE	321	SE
PARK LA	323	NE
PARK PL	321	SE
PARK ST	320	SE
PARK TERR E.	317	SW
PARKDALE ST	322	NE
PARKER ST	322	NW
PARK MEADOWS DR	329	SW
PARKVIEW LA	322	NW
PARKVIEW ST	322	SW
PARKWAY DR	321	SW
PARK WEST DR	320	NW
PARKWOOD DR	320	NW
PATTENGILL AVE	321	NW
PAUL AVE	316	NW
PAULSON ST	316	NE
PEARL ST	317	SW
PECOS DR	320	NE
PEGGY PL	321	SE
PEMBROKE RD	316	SW
PEMBROOK PL	320	NW
PENDLETON DR	316	SW
PENNSYLVANIA AVE N.	322	NW
PENNSYLVANIA AVE S.	322	NW
PENNSYLVANIA CT 32	322	NW
PENNWAY DR	328	NW
PENROD CT	322	NE
PENROSE DR	322	NE
PEONY PL	327	NE
PEPPERHILL DR	315	SE
PEPPERTREE LA	317	SE
PERE MARQUETTE DR	322	NW
PERKINS ST	322	NE
PERSHING DR	322	SW
PERSONS CT	317	SW
PETTIS ST	321	NE
PHEASANT AVE	327	SW
PHYLLIS ST	315	NE
PICARDY ST	327	SW
PICKETTS WAY	320	NW
PICKTON DR	320	NE
PICKWICK PL	316	SW
PICO AVE	321	SE
PIERCE RD	327	NE
PIERPONT ST	328	NE
PIERSON HWY	320	SW
PINE CIR	329	SW
PINE ST N.	321	NE
PINE ST S.	321	NE
PINE DELL DR	329	SW
PINE-DELL DR N.	329	SW
PINE-DELL DR S.	329	SW
PINETREE RD	327	NW
PINEWOOD	327	NE
PINEY POINT DR	315	SW
PINGREE ST	321	SE
PINO	326	NW
PIPER	330	NW
PLAINFIELD DR	327	SW
PLAZA DR	316	NW
PLEASANT ST	321	SW
PLEASANT GROVE RD	322	SE
PLEASANT VIEW AVE	327	NE
PLUM HOLLOW DR	315	SE
PLYMOUTH DR	322	NW
POLLARD RD	327	NW
POLLY AVE	317	SW
POMPTON CIRCLE	327	NW
PONTIAC ST	322	SW
PONY TR	315	SW
POPLAR ST	321	SE
PORTER ST	317	SW
POST OAK LA	317	SE
POTOMAC CIRCLE	321	SW
POTTER ST	328	NW
POXSON AVE	321	SE
PRINCETON AVE	316	SW
PRINCETON DR	320	NW
PRIVATE DR	316	NE
PRIVATE RD A	322	SW
PRIVATE RD B	322	SW
PROSPECT ST	322	NE
PROVINCIAL HOUSE DR	322	SE
PULASKI ST	321	SW
QUADRILLA LA	329	SW
QUEEN ST	316	SE
QUENTIN AVE	321	SE
QUINCY LA	321	SE
RACE ST	317	SW
RADFORD DR	328	NW
RADFORD RD	327	SW
RAIDER ST	322	NW
RAMADA DR	328	SW
RAMPARTE PATH	329	SW
RANDALL ST	317	SW
RANDOLPH ST	316	SE
RANGER RD	316	NE
RAPIDAN	328	NW
RARITAN RD	328	NW
RAVENSWOOD DR	316	SE
RAYMOND ST	316	SE
RAYNELL	327	SW
RAY ST	317	SW
REASONER ST	317	SW
RED CT	322	SW
RED RD	322	SW
REDNER ST	320	NE
REDWOOD DR	320	NE
REED DR	328	NE
REGEN ST	322	NE
REMY DR	316	NE
RENEE ST	317	NW
RENFREW WAY	321	NE
RENKER RD	320	NE
RENNER ST	321	NE
REVERE PL	321	NE
REX ST	328	NE
R.G. CURTIS AVE	320	SW
RHEAMOUNT AVE	317	SW
RICE CT	321	SW
RICHARD AVE	322	NE
RICHARD RD	327	SW
RICHMOND ST	327	SW
RICHWOOD ST	322	SW
RIDGEFIELD RD	316	SW
RIDGELINE DR	317	SE
RILEY ST	322	SW
RILEY RIDGE	315	SW

Street	Pg	Dir	Street	Pg	Dir	Street	Pg	Dir
RISDALE AVE	327	NW	SPOKANE AVE	328	NW	WADSWORTH DR S.	327	NW
RISLEY DR	316	SE	SPRING ST	322	NW	WAGONWHEEL LA	315	SE
RITA ST	322	SW	SPRINGBROOK LA	316	SW	WAINWRIGHT AVE	327	NW
RIVER CT	315	SE	SPRINGBROOK RD	316	SW	WAKEFIELD AVE	321	SE
RIVER ST	322	NW	SPRINGFIELD LA	317	SE	WALKER ST	317	NW
RIVER RIDGE DR	315	SE	SPRUCEWOOD AVE	327	SE	WALKER ST	317	SW
RIVERSHELL LA	326	NE	STABLER ST	328	NW	WALMAR DR	315	SW
RIVERSIDE CT	316	SE	STAFFORD AVE	328	NW	WALSH ST	322	NE
RIVER VIEW HGTS	321	NW	STANLEY CT	322	NE	WALTON DR	327	NE
ROBERTS ST	328	NW	STANLEY ST	316	SE	WARBLER WAY	328	SE
ROBERTS LANE	322	SW	STARLIGHT LA	321	SW	WARREN AVE	321	NW
ROBERTSON AVE	316	SE	STARR AVE	327	NW	WARRINGTON ST	328	SW
ROBINS RD	315	SE	STATE RD	315	NW	WARWICK DR	327	NE
ROBINSON ST	322	SW	STATE ST	316	SE	WASHINGTON	315	NW
ROCKDALE AVE	315	SW	STATEN AVE	322	SW	WASHINGTON AVE N.	317	SW
ROCKFORD RD E.	322	SW	STERLING AVE	321	SE	WASHINGTON AVE S.	322	SW
ROCKINGHAM DR	326	SE	STIEFFEL ST	320	NE	WASHTENAW ST	321	NW
ROCKLEDGE DR	320	NW	STILLWELL	327	NW	WATER ST	317	SW
ROCKWAY	321	SE	STOCKMAN CT	316	SE	WAVERLY RD	311	NW
ROLFE RD	317	NW	STOCKWELL RD	317	NW	WAVERLY HILL RD	321	SW
RONALD ST	327	NN	STOLL RD	320	NE	WAYBURN RD	322	SW
ROOSEVELT AVE	316	SE	STONEHEIGH DR	320	SW	WAYCROSS DR	328	SW
ROSADELL AVE	321	SE	STONER RD	321	NW	WAYFARER LA	322	SW
ROSAMOND ST	322	NE	STONE RIDGE DR	320	NW	WAYLAND DR	315	SE
ROSCOMMON DR	326	NE	STONEWOOD DR	318	SW	WAYNE ST	328	NE
ROSE CT	316	SE	STONEY POINT DR	315	SW	WEALD WAY	328	SE
ROSEDALE RD	328	SW	STRATFORD	327	NW	WEBER DR	312	SW
ROSELAWN AVE	316	SE	SUMMERVILLE AVE	316	SE	WEBSTER ST LANS.	315	SW
ROSEMARY ST	321	NN	SUMMIT ST	317	SW	WEBSTER DELTA	327	SW
ROSENEATH AVE	316	SW	SUMPTER ST	327	NW	WEDGEWOOD DR	327	NW
ROTH DR	328	SW	SUNDERLAND RD	321	SW	WEGER PL	328	SW
ROUSE ST	328	NW	SUNNY LA	316	SW	WEISSMAN DR N.	316	NE
ROYALE DR	329	SW	SUNNYSIDE AVE	322	SW	WEISSMAN DR S.	316	NE
RUBINA WAY	316	EW	SUNROSE AVE	327	NE	WEISSMAN DR W.	316	NE
RUBY GLASS RD	315	SW	SUNSET AVE	316	SE	WELLESLEY	321	SE
RULISON ST	321	NE	SUPERIOR ST	327	SE	WELLINGTON ST	321	SE
RUMSEY AVE	322	SW	SUSAN DR	317	NW	WENDY CIR	327	NE
RUNDLE AVE S.	321	SE	SUSSEX	321	NW	WESLEY PL	316	NW
RUNDLE AVE W.	321	SE	SWANEE DR	327	NW	WEST RD	316	NW
RUSSELL ST	317	SW	SWEET RD	316	NE	WEST ST	321	NE
RUTH AVE	328	SW	SYCAMORE ST S.	321	NE	W. BICKETT BLVD	328	SE
SABLAIN PARKWAY	322	SW	SYCAMORE ST	316	SE	WESTBRIDGE CIR	320	NE
SADIE CT	316	SE	SYLVAN RD	316	SW	WESTBURY RD	316	SW
SAGEBRUSH	315	SE	SYLVESTER AVE	327	NW	WESTCHESTER RD	321	SW
SAGINAW ST E.	317	SE	SYRINGA DR	328	NW	WESTCHESTER RD E.	321	SW
SAGINAW ST W.	315	SW	TAFFY	330	NE	WESTERN AVE	321	NW
ST CLARE ST	321	NE	TAFT ST	317	SE	WESTFIELD RD	316	SW
ST JOSEPH ST W.	320	NW	TAMMANY AVE	322	SE	WEST GATE	317	NE
ST MARYS CT	327	NE	TAYLOR ST	316	SE	WESTGATE RD	321	SW
SAMANTHA ST	328	NW	TECUMSEH AVE	316	NE	WEST HANGER DR	316	SW
SANDERS RD	320	SW	TECUMSEH RIVER RD	316	SW	WESTHAVEN BLVD	320	NE
SANFORD ST	317	NW	TEEL AVE	322	SW	WESTHILL DR	320	SE
SANDHILL RD	329	SW	TEEL CT	322	SW	WEST LEDGE DR	320	NW
SANDHURST DR	321	SW	TELLER TR	326	NE	WESTMONT	316	NW
SANDLYN	321	NW	TENNY ST	322	SW	WEST MORELAND AVE	316	SE
SAND POINT DR	315	SE	TENNYSON LA	327	NW	WESTON ST	320	NE
SAN GABRIEL	315	SE	TERMINAL RD	316	NE	WESTPORT DR	316	SW
SARATOGA WAY	326	SW	THACKIN DR	320	SE	WESTVALE CIR	320	NE
SAVOY CT	321	NE	THEO AVE	320	NE	WESTWOOD AVE	316	NE
SCARBOROUGH DR	322	SW	THEODORE ST	316	SE	WEXFORD DR	327	NW
SCHAFER RD	327	SE	THOMAS ST	317	SW	WEYMOUTH CT	327	NE
SCHLEE ST	317	SW	THOMAS L PKWY	315	SE	WHISPERING LA	320	NW
SCOTTMAR DR	328	SE	THOMAS L PKWY E.	315	SE	WHITELEY CT	328	SW
SCOTT PARK DR	322	NW	THOMAS L PKWY W	316	SE	WHITE OAKS DR	315	NE
SEAWAY DR	326	NE	THOMPSON ST	317	SW	WICKHAM DR	316	SW
SELFRIDGE BLVD	327	SE	THORNAPPLE LA	320	SE	WIELAND RD	317	NW
SELLER	323	NE	TIFFANY LA	329	SW	WIELAND ST	317	SW
SELMA ST	328	SE	TIMBER DR	316	SW	WILDWOOD AVE	320	NE
SENATE DR	317	SE	TINDALALAYA DR	320	NE	WILDWOOD WAY	328	NW
SEVENTH AVE N.	317	NW	TINLEY DR	328	SW	WILLARD AVE	321	SE
SEYMOUR AVE	317	SW	TISDALE AVE	322	SW	WILLEMAN ST	328	NW
SHADYHILL LA	315	SE	TOBOGGAN LA	322	SW	WILLIAMS RD	326	SE
SHAFFER CT	316	SW	TODD AVE	322	SW	WILLOUGHBY RD	327	SE
SHANNON LA	315	SW	TORRENCE CT	328	SW	WILLOW ST	316	SW
SHARON CT	321	NE	TOWNSEND ST	328	NW	WILLOW HWY	323	SW
SHEFFER AVE	321	NW	TRANTER ST	316	NW	WILLOWAY LA	329	SW
SHEFFIELD BLVD	326	NE	TRAPPERS COVE TR	320	NE	WILLOW BEND DR	315	SW
SHELDON ST	317	SE	TRENT ST	327	SW	WILLOWBROOK DR	315	SW
SHELTER LA	318	SW	TRENTON PL	329	NW	WILLOW RIDGE DR	329	SW
SHEPARD ST	322	NE	TRESSA DR	322	NE	WILSON AVE	322	SW
SHERIDAN RD	317	NW	TRIANON TR	323	SW	WILSON ST	316	NW
SHERWOOD LA	315	NE	TRUCK CT	323	NW	WINDIMERE DR	326	NE
SHETLAND RD LANS.	315	NE	TRUDY LA	327	SW	WINDMILL LI	328	SE
SHETLAND DEWITT	321	NE	TRUMAN CIR	326	SW	WINDSOR DR	321	SE
SHIAWASSEE ST E.	322	NW	TRUMBULL ST	317	SW	WINDSOR ST	316	NE
SHIAWASSEE ST W.	321	NW	TRUXTON LA	327	SE	WINDWARD DR	316	NE
SHILOH WAY	320	NW	TULANE DR	317	SE	WINIFRED AVE	320	NE
SHIPPEL ST	328	SE	TULIP AVE	317	NE	WINSTON AVE	317	SW
SHIRANN	316	SE	TURNER RD	323	NW	WINTERSET DR	327	SE
SHIRLEY ST	328	NW	TURNER ST	316	NW	WISCONSIN AVE	316	SW
SHORT ST	321	NE	UPTON RD	316	SW	WISE RD	327	SW
SHREVE ST	327	SE	VALENCIA BLVD	327	SE	WOOD DR	320	NW
SHUBEL AVE	322	SW	VALLEY RD	317	NW	WOOD RD	317	NE
SHULTZ ST	317	NW	VANCE ST	317	SW	WOOD ST	317	NE
SIDNEY ST	327	NW	VANS CT	328	NW	WOODBINE AVE	321	SE
SILVER BAY LA	326	NE	VASSAR DR	317	SE	WOODBRIDGE DR	326	NE
SIMS CT	316	SE	VELTEMA DR	329	SW	WOODBURY AVE	317	SW
SKYE RD	321	SW	VERLINDEN AVE	316	SE	WOODCREEK LA	326	NE
SKYWAY LA	320	SE	VERMONT AVE LANS.	317	SW	WOODGATE DR	327	SE
SNOW RD	321	SE	VERMONT DELTA	315	NW	WOODHAVEN DR	320	NE
SNOWGLEN LA	316	SW	VERNON AVE	322	SW	WOODLAWN AVE	321	SE
SOAPSTONE DR	315	SW	VERNSON DR	327	SE	WOODLYN	321	NW
SOMERCROFT DR	317	SE	VICKIE CT	328	NW	WOODMAN RD	322	NE
SOMERSET RD	328	SW	VICTOR AVE	321	NE	WOODRUFF AVE	317	SE
SOUTH ST E.	322	NW	VICTORIA DR	327	SE	WOODVIEW DR	321	SW
SOUTHBROOK AVE	328	NW	VIKING RD	321	SW	WORDEN DR	328	SW
SOUTHGATE AVE	328	NW	VILLAGE DR	328	NW	WORTHMORE AVE	315	SW
SOUTHFIELD CT	327	SW	VINCENT CT	327	NE	WREN	320	NW
SOUTHLAND AVE	321	SW	VINE ST	322	NE	WYETH DR	320	NW
S PARK BLVD	322	SW	VIOLA DR	327	NN	YORK RD	321	SW
SOUTHWICK CIR	320	NE	VIOLET CT	322	SW	YOUNG AVE	316	NW
SPARROW AVE	321	SE	VIRGINIA ST	322	NE	YUNKER ST	327	SE
SPEARBERRY LA	315	SE	WABASH RD	321	SW			
SPENCER ST	321	NE	WACHTEL DR	319	SW			
SPIKE ST	316	SE	WADDEL RD	376	NE			
			WADSWORTH DR N.	327	NW			

Street	Page	Dir
ABBOTT RD	318	SE
AKERS RD	324	NE
ALBERT AVE	323	NE
ALGONQUIN WAY	324	NE
ALTON ST	318	SE
AMBER DR	324	NW
ANDERSON WAY	318	SE
ANN ST	323	NE
APACHE DR	324	SW
APPLEGATE LA	318	SE
ARAPAHO TR	324	NE
ARBOR DR	323	NW
ARDMORE AVE	324	NW
ARDSON RD	323	NW
ARROW HEAD RD	324	SE
ATHERTON DR	323	NE
AUDITORIUM RD	323	NE
AUDUBON RD	318	SE
BAILEY ST	318	SW
BAINBRIDGE DR	318	SW
BAKER ST	322	SW
BALDWIN CT	318	SE
BARCLAY	323	NE
BASSWOOD CIR	318	SW
BASSWOOD ST	318	SW
BAYMEADOWS CT	325	SW
BEAL ST	321	SE
BEAUMONT RD	323	SE
BEDFORD RD	319	SW
BEECH ST	323	NE
BEECHLAWN CT	318	SW
BELDING CT	324	SE
BELMONTE CIR	324	SE
BENNETT RD	324	SE
BERKSHIRE LA	324	SE
BESSEMAUR DR	318	SE
BIBER ST	318	NE
BIRCH RD	323	NE
BIRCH ROW DR	318	SW
BIRCHWOOD DR	325	SW
BLACK FOOTE WAY	325	SW
BLACK STONE TR	325	SW
BLANCHETTE DR	318	SW
BLOOMFIELD DR	325	NW
BLOSSOM LA	324	SW
BLUE HAVEN CT	318	SW
BLUE HAVEN DR	324	SW
BLYTHEFIELD DR	319	SW
BOGUE ST	323	NE
BOLTWOOD DR	318	SE
BONITA CIR	319	SW
BOULEVARD DR	325	SW
BOXTREE LA	318	SE
BOXWOOD LA	318	SE
BRAMBLE DR	318	SW
BRENTWOOD AVE	324	NW
BRIARCLIFF DR	324	SW
BRIARWICK CT	329	SW
BRIARWICK DR	324	SW
BRODY RD E	325	NW
BRODY RD N	323	NW
BRODY RD S	323	NW
BRODY RD W	323	NW
BROOKLINE CT	319	SW
BRYANT DR	318	SE
BUCKDEN WAY	319	SW
BUGLERS WAY	319	SW
BURCHAM DR	318	SE
BURGUNDAY SQ	318	SE
BURNING BUSH DR	324	SW
BURROWS AVE	318	SE
BURRWOOD DR	324	NW
BUTTERFIELD DR	323	SE
BUTTERNUT DR	324	SW
CAHILL DR	324	NW
CALGARY BLVD	325	SW
CAMBRIA DR	319	SW
CAMELOT DR	318	SW
CAMPUS HILL DR	324	SE
CAPESIDE DR	324	SE
CAPTAINS WAY	318	SE
CARINO CT	318	SW
CARRIAGE HILLS CT	319	SW
CARRIAGE DR	319	SW
CEDAR ST	323	NE
CEDAR HILL DR	319	SW
CENTERLAWN ST	318	SE
CHANNING WAY	325	SW
CHARLES ST	323	NE
CHARTWELL CARRIAGE WAY N	318	SW
CHARTWELL CARRIAGE WAY S	318	SW
CHARTWELL DUAL CARRIAGE WAY	318	SW
CHEBOYGAN RD	325	SE
CHEROKEE WAY	323	SE
CHERRY LA	323	NE
CHERRY HILL DR	325	SE
CHERRYWOOD DR	324	SE
CHESTERFIELD PKWY N	323	NW
CHESTNUT RD	323	NW
CHIEF OKEMOS CIR	325	SW
CHIPPEWA DR	323	SW
CHITTENDEN DR	323	NE
CLARENDON DR	318	SE
CLIFTON BLVD	322	NW
CLINTON ST	324	SE
COACH HOUSE DR	319	SW
COBBLERS DR	319	SW
COCHISE LA	324	SW
COLLEGE RD	323	SE
COLLINGWOOD DR	318	SE
COLONY DR	319	SE
COLORADO DR	318	SE
COLUMBINE DR	318	SE
COMANCHE DR	324	SE
CONIFER CIR	324	SE
COOPER	323	SE
GOODBROOK RD	318	SE
CORNELL AVE	324	NW
CORNELL RD	325	SW
COUNTRY WAY	324	NW
COVE CT	325	SE
COVENTRY	318	SW
COWLEY AVE	318	SW
CRANSTON CT	319	SW
CRANWOOD CT	325	SW
CRESCENT RD	323	SE
CRESENWOOD RD	319	SW
CRIMSON CT	318	SW
CRIMSON DR	318	SW
CROWN BLVD	318	SW
CURTIS RD	318	SW
CYPRESS LA	318	SW
DAISY LANE	323	NW
DARLINGTON AVE	318	SE
DAWN AVE	319	SW
DEL MAR DR	324	SW
DELRIDGE RD	319	SW
DELTA ST	323	NE
DENNISON RD	318	SE
DIVISION ST	323	NE
DIXON CIR	325	SE
DOBIE CIR	324	SE
DORMITORY RD	323	NE
DROSTE CIR	324	NW
DUNBAR CT	318	SW
DURAND ST	318	SE
E. BROOKFIELD DR	324	NW
EAST CIRCLE DR	323	NE
EASTKNOLLS	324	SW
E. POINTE LANE	318	SE
E. SLEEPY HOLLOW	319	SW
EASTWAY DR	324	SW
EASTWOOD DR	318	SW
ELIZABETH ST	323	NE
ELM ST	323	NW
ELM PL	323	NE
ELMWOOD DR	325	SE
ENDENHALL WAY	325	SE
ENGINEERING RD	323	NE
ESPERANZA CT	318	NE
ETHEL ST	325	SE
EVERGREEN AVE	318	SE
FAIROAKS CT	318	SW
FAIRWAY RD	323	SW
FARM LA	323	NE
FARRINGTON CT	324	SE
FARWOOD DR	318	SW
FEE RD	324	NW
FERN ST	319	SW
FERNDALE	319	SW
FOOTMAN DR	319	SW
FOREST HILLS DR	324	SW
FOREST RD	318	SE
FOREST ST	318	SE
FOX CHASE	325	SW
FOXCROFT RD	319	SW
FOXFIRE	324	SW
FOX HILLS DR	319	SW
FRATERNITY RD	323	NE
FRY AVE	324	NW
GAINSBOROUGH DR	318	SW
GIBSON AVE	318	SE
GILCREST AVE	318	SE
GLENHAVEN AVE	318	SW
GLEN MEADOW LA	319	SW
GLENMOOR DR	323	NE
GOSSARD AVE	318	NE
GRANADA WAY	318	SE
GRAND RIVER AVE	323	NE
GRAND RIVER RD	324	NW
GRANDVIEW AVE	318	SE
GRAYSTONE DR	324	SW
GREENCLIFF DR	324	NW
GREENCREST AVE	318	SW
GREENFIELD PKWY	324	SW
GREEN TREE LA	318	SW
GREENVIEW AVE	318	SW
GROTON WAY	318	SW
GREENWOOD DR	325	SW
HAGADORN AVE	319	SW
HAGADORN RD	324	NW
HAMILTON ST	319	SW
HARBOR CUT	325	SE
HARDY AVE	318	NE
HARKSON DR	318	SE
HARRISON RD	318	SE
HART ST	319	SW
HARVARD ST	318	SW
HASLETT RD	319	SW
HATCH RD	325	SW
HAWTHORNE LA	324	SW
HEATHER DR	319	SW
HERMANDAD CT	318	SW
HERRON RD	324	SW
HICKS DR	323	NW
HIGHGATE AVE	318	SW
HIGHLAND AVE	323	NW
HILL CREST AVE	323	NE
HILLCREST AVE	323	NE
HILLSIDE CT	323	SW
HILLSIDE DR	323	SW
HITCHING POST RD	318	SW
HORIZON DR	319	NW
HUBBARD RD	324	NW
HULETT RD	324	NW
HUNTINGTON RD	323	NW
HURON HILL DR	324	SE
INDIAN GLEN DR	325	SW
INDIAN HILLS DR	324	SW
INDIAN WAY	325	SW
INNKEEPERS CT	318	SE
INNSBROOKE WAY	324	SE
IROQUOIS DR	324	NE
IVANHOE DR	323	NW
IVANHOE ST	324	NW
JANICE TR	318	NW
JAYWOOD DR	319	SW
JO DON	325	SW
JOHN R. ST	324	NW
JONQUIL LA	325	SW
KALAMAZOO ST E.	323	NW
KAREN ANN	324	SW
KARLIN CT	319	SW
KEDZIE DR	323	NE
KENBERRY DR	324	NW
KENDALE BLVD	318	SW
KENMORE DR	324	SW
KENNETH	324	SW
KENOSHA	325	SW
KENSINGTON RD	325	NW
KENT ST	318	NW
KEWANEE WAY	324	SE
KINAWA DR	324	SE
KING CT	318	SW
KINGSWOOD CIR	325	SW
KINGSWOOD DR	318	SW
KNOLL RD	324	SE
LAC LA MONT DR	319	SE
LAGOON DR	325	SE
LAKESIDE DR	324	SW
LANTERN HILL DR	319	SW
LARKSPUR DR	323	NW
LAUREL LA	318	SW
LEE CIR	323	NE
LEE ST	322	NE
LEEWARD DR	325	SE
LELAND CIRCLE	324	NW
LEXINGTON AVE	318	NE
LIBRARY LA	323	SE
LILAC AVE	323	NW
LINDELL DR	318	SW
LINDEN ST	323	NE
LIVERANCE ST	318	NW
LONGFELLOW DR	318	SW
LONG LEAF TR	324	SE
LOREE DR	323	NE
LOUIS ST	328	NW
LUFF CT	325	SE
M.A.C. AVE	323	NE
MACKINAC DR	325	SE
MANITOU DR	325	SW
MANSFIELD DR	319	SW
MAPLE RIDGE RD	325	NW
MAPLEWOOD DR	324	NW
MARBLE RD	319	SW
MARGARET ST	324	NW
MARGATE	324	NW
MARIGOLD AVE	323	SW
MARLBOROUGH RD	323	SE
MARSH RD	324	SE
MARSHALL ST	323	NW
MAUMEE DR	324	SW
MAYFAIR DR	318	SW
MEADOW BROOK LA	318	SW
MEADOWLAWN AVE	318	SE
MEADOW RUE	318	SW
MELLING WAY	324	SW
MELROSE AVE	324	NW
MELVILLE DR	324	NW
MENDOTA CIR	318	SW
MERCER DR	325	SE
MERRITT RD	318	SW
METHODIST ST	324	NE
MIDDLEVALE RD	323	NW
MILFORD ST	325	SW
MINOKA TR	325	SW
MIRABEAU DR	324	NE
MOHAWK	324	NE
MOHICAN LA	324	SW
MOJAVE CT	324	SW
MONTROSE AVE	323	NE
MOORE ST	324	SW
MOORLAND DR	324	SW
MT HOPE RD	318	SW
MULBERRY	324	NW
MURPHY CIR	324	NW
NAKOMA DR	324	NE
NARCISSUS	323	NW
NAVAHO TR	324	SE
NAUBINWAY RD	325	SE
NEMOKE CT	325	NW
NEMOKE TR	325	NW
NEWTON RD	319	SE
NORMANDY	324	SW
NORTHGATE DR	318	SW
NORTHLAWN ST	318	SE
N OKEMOS RD	325	SE
N SHAW LA	323	NE
NORTHVIEW DR	323	NE
NORTHWIND DR	324	NW
OAK ST	323	NE
OAK HILL AVE	323	NW
OAKLAND DR	324	NW
OAKLAWN RD	325	SW
OAK RIDGE AVE	323	NW
OAKWOOD DR	323	NW
OAKWOOD DR E.	318	SW
OAKWOOD DR W.	318	SW
OKEMOS RD	324	NW
OLD CANTON LA	318	NW
OLD HICKORY LANE	318	SE
OLD MILL RD	318	SE
OLIN AVE	323	NW
ONEIDA DR	325	SW
ONERIAL PL	325	SW
ORCHARD ST	328	SW
OSAGE DR	324	SW
OSCODA RD	325	SE
OTTAWA DR	324	NE
OXFORD RD	318	SW
PADDOCK DR	318	SW
PALMER LA	327	NE
PARK LAKE RD	319	SW
PARK TRACE	324	SE
PARKVALE AVE	319	SW
PATRIOTS WAY	319	SW
PAWNEE CIR	324	SE
PAWNEE TR	324	SE
PEBBLEBROOK LA	318	SE
PEBBLE CREEK BLVD	318	SE
PEBBLESTONE DR	325	SW
PENOBSCOT DR	325	SW
PHYSICS RD	323	NE
PIMLICO PL	325	SE
PINECREST DR	318	SW
PINE FOREST DR	318	SW
PINOAK LA	318	SW
PIONEER TR	324	SW
POLLARD AVE	318	SE
PONTCHARTRAIN DR	325	SW
POPLAR LA	318	SW
PORTAGE PATH	317	SE
PORTER AVE	318	SE
PRESCOTT DR	318	SE
RABY RD	318	SW
RAINDROP RD	318	SW
RAMBLEWOOD DR	318	SW
RAMPART WAY	318	SW
RAPHAEL RD	324	NW
RAVIN CIR	325	SW
REBECCA RD	323	NW
RED CEDAR RD	323	NE
RED LEAF LA	318	SW
REDOAK LA	318	SW
RENIGER CT	323	NW
RESEARCH CIR	318	NW
RIDGE ST	318	SE
RIDGEWOOD DR	318	SW
RIVER TERRACE DR	314	NW
RIVERWOOD DR	319	SW
RIVIERA DR	318	SW
ROBB ST	319	SW
ROCKWOOD DR	324	NW
ROLLING BROOK	318	SW
ROLLING HILLS DR	325	NW
ROSELAND AVE	318	SW
ROSEWOOD AVE	318	SW
ROTHBURY WAY	319	SW
ROWENA DR	323	NW
ROXBURGH AVE	318	SW
RUDGATE LA	318	SW
RUTGERS CIR	318	SW
RUTHERFORD AVE	318	SW
SABRON RD	318	SW
SAGINAW ST	318	SW
SAGO WAY	325	SW
SANDOWN CT	325	SE
SAND RIDGE	324	SE
SARAN DR	324	SW
SARANAC LA	324	NW
SAVILLE DR	324	NW
SCIENCE PKWY	324	SW
SCIENCE RD	323	NE
SCOTT DR	323	NW
SEEBEWAING RD	324	NE
SEMINOLE DR	324	NE
SEMINOLE PL	324	NE
SENECA DR	325	SW
SEQUOIA TR	324	SW
SEVEN TRAILS CT	325	SW
SEVER DR	323	NW
SHADOW LAWN CT	319	SW
SHADOW LAWN DR	319	SW
SHAKER BLVD	325	SW
SHAW LANE	323	NW
SHAWNEE TRAIL	324	SE
SHERWOOD DR	319	SW
SHOALS DR	325	SE
SHORT ST SW OKEMOS	324	SE
SHORT ST E. LANS.	323	NE
SIOUX WAY	324	NE
SIRHAL DR	324	NW
SKYLINE CT	319	SW
SKYLINE DR	319	SW
SMALL ACRES LA	324	SW
SMITH AVE	319	SE
SMITHFIELD AVE	319	SW
SNYDER RD	323	NE
SOMERSET CLOSE	318	SW
SOUTHLAWN ST	318	SE
S. SERVICE RD	323	NE
S. SHAW LANE	323	NE
SOUTHWOOD DR	319	SW
SOWER BLVD	324	SW
SPARTAN ST	323	NE
SPRUCE HILL RD	318	SW
STADIUM RD	323	NE
STAN LAKE	323	SW
STILL VALLEY CT	323	SW
STILL VALLEY DR	323	SW
STODDARD AVE	319	SW
STONEGATE LA	318	SE
STONEYCROFT DR	325	SW
STUART AVE	318	SE
SUGAR MAPLE LA	324	SE
SUNRISE CT	324	SE
SUNSET LANE	318	SE
SWART ST	318	SE
SYCAMORE LA	324	SE
SYLVAN GLEN RD	325	SW
TACOMA CIR	324	SE
TACOMA BLVD	325	SW
TAHOE CIR	325	SW
TAHQUAMENON RD	324	SE
TAMARISK DR	318	SW
TANAGER LA	318	SW
TANFORM PL	324	SE
TANGLEWOOD LA	324	SE
TARLETON AVE	318	SE
TARLETON DR	318	SE
TAYLOR DR	318	SE
TEKONSHA TR	324	NW
TERRI TER	318	SW
THISTLEDOWN PL	325	SW
TIHART RD	325	NW
TIMBERLANE ST	319	SW
TOMAHAWK CIR	324	SE
TOMAHAWK RD	324	SE
TONAPAH TR	324	NW
TOURAINE AVE	318	SW
TOWAR AVE	318	SE
TOWAR GARDENS CIR	317	SE
TRAFALGER	317	SE
TROWBRIDGE ST	323	NW
TWYCKINGHAM LA	318	SE
UNIVERSITY DR	323	NW
VALLEY CT	323	NE
VAN DYCK DR	324	NE
VICTOR ST	324	NW
VILLAGE ST	324	NW
VIRGINIA AVE	324	NW
VOUVRAY DR	318	SW
WABEEK DR	318	SW
WALBRIDGE DR	318	SE
WALNUT HTS DR	318	SW
WARANINGO RD	325	SW
WARDCLIFF DR	324	SW
WASHINGTON SQ.	323	NW
WATER ST	324	SE
WATERFORD CT	318	SW
WATERS EDGE DR	323	NE
WAUSAU RD	324	SE
WAYLAND AVE	324	NW
WEMBLEY WAY	318	SW
WEST CIRCLE DR	323	NE
WEST CIRCLE	323	NE
WESTLAWN ST	318	SE
W. SLEEPY HOLLOW LA	319	SE
WESTVIEW AVE	323	NW
WHISTLER DR	324	NW
WHITEHILLS DR	318	SE
WHITE OAKS DR	325	SE
WHITE POND RD	318	SE
WHITETAIL CIR	325	NW
WHITMAN DR	318	SE
WHITTIER DR	324	NW
WICK CT	318	SE
WILDWOOD DR	318	SE
WILLOW LANE	323	NW
WILSON RD	323	NE
WINCHESTER DR	324	SW
WINDGATE	319	SW
WINTERCREST LA	319	SW
WOLF CT	324	SW
WOODBROOK DR	318	SE
WOODDRAFT RD	324	NE
WOODCREST LA	318	SW
WOOD GLEN LA	319	SW
WOODHILL DR	326	SW
WOODINGHAM DR	318	SE
WOODLAND DR	318	SW
WOODLAND PASS	318	SW
WOODMERE AVE	324	SW
WOODSIDE DR	319	SW
WOODVILLE RD	320	SE
WYNGARDEN LA	329	SW
YUMA TR	324	SE

NOTES

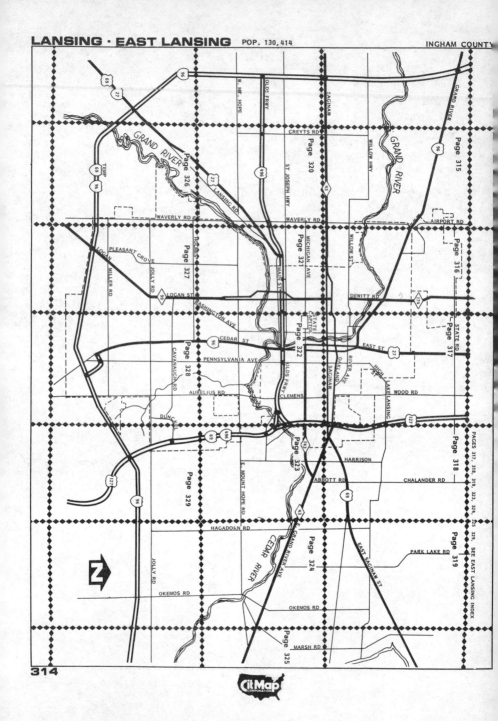

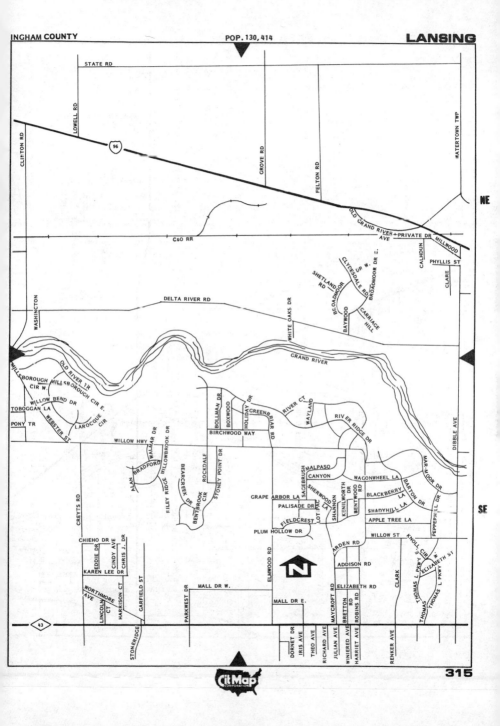

STATE RD

LOWELL RD

CLIFTON RD

96

WATERTOWN TWP

GROVE RD

FELTON RD

NE

OLD GRAND RIVER + PRIVATE DR   MILLWOOD
AVE

C&O RR

CALHOUN

PHYLLIS ST

CLARE

UP W.

CLYDESDALE RD

BROADMOOR DR E.

SHETLAND RD

BROADMOOR RD

WASHINGTON

DELTA RIVER RD

BELOADMOOR

BAYWOOD

CARRIAGE HILL

WHITE OAKS DR

GRAND RIVER

OLD RIVER TR

HILLSBOROUGH MILL
CIR W.

HILLSBOROUGH CIR E.

WILLOW BEND DR

TOBOGGAN LA

LAROCQUE CIR

PONY TR

WEBSTER ST

BOLLMAN DR

BOXWOOD

HOLIDAY DR

GREENBRIAR RD

RIVER CT

WAYLAND

RIVER RIDGE DR

DIBBLE AVE

BIRCHWOOD WAY

WILLOW HWY

WALMAR DR

WILLOWBROOK DR

BRADFORD

ALAN

FILEY RIDGE

BEARCREEK DR

ROCKDALE

STONEY POINT DR

SAGEBRUSH

MALPASO CANYON

WAGONWHEEL LA

VAN MOOR DR

CREYTS RD

BENTBROOK CIR

GRAPE ARBOR LA

SHERWOOD

KENILWORTH

BENTWOOD RD

BLACKBERRY

BARTON DR

SE

PALISADE DR E.

LOT PKY

SHANNON

SHADYHILL LA

PEPPERHILL DR

FIELDCREST

APPLE TREE LA

PLUM HOLLOW DR

WILLOW ST

KNOLL CIR

CHIEHO DR

ARDEN RD

CLARK

EDDIE DR

CINDY AVE

CHRIS J. DR

KAREN LEE DR

ADDISON RD

THOMAS L PKWY E.

ELIZABETH ST

WORTHMORE AVE

GARFIELD ST

MALL DR W.

ELMWOOD RD

MAYCROFT RD

ELIZABETH RD

BRETTON RD

ROBINS RD

THOMAS L PKWY W.

LINCOLN CT

HARRISON CT

PARKWEST DR

MALL DR E.

THOMAS

43

STONERIDGE

DORNET DR

IRIS AVE

THEO AVE

RICHARD AVE

JULIAN AVE

WINIERED AVE

HARRIET AVE

RENKER AVE

CitMap

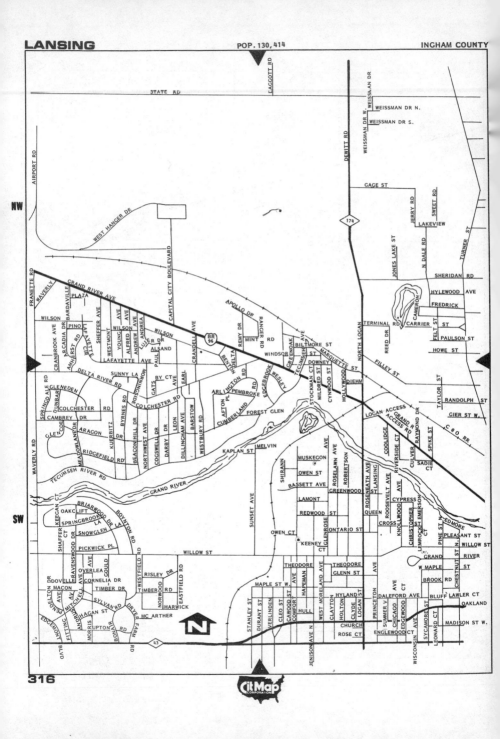

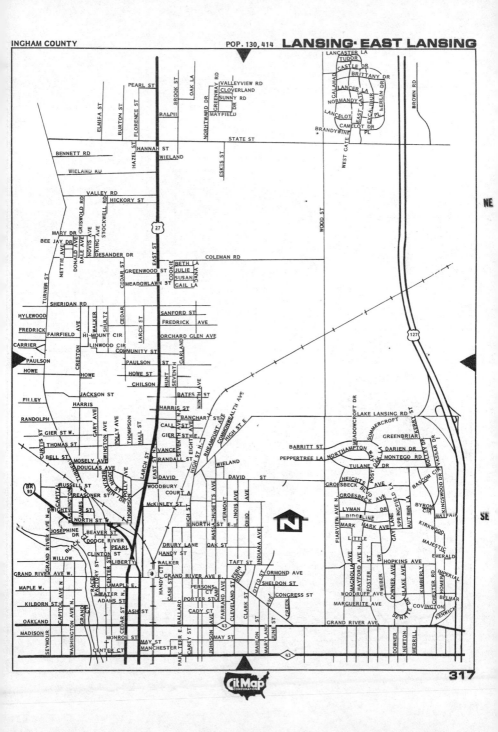

NE

SE

CitMap
CORPORATION

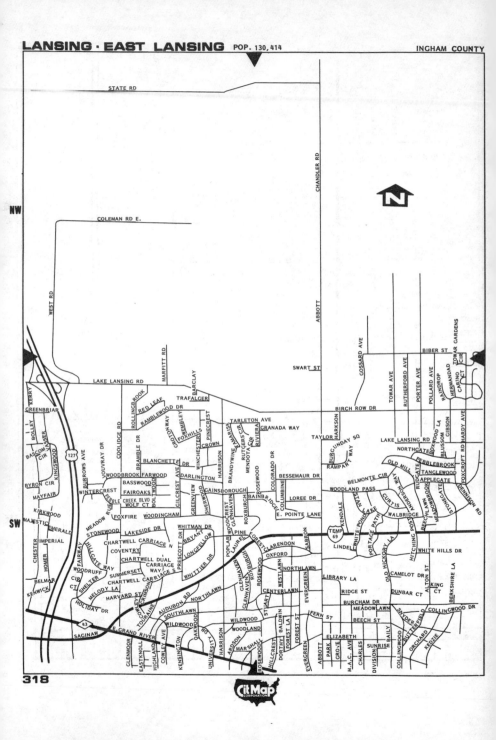

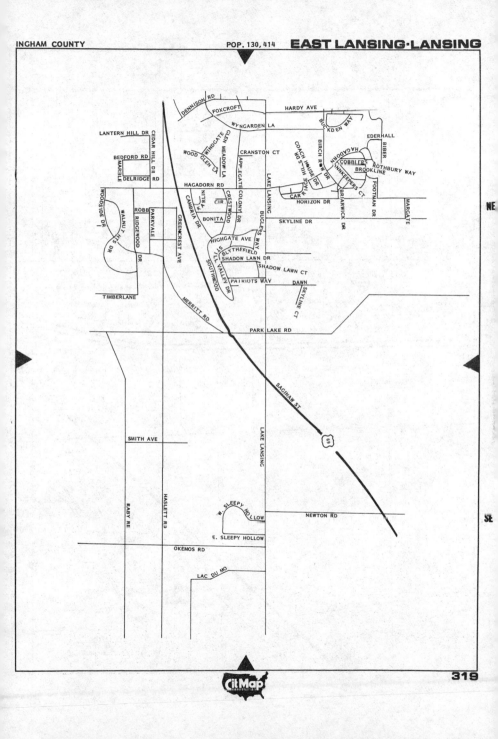

NE

SE

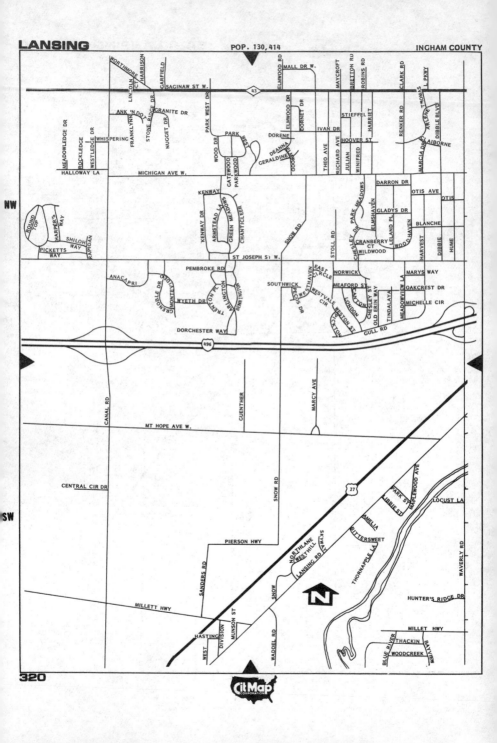

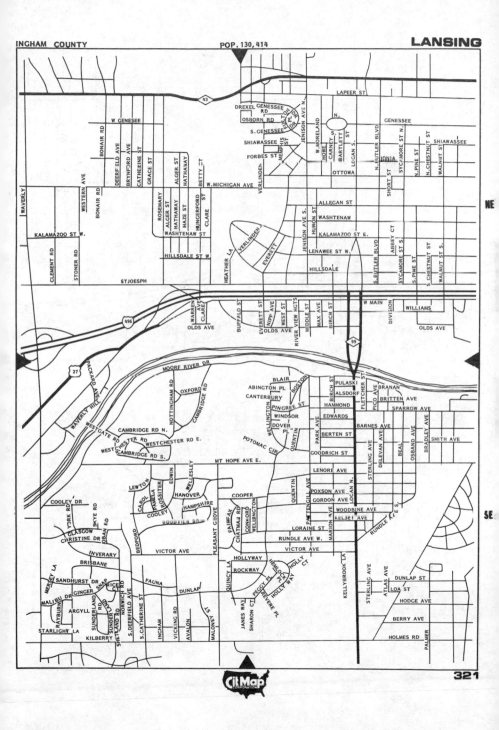

NE

SE

CitMap
CORPORATION

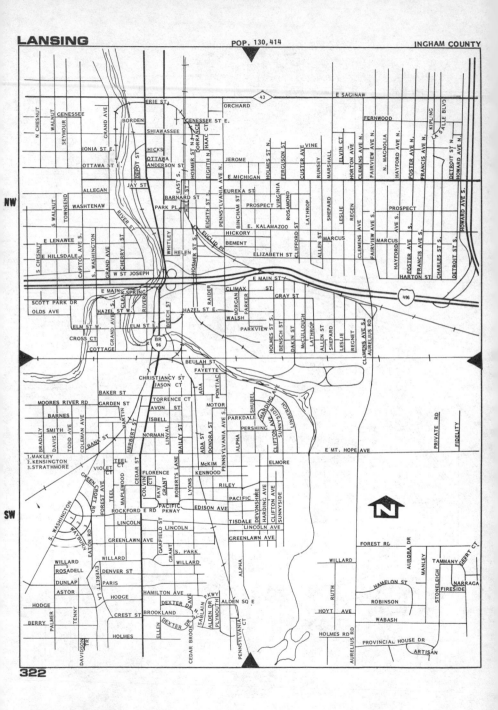

NW

SW

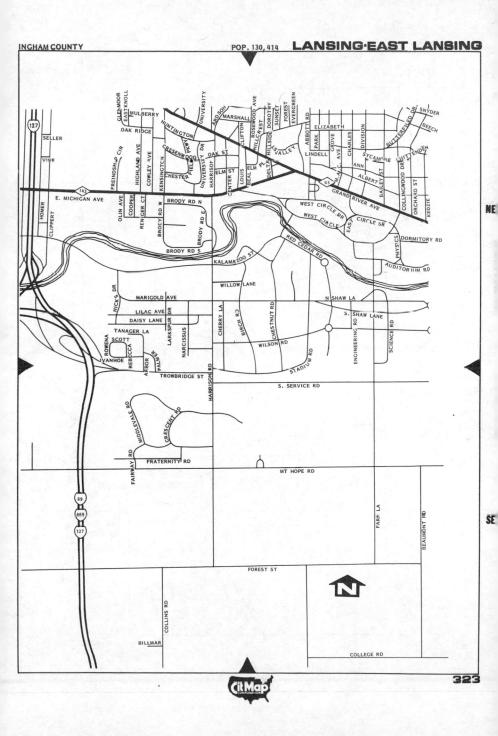

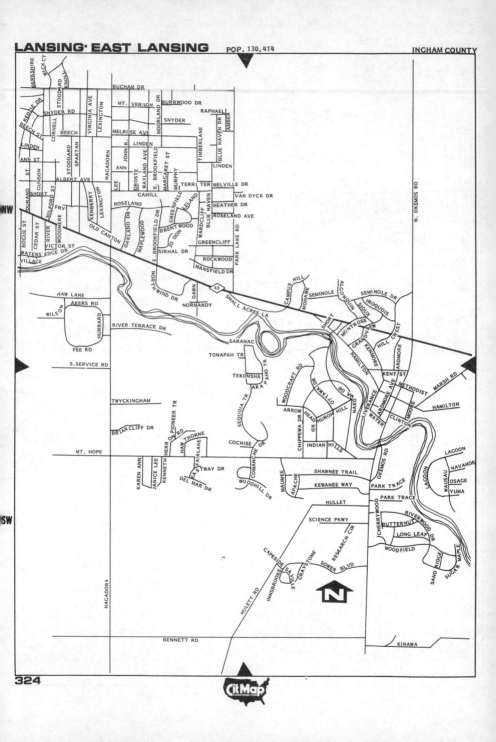

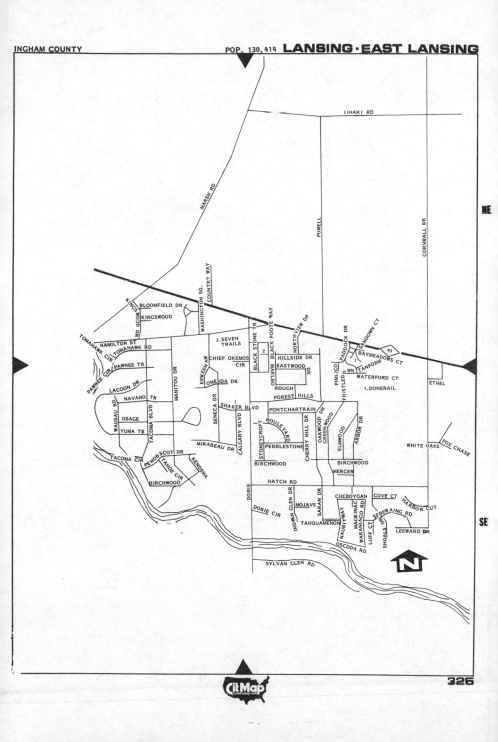

NE

SE

TIHART RD

MARSH RD

POWELL

CORNWALL DR

COUNTRY WAY

WASHINGTON SQ.

BLOOMFIELD DR

KINGSWOOD

KINGSCOM RD

TOMAHAWK CIR

HAMILTON ST

TOMAHAWK RD

PAWNEE TR

PAWNEE CIR

LAGOON DR

NAVAHO

WAUSAU RD

OSAGE

YUMA TR

TACOMA BLVD

MANITOU DR

KEWEENAW

CHIEF OKEMOS CIR

ONEIDA DR

SENECA DR

SHAKER BLVD

CALGARY BLVD

MIRABEAU DR

TACOMA CIR

PENOBSCOT DR

TAHOE CIR

KENOSHA

BIRCHWOOD

2. SEVEN TRAILS

BLACK STONE TR

BLACK FOOTE WAY

NORTH VIEW DR

HILLSIDE DR

EASTWOOD

MAFLBO

ROUGH

FOREST HILLS

PONTCHARTRAIN

STONEYCROFT

BOULEVARD

PEBBLESTONE

BIRCHWOOD

CHERRY HILL DR

OAKWOOD DR

GREENWOOD

ELMWOOD

ARBOR DR

BIRCHWOOD

MERCER

DOBIE

HATCH RD

DOBIE CIR

INDIAN GLEN DR

MOJAVE

SARAN DR

TAHQUAMENON

CHEDOYGAN

MAUBY WAY

MACKINAC

WARANING RD

LUFF CT

SHOALS DR

SEBEWAING RD

NAUBY WAY

COVE CT

HARBOR CUT

LEEWARD DR

OSCODA RD

SYLVAN GLEN RD

PADDOCK DR

SANDOWN CT

BAYMEADOWS CT

TANFORM CIR

WN

PHLICO

THISTLED

WATERFORD CT

1. DONERAIL

43

1

2

ETHEL

WHITE OAKS

FOX CHASE

N

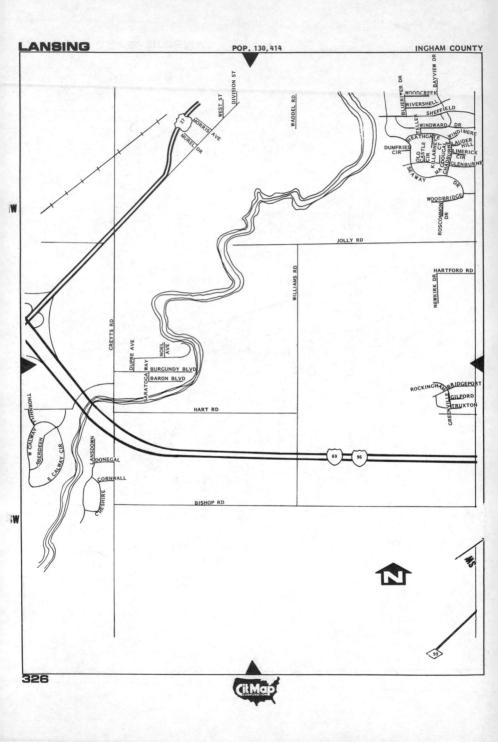

BAYVIEW DR
BLUEHEATHER DR
WOODCREEK
RIVERSHELL
SHEFFIELD
WINDWARD DR
WINDMERE
HEATHGATE
LAUDER HILL
DUMFRIES CIR
OLD CASTLE CIR
K LANNET CT
LIMERICK CIR
MACDOUGAL
CHADBURN
GLENBURNE
SEAWAY
DR
WOODBRIDGE
ROSCOMMON DR

WEST ST
DIVISION ST
WADDEL RD
MORRIS AVE
MUREL DR
77

JOLLY RD

WILLIAMS RD
HARTFORD RD
NEWKIRK DR

CREYTS RD
DUPRE AVE
NOEL AVE
SARATOGA WAY
BURGUNDY BLVD
BARON BLVD

HART RD

ROCKINGHAM BRIDGEPORT
GILFORD
GREENVILLE
TRUXTON

W CALWAY
THORNHILL
ABERDEEN
E CALWAY CIR
LANSDOWN
DONEGAL
CORNWALL
CHESHIRE

BISHOP RD

69 96

N

MS

99

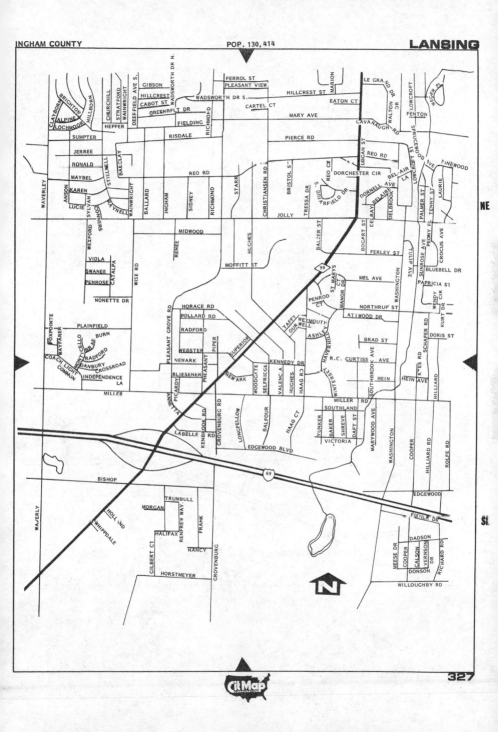

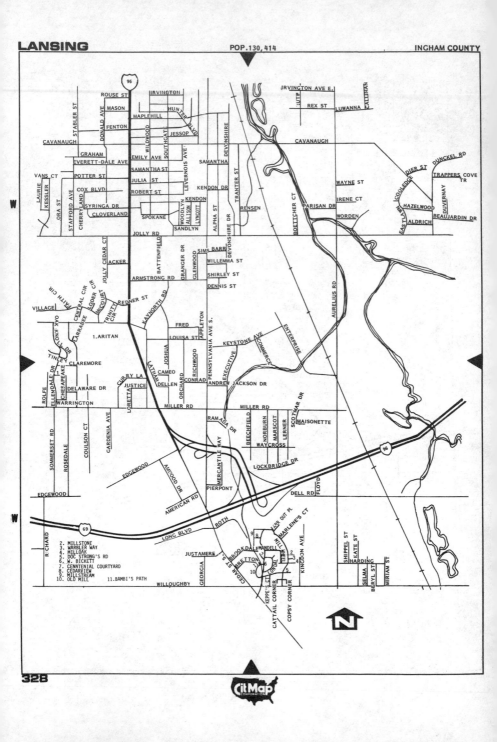

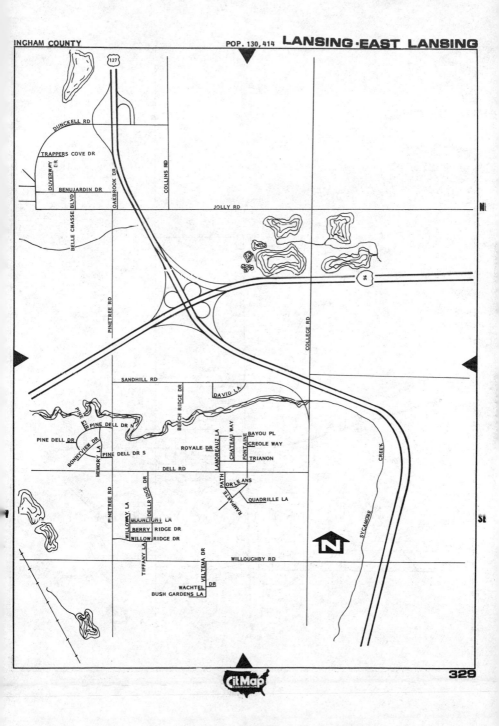

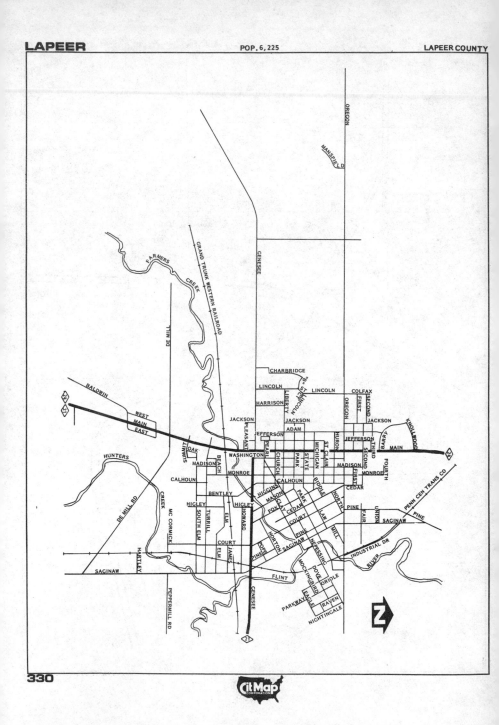

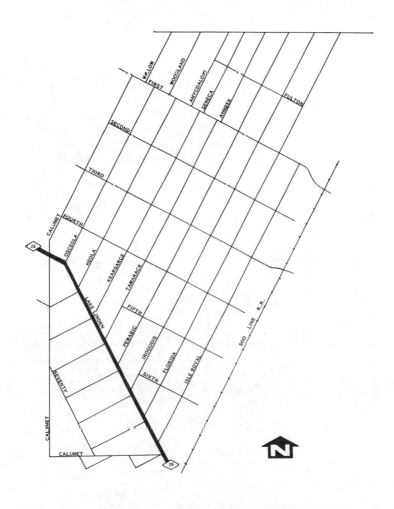

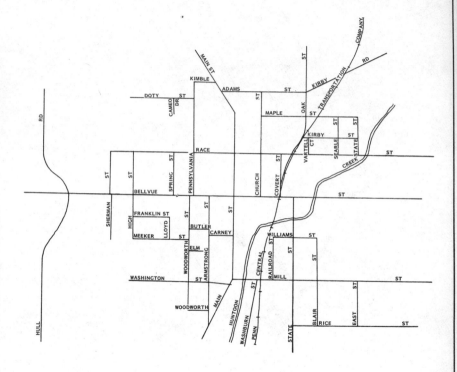

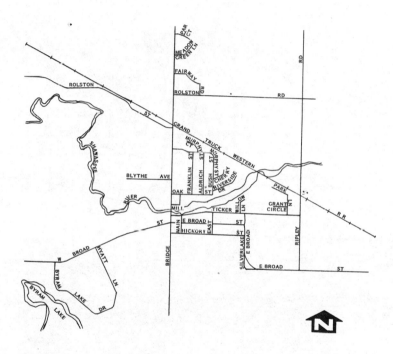

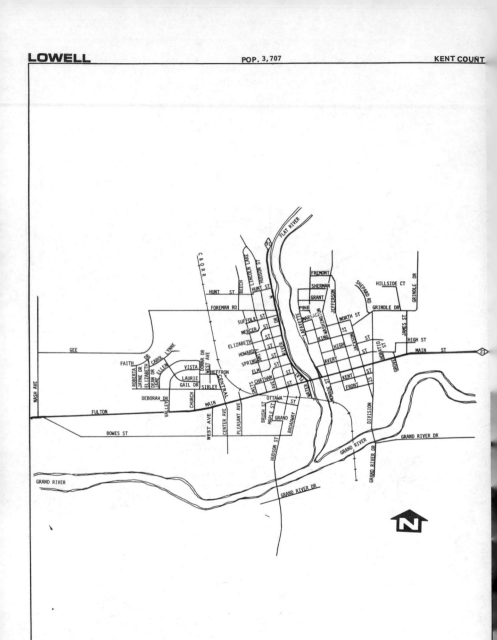

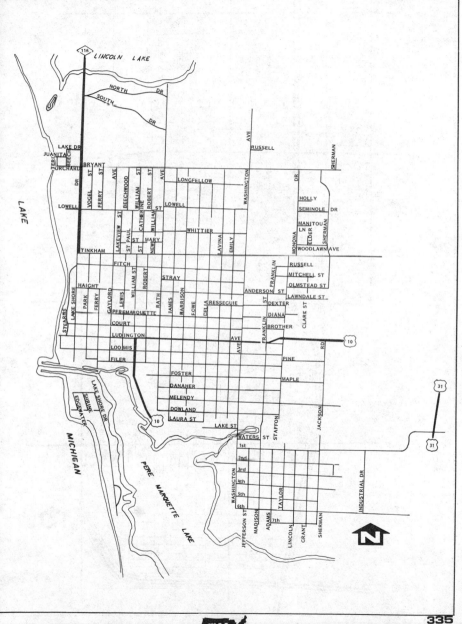

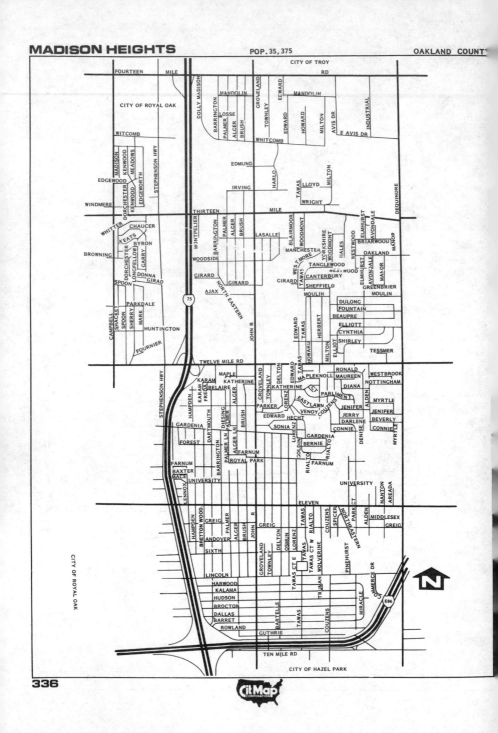

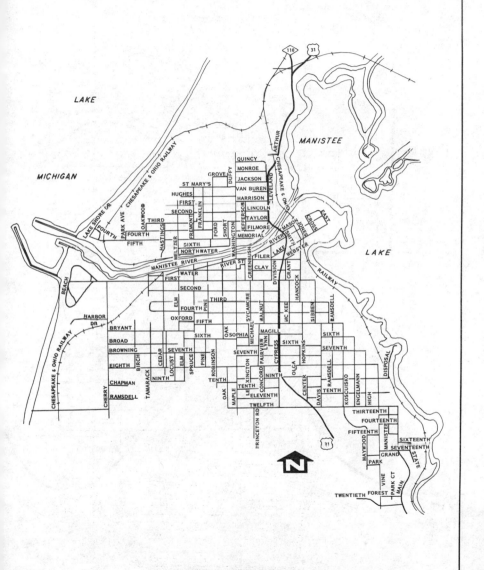

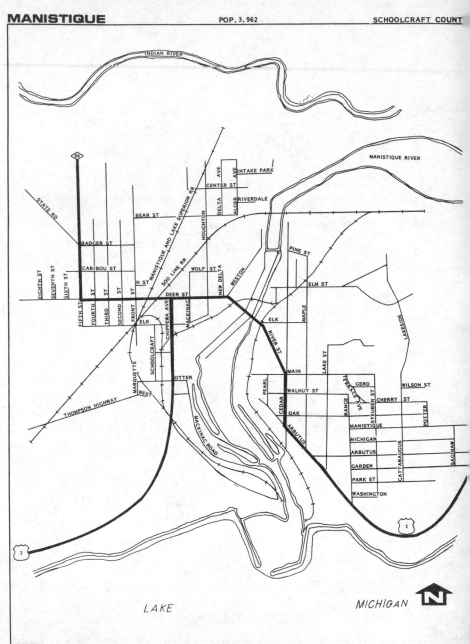

INDIAN RIVER

MANISTIQUE RIVER

STATE RD

INTAKE PARK

CENTER ST

DELTA AVE

ALGER AVE

RIVERDALE

BEAR ST

HOUGHTON

BADGER ST

MANISTIQUE AND LAKE SUPERIOR RR

CARIBOU ST

SOO LINE RR

PINE ST

EIGHTH ST

SEVENTH ST

SIXTH ST

FIFTH ST

FOURTH ST

THIRD ST

SECOND ST

FRONT ST

H ST

WOLF ST

NEW DELTA

WESTON

DEER ST

MACKINAC

ELM ST

ELK

CHIPPEWA AVE

MAPLE

ELK

RIVER ST

LAKESIDE

SCHOOLCRAFT

MARQUETTE

POTTER

MAIN

LAKE ST

GERO

WILSON ST

WEST

PEARL

WALNUT ST

TERRACE AVE

STEUBEN ST

CHERRY ST

POTTER

THOMPSON HIGHWAY

CEDAR

OAK

RANGE

MANISTIQUE

MACKINAC ROAD

ARBUTUS

MICHIGAN

ARBUTUS

CATTARAUGUS

SAGINAW

GARDEN

PARK ST

WASHINGTON

2

LAKE   MICHIGAN   N

94

2

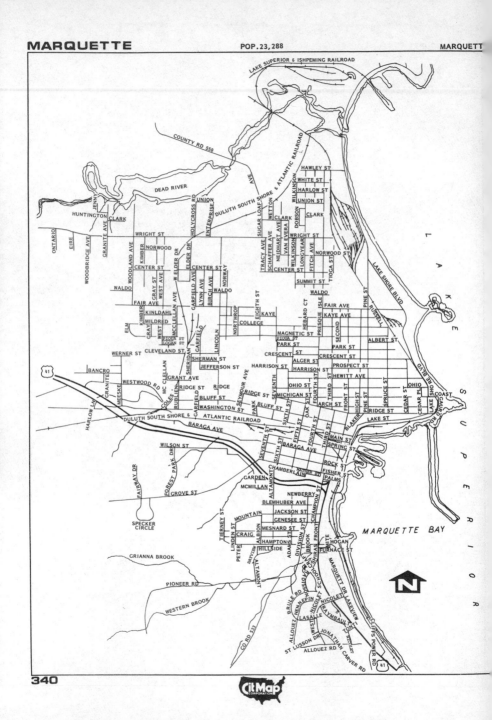

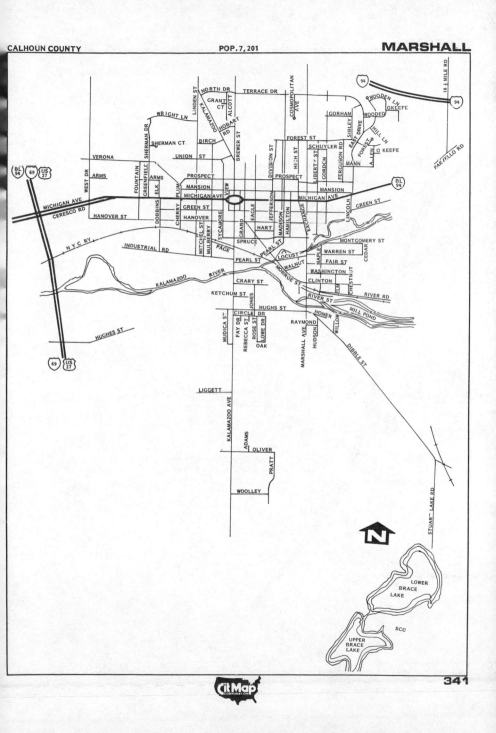

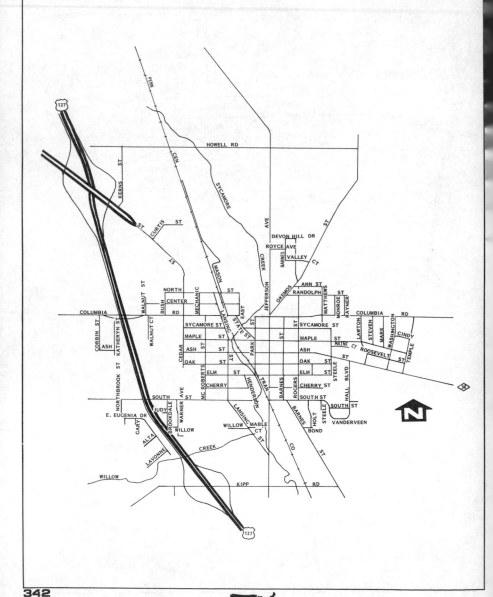

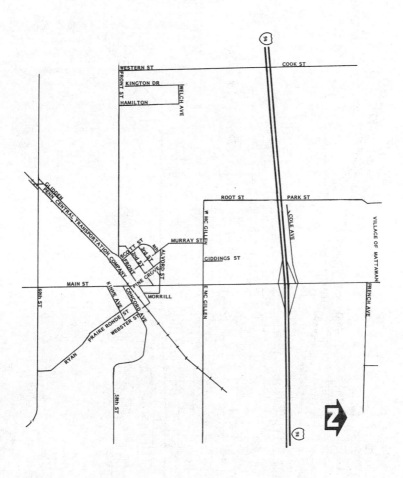

POP. 10,099

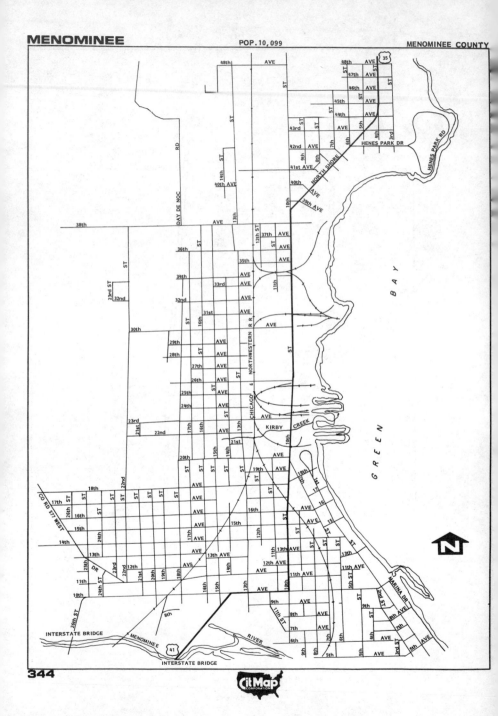

Street	Grid	Street	Grid	Street	Grid	Street	Grid
ABBOT	346 SW	CRONKRIGHT	345 SE	JAMES	346 NW	SALEM	346 NW
ADAMS DE.	346 NW	CRUZ	346 NW	JAMES SARAGE RD.	346 SE	SANDYRIDGE	345 NE
ACELAIDE	345 SE	CYPRESS	345 SE	JAY	346 SW	SAUVE	346 SW
AIRCRAFT	346 SW	DALE	346 SW	JEFFERSON	346 NW	SAYRE	346 SW
AIRPORT RD.	345 NW	DAMON	345 NW	JEROME	346 SW	SCHUELETTE	346 SW
ALBEE LN	345 SW	DAN	345 SW	JOANNE	346 NW	SCOTT	346 SW
ALLEN	345 SE	DANER	345 SE	JONIEL	346 SE	SEMIDIF	346 NW
ALOHA	345 NE	DARTMOOR	345 SW	JUDITH	345 SE	SERVICE RD.	346 NW
ALTA	346 SW	DARTMOORE	346 SW	KENNY CT.	345 NE	SHARON	346 NW
ANDRE	346 NW	DARTMOUTH	346 SW	KENT ST.	346 NW	SHAWNEE	346 NW
ANN	345 SE	DAUN	346 NW	KENTWOOD	345 NE	SHERWOOD	345 NE
APPLEWOOD	345 NW	DAWN	345 NW	KENTUCKY	346 NW	SHREEVE	345 SE
ARBOR	345 NE	DEERFIELD	345 NE	KILT	345 NE	SIAS	345 SE
ARBURY	346 NW	DENNIS	345 SE	KIM CT.	345 NE	SIEBERT	345 NE
ARDMORE	346 NW	DETROIT	345 SE	KINGSBURY	345 SE	SINCLAIR	345 SE
ARLINGTON	346 NW	DEVONSHIRE	346 NW	KINGSTON	346 NW	SIXTH	345 NE
ARRON	345 NW	DICK	345 NW	KIRKLAND	346 SE	SMITH	345 NE
ARTCREST	345 NW	DILLOWAY	345 NW	KNOLLWOOD	345 SE	SNOWFIELD CT.	345 NE
ASHLY WAKEFIELD	345 NE	DINA	345 NE	KOERNER	346 NW	SPRINGFIELD	346 SE
ASHMAN	345 SE	DRAKE	345 SE	KORRNER	345 NW	SPRUCE	345 NE
ATWELL	345 SW	DUBLIN RD.	345 SW	LAMBUOS	345 NW	ST. ANDREWS	346 NW
AUBURN	345 SE	E. ASHMAN	345 SE	LAMPLIGHTER	346 NW	ST. CHARLES	345 NW
AUSTIN	345 SE	E. HALEY	345 SE	LANDCASTER	346 NW	ST. MARYS	345 NW
AUSTIN	345 SW	E. MEADOW	345 SW	LARRET	346 NW	STANDREWS	346 NW
AVALON	346 NW	E. SUGNET	346 NW	LARRIN	346 NW	STATE	345 NE
AVON	345 SW	E-PARK	345 SW	LAWNDALE	345 SE	STERLING	345 NE
BACKER	345 SW	EAST LAWN ST.	346 SW	LEONARD LN.	346 NW	STONE CR. DR.	345 NW
BALDWIN	346 NW	EAST LAWN ST.	346 SW	LESSA	346 SE	STURGEON	345 NW
BALFOUR	345 SE	EASTMAN	345 SE	LEXINGTON CT.	345 SE	STURGEON CREEK PKWY.	345 NW
BARTH	346 SW	EASTMAN	346 SW	LINCOLN	345 NE		
BARTON	345 NE	EDGEWOOD	345 NE	LINOY	346 SW	SUDBURRY	345 NW
BAUSS	345 NE	EDWIN	346 SW	LINGLE LA	346 SW	SUMMERSET	345 NE
BAY CITY	345 SE	ELGIN	345 SE	LIVINGSTON	346 SW	SUNCREST	345 SE
BAY CITY RD.	346 SW	ELIZABETH	346 SW	LOVE	345 SE	SUNSET	345 NE
BAYBERRY	345 NE	ELLSWORTH	345 NE	LOWELL	345 SE	SUTTON	345 NW
BAYLISS	345 NE	ELM	345 SE	LUCKY	346 NE	SWEDE	345 SW
BEEBE	346 SW	ERIE	346 SW	LUHRING	346 SE	SWEETBRIER	345 NE
BEECH ST.	346 SW	EVAMAR	346 SW	LUND	345 NE	SYLVAN	345 NE
BELMONT	345 NW	EVART	345 NW	LYON	346 NW	TANWOOD	345 NW
BENSON	345 SE	EVERGREEN	345 SE	MAIN	345 SE	TENNESSE	346 SW
BERKSHIRE	345 NE	FAIRLANE	345 NE	MANOR	346 NW	TERRA LINDEN	345 SE
BIRCH	346 NW	FAIRWAY	345 NE	MAPLE	345 NE	THIRD	345 SE
BIRCHFIELD	346 NW	FARNSWORTH	346 NW	MARK TWAIN	346 NW	THURLOW CT.	346 SW
BLAIRMONT	346 NE	FEDERAL	346 NE	MARRYLAND	346 SW	TIBBS	346 SW
BLOOMFIELD	346 NW	FERNSIDE	346 NW	MARVO	345 NE	TIMBER	345 NE
BOND	345 NE	FIFTH	345 NE	MCDONALD	345 SE	TODD	345 SE
BOOKNESS	345 SE	FITZHUGH	345 SE	MCKERTH	345 SE	TOWNSEND	345 SE
BOSTON	346 NW	FLAZMOORE	346 NW	MEADOWBROOK	345 NW	TOWSLEW	345 SE
BRADFIELD	345 SW	FOREST	345 SE	MERTZ	346 NW	TRAVIS	346 NE
BRADLEY	345 NE	FOSTER	345 SE	MEOILL	345 NE	TRINITY	345 NE
BRADLEY RD.	346 SW	FOURNIE	346 SW	MEYERS	345 SE	TUCKER	345 NE
BRMBLERIDGE	345 NW	FOURTH	345 NW	MICHIGAN	346 NE	TYLER	346 NW
BRENTWOOD	345 NE	FOXCROFT	345 NE	MIDLAND	346 NE	VAIL	345 NE
BRISTOL	345 NE	FRANKLIN	345 NE	MILFORD	345 SE	VALLEY RD.	345 NW
BROOKFIELD	346 NW	FRIAR	346 NW	MILL	346 NW	VALORIE	345 NW
BROWN CT.	345 SE	FULLER	345 SE	MOORELAND	346 NW	VANBUREN	345 SW
BUCHANAN	346 NW	GARDENBROOK	346 NW	MYRTLE	346 NE	VANCE	345 SW
BURCH	345 SE	GARLAND	345 SE	NOKOMA	345 SE	VARNER	345 SW
BURGRESS	346 SW	GEORGE	346 SW	NICKELS	345 SE	VIRGINIA	346 SW
BURLINGTON DR.	346 NW	GEORGE TOWN	346 NW	NOESKE	346 NE	W 1/8 LINE RD.	345 SW
BURRELL CT.	345 SE	GERALD CT.	346 NW	NORFOLK	345 NE	W. SUGNET	345 NW
BUTTLES	345 SE	GIBSON	345 SE	NORWICH	345 NW	W-PARK	345 SE
BYRD	346 SW	GLADDING CT.	346 NW	NOTTINGHAM	345 SE	WACKERLY	345 NW
CAMBRIDGE	346 NW	GLENCOE	346 NW	NORWOOD	345 NW	WALBO	346 SE
CAMPAU	345 NE	GLENDALE	345 NE	NOVAK	346 SE	WALLBRIDGE	345 NE
CAMPBELL	346 NW	GOLFSIDE	346 NW	NURMI DR.	345 SE	WALLEN	346 NW
CANDLESTICK	346 NW	GORDON	346 NW	OAK	345 SE	WANETAH	345 SE
CANTERBURY	346 NE	GRAHAM	345 NE	OHIO	346 SW	WARWICH	345 NE
CAPITAL	346 NW	GRANT LN.	346 NW	OLIVE	345 SE	WASHINGTON	345 SW
CARLE DR.	345 NW	GREEN BRIER	345 NW	ORCHARD	346 NE	WEST MAIN	346 NW
CAROL	346 SW	GREEIIFIELD	346 SW	OTTAWA	346 NW	WESTBERRY	346 NE
CAROLINA	346 SW	GREENWAY	346 SW	PAINE	346 NW	WESTBRIER	346 NE
CARPENTER	345 SE	GROVE	345 SE	PARKWAY	345 SE	WHEELER	346 NW
CARRIE PKWY.	346 NW	HAKER	345 NE	PARKWOOD	345 NU	WHITEHALL	346 NW
CASH	345 NE	HALEY	345 SE	PARSONS	346 SE	WHITEWOOD	345 SS
CASTLE	345 NE	HAM DR.	345 NE	PARTRIDGE	346 NW	WHITEMAN	345 SW
CEDAR	345 SW	HAMILTON	345 SE	PATFICK RD.	346 SE	WILDES	345 SS
CHAPELL	345 SE	HAMPDEN	345 SE	PATTERSON	345 NE	WILDWOOD	345 NW
CHARLES	345 SE	HAMPSHIRE	345 SE	PAUL CT.	345 SE	WILLIAMS	345 SE
CHAT	346 NW	HANCOCK	346 SE	PEPPERIDGE CT.	346 NW	WILMINGTON	346 NW
CHELSEA CT.	345 NW	HANNAH	346 NW	PHEIFFER	345 NW	WILLOW	346 SE
CHERRY	346 SW	HARDING	346 SW	PINE RIVER RD.	345 NW	WILSON	346 NW
CHESTERFIELD	345 NE	HARLOW	345 NE	PINEHURST CT.	345 SE	WINGATE	346 NW
CHESTNUT HILL	346 NW	HAROLD	345 SE	PLAINFIELD	345 NE	WINSOR	345 NW
CHRISTY CT.	345 NW	HARPER LN.	345 NW	PLYMOUTH	346 NE	WINTERGREEN	345 NW
CHURCH	345 SE	HARRISON	345 NE	POMRANKY RD.	346 NW	WISCONSIN	346 SW
CLAREMONT	347 NW	HARTFORD	345 SE	POST	346 SE	WOOD	346 SW
CLAY ST.	346 SE	HARWOOD	345 SE	PRINCETON CT.	345 NW	WOODLAND	345 NE
CLEVELAND	346 SW	HASKIN	345 NE	RAPANO	346 NW	WOODPARK	345 NE
CLOVER CT.	345 NE	HEATERMOOR DR.	346 NW	REARDON	345 SE	WOODVIEW	345 SW
COBB	346 SE	HEDGEWOOD	345 NW	REVERE	345 SE	WYLLYS	346 SW
COLL	345 SE	HELEN	345 SE	RICHARD	345 SE	WYMAN	345 SE
COLORADO	346 NW	HEMLOCK	346 SE	RIDGEMONT	346 NE		
COLUMBIA	345 NE	HENRY	345 NE	RIDGEWOOD	345 NE		
CONCORD ST.	346 NW	HIGH RIDGE CT.	346 NW	RIGGIE	345 SW		
CONES CT.	345 SW	HIGHBROOK	345 SW	RIPLEY	345 SE		
CONGRESS	346 NW	HIGHLAND	346 NW	ROANOKE	345 SE		
COOK	345 NW	HILL	345 NW	ROBIN CT.	345 NE		
COOLIDGE	346 SW	HILL GROVE	346 SW	ROBINLAND	346 NW		
CORNING LN.	346 SW	HILL GROVE CT.	346 SW	ROCKWELL	346 SE		
CORRUNE	346 NW	HINES	346 NW	ROLLCREST	345 NE		
CORTLAND	346 NW	HINES	346 NW	ROMAN	345 SW		
COTTONWOOD	346 SE	HOLLYBROOK	346 SE	RONAI	345 SE		
COUNTRY LINE	345 SW	HOLYROOD	346 SE	ROOD	345 SE		
COVENTRY CT.	346 NW	HUBBARD	346 NW	ROSEMARY CT.	345 NE		
CRANBROOK	346 NW	HUNTERSRIDGE	346 NW	ROSEVILLE	345 SE		
CRANE CT.	345 SE	ILLINOIS	345 SE	ROSS	345 SE		
CRESCENT	345 NE	INDIAN	345 SE	RUMPLE CT.	345 NE		
CRESCENT	345 NE	INS	345 NE	RUSSELL	345 NE		
CRESTWOOD	345 NE	IONIA	346 SW	SAGINAW RD.	346 SW		
CRISSEY	345 NE	IVY	345 SE				

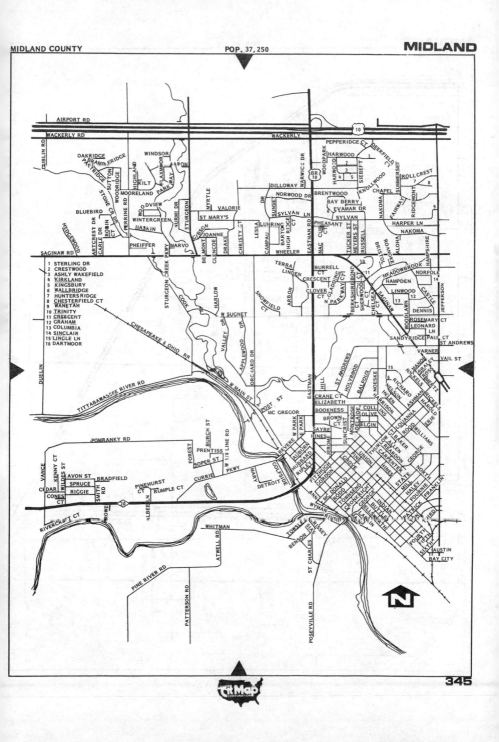

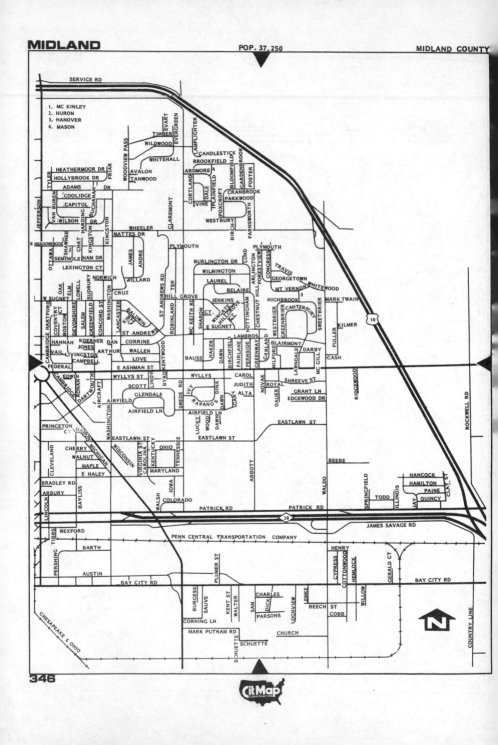

1. MC KINLEY
2. HURON
3. HANOVER
4. MASON

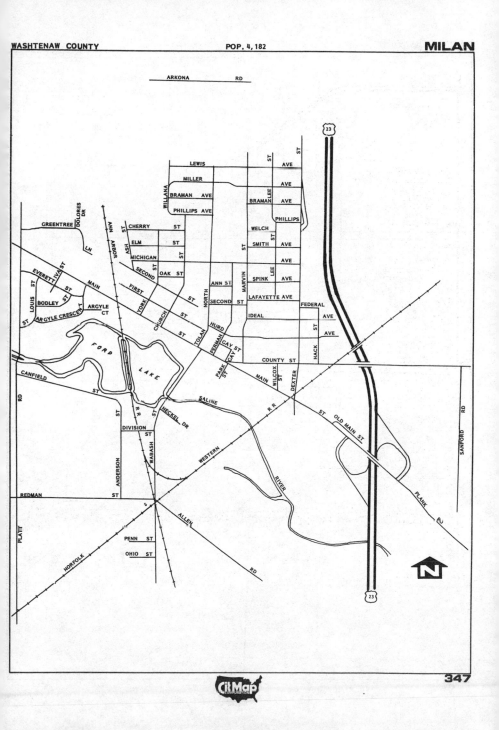

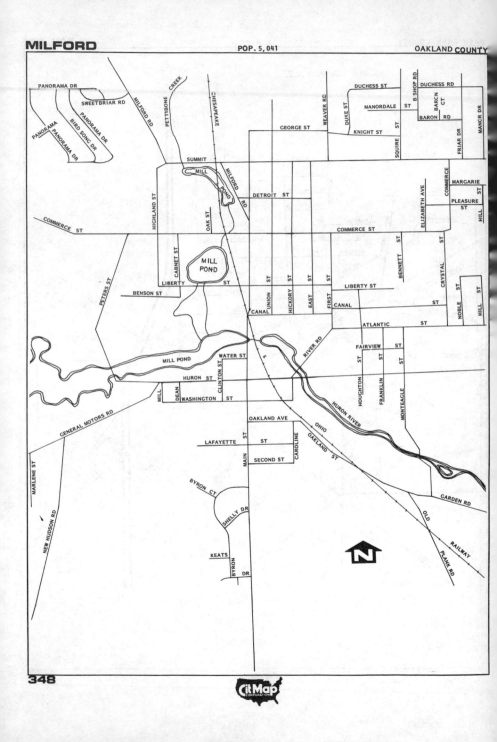

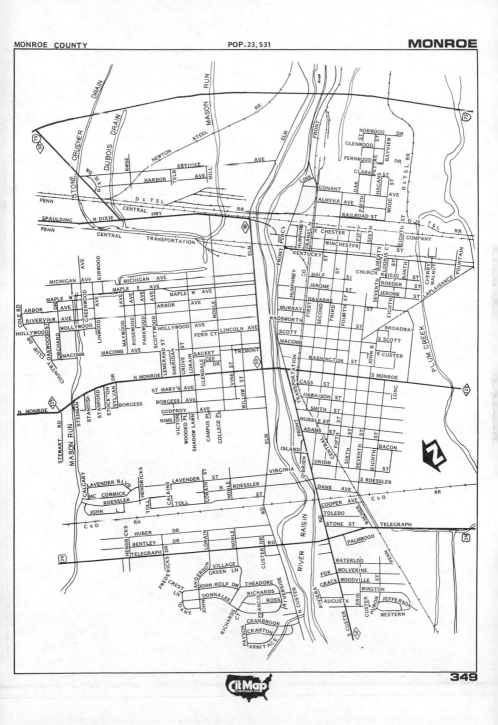

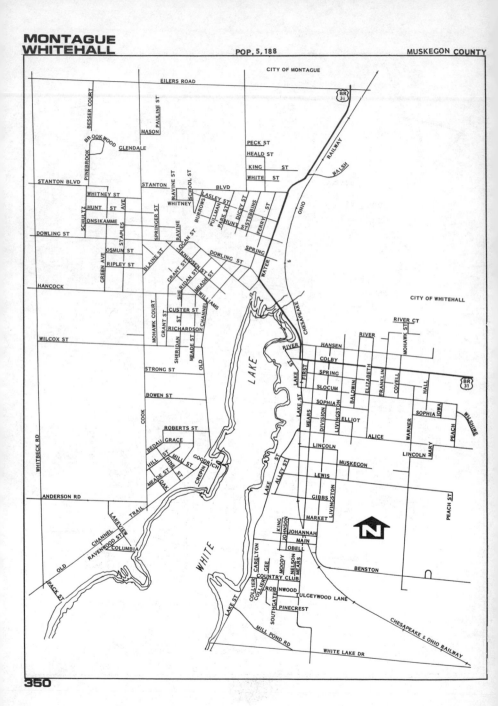

CITY OF MONTAGUE

EILERS ROAD

BR 31

BESSER COURT

PAULINE ST

MASON

BROOKWOOD

GLENDALE

PINEBROOK

PECK ST

HEALD ST

KING ST

WHITE ST

RAILWAY

WALSH

STANTON BLVD

STANTON

RAVINE ST

SCHOOL ST

BLVD

WHITNEY ST

WHITNEY

LASLEY ST

BURROWS

PULLMAN ST

DICEY ST

STEBBINS ST

HUNT ST

AVE

SCHULTZ

ONSIKAMME

STAPLES

SPRINGER ST

RAVINE

PARK ST

HUNT ST

FERRY ST

OHIO

DOWLING ST

OSMUN ST

BLAINE ST

LOGAN ST

DOWLING ST

SPRING

WATER

GREEN AVE

RIPLEY ST

GRANT ST

KNUDSEN ST

MEADE ST

HANCOCK

MOHAWK COURT

SHERIDAN ST

WILLIAMS

CITY OF WHITEHALL

CUSTER ST

CHANNEL ST

RIVER CT

MOHAWK ST

GRANT ST

RICHARDSON

RIVER

RIVER

SHERIDAN

MEADE ST

HANSEN

WILCOX ST

COLBY

FIRST

STRONG ST

OLD

SPRING

ELIZABETH

FRANKLIN

COVELL

HALL

BR 31

SLOCUM

BALDWIN

COOK

BOWEN ST

SOPHIA

LAKE ST

MEARS

DIVISION

LIVINGSTON

ELLIOT

SOPHIA

IOWA

WARNER

PEACH

WILSHIRE

ROBERTS ST

BEDAU

GRACE

HILL ST

STONE ST

MILL ST

GOODRICH

ALICE

WHITBECK RD

MEADE ST

OAK

CREPIN

ALLEY ST

LINCOLN

MUSKEGON

LINCOLN

MARY

ANDERSON RD

LAKEVIEW

TRAIL

LEWIS

PEACH ST

LAKE ST

GIBBS

LIVINGSTON

CHANNEL

RAVENWOOD ST

COLUMBIA

OLD

PACK ST

MARKET

N

KING

JOHNSON

JOHANNAH

MAIN

WHITE

OBELL

COLLIER

CARLETON

GEE

MOODY

NELSON

MEARS

BENSTON

LAKE ST

COUNTRY CLUB

COLLIER

ROBINWOOD

SOUTHGATE

TULGEYWOOD LANE

PINECREST

CHESAPEAKE & OHIO RAILWAY

MILL POND RD

WHITE LAKE DR

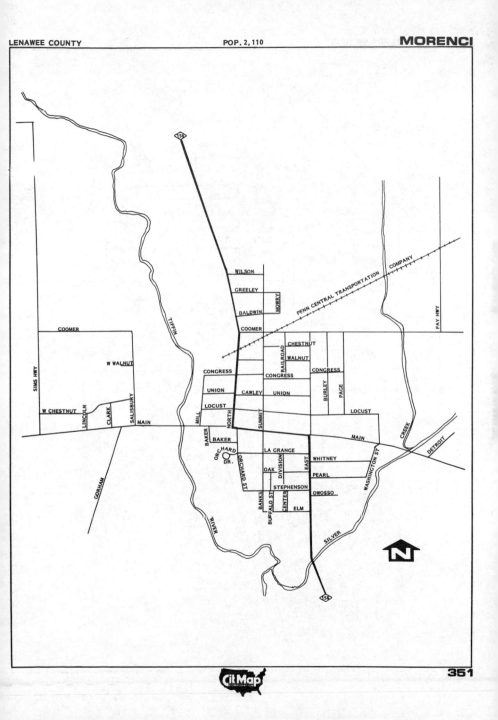

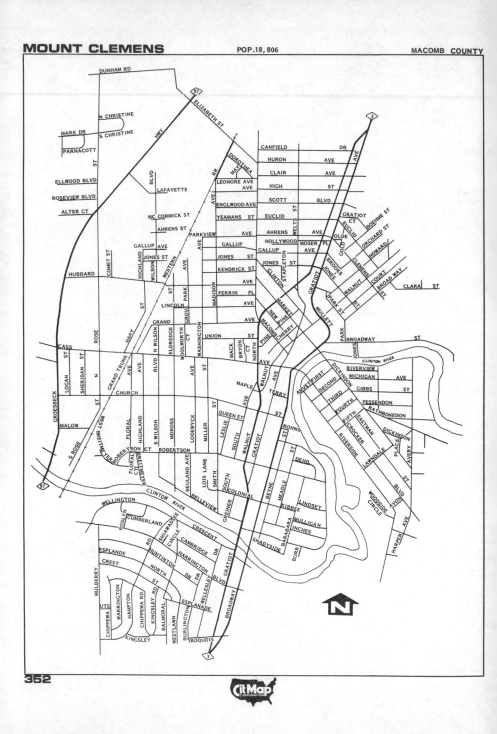

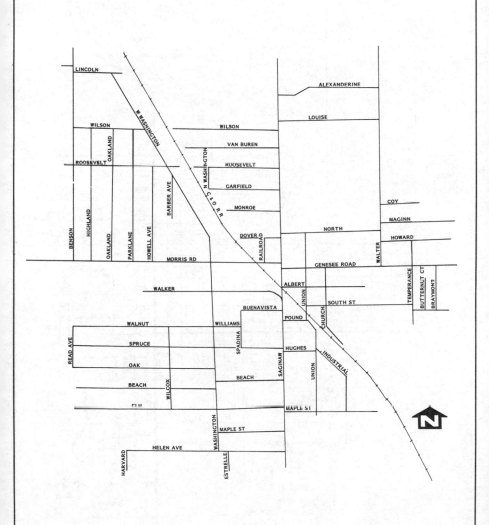

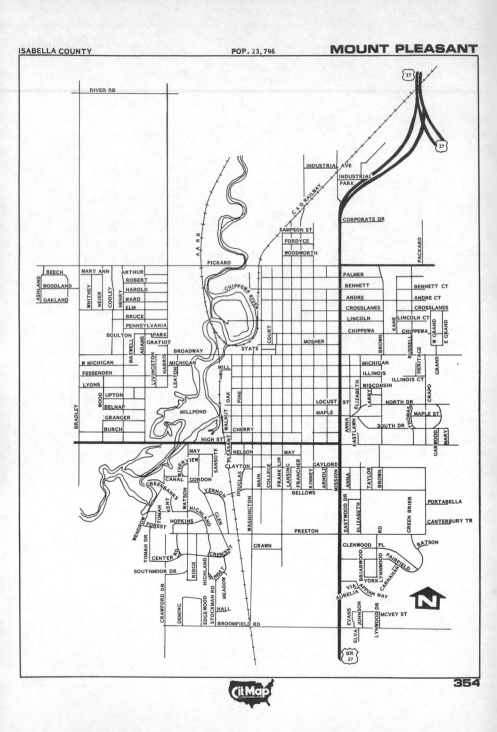

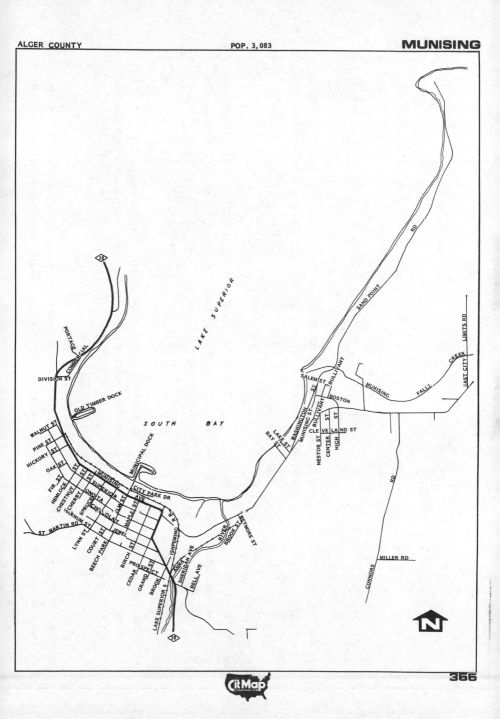

MUSKEGON

STREET INDEX

ABBEY RD	369	NW
ABBEY ST	362	SE
ACCESS RD	362	SE
ACORN	360	SW
ADA AVE	366	NW
ADAMS AVE	362	SW
ADDISON ST	365	SW
AGNES ST	362	SE
AIRLINE DR	371	SW
AIRLINE RD	370	NW
AIRPORT RD	370	NE
ALBERT AVE	362	SW
ALBERTA AVE	365	SE
ALGONQUIN CT	365	SE
ALGONQUIN DR	369	NW
ALLEN AVE	366	NW
ALLENDALE	361	NW
ALPHA AVE	365	SE
ALVA ST	362	SW
AMANDA ST	371	NW
AMBROSIA ST	366	NW
AMHERST RD	369	NW
AMITY AVE	366	NW
AMSTERDAM AVE	369	NE
AMY ST	360	SE
ANDERSON	369	NW
ANDREE RD	361	NW
ANN ST	361	NE
ANNA RD	362	NE
ANNETTA ST	369	NW
ANTISDALE RD	368	SE
ARLINGTON AVE	364	NW
ARMSTRONG RD	369	SE
ARNOLDI AVE	361	NW
ARTHUR ST	360	NW
ASHLAND ST	365	SE
ASPASIA ST	361	NW
ATHENS ST	371	NW
AUBLE RD	361	NW
AUE RD	369	SE
AUGUST AVE	370	SW
AUGUST RD	369	SE
AUGUSTINE ST	369	NW
AURORA AVE	366	NE
AUSTIN ST	366	SE
AVONDALE	368	NE
BAILEY ST	366	SE
BAKER ST	366	SW
BAKKER RD	370	NE
BANK ST	362	SW
BARBARA ST	367	SW
BARCLAY ST	365	NW
BARLOW ST	367	NW
BARNEY AVE	365	SE
BAUER AVE	366	NW
BAY LANE	360	SE
BAYOU ST	362	SW
BAYVIEW DR	369	SW
BEARDSLEY AVE	365	SW
BEAR LAKE RD	361	SW
BECKER RD	362	NE
BEACH ST	364	NW
BEECHTREE CT	360	SW
BEIDLER ST	365	NE
BELLAIRE CT	368	NE
BELLEVUE RD	364	SE
BELLUM AVE	365	SW
BELLWAY AVE	370	SE
BELMONT DR	369	NW
BELTON AVE	369	NE
BENJAMIN RD	359	NE
BENNET ST	369	NE
BENNETT ST	362	SE
BERNADINE AVE	360	SE
BEULAH	366	SW
BEXLEY RD	371	NW
BIRCH DR	370	NW
BIRCH DR	360	SW
BLACK CREEK RD	367	SW
BLISSFIELD CT	368	NE
BLODGETT ST	365	SW
BLOOMFIELD	365	NE
BLUFF ST	364	NW
BLUFFTON AVE	364	SW
BOLTWOOD DR	364	SW
BONNETA RD	363	SE
BONNEVILLE DR	365	SW
BOURDON ST	365	SW
BOYLE ST	364	SW
BRADFORD ST	370	NW
BRADLEY AVE	369	NE
BRAEBURN DR	369	NW
BRENTWOOD ST	369	NW
BREWER ST	371	SW
BRIAR AVE	371	NW
BRIGHTON AVE	364	NW
BROADMOOR ST	362	SE
BROADWAY AVE	365	SW
BROOK CT	370	NW
BROOKDALE DR	369	SW
BROOKFIELD RD	369	NW
BROOKWOOD DR	369	SW
BROWNE AVE	369	NE
BROWNE ST	364	NW
BRUNSWICK ST	366	SE
BRUSSE AVE	362	SE
BUNDT DR	365	SW
BURKE ST	367	NW
BURTON ST	366	NE
BUSH AVE	366	NE
BUSHNELL DR	368	NW
BUTLER DR	369	NW
BUTLER ST	362	SW
BUYS RD	360	SE

CADILLAC DR	361	NW
CALIFORNIA AVE	360	SE
CALVIN AVE	366	NE
CAMBRIDGE DR	370	NW
CAMELOT DR	361	NW
CAMPBELL DR	368	NE
CAMPBELL CT	362	SW
CAMPUS	365	NE
CENTERBURY ST	360	NE
CARLTON ST	367	NW
CAROL AVE	369	SW
CAROLYN ST	371	SW
CARRIAGE RD	367	NW
CARTER DR	368	NE
CASANELLI AVE	360	SE
CASTLE AVE	365	SW
CATAWBA AVE	366	NW
CATHERINE AVE	366	NW
CAVALIER DR	361	NW
CEDAR ST	366	NW
CEDAR ST	361	SE
CEDARCREEK	363	SW
CELERY LA	361	NE
CENTER	367	SW
CENTER ST	361	SE
CENTER ST	367	NW
CENTER ST	366	SW
CENTRAL AVE	368	NE
CENTRAL AVE	361	SW
CHADWICK DR E	361	SW
CHADWICK DR W	361	SW
CHANNEL AVE	364	NW
CHANNEL RD	368	SE
CHANNEL RD	360	SE
CHAPEL CT	369	NW
CHAPEL RD	369	NW
CHARLES AVE	364	SE
CHARLES ST	361	NE
CHARLES ST	362	SW
CHARLES ST	371	NE
CHEBOYGAN DR	361	NW
CHELMSFORD DR	360	SE
CHERRY ST	365	SE
CHERRY ST	370	SE
CHERRY ST	364	NW
CHESTER AVE	371	NW
CHESTNUT ST	366	NW
CHIAK ST	360	SE
CHILTON DR	370	NW
CHIPPEWA	369	NW
CHURCHILL DR	369	SE
CIRCLE DR	361	SW
CIRCLE PL	370	NE
CLARK ST	367	NW
CLARK ST	368	NE
CLAY AVE	365	NE
CLAYTON AVE	369	NW
CLEARWATER CTS	369	SE
CLEARWATER ST	369	SE
CLEVELAND AVE	369	NE
CLIFFORD ST	364	SE
CLINE RD	371	NW
CLINTON ST	366	NW
COLLINS AVE	366	SW
COLONIAL RD	369	NW
COLUMBIA AVE	365	SE
COLUMBIA AVE	367	SW
COLUMBUS AVE	368	NE
COMMERCE ST	365	SE
CONCORD AVE	366	NW
CONNECTICUT AVE	360	SE
CONTINENTAL ST	366	SE
CONVOY AVE	365	SW
COOLIDGE PKWY	370	SE
COOLIDGE RD	369	NW
CORNELL CT	365	SW
CORNELL RD	365	SW
CORRINE AVE	371	NW
COTTAGE GROVE ST	364	SW
COUNTRY CLUB DR	364	SW
COUNTRY CLUB DR	364	SW
COVENTRY RD	369	NW
COWLES ST	360	SE
CRANBROOK AVE	360	SW
CRANBROOK RD	369	NE
CRANDALL AVE	369	NW
CREEK DR	365	SW
CRESCENT AVE	370	NW
CRESS CREEK DR	371	NW
CRESTBROOK AVE	370	NE
CRESTON RD N	362	NE
CRESTON ST	366	NE
CRESTWOOD LA	368	NE
CROSS ST	362	SW
CROWLEY ST	365	SE
CROZIER AVE	365	SW
CUMBERLAND ST	365	SW
CURTIS AVE		
NORTON SHORES	369	NW
CURTIS AVE		
N.MUSKEGON	361	NE
CURVECREST	361	NE
CUTLER AVE	364	SE
DALE AVE	365	NE
DANGL RD	363	SE
DATTNER ST	365	SW
DAVID ST	371	NW
DAVIS ST		
MUSKEGON	365	NW
DAVIS RD		
NORTON SHORES	369	SW
DAVIS RD		
ROOSEVELT PK	369	NW
DAWES RD	365	SW

DEANER DR	362	SW
DEBAKER RD	367	NE
DEFENSE AVE	365	SW
DE FEYTER ST	371	NE
DELANO AVE	365	SE
DELAWARE AVE	366	NW
DELZ DR	361	NW
DENMARK ST	364	SE
DENSMORE ST	363	SW
DEVONSHIRE DR	369	SW
DE VOWE	367	SE
DEWEY ST	364	NW
DIANA AVE	366	NW
DIVERSEY ST	369	NW
DIVISION ST	365	NE
DONALD AVE	367	NE
DONALD ST	363	SW
DONNA AVE	369	SE
DOROTHY ST	369	SE
DORSET LA	369	SE
DOUGLAS LA		
FRUITPORT TWP.	371	NW
DOUGLAS ST		
N. MUSK.	361	NE
DOWD ST	365	SE
DRATZ ST	362	SE
DREXEL RD	369	NW
DUCEY AVE	362	SE
DUDLEY AVE	366	NE
DUNE ST	364	SW
DUNECREST	368	NE
DURHAM RD	369	NE
DYKSTRA RD	361	NW
DYSON ST	366	NW
EARL ST	369	SE
EAST ST	363	SW
EASTERN AVE	366	NW
EASTGATE ST	366	NE
EASTHILL CT	368	NE
EASTHILL DR	368	NE
EAST LAKE RD	370	NE
EASTLAND RD	365	SW
E WEDGEWOOD DR	361	NW
EASTWOOD DR	366	NE
EDENBROOK CT	369	SE
EDGEBROOK ST	365	SE
EDGEWATER ST	364	NW
EDINBOROUGH DR	369	SW
EDMUNDS AVE	364	SW
EDNA ST	362	NE
EDWARDS ST	368	NE
EDWIN ST	366	NE
EIGHTH ST	365	NE
EIGHTH ST	365	SE
MUSK. HTS		
ELMER ST	361	SE
ELIZABETH CT	366	SW
ELLEN ST	371	NW
ELLIFSON AVE	362	SW
ELLIS RD	370	SW
ELM	360	SW
ELM AVE	365	NW
ROOSEVELT PK		
ELMWOOD ST	369	SW
ELOISE DR	370	NE
ELSA AVE		
NORTON SHORES	369	NW
ELSA AVE		
N. MUSKEGON	361	NE
ELWOOD ST	366	NW
EMENS DR	371	SW
EMERALD AVE		
NORTON SHORES	370	SE
EMERALD ST	366	NW
EMERSON AVE	365	SE
ENGLAND AVE	360	SW
ENGLEWOOD AVE	370	SE
ENGMAN RD	362	NW
ERIC AVE	369	NE
ERICKSON ST	362	SW
ERIE	365	SE
ESSEX RD	369	NE
ESTES ST	365	SW
ESTHER AVE	370	SE
EUGENE AVE	364	SE
EVALINE DR	371	NW
EVANSTON AVE	366	NE
EVART AVE	366	NE
FAIR AVE	365	SW
FAIRFIELD ST	365	SE
FAIRLAWN CT	364	SW
FAIRVIEW ST	365	SE
FAIRWOOD DR	368	NE
FARNSWORTH AVE	367	NW
FENNER RD	361	SW
FENNWOOD CIR	361	NW
FERGUSON CT	364	NW
FERN HILLS DR	371	NW
FETT AVE	371	SW
FIFTH ST	365	NE
FIGGE RD	362	NE
FILINOW	371	NW
FINK ST	370	NE
FIRST ST	365	NE
FIRST ST	361	SW
N. MUSKEGON		
FISCHER AVE	370	NW
FLEMING AVE	366	NE
FLEMING ST	361	SW
N.MUSKEGON		
FLOWER AVE	366	NE
FORD RD	359	NW
FORDHAM CT	369	NE
FORDHAM RD	369	NW
FOREST	365	NE

FOREST DR	362	SE
FOREST HILLS RD	364	SE
FOREST PARK RD	369	NW
FORK ST	366	NW
FOUNTAIN ST	364	SE
FOURTH ST	365	NE
FOURTH ST		
N.MUSKEGON	361	SW
FOWLER ST	361	SE
FRANCIS AVE	366	NE
FRANKLIN ST	365	NE
FRANKLIN ST		
N.MUSK.	361	SW
FREMONT ST	361	NE
FRISBIE ST	365	SW
FROST ST	267	NE
FULTON AVE	364	NW
FURHMAN ST	369	NW
GARBER RD	361	SW
GARDEN AVE		
NORTON SHORES	370	NE
GARDEN ST	366	NE
GARDNER ST	363	SE
GARLAND DR	368	NE
GARY ST	362	NW
GAY ST	369	SW
GAYLORD DR	361	NW
GENESEE AVE	367	NE
GEORGE ST	371	NE
GEORG'S LANE	366	SW
GERMAINE RD	369	NW
GETTY AVE	366	NW
GETTY RD N	362	NE
GETZ RD	369	SW
GIDDINGS AVE	362	SW
GILES RD	361	NE
GIN CHAN AVE	369	NE
GLADE ST	365	NE
GLADE ST		
NORTON SHORES	369	SE
GLADSTONE DR	361	NW
GLEN AVE	365	SW
GLENDALE ST		
MUSK. HTS	370	NW
GLENRICK AVE	367	NE
GLENSIDE BLVD	365	SW
GLENWOOD AVE	361	SW
GOODY RD	369	SW
GORDON AVE	367	NW
GRACE AVE	366	NE
GRAF ST	366	NE
GRAHAM ST	367	NW
GRAND AVE	365	NE
GRAND AVE	370	SE
NORTON SH.		
GRAND HAVEN RD	370	NE
GREELEY ST	365	NW
GREEN	360	SW
LAKETON TWP.	360	SW
GREEN RD		
GREEN ST	366	NE
GREENBRIAR DR	361	NW
GREEN CREEK RD	360	SW
GREENFIELD ST	369	SW
GREEN RIDGE AVE	360	SW
GREENWICH RD	369	NW
GREENWOOD ST	365	SW
GRIESBACH ST	368	NE
GRIFFIN ST	367	SW
GROVE ST	364	SE
GRUBER CT	364	SW
GRUELING RD	369	NW
GUNN ST	362	SW
HACKLEY AVE		
MUSK. HTS	365	SE
HACKLEY AVE	367	SW
HACKLEY LA		
NORTON SH.	369	SW
HADDEN ST		
MUSK. TOWNSHIP	365	SW
HAIGHT		
FRUITPORT TWP.	371	NE
HAIGHT ST	367	SE
HALL AVE	362	SW
HALL RD	363	SW
HAMILTON AVE	366	NW
HAMPDEN RD	369	NW
HANCOCK AVE	365	SE
HANLEY	369	NW
HANLEY	365	SE
ROOSEVELT PK		
HANOVER DR	360	SE
HANSEN ST	361	NW
HARBOR	365	SW
HARBOR DR	369	NW
HARBOR POINT DR	369	NW
HARDING AVE	370	SE
HARDING AVE		
NORTON SHORES	364	SE
HARMONY LANE	360	SW
HARNAU ST	366	NW
HAROLD ST	363	SE
HARRISON AVE	365	SW
HARRISON BLVD		
MUSKEGON HTS	370	NW
HARRISON CT	364	SE
HARTFORD AVE	366	NW
HARTS LA	363	NW
HARVEY ST	362	SE
HATHAWAY CT	368	NE
HAVENGA ST	361	NW
HAVERHILL CT	369	NW
HAVERHILL RD	369	NW
HEIGHTS RAVENNA	371	NW
HEINICKE RD	369	SE

HELEN DR	369	SW
HENDRICK RD	368	SE
HENRY ST	365	NE
HERRICK ST	362	SW
HESS	370	NE
HIAWATHA DR	369	NW
HIGH ST	365	NW
HIGHGATE RD	370	NW
HIGHLAND AVE	368	NW
HILE RD	369	SW
HILL AVE	364	NW
HILL ST	366	NW
HILLCREST DR	366	NE
HILLSIDE DR	368	NE
HILLVIEW DR	369	SW
HOLBROOK AVE	366	NW
HOLT ST	366	NW
HOLTON RD	361	NE
HOME ST	366	NE
HORTON RD	361	NW
HOUSTON AVE	365	NE
HOVEY AVE	366	SW
HOWARD AVE	366	NE
HOWDEN ST	366	SW
HOWELL AVE	366	SW
HOYT ST	366	NW
HUDSON ST	365	NE
HUETHER AVE	360	SE
HUGHES AVE	364	SE
HUGHEY ST	360	SW
HUGO AVE	366	NW
HUIZENGA ST	366	NE
HULKA AVE	371	NE
HUME AVE	366	SW
IDA	370	SW
IDAHO	366	SE
IDLEWILD RD	364	SW
INDIANA AVE	364	NW
INDUSTRIAL	366	SE
INTERWOOD ST	367	SW
IONA AVE	366	NW
IONE AVE	369	SW
IRELAND AVE	365	NW
IRWIN AVE	366	NW
ISABELLA AVE	366	NW
IVANHOE DR	361	NW
IVORY AVE	366	SW
IVY LA	362	NW
IVY ST	365	NW
N.MUSK		
JACKSON AVE	362	SW
JACKSON DR	360	SE
JAMES AVE	362	SE
JANE CT	366	SE
JARMAN ST	366	NW
JAY ST	366	NW
JEFFERSON ST	365	NE
JEFFREY ST	369	NW
JENSEN RD	371	SW
JEROME AVE	367	NW
JIROCH ST	366	NW
JOHN AVE	369	SE
JOHN AVE	361	SW
JOHN ST	361	NE
JONES ST	367	NE
JOSEPHINE AVE	371	SW
JOSLYN RD	362	NW
JUDY LANE	360	SW
JULIA CT	370	SE
KAMPENGA AVE	366	NE
KANITZ ST	365	SE
KAREN AVE	371	NW
KATHERINE ST	368	NW
KATHERINE ST W	368	NW
KATHRYN ST	371	SW
KATY AVE	371	NE
KEATING AVE	365	SE
KEATON CT	364	SW
KEATING AVE	365	SE
KEATON CT	364	SW
KEENER ST	371	SW
KELLER ST	369	SE
KENNETH ST	366	NW
KENT ST	367	NW
KERN RD	360	SW
KIMBERLY DR	371	NW
KINGS CT	362	NE
KINGSBURY	361	NW
KINGSLEY ST	366	NE
KINSEY ST	365	SE
KNOLLWOOD CT	364	SW
KOOI ST	366	SE
KRAFT ST	362	SE
KREGEL AVE	366	NE
KRUGER	367	SW
KUNZ ST	369	SE
LAFOND ST	371	NW
LAKE AVE	361	SW
LAKE DR	369	NE
LAKE DR	361	SW
LAKE ST	361	SW
LAKETON TWP		
LAKE HARBOR RD	369	SW
LAKESHORE	370	NW
LAKE SHORE DR	365	NW
LAKETON AVE	365	NE
LAKEVIEW AVE	370	NW
LAMBERT DR	369	NW
LANCELOT DR	361	NW
LANGELAND AVE	366	NE
LANGLEY ST	362	SW
LANNING AVE	363	SW
LARCH AVE	365	NE
LARKIN ST	364	SW
LARUE ST	364	SE

CitMap CORPORATION

Street	Pg	Dir
LATIMER DR	367	SW
LAUREL ST	369	SW
LAWNEL AVE	368	SW
LAWRENCE	361	SW
LAWRENCE AVE	366	NE
LEAHY ST	366	NW
LE BOEUF ST	368	NE
LEBOUY	364	SE
LE CLARE ST	371	NW
LEE ST	371	NW
I FIF AVE	368	NE
LEMUEL ST	365	SE
LENEDO ST	371	NE
LENORE AVE	367	NE
LEON ST	368	NE
LEONARD AVE	362	SW
LEORIE AVE	361	NE
LEROUX RD	369	NE
LETARTE AVE	364	SE
LEXINGTON AVE	365	NE
LIBERTY HD	564	SC
LINCOLN NORTON SHORE	368	NW
LINCOLN AVE	369	NW
LINCOLN CT	370	NW
LINCOLN ST	369	NW
LINCOLN PARK DR	364	SW
LINDA ST	366	SW
LINDBERG DR	365	NW
LINDEN DR	360	SW
LINDEN ST	362	NW
LINDERMAN RD	369	NW
LIN-NAN LANE	369	SW
LOGAN RD	362	NE
LOIS CT	364	NE
LOOMIS DR	370	NW
LOOP RD	365	SW
LOUISE ST	366	NW
LYMAN AVE	365	SE
LYNCOTT ST	361	SW
MAC LANE	368	NE
MAC ARTIIIUR RD	366	NE
MACKLIN AVE	366	NE
MADALENE AVE	367	NW
MADISON ST	366	SW
MAFFETT ST	366	SW
MALCOLM DR	369	SW
MANAHAN AVE	365	SW
MANCELONA DR	370	NW
MANGIN AVE	366	NE
MANHATTAN AVE	364	NW
MANISTEE RD	368	NE
MANITOU BLVD	368	NE
MANITOU HTS MUSK. HTS		
MANN ST	364	SE
MANNING ST	371	NW
MANOR DR	365	SW
MANZ ST	369	NE
MAPLE AVE ROOSEVELT PK	369	NW
MAPLE CT	369	NW
MAPLE ST	365	NW
MAPLE GT	369	SE
MAPLE GROVE NORTON SHORES	364	SW
MAPLEGROVE RD ROOSEVELT PK	365	SW
MAPLE GROVE RD NORTON SHORES	370	SE
MAPLERIDGE ST	360	NE
MAPLEWOOD AVE	369	NE
MARANATHA DR	365	SE
MARCOUX AVE	366	NW
MARGARET ST	362	SW
MARIWOOD AVE	361	NW
MARK AVE	371	NE
MARLANE CT	363	SW
MARLBORO RD	369	NW
MARQUARD AVE	366	SE
MARQUETTE AVE	362	SW
MARSH ST	366	NW
MARSHALL RD NORTON SHORES	370	SE
MARSHALL ST	362	SW
MARTI RD	365	NE
MARTIN RD	370	SW
MARVA AVE	371	SW
MARVIN AVE	376	NW
MARY AVE FRUITPORT TWP.	371	SW
MARY ST	362	SW
MARYLAND DR	368	NE
MARYLAND ST	360	SE
MASON AVE	365	NE
MASON BLVD	366	SW
MASSACHUSETTS	360	SE
MAXPAULSEN DR	371	NE
MAXWELL AVE	361	NE
MAYFAIR AVE	364	SW
McARTHUR ST	367	SW
McCONNELL AVE	360	SE
McCRACKEN ST	366	SE
McDERMOTT ST	366	SE
McDOWELL ST	365	NW
McGRAFT ST	365	NW
McGRAFT PARK RD	365	NW
McILWRAITH ST	365	NW
McKINLEY CT	370	SE
McLAREN ST	362	SW
McLAUGHLIN AVE	366	NE
MEDEMA ST	371	NW
MEEKING ST	362	SE
MELMAX ST	369	SE
MELODY LANE	360	SE
MEMORIAL CA WAY	362	SE
MEMORIAL DR	360	SE
MERRIAM ST	370	NW
MERRILL AVE	365	NE
MERTESE ST	367	NE
MESSLER ST	365	NE
METRO	361	NW
MEUER CT	364	SE
MICHAEL ST	370	NE
MICHIGAN AVE	365	NW
MICKA ST	371	NE
MIDDLEBROOK	369	NW
MID OAK DR	361	SW
MILLARD ST	364	SW
MILLER DR	361	SW
MILLER ST	369	SE
MILL IRON RD	363	SE
MILLS AVE	361	NE
MILTON AVE	367	NW
MINER AVE	361	BE
MINK AVE	367	SE
MITZI AVE	361	NE
MOHAWK DR	369	NW
MONA LA	369	NW
MONA ST	369	NE
MONA BROOK RD	369	SE
MONA LAKE PARK	370	NW
MONA VIEW DR	370	NW
MONROE AVE	369	NE
MONTAGUE AVE	365	NW
MONTANA ST	366	SE
MONTE AVE	371	SW
MONTEVIEW DR	368	NE
MONTGOMERY	365	SW
MOON ST	365	SW
MOORE ST	365	SW
MOORE ST NORTON SH.	369	SW
MORGAN	362	SE
MORNINGSIDE ST	367	NE
MORRIS ST	363	NC
MORTON AVE	366	NE
MORTON AVE	370	NW
MOULTON ST	361	SW
MULDER DR LAKETON TWP.	361	NE
MULDER ST	362	NW
MURL AVE	367	SE
MURPHY ST	366	NW
MUSKEGON AVE	365	NE
MYRTLE AVE	366	NW
NANCY LANE	360	SW
NASSAU ST	363	SW
NEECE DR	369	SW
NELSON ST	364	NW
NELSON ST N.MUSKEGON	361	SE
NEVADA ST	363	SW
NEW ST	366	NE
NIMS ST	366	NW
NINTH ST	365	SW
NINTH ST MUSK. HTS	365	SE
NOB HILL DR	368	SE
NOLAND ST	362	NE
NORCREST DR	368	NE
NORLOCK ST	369	NE
NORMAN DR	364	SE
N BROOKSIDE	369	SE
N LANDCASTER	368	NE
N MANITOU CIR	368	NE
NORTH PARK LA	368	SE
NORTON AVE	368	NW
NORTON HILLS	368	NW
NORWICH AVE	368	NW
NOTTINGHAM CT	361	SE
OAK AVE	361	SE
OAK AVE MUSKEGON	366	NW
OAKDALE ST	370	NW
OAKGROVE ST	366	NE
OAK HILL	362	SE
OAK KNOLL	366	SE
OAKLANE	366	SE
OAKLEA AVE	367	NW
OAKMERE PL	364	SE
OAK PARK DR	366	SE
OAKRIDGE RD	365	SE
OAKWOOD LA	370	NW
OCTAVIUS ST	362	SW
OHIO AVE	364	SW
OLTHOFF DR	367	SW
ORCHARD AVE	366	NW
ORCHARD ST	370	NE
OREGON AVE	366	SW
ORIOLE ST	371	SW
ORSHAL RD	359	NW
OSCAR AVE	361	NE
OSCEOLA DR	368	NE
OTTAWA ST	362	NE
OVERBROOK	370	NW
PADELT ST	369	NW
PALMER AVE	365	NW
PANZL ST	367	SW
PAPPAS ST	362	NE
PARK DR	365	NE
PARK DR N.MUSKEGON		
PARK PL	364	SW
PARKWAY	364	SW
PARSLOW ST	369	SE
PARSONS ST	364	NE
PATRICIA DR	366	NE
PATTERSON DR	363	SE
PECK ST	377	NW
PENINSULAR DR	370	NW
PENN AVE	367	SW
PENN LA	360	SE
PENNSYLVANIA	360	SW
PETERSON RD	360	SW
PETOSKEY DR	361	NW
PETRIE AVE	370	SE
PHILIP SMITH ST	365	SW
PHILO AVE	364	SE
PIERCE RD	360	NW
PINE ST	366	NW
PINE GROVE ST	365	SW
PINEHURST RD	364	SE
PINE RIDGE DR	369	SE
PINEWOOD DR LAKETON TWP	360	SW
PINEWOOD RD	361	SE
PIPER AVE	361	NW
PLAIN ST	371	NE
PLUILIN S1	364	SW
PLAINFIELD AVE	361	BE
PLUM AVE	364	SW
PLUMB AVE S	365	SW
PLUMB ST W	365	SW
PLYMOUTH AVE	366	SW
PLYMOUTH DR NORTON SHORES	370	NW
PLYMOUTH DR	364	SW
PONTIAC AVE	369	NE
PORT CITY BLVD	367	SW
PORTER RD	360	SW
POST RD	365	SW
POULIN S1	370	NE
PRESCOTT ST	368	SW
PRINCETON CT	365	SW
PRINCETON RD	365	SW
PULASKI AVE	365	SE
QUAINTON RD	370	NW
QUARTERLINE RD N	363	NW
QUARTERLINE R	363	NW
RAFFIE ST	371	NE
RANCII DR	369	NE
RANDALL RD	369	NW
RANDOLPH AVE	361	NE
RANSFORD	366	NW
RANSOM ST	366	NW
RATHBONE ST	366	NW
RAY ST	366	NW
RAY ST N.MUSKEGON	361	SW
REETH CT	362	NE
REGINALD DR	371	NE
RENEER AVE	368	NE
RESORT AVE	364	SW
REYNOLDS ST	366	SW
RIBLET ST	362	NW
RICHARD ST	365	SW
RICHARDS ST	365	SW
RIDGE AVE	365	SW
RIEGLER RD	366	NW
RIORDAN ST	369	SW
RITTER DR	369	NW
RITTER HILLS	369	NW
RIVERVIEW AVE	361	NE
ROBERTS RD N	362	NE
ROBERTS ST	362	SE
ROBINHOOD DR N	361	NW
ROBINHOOD DR W	361	NW
ROBINSON ST	265	NW
ROBLANE	363	SW
ROCKLAND RD	369	NW
RODGERS AVE	364	NW
ROILSON ST	369	SE
ROMEDIUS ST	367	SE
ROOD RD	369	NW
ROOD POINT RD	369	NE
ROOSEVELT CT	370	SE
ROOSEVELT RD	369	NW
ROSS RD	369	SE
ROTTERDAM AVE	369	NW
ROUSE ST	369	SW
ROUSELL	369	SW
ROY AVE	366	SW
ROYAL OAK RD	369	NW
RUDDIMAN AVE	365	NW
RUDDIMAN AVE	365	NW
RUDOLPH CT	370	NW
RUSSELL RD	367	NW
RUTH ST	361	NW
SALEM DR W	361	NW
SAMBURT ST	366	NE
SAMPSON AVE	364	NW
SAND ST	364	NW
SANDYBROOK	370	NW
SANFORD ST	366	NW
SARASOTA CT	368	SE
SAUTER AVE	364	NW
SCENIC DR	359	NW
SCHOOL ST	362	SE
SCHULER ST	365	NW
SCHUYLER ST	365	NW
SCOTT ST	369	SW
SCRANTON DR	369	SW
SEABOLT AVE	360	SW
SEAWAY DR	369	NE
SECOND AVE NORTON SH	370	NW
SECOND ST	362	SW
SECOND ST N. MUSK	361	SW
SEMINOLE RD	369	NW
SENECA DR	368	NE
SENG RD	369	NE
SEVENTH ST	365	SW
SEVENTH ST MUSK. HTS	365	SE
SHELBY ST	369	NE
SHEFFIELD ST	365	SE
SHERIDAN RD	363	SW
SHERIDAN RD N	363	SW
SHERIN ST	364	SE
SHERINGER RD	371	NW
SHERMAN AVE	361	NE
SHRMAN BLVD	365	SE
SHERWOOD LAKETON TWP	361	NW
SHERWOOD CT N	364	SW
SHERWOOD CT S	364	NW
SHERWOOD RD ROOSEVELT PK	369	NW
SHETTLER RD	370	NE
SHIRLEY BLVD	367	NW
SHONAT ST	363	SW
SHOREWOOD	368	SE
SHORROCK ST	367	SE
SICORD ST	364	SW
SIDELL BLVD	367	NW
SIMONELLI RD	359	NE
SIMPSON AVE	364	NW
SISSON AVE	364	SE
SIXTH ST	365	SW
SIXTH ST MUSKEGON HT	365	SE
SKY LINE CIR	371	NW
SKYLINE DR	367	NW
SMITH ST	366	NW
SOMERSET CT	309	SW
SOPHIA ST	366	NW
SOUTH CT	370	NE
S BROOKSIDE DR	369	SE
SOUTHERN AVE	365	NE
SOUTHLAND DR	366	NW
S MANITOU CIR	368	NE
SOUTHWOOD AVE	369	NW
SPENCER DR	368	NE
SPENCER DR MUSK. TWP.	362	NW
SPIERS ST	369	NE
SPRING ST	366	NW
SPRUCE AVE	371	NW
STAFFORD DR	361	SW
STANTON ST	370	NW
STANWOOD ST	369	SE
STAR AVE	371	NE
STERBINS RD	363	NW
STEIN ST	365	SW
STERNBERG RD	363	NW
STEVENS ST	366	NE
FRUITPORT TWP.	371	NW
STEWART ST	361	SW
STRALEY ST	366	SE
STRATFORD ST	366	SE
STRONG AVE	369	NW
STRYKER DR	363	SW
SUELANE	363	SW
SUMAC ST	362	NW
SUMMIT AVE ROOSEVELT PK	365	SE
SUMMIT AVE	362	SW
SUMNER AVE	370	NE
SUNBURY AVE	370	NE
SUNNY RIDGE ST	369	SE
SUNSET DR	361	NE
SUNSET DR FRUITPORT TWP	371	NE
SUNSET LA	361	NW
SUNVIEW ST	361	NW
SUPERIOR ST	366	NW
SURFSIDE	363	NE
SURFWOOD DR	364	SW
SURREY	367	NW
SUSAN CT	366	SE
SUSAN ST	366	SE
SUSIE AVE	371	NE
SYLVAN AVE	367	NE
TAFT CT	370	SE
TAYLOR ST	364	SW
TAYLOR ST	370	NE
TEMPLE ST	365	SW
TERRA CIRCLE DR	360	SE
TERRACE ST	365	NE
TERRY ST	363	NE
THAVEL LI	303	NL
THERESA ST	366	SE
THIRD ST N.MUSKEGON	361	SW
THIRD ST	365	NE
THOMAS AVE	361	NW
THOMPSON AVE MUSK.	370	SE
THOMPSON RD	364	NW
THONA ST	371	NW
THRUSH ST	369	NE
TIBET	369	NE
TIMBERLANE AVE	360	NE
TOLSON DR	371	SW
TORRENT ST	365	SW
TOSTENABE LA	370	SE
TOWNER ST	370	NE
TRYON AVE	371	SW
TWIGS AVE	362	NW
TWIGS LA	362	NW
TWIN OAK RD	362	SW
UTAH ST	366	SW
VALK ST	366	SE
VALLEY ST	366	SE
VAN ALLEN DR	371	NW
VANDERBERG RD	363	NE
VANDERLINDE ST	365	SW
VANDER WERP	361	SW
VERNA AVE	367	SE
VERNON PL	365	NW
VICK RD	370	SE
VINCENT	366	NE
VINE AVE	366	NE
VINE ST	361	SW
VIOLET AVE	367	NE
VIRGINIA DR E FRUITPORT	371	NW
VIRGINIA DR S	371	NW
VIRGINIA ST LAKETON TWP	361	NW
VISTA ST	365	NE
VULCAN ST	366	NE
WAALKES ST	365	SE
WALKER RD	363	SE
WALKER RD FRUITPORT	371	NE
WALKER ST FRUITPORT	371	NE
WALNUT ST	365	SW
WALTON AVE	368	HW
WANDA AVE	365	NE
WARREN AVE	364	SE
WASHINGTON	365	NE
WASHINGTON ST	361	NE
WATERWORKS RD	364	SW
WATSON AVE	364	NW
WAYNE ST	370	NW
WEALTHY ST	370	NE
WEBER RD	360	SW
WEBSTER AVE	365	NE
WELLESLEY DR	370	NW
WELLWOOD ST	368	NE
WENDOVER BLVD	370	NW
WERNER ST	370	NE
WESLEY AVE	363	SW
WEST LA NORTON SH	367	NW
WEST ST	363	NW
WESTERN AVE	362	SW
W BYRION RD	369	SE
W. LANCASTER	360	SE
WESTLAND RD	365	SW
W WEDGEWOOD	361	NW
WESTWIND DR	361	NW
WESTWOOD RD	365	SW
WHITE AVE	366	SW
WHITE ST FRUITPORT	371	NW
WHITEHALL RD	361	NE
WICKHAM DR	365	SW
WILCOX AVE	364	SW
WILFRED ST	371	SW
WILLIAMS ST	366	NW
WILSON AVE	365	SW
WILSON AVE	367	NW
WILSON CT	370	SE
WINCHESTER DR	365	SE
WINDSOR AVE	365	SW
WINDWARD ST	364	NW
WINNETASKA RD	368	NW
WINGLOW CT	303	NC
WINTERS ST	366	NE
WISCONSIN AVE	360	SE
WITHAM RD	361	NE
WITHKOPP ST	365	SW
WOOD RD N	362	NW
WOOD ST	365	SW
WOODCLIFFE	366	NW
WOODHAVEN ST	362	NW
WOODLAND ST	363	SE
WOODLAND	364	NW
WOODLAWN ST FRUITPORT	371	NW
WOODLAWN AVE	364	SW
WOODLAWN CT	364	SW
WOODSIDE DR	369	NW
WOODSIDE RD ROOSEVELT PK	369	NW
WOODWARD ST	367	SW
WORDEN ST	366	SE
YARMOUTH AVE	366	NW
YOUNG AVE	365	SE
YORK ST	369	SE
YORKSHIRE DR	369	SE
ZAHL AVE	369	SE
ZUDER ST	369	SE

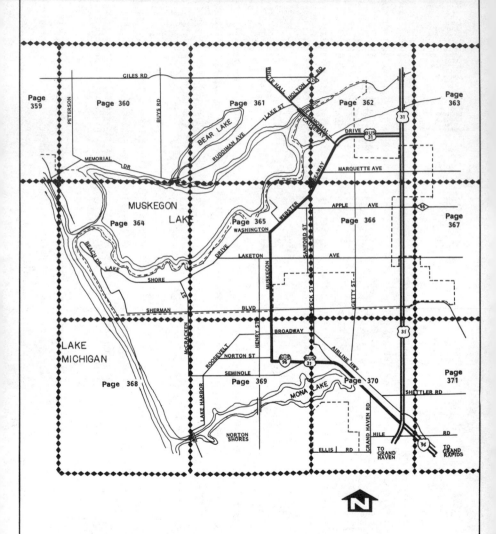

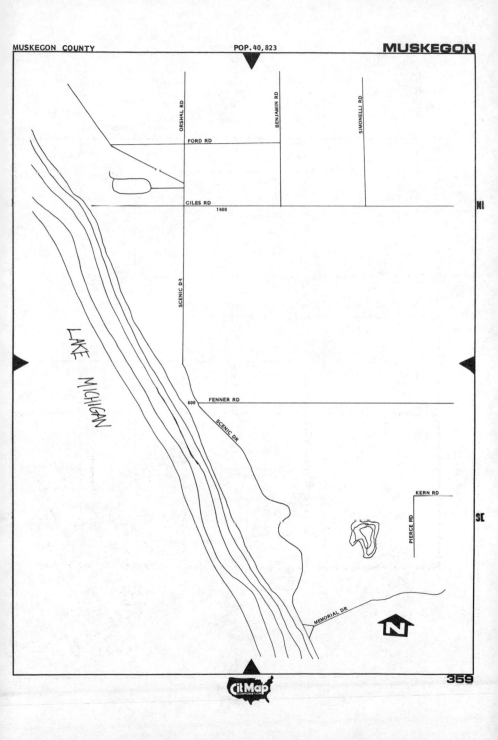

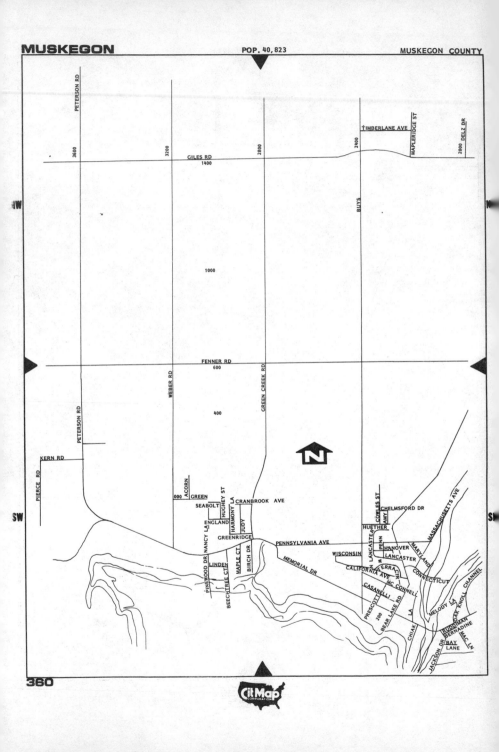

PETERSON RD

TIMBERLANE AVE

MAPLERIDGE ST

DELZ DR

3600

3200

2800

2400

2000

GILES RD
1400

W

N

BUYS

1000

FENNER RD
600

WEBER RD

GREEN CREEK RD

400

PETERSON RD

N

KERN RD

PIERCE RD

ACORN

000 GREEN

HUGHEY ST

HARMONY LA

SEABOLT

CRANBROOK AVE

COWLES ST

AMY

CHELMSFORD DR

MASSACHUSETTS AVE

ENGLAND

JUDY

HUETHER

SW

GREENRIDGE

PENN

HANOVER

MARYLAND

SW

PINEWOOD DR

NANCY LA

LINDEN

MAPLE CT

BIRCH DR

PENNSYLVANIA AVE

WISCONSIN

LANCASTER

LANCASTER

CONNECTICUT

BEECHTREE CT

MEMORIAL DR

CALIFORNIA AVE

TERRACE

MC CONNELL

MELODY LA

OAK KNOLL CHANNEL

CASANELLI

PRESCOTT

200

BEAR LANE RD

CHIAK

RUDDIMAN

BERNADINE

JACKSON DR

MAC LN

BAY
LANE

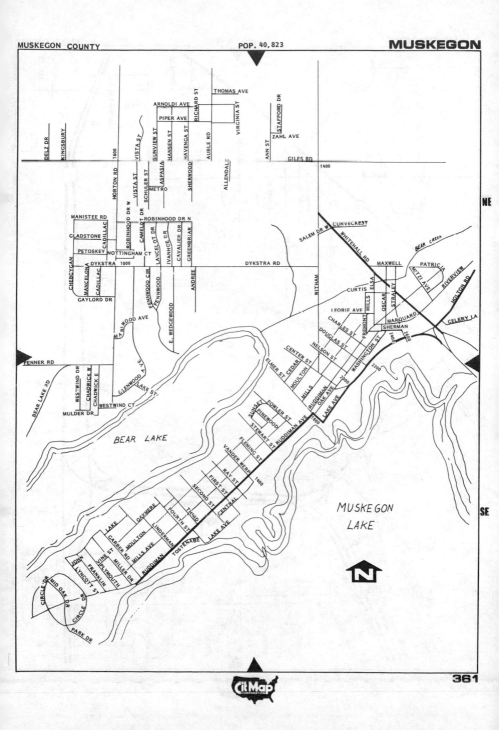

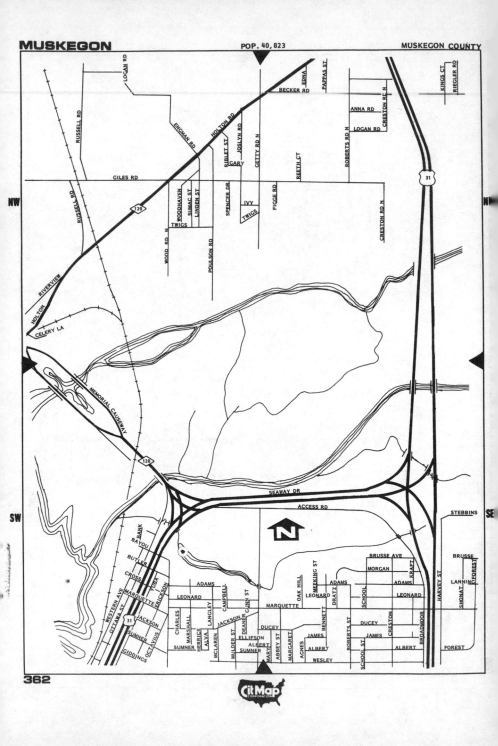

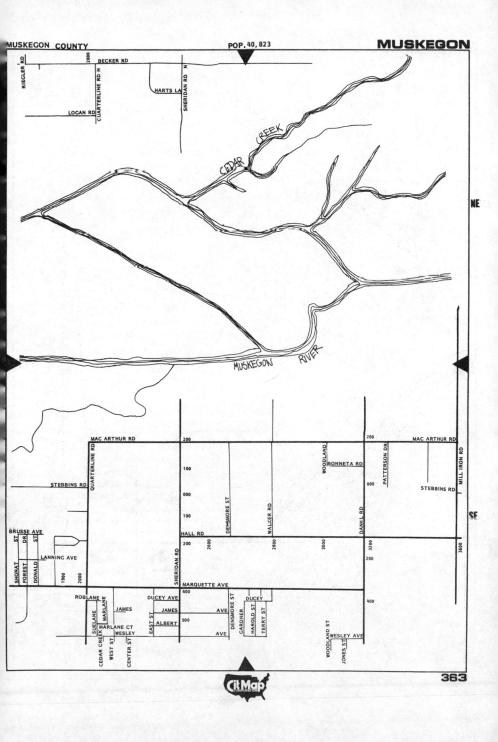

NE

SE

LAKE MICHIGAN

MUSKEGON LAKE

NW

LAKE MICHIGAN

SW

CHANNEL AVE

FULTON AVE
SAND
RODGERS
WATSON AVE
BLUFF
GIBBONNE ST
SIMPSON

BRIGHTON AVE
WINDWARD DR
ARLINGTON AVE
PARK PL

INDIANA
OHIO
DEWEY
NELSON
WOODLAND
FERGUSON CT

WILCOX
WATERWORKS
WALNUT
CHERRY
EDGEWATER
PLUM THOMPSON
PARSONS
KEATON
GRUBER
MILLARD
CRU
MILLARD ST

BEACH ST

SAMPSON
EDMUNDS
BLUFFTON
SURFWOOD
STONE
RESORT
BOYLE
PIGEON
COTTAGE
GROVE
LARKIN ST
COUNTRY CLUB
PARKTOWN BEACH
BOLTWOOD
SHERWOOD

LAKESHORE DR   C & O RR
RICHARDS
LAKESHORE DR
MANN ST

SHERIN
LARUE
CLIFFORD
LINCOLN
HARRISON AVE
HARRISON CT
MINER AVE
MINER AVE
MORTON AVE
FOUNTAIN
GROVE
HARDING AVE
CROZIER AVE
LEON ST
HARDING AVE
SISSON
TORRENT
CUTLER
CUTLER
CROZIER AVE
PHILO AVE
LETARTE AVE
LEBOUT
DENMARK ST
PHILO AVE
LETARTE AVE

KNOLLWOOD CT

IDLEWILD

MAPLEGROVE

SHERMAN BLVD

N

WARREN
CHARLES
HUGHES AVE
NORMAN DR
FOREST
PINEHURST
LIBERTY
LEVUR DR
LINDBERG DR
BUNDT
MANOR
HARBOR
ESTES

WINNETASKA
LINCOLN ST
LINCOLN PARK
LOIS CT
CASTLE AVE
LEON ST
WELLWOOD
PLAINFIELD AVE
MAYFAIR
McCRACKEN ST
BONNEY
VILLE DR
CASTLE

CitMap CORPORATION

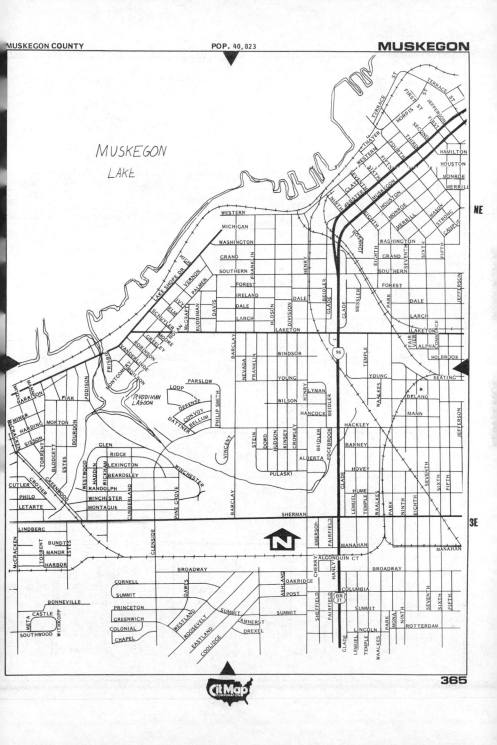

MUSKEGON LAKE

NE

3E

POP. 40,823

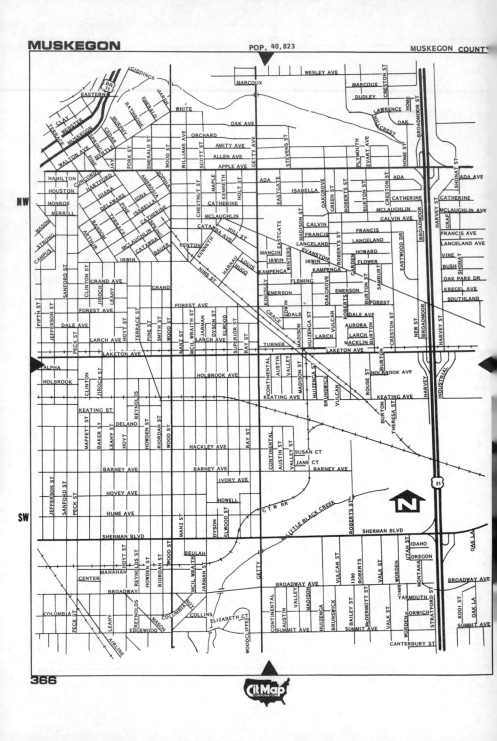

NW

SW

N

366

CitMap
CORPORATION

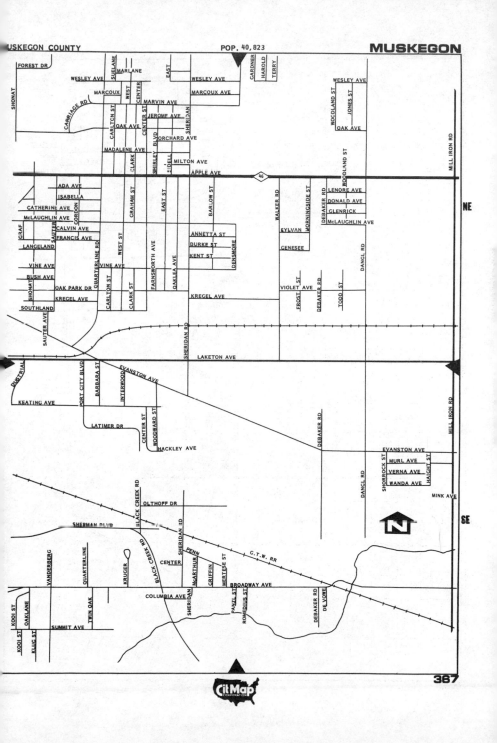

CitMap
CORPORATION

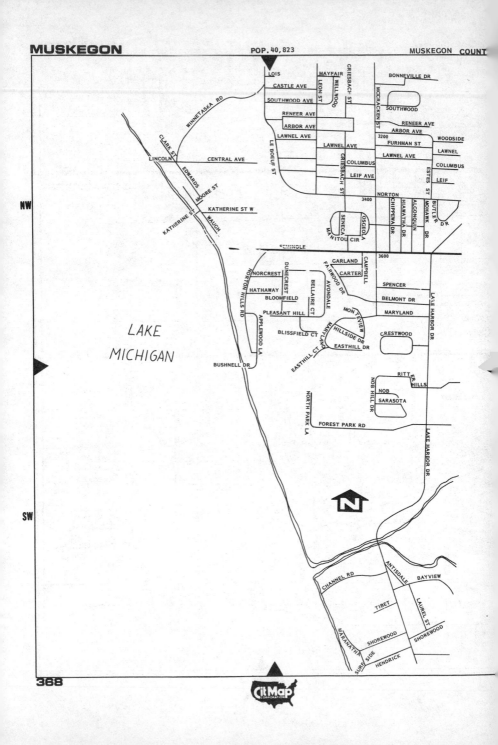

LAKE
MICHIGAN

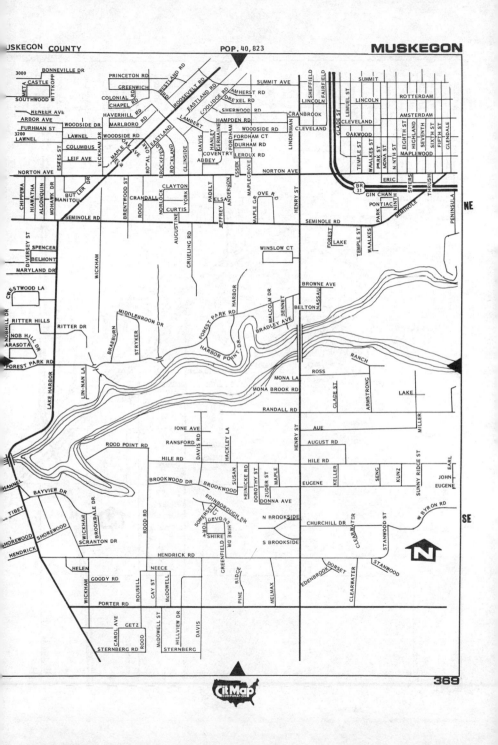

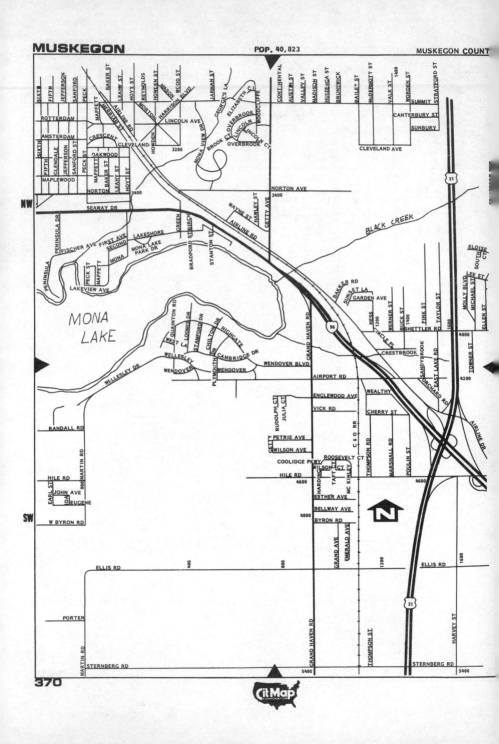

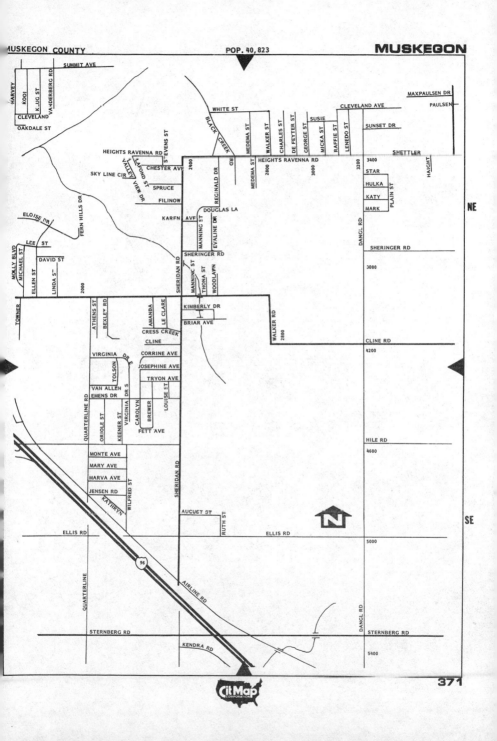

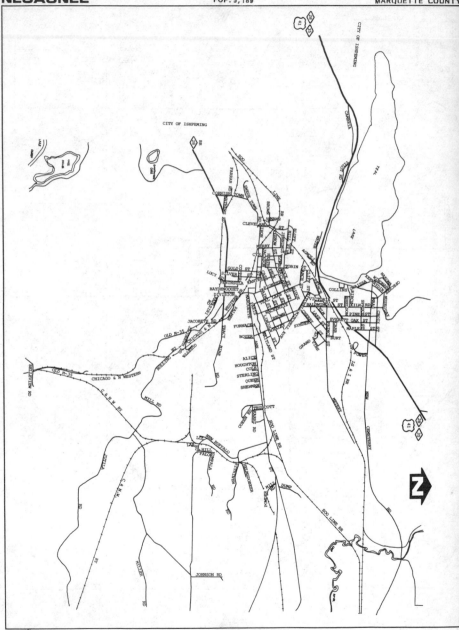

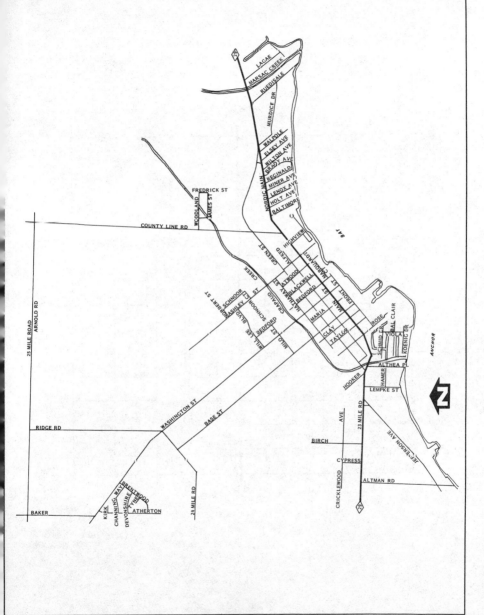

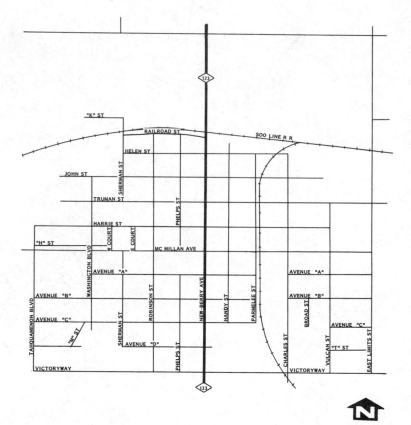

NEWBERRY

POP. 2,120

LUCE COUNTY

123

"K" ST

RAILROAD ST

SOO LINE R R

HELEN ST

JOHN ST

SHERMAN ST

TRUMAN ST

PHELPS ST

HARRIE ST

W COURT

E COURT

"H" ST

WASHINGTON BLVD

MC MILLAN AVE

AVENUE "A"

AVENUE "A"

TAHQUAMENON BLVD

AVENUE "B"

ROBINSON ST

NEW-BERRY AVE

HANDY ST

PARMELEE ST

AVENUE "B"

BROAD ST

AVENUE "C"

SHERMAN ST

"M" ST

AVENUE "C"

VULCAN ST

"T" ST

EAST LIMITS ST

AVENUE "D"

PHELPS ST

CHARLES ST

VICTORYWAY

VICTORYWAY

123

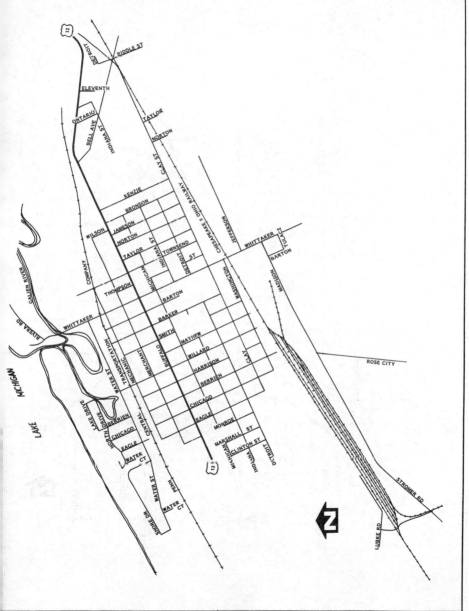

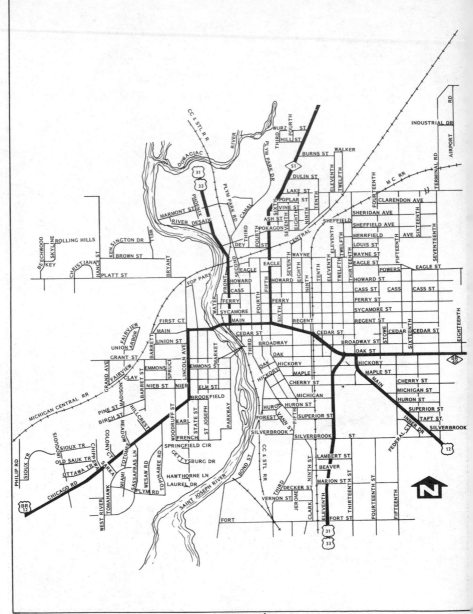

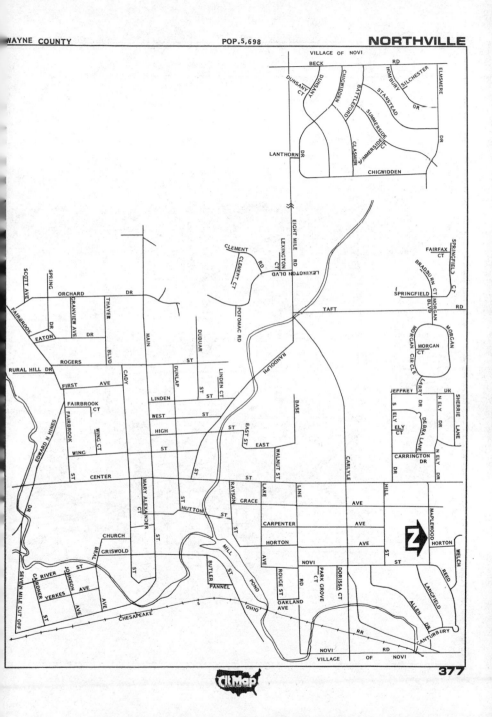

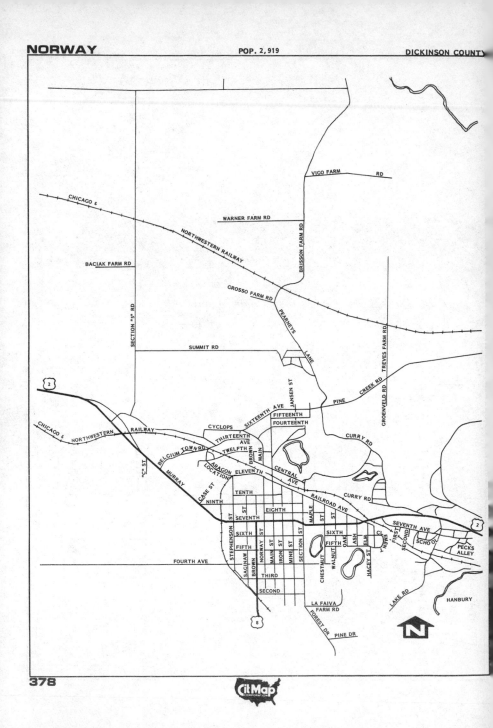

NOTES

ADELL	379	NE
APPLE CREST	380	NW
ARBOR LN	380	SE
ASPEN RD	380	NW
AUSTIN	379	NE
BALCOMBE DR	380	SW
BECK	379	SW
BERNSTADT	379	NE
BORCHART	380	NW
BROOK FOREST	380	SE
BUFFINTON	379	NE
BURNE	379	SW
BURNE CT	379	SW
BURNTWOOD	379	SW
BURTON CT	380	NE
BURTON RD	380	NE
CEDARWOOD	379	SW
CENTER	379	SW
CHAPMAN	379	NE
CHARLOTTE	379	NE
CHATTMAN DR	380	NW
CHERRYHILL	380	NW
CHERRYHILL RD	380	NW
CHESTNUT TREE WAY	380	SE
CIRCLE	380	NE
CLARK RD	379	SE
CLEWELYN	380	SE
CLEWELYN CT	380	SE
CLORAC	380	SE
CLOVER	380	SE
CLOVER LN	380	SE
CONNEMARA	379	SW
COTTIS	380	SW
COTTISFORD	379	SE
CRANBROOK	380	SE
CROWN	379	NE
CUMBERLAND	379	SW
DEERFIELD	380	SE
DEGROSS	379	NE
DIXON RD	379	NW
DUANA	379	NE
DURSON	379	NE
DURSON	379	NE
EIGHT MILE	379	SE
EIGHT MILE RD	380	SW
ELEVEN MILE RD	379	NW
ELEVEN MILE RD	379	NE
ELM	379	NE
EMERY	379	SE
ENDWELL	379	NE
ENNISHORE DR	380	SW
ERMA	379	NE
EUBANK	379	NE
FENWAY	379	SE
FONDA	379	NE
FOOTHILL	379	SW
FOREST CT	380	SE
FOURTEEN MILE RD	379	NE
FRANKLIN MILL	380	NE
GALWAY	380	SW
GALWAY	379	SW
GARFIELD	379	SW
GILBAR DR	380	SW
GLENDA	379	SW
GLENRIDGE CT	380	NE
GLYME DR	380	SW
GRAND RIVER	380	NW
GRAND RIVER	379	NW
GREENTREE	380	SE
GUILFORD RD	380	SE
HAGGERTY	379	SE
HAGGERTY HWY	380	NE
HAMPTON HILL	380	NW
HAVEN	379	NW
HEARTHWOOD	379	SW
HEATHERBROOK	380	SE
HEATHERWOOD	380	SE
HELSIP	379	SE
HELSIP DR	380	SW
HENNING	379	NE
HERMAN	379	NE
HIGHLANDS	380	NW
HILL DR	380	NE
HOLLYDALE	380	NE
IRA	379	NE
JASON CT	380	NE
KINGS POINTE DR	380	NW
KNOLLWOOD	380	NW
LADENE LN	380	SE
LANNEYS RD	379	NW
LASHBROOK	379	NE
LEBOST	380	NE
LEBOST DP	380	NE
LEMAY	379	NW
LILAC	379	NE
LINHART	379	NE
LOGAN	380	NW
LOGAN BERRY RIDGE N	380	NW
LONDON FERRY	380	NE
LYNWOOD	379	SW
MALLOTT	380	NE
MARLSON	379	SE
MARLSON	380	NE
MARTIN	379	NE
MAUDE-LEA CIR	380	NE
MAUDLIN	379	NE
MAYD	379	SW
MCMAHON	380	NE
MEADOWBROOK	380	SW
MEADOWBROOK	380	SW
MILL RD. CT	380	SE
MONTICELLO	379	NE
MORNINGSIDE	380	NE
NILAN	380	NE
NINE MILE RD	379	SW
NORTH HILLS	379	SE
NOVI RD	379	SE
OAK TREE RD	380	NE
OAKWOOD	380	NE
OWENTON	379	NE
PARAMOUNT	379	NE
PARK RIDGE	380	NW
PARKLON	379	NE
PEMBINE	379	NE
PENTON RISE CT	380	SW
PEPPERMILL CT	380	SE
PINE CREST	380	NW
RATHRONE, E	379	SW
RIDGE RD. E	380	NW
RIDGE RD. N	380	NW
RIPPLE CREEK RD	380	NE
ROCKHILL	380	NE
ROSEDALE	379	SW
RUSHWOOD	379	SW
SANFORD	379	NW
SHADOW PINE	380	SE
SHADYBROOK	380	SE
SHADYBROOK DR	380	SE
SHAMROCK HILL	379	NE
SHAWOOD	379	NE
SHERIDAN	380	SE
SIERRA	379	NW
SILVERY RD	380	NE
SIRATH	379	NW
SIXTH GATE	380	NW
SQUIRE	380	NE
STASSEN	379	NE
STATE	379	NE
SUMMIT	379	NE
SUMMIT DR	379	NE
SUNRISE BLVD	380	SE
SYCAMORE	380	NW
TEN MILE RD	379	SW
THIRTEEN MILE RD	379	NE
TOMERA	380	NW
TWELVE & ½ MILE RD	379	NE
TWELVE MILE RS	379	NW
TWELVE MILE RD	379	NE
UPLAND	380	NW
VALLEY STARR	380	NE
VILLAGE LAKE WAY	380	SE
VILLAGE OAK RD	380	SE
VILLAGEWOOD	380	NE
VINCENTI	379	NE
W. LEBOST	380	NE
W. LEBOST	380	NE
WAINRIGHT	379	NE
WEST RD	379	NW
WEST RIDGE	380	SW
WEST RIDGE	379	SE
WINEFIELD	379	SW
WIXOM	379	SW
WIXOM RD	379	NW
WOODGLEN	380	NW
WOODHAM	380	NE
WOODLAND CREEK	380	NW
WOODSIDE	379	SW

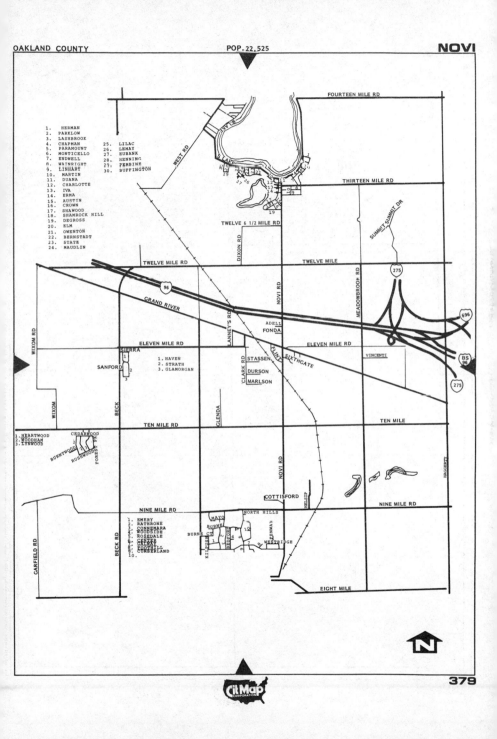

1.   HERMAN
2.   PARKLOW
3.   LASHBROOK
4.   CHAPMAN   25. LILAC
5.   PARAMOUNT   26. LEMAY
6.   MONTICELLO 27. EUBANK
7.   ENDWELL   28. HENNING
8.   WAINRIGHT   29. FENBINE
9.   LINHART   30. BUFFINGTON
10. MARTIN
11. DUANA
12. CHARLOTTE
13. IVA
14. ERMA
15. AUSTIN
16. CROWN
17. SHAWOOD
18. SHAMROCK HILL
19. DEGROSS
20. ELM
21. OWENTON
22. BERNSTADT
23. STATE
24. MAUDLIN

1. HAVEN
2. STRATH
3. GLAMORGAN

1. HEARTWOOD
2. WOODHAM
3. LYNWOOD

1. EMERY
2. RATHRONE
3. CONNEMARA
4. WOODSIDE
5. ROSEDALE
6. CRETES
7. FOXHILL
8. CUMBERLAND
9.
10.

FOURTEEN MILE RD
THIRTEEN MILE RD
TWELVE & 1/2 MILE RD
TWELVE MILE RD
TWELVE MILE
ELEVEN MILE RD
ELEVEN MILE RD
TEN MILE RD
TEN MILE
NINE MILE RD
NINE MILE RD
EIGHT MILE

WEST RD
DIXON RD
NOVI RD
MEADOWBROOK RD
SUMMIT DR
WIXOM RD
BECK
GLENDA
NOVI RD
HAGGERTY
GARFIELD RD
BECK RD
CLARK RD
LANNEY'S RD

GRAND RIVER
ADELL
FONDA
STASSEN
DURSON
MARLSON
SIXTHGATE
VINCENTI
SANFORD
SIERRA
COTTISFORD
NORTH HILLS
WESTRIDGE
BEDFORD
MAYO
BURNE

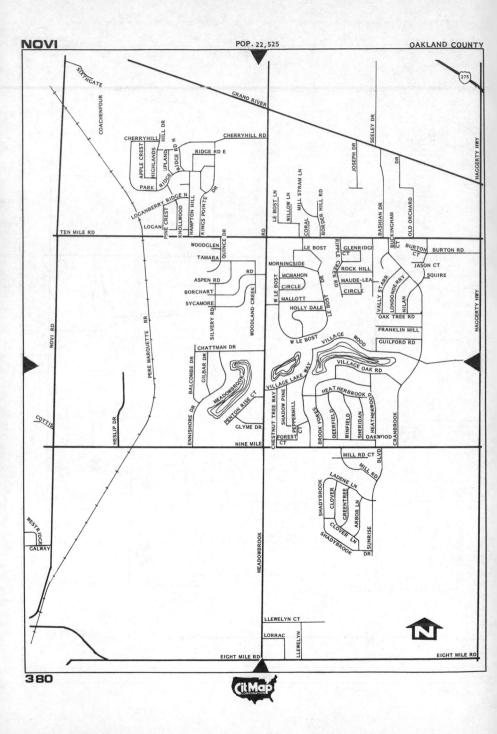

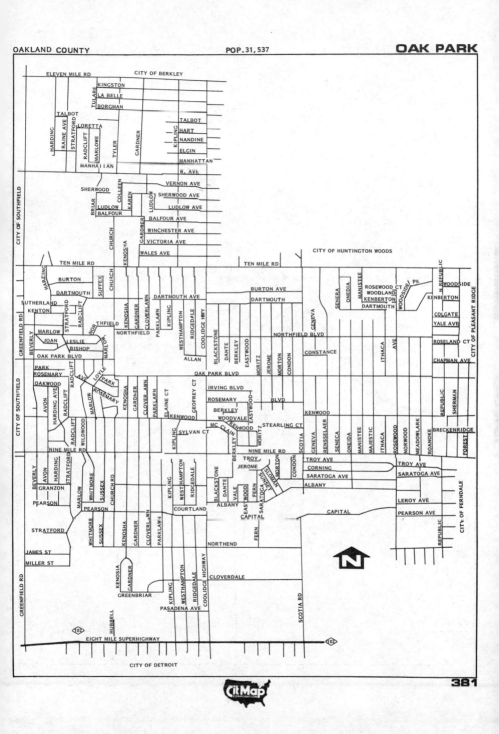

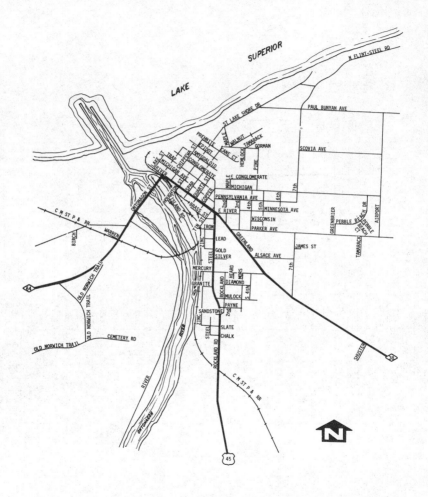

LAKE SUPERIOR

N FLINT-STEEL RD

PAUL BUNYAN AVE

ST LAKE SHORE DR

PREHNITE
KANE CT
WALNUT
TAMARACK
GORMAN
EPIDOT
CRYSTAL
MAPLE ST
ZINC
HEMLOCK

SCOVIA AVE

CONGLOMERATE
MAPLE CONGLOMERATE
MICHIGAN
7th
PENNSYLVANIA AVE
2nd 3rd 4th 5th 6th
E RIVER
MINNESOTA AVE
WISCONSIN
GREENBRIER
PEBBLE BEACH DR
PEBBLE BEACH
AIRPORT
PARKER AVE
CT

C M ST P & RR
WARREN
BIRCH
IRON
LEAD
GREENLAND
JAMES ST
TAMARACK
ONTONAGON ST
HOSPITAL
ISLAND RD
BRASS ST
TIN
ZINC
GOLD
SILVER
ALSACE AVE
7th
STEEL
MERCURY
HEARD
MORS
GRANITE
DIAMOND
ROCKLAND
45
OLD NORWICH TRAIL
MULOCK
S 4th
PAYNE
SANDSTONE
ZINC
SHUSTER
45
STEEL
SLATE
ROCKLAND RD
CHALK
OLD NORWICH TRAIL
CEMETERY RD
RIVER
C M ST P & RR
ONTONAGON

N

45

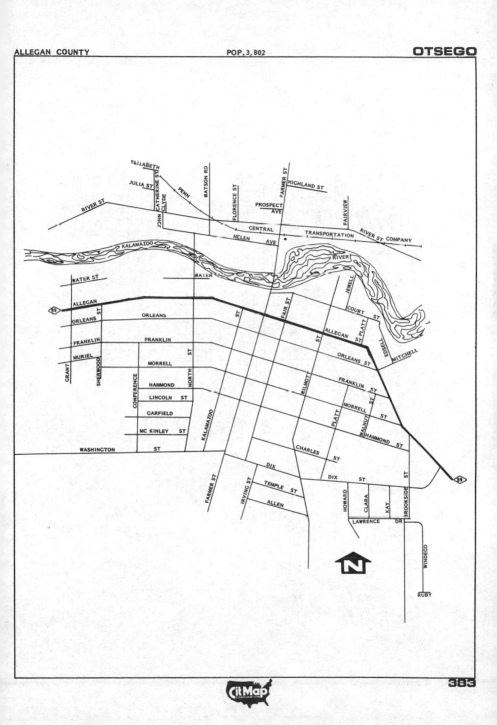

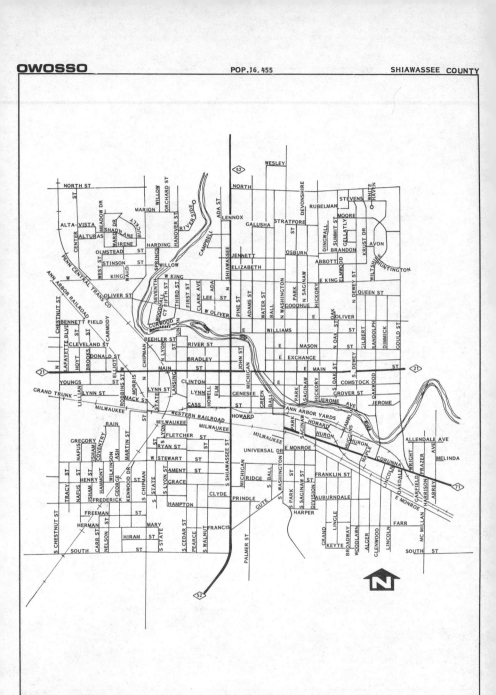

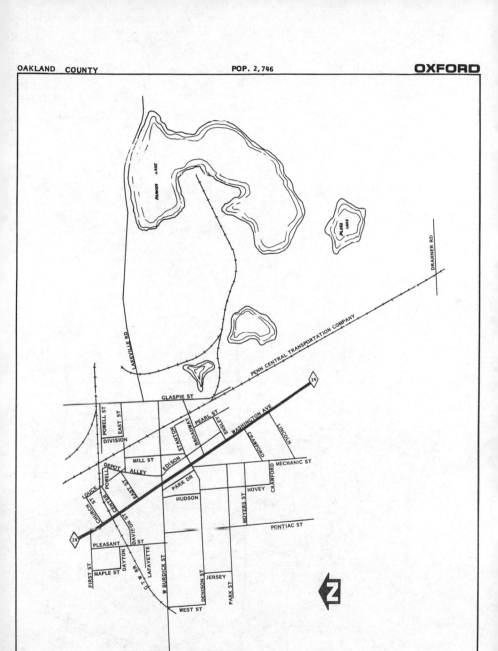

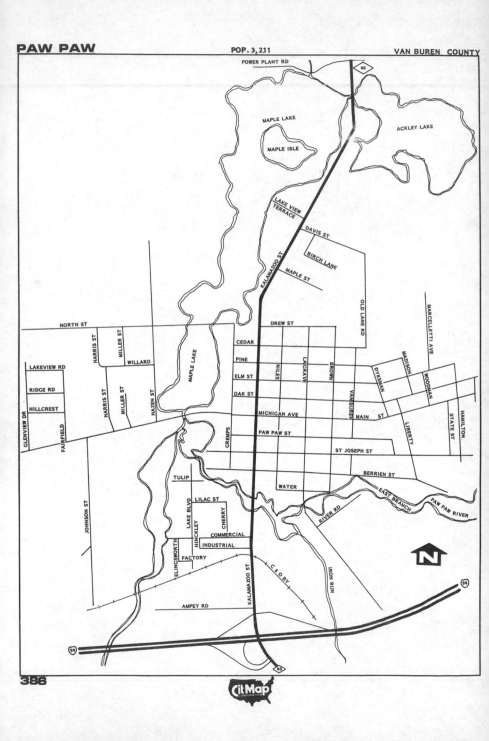

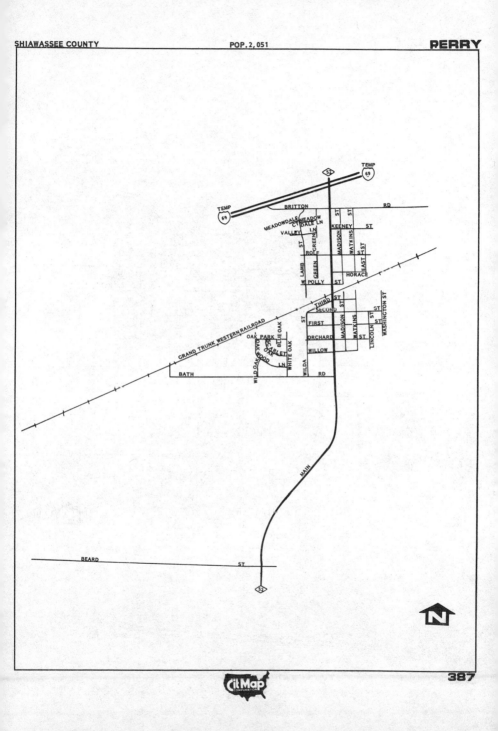

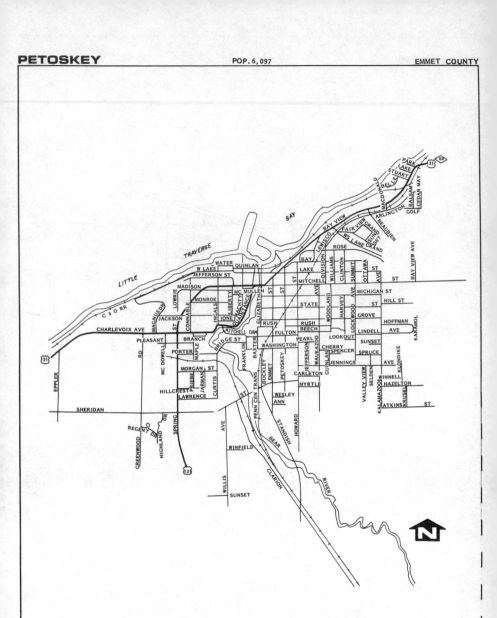

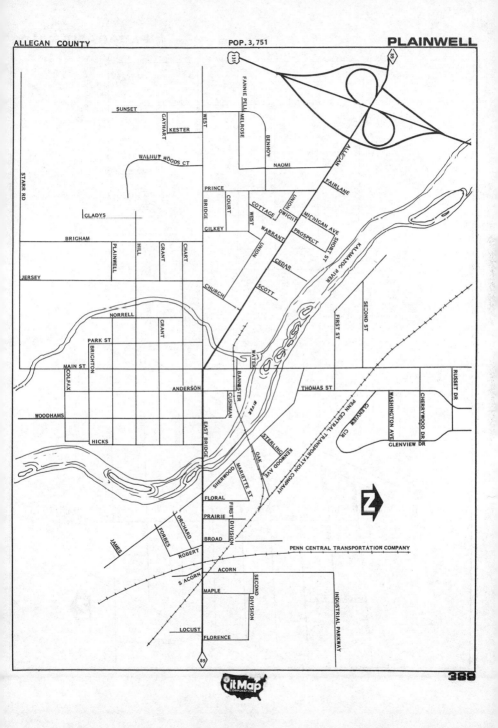

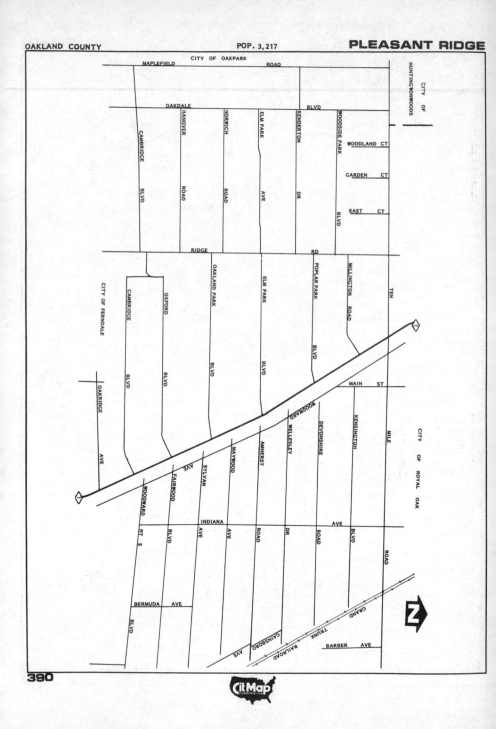

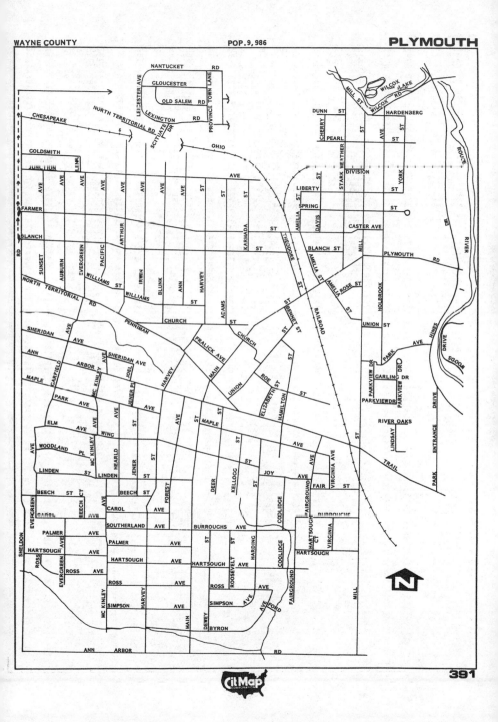

Street	No.	Dir.
A ST	317	NW
ABERDEEN	401	NW
ACORN CT	399	SW
ACORN RD	400	SW
ADAMS RD		
AVON TWP.	398	SE
ADAMS ST		
PONTIAC	400	NW
ADELAIDE ST	401	SE
ALDGATE DR	400	SW
ALFRED ST	400	NW
ALGONQUIN RD	399	NW
ALICE BLVD	400	NW
ALLEN ST	400	NW
ALLERTON RD	398	NW
ALLIANCE AVE	401	SE
ALPHA AVE E	397	SW
ALPHA PKWY E	396	SW
ALPHA PKWY W	396	SW
ALTER RD	401	SW
ALTON AVE	400	NW
ALVESTON	401	NW
AMOS ST	397	SE
ANDERS DR	396	NW
ANDERSON ST	400	NW
ANDOVER CT	401	SE
ANDOVER RD	401	SE
ANDRE	399	SW
ANGLIA CT	399	SW
ANN ARBOR AV E	397	NW
ANN ARBOR AV W	396	NW
ANNIE LA	400	SE
ANSLOW	401	SW
ANTOINETTE DR	398	NW
APPLE CT	399	SE
APPLE LA		
BL-FIELD TWP.	396	NE
APPLE LA PONT.	399	SE
APPLEWOOD	400	SE
AQUINAS	398	NE
ARCADIA CT	397	SW
ARDMORE ST	397	SW
ARGYLE AVE	399	NE
ARLENE AVE	397	SW
ARLUND WAY	401	SE
ARMADA	398	NW
ARTHUR AVE	400	NW
ASHBORNHAM RD	400	NW
ASHOVER CIR	401	SW
ASHOVER CT	401	SW
ASHOVER DR	401	SW
ASPEN LA	400	SW
ASTOR ST	397	SW
ASTORWOOD ST	400	NW
ATKINSON AVE	399	NW
ATLAS	397	SW
AUBURN TROY	401	NW
AUBURN RD.		
PONTIAC	400	NW
AUGUSTA AVE	396	SW
AVALON	401	NE
AVIS	397	SW
AVON RD	399	NW
AVONDALE AVE	399	NW
AYRSHIRE DR	400	SW
B ST	397	SW
BAGLEY	400	NW
BALBOA PL	397	SW
BALD MOUNTAIN	398	NW
BALDWIN AVE	396	SW
BALFOUR DR	400	SE
BALTIMORE	397	SW
BARKELL ST	397	NW
BARLYN LA	400	SW
BARNABY CT	399	SW
BARNES	396	NW
BARRINGTON RD	400	SW
BARTLETT ST	399	NE
BASSETT AVE	400	NW
BASSWOOD	400	SW
BATAAN DR	399	SW
BAXTER ALLEY	400	NW
BAY ST	397	SW
BAYOU	399	SW
BEACH RD TROY	401	SW
BEACH ST PONT.	397	SW
BEACHAM DR	396	NW
BEACHLAND BLVD	399	NW
BEACH VIEW LA	399	SW
BEAUDETTE ST	399	NE
BEAVER CT	399	SE
BEDFORD	400	SE
BEECHCROFT ST	399	NW
BEECHFIELD ST	399	NW
BEECHWOOD	399	SW
BEECHWOODE LA	397	NE
BELAIRE AVE	399	NW
BELAND AVE	399	NW
BELFANTINE DR	397	SW
BELLARMINE	398	NE
BELLEVUE ST	397	SW
BELLROI CT	400	SE
BELTON RD	397	SW
BELVIDERE DR	397	SW
BENNETT ST	396	SE
BENSON	397	SE
BENVENUE AVE	399	NW
BERKLEY AVE	399	NE
BERKSHIRE RD E	400	SW
BERKSHIRE RD N	400	SW
BERKSHIRE RD S	400	SW
BERRY	400	SW
BERRICK BLVD	400	SE
BESSIE ST	401	NW
BEVERLY AVE		
SYLVAN LAKE	399	NW
BEVERLY AVE E		
PONTIAC	397	NW
BEVERLY AVE W		
PONTIAC	396	NE
BIGMAN AVE	397	SE
BING HAMTON DR	401	NW
BIRCH CREEK LA	399	NW
BIRCHCREST ST	396	NW
BIRCHFIELD	398	NW
BIRCH HAR. LA	399	SW
BIRCHLAND	399	NW
BIRWOODE DR	397	NE
BLAINE AVE	396	SE
BLOOMFIELD AVE		
PONTIAC	400	NW
BLOOMFIELD BLVD		
BLOOMFIELD LA		
PONTIAC TWP	400	NW
BLOOMFIELD LA		
PONTIAC TWP	400	NW
BLOOMFIELD VIL.		
BOULEVARD	401	NW
BLOOMFIELD WDS.	399	SE
BLOSSOM LA	399	SE
BLUE SKY	398	NW
BONDALE AVE	400	NW
BOOTMAKER LA	401	SE
BOSTON AVE	396	SW
BOYD ST	397	SE
BOYDSTON	401	NW
BRADFORD ST	401	NW
BRADY DR	400	SE
BRAMBLE BUSH	401	SE
BRANCH ST	399	NE
BRATTON AVE	400	NW
BRENTHAVEN CT	401	SW
BRENTHAVEN LA	401	SW
BRETBY DR	401	SW
BRIARCLIFF AVE	399	NW
BRIARVALE	401	SW
BRIARVALE N	401	NE
BRIARWOOD	397	SE
BRIDLE	400	SE
BRIMFIELD	401	NE
BROADWAY AVE	397	NW
BROCK BLVD	399	SW
BROOKLYN AVE E	397	NW
BROOKLYN AVE W	396	NE
BROOKS AVE	397	NW
BROOKSHEAR	398	NE
BROOKVIEW CIR	401	SW
BROOKVIEW CT	401	SW
BROOKWOOD		
BIRMINGHAM	401	SW
BROOKWOOD LA		
PONTIAC	397	NE
BROOKWOOD		
WALKE	401	SW
BRUSH ST	400	NW
BUICK AVE	396	SW
BURT AVE	396	SE
BUTLER RD	398	SE
BYNAN LA	397	NE
C ST	397	SE
CADILLAC AVE	396	SE
CALIFORNIA AVE	400	NW
CALVERT ST	399	NW
CAMERON AVE	397	NE
CAMLEY ST	399	NE
CAMPUS DR N	396	SW
CAMPUS DR S	396	SW
CANAL DR	396	SW
CANDLELIGHT LA	396	NE
CANDLESTICK CT	401	SE
CANTERBURY DR	399	NE
CARLETON CT	397	SW
CARLISLE ST	396	SW
CAROLINE ST	401	NW
CARPENTER AVE	396	SW
CARR	399	SW
CARRIAGE CIR	400	NW
CARRINGTON	399	SE
CARTER ST	397	SW
CASS AVE	396	SE
CASS LAKE	399	NW
CASS LAKE RD	399	NW
CASS LAKE FRONT	399	NW
CATALPA		
BIRMINGHAM	401	SE
CATALPA CT		
PONTIAC TWP	397	SE
CEDAR ST	397	SE
CEDARDALE AVE	400	NW
CEDARHOLM LANE	400	NW
CENTER ST	401	NW
CENTRAL AVE		
SYLVAN LAKE	399	NW
CENTRAL AVE		
PONTIAC	400	NW
CENTURY OAK LA	399	NW
CERDON	396	SW
CHADWICK DR	399	NW
CHALGROVE	401	SE
CHALMERS	396	SW
CHAMBERLAIN ST	397	SE
CHAMPION	400	SE
CHAMPLAIN DR	401	SE
CHANDLER AVE	397	SW
CHAPMAN ST	399	NE
CHAREL CT	399	SW
CHARLES LA	400	SW
CHARLESTON	396	NE
CHARLOTTE ST	397	SE
CHARNWOOD	401	SE
CHARTER OAK CT	398	SE
CHATA DR	399	SW
CHELTINGHAM AV	399	NW
CHEROKEE		
WATERFORD	396	SW
CHEROKEE RD		
PONTIAC	399	NE
CHERRY HILL	396	NE
CHERRYLAND AVE	401	NW
CHERRYLAWN ST	399	SE
CHESTNUT ST		
BL-FIELD HILLS	400	SE
CHESTNUT DR		
BL-FIELD HILLS	400	SE
CHEVROLET AVE	396	SW
CHICAGO AVE E	397	NW
CHICAGO AVE W	396	NE
CHICKERING	400	SW
CHICKERING CT	400	SW
CHIPPEWA RD	399	NE
CHRISTOPHER LA	399	SW
CHRYSLER AVE	396	SW
CHURCHILL CT	401	NW
CHURCHILL RD	398	SW
CIRCLE CT		
PONTIAC	397	NE
CITY LINE RD	396	NE
CLAIRMONT PL	397	SE
CLARA AVE	397	NW
CLARENCE ST	397	SW
CLEARVIEW DR	401	SE
CLIFFORD AVE	400	NE
CLINTON ST	397	SW
CLINTON RIV. DR	398	NW
CLOCK GATE CIR	401	SE
CLOSE ST	396	SE
CLOVERLAWN ST	396	NE
CLOVERLAWN	399	SE
CLOVESE ST	399	NE
CLUB DR	400	SW
CLUBVIEW AVE	399	SE
COCHRANE PL	396	SE
COE ST	397	NE
COLBY	400	SE
COLDSPRING DR	400	SE
COLEMAN	396	SW
COLGATE AVE E	397	NW
COLGATE AVE W	396	SW
COLLEGE DR	401	SW
COLLIER DR	397	NW
COLLINGWOOD AV	400	NW
COLONIAL PARK	401	SW
COLONIAL TRAIL	400	SE
COLONIAL WAY	400	SE
COLONIAL VILLAGE		
WAY	396	NW
COLORADO	400	NW
COLUMBIA AVE E	397	NW
COLUMBIA AVE W	396	NE
COLUMBIA WAY	397	NW
COMMONWEALTH		
AVENUE	397	NE
CONGRESS	400	NE
CONNOLLY DR	401	SE
COOLEY ST	396	SW
COOLIDGE	401	NW
COOPER	396	SE
CORDELL AVE	399	NW
COREY	396	SW
CORNELL AVE E	397	NW
CORNEL. AVE W	396	SW
CORTEZ PL	397	SE
CORTWRIGHT	396	SE
CORWIN DR	396	SE
CORWIN AVE	396	SW
COSGROVE	396	SW
COTTAGE ST	400	NW
COUGHLAN	401	NW
COUNTY CENTER		
DRIVE E	396	SW
COUNTY CENTER		
DRIVE W	396	SW
COUNTRYSIDE CT	398	NW
COURT DR	397	SW
COURT TOWER		
BLVD N	396	SW
COURT TOWER		
BLVD S	396	SW
COURT VILLA DR	400	SW
CRANDIE	396	SW
CRAWFORD ST	399	NE
CRESCETN DR		
PONTIAC	400	SW
CRESCENT DR		
PONTIAC TWP	397	SW
CRESTVIEW AVE	399	NW
CRESTWOOD ST	397	SS
CROFTON	396	SE
CROFT	399	SW
CROFTHILL	401	SW
CRYSTAL LK DR	400	NW
CULVER	396	NW
CULV ST	397	NW
DAKOTA DR	399	NE
DALESFORD	401	SW
DEARBORN RD	396	SW
DEDHAM CT	401	SW
DELAND ST	396	SW
DELAWARE DR	396	SW
DELCO DR	397	SW
DELL ROSE DR	399	NE
DELLWOOD AVE	400	NW
DEL RAY DR	397	SW
DENISON CT	400	SW
DEPEW DR	399	SW
DERBY	398	SW
DESIAX AVE	399	NE
DE SOTA PL	397	NE
DEVON RD	400	SW
DEVON BROOK	400	SW
DEVONBROOK CT	400	SW
DEVONWOOD	400	SW
DEWEY ST	396	NE
DEXTER RD	398	NW
DICK AVE	399	NW
DISTON AVE	400	NW
DITMAR	400	NW
DIXIE HIGHWAY	396	NW
DOBSON LA	401	SW
DONEGAL		
AVON TWP	398	NE
DONEGAL DR		
TROY	401	SE
DORCHESTER AVE	399	NW
DORIS CT	401	NW
DORIS RD	398	SW
DOUGLAS DR		
BL-FIELD TWP	400	SE
DOUGLAS ST		
PONTIAC	397	SE
DOVER RD	397	NE
DOWNDERRY CT	401	SW
DOWNING	396	SW
DRAPER AVE	399	NW
DRESDEN AVE	396	NE
DREXEL AVE	400	NW
DUANE ST	397	NW
DUBLIN FAIR RD	401	SE
DUCHESS CT	401	SW
DUDLEY AVE	397	SE
DUFRAIN AVE	397	SW
DUNNING	401	NE
DURANT AVE	396	SE
DWIGHT AVE	396	SW
EAMES ST	400	NE
EARL ST	401	NW
EARLMOOR BLVD	400	NW
EAST BLVD	400	NE
E.CEDARWOOD CR	401	SE
E.HAMMOND LAKE		
DRIVE	399	NE
EAST POINT LANE	400	NE
E. PONTIAC RD	398	NE
E.SPINNINGWHEEL		
LANE	401	SW
EASTWAY DR	397	SE
E.WIDE TRACK DR	400	NW
EASTWOOD	401	SW
E. VALLEY RD	400	SE
ECKMAN AVE	397	SE
EDDY ST	397	SE
EDGEFIELD DR	396	SW
EDGEWATER	396	SW
EDINBOROUGH DR	396	NW
EDISON ST	401	NW
EDISON ST	399	NE
EDITH ST	400	NW
EDMUND CT	400	NW
EDNA AVE	399	NW
EDNA JANE	398	NW
EDWARD CT	397	SW
EDWARD ST	399	NW
EILEEN DR	399	NW
ELAM CT	399	SW
ELIZABETH ST		
PONTIAC	400	NW
ELIZABETH LK RD	396	NW
ELLWOOD AVE	397	SW
ELM ST	400	NW
ELSINORE DR	399	NW
EMERSON AVE	400	SW
EMILEY CT	397	SE
EMIRY ST	396	SE
EMPIRE DR	399	SW
ENGLEWOOD CT	399	SW
ERIE DR	401	SE
ERIN WAY	401	SE
ERNEST CT	396	NE
ESTHER ST	399	NE
ESTON	397	SE
EUCLID AVE	396	SE
EVELYN CT	396	SE
EXCHANGE ST	396	SE
FILDEW AVE	400	NW
FIREWOOD DR	398	NE
FIRST AVE	397	NW
FISHER AVE	400	SW
FLORENCE AVE	396	SE
FORDCROFT DR	398	NE
FORDHAM	399	SW
FOREST ST	397	SW
FORESTER	401	NE
FOREST GLEN CT	401	SE
FOREST HILL	400	SE
FOUNDATION	398	NE
FOURTH AVE	397	NW
FOXCHASE	401	SE
FOX GLEN CT	401	SE
FOXHALL RD	401	SE
FOX HILLS DR E	401	SW
FOX HILLS DR N	400	NE
FOX HILLS DR S	400	SE
FOX RIVER DR	400	NE
FRANCIS ST	400	NW
FRANK ST	397	SW
FRANKEL LA	400	SW
FRANKLIN BLVD		
PONTIAC	396	SE
FRANKLIN RD		
BL-FIELD TWP	400	NW
FREMONT ST	400	NW
FULLER ST	397	NW
FULTON ST	400	NW
FURSE	400	SW
GAGE ST	397	SE
GALLOWAY	397	NE
GAMBRELL DR	397	NE
GANNON	398	SE
GARDEN CT	397	NW
GARLAND AVE	399	NW
GARNER AVE	397	SW
GENE CT	397	SW
GENES	398	NW
GENESSEE AVE	399	NE
GEORGETOWN	401	NW
GIDDINGS RD	397	NE
GILLESPIE ST	399	NW
GILROY AVE	396	SW
GINGELL CT	397	SW
GLADSTONE PL	397	NW
GLEN CT		
BL-FIELD TWP.	401	SE
GLEN DR TROY	399	SE
GLENBROKE	399	SW
GLENDALE AVE	399	NW
GLENGROVE DR	399	SE
GLENROSE	397	NE
GLENSHIRE LA	396	NW
GLENVIEW ST	397	SW
GLENWOOD AVE	397	NW
GLYNDE BOURNE	401	SE
GOING ST	400	NW
GOLF DR	300	NE
GOLFHILL	396	NW
GRACE AVE	397	NW
GRACEVIEW CT	396	NW
GRANADA DR	396	NW
GRANVIEW BLVD	399	NW
GRANDVILLE CT	397	SW
GRANT ST	399	NE
GRANTOUR CT	397	SW
GRASMERE AVE	400	NW
GRAYTON DR	400	NW
GREAT OAKS DR	401	SE
GREENDALE AVE	400	NE
GREENLAWN AVE	399	NW
GREENSPRING LA	398	SE
GREENVIEW	401	SE
GREENWOOD		
BIRMINGHAM	401	NE
GREENWOODE LA		
PONTIAC	397	SE
GREER BLVD	399	SW
GRENADIER DR	401	NE
GRETCHEN CT	399	SW
GREY RD	401	NW
GROVE		
KEEGO HARBOR	399	NW
GROVE		
BL-FIELD TWP	399	SE
GUANONEQUE	401	SW
GUNDER CT	398	NE
GUNDER DR	398	NE
HADDRILL CT	396	NW
HADSELL DR	400	NW
HALLMAN AVE	396	SW
HAMILTON DR		
BL-FIELD TWP	399	SE
HAMILTON ST		
PONTIAC	400	SW
HAMLET ST	401	NW
HAMLIN RD	398	SW
HAMMOND ST	397	SW
HAMMOND LK CT	399	SE
HARPER ST	397	SW
HARRIET ST	396	SE
HARRIS ST	399	SW
HARRISON AVE	400	NW
HARTFORD CT	397	NW
HARTUNG CT	397	NW
HARVARD		
AVON TWP	398	SW
HARVARD		
W.BL-FIELD TWP	399	SW
HARVEST LA	399	NW
HARVEY AVE	400	NW
HATTON	397	NE

Street	No.	Dir.
HAVENS	401	NW
HAVERFORD RD	401	SE
HAZEL AVE	399	NW
HEATHERWOOD CT	398	NE
HEMPSTEAD DR TROY	401	NW
HEMPSTEAD RD PONTIAC TWP	400	NE
HENDERSON WATERFORD TWP	396	SW
HENDERSON ST PONTIAC	396	SE
HENLEY	400	SE
HENLEY CT	400	SE
HENRYDALE ST	401	NW
HENRY CLAY	396	SW
HENSMAN DR	396	SW
HERBELL	396	SW
AUBURN HTS.	401	NW
HERNDON AVE	399	NE
HERRINGTON LA	397	SE
HESS ST	399	NE
HIBBARD ST	400	NW
HICKORY CT BL-FIELD TWP	399	SW
HICKORY TR AVON TWP	398	SE
HICKORY BARK LANE	401	SW
HICKORY GROVE COURT	400	SE
HICKORY GROVE ROAD	398	SE
HIGH ST	356	SE
HIGHLAND AVE PONTIAC	400	NW
HIGHLAND DR BL-FIELD TWP	398	NE
HIGH POINTE CT	400	SW
HIGHWOOD DR	397	NW
HILL PONTIAC	396	SW
HILL RD PONTIAC	397	NW
HILL CIRCLE	396	SW
HILLCREST PONTIAC TWP	399	SE
HILL CREST INDEPEND. TWP	401	NW
HILLDALE DR	397	SE
HILLFIELD RD	397	SE
HILLPOINTE	401	SW
HILLSDLAE RD	400	SE
HILLSIDE AVE BL-FIELD TWP	400	SW
HILLSIDE DR PONTIAC	396	SE
HILLSMONT AVE	400	NW
HOLBROOK AVE	396	SW
HOLLISTER	396	SE
HOLLY	396	NE
HOLLYWOOD AVE	396	NE
HOME ST	397	SW
HOMESTEAD DR	400	NE
HOOD BL-FIELD TWP	399	NE
HOOD ST PONT.	397	SW
HOPKINS AVE E	397	NW
HOPKINS AVE W	396	NE
HOSPITAL DR	396	SW
HOTCHKISS	397	SE
HOUNDS CHASE	401	SE
HOUSTON ST	399	SW
HOVEY ST	400	NW
HOWARD ST E	397	SW
HOWARD ST W	396	SE
HOWARD McNEILL STREET	399	NE
HOWLAND AVE	400	NW
HUDSON AVE	396	SE
HUMPHREY AVE	399	NE
HUNTERS GATE	401	SW
HUNTERS HILL RD	401	SW
HUNTERS RIDGE ROAD	400	SW
HUNTERS WAY	401	SW
HUNTINGTON PK DRIVE	396	NW
HURON ST E	397	SE
HURON ST W	396	SE
ILLINOIS AVE	399	NE
INDIAN SUMMER	399	SE
INDIANWOOD CT	399	SE
INDUSTRIAL CT BL-FIELD TWP	399	SW
INDUSTRIAL DR AVON TWP	398	SE
INGLEWOOD AVE	396	SE
INNSBROOK CT	398	NE
INTERLAKEN	399	SW
INVERNESS CT	398	NE
INWOODS RD	399	NW
IRENE	400	NW
IRONTON DR	396	NW
IROQUOIS RD E	399	NE
IROQUOIS RD W	399	NE
IRWIN AVE	400	NW
ISLAND CT SYLVAN LK	399	NW
ISLAND LANE BL-FIELD TWP	399	SE
IVANHOE	397	SE
IVY ST	397	SW
IVYGLEN	401	SE
JACKSON ST	400	NW
JAMES ST	398	NW
JAMES K. BLVD	399	NW
JAMES K. CT	399	NW
JAMESTOWN RD	401	NW
JEFFERSON ST	396	SE
JESSIE ST N	397	SW
JESSIE ST S	400	NW
JOHNATHON DR	401	SE
JOHNSON AVE N	399	NW
JOHNSON AVE S	399	NW
JORDON	397	SE
JOSEPHINE AVE	399	NW
JOSLYN AVE	397	NW
JOSWICK RD	398	NW
JOTHAM	396	NE
JOY RD	397	NE
JUDSON ST	400	NW
JUNIPER AVE		
KAREN CT	399	NE
KEELEY CT	396	SW
KEMP	399	NE
KEMP	397	NE
KEMPER AVE	399	NE
KENDALL	399	SW
KENDRY AVE	400	SW
KENDRY CT	400	SW
KENILWORHT AVE	397	NE
KENNITT RD E.	397	SW
KENNETT RD W.	397	SW
KENRICK AVE	399	SW
KENSINGTON RD	400	SE
KENTMOOR	401	SW
KENWOOD RD	398	SE
KEELLER DR	399	NW
KETTERING AVE	397	NE
KILLARNEY LA	401	SE
KIMBALL ST	396	SE
KINGSWAY CT	399	SE
KINNEY RD	396	SE
KIRCHER CT	397	NE
KISE AVE	397	NE
KLEIST CT	399	SE
KNOLLCREST	399	SC
KNOLLWOOD PONTIAC TWP	400	NE
KNOWLSON AVE	399	NW
KOMOKA DR	396	NW
KOPSON CT	400	SE
KUHN ST	397	NE
LABROSSE	399	NW
LACOTA	396	SW
LAFAY DR	399	SE
LAFAYETTE ST	399	NE
LAHSER RD	400	SE
LAKE	399	SW
LAKE DR	400	SE
LAKE ST	399	NE
LAKE CHARNWOOD BLVD	401	SE
LAKELAND	400	NW
LAKELAND AVE	399	NW
LAKEVIEW AVE SYLVAN LAKE		
LAKEVIEW N WATERFORD TWP	396	SW
LAKEVIEW BLVD BLOOMFIELD TWP	399	SE
LAKEWARD	399	SE
LAKEWAY DR	399	NE
LAKEWIND	399	NE
LAMP LIGHTER LA	401	NW
LAMPOST LA	401	NW
LAMPWICK CT	401	SE
LANA DR	398	NE
LANCASTER LA	400	SE
LANTERN	396	NE
LAPEER RD	398	NE
LARCH DR	399	SE
LARKWOOD	400	SW
LA SALLE AVE	396	SE
LAUREL AVE	397	NE
LEACH	401	NE
LEANEE LA	396	NE
LE BARON AVE	397	NW
LEDBURY DR	401	SW
LEE CT	397	NW
LE GRAND BLVD	396	SE
LEHEICH AVE	397	NW
LEINHALH AVE	399	NW
LENHILL CT	401	SE
LENOX AVE	397	NW
LENOX RD PONTIAC BLOOMFIELD TWP	401	SW
LEONARD LA	397	SW
LESTER CT	400	NW
LETCHWORTH	400	SW
LEWIS ST	397	SW
LEXINGTON PL PONTIAC	397	SW
LEXINGTON RD PONTIAC	397	SW
LIBERTY ST PONTIAC	396	SE
LIMERICK LA	401	SE
LINCOLN AVE	396	SE
LINCOLNVIEW	397	SE
LINDA VISTA DR	397	SE
LINDEN	399	NW
LINFERE ST	400	NW
LITTLETELL AVE	399	SW
LIVERPOOL RD	401	NW
LIVINGSTONE	396	SW
LOCKE ST	397	SE
LOCKRIDGE	399	SE
LOIS CT	396	NW
LONDON WALL	400	SW
LONEDALE	398	NE
LONE OAK RD	399	SE
LONGFELLOW AVE E PONTIAC	397	NW
LONGFELLOW DR TROY	396	NW
LONG LAKE SHORE	398	SE
LONG POINT	399	SE
LONGVIEW	399	SE
LONGWOOD DR	400	SE
LOOKOUT DR	400	SE
LORGILL	400	SE
LORRAINE CT	396	SE
LOST TREE WAY	401	SW
LOUNSBURY AVE	396	SE
LOWELL ST	397	SW
LUCILLE	397	SW
LULL ST	399	NE
LUTHER AVE	400	NW
LYNCH ST	397	SW
LYNN AVE	396	SW
MALAINTOSH LANE	400	NE
MADDY LANE	399	NW
MADISON AVE E	399	NW
MAE ST	396	SE
MAINES AVE	397	SW
MALLARD CT	399	SW
MALVERN	401	SE
MANDEFORD	401	SE
MANHATTAN AVE	397	SW
MANITOU RD	399	NE
MANORWOOD DR	400	SE
MANSFIELD AVE E	397	NW
MANSFIELD AVE W	396	NE
MAPLERIDGE DR	398	NE
MAPLEWOOD AVE BL-FIELD TWP	399	SE
MAPLEWOOD W SYLVAN LAKE	399	NW
MARCY CT	400	SW
MARIAN AVE	396	SW
MARIE CIR	399	SE
MARIVA ST	397	NE
MARK AVE	396	SE
MARKLE AVE	397	SW
MARLBOROUGH DR	400	SW
MARQUETTE ST	397	SW
MARSHALL ST	400	NE
MARTELL DR	401	NE
MARX AVE	399	SW
MARY DAY AVE	396	SW
MASEFIELD DR	401	SW
MATHEWS ST	397	SW
MATTIE LU	398	NW
MAURER AVE	397	SW
MAXWELL RD	397	SE
MAYNARD DR	397	SW
MAYWARD	397	NE
McCORMICK DR	396	NW
McDONALD CT	396	NW
McDOWELL DR	396	NW
McGLINTOCK		
McGREGON ST	397	SW
McINTOSH DR	401	SE
MaKINLEY ST	397	NW
McNEIL ST	396	SW
MEADER AVE	396	SW
MEADOW AVE PONTIAC	400	NE
MEADOW CT BL-FIELD TWP	399	SE
MEADOWBROOK	399	NE
MEADOWLAWN ST	396	NE
MEATH HUNT CIR	401	SE
MECHANIC ST	397	SE
MELROSE AVE	397	SE
MENOMINEE RD	397	SE
MERRIMAC ST	396	SE
MIAMI	396	SE
MIAMI RD	399	NW
MIDDLE BELT RD	396	SE
MIDLAND DR	397	SE
MID PINE	399	SW
MIDWAY AVE	400	NW
MILES	396	SW
MILL ROCHESTER	396	SW
MILL ST PONTIAC	397	SW
MILLER ST	397	SW
MILLINGTON	400	SE
MILLINGTON CT	400	SE
MILLWALL AVE	397	SE
MOHAWK RD	396	SE
MONROE ST	396	SE
MONTANA AVE	400	NW
MONTCALM ST W	396	SE
MONTCLAIR	397	SW
MONTEREY AVE	397	SW
MONTICELLO AVE	396	NW
MONTROYAL AVE	396	NW
MOON LAKE DR	399	SW
MOORE ST	397	SE
MORELAND ST	397	SW
MORINGSIDE	399	SE
MOSS	397	SW
MOTOR ST	400	NW
MOTT AVE WATERFORD TWP	396	SW
MULBERRY RD	400	NE
MURPHY AVE	399	NW
MURPHY PARK DR	400	NW
MURRAY	397	SE
MUSKOVIE	396	NW
MYRA AVE	399	NE
MYRTLE	399	NE
BL-FIELD TWP	396	SW
NAGEL CT	399	SW
NASH AVE	396	SW
NAVAJO	399	SW
NEAFIE AVE	397	SE
NEBRASKA AVE	400	NW
NELSON ST	397	SW
NEOME DR	396	SE
NEVADA AVE	400	NW
NEWARK AVE	396	NE
NEVA DR		
NEWBERRY ST	398	SE
NEW HAVEN	396	NE
NEWLAND E	399	SW
NEWLAND W	399	SW
NEWPORT TROY	396	NE
NEWPORT AVE PONTIAC	397	NW
NEWTON PL	397	SW
NEW YORK AVE E	397	NW
NEW YORK AVE W	396	NE
NIAGARA AVE	399	NE
NICHOLS DR	401	NW
NOB LA	397	NE
NORCOTT AVE	399	NW
NORKADALE	396	NW
NORTHFIELD AVE	397	NW
N.HAMMOND LK DR	399	NW
N. MERRIMAC ST	396	NE
NORTHVIEW CT	396	SW
NORTHWAY DR	397	SE
N. WESTVIEW CT	401	SW
NORTON AVE	396	SE
NORWOOD RD	400	SW
NOVARA AVE	396	SW
NOYLE DR	396	SW
OAK BROOK DR	400	NE
OAK HILL ST	397	SW
OAK KNOLL	400	NE
OAKLAND AVE	396	SE
OAKMONT	401	NE
OAKWAY DR	399	SW
OAKWOOD AVE	396	SE
OCEMAN RD	399	NE
ODETTE DR	396	NW
OJESTA AVE	399	SW
OLDEN OAK	399	NW
OLD OAK CT	397	NE
OLD ORCHARD DR	396	SW
OLD RIDER	398	NE
OLD SALEM BIRMINGHAM	401	NW
OLDSMOBILE AVE	396	SW
OLD SQUIRREL CT	398	SE
OLD TREE	398	NE
OLIVER ST	397	SW
OMAR ST	397	SE
OMIRA DR	396	NW
ONAGON	396	SW
ONAGON CT	396	NW
ONORADO RD	399	NE
ONTARIO PONTIAC TWP	399	NE
OPDYKE RD	400	NE
ORBERTA	396	SW
ORCHARD LK AVE	400	NW
O'RILEY CT	400	NW
O'RILEY ST	400	NW
ORIOLE RD	399	SW
ORLANDO AVE	396	NE
ORTON ST	399	SE
OSAGE CIRCLE	396	SW
OSHANA CIRCLE	396	SW
OSMUN ST	400	NW
OSTRUM ST	396	NW
OTSEGO	396	SW
OTTAWA DR	399	NW
OTTER AVE	399	SW
OWEGO DR	399	NE
OXFORD RD	399	NE
OXLEY DR	399	NE
PACKER	399	SW
PADDOCK ST N.	397	SW
PADDOCK ST S.	400	NW
PAIGE	399	SW
PALMER RD		
PAMELA CT	399	SW
PARCELLS CIR	400	SW
PARK ST	400	NW
PARK PL	400	NW
PARKCREEK CT	398	SE
PARLDALE AVE	396	NW
PARKHURST ST	400	NW
PARKINSON DR	396	NW
PARK RIDGE	401	SW
PARKVIEW	401	SE
PARKWAY	399	NW
PARKWOOD AVE	397	SE
PATRICK HENRY	396	SW
PATTY ANN	397	SE
PEACOCK AVE	397	SE
PEARSLAL AVE	400	NW
PEERLESS AVE	396	SW
PEGGY AVE	397	SW
PENDLETON	400	NE
PENNA DR	399	SW
PENNSYLVANIA AVE	397	SE
PENSACOLA AVE	396	SW
PEPPER	398	NE
PERRY ST	397	NE
PERRY PLACE DR	397	NE
PERSHING AVE	396	SE
PERVERIL RD	401	SW
PHILLIP	397	SE
PHILLIPS RD	398	NW
PIKE ST E.	397	SW
PIKE ST W.	397	SW
PINE ST	397	SW
PINE CENTER DR N	399	SW
PINE CENTER DR S	399	SW
PINE ESTATES DR	399	SW
PINEGROVE AVE	398	NE
PINE HGTS	399	SW
PINEHURST DR	398	NE
PINE LAKE AVE	398	NE
PINE LAKE RD	399	SW
PINE RIDGE	399	SW
PINERIDGE DR	400	SE
PINE VIEW DR	399	SW
PINGREE AVE	396	SE
PIONEER DR	399	SW
PIPPIN CT	401	SE
PITTSFIELD AVE	396	NE
PLAINFIELD AVE	400	NE
PLEASANT ST	396	SE
PLEASANT VIEW DR	400	NW
PONTIAC AVE	399	NW
PONTIAC RD	397	NE
PONTIAC LAKE RD	396	SW
PONTIAC PLAZA	397	NE
POPLAR ST	397	SE
PORTAGE ST	399	NE
PORTER ST	396	SE
PORTERS LANE	400	SW
PORTLAND ST	397	GW
PORTMAN	399	SW
POST CHASE CT	401	SW
POST HOUSE CT	401	SW
POWER HOUSE DR	396	SW
PRESTON AVE	396	SW
PRICE ST	397	NW
PRIDHAM AVE	399	SW
PRIMARY	397	SW
PRINCETON AVE F.	397	NW
PRINCETON AVE W.	399	NW
PRIVATE	400	SE
PROSPECT ST	400	NW
PROVINCETOWN RD	400	NE
PUBLIC WORKS DR	398	SE
PURDUE	398	SE
PUTNEY	398	SE
PYRNNE DR	399	NW
QUAIL HOLLOW	399	SW
QUAIL RIDGE CIR	399	SW
QUICK CT	397	SW
QUICK ST	399	NE
RAEBURN ST	400	NW
RAINTREE DR	398	NE
RAMBLING WAY	400	SW
RAMONA TER N.	396	SW
RAMONA TER S.	396	SW
RAPID ST	400	NW
RASKOB AVE	399	SW
RATHMOR RD	400	SE
RAVINVIEW		
RAYMOND PONTIAC	397	EE
READING CT	401	SW
READING N.	401	SW
READING S.	401	SW
RED	399	SW
RED HILL	397	SE
REDMAPLE LANE	401	SE
RED OAK	401	SE
REDWOOD	396	NE
REED RD	400	NE
RENFREW AVE	399	NW
RICHARD	396	SW
RICHMOND AVE	396	NE
RICHTON AVE	397	SE
RICHWOOD RD	398	NW
RIDGE RD	401	SE
RIDGEDALE	401	SW
RIDGEMONT	397	NW
RIDGEMOOR DR	399	NW
RIDGEVIEW CT	399	SE
RIDGEWOOD RD	399	SW
RIVERBANK DR	399	SW
RIVERSIDE	398	SW
RIVERSIDE DR	397	SE
ROBERT CT	398	SW
ROBINDALE	399	SW
ROBINWOOD AVE	397	SW
ROBSON LANE	401	SW
ROCKLEDGE LA	401	SW
ROCKWELL AVE	399	NW
ROGERS AVE	396	SW
ROLAND DR	399	NE
ROLLING GREEN	398	NE
ROLLING ROCK DR	400	NE
ROMNEY RD	401	SW
ROSE CT	396	SE
ROSE ANN	396	NW
ROSEDALE	399	SW
ROSELAWN DR	397	SE
ROSEMARY AVE	399	NW
ROSEWOOD DR	396	NW
ROSEWOOD PL	397	SE
ROSSMOOR CIR	400	SE
ROSWELL	400	SE
ROTSEL	399	NE
ROXIE	400	SE
RUBY CIR	400	SE
RUNDELL ST E.	398	NE
RUNDELL ST W.	398	NE
RUSSELL ST	400	NE

Street	Page	Dir
RULLET DR	401	SE
RUSTIC LA	399	NE
RUTGERS AVE E.	397	NW
RUTGERS AVE W.	396	NE
RUTH AVE	400	SE
SAGINAW ST N.	400	NW
ST CLAIR	401	NE
ST JUDE	396	NW
ST JOSEPH ST	399	SW
ST LOUIS AVE	396	NE
SALLEE LA	396	NE
SALMER AVE	399	NE
SANDERS CIRCLE	400	SW
SANDERSON AVE	396	SE
SANFORD ST N.	397	SW
SANFORD ST S.	400	NW
SARASOTA AVW	396	NE
SAWYER	396	SE
SCHOOLCRAFT	401	NW
SCOTCH PINE	399	SW
SCOTT LAKE RD	396	SW
SCOTTWOOD AVE	397	SE
SEABRIGHT	399	NW
SECOND AVE	397	NW
SEDGEFIELD DR	400	NE
SEMINARY RD	396	SE
SEMINOLE AVW	399	NE
SENECA ST	397	SW
SEVERN LA	401	SW
SEWARD ST	400	NE
SHAGBARK	401	SE
SHAGBARK DR	401	SE
SHALLOW BROOK DR	400	SW
SHAWNEE LA	396	NW
SHEFFIELD AVE E.	397	NW
SHEFFIELD AVE W.	396	NE
SHEFFIELD RD	401	NW
SHELLBOURNE DR	398	NE
SHERIDAN ST	397	SW
SHERMAN PL	397	NE
SHERWOOD RD	399	NW
SHIMMONS RD	398	NW
SHIRLEY AVE	400	NW
SHORE HILL CT	399	SW
SHORE HILL DR	399	SW
SHOREVIEW CT	399	SE
SHORT ST	399	NW
SILVER CIRCLE	396	NW
SILVERDOWN DR	396	NW
SILVERHILL DR	398	NE
SILVER LAKE RD	396	NW
SILVER SIDE CT	396	NW
SILVER SIDE DR	396	NW
SILVERSTONE LA	396	NW
SILVERVALVE DR	398	NE
SIMMONS	397	NE
SINCLAIR	396	SW
SLOCUM RD	401	NW
SMITH DR	399	NW
SHELLBROOK RD	396	SW
SOMERSET RD	400	SE
SOUTER BOVD	401	NW
SOUTH BLVD	400	NW
SOUTHAMPTON RD	401	NW
S. HAMMOND LAKE DR	399	SW
S. MERRIMAC ST	396	SE
S. SPINNINGWHEEL LA	401	SW
SPANISH OAKS DR	399	SW
SPENCE ST	397	SW
SPINNAKER	399	SW
SPOTSWOOD	396	SE
SPRING GROVE RD	401	SW
SPRUCE ST	397	SE
SQUARE LAKE RD	400	SW
SQUIRREL CT	401	NW
SQUIRREL RD	398	SE
SQUIRREL VALLEY DR	401	SW
STANLEY AVE	396	NE
STAPLETON CT	399	NW
STAPLETON DR	399	NW
STARLIGHT DR	396	NE
STARR AVE	399	NW
STATE ST	396	SE
STEGMAN LA	396	NE
STEINBAUGH CT	396	SE
STENNETT AVE	399	NW
STEPHANIE CT	397	SW
STEPHENS CT	397	SW
STIRLING AVE	397	NE
STOCKWELL ST	397	SW
STONE HOLLOW CT	400	NE
STONETREE CIR	398	NE
STOUT PL	397	SW
STOUT ST	399	NE
STOWELL ST	397	SW
STRATFORD AVE	399	NW
STRATHMORE AVE E.	397	NW
S. RATHMORE RD	396	NE
STRATTON DR	399	NW
TACOMA CT	396	SE
TALLAHASSEE	396	SW
TAMARRON DR	398	NE
TANGLEWOOD CT	401	SE
TANGLEWOOD DR	401	SE
TANNAHILL	401	NW
TASMANIA AVE	397	SW
TAYLOR ST	397	SW
TELEGRAPH RD	400	SW
TENNYSON AVE E	397	NE
TENNYSON AVE W	396	NE
TERRY AVE	396	NE
TEWKSBURY	401	SE
TEX AVE	400	NE
THE CROSS RD	400	SW
THDFORD	401	SE
THIRD AVE	397	NW
THOMPSON CT	397	SW
THORPE ST	396	SE
THORS ST	397	SE
TILDEN AVE	399	NW
TILMOR	396	SW
TIMBERVIEW	401	SW
TINA MARIE DR	396	NW
TRAYMORE DR	400	NE
TREGENT ST	397	SW
TRENTON	396	NE
TRINITY CT	396	NW
TULANE	398	SW
TURK ST	400	NW
TURTLE LAKE RD	399	SE
TUTBURY LA	401	SE
TYRONE	396	SW
UNION ST	397	SW
UNIVERSITY DR	398	NW
UNIVERSITY DR PONTIAC	397	SW
UNIVERSITY DR PONTIAC TWP	397	SW
UPLAND AVE	397	NW
UPLONG DR	399	SW
UTICA RD	396	SE
VALENCIA DR	397	SE
VANEL DR	399	SW
VARJO CT	399	SW
VAUGHT	396	SW
VERNON DR	397	SW
VHAY LANE	401	SE
VICTORY CT	397	SW
VICTORY DR	397	SW
VILLAGE DR	396	SW
VINEWOOD	396	SW
VINEYARD AVE	396	NW
VIRGINIA AVE	399	SW
VISTA	400	SE
VOORHEIS RD	399	NE
WABEEK LK DR E	399	SE
WABEEK LK DR W	399	SE
WAGNER AVE	399	NE
WAKEROBIN	399	SE
WALDO ST	396	SE
WALL KEEGO HARBOR	399	NW
WALL ST PONTIAC	400	NW
WALNUT RD		
WALNUT ST PONTIAC TWP	398	NW
WALNUT ST PONTIAC	399	NE
WALSH	399	SW
WALTON BLVD E	397	NW
WALTON BLVD W	396	NE
WALTON CT	397	SW
WANAMAKER AVE	396	NW
WARD RD	399	NE
WARNER ST	399	NE
WAREEN	397	SW
WARWICK BL-FIELD TWP	400	SE
WARWICK AVE SYLVAN LAKE	399	NW
WARWICK CT BL-FIELD TWP	400	SE
WASHINGTON ST	396	SE
WATER	397	SW
WATERLY ST	399	NW
WATKINS LK RD	396	SW
WAUKEGAN	401	NW
WAYNE ST	397	SE
WEBB AVE	397	SE
WEGEWOODE LA	397	NE
WELLINGTON AVE	399	NE
WENDOVER	400	SW
WENDY LA	400	SE
WENONAH DR	399	NE
WESBROOK AVE	397	NW
WESSEN ST	399	NE
WEST BLVD PONTIAC	396	NW
WEST DR BL-FIELD TWP	400	SW
W. BEND ST	399	SW
W. BEND DR	399	SE
WESTEND AVE	396	SW
WESTLAKE CT	399	SW
W. SHORE HILL DR	399	SW
W. SPINNINGWHEEL LANE	400	NE
W. VALLEY RD	400	SW
WESTVIEW DR	401	SW
WESTWAY DR	397	SE
W. WIDE TRACK DR	397	SW
WEYBRIDGE DR	400	NE
WHITFIELD ST	397	SW
WHITMORE	401	SE
WHITTEMORE ST	400	NW
WHITTIER DR	401	SW
WICKFORD CT	400	NE
WILBUR ST	399	NW
WILLARD ST	400	NE
WILLET	401	NE
WILLIAMS AVE WATERFORD TWP	396	NW
WILLIAMS ST PONTIAC	396	SE
WILLIAMSBURG CT WATERFORD TWP	401	NW
WILLIAMSBURG CT AVON TWP	398	NE
WILLIAMSTOWN CT	401	SW
WILLIS	397	NE
WILLOT RD	397	NE
WILLOW BEACH AV	399	SW
WILSHIRE DR	400	SW
WILSON WATERFORD TWP	400	NW
WILSON AVE E PONTIAC	400	NW
WILSON AVE W	400	NW
WINCHCOMBE	401	SW
WINDRUSH	401	SE
WINDY HILL	397	SE
WING ST	397	SW
WINKLEMAN DR	396	NW
WINTERSET ST	399	SW
WINTHROP RD	400	NE
WINTON	396	NW
WISHBONE	400	SE
WISNER ST	396	SE
WOLFE ST	397	SW
WOODBINE DR	400	SE
WOODCHESTER DR	401	SW
WOODCREEK WAY	401	SW
WOODCREST	401	NE
WOODEDGE DR	400	SE
WOODFORD AVE	400	NE
WOODGLEN	401	SE
WOODLAND PONTIAC	396	SE
WOODLAND AVE SYLVAN LAKE	399	NW
WOODLAWN	399	SE
WOODROW WILSON DRIVE	399	SW
WOODWARD AVE	400	NW
WOODWAY CT	400	SE
WORTHINGTON CT	398	NE
WRENN ST	400	NW
WYMAN DR	399	NW
WYOMING AVE	400	NW
YALE AVE E	397	NW
YALE AVE W	396	NE
YORK ST	401	NE
YORKSHIRE	401	NE
YOUNG ST	397	SW
YPSILANTI AVE E	397	NW
YPSILANTI AVE W	396	NW
ZAHN RD	398	NE
ZELMA	397	NE

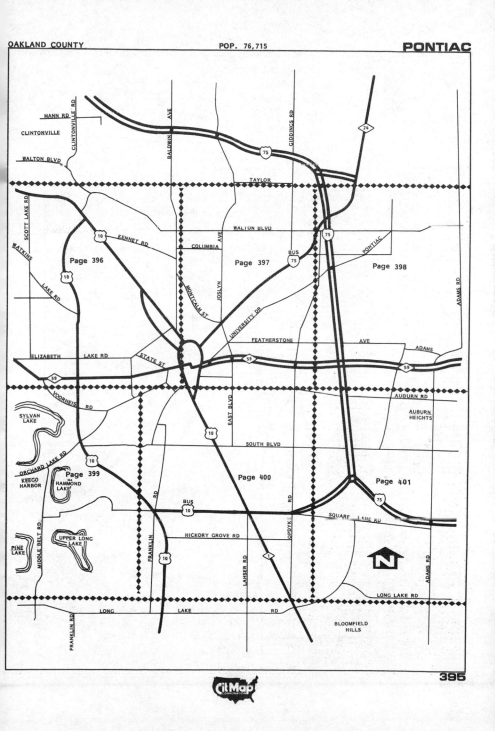

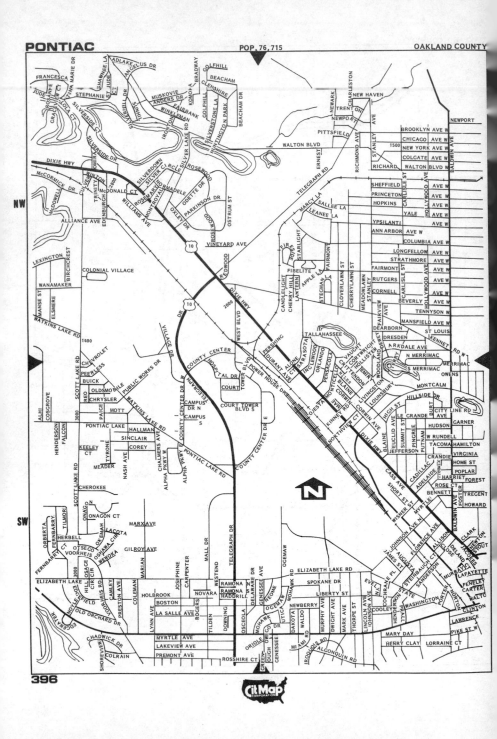

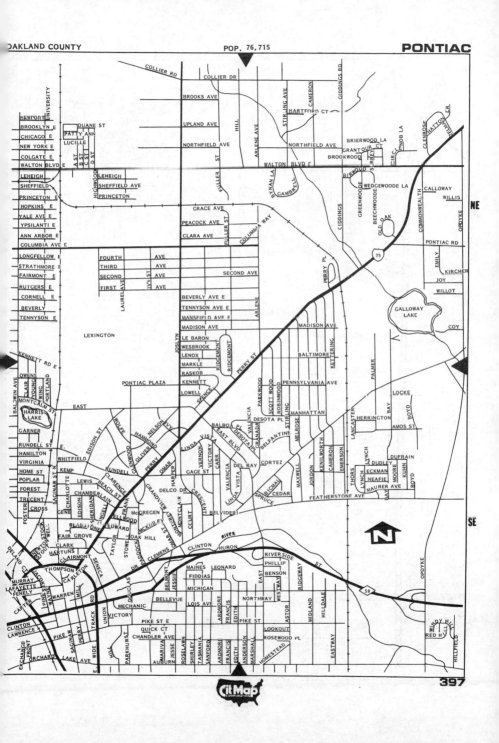

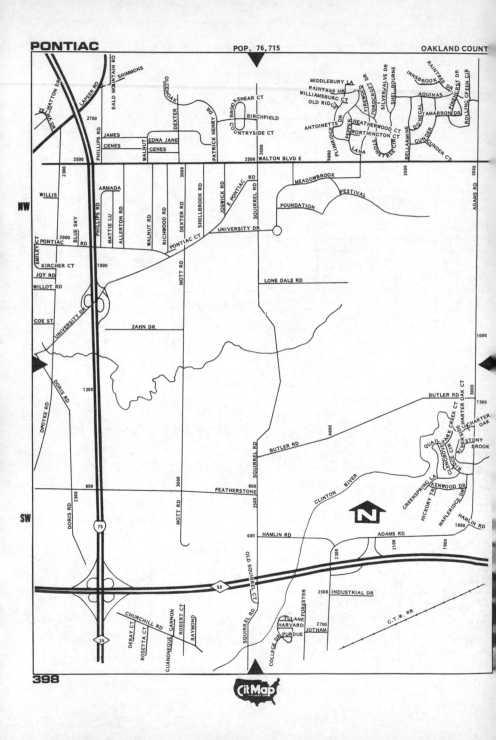

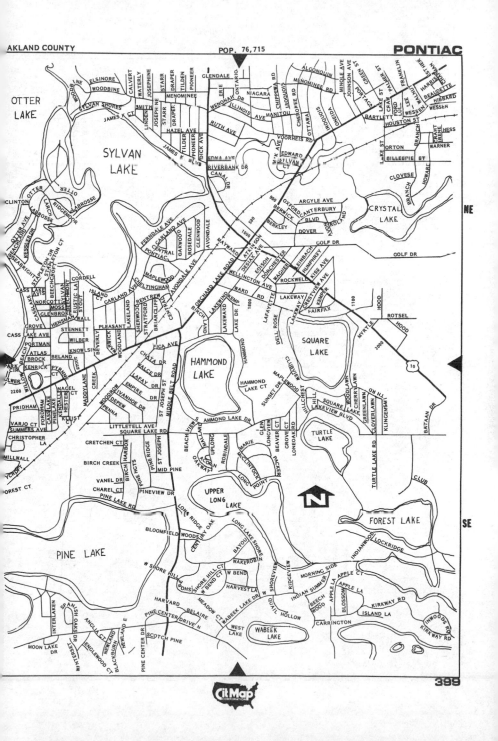

OTTER
LAKE

SYLVAN
LAKE

CRYSTAL
LAKE

NE

OTTER

CASS LAKE

HAMMOND
LAKE

SQUARE
LAKE

10

TURTLE
LAKE

UPPER
LONG
LAKE

FOREST LAKE

SE

PINE LAKE

WABEEK
LAKE

WEST
LAKE

MOON LAKE
DR

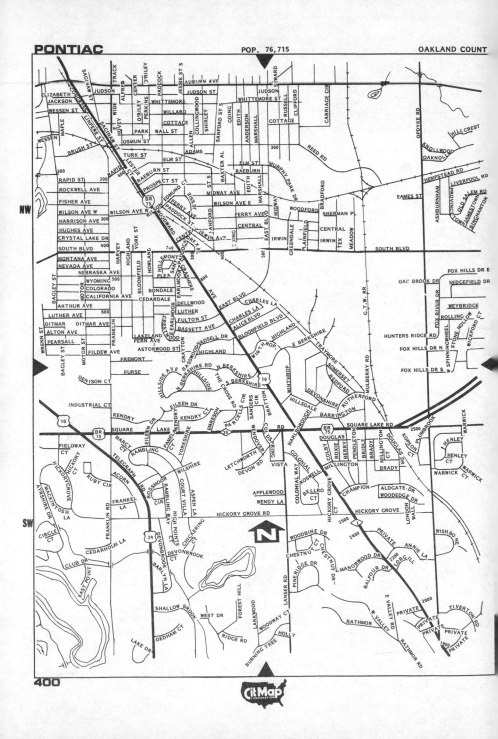

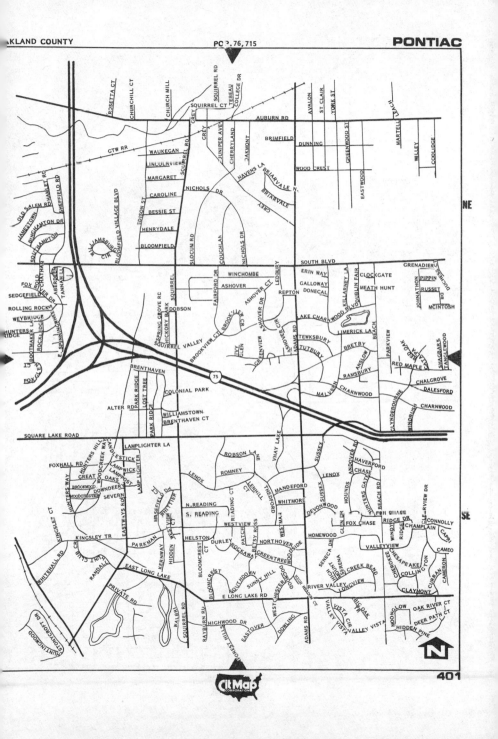

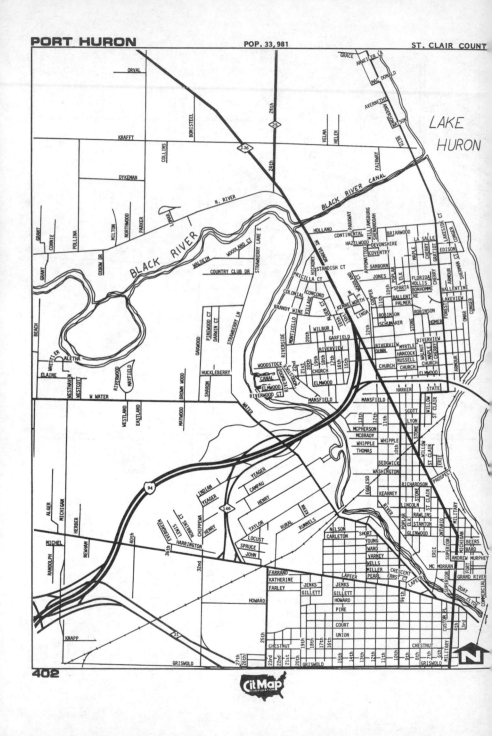

LAKE
HURON

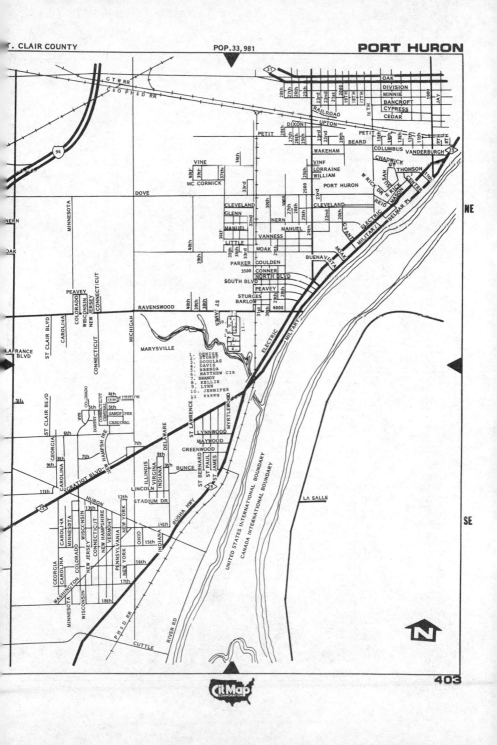

Street	Grid	Street	Grid	Street	Grid	Street	Grid
ALDEN CT	402 NE	HENRY	402 SW	RIVERWOOD	402 SW	23RD	403 NE
ALETHA	402 SW	HERBER	402 SW	RIVERWOOD CT.	402 SE	24TH	403 NE
ALGER	402 SW	HICKORY	402 NE	ROBBINS CT.	402 SW	24TH	402 NE
ANDERSON	402 SW	HOLLAND	402 NE	ROBINSON	402 NE	25	402 SE
ANDREW	402 SE	HOLLIS	402 NE	RUSSEL	402 SE	25TH	403 NE
ANWEILER LA	402 NE	HOMER	402 NE	RUSSEL	402 NE	26	402 SW
APPOMATTOX	402 NE	HOWARD	402 SE	SANBORN	402 NE	26TH	403 NE
ARMOUR	402 SW	HUCKLEBERRY	402 SW	SAND PIPER	403 SW	27	402 SE
AVERNETHY	402 NE	HURON	403 SW	SCHUMAKER	402 NE	27TH	403 NE
BALLENTINE	402 NE	ILLINOIS	403 SW	SCOTT	402 SE	28TH	402 SE
BANCROFT	403 NE	INDIAN	402 SW	SEDGWICK	402 SW	29TH	403 NE
BAR	403 NE	INDIANA	403 SW	SHARON	402 SW	3	402 NE
BARD	402 SE	JAY	403 NE	SHENANDOAH	402 NE	30TH	403 NE
BARLOW	403 NE	JENKS	402 SE	SHERMON CT.	402 NE	31ST	403 NE
BEACH	402 NW	JENNIFER	403 NE	SHORT	403 NE	32	402 SW
BEARD	403 NE	JOHN	403 NE	SOUTH BLVD	403 NE	33RD	403 NE
BEERS	402 SE	JONES	402 NE	SPARTA	402 NE	34TH	403 NE
BELMAR	403 NE	KAREN	403 NE	SPRUCE	402 SW	35TH	403 NE
BETH	402 NE	KATHERINE	402 SE	ST. CLAIR	402 SE	36	403 NE
BONHOMME	402 NE	KEARNY	402 SE	ST. JAMES	402 SW	37	403 NE
BONISTEEL	402 NW	KEARNY	402 SE	ST. BERNARD	403 SW	38	403 NW
BRANDY	403 NE	KELLIE	403 NE	ST. CLAIR BLVD.	403 NW	39	403 NW
BRANDY WINE	402 NE	KENNELWORTH	402 NE	ST. JAMES	403 SW	4	402 SE
BRENDA	403 NW	KNAPP	402 SW	ST. LAWRENCE	403 SW	40	403 SW
BRIARWOOD	402 NE	KRAFT	402 NW	ST. PAUL	403 SW	40	402 SW
BROWN WOOD	402 SW	LA SALLE	403 SE	STADIUM DR.	403 SW	5	403 SW
BUENAVISTA	403 NE	LA SALLE	402 NE	STANDISH CT.	402 NE	6	403 SE
BUNCE	403 NE	LA FRANCE	403 NW	STANTON	403 NW	6	402 SE
BUSHA HUY	403 SW	LAKESIDE CT	403 SW	STATE	402 SE	7	403 SW
CAMPAU	402 SW	LAKEVIEW	402 SW	STONE	402 SE	7	402 SE
CANAL	402 SE	LAPEER	402 SE	STONE	402 NE	8	403 NE
CARDINAL	403 SW	LEWIS	402 SW	STRAWBERRY LANE	402 SW	8	402 SE
CARLETON	402 SE	LINCOLN	403 SW	STRAWBERRY LANE E	402 NW	8TH	403 NE
CAROLINA	402 NE	LINCOLN	402 SE	STUART	403 NE	9	403 SW
CEDAR	403 NE	LINDA	402 NE	STURGES	403 NE	9	402 SE
CENTER	403 NE	LINDA E	402 NE	SUPERIOR	402 SE	9 1/2	402 NE
CENTRAL	403 SW	LINDA N	402 NE	SUSAN	403 NE	9TH	403 NE
CHADWICK CT.	403 NE	LITTLE	403 NE	TAYLOR	402 SW		
CHERRY	402 NE	LOCUST	402 SW	THOMAS	402 SE		
CHIPPEWA	402 SW	LOMAR	402 NW	UNION	403 NE		
CHURCH	403 SE	LORRAINE	403 NE	UPTON	403 NE		
CLEVELAND	403 NE	LYNN	402 SE	VANDERBURGH	403 NE		
CLYDE	402 SE	LYNNWOOD	403 NE	VANNESS	403 NE		
COLLINS	402 NW	LYON	402 SE	VARNENY	402 SE		
COLONIAL	402 NE	MAC DONALD	402 NE	VELMA	402 NE		
COLORADO	403 SW	MANSFIELD	402 SE	VERMONT	403 SW		
COLORADO	403 SW	MANUEL	403 NE	VILLAGE	402 NE		
COLUMBUS	403 NE	MAPLE	402 NE	VINE	403 NE		
COMMERCIAL	402 NE	MARYWOOD	403 SW	VINE	403 SW		
CONCORD	402 NE	MASON	403 NE	VIRGINIA	403 SW		
CONGER	402 NE	MATHEW CIR.	402 SW	W. RICK DR.	403 NE		
CONNETICUT	403 SW	MAYFIELD	402 SW	WAKEHAM	403 NE		
CONNER	403 NE	MC BRANDY	403 NE	WALDEIM	402 SE		
CONNIE	402 NW	MC CORMICK	403 SW	WALNUT	402 NE		
CONSTITUTION	403 SW	MC MORRAN	402 SE	WARD	402 SE		
CONTINENTAL	402 NE	MC PHEREON	402 SW	WASHINGTON	403 SW		
COPPER	402	MICHEL	402 SW	WASHINGTON	402 SW		
COOPER	402 NE	MICHIGAN	402 SE	WATER	402 NE		
COUNTY CLUB DR.	402 NW	MILITARY	403 NE	WATSON	402 NE		
COURT	402 SE	MILITARY	403 NE	WEST WATER	402 SW		
COVENTRY	402 NE	MILLER	402 NE	WESTCOT	402 SW		
CRESCENT	402 SE	MILTON	402 NW	WESTHAVEN	402 SW		
CUSTOM PL	402 SE	MINNESOTA	403 SW	WESTLAND	402 SW		
CUTTLE	403 SW	MINNIE	403 NE	WHIPPLE	403 NE		
CYPRESS	403 NE	MOAK	403 NE	WHITTIER	402 NE		
DARWIN CT	402 NW	MONTICELLO	403 NE	WILBER	402 NE		
DAVIS	403 NE	MT. VERNON	402 SE	WILLIAM	403 NE		
DELAWARE	403 SW	MURPHEY	402 SE	WILLIAMSBURG	402 NE		
DENISE	403 NW	MYRTLE	402 NE	WILLOW	402 SE		
DEVONSHIRE	403 NE	MYRTLEWOOD	403 NE	WISCONSIN	403 SW		
DIVISION	403 NE	NELSON	402 SE	WOODLAND	402 NW		
DIXON	403 NE	NERN	403 NE	WOODLAND CT.	402 NW		
DOROTHY	403 SW	NEW HAMPSHIRE	403 SW	WOOODSTOCK	402 SE		
DOUGLAS	403 NE	NEW JERSEY	403 SW	YEAGER	402 SE		
DOVE	403 NW	NEW YORK	403 SW	YOUNG	402 SE		
DUNN	402 NE	NEWHAM	402 SW	10	402 SE		
DYKMAN	402 NW	NORTH BLVD.	402 SW	10TH	403 NE		
E. RICK	403 NE	NORTH RIVER	402 NW	10TH	403 SW		
EASTLAND	402 SW	NORTHWOOD	402 NW	11	402 SE		
EDISON	402 NE	OAK	403 NE	11TH	402 SE		
EGGLESO	402 SE	OAKWOOD	402 NW	11TH	403 NE		
ELAINE	402 SW	OHIO	403 SW	12	402 NE		
ELECTRIC	402 SE	OMAR	402 NE	12	402 SE		
ELK	402 SE	ONTARIO	402 SE	12TH	403 NE		
ELMWOOD	402 SE	ORVAL	402 NW	12TH	402 NE		
ERIE	402 SE	OXBOW	402 NW	13	402 SE		
ERNST CT.	402 SE	PALMER	402 SE	13	402 SE		
EVERGREEN	402 SW	PARKER	403 NE	13TH	403 NE		
FAIRWAY	402 NE	PARKER	402 NW	14TH	403 NE		
FARLEY	402 SE	PARKWAY	402 SE	15	402 SE		
FARRAND	402 SE	PEARL	402 SE	15	402 NE		
FLORIDA	402 NE	PEAVY	403 NE	15TH	403 NE		
FOREST	402 NE	PENNSYLVANIA	403 SW	15TH	402 NE		
FORT	402 SE	PETIT	403 NE	16	403 SW		
GARFIELD	402 NE	PINE	402 SE	16	402 SE		
GEORGIA	403 SW	PINEWOOD CT.	402 NW	16TH	403 NE		
GILLET	402 SE	POLLINA	402 NW	16TH	402 NE		
GLENN	402 NE	POPLAR	402 NE	17	402 SE		
GLENNWOOD	402 NE	POPLAR	402 NE	17TH	402 SE		
GOULDEN	403 NE	PRICILLA	402 NE	18	403 NE		
GRACE	402 NE	QUAY	403 NE	18TH	403 SW		
GRAND RIVER	402 SE	RAILROAD	403 NE	19	403 NE		
GRANT	403 NE	RANDOLPH	402 NE	19TH	403 NE		
GRANT	402 NW	RAWLINS	402 NE	20	402 SE		
GRATIOT	403 SW	REID	403 NE	20TH	402 NE		
GREENWOOD	403 SW	RICHARDSON	402 SE	21	402 SE		
GRISWOLD	403 NE	RIVER	402 SE	21TH	402 SE		
HANCOCK	403 NE	RIVER RD.	402 SW	21ST	401 NE		
HARKER	403 SE	RIVERSIDE	402 NE	22	402 NE		
HARRINGTON	402 SW	RIVERVIEW	402 NE	22ND	401 NE		
HAZLEWOOD	403 NE	RIVERVIEW	402 NE	23	402 SE		
HELEN	402 NE	RIVERWOOD	402 SE				
HENRY	402 SW						

NOTES

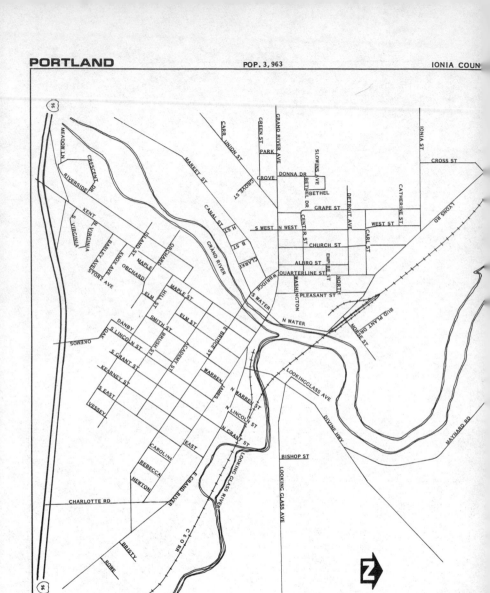

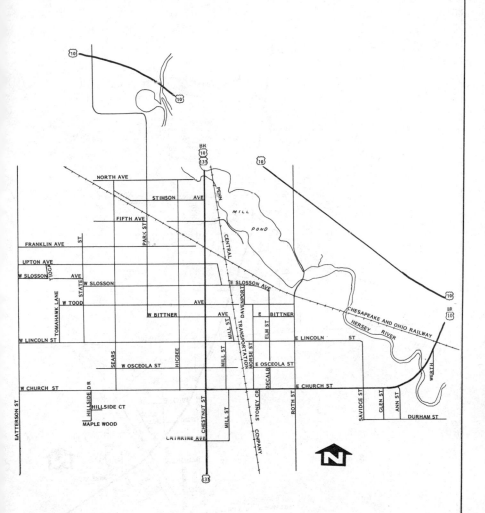

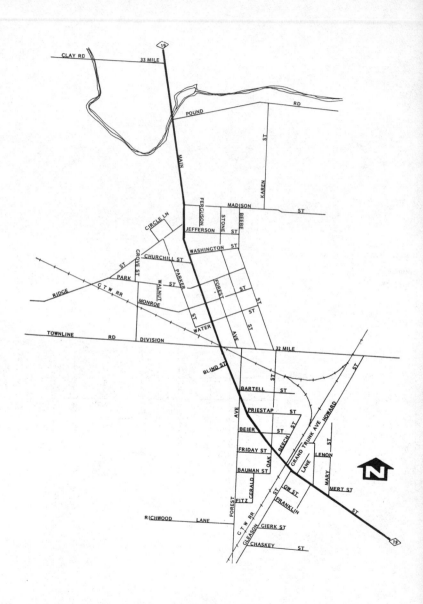

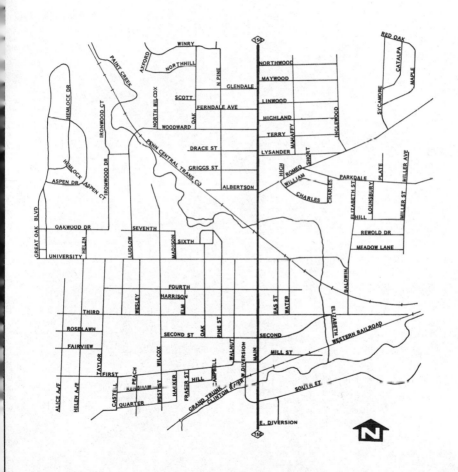

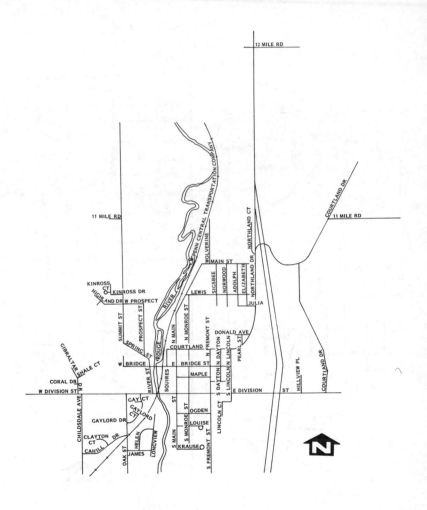

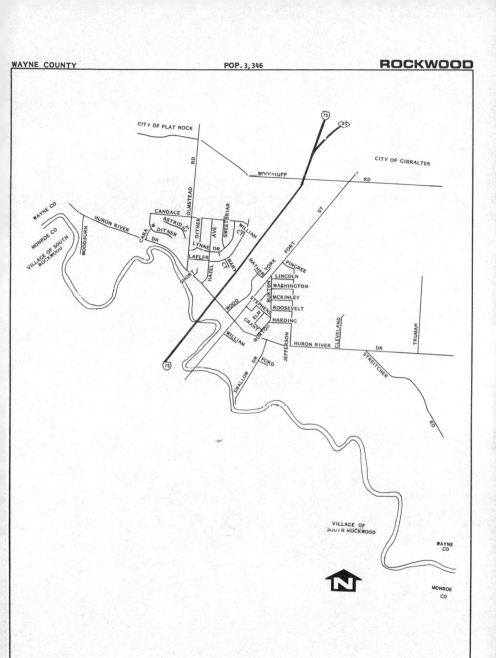

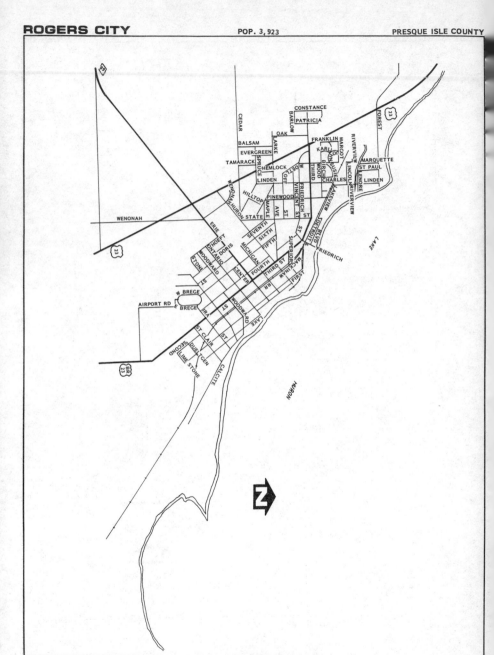

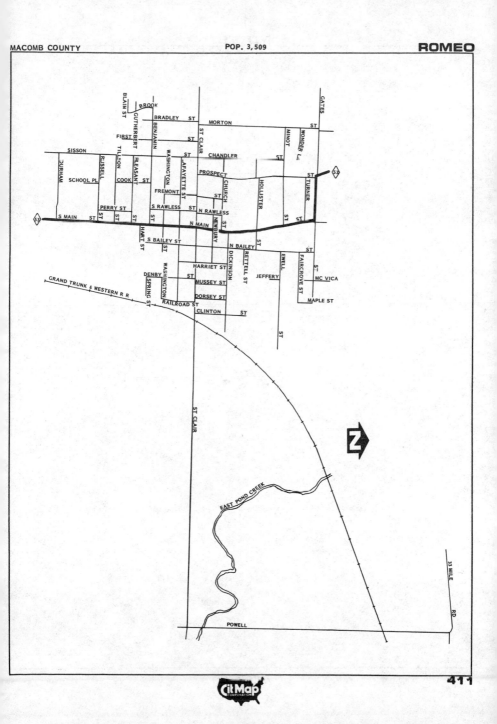

NOTES

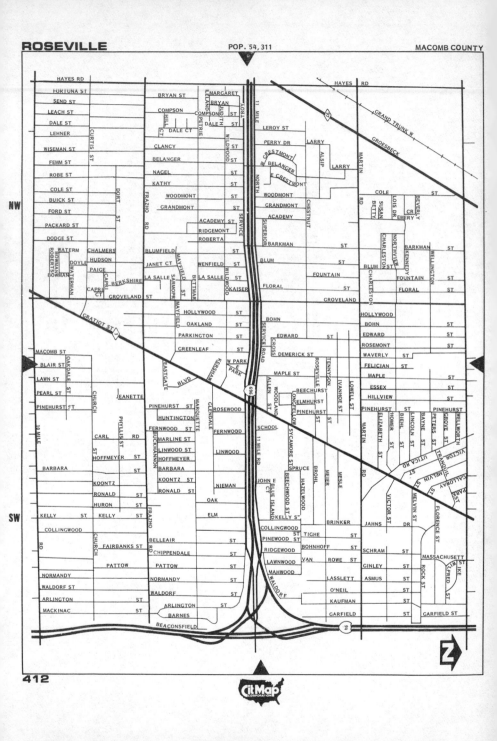

ROSEVILLE

POP. 54,311

MACOMB COUNTY

412

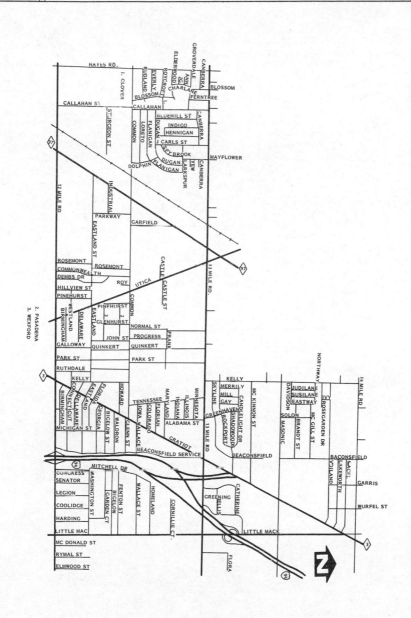

AAVA	414 NW	GAINSBORO	414 NE	RAVANA	415 NE
ABERDOVEY	415 SW	GALPIN	414 NW	RED RUN	415 NE
ALBERT	415 SE	GARDEN	415 SE	REMBRANDT	415 SE
ALEXANDER	414 SE	GARDENIA AVE.	414 NE	ROBINWOOD	415 NW
ALFRED	414 SW	GIRARD	415 SW	ROCHESTER	415 NE
ALICIA	414 NW	GLAPIN	414 NW	ROSEDALE	414 NE
ALICIA LANE	414 NW	GLENDALE	415 NW	ROSELAND	414 NW
ALTADENA	415 SW	GLENVIEW	414 NW	ROSEWOOD	415 NW
AMELIA	415 SE	GLENWOOD	415 SW	ROSZEI	414 NE
AMHERST	415 NE	GOLF AVE.	414 NE	ROYAL	415 SE
ARDEN PL.	415 SE	GRANDVIEW	415 SW	SAGAMORE	415 SW
ARDMORE	414 NE	GREENFIELD	414 NW	SAMOSET	415 NW
ARLINGTON	415 NE	GREENWAY	415 SW	SECOND	414 SE
AUBURN	415 NE	GREENWAY	415 SW	SEDGEMORE	415 NW
AUSTIN	414 NW	GROVELAND	415 NW	SEMINOLE	415 NE
BAKER	414 SW	GUILFORD	415 NE	SEVENTH	414 SE
BALDWIN	414 NE	HAMILTON	414 SE	SHAW	415 SW
BAMLET	415 SW	HAMPTON	415 SW	SHEFFIELD	415 NE
BASSETT	414 NW	HARRISON	414 SE	SHENANDOAH	415 SW
BATAVIA	414 SW	HARTRICK	414 SW	SHERIDAN	415 NE
BAUMAN	415 SE	HARVARD	415 SE	SIMON	414 SW
BAXTER AVE.	414 SE	HARWOOD	414 SE	SPRINGER	415 SW
BELLAIRE	414 NE	HAWKINS	414 NW	ST. CHARLES	414 SE
BAMBRIDGE	415 SW	HAWTHORNE AVE.	414 NE	STANLEY	415 NW
BENJAMIN	415 SW	HENENE	414 SE	STARK	415 SW
BERKSIRE	415 NE	HIGHFIELD	415 NE	STEPHENSON SUPER HWY.	
BETSY	415 NE	HIGHLAND	414 NE		414 NE
BLAIR AVE.	414 SE	HILLCREST	415 NE	SUNNY BROOK	415 NE
BONNIEVIEW DR.	414 NW	HILLDALE	414 NW	SUNSET BLVD.	414 NW
BRINKLEY	414 SE	HILLSIDE CT.	415 NE	SYCAMORE	414 NW
BUCKINGHAM	415 NE	HOFFMAN AVE.	414 SE	SYLVAU	415 SE
BURNAM	415 SW	HOUSTONIA	414 NW	TARTFORD	414 SE
BUTTERNUT	415 SE	HUWSTONIA	414 NE	TAYLOR	414 SE
BWERLY	415 NE	HUDSON	414 SE	TEN MILE	414 SE
CALIFORNIA	414 SE	HUNTER	415 SW	THIRD	414 SE
CAMBRIDGE RD.	414 SW	HURON	415 SW	THIRTEEN MILE	414 NE
CAMPBELL	414 SE	INDIANA	414 SE	THORNCROFT	415 NW
CANMAN	414 NW	INSETTA	414 NW	TONANWANDA	415 NW
CATALPA	414 NW	IROQUIS BLVD.	414 NW	TORQUAY	415 NW
CEDAR	414 NW	IRVING AVE.	414 SE	TRAFFORD	415 SW
CEDAR HILL	414 NW	JEFFREY	415 SE	TROY	414 SE
CENTER	414 NW	JOSEPHINE	414 SE	TUFTS	414 NE
CHAMBERS	414 SE	JUDSON	415 NE	TWELVE MILE	414 NE
CHARLOTTE	415 SE	KAYSER	414 SE	UNIVERSITY	414 SE
CHEROKEE AVE.	414 SE	KENIWORTH	414 SW	UPTON	414 NW
CHERRY	414 NW	KENSINGTON	415 SW	VERMONT	415 SE
CHESTER	415 SE	KENT	415 SE	VERONA CIRCLE	414 NW
CHESTER	415 SE	KENWOOD	414 SE	VINSETTA	414 NW
CHIPPAWA	415 SE	KNOWLES	414 SE	VINTON	414 NW
CLAWSON	414 NW	LA-PLAZA	414 NW	VIRGINIA	414 SE
CLIFTON	414 NE	LAFFAYETTE	414 NW	WARICK	415 SE
CLOVERDALE	414 NW	LAKESIDE DR.	414 NE	WASHINGTON	414 NW
CODY	414 NE	LASALLE	415 SE	WAVERLY	414 NW
COLONIAL	415 NE	LAUREL	414 SW	WEBSTER	414 NW
COLUMBUS	415 SE	LAWNDALE	414 NW	WEST	414 NW
CONNECTICUT	415 SE	LAWRENCE	415 SW	WESTGATE	414 SW
CONNECTICUT	414 SE	LAWSON	414 SW	WHITCOB	415 SE
COOLIDGE HWY.	415 NW	LEAFDALE	415 NW	WILLESLEY	414 SE
COOPER	415 NW	LENOX	414 SE	WILSON	415 SE
CRANE	414 NW	LEXINGTON	415 SE	WILSON	414 NW
CROOK	415 SW	LINCOLN	415 SW	WINDEMERE	415 SE
CROOK	415 NW	LINDEN	415 SE	WOODCREST	414 NW
CROOK RD.	414 NW	LINWOOD	rqr NW	WOODLAND	415 SW
CURRY	414 SE	LLOYD	414 NW	WOODLAWN	415 SE
CUSTER	415 SE	LOCKWOOD	414 NW	WOOSBORO	414 NW
DE VILLEN	415 SE	LONGFELLOW	414 SE	WOODSIDE	414 NW
DELAWARE	414 SE	MACE	414 SE	WOODSLEE	415 SW
DELEMERE	415 SW	MAIN	414 NW	WOODWARD	414 NW
DETROIT	414 NE	MANDALAY	415 SW	WRENFORD	415 NE
DEVON	415 SW	MANITOU	415 SE	WYANDOTTE	414 SE
DEWEY	414 NE	MANKATO	415 SW	YALE	414 SW
DONALD	414 SE	MANOR	415 SW	YORBA	415 NE
DORCHESTER	414 SE	MANSFIELD	415 NW	YORBA LINDA	415 NE
DUKESHIRE HWY.	415 NE	MAPLE	414 NW	YORK	414 NE
DUNDEE	414 SW	MAPLEGROVE	414 NW		
DUNHAM	415 SW	MAPLEWOOD	414 NW		
EDGELAND	415 SW	mark orr	414 NE		
EDGELAND	415 SW	MARLIN	414 NE		
EDGER	415 SW	MARWELL	414 NW		
EDGEWOOD	414 NW	MARY	414 NW		
EDGEWORTH	414 SE	MARYWOOD	414 NW		
EDISON	414 SE	MASON	414 SE		
EDMUND	415 SE	MASSOIT	415 SW		
ELEVEN MILE	414 SE	MCLEAN	414 SE		
ELIZABETH	414 NE	MEIJER	415 NW		
ELLEN	415 SE	MERRILL	415 SE		
ELMHURST	414 NW	MIDLAND	415 SE		
ELM WOOD	415 SW	MILLARD	415 SE		
ENGLEWOOD	415 SE	MINERVA	414 SE		
ESSEX	415 SW	MOHAWK	414 SE		
ETON CROSS	415 SW	MONTROSE	415 SE		
ETOWAH	414 SE	MORSE	414 SE		
EUCLID	414 NE	MT. VERNON	415 SE		
EVERGREEN	414 NW	NAKOTA	415 SE		
EXINGTON	414 SE	NORMANDY	415 NE		
FAIRGROVE	525 SE	NORTHWOOD	414 NW		
FAIRWAY	414 NW	OAKMOUNT	414 NE		
FARNUEN	414 NW	OAKRIDGE	414 SE		
FARNUM	414 NE	OLIVIA	415 NW		
FERN	415 SE	ORCHARD	415 SE		
FERN	415 SE	ORCHARD GROVE	414 NW		
FERNCLIFF	414 NW	OTTAWA	415 SE		
FERNLEE	415 NW	PARENT	415 SE		
FERRIS	415 SE	PARKER	415 SE		
FERRIS AVE.	414 NE	PARKVIEW	415 NE		
FORESTDALE	414 NW	PARMENTOR	415 NW		
FOURTEEN MILE	415 NE	PHILLIPS	415 SE		
FOURTH	414 SW	PLEASANT	414 NW		
FREDERICK	414 SE	POPLAR	415 SE		
FULTON	415 NE	PORTTER	414 NE		
		POTAWTOM	414 NW		
		PRAIRIE	415 SE		

POP. 70,893

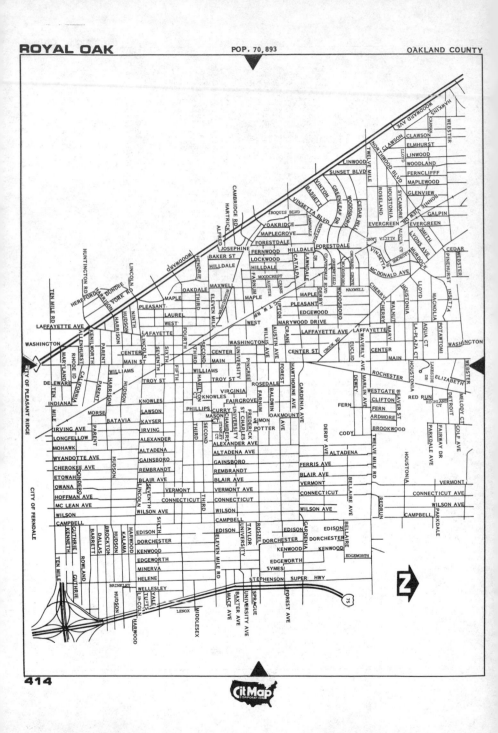

CitMap
CORPORATION

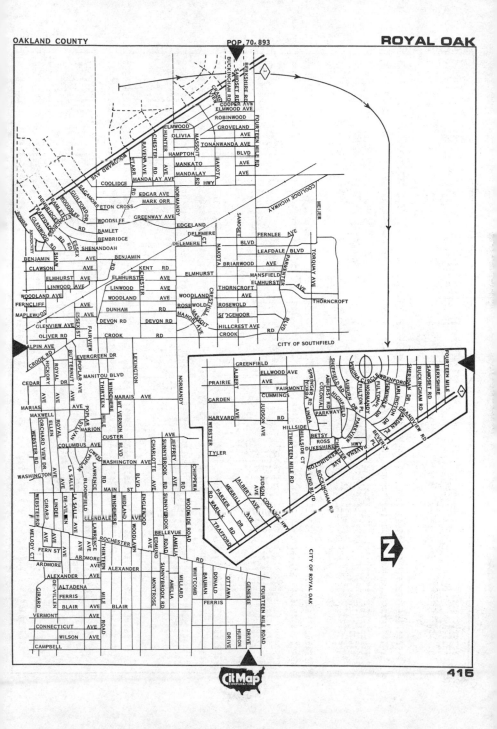

CITY OF SOUTHFIELD

CITY OF ROYAL OAK

ACACIA ST	424	SW
ACORN DR	423	SE
ADA PL	419	SW
ADAM ST		
THOMAS TWP.	424	SE
ADAMS AVE		
SAGINAW	424	NW
ADAMS BLVD		
SAGINAW	424	NE
ADAMS ST		
SAGINAW	424	NW
ADAMS ST		
ZILWAUKEE	421	NE
ADRIAN ST	419	SE
AGRICOLA DR	421	NW
AKRON ST	428	NE
ALABAMA AVE	428	NW
ALAMO CT	426	NW
ALBANY ST	427	NW
ALBERT ST	423	SE
ALBRECHT DR	421	NW
ALCONA ST	421	SW
ALCOTT RD	421	NW
ALDORAN RD	423	NE
ALEXANDER ST N	424	SE
ALEXANDER ST S	424	SE
ALGER ST	425	SE
ALICE ST	424	SW
ALLEGAN ST	424	SW
ALLENDALE DR	423	NW
ALLINGTON	419	SE
ALLISON ST	428	NW
ALMIRA	425	NW
ALPINE DR	427	NE
ALTON CT	419	SW
ALURA PL	421	NW
ALVIN ST	419	SE
AMANDA DR	423	NW
AMBASSADOR	419	SW
AMELIA DR	427	SW
AMES ST	424	SE
AMHERST	420	SE
ANDERSON RD	419	SE
ANDRE ST N	424	SE
ANDRE ST S	424	SE
ANDREW ST	423	SE
ANGEL DR	428	SW
ANGUS DR	419	SW
ANN ST	420	SW
ANNCHESTER DR	420	NE
ANNESLEY ST	426	SW
ANNMARY ST	428	NW
APPLE ST	428	NW
APPOLO DR	420	SW
APOLLO ST	428	NW
AQUA PL	420	SE
ARBOR LANE	423	NE
ARBORETUM DR	423	SE
ARBORETUM DR N	423	SE
ARBORETUM DR S	423	SE
ARBUTUS DR	219	SE
ARCHIE	425	NW
ARCHWOOD PL	420	NW
ARCLAIR PL	423	NE
ARDMORE PL	420	NW
ARCLAIR PL	423	NE
ARDMORE PL	420	SW
ARDUSSI AVE	424	SW
ARLINGTON DR	428	NW
ARNETTE ST	425	SE
ARNOLD ST	427	NW
ARVIN DR	427	NE
ARVIN DR S	427	NE
ASBURY CT	420	SE
ASH ST		
CARROLLTON TWP	421	SE
ASH ST SAGINAW	425	NW
ASHLAND DR	423	NE
ASHTON DR	419	SE
ASHWOOD W	419	NW
ASPEN ST	427	NE
ASTOR	425	NE
ATHENS ST	426	NW
ATLANTA ST	421	SW
ATWATER ST	425	SW
ATWOOD LA	428	SW
AUBURN DR S	427	NE
AUBURN DR W	427	NE
AUDUBON DR	423	NE
AUGSBURG ST	419	SE
AUGUSTINE ST	423	SE
AURELIA CT	419	SE
AUSTIN ST	427	NW
AVALON AVE	420	SW
AVON ST	424	NE
BADGER PL	419	SE
BAGLEY ST	425	SE
BAGSHAW DR	427	NE
BAINBRIDGE RD	423	SE
BAINES DR	423	NW
BALDWIN AVE	428	NW
BALSAM ST	421	SE
BANCROFT ST	425	SE
BANNER RD	427	NW
BARBEAU	423	NW
BARBERRY LA	419	SW
BARCLAY DR	420	SW
BARNARD RD	420	NE
BARNARD ST	424	NE
BARNET	426	NW
BARTOW	425	NE
BASKINS PL	423	NE

BASSWOOD DR	419	SE
BATES ST N	424	SE
BATES ST S	424	SE
BAUER DR	421	SW
BAUM ST N	425	NE
BAY RD	420	NE
BAY CITY RD	422	NW
BAYLOR CT	421	NW
BAYWOOD PL	420	NW
BEACH RD	423	SE
BEAUMONT	423	NE
BECKER RD	422	NE
BECKETT PL	419	NE
BEDFORD ST	428	NW
BEECH ST	424	SW
BEECHWOOD AVE	427	NE
BELAIR DR		
SAGINAW TWP.	424	SW
BEL AIR ST		
CARROLLTON TWP	421	SW
BELDING ST	427	NW
BELLENCA DR	421	SW
BELLEVIEW AVE	428	NW
BELMAR DR	419	SW
BELMONT PL	419	SW
BENED PL	423	SE
BENJAMIN ST	425	NW
BENNINGTON	419	NE
BENTON RD	424	SW
BERBEROVICH DR	419	SE
BERGER RD	420	SE
BERKELEY CT	426	SW
BERL DR	420	
BERNICE DR	428	SW
BERRYWOOD	419	NW
BERTHA DR	428	NE
BERTRAM	419	NE
BETHANY ST	426	NW
BEULAH ST	427	NE
BEWICK AVE	428	NW
BINSCARTH AVE	420	SW
BIRCH ST	425	SW
BIRCHCREST DR	423	SW
BIRCHVIEW DR	423	SW
BIRNEY ST	424	SW
BISHOP	427	NE
BISMARCK ST	422	SW
BITTERSWEET LA	421	NE
BLACKMORE ST	420	SW
BLAINE RD	420	SE
BLAKE ST	420	SE
BLISS ST	424	SW
BLOOMFIELD BLVD	427	NW
BLUEBERRY PL	419	NW
BLUEBIRD DR	427	SE
BOBENDICK DR	421	SW
BOCL RD	419	SE
BOEHLKE ST	425	SE
BOEING DR	421	SW
BOND ST N	425	NW
BOND ST S	425	SW
BONDALYN	426	SE
BORLAND AVE	424	NW
BORLAND CT	424	NW
BOXWOOD ST	425	SE
BRADFORD DR	419	SE
BRADINGTON DR	421	NE
BRALEY ST	424	SW
BRAMBLE DR	420	NW
BRANDON PL	420	SW
BRENNER ST	424	NW
BRETTON CT	420	SW
BREWSTER ST	425	SW
BRIAN SCOTT PL	424	SW
BRIARSON DR	423	NW
BRIARWOOD DR	428	SW
BRIDGTON RD	427	SW
BRISTOL ST E	425	SW
BRISTOL ST W	425	SW
BROADWAY ST	428	NW
BROCKTON PL	420	SW
BROCKWAY PL	424	SW
BROCKWAY RD	419	SW
BROCKWAY ST	424	SE
BRO-MOR PL	424	NE
BRO-MOR ST	420	SE
BROOK DR	423	NE
BROWN ST	425	SW
BRUCE ST	419	SE
BRUNKOW CT	428	NW
BRUNSWICK ST	420	NE
BRYN MAWR PL	423	NW
BUCKTHORNE DR	419	SE
BULLOCK ST	424	SE
BUNDY ST	427	NW
BURBANK PL	423	NE
BURLINGTON DR	428	NW
BURROWS ST	424	SW
BURT ST	426	SW
BUSH ST	421	NE
BUTLER RD	426	NE
BUTTERNUT RD	420	NW
CABARET TR S	420	NE
CABARET TR W	420	NW
CABOT ST	428	NE
CACTUS DR	419	NE
CADILLAC PL	421	NW
CALDWELL ST	428	NE
CALETTE DR	427	SW
CALIFORNIA AVE	428	NW
CALUMET DR	420	NE
CAMDEN DR	420	SW
CAMELOT	423	SE
CAMPBELL ST	425	SW

CAMP WILLOWS DR	424	SE
CAMMIN DR	423	NE
CANARY DR	428	SW
CANTON DR	419	SW
CANYON DR	419	NE
CAPEHART DR	427	NE
CAPITOL ST	421	NE
CARAVELLE DR	421	SW
CARBECK DR	420	NE
CARDINAL DR	428	SW
CARDINGTON DR	419	SE
CARLA DR	421	SW
CARLISLE ST	426	NW
CARMAN DR	424	SW
CARNEGIE ST	428	NE
CAROLINA ST N	424	SE
CAROLINA ST S	424	SE
CARRIE MARIE CT	426	SW
CARROLL ST	425	NE
CARROLLTON RD	421	SE
CARROLLYN LA	421	NW
CARTER ST	425	SE
CARVER DR	420	NW
CARY ST	425	SW
CASIMIR ST	426	NW
CASS RIVER DR	428	SE
CASS ST	424	SE
CATALINA ST	421	SW
CATERBURY DR	423	NE
CATHAY ST	426	NW
CATHEDRAL DR	419	SW
CATHERINE ST	425	NW
CATTERFELD LA	428	NE
CECELIA ST	425	NW
CEDAR ST	425	SW
CENTENNIAL DR	423	NE
CENTER SAGINAW	419	NE
CENTER RD N		
SAGINAW TWP.	423	NE
CENTER RD S		
SAGINAW TWP.	423	SE
CENTER ST		
CARROLLTON	421	SE
CENTER WOODS DR	423	NE
CENTURY DR	423	NE
CHALMERS RD	428	NE
CHAMBER ST	426	NW
CHAPEL DR E	419	SW
CHAPEL DR S	419	SW
CHAPEL DR W	419	SW
CHARLES ST		
SAGINAW TWP	420	SE
CHARLES ST N	424	SE
CHARLES ST S	424	SW
CHATHAM DR	427	NW
CHENEY ST	428	NW
CHEROKEE RD	421	NW
CHERRY ST	426	NW
CHESTERFIELD	419	NE
CHESTNUT ST	424	SW
CHEVEL DR	428	SE
CHEYENNE PL	419	SE
CHICAGO ST	428	NW
CHICKASAW TRAIL	421	NW
CHILTON DR	420	SW
CHIPPEWA CT	424	SW
CHRISTY WAY	420	NW
CHRISTY WAY E	420	NE
CHRISTY WAY N	420	NW
CHRISTY WAY W	420	NW
CHURCH ST	421	SW
CINDY DR	421	SW
CLAIRMOUNT DR	420	SW
CLARA DR	423	NE
CLARK ST	425	NW
CLAYBURN RD	420	SW
CLAYTON CT	426	NW
CLEMATIS DR	420	NW
CLEMENT CT	420	NW
CLEMENT DR	419	NE
CLEMSON CT	419	SE
CLEVELAND		
SAGINAW	424	SE
CLEVELAND ST		
CARROLLTON	421	SE
CLIFFORD DR	423	NW
CLIFFORD PL	423	NW
CLINTON ST N	424	NE
CLIPERT DR	421	SW
CLOVER LA	424	SW
CLUNIE ST	423	SE
CLUTIER RD	428	NE
CLYDESDALE LA	419	SE
COLFAX DR	427	SW
COLLINGWOOD AVE	427	NE
COLONIAL DR	419	SE
COLONY BLVD	423	NE
COLONY DR N	423	NW
COLONY DR S	423	NW
COLUMBINE DR	419	SE
COMMONWEALTH	421	NE
COMPTON ST	420	SE
CONCORD ST	419	SE
CONGRESS	424	NW
CONGRESS AVE	425	NW
CONGRESS CT A	420	SE
CONGRESS CT B	420	SE
CONGRESS CT C	420	SE
CONGRESS CT D	420	SE
CONKLIN DR	420	SW
CONLEY DR	419	SW
CONRAD RD	427	NW
CONSTANCE DR	419	NE
COOLIDGE AVE	420	SW
COOPER	424	NE

CORA ST	427	NE
CORALBERRY RD	420	NW
CORCORAN ST	419	SE
CORNELIA ST	425	SE
CORNELL ST	421	NE
CORRAL DR E	424	SW
CORRAL DR W	424	SW
CORVAIR LA	420	SW
COTTAGE GROVE	420	NW
COUNTRY WAY S	419	NW
COURT ST	424	SE
COURTLAND PL	420	SW
CRANBROOK DR	423	NW
CRANSTON PL	419	SW
CRAPO ST	425	SE
CREEKWOOD DR	428	SW
CREGO BLVD	426	NW
CRESCENT DR	421	NW
CRESSWELL ST	425	SW
CRESTMONT DR	420	SW
CRISTOM PL	420	NW
CRONK ST	420	SE
CROSS ST	425	NW
CROW ISLAND RD	422	SW
CRUTCHFIELD	423	NE
CUMBERLAND ST	428	NW
CUSTER ST	424	SW
CYPRESS ST	424	SW
DALE RD	420	SW
DANA DR	421	NE
DARTMOUTH DR	423	SE
DARWIN LA	419	SW
DATE ST	428	NW
DATONA RD	423	NW
DAVENPORT AVE	420	SW
DAVID	420	SW
DAVIS RD		
SAGINAW TWP.	421	NW
DAVIS RD		
KOCHVILLE TWP	424	SW
DAWSON DR	419	SE
DAYTON ST	427	NW
DEAN ST	427	NW
DEARBORN ST	424	SE
DEERFIELD DR	419	SE
DEIBEL DR	420	NW
DEINDORFER ST	420	SE
DELAWARE BLVD	424	NE
DELEVAN CT. #1	419	NE
DELEVAN CT. #2	419	NE
DELEVAN DR	419	NE
DELORES ST	426	NW
DELRAY ST	427	NE
DELTA DR	423	NE
DELTA DR W	423	NE
DELTON DR	428	NE
DENBY DR	419	SE
DE PAUL PL	428	SE
DESER DR	419	NE
DEVONSHIRE RD	419	SE
DEWBERRY CT	419	NE
DEWBERRY DR	419	NE
DEWHIRST DR	423	NW
DEXTER DR	420	SE
DEXTER DR E	420	SE
DEXTER DR W	420	SE
DIAMOND ST	428	SW
DIAMONDALE DR	428	SW
DIAMONDALE DR E	428	SW
DIAMONDALE DR W	428	SW
DICKINSON DR	420	NW
DILLON ST	426	NW
DIRKER RD	423	NE
DIVISION ST	426	SW
DIXIE CT	428	SW
DIXIE HWY	428	NW
DOERR ST	427	NE
DOGWOOD LA	419	NE
DON CASTER	419	NE
DONNA DR	423	NE
DORO LA	421	NE
DORSET PL	419	SE
DOVER PL	423	NE
DOW PL	420	SW
DRAKE DR	427	NW
DRAPER DR	423	NE
DRESDEN CT	428	NW
DREXEL DR	427	NE
DRIFTWOOD LA	428	SW
DUANE DR	420	SW
DUCK PL	425	NW
DUNDALE CT	423	NE
DUNDEE DR	420	NW
DUNKIRK DR	420	SW
DUNMORE DR	420	SW
DUNROVIN DR	423	NW
DUPONT ST	425	SW
DURAND CT	420	SE
DURAND ST	424	NE
DUSTINE DR E	419	NE
DUSTINE DR N	419	NE
DUSTINE DR W	419	NE
DUTCH RD	423	SW
DUTTON ST	420	SE
DWIGHT ST	425	NE
EAST ST	427	SW
E. MCLEOD DR	420	NE
EATON ST	425	SW
EDDY ST	425	NW
EDGAR ST	426	NW
EDGEWOOD RD	424	SW
EDISON RD	421	NE
EDWARD PL	420	SE
EGAN ST	428	SE

EIGHTEENTH ST N	426	NW
EIGHTH ST	425	NE
ELDER LA	420	NW
ELEANOR AVE	425	SW
ELEVENTH ST N	425	NE
ELEVENTH ST S	425	NE
ELIZABETH ST	427	NW
ELLSWORTH ST	425	NW
ELM ST		
CARROLLTON TWP	421	SW
ELM ST SAGINAW	424	SW
ELM ST N SAGINAW	424	SW
ELMDALE DR	424	SW
ELMERS DR	428	NW
ELMHURST ST	419	SE
EL MONTE ST	424	SW
ELMPORT ST	428	SE
ELMVIEW CT	424	NW
ELMWOOD AVE	427	NE
ELSIE ST	427	NW
EMERICK ST	424	SW
EMERSON ST	425	SW
EMILY ST	425	SE
EMPIRE DR	423	NW
ENTERPRISE CT	420	NE
ENTERPRISE DR	420	NE
ERIC JAMES CT	420	SW
ERIE ST	427	NW
ERNA DR	420	SE
ERNEST ST	421	SW
ERWIN ST	421	SW
ESSEX ST	420	SE
ESSLING ST	426	NW
ETHEL AVE	420	SW
ETON PL	420	SW
EUCLID ST	425	SW
EVA ST	428	NE
EVERGREEN LA	421	SW
EXETER PL	426	NW
EYMER ST	424	SW
EZOP ST	422	SW
EZRA RUST DR	425	SW
FABIAN DR	419	SW
FAIRCREST LA	423	NE
FAIRFAX ST	425	SE
FAIRFIELD ST	420	SW
FAIR OAKS DR	423	NE
FAIRVIEW ST	427	NE
FAIRWAY DR	424	SW
FARMBROOK DR	423	NE
FARMER ST	428	NW
FARMINGTON DR	424	NW
FARWELL ST	425	NE
FASHION SQ. BLVD	420	NE
FAYETTE ST N	424	SE
FAYETTE ST S	424	SE
FEDERAL AVE	425	NW
FENTON ST	425	SE
FERNDALE DR	419	SE
FERRIS RD	420	SE
FIFTEENTH ST N	425	NE
FIFTEENTH ST S	425	NE
FIFTH AVE N	425	NE
FIFTH AVE S	425	NE
FINCH DR	428	SW
FIRETHORN DR	420	NW
FIRST ST		
CARROLLTON	421	SE
1ST ST SAGINAW	425	NE
FISHER DR		
BRIDGEPORT TWP	427	SE
FISHER ST		
ZILWAUKEE	421	NE
FITZHUGH ST	425	NE
FIVE OAKS DR	423	SW
FLAMINGO DR	428	SW
FLANDERS DR	421	NW
FLAXTON	419	NE
FLEETWOOD DR	421	SW
FONTAINE BLVD	419	SE
FORDNEY PARK DR	424	SW
FOREST ST		
BRIDGEPORT	424	SW
FOREST ST		
SAGINAW	424	SW
FORSYTHE RD	423	NE
FORTUNE BLVD	420	NW
FOSS CT #1	419	SE
FOSS CT #2	419	SE
FOSS DR	419	NE
FOURTEENTH ST N	425	NE
FOURTEENTH ST S	425	NE
FOURTH AVE N	425	NE
FOURTH AVE S	425	NE
FOXBORO RD	423	NE
FRANDOR PL	420	NW
FRANKLIN ST		
ZILWAUKEE	421	NE
FRANKLIN ST N		
SAGINAW	425	NE
FRANKLIN ST S	425	NE
FRASER ST	424	SE
FRENCH ST	422	NW
FROMM DR	423	NE
FRONT ST	421	NE
FRONTIER LA	419	NE
FROST DR	423	NW
FROVAN PL	423	NE
FRUEH ST	426	SW
FULLER ST	426	NW
FULTON ST	426	SW

Street	Code	Dir
GAGE ST	425	SE
GALAXY DR	428	SW
GALEN ST	422	SW
GALLAGHER ST	427	NW
GARDEN LANE	424	SW
GAREY ST	425	SE
GARFIELD ST	421	SE
GARLAND DR	424	NE
GATESBORO DR S	419	SE
GATESBORO DR S	419	NE
GATESBORO DR W	419	NE
GAVIT ST	427	NW
GAYLORD ST	420	SE
GEMINI ST	428	NW
GENESEE AVE E	428	NW
GENESEE AVE W	420	SW
GENEVA CT	426	NW
GEORGE ST	419	SW
GERHARD CT	410	SW
GERMAIN ST	428	SW
GHIA CT	420	NW
GLACIER DR	420	SE
GLADSTONE ST	421	NE
GLADWIN ST	421	SW
GLASBY	427	NW
GLENDALE AVE	420	SW
GLENFIELD DR	423	NE
GLENMEADOW CT	426	SW
GLEN OAK PL	419	NE
GLENWOOD AVE	427	NW
GOETZ RD KOCHVILLE TWP.	424	NE
GOETZ ST SAGINAW	424	SW
GOLFVIEW DR	423	NE
GOOD ST	425	SW
GORHAM PL	422	SW
GRACE CT	426	NW
GRACERIDGE PL	425	NW
GRAEBNER LANE	420	SW
GRAHAM ST	424	NW
GRANADA LA	419	SW
GRANGER ST N	424	SE
GRANGER ST S	424	SE
GRANT ST. CARROLLTON	421	SE
GRANT ST BRIDGEPORT	428	SE
GRANT ST SAGINAW	427	NW
GRATIOT AVE	424	SW
GRATIOT CT	424	SW
GRATIOT RD	423	NE
GREEN ST	424	SW
GREENBRIAR DR	424	SW
GREENBUSH PL	419	SW
GREENDALE DR E	419	SW
GREENDALE DR W	419	SW
GREEN ISLE WAY	426	NE
GREENWICH ST	424	SW
GREGORY PL	423	NE
GREGORY ST N	424	NW
GREGORY ST S	420	NW
GRETCHEN CT	420	SE
GROVE ST	424	SW
HACIENDA CT	424	SW
HACK RD	422	SW
HACKBERRY ST	425	SE
HADLEY ST	425	SE
HAENLEIN DR	420	SW
HALLMARK CT	420	SW
HAMILTON ST N	424	SE
HAMILTON ST S	424	SE
HAMLET DR	419	NE
HAMLET DR N	419	NE
HAMLET DR S	419	NE
HAMMEL ST	425	SE
HAMMOND RD	420	SE
HAMPSHIRE ST	427	NE
HANCHETT AVE	425	NW
HANCHETT ST CARROLLTON TWP	421	SE
HANCOCK ST	424	SE
HANDLEY ST	424	SE
HANNUM BLVD E	424	SW
HANNUM BLVD W	424	SW
HANOVER PL	419	SE
HARBOR TOWNE DR	420	NE
HARDIN ST	424	NE
HAROLD ST	426	SW
HARRIS ST	425	SE
HARRISON ST N	425	SW
HARRISON ST S	425	SW
HARROW LA	423	NE
HARRY ST	420	SW
HARTFORD DR	420	NW
HARTFORD DR N	420	NW
HARTFORD DR S	420	NW
HARTSTUFF ST	426	NW
HARVARD AVE	424	SW
HAWTHORNE DR	423	NE
HAYDEN ST	425	NW
HAYES ST	424	SW
HAZELWOOD AVE	427	NW
HEATHER LA	424	SW
HEDDILA	421	NW
HELGA ST	419	SE
HEMMETER RD	419	NE
HEMMETER CT	419	NE
HEMSTEAD PL	419	NE
HENRY DR	423	NE
HENSLER PL	420	NW
HEPBURN RD	419	SE
HERITAGE DR	419	NE
HERMANSAU ST	420	NE
HERRINGTON DR	419	NE
HESS AVE	427	NW
HETZNER DR	420	NE
HEYN AVE	424	SW
HIALEAH LA	428	SW
HIAWATHA DR	421	NW
HICKORY LA KETTERING RD	430	NW
HICKORY PL SAGINAW TWP.	419	NE
HICKORY ST CARROLLTON	419	NE
HIDDEN LA	428	NW
HIGH ST	425	SW
HILAND ST	425	SW
HILL ST	425	NW
HILLCREST DR	423	NE
HILLSDALE PL	423	NE
HILRAY DR	428	SW
HOLBROOK LA	423	NE
HOLCOMB ST	424	SW
HOLDEN ST	421	NW
HOLLAND AVE E	426	SW
HOLLAND AVE W	425	SW
HOLLAND CT	425	SW
HOLLAND RD	426	SE
HOLLY LA	426	SE
HOMEDALE ST	419	SW
HORTON AVE	427	NE
HOSMER ST	425	SW
HOWARD ST	425	SW
HOWLEY CT	425	SW
HOYT AVE	425	SW
HOYT PK. LOWER	425	SW
HOYT PK. UPPER	425	SW
HUBER ST	424	SW
HUDSON AVE	420	SE
HUGHES ST	42	NW
HULL ST	428	NE
HUNTER ST	424	SW
HUNTINGTON RD	427	SW
HUNTLEY CT	427	NW
HUNTLEY RD	427	NW
HURON ST	420	NW
INDIANA AVE	428	NW
INDIAN TRAIL	423	NE
INDUSTRIAL DR	424	SW
IOTA PL	425	SW
IOWA AVE	427	NE
IRONWOOD ST	423	NE
IRIS DR	419	NW
IRVING ST	425	NW
IRVING PARK AVE	426	NW
IRVING PARK PL	426	NW
IVANHOE	423	NE
IVY ST	424	SW
JACKSON ST CARROLLTON TWP	421	SE
JACKSON ST SAGINAW	425	NW
JACKSON ST CARROLLTON	425	SE
JAMESON PL	420	SW
JAMESON ST	420	SW
JANES RD	426	NE
JANES RD	426	NE
JARABEC RD	423	SW
JASMINE DR	424	SW
JAY ST	425	SW
JEFFERS ST	424	SW
JEFFERSON AVE N SAGINAW	425	SW
JEFFERSON AVE S SAGINAW	427	NW
JEFFERSON CT	425	SW
JEFFERSON ST SAGINAW	425	SW
JEFFERSON ST CARROLLTON	421	SE
JEFFERSON ST ZILWAUKEE	426	NE
JIM DR	428	SE
JO DR	425	SW
JOHN ST	420	SW
JOHNS DR	420	SE
JOHNSON ST SAGINAW	425	NW
JOHNSON ST CARROLLTON	421	SE
JOHNSON ST ZILWAUKEE	426	NE
JONES ST	421	NE
JONQUIL DR	420	NW
JORDAN DR BRIDGEPORT	428	SE
JORDAN ST SAGINAW	424	SW
JOSEPH ST	423	SW
JOY RD	428	NE
JOYCE DR	419	SE
JULIANNE DR	419	NW
JULIUS ST	427	NW
JUNIPER LA	419	SW
KANSAS AVE	427	NE
KATHERINE CT	419	SW
KATHERINE WAY	419	SW
KELLY DR	423	SW
KENCLIFF DR	423	NE
KENDORA DR	421	NW
KENDRICK ST	424	SW
KENROSS	423	NE
KENSINGTON DR	424	SW
KENT ST	421	SE
KENTFORD DR E	423	NE
KENTFORD DR N	423	NE
KENTFORD DR W	423	NE
KENTON DR	423	NE
KENWOOD DR	427	SW
KERBY PL	419	SE
KETCHAM ST	426	SW
KETTERING RD	430	NW
KIMMEL ST	424	NW
KING RD	428	SW
KINGSTON DR	423	NW
KINNEY BLVD	420	NW
KIPLING DR	420	SW
KIRBY ST	425	SE
KIRK ST	426	NW
KIRKWOOD DR	423	NE
KISS ST	425	NW
KITTY ST	427	BE
KNOX ST	421	SW
KOCHVILLE RD	421	NW
KOLLEN ST	424	SW
KRISS PL	419	SE
KRUEGER PL	419	NW
KUEHN AVE	428	SW
KUEHN DR	420	SW
LAKEVIEW DR	421	NW
LAMONT PL	428	NW
LAMSON ST	421	SW
LAPEER AVE	426	NW
LARCH ST	424	SW
LARRY TIM DR	428	SW
LATHRUP AVE	470	SW
LAUER RD	420	NW
LAUREL ST	425	SE
LAWNDALE RD	419	SW
LAWRENCE	424	SW
LAWSON ST	419	SE
LEASIDE DR	419	SE
LEDYARD ST	419	SE
LEE ST	424	SE
LELIA ST	423	SW
LENWOOD DR	423	SE
LEO ST	423	SW
LEON SCOTT CT	426	NW
LESSANDRO ST	419	SW
LESSUR ST	424	NW
LETA PL	420	NW
LETCHER ST	426	SW
LEXINGTON DR	427	NE
LIBERTY ST	428	SE
LILLY ST	421	SW
LIMERICK ST	426	SW
LINCOLN ST SAGINAW	427	NW
LINCOLN ST CARROLLTON	421	SE
LINDA AVE	420	SW
LINDBERCH ST	421	NE
LINDEN PL	423	NE
LINDSAY DR	424	SW
LINGER LA	428	SW
LINTON ST	424	SW
LIONS HEAD LA	428	SW
LITTLE ST	424	SW
LIVINGSTON DR	427	NE
LLOYD ST	426	NE
LOCHMOOR PL	419	SE
LOCKWOOD ST	424	SW
LOCUST RD	420	NW
LODGE ST	424	SW
LOGANBERRY DR	419	NE
LOIS DR	427	SW
LONGMEADOW BLVD	419	NE
LONGVIEW AVE	428	NW
LOOMIS ST	426	SW
LORETTA ST	419	SW
LORRAINE AVE	427	NW
LOUISE ST	420	SW
LOWELL AVE	427	NW
LUELLA ST	419	SE
LUTHER RD	425	SE
LYMAN ST	425	NE
LYNN ST	421	SW
LYNNDALE ST	113	SE
LYNNWOOD AVE	427	NW
LYON ST	424	SW
MACK RD	428	SW
MACKINAW ST SAGINAW	420	SW
MACKINAW RD SAGINAW TWP.	420	NW
MACKINAW ST SAGINAW	424	SW
MADISON ST SAGINAW	424	SW
MADISON ST CARROLLTON	421	SE
MAINE ST	424	SW
MALDEN PL	420	SW
MALZAHN ST	424	SW
MANGROVE DR	420	SW
MANISTEE ST	419	SW
MANNION RD	423	NE
MANOR DR	419	SW
MANSFIELD PL	420	NW
MAPLE ST	424	SW
MAPLEPORT	428	SE
MAPLE RIDGE	421	SE
MAPLEWOOD AVE	427	NE
MARGARET LA	423	NE
MARION ST	419	SE
MARKHAM ST	419	SE
MARKLE PL	426	SW
MARLEA	428	SW
MARLOU CT	419	SE
MARLYN AVE	420	SW
MARQUETTE ST	424	SW
MARSHALL CT	420	SW
MARTHA ST	425	SE
MARTINDALE ST	427	NW
MARTZ PL	420	SW
MARY CT	424	NW
MARY JANE CT	424	NW
MASON ST N	424	SE
MASON ST S	424	SE
MATTEN DR	419	SE
MATTHEW ST	427	NW
MAXSON	419	NE
MAYBROOK DR	428	SW
MAYFIELD RD	427	SW
MAYFLOWER DR	423	NE
MCARTHUR ST	419	SE
McCARTY RD	419	NW
McCOSKRY ST	425	SE
McEWAN ST	420	SE
McGILL ST	426	SW
McGREGOR ST	424	SE
McKINLEY ST	421	SE
McLEAN ST	427	NW
MEADOW LA	419	NE
MEADOWDALE DR	419	SW
MEADOW LAWN ST	424	SE
MEADOWVIEW LA	100	GW
MELBOURNE RD	422	NW
MELODY LA	428	NE
MELROSE DR	428	NE
MEREDITH ST	425	SW
MERRILL ST	425	SE
MERSHON ST	424	NE
METZGER CT	419	NW
MEYER PL	420	NW
MICHELLE ST N	428	NW
MICHELLE ST S	428	NW
MICHIGAN AVE N	425	SW
MICHIGAN AVE S	425	NW
MICHIGAN AVE W	420	NW
MIDDLE ST	420	NW
MIDLAND RD	419	NW
MIDWAY ST	419	SE
MIA CT	428	NW
MILFORD DR	419	SE
MILLARD	425	SW
MILLER ST	424	SE
MILTON ST	427	SW
MISSION DR	419	SE
MITCHELL ST	419	NE
MOFFET ST	427	NE
MONMOUTH ST	426	NW
MONROE ST CARROLLTON TWP	421	SE
MONROE ST CARROLLTON	424	NE
MONROE ST SAGINAW	427	NW
MONTANA AVE	428	NW
MONTGOMERY ST	426	SW
MOONGLOW DR	420	SW
MOORE ST	424	SW
MORAN ST	421	NE
MORELAND LA	419	SW
MORGAN ST	420	SE
MORGANPORT DR	419	SE
MORRIS ST	427	NW
MORSON	420	NW
MOTON DR	426	SE
MOTT ST	425	SE
MT. VERNON RD	427	SW
MURRAY HILL DR	428	SW
MYRTLE	425	NE
MYSTVLIA DR	420	NE
NAHMONIE DR	423	NW
NANCY DR	427	SW
NARCISSUS DR	419	NE
NARLOCH ST	426	NW
NEBRASKA AVE	426	NW
NEEDHAM ST	426	NW
NEWBERRY ST	424	SW
NEWBRIGHT PL	423	NE
NEWTON ST	424	SW
NIAGARA ST N	424	SE
NIAGARA ST S	424	SE
NICOL ST	419	SE
NIMITZ ST	419	SE
NINETEENTH ST N	426	SW
NINETEENTH ST S	426	SW
NINTH ST N	425	NE
NINTH ST S	425	SE
NODULAR DR	419	SW
NOEL CT	419	SW
NORMA JEAN DR	423	SW
NORMAN ST	424	SW
N. BERKSHIRE DR	419	SW
N. GLEN OAK DR	419	NE
N. KEARNEY DR	419	SW
NORTHLAWN CT	424	SW
N MCLEOD DR	419	SW
NORTHMOORE	420	SW
NORTHPORT DR	428	NW
NORTHRIDGE DR	426	SW
N. SOUTHFIELD DR	419	SW
N. 10TH ST	425	SE
N. 13TH ST	425	SE
N. 31ST ST	425	SW
N. TOWERLINE RD	422	NE
N. 12TH ST	425	SE
N. 25TH ST	422	SW
N. 24TH ST	422	SW
N. 26TH ST	422	SW
NORTHWEST DR	420	SW
NORTHWEST DR W	420	SW
NORWICH ST	420	SW
NORWICH ST	420	SW
NOTTINGHAM DR E	419	SE
NOTTINGHAM DR N	419	GE
NOTTINGHAM DR W	419	SE
NYLON ST	421	SW
OAK ST	425	NW
OAK LEAF	419	NW
OAKLEY ST N	424	SE
OAKLEY ST S	424	SE
OAK VIEW DR	421	SW
OAKWOOD AVE	427	NW
O'CONNER RD	420	SW
OHIO AVE	428	NW
OLDS AVE	420	SW
OLIVE ST	427	SE
OMEGA DR	423	SW
ORANGE ST	428	NW
ORCHARD CT	428	NW
OREGON AVE	428	NW
OSBORN ST	424	SW
OSCODA ST	421	NE
OSCODA ST	425	NW
OSLER AVE	420	SW
OTTAWA BLVD	420	SW
OTTAWA ST	424	SW
OUTER DR BUENA VISTA TWP	426	NW
OUTER DR SAGINAW	422	SW
OVERHILL DR	419	SE
OWEN ST	427	NW
OXFORD	420	SE
PACELLI AVE	423	SE
PACKARD DR E	419	SE
PACKARD DR W	419	SE
PADDOCK LA	419	SW
PALMETTO DR	421	SW
PARK AVE N	425	NE
PARK AVE S	425	SE
PARKSIDE CT	427	NW
PARKWOOD AVE	427	NW
PASAUENA PL	420	NW
PASSOLT ST	424	NW
PATRICIA DR BRIDGEPORT TWP	428	SE
PATRICIA PL SAGINAW	420	SW
PAULINE ST	422	SW
PAWLICK	421	NW
PAYSON DR	427	NW
PEACH ST	428	NW
PEALE DR	420	SW
PEAR ST	428	NW
PEARL ST	420	SW
PEGGY DR	427	SW
PEMBERTON ST	400	SW
PENNSBURG PL	427	NW
PERKINS ST	424	SE
PERRY ST	428	SE
PERSIMMON DR	410	NE
PERWOOD DR	423	SE
PETERSON ST	428	NE
PETTIBONE AVE	428	NW
PHEASANT RUN DR	419	SE
PHELON ST	425	SE
PHOENIX ST	426	SW
PILGRIM DR	423	NW
PINE ALLEY	422	NW
PINE ST	426	SW
PINEHAVEN DR	423	NE
PINEPORT ST	428	SE
PIONEER TRAIL	421	SW
PIPER DR	421	SW
PIUS AVE	423	SW
PLAINVIEW DR	420	SE
PLEASANT ST	420	SE
PLUM ST	428	NW
PLYMOUTH RD	423	NW
POINSETTIA DR	419	NE
PORLAS ST	420	SE
PORTER ST N	424	SW
PORTER ST S	424	SW
POST ST	424	SW
POTTER ST	425	SE
PRESCOTT AVE	427	NW
PRESCOTT CT	427	SW
PRESTWICK	419	NE
PRIMROSE DR	420	NW
PROSPECT ST BRIDGEPORT	428	SE
PROSPECT ST BUENA VISTA TWP	423	NE
PROVINCIAL CT	423	NE
PRUETER RD	426	SW
PURDUE ST	421	NE
QUEEN	424	SW
QUINCE ST	428	NW
RAMADA DR	420	SE
RAMSEY ST	422	SW
RANDOLPH ST	427	NW
RAINBOW DR	420	SW
RAINIER ST	420	SW
RAY ST	427	NE
RAYMOND ST	428	SW
RAYJAC PL	425	NE
REDBROOK	419	SW
REDWOOD DR	419	SW
REED ST	420	SE
REINHARDT ST	425	NW

Street	Grid	Dir
REMINGTON ST E	425	SW
REMINGTON ST W	425	SE
REO AVE	420	SW
REPPUHN DR	420	SW
RESERVE AVE	421	SW
RESMER ST	421	SW
REVERE DR	419	SW
REYNICK AVE	424	NW
RIBBLE ST	428	NE
RICHARD	420	SW
RIDGELAND DR	421	SW
RISER DR	423	NE
RIVER FOREST DR	423	NE
RIVIERA ST	421	SW
RO.NOKE ST	422	SW
RC BERGE ST	421	SW
RC BERTS ST	425	SE
ROBINWOOD AVE	427	NW
ROETHKE CT	424	SW
ROLLING GREEN PL	419	SE
ROOSEVELT ST	421	SE
ROSEDALE PL	419	SE
ROSEHILL	419	NW
ROSELAWN CT	424	SW
ROSEMARY ST	424	NW
ROSEWOOD DR	420	NW
ROSS DR	423	SW
ROWAN PL	423	NE
RUCKLE ST	425	SW
RUGGLES RD	420	SE
RGHLIC CT	420	SW
RUSHMORE ST	420	SE
RUSKVIEW DR	420	NW
RUST AVE	425	SE
RUST LANE	423	SE
RUSTIC RD	421	SW
RUTH ST	427	NW
RUTTMAN CT	419	SW
RYAN ST	421	SW
SAGE LA	419	SE
ST. ANDREW RD	423	NE
ST. CLAIR	421	SE
ST. PAUL DR	427	NW
SAGINAW ST	424	SE
SALEM CT	425	NE
SALINA ST	427	NW
SALLY LA	421	NW
SAMUEL DR	428	NW
SANDRA CT	424	SW
SANFORD ST	425	NE
SANGEMON DR	419	SW
SARGENT LA	423	NE
SAUK LA	423	NE
SAVOY LA	421	NW
SAXTON DR	419	SE
SCARLET OAK DR	420	SW
SCHAFFER ST	425	NW
SCHAUMAN DR	428	SW
SCHEMM ST	424	NW
SCHNEIDER ST	419	SE
SCHUST ST	421	NW
SCHUST RD	420	NW
SCOFIELD DR	427	NW
SCOTT ST	422	SW
SEARS ST	426	NW
SEAWAY DR	421	SE
SECOND ST N	425	NE
SECOND ST S	425	NE
SEIDEL PL	424	SW
SEIDEL RD	423	NW
SELDEN ST	419	SE
SEMINOLE LA	419	SE
SEVENTH ST N	425	NE
SEVENTH ST S	425	NE
SEVENTEENTH ST N	425	NE
SEVENTEENTH ST S	426	SW
SEVERANCE CT	427	NW
SHADYSIDE CT	424	SW
SHAHEEN DR	428	NW
SHARP ST	424	SW
SHASTA	419	NW
SHATTUCK RD	421	SW
SHATTUCK ARMS BLVD	420	SW
SHEAR ST	427	NE
SHEFFIELD PL	423	NE
SHELLEY CT	424	SW
SHEPARD ST	421	NE
SHERAFIELD	423	SE
SHERBROOKE PL	423	NE
SHERIDAN AVE	425	SE
SHERIDAN PL	425	SE
SHERMAN RD CARROLLTON	421	NE
SHERMAN ST BRIDGEPORT	428	SE
SHREVE ST	428	SE
SILVERCREST LA	423	NE
SILVER LEAF	419	NW
SIMONEAU ST	425	SE
SIOUX PL	423	NE
SIXTEENTH ST N	426	NW
SIXTEENTH ST S	426	NW
SIXTH ST N	425	NE
SIXTH ST S	425	NE
SKYHAVEN CT	419	SW
SKYHAVEN DR	421	SW
SNELLING PL	426	NW
SNOW AVE	424	NW
SNOWBERRY DR	428	SW
SNOWEY RD	419	SW
SOMERSET RD	423	SE
SOUDERTON DR	427	NW
SOUTH ST	428	NW
SOUTHFIELD CT	428	SW
S. GLEN OAK DR	419	NW
SOUTHFIELD DR W	428	SW
SOUTHLAWN CT	419	SW
S. MARCUS ST	419	NE
S. MCLEOD DR	420	NE
S. TOWERLINE RD	426	SE
SOUTH VIEW ST	427	NW
SPATZ CT	425	NW
SPICER DR	419	NE
SPRING	426	NE
SPRINGBROOK	410	NW
SPRUCE ST	425	SW
STAGHORN DR	423	SE
STAMFORD	419	NE
STANOCA ST	421	NE
STANSBURY LA	419	SW
STANTON ST	428	NW
STARDUST LA	420	NE
STARK ST	425	NW
STARLITE DR	420	SE
STATE ST SAGINAW	420	SW
STATE ST BRIDGEPORT	428	SE
STATE RD SAGINAW TWP	419	SW
STEPHENS ST	424	SE
STINSON DR	421	SW
STOBBE ST	419	SW
STOKER DR	425	NW
STONE ST	425	NW
STONEYBROOK DR	420	NW
STONEHAM RD	423	SE
STORCH ST	424	NW
STORK RD	421	SW
STOUT ST	421	NE
STRATHMOOR ST	428	NW
STROEBEL RD	423	SW
STUART CT	425	NW
STUDOR RD	427	SE
SUDBURY DR	423	SE
SUFFOLL ST	428	NE
SUGAR ST	421	SW
SULLIVAN DR	419	SW
SUMMER LA	428	NW
SUMMIT DR	419	SE
SUNNY LA	423	NE
SUNNYVIEW DR	421	SW
SUNSET LANE	425	NW
SUNVALLEY DR	428	SW
SUPERIOR ST	424	SW
SUSANNA ST	422	SW
SWARTHOUT DR	423	NE
SWEET ST	424	SE
SWEETBRIAR DR	420	NW
SYMPHONY LA	425	NW
SYRACUSE ST	425	NW
TAFT ST CARROLLTON	421	SE
TAFT ST SAGINAW	420	SE
TAMARIX LA	419	SW
TANAGER DR	423	SW
TATHAM AVE	428	NW
TATHAM RD	428	NW
TAUSEND ST	427	NE
TAYLOR ST	421	SE
TENTH ST N	425	NE
TENTH ST S	425	NE
TERMINAL ST	426	NE
TERRY ST	421	SW
THATCHER ST	427	NW
THAYER ST	421	NW
THIRD AVE N	425	NE
THIRD AVE S	425	NE
THIRTEENTH ST N	425	NE
THIRTEENTH ST S	425	NE
THISTLE DR	423	NW
THOMPSON ST	425	NW
THORNE PL	420	SW
THORNEHURST PL	419	SW
THORN TREE RD	421	SW
THREASA ST	419	SW
THROOP ST	424	SW
THURBER ST	427	NW
THURMAN ST	424	SW
TIFFTON DR	419	NE
TILDON ST	426	SW
TIMOTHY ST	423	SE
TITTABAWASSEE RD	421	NW
TOTH RD	427	SE
TOWERLINE RD	428	SW
TRAUM DR	420	SW
TREANOR ST	421	SW
TRENTON ST	420	SE
TRIER ST	424	NW
TRIWOOD LA	428	NW
TROUT DR	423	NE
TROY ST	425	SE
TULANE ST	421	SW
TULIP DR	428	SE
TULLER PL	419	NW
TURNER DR	428	SE
TUSCOLA ST	425	NE
TWELFTH ST N	425	NE
TWELFTH ST S	425	NE
TWENTIETH ST N	426	NW
TWENTIETH ST S	426	SW
TWENTY-EIGHTH ST	426	SW
TWENTY-FIFTH ST	426	SW
TWENTY-FIRST ST N	426	NW
TWENTY-FIRST ST S	426	SW
TWENTY-FOURTH ST	426	SW
TWENTY-NINTH ST	426	NW
TWENTY-SECOND N	426	NW
TWENTY-SECOND S	426	SW
TWENTY-SEVENTH	426	SW
TWENTY-SIXTH ST	426	SW
TWENTY-THIRD ST N	426	NW
TWENTY-THIRD ST S	426	SW
TWIN OAKS BLVD	419	SW
TYLER ST	421	SE
UNION AVE	420	SE
UNIVERSAL DR	420	SW
UNIVERSITY AVE	425	NW
VALENTINE CT	423	SW
VALLEY DR	420	SW
VANALLEO DR	423	NE
VAN BUREN ST	424	NE
VANCOUVER DR	423	NE
VAN ETTEN ST	427	NW
VANGUARD DR	421	SW
VAN WAGONER DR	423	NE
VEAN ST	420	SW
VENOY RD	421	NE
VENTURA DR	421	SE
VERA ST	419	SE
VERMONT ST	424	SW
VERNON ST	424	SW
VESSY DR	428	SW
VESTRY DR	427	SW
VETERANS MEMORIAL PARKWAY	422	SW
VICTORY CT	424	NW
VIDO DR	426	SW
VILLAGE DR	423	NE
VINE ST	424	SW
VIRBURNUM DR	420	NW
VIRGINIA AVE	428	NW
VOGUE BLVD	420	SE
VOIGHT PL	420	NW
WABASH ST	421	NE
WACKER RD	426	NE
WADSWORTH RD	426	NE
WAKE ST	419	SE
WALCOTT ST	427	NE
WALL ST	419	SE
WALLER ST	424	SE
WALLGREN CT	420	SW
WALLINGFORD	419	NE
WALNUT ST CARROLLTON	421	SE
WALNUT ST SAGINAW	426	SW
WALTERS DR	427	NE
WALTON PL	419	NE
WARD ST	425	SE
WARNER RD	420	SW
WARREN AVE N SAGINAW	425	NE
WARREN AVE S SAGINAW	425	SE
WARREN ST BRIDGEPORT	428	SE
WARTENBURG AVE	422	SW
WARWICK ST	420	SW
WASHBURN PL E	424	SW
WASHBURN PL W	424	SW
WASHINGTON AVE E BUENA VISTA TWP	422	SE
WASHINGTON AVE N SAGINAW	422	SW
WASHINGTON AVE S SAGINAW	422	SW
WASHINGTON RD SPAULDING TWP	427	NW
WASHIGTON ST BRIDGEPORT	425	NE
WATER ST ZILWAUKEE	422	NW
WATER ST N	425	NW
WATER ST S SAGINAW	425	NW
WATERFORD DR	420	SW
WATERLOO	420	NW
WAUKEE LA	421	NE
WAVERLY AVE	424	SW
WAYNE ST	424	SE
WAYSIDE DR N	420	SW
WAYSIDE DR S	420	SW
WAYWARD LA	428	SW
WEADOCK AVE N	425	NE
WEADOCK AVE S	425	NE
WEBBER ST	426	SW
WEBSTER ST N	424	SE
WEBSTER ST S	424	SE
WEIGL RD	423	SW
WEISS RD	419	SW
WEISS ST	425	SW
WELBY DR	421	NW
WELCH ST	425	NW
WELLAND DR BUENA VISTA TWP	428	NW
WELLAND ST SAGINAW	425	SE
WELLESLEY DR	419	SE
WELLINGTON ST	421	SE
WELLS ST	424	SW
WENMAR DR	420	NE
WENONAH LA	419	SE
WESLEY DR	427	NE
WEST PL	426	NW
WESTBRIDGE CT	425	SE
WESTBROOK ST	419	SW
WESTBURY DR	419	SW
W. CENTER ST	423	NE
WESTERN DR	423	NW
WESTERVELT AVE	421	NE
WESTFIELD ST	424	SW
WESTVIEW CT	420	SW
WESTVIEW DR	420	SW
W. WINFIELD DR	419	NE
WESTWOOD DR	419	SE
WESTWOOD DR N	419	SE
WESTWOOD DR S	419	SE
WEXFORD DR	420	SW
WEXFORD DR N	420	SW
WEYMOUTH CT	428	NW
WHEELER ST	424	SW
WHISPER LA	420	SW
WHITCOMB DR	419	SW
WHITE ST	425	SE
WHITEMORE PL	420	SW
WHITFIELD DR	420	SW
WHITTIER ST	425	NE
WHITTINGTON DR	425	NE
WICKLOW DR	420	SW
WIENEKE RD	419	SW
WIGEN ST	428	NW
WILDER DR	421	NW
WILDOAK DR	419	NW
WILDWOOD DR	419	SW
WILKINS ST	422	SW
WILLARD ST	427	NE
WILLIAMS ST	424	SE
WILLIAMSON RD	428	SW
WILLOW LA	427	NE
WILLOWBROOK DR	423	NE
WILMETTE ST	421	SE
WILSON AVE	423	NE
WILTSE CT	420	SW
WINIFIELD DR	420	NW
WINIFRED PL	420	SW
WINSTON DR	419	SW
WINTER ST	421	SW
WINTERBERRY	419	NW
WINTERGREEN DR	419	SW
WINTERGREEN DR E	419	SW
WINTERGREEN DR N	419	SW
WINTERGREEN DR S	419	SW
WINTERGREEN DR W	419	SW
WINTHROP LA	423	NE
WISNER ST	428	NW
WITTERS ST	425	SE
WOLF RD	422	SW
WOLVERINE DR	419	SE
WOODBRIDGE ST N	424	SE
WOODBRIDGE ST S	428	SE
WOODLAND CT	428	SE
WOODSIDE ST	428	NW
WOODWARD DR	427	NE
WRIGHT	424	SE
WYLIE CT	424	NE
WYLIE ST	424	NE
WYNES ST	424	SW
YALE ST	428	NE
YAUCK RD	428	NE
YAWKEY ST	425	SW
YELLOWSTONE ST	420	SE
YORK DR	427	NW
YOSEMITE ST	420	SE

NOTES

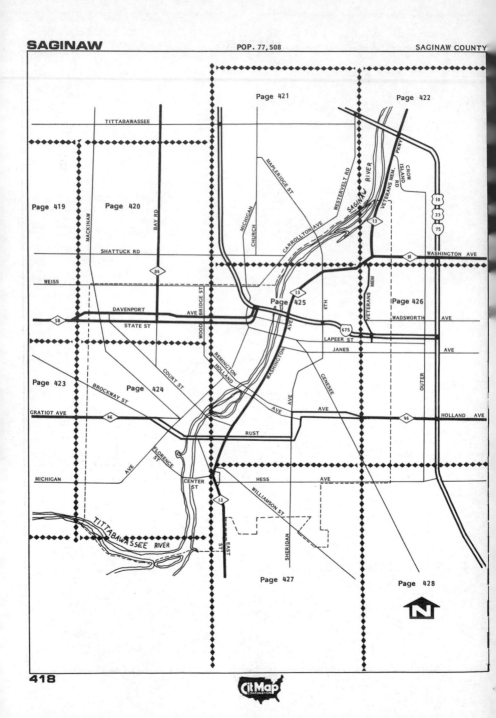

Page 421

Page 422

TITTABAWASSEE

MAPLERIDGE ST

WESTERVELT RD

SAGINAW RIVER

VETERANS MEM. RD

CROW ISLAND

PKWY

Page 419

Page 420

MACKINAW

BAY RD

MICHIGAN

CHURCH

CARROLLTON AVE

10
23
75

SHATTUCK RD

WASHINGTON AVE

WEISS

84

13

DAVENPORT

AVE

WOOD

BRIDGE ST

Page 425

6TH

VETERANS

MEM

Page 426

WADSWORTH AVE

58

STATE ST

675

LAPEER ST

JANES

AVE

REMINGTON

HOLLAND

WASHINGTON

AVE

GENESEE

OUTER

Page 423

BROCKWAY ST

Page 424

COURT ST

AVE

AVE

AVE

GRATIOT AVE

46

46

HOLLAND AVE

RUST

FLORENCE ST

AVE

MICHIGAN

CENTER ST

HESS

AVE

13

WILLIAMSON ST

EAST

ST

SHERIDAN

Page 427

Page 428

N

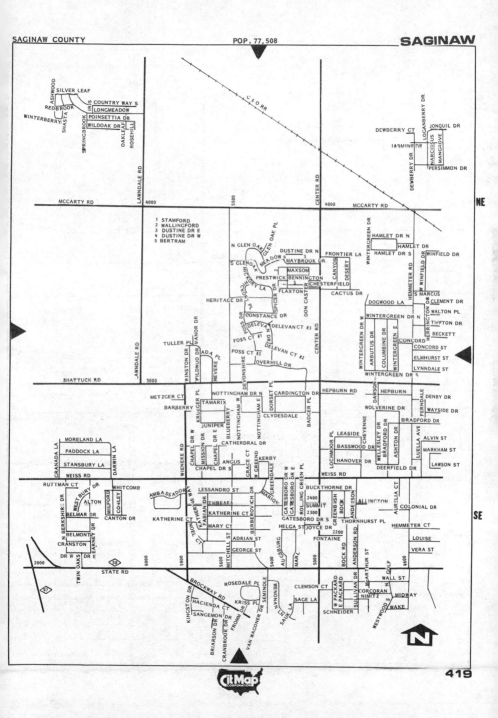

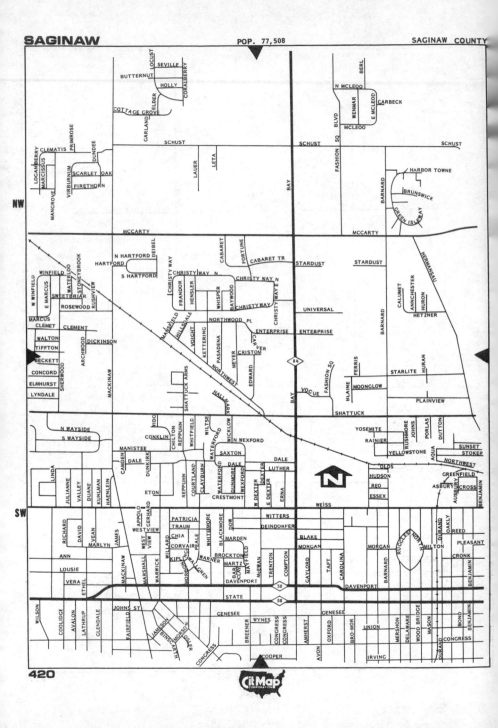

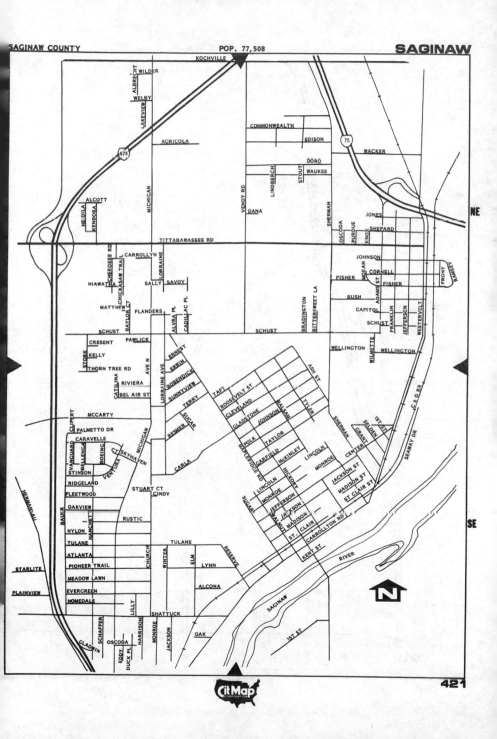

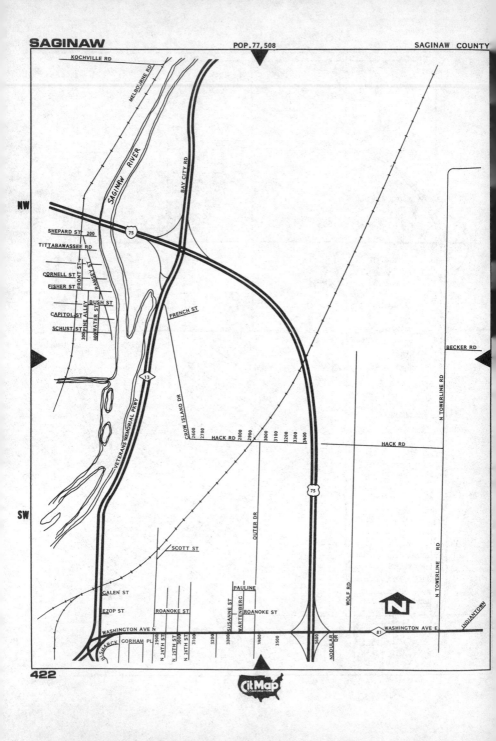

NW

SW

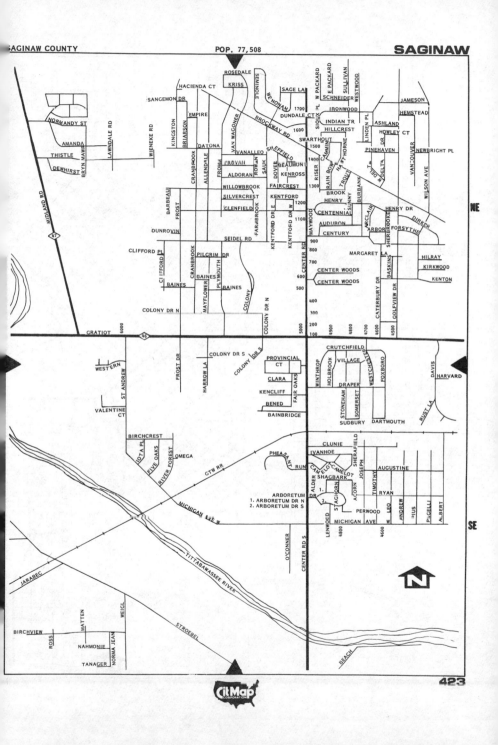

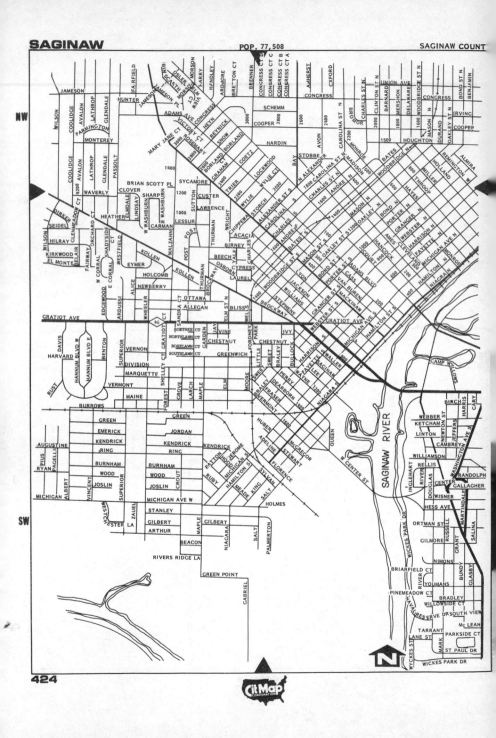

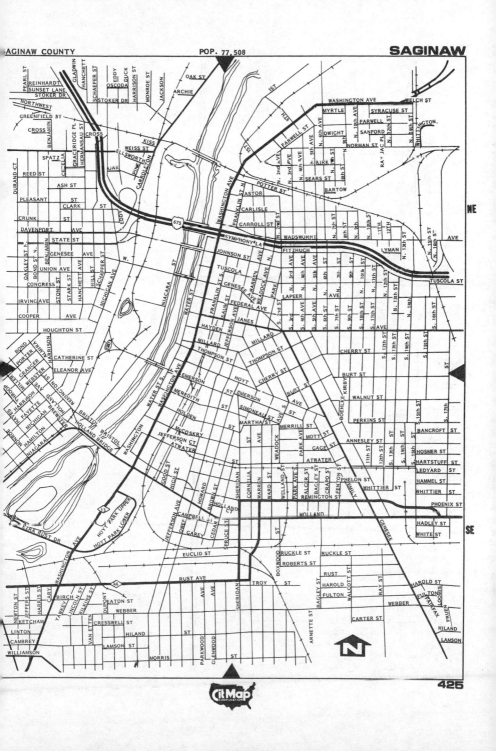

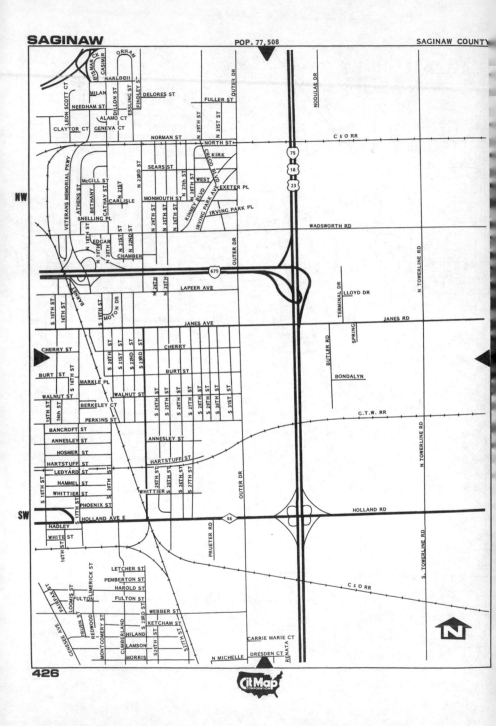

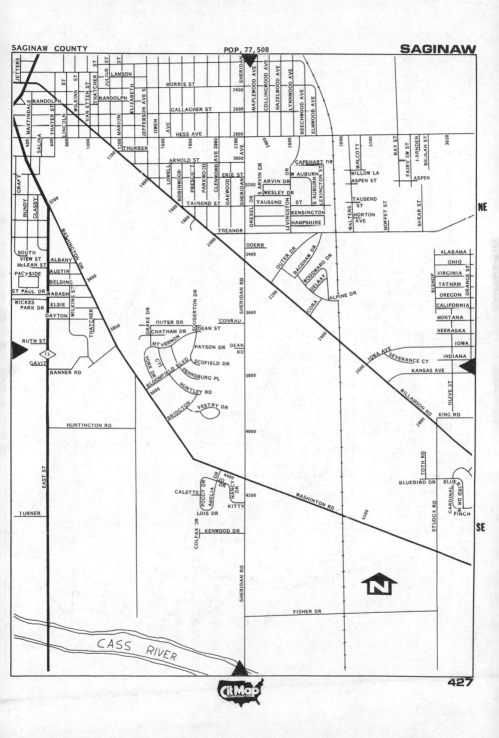

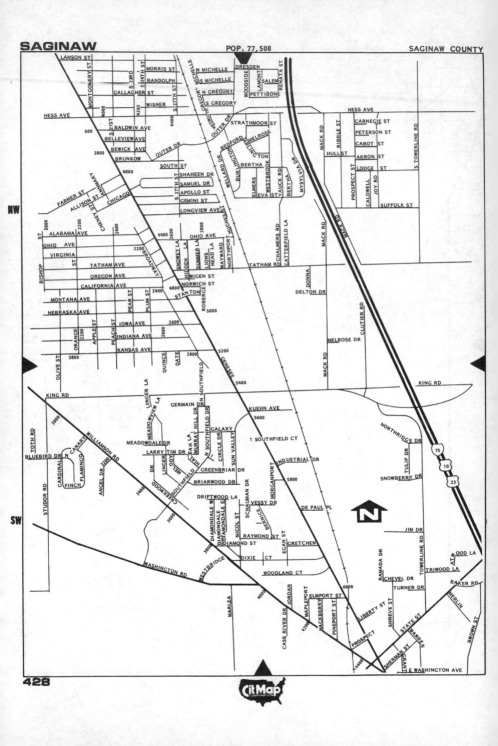

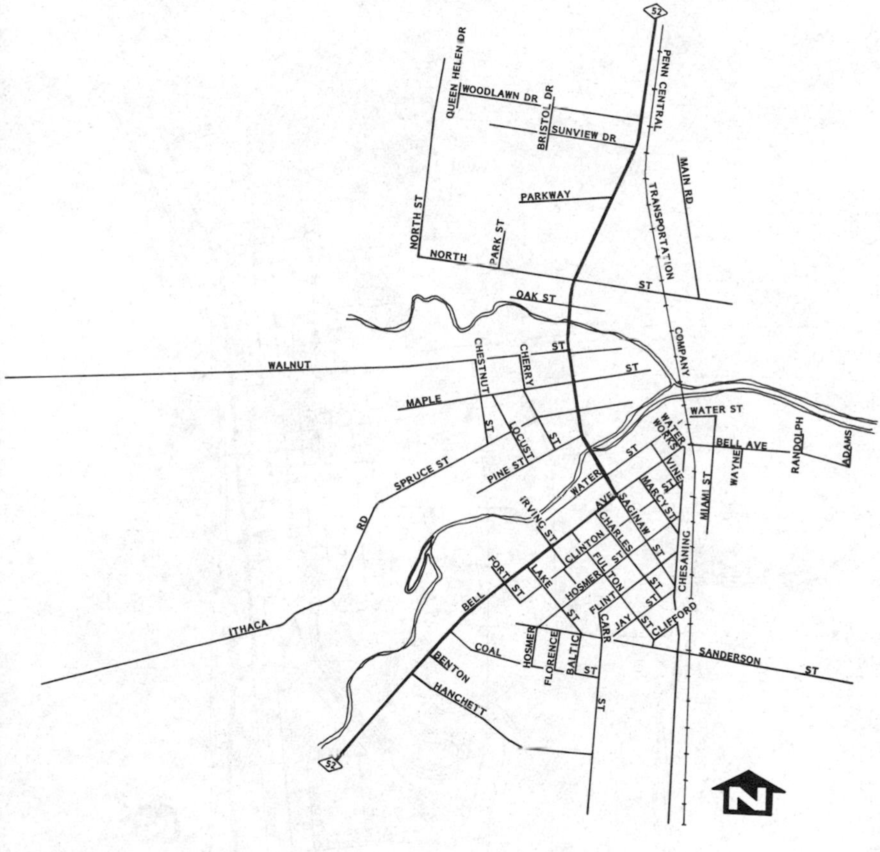

QUEEN HELEN DR

WOODLAWN DR

BRISTOL DR

SUNVIEW DR

PENN CENTRAL

MAIN RD

PARKWAY

NORTH ST

PARK ST

NORTH

TRANSPORTATION

OAK ST

COMPANY

ST

WALNUT

CHESTNUT

CHERRY

ST

ST

MAPLE

WATER ST

WATER WORKS

BELL AVE

RANDOLPH

ADAMS

LOCUST

PINE ST

SPRUCE ST

ST

ST

WATER

VINE

MIAMI ST

WAYNE

IRVING ST

SAGINAW

MARCY ST

CHARLES

AVE

CLINTON

FULTON ST

CHESANING

ST

RD

FORT ST

LAKE

HOSMER

FLINT ST

JAY

CLIFFORD

BELL

ST

CARR

ITHACA

COAL

HOSMER

FLORENCE

BALTIC

ST

SANDERSON

ST

BENTON

HANCHETT

N

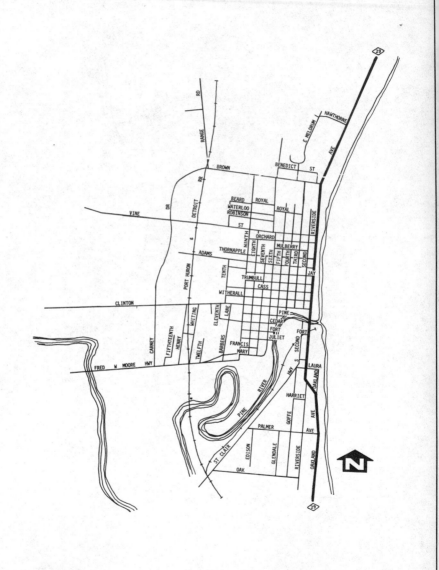

LAKE

ST. CLAIR

1. TANGLEWOOD
2. BRIARCLIFF
3. HEATHWOOD
4. TIMBERIDGE
5. S. BRIARCLIFF
6. LAKEBREEZE
7. ARROWHEAD
8. EVERGREEN

9. WINSHALL
10. SHERRY
11. SCARSDALE
12. SUSEX

13. LANGE AVE
14. CANTERBURY
15. CLAIRWOOD AVE
16. EDGEWOOD
17. HARMON
18. ELAINE
19. GROVE
20. NORCREST
21. GREENCREST
22. MIDDLESEX
23. COLONIAL

24. URSULINE
25. CUMBERNESS

26. RUEHLE
27. BOSTON
28. CHAMPINE

29. LARMOOR
30. GREENLAWN
31. BERKSHIRE
32. VANDOVER
33. RHODE

34. B AVE
35. C AVE
36. D AVE
37. E AVE
38. F AVE

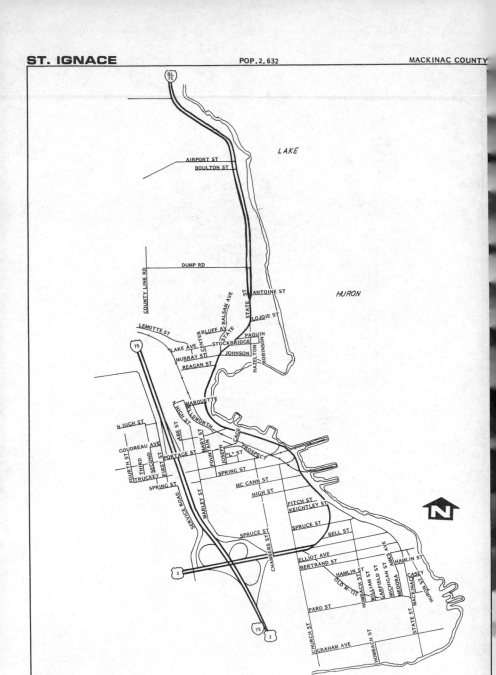

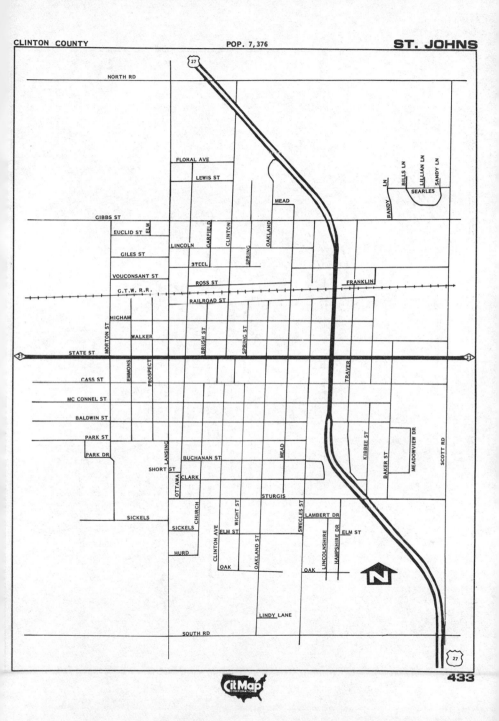

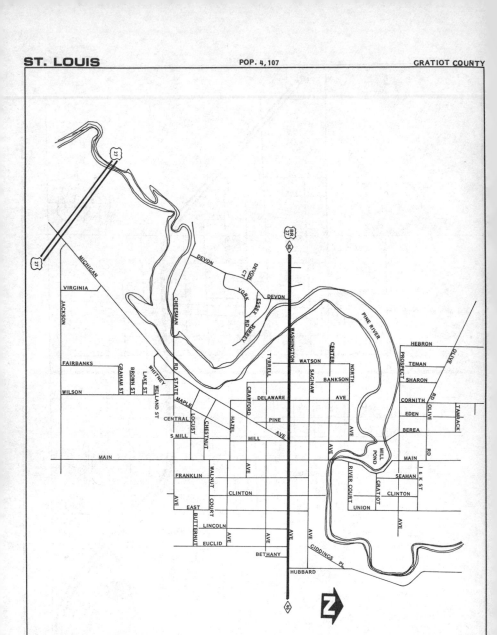

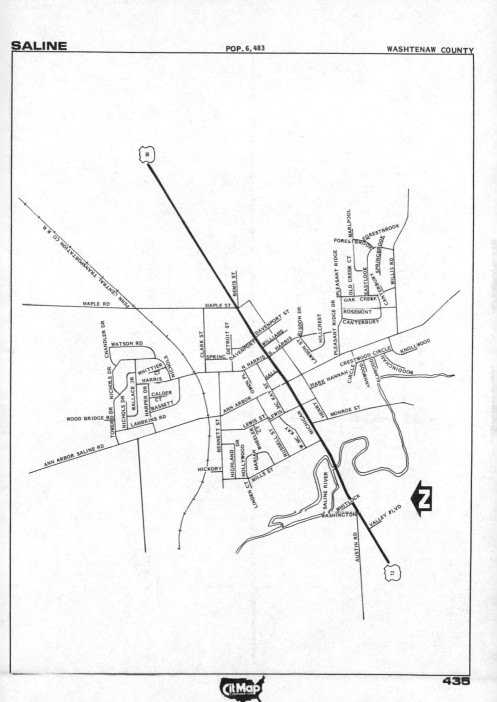

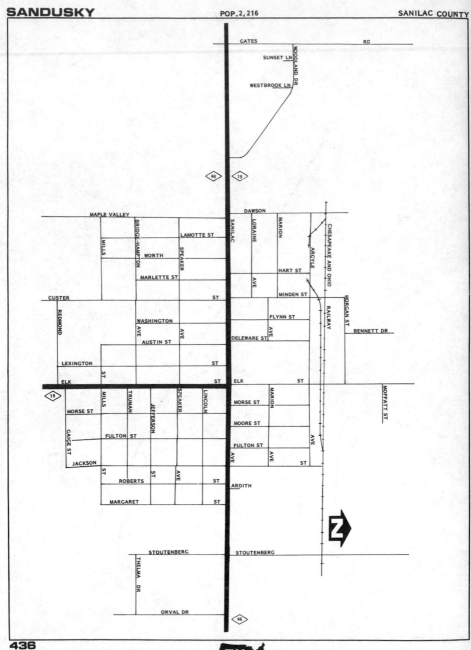

NOTES

436A

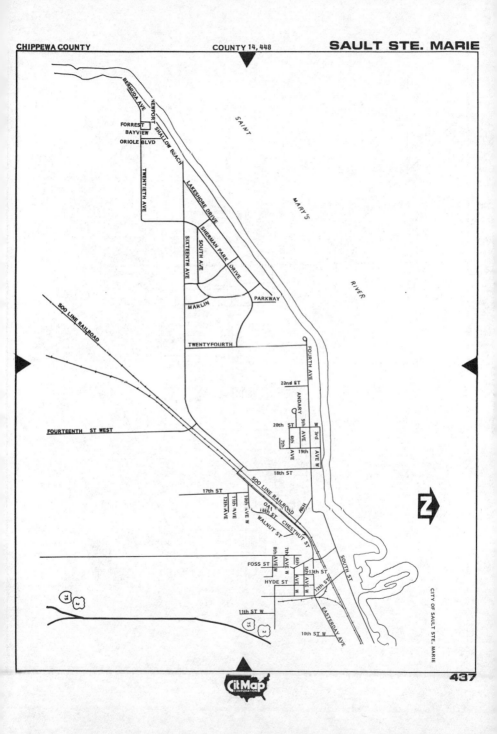

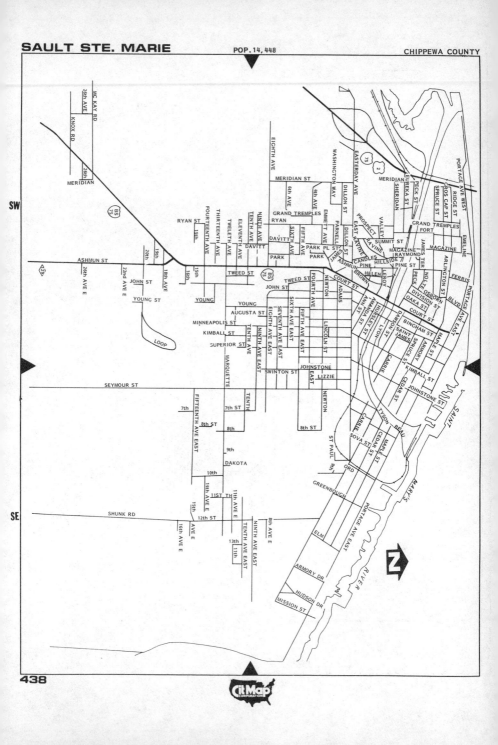

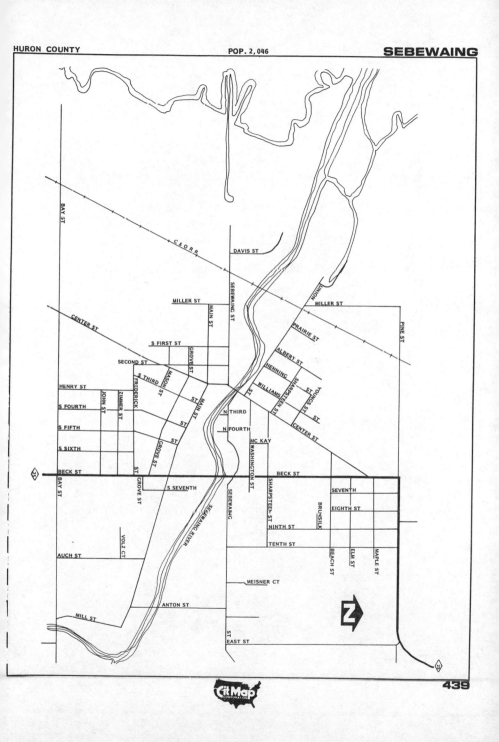

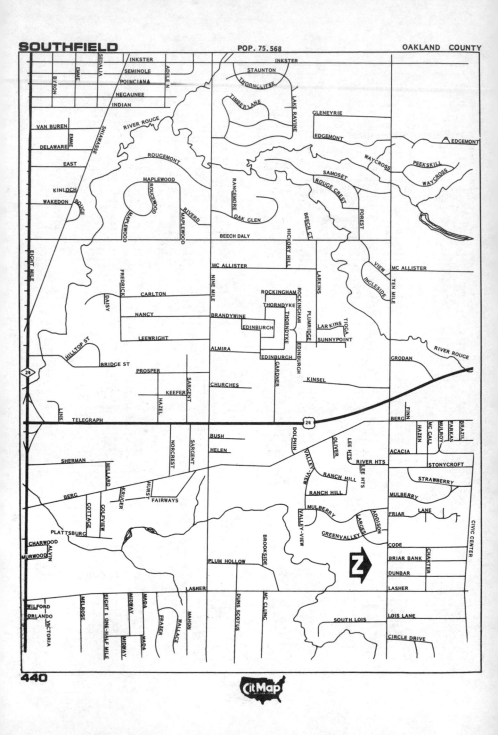

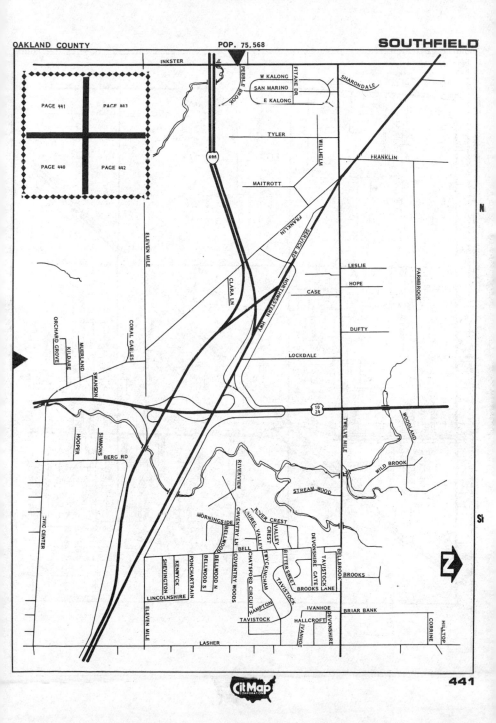

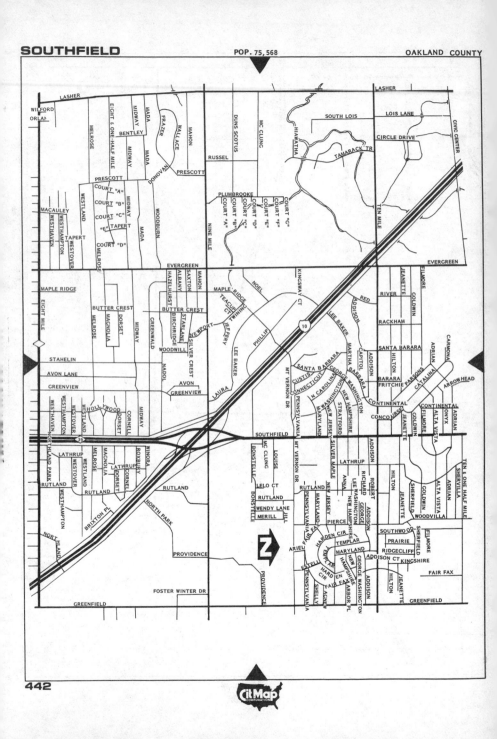

CitMap
CORPORATION

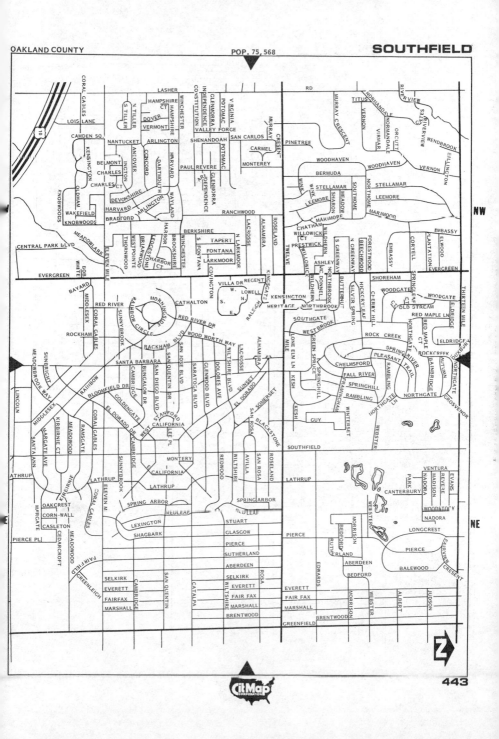

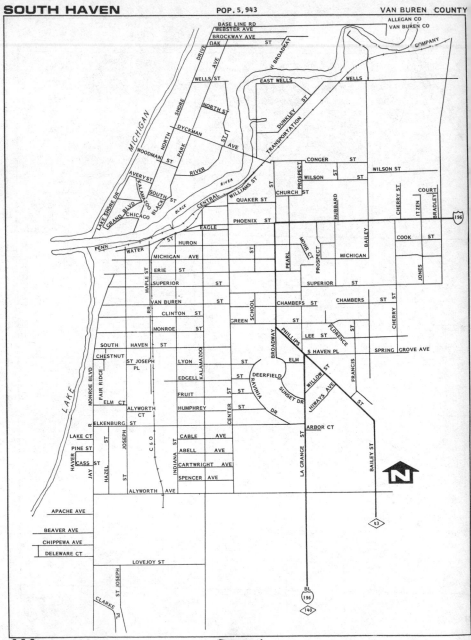

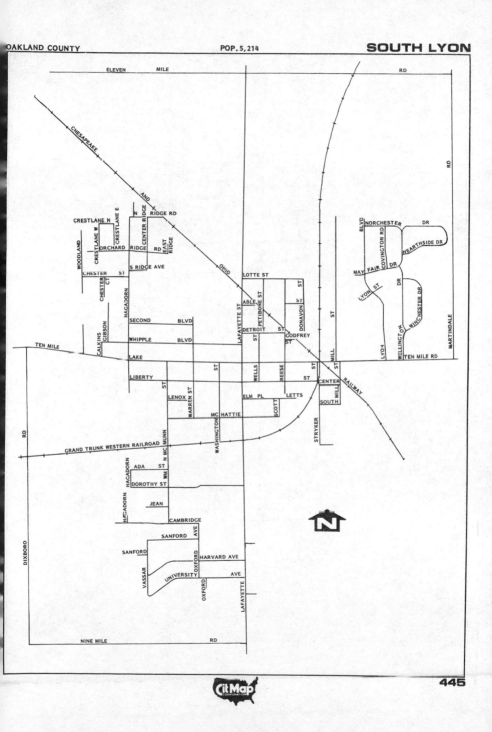

POP. 3,373

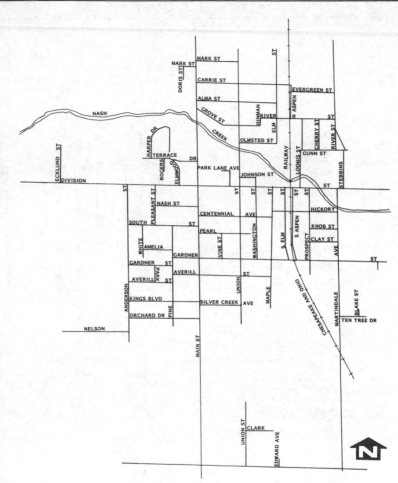

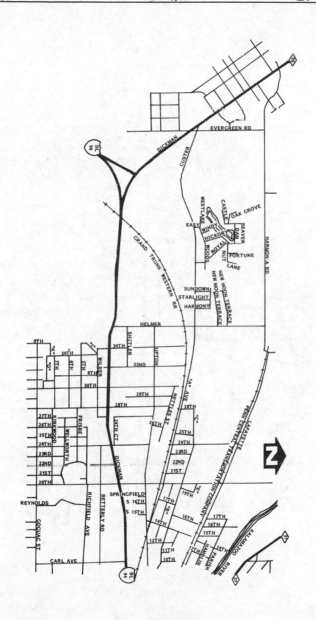

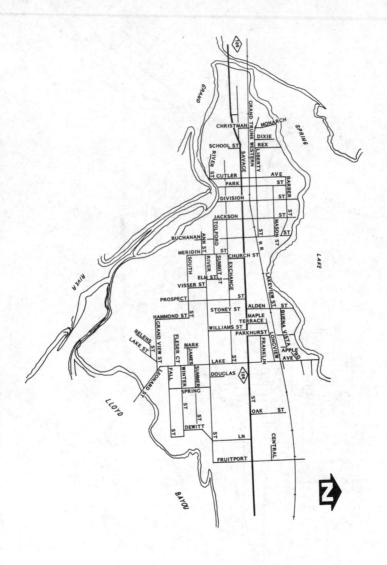

ADMIRAL	449 NW	EASON	452 SW	HEADLEY	450 NW
ALICE	450 NW	EASTATE	452 SW	HEDGE	451 SW
ALWAROT	450 NW	EBONY	452 SW	HEINDALE	449 NE
AMHURST	451 NE	ECHO	449 SE	HELENA	452 SW
AMSTERDAM	452 SW	EDEN	450 NW	HEMLOCK	452 SW
ANNETTE	451 NW	EDGEMONT	449 NW	HENSLEY	450 NW
ANNOPOLIS	450 NE	EDGEVALE	452 NW	HERTIAGE	452 SW
ANUIL	450 SW	EDSHIRE	452 SE	HIBER	451 NW
ASHBURTON	451 SW	EL CAMINO	452 SW	HIGGINS	451 SW
ASHTON	450 NE	ELDORADO	452 SW	HILLSDALE	452 SW
AUGUSTINE	451 SW	ELECTRA	452 SW	HILLVIEW	452 SW
AVIS	451 SW	ELFROD	450 SW	KIHLOCK	452 NE
AWDEY	452 SW	ELGIN	451 SW	KILBORNE	451 SW
BAKER	449 SE	ELLICO	452 SW	KINGS	452 SW
BECREST	452 NW	ELLSWORTH	452 SW	KINGS CT	452 SW
BEDFORD	450 SW	ELMCREST	451 NW	KINGSBURY	450 SW
BELLA VISTA	450 SE	ELTON	452 SW	KINGSVILLE	452 SE
BENDER	450 SE	EMBASSY	450 NW	KINLOCK	450 NW
BERNARD	450 SE	ENGLISH	452 NW	KIPLING	449 SW
BLABUN	450 SW	ENSIGN	452 SE	KIRKWOOD	451 SW
BONNEH	450 SW	ERDANN	452 NW	KLEINO	452 NE
BONNEVILLE	452 SW	ESPER	452 SW	KOCH	451 SE
BRIARCLIFF	452 SW	ESSEN	450 NW	KOPPER	451 SW
BRIDGEWOOD	449 SE	ETON	451 NW	KOZAK	452 NE
BRIERSTONE	450 SE	EUNICE	451 SW	KRAFT	449 SW
BROOKSHIRE	452 SW	EVANSTON	451 SW	KREGER	452 NW
BUCKNELL	450 NE	EWALD	452 SW	KYRO	451 NE
BUTLER	450 SE	EXECUTIVE	450 SE	LA MARRA	450 SW
CAGE CRESENT	449 NE	FABLE	449 SW	LAFAYETTE	450 SW
CALVERT	450 SW	FAIRFAX	452 SW	LAMANNA	452 SW
CALVERT	450 SE	FAIRFIELD	452 SW	LANA	452 SW
CAPITOL	450 SE	FAIRMONT CT	451 SE	LANCASTER	450 SW
CARDENER	449 SW	FAIRVIEW	452 NW	LANGER	450 SW
CARRNATION	450 NE	FAIRWAY	452 NW	LANIGAN	452 NW
CASIMIRA	452 SE	FALCON	450 SW	LAUREL CT	452 NW
CATHEDRAL	452 SE	FANNING	452 NW	LEA	452 SW
CHARLES CT.	452 SW	FARGO	452 SW	LEAH	450 SW
CHERRYLAWN	450 NE	FARMHILL	452 SE	LEASON	450 SW
CHESTERFIELD	450 NE	FARNSWO	452 SE	LEDGATE	449 SW
CLINTON	450 SW	FARTHING	450 NW	LECCII	452 NC
COACHWOOD	452 SE	FELSTONE	450 NW	LESLIE	450 NW
COLOGNE	440 NW	FEMMORE	452 NW	LESURE DR	451 NW
COLONY	450 SW	FERRIS	451 NE	LEU	452 NW
COLONY	450 SW	FILER	451 NW	LEWIS	451 NE
COMSTOCK	451 SW	FIRST ONE	452 SW	LEWLAND	450 NW
CONGRESS	450 SE	FLAGSTAFF	450 SW	LEXINGTON	450 SW
CONSTITUTION	450 SW	FLEET	452 SW	LIN	450 SW
COREY	451 SE	FLEMING	452 SW	LINDELL	451 SW
CORNELISSEN	452 SE	FORDHAM	450 NE	LINDOW	451 SW
CREEK	449 NE	FORESTER	451 SW	LINDALE	451 SW
CUSMIRA	452 NE	FORMAN	451 SW	LITTLE GIELD	451 NW
DAILY	450 NE	FORRER CT	452 SW	LITTLE JOHN	451 SW
DANE	450 NE	FORTNER	452 SW	LIZABETH	450 SW
DANIEL	452 SW	FOX HILL	449 SW	LOCODALE	451 SE
DANSWORTH	452 SW	FOXBORO	452 SF	LODGE	452 NE
DAREY	452 SW	FOX HILL	449 SE	LOLA	452 SW
DART	452 NW	FRANCIS	452 NW	LONDON	452 NW
DART CT.	452 SW	FRANKFURT	452 SW	LONGACRE	450 NW
DARTMOUTH	451 NE	FRANKLIN PARK	452 SW	LONI	450 NW
DASHER	451 SE	FREDRICK	449 SE	LORI	452 NW
DAVISON	452 SW	FREEDOM	450 SE	LORMAN	452 SW
DAWN	450 NW	FURY CT	452 SW	LOYOLA	450 NE
DAWN	449 NE	GAGE CRESENT	449 NE	LOZEN	450 SW
DAYTONA	452 NE	GAINSLEY	452 SW	LUCERNE	451 NW
DAYTONA	450 SW	GARDNER	452 SW	LVRORD	452 SW
DE COOK	450 NW	GAYLORD	452 SW	MAAS	451 SW
DE QUINDRE	451 SW	GEORGETOWN	452 SW	MAC DONALD	451 SW
DEARING	452 SW	GERTRUDE PALMER WOODS		MAC-RAE	450 NW
DEBBIE	452 SW			MAEWOOD	452 NE
DECLERK	452 NW	GETTYSBURG	450 SW	MAHOGANY	451 NW
DEFOUR	451 SE	GIBSON	452 SW	MAIR	450 NE
DEGROVE	452 SW	GLADSTONE	452 SW	MAISANO	450 SW
DEL RAY	450 NW	GLENFRELD	452 SW	MALBECK	452 NE
DELCG	450 NW	GLENGARY	452 SW	MALIBU	452 SW
DELVIN	452 NW	GLENIS	452 SW	MALOW	452 SW
DELVIN	450 NW	GOETZ	452 SE	MANDALE	452 SW
DENO	452 NW	GOFF	449 NE	MANNIN	452 NE
DENOTER	450 SE	GOLDBERG	450 SW	MANSFIELD	452 NE
DENSON	451 NW	GORDON	451 NW	MAPLE LAND DR	452 SW
DENSON	450 SE	GRAND HAVEN	450 SW	MAPLECREST	452 SW
DENWOOD	452 SW	GRAND PRIX	452 SW	MARC	451 NW
DERBY	452 NW	GRAY	451 NW	MARFORD	451 SE
DERBY	450 NW	GRAYFIELD	450 SW	MARIE	452 NW
DERNING	452 SW	GREENDALE	452 SW	MARINA	452 SE
DEVILLE	452 SW	GREENTREEO	452 NE	MARIO	452 SE
DEVONSHIRE	451 NW	GREGORY	452 SW	MARION	452 NW
DIAMOND	450 NW	GRENADA	450 SW	MARKREY	452 NW
DIANE	452 NW	GRIGG	451 SW	MARLENA	452 SW
DICKSON	451 NE	GRINDLEY	452 NW	MARNE	452 SE
DIEHL	452 NW	GROTH	452 SE	MAROLD	449 NE
DILL	452 NW	GROVES	451 SW	MARTHA	451 SW
DILL CT.	452 NW	GUNTHER	451 NW	MARY ANN	450 SW
DILL CT.	450 SW	HACKER	451 NE	MARY GROVE	450 SE
DILL DR.	450 SW	HALL RD	450 NW	MASON	452 NW
DINCIANNA	452 NW	HAMILTON	450 NW	MAYHEM	450 SW
DOCKSIN	450 NE	HAMPTON	449 SW	MC COY	452 SE
DODGEBARK	452 SW	HANKS LN	449 NE	MEADE	450 SW
DONCASTER	452 SW	HANNA	452 SW	MEDVILLE	450 NW
DONCASTER	450 SW	HANSON	451 SW	MELANIE	450 NE
DORIAN	449 SW	HANUS	451 SW	MELLOWWOOD	449 SW
DOYLE	451 SE	HARTHSTONE	452 NW	MEMORIAL	450 SE
DOYLE	452 SW	HARTWELL	452 NW	MENDELL	452 NE
DRUENS	452 NE	HARTWICK	452 NW	MERRILL	452 NW
DRYDEN	451 SW	HARVARD	450 NW	METEOR	452 NW
DUBLINE WAY	450 NW	HARVEY	450 NW	METROPOLITAN PARKWAY	
DUFFIELD	452 SW	HAVANAU	450 NW		
DUKES	451 NE	HAVERHILL	452 NE	MICHIGAN	452 NE
DUNDEE	451 NW	HAVPERT	451 SE	MILLFR	450 NE
DUPON	452 SW	HAWKE	452 SE	MILLINGTON	452 NE
DURAND	449 SW	HAYES	452 SE	MINA	452 NE
DYAR	451 SW	HAYES RD	450 SW	MINT	452 NW
				MIRS CT	

MOERS	450 NW	RIVERWOOD			
MONA	452 SW	ROB	452 SE		
MONACO	449 NE	ROBIN NEST	450 SW		
MONSBRADE	452 NW	ROBINSON	451 SW		
MONTEGO	452 SW	ROCKDALE CT	452 SW		
MONTEREY	450 NW	ROCKFORD	452 SW		
MONTROY	452 SW	ROCKINGHAM	451 SW		
MONZA	452 SW	ROGER	451 SW		
MORANG	450 NW	RORAN	452 SW		
MORAVIUN	452 SE	ROSEANN	449 NW		
MORIANO	450 SW	ROSEBUSH	451 NW		
MORLEY	452 NE	ROSEMARY	451 NW		
MORRISON	452 SE	ROSLYN	450 NW		
MOUND	450 SE	ROWE	452 NE		
MT. PLEASANT	452 SW	ROXBURY	450 SE		
MT. VERNON	450 SE	ROYAL	450 SE		
MURIEL	452 SE	ROYCE	452 SW		
MUSTANG	452 SW	RUTH	452 NW		
MYLES	450 NW	RUTHLAND	450 SE		
NADINE	449 SW	RYAN RD	449 SW		
NANTUCKET	450 NE	S. AVIS	451 SW		
NATHAN	449 SE	SAAL	450 SE		
NATIONAL	451 SW	SALEM	451 NW		
NEW BRADFORD	450 SW	SALISBURY	450 NE		
NEWBURG	449 SW	SALVADOVE	452 NW		
NEWBURY	452 NW	SAN MARCO	452 SW		
NEWPORT	451 SW	SAND CT	451 SW		
NIAGARA	450 NW	SANDWOOD	451 SW		
NICKOLAS	451 SW	SANTA ROSE	452 SW		
NORMANDALE	452 SW	SARATINA	452 NW		
NORTH CENTRAL	450 NE	SARR	450 NW		
NORTH YORK	452 SW	SAVAGE	452 SW		
NORTHLAWN	451 SE	SAXONY	451 NE		
NORTHWOOD CT	452 SW	SEBASTIAN	451 SW		
NOWAK	451 SW	SERRA	450 NW		
NOWAK CT	451 SW	SHANNON	450 NW		
O'HARA CIRCLE	450 NW	SHEARING	452 SW		
OCEAN	449 SW	SHEFFIELD	450 SE		
OENEVIEVE	452 NW	SHELLY LYNNE	452 SW		
OGDEN	450 NW	SHETLAND	450 NW		
OLD FROGE	452 SE	SHILLING	450 NW		
OLEANDER	450 NE	SHOENHERR	450 SE		
ONTARIO	451 NW	SILVER	450 SE		
OREGON	451 NE	SIMETHWICK	452 NW		
OSMOND	449 SW	SIMS	449 SE		
OWASSO	450 SW	SMETHWICK	452 SW		
OWENDALE	449 SW	SMILE	452 SW		
PAIGN	451 SW	SMITH CT	451 SW		
PALL MALL	451 SW	SMITH CT	451 SW		
PARIS	451 NE	SOLOSOM	451 SW		
PARKLAWN	450 SW	SOMERSET	452 SW		
PARKWOOD	450 SE	SORRENTO BLVD	452 SW		
PARILAMENT	450 SW	SOUTHGATE	452 SW		
PARSONS	451 SE	SOUTHLAWN	451 SF		
PATRICK	450 NE	SPALDING	450 SW		
PAVINA	452 SW	SPITZ	452 NW		
PEACHTREE	449 SW	SPULDING	452 NW		
PELLA ROSA	452 NW	ST. JOSEPH	452 SW		
PEMBERTON	452 NW	STACY	449 NE		
PEPPERMILL CT	452 SE	STADLER	450 SE		
PEPPERMILL RD	452 SW	STANSBERRY	450 NW		
PESO	450 NW	STANFORD	451 SW		
PEXTON	452 SW	STARLITE	452 SW		
PHEASANT	450 NE	STEEL	450 SW		
PICADILLY	450 SE	STEPHANIE	451 NW		
PICKETT RIDGE	450 SW	STERRITT	452 SE		
PICKWICK	451 NW	STONER	452 SE		
PINEBROOK	449 SW	STONEWOOD	452 SE		
PLAINVIEW	450 NW	STRATFORD	450 NE		
PLEASANT	452 NW	STROM	452 SW		
PLUMBROOK	450 SW	STURBRIDGE	449 SW		
PLUMRIDGE	452 NW	SUINELA	452 SW		
PLYMOUTH	451 SE	SUMMERSET	452 SE		
POINCIANNA	450 SW	SUNCREST	450 SE		
POKLEY	452 SW	SUNSET	452 SE		
POLARA	452 SW	SUPREME	452 SW		
POLLARD PEPPER	452 NE	SURREY WAY	452 SW		
POMONA	451 NW	SUSAN	451 NW		
POMPANA	449 NE	SWAN	452 SW		
POPLAR	451 NW	TACOMA	450 NE		
POTEREK	451 SE	TAHITA	452 NW		
POTOMAC	452 SE	TAMATACK	452 NW		
PRESDEN	452 SE	TARPON	452 NW		
PRESTON	452 SE	TARRY	451 SW		
PRIFHS CT	452 SE	TATLEY	451 SE		
PRINCE	451 SE	TEAK	452 SW		
PRODUST	451 NE	TEMPLE	451 SE		
PUCHESS	449 SW	TERRA SANTA	452 SW		
PURCELL	450 NE	TESSMER	449 NE		
PURDUE	450 NW	THERESA	452 SW		
QUAKER	452 SE	THOMAS	452 NW		
QUEENS	451 NE	THORNTON	451 NW		
QUINN	449 SW	TIFFANY	452 SW		
RADCLIFF	450 SW	TIMBERLANE	452 SW		
RADNER	452 SE	TIMMY	451 SW		
RAINBOW	450 NE	TINDELL	452 SE		
RALIEGH	452 NW	TINKLER	452 NW		
RAMBLER	450 NE	TORRINGTON	452 SW		
RANDALL	450 NW	TOTTENHAM	450 SW		
RED RUN	449 SW	TRACY	449 SW		
REESE	450 SE	TRAFLAGGAR	452 NW		
REGAL	452 NW	TRICIA	451 NW		
REGENCY	451 NW	TRINITY	452 SW		
RHEA	452 NW	TRUNS	452 SW		
RHOTEN	451 SW	TUANE	452 NW		
RICE	450 NE	TUDOR CT	452 SE		
RICHARD	451 SW	TWIN CT	452 NW		
RIDGECROFT	450 SW	TYLER	451 SE		
RINALDI	450 SW	UNIVERSITY	449 SE		
RIVERCREST	452 SE	UPDALE	451 NE		
RIVERLAND	450 NW	UTAH	450 NE		
		UTICA	452 NE		

UTICA RD	450 SE
VALIANT	452 NW
VALUSEK	452 SE
VAN DYKE	450 NW
VAN DYKE RD	449 SE
VANESS	452 NW
VEGA	449 SW
VERNON	451 NE
VEVONICA	451 NW
VICEROY	451 SW
VILLAGE	452 NW
VINE	452 NW
VIOLA	452 SE
VIRGINIA	449 SW
VISTA	452 SE
VISTA	452 NW
VISTA CT	451 SE
VITO	451 SW
WAITELEY	450 NW
WALDO	449 NE
WALL	451 NE
WALTHAM	451 NW
WANDA	452 NE
WANDA	450 SE
WARRINGTON	449 SW
WARSAW	452 SW
WARWICKSHINE	452 NW
WAYNE	452 NW
WEBB	452 NW
WEBER	451 NE
WEDGEWOOD	452 SE
WEIN	451 SW
WELLSTON	452 SW
WESSEL	450 SE
WEST POINT	450 NE
WESTCHESTER	451 NE
WESTMINSTER	450 NE
WESTWOOD	452 NE
WHEATON	450 NW
WHITEFIELD	452 NE
WHITEHALL	452 NW
WHITEFIELD	450 SE
WHITHORN	450 NW
WICKES LN	452 SW
WILKE	451 SW
WILLESDON	450 SW
WILLIAM	450 SW
WILLSHARON	449 NE
WILMINGTON	450 NE
WILSECK	450 NW
WINOMA	450 SE
WINSTON	451 SW
WITT CT	452 SW
WOODMONT	451 NE
WOODVILLA	452 SE
YARDLY	451 SW
ZIMMER	451 SW
14 MILE	451 SW
15 MILE	452 SW
16 MILE	451 NW
16 ½ MILE	452 NW
17 MILE RD	449 SW
18 MILE RD	449 SW
18½ MILE RD	449 NW
19 MILE RD	450 NE
19 ½ MILE RD	449 NE
53 RD	451 SE

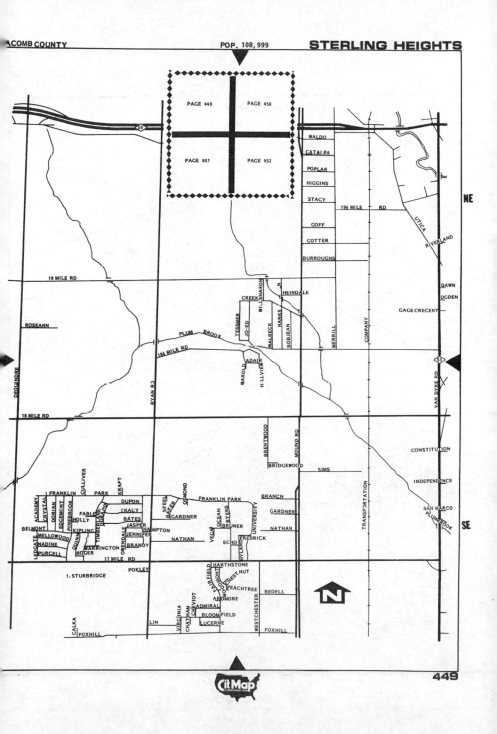

PAGE 449   PAGE 450

PAGE 451   PAGE 452

WALDO
CATALPA
POPLAR
HIGGINS
STACY

NE

19½ MILE RD

GOFF
COTTER
BURROUGHS

UTICA
RIVERLAND

19 MILE RD

DAWN
OGDEN

GAGE CRECENT

ROSEANN

CREEK
WILLSHARON
HEINDALE

TESSMER
JO-ED
MALBECK
HANKS
BOBJEAN
MERRILL
COMPANY

PLUM BROOK

18½ MILE RD

DEQUINDRE

ADAIR
HAROLD
HILLVIEW

RYAN RD

VAN DYKE RD

18 MILE RD

BRENTWOOD
MOUND RD

CONSTITUTION

BRIDGEWOOD   SIMS

INDEPENDENCE

CULLIVER
PARK
KRAFT

SAN MARCO
PLUMBROOK

SE

FRANKLIN
DUPON
OSMOND
FRANKLIN PARK
BRANCH

ACADEMY
CRYSTAL
DORIAN
EDGEMONT
PINEBROOK
FABLE
HOLLY
TRACY
STEEL
BAKER
GARDNER
OCEAN
BYERS
UNIVERSITY
GARDNER

BELMONT
KIPLING
BATES
JASPER
HAMPTON
VEGA
BRUNER
NATHAN

MELLOWOOD
QUINN
TIMBER
JENNIFER
NATHAN
ECHO
FREDRICK

LEDGATE
NADINE
PURCELL
WARRINGTON
OWENDALE
BRANDY
RYLAND

ROGER

17 MILE RD

TRANSPORTATION

1. STURBRIDGE
POKLEY

HARTHSTONE
CHESTNUT
PEACHTREE
BEDELL

FAIRFIELD
BELMONT
GOLDCREST
ARDMORE

N

CALKA
FOXHILL

VIRGINIA
CHATHAM
CHEVIOT
ADMIRAL
BLOOMFIELD
LUCERNE

WESTCHESTER

LIN

FOXHILL

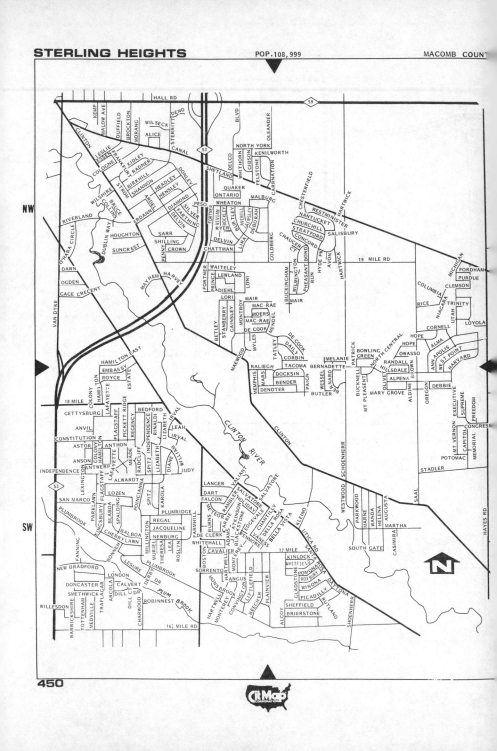

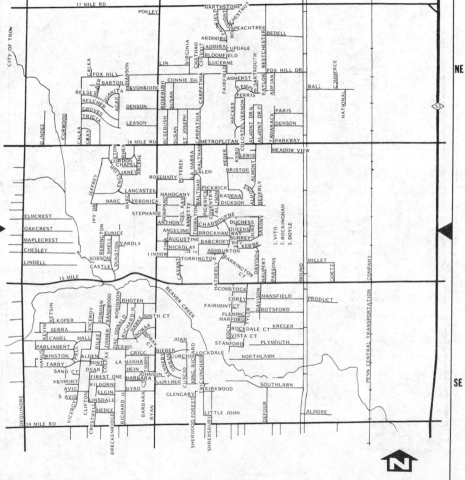

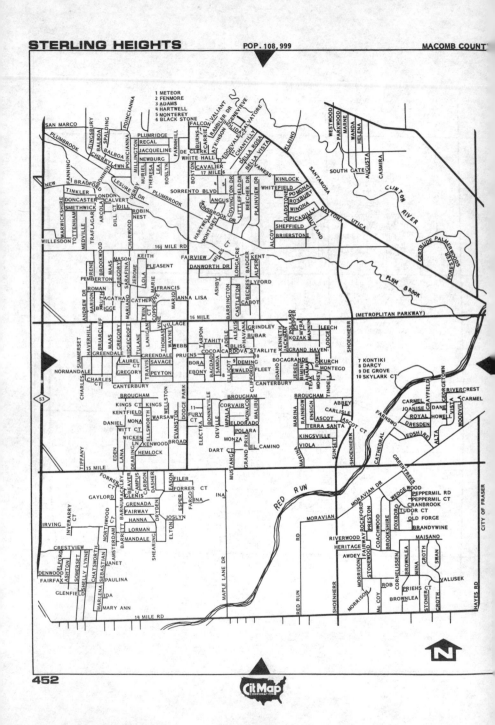

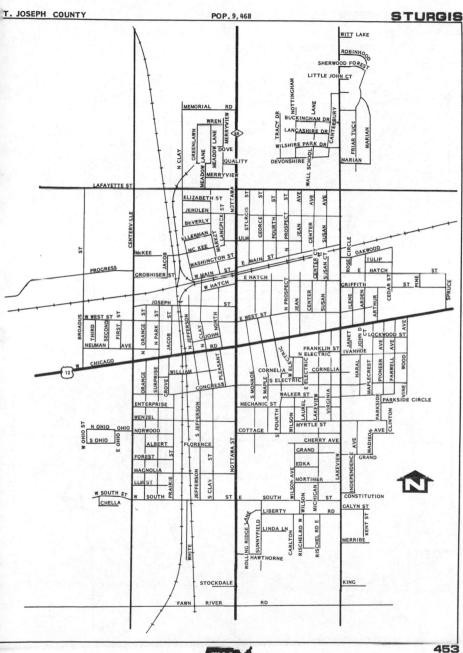

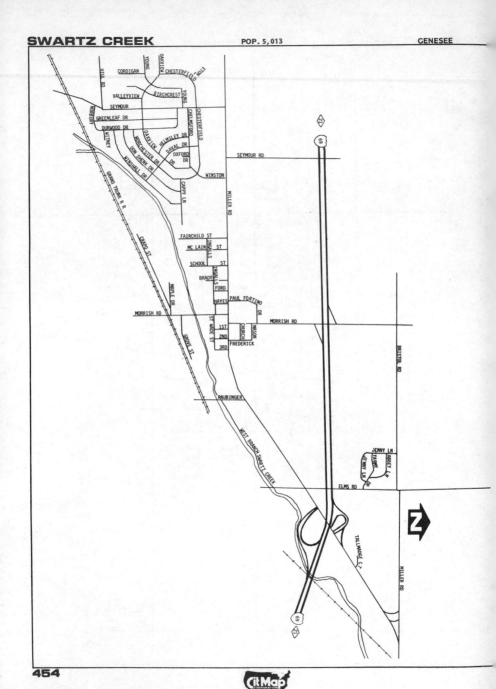

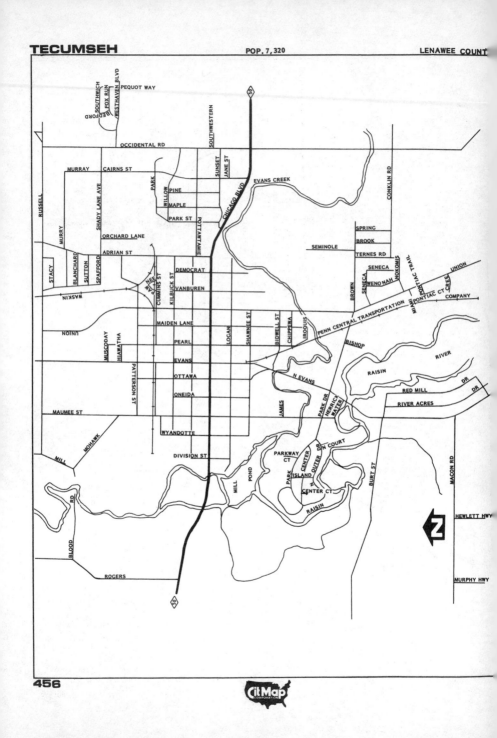

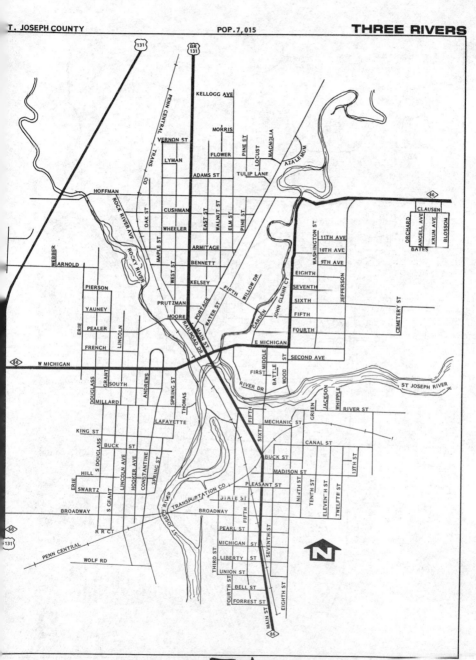

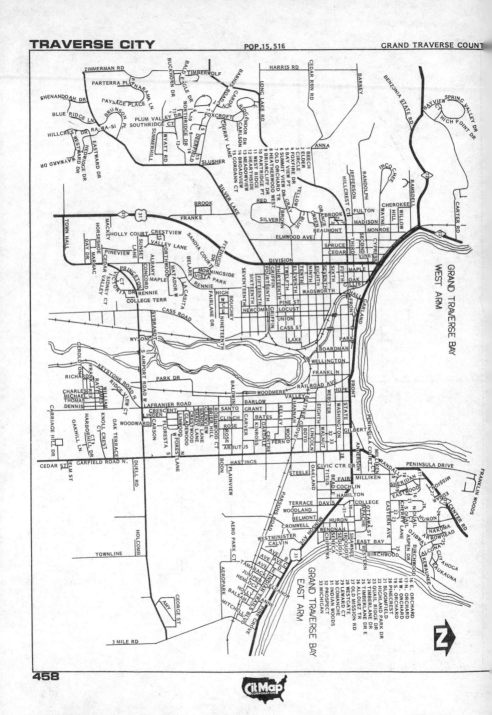

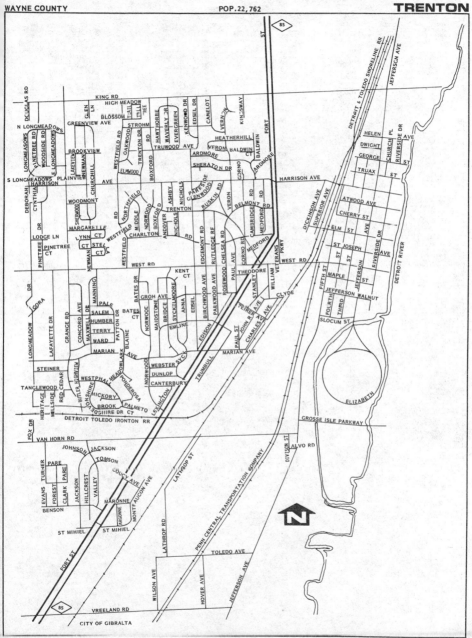

ABBEY . . . . 463 NE
ABBOTSFORD . . . 461 SE
ABERDEEN . . . 460 SE
ADINGTO . . . 461 EW
ACACIA . . . 460 NW
ACADEMY . . . 463 NW
ADAMS . . . 462 NW
ADONIS . . . 463 SE
ADRIENNE . . . 461 SE
ALEXANDER . . . 463 SE
ALFERD . . . 461 NE
ALGANSEE . . . 463 SW
ALGANSEE . . . 463 SE
ALGER . . . 461 SE
ALLEGHENY . . . 463 SW
ALLEN RD . . . 463 SW
ALTON CT. . . . 461 SE
ANDOVER . . . 460 NW
ANSLOW . . . 461 NE
ANVIL . . . 461 NE
ARDMORE . . . 463 NW
ARLUNDWAY . . . 461 NW
ARROWHEAD . . . 463 SW
ARTHUR . . . 463 SW
ASHLEY . . . 461 SW
ASPINWALL . . . 460 NE
ASPINWALL . . . 460 NE
ASTER . . . 461 SE
ATHENA . . . 463 SE
ATLAS . . . 463 SE
AUBURN . . . 463 NE
AUSTIN . . . 463 SW
AVERY . . . 461 SE
AVONHURST . . . 462 SW
AXTELL . . . 461 SE
BABBIT . . . 461 SW
BABCOCK . . . 461 NE
BADDER . . . 463 NW
BALFOUR . . . 461 SW
BANKLE . . . 461 SE
BANMOOR . . . 462 NE
BARBARA . . . 461 SW
BARCLAY . . . 461 NW
BARILANE . . . 462 NE
BARRTON . . . 463 SW
BARRTON . . . 460 NE
BAYLORD . . . 460 SW
BAYSIDE . . . 461 NE
BEACH . . . 460 SW
BEATTI . . . 461 SW
BEECH LANE . . . 463 SW
BELDALE . . . 461 SW
BELHAVEN . . . 461 SW
BELLINGHAM . . . 463 SW
BELLOWS . . . 461 SW
BELZAIR . . . 463 NE
BERKSHIRE . . . 461 SW
BERWICK . . . 461 SW
BERWICK . . . 461 SW
BEV . . . 461 SW
BIG OA TRAIL . . . 460 SW
BILTMORE . . . 462 SE
BINBROOK . . . 462 NE
BINGHAM . . . 461 NE
BIRCHWOOD . . . 463 NW
BISHOP . . . 463 NW
BLACK PINE . . . 460 SW
BLACKWALL . . . 460 NE
BLACKWALL . . . 460 NE
BLAIR . . . 461 SE
BLANCHE . . . 460 SE
BLANEY . . . 460 SE
BOLLING BROOK . . . 462 SE
BONITO . . . 461 NE
BONNIEBROOK . . . 460 SE
BOOTH . . . 461 NW
BORDEN . . . 463 SW
BOROS . . . 461 SW
BOULAN . . . 462 SW
BOULDER . . . 462 SW
BOYD . . . 463 NW
BRADLEY . . . 461 NW
BRAEMAR . . . 462 SW
BRAMFORD . . . 461 SE
BRANCH . . . 461 NE
BRANDYWYNE . . . 460 SW
BREEZE HILL . . . 460 NE
BRENTWOOD . . . 460 SW
BRETBY . . . 460 SW
BRIARGROVE . . . 460 SW
BRIDGE PARK . . . 460 NE
BRIDGE PARK . . . 460 NE
BRINSTON . . . 463 SW
BRINSTON . . . 463 NW
BRINSTON . . . 463 NW
BRISTOL . . . 463 NW
BRISTOL . . . 463 NW
BRONSON . . . 463 SW
BROOKLAWN . . . 462 NW
BUCKINGHAM . . . 460 NE
BURDIC . . . 461 NE
BURKOFF . . . 462 NW
BURNS . . . 461 SW
BURTMAN . . . 461 SW
BUTLER . . . 461 SE
BUTTERFIELD . . . 462 NE
BUTTERNUT HILL . . . 462 SW
BYRON . . . 460 SE
CADMUS . . . 461 NW
CAHILL . . . 460 SE
CALIPER . . . 462 NW
CALVERT . . . 461 SE

CAMARON . . . 460 SW
CAMBRIA . . . 461 NW
CAMBRIDGE . . . 461 SW
CAMEO . . . 460 EW
CAMARON . . . 460 SW
CAMBRIA . . . 461 NW
CAMBRIDGE . . . 461 SE
CAMEO . . . 460 SW
CAMERON . . . 460 SW
CAMILLA . . . 463 NE
CANARY . . . 462 NW
CANHAM . . . 460 NE
CANHAM . . . 460 NE
CANMOOR . . . 460 NE
CANNOOR . . . 460 NE
CAPRI . . . 460 SW
CARDINAL . . . 460 SW
CARMEL . . . 463 NE
CARNABY . . . 460 SW
CAROL . . . 461 SE
CARR . . . 461 SE
CARSON . . . 461 SE
CARTER . . . 461 SE
CASPER . . . 461 SW
CASTLETON . . . 463 SE
CASWEL . . . 462 NW
CATALPA . . . 460 SW
CATTERMOLE . . . 462 SW
CHALGROVE . . . 460 NW
CHAMPLAIN . . . 460 SW
CHANCERY . . . 461 NE
CHAPEL . . . 461 SE
CHARNWOOD . . . 460 NW
CHARRINGTON . . . 463 NW
CHASE . . . 460 SW
CHATHAM . . . 460 SW
CHAUCER . . . 460 SW
CHELSEA . . . 462 NW
CHELTMAN . . . 461 NE
CHEROKEE . . . 462 SE
CHERRY . . . 463 NW
CHERRYWOOD . . . 460 SW
CHESAPEAKE . . . 460 NW
CHESTERFIELD . . . 463 SE
CHESTNUT HILL . . . 461 SW
CIVIC CENTER DR. . . . 462 NE
CLARK . . . 461 SW
CLAYMONT . . . 461 NE
CLAYTON . . . 463 NE
CLIFFSIDE . . . 461 NE
CLOCKGATE . . . 461 NW
CLOVER RIDGE . . . 462 SE
COLEBROOK . . . 463 NW
COLIDGE . . . 460 NW
COLLEEN . . . 461 NE
COLLINGTON . . . 460 NW
COLONIA . . . 461 SE
COLUMBIA . . . 463 NE
COLWELL . . . 463 NE
COMBERMERE . . . 461 SW
CONDOR . . . 462 NW
CONNOLLY . . . 460 SW
COOK CT. . . . 463 SW
COOLIDGE . . . 460 SW
CORAL . . . 460 SW
CORBIN . . . 460 SW
COTSWOLD . . . 461 NW
COVENTRY . . . 463 SE
CRANBROOK . . . 460 NE
CREEKBEND . . . 460 SW
CRESENT . . . 461 NE
CRESENT WAY . . . 461 NE
CRESTFIELD . . . 461 SW
CRESTLINE . . . 461 NE
CRESTMONT . . . 460 SW
CRESTON . . . 461 SW
CRIMSON . . . 463 NE
CRIMSON . . . 463 NE
CROOKS . . . 462 SE
CUMBERLAND . . . 461 SE
CURRAN . . . 460 SW
CUTTING . . . 461 SE
CYNTHIA . . . 461 SE
CYPRESS . . . 461 NE
DALESFORD . . . 460 NW
DALEY . . . 463 NW
DANBURY . . . 461 SE
DANIELS . . . 461 SE
DARLEEN . . . 462 NE
DASHWOOD . . . 461 SE
DAYTON . . . 461 SE
DE ETTA . . . 461 NW
DEINMORE . . . 461 SE
DELEWARE . . . 462 NE
DELOY . . . 461 SE
DEMARE . . . 461 SW
DENISE . . . 461 SE
DEQUINDRE . . . 461 SE
DERBY . . . 461 NE
DEVOWOOD . . . 460 SW
DEWULF . . . 461 SE
DIAMONS . . . 461 SW
DIANE . . . 461 SE
DINBOROUGH . . . 462 SW
DOENGES . . . 461 NE
DONALDSON . . . 461 NW
DONEGAL . . . 460 SW
DORCHESTER . . . 460 SW
DORSET . . . 461 SW
DORSHIRE . . . 461 SW
DOWNEY . . . 463 NE
DUBLIN FAIR . . . 460 NW
DUCHESS CT . . . 460 NW

DUKE . . . 461 SE
DUNCAN . . . 460 SE
DURHAM . . . 461 SE
E. CEDARWOOD . . . 460 SW
EAGLE . . . 463 NE
EAST BOURNE . . . 462 NW
EAST BOURNE . . . 462 NW
EASTPORT . . . 463 SW
ECKERMAN . . . 461 NE
ECKFORD . . . 461 SW
EDGEMONT . . . 462 NW
EDITH . . . 461 NE
ELANOR . . . 461 SE
ELGIN . . . 461 SE
ELIZABETH . . . 462 NE
ELLENBORO . . . 463 NW
ELLERY . . . 461 SE
ELLIOT . . . 463 SE
ELLIS . . . 461 NE
ELM . . . 460 NW
ELMOOR . . . 460 NE
ELMOOR . . . 460 NE
ELMSFORD . . . 463 NE
ELMWOOD . . . 463 SW
ELSEY . . . 460 NE
ELSEY . . . 460 NE
ELVER . . . 462 SE
EMERALD . . . 461 NE
EMERALD SHORES . . . 461 NE
ENDICOTT . . . 461 NE
ENGLE . . . 462 NW
ENGLISH . . . 461 SE
ENTERPRISE . . . 463 SW
ERIN WAY . . . 460 NW
ESSEX . . . 461 SE
ESTATES . . . 462 NW
ETON . . . 462 SW
EVALINE . . . 461 SW
EVANSWOOD . . . 461 SE
EXECUTIVE . . . 463 SE
FABIUS . . . 460 SW
FAIRMONT . . . 461 SE
FALCON . . . 460 NE
FALCON . . . 460 NE
FARMBROOK . . . 460 SW
FAWN . . . 461 SE
FEDORA . . . 461 SE
FERNLEIGH . . . 463 NE
FINCH . . . 462 NE
FLAMOUTH . . . 461 SW
FLEMINGTON . . . 460 SW
FLINT . . . 460 SW
FLORA . . . 461 NE
FLORENCE . . . 460 SW
FLOYD . . . 461 NW
FOLKSTONE . . . 461 SW
FORDHAM . . . 460 SW
FOREST PARK . . . 460 NW
FOREST TRAIL . . . 460 NW
FORGE . . . 463 NE
FORSYTH . . . 463 NE
FORTHTON . . . 462 SE
FOUNTAIN . . . 461 SW
FOURTEEN MILE RD. . . . 461 NW
FOXCHASE . . . 460 SW
FOXCROFT . . . 461 NW
FRANKTON . . . 460 SW
FREDMOOR . . . 460 NE
FREDMOOR . . . 460 NE
FREEMONT . . . 461 SW
FROSTWOOD . . . 460 NE
FULTON . . . 460 NE
FULTON . . . 460 NE
GALLOWAY . . . 461 SW
GAMBER . . . 461 SE
GARDEN . . . 460 NW
GARFIELD . . . 462 SW
GARRY . . . 463 NE
GATE . . . 463 NE
GATESFORD . . . 460 SE
GEORGIAN CT. . . . 460 SE
GEORGIAN CT. . . . 460 SE
GLASER . . . 461 SW
GLASGLOW . . . 461 NW
GLEN . . . 460 SW
GLENDALE . . . 463 SW
GLENDALE . . . 463 SW
GLENWOOD . . . 463 NW
GLYNDERBORNE . . . 461 SW
GOLFVIEW . . . 462 NW
GORDON . . . 461 SE
GRANGER . . . 461 SW
GRANGER . . . 461 SW
GRANT . . . 463 SW
GREENSBORO . . . 461 NW
GRENADIER . . . 460 NW
GROVE . . . 461 SE
GULLIVER . . . 461 NE
HABRAND . . . 460 SE
HALDANE . . . 461 SW
HALE ABINGTON . . . 461 SE
HAMES . . . 463 NE
HAMMAN . . . 461 SW
HAMPSHIRE . . . 461 SW
HAMPSTEAD . . . 461 SW
HAMPTON . . . 461 SW
HANNAH . . . 461 NW
HANOVER . . . 461 SE
HARBOR . . . 461 NE
HARMONY . . . 463 NE
HARNED . . . 463 NE
HAROLD . . . 463 NE
HARRIS . . . 463 NW
HART . . . 460 SE

HARTLAND . . . 463 NW
HARTSHORN . . . 463 SW
HARTWIG . . . 461 NW
HARWICH . . . 461 SW
HAVERFORD . . . 460 SW
HAWTHORNE . . . 461 SW
HEATHERBROOK . . . 460 SE
HFIDFS . . . 462 SE
HELENA . . . 463 NW
HENDRICKSON . . . 463 SW
HENHAWK . . . 462 NW
HERBMOOR . . . 460 NE
HERBMOOR . . . 460 NE
HERIETTA . . . 461 SW
HERTFORD . . . 463 NW
HICKORY . . . 463 NW
HICKORY . . . 462 SE
HIGH OAK . . . 460 NE
HIGH OAK . . . 460 NE
HIGHBURY . . . 461 SE
HIGHMOUNT . . . 460 NE
HILL . . . 461 SE
HILL CRESENT . . . 461 SE
HILL CT. . . . 461 SE
INDUSTRIAL ROW . . . 462 SW
IOWA . . . 463 SE
ISABELL . . . 461 NE
IVANHOE . . . 461 SE
JACK . . . 461 NW
JADE . . . 461 SE
JAMACIA . . . 460 NW
JANDALE . . . 460 NE
JARMEN . . . 461 NE
JASON . . . 461 SW
JASPER . . . 461 SE
JEFFERY . . . 461 SE
JILL . . . 462 NW
JOANNE . . . 462 NW
JONATHON . . . 460 NW
JUNIPER . . . 460 SW
KEATON . . . 460 NE
KEATON . . . 460 NE
KELLY . . . 463 SW
KENT . . . 461 NW
KENWYCH . . . 461 SE
KENYON . . . 461 SW
KERRY . . . 462 NW
KETTLE . . . 461 SE
KILLARNEY . . . 460 NW
KILMER . . . 463 NW
KINGS POINT. . . . 463 NW
KINGSBURRY . . . 460 SW
KINGSLEY . . . 461 SW
KINGSTON . . . 462 NW
KINLOCK . . . 463 SW
KINLOCK . . . 460 NE
KIRKTON . . . 463 SW
KIRKTON . . . 463 SW
KIRTS . . . 462 SE
KNIGHTS . . . 463 NW
KRISTIN . . . 462 NW
LAKES DR. . . . 461 NE
LAKEWOOD . . . 463 NE
LAMB . . . 461 SW
LANCASHIRE . . . 461 SE
LANCER . . . 462 SW
LANERGAN . . . 462 NW
LANGE . . . 463 NE
LAPP CT. . . . 461 NW
LARAVNE . . . 461 NW
LARCHWOOD . . . 463 SW
LARKINS . . . 461 SW
LATA . . . 461 NW
LAURAL . . . 461 SW
LAWSON . . . 462 NE
LEAFGREEN . . . 463 SE
LEDGE . . . 462 NW
LEDWIN . . . 460 NW
LEETONIA . . . 463 SE
LEGHORN . . . 461 NW
LEHIGH . . . 461 SW
LENOX . . . 460 SW
LESDALE . . . 461 NW
LIDIA . . . 463 SW
LILA . . . 461 SE
LIMERICK . . . 460 NW
LIMESTONE . . . 461 NE
LINCOLN . . . 461 NE
LINDA . . . 461 NE
LITTLE CREEK . . . 461 NE
LITTLER . . . 461 SW
LIVERNOIS . . . 461 NE
LIVERNOIS . . . 461 NE
LIVERNOIS . . . 461 NE
LIVERPOOL . . . 461 SW
LOCUST . . . 461 SE
LONDON . . . 461 SE
LONG LAKE RD . . . 461 SW
LONGFELLOW . . . 461 SW
LONGVIEW . . . 460 SW
LOUIS . . . 461 SW
LOVELL . . . 461 NE
LOVINGTON . . . 463 SE
LYONS . . . 463 NE
LYSTER . . . 461 NE
LYSTER CT. . . . 461 NE
MAC LYNN . . . 460 SE
MADISON . . . 463 NW
MAJESTIC . . . 461 SW
MANDALE . . . 461 NE
MANHATTEN AVE. . . . 463 NW
MAPLE . . . 462 SE

MAPLELAWN . . . 462 SE
MARBEL . . . 461 NE
MARBEL CT. . . . 461 NE
MARCUS . . . 463 NE
MARENGO . . . 461 NW
MARTEL . . . 461 NW
MARTINQUE . . . 462 NW
MARYLIN . . . 461 NE
MARYWOOD . . . 463 SW
MASTIN . . . 462 NW
MAXWELL . . . 461 SE
MAYBERRY . . . 461 SW
MAYFAIR . . . 462 NW
MC MANUS . . . 462 NE
MCCLURE . . . 461 SE
MCINTOSH . . . 460 NW
MCKINLEY . . . 460 SE
MEADOWBROOK . . . 462 NE
MEATH HUNT . . . 462 SW
MEDFORD . . . 463 SW
MERRICK . . . 461 SE
MICHELE . . . 461 SE
MIDDLEBURY . . . 461 SE
MILL POND . . . 461 SE
MILVERTON . . . 463 SE
MINER . . . 462 NE
MINNESOTA . . . 463 SE
MIRACLE . . . 462 NE
MONTCLAIR . . . 461 NW
MORSE . . . 462 SE
MOUNTAIN . . . 460 NW
MUER . . . 462 NE
MUNTERSGATE . . . 462 NW
MYDDLETON . . . 462 NW
NAMPA . . . 462 NW
NAPIER . . . 460 NE
NAPIER . . . 460 NE
NASH . . . 463 NW
NAUGHTON . . . 462 NW
NEW BEDFORD . . . 461 SE
NEWGATE . . . 462 NW
NEWPORT . . . 462 NW
NEWTON . . . 463 NE
NIAGRA . . . 461 SW
NICKLAUS . . . 461 SE
NILES . . . 461 SW
NILES . . . 461 SW
NILO . . . 461 SW
NORTH HAMPTON . . . 463 SE
NORTHFIELD . . . 462 NW
NORTHFIELD . . . 462 NW
NORTHFIELD PARKWY. . . . 462 NW
NORTHLAKE . . . 463 NE
NORTHPOINT . . . 461 NE
NORTHWOOD . . . 462 SE
NORTON . . . 461 NW
NORWICH . . . 462 SW
NOTTINGHAM . . . 461 SW
OAK HILL . . . 462 SW
OAKCREST . . . 463 NE
OAKLAND . . . 460 NE
OAKLAND . . . 460 NE
OGDEN . . . 461 SW
OHAIR . . . 463 NW
OLIVER . . . 462 SE
OLYMPIA . . . 461 SW
OPAL . . . 461 SE
ORCHARD . . . 460 SE
ORCHARD RIDGE . . . 460 SW
ORCHARD RIDGE . . . 460 SW
ORIOLE . . . 462 SE
ORPINGTON . . . 461 SW
OTTER . . . 463 NE
OWRNDALE . . . 463 NW
OXFORD . . . 462 NW
OXLEY . . . 461 SE
PADDINGTON . . . 462 NW
PALMERSTOWN . . . 462 NW
PARAGON . . . 462 SE
PARK ST. . . . 461 SW
PARK ST. . . . 462 SE
PARKTON . . . 463 NW
PARKVIEW . . . 460 NW
PARLIAMENT . . . 462 NW
PASADENA . . . 463 NE
PATTERSON . . . 461 SE
PEACH TREE . . . 461 NW
PEARL . . . 461 NE
PEBBLE POINT . . . 461 NE
PELICAN . . . 462 NW
PENTON . . . 460 NE
PENTON . . . 460 NE
PERRI . . . 461 NW
PHILATHA . . . 461 NW
PICKENS . . . 463 NW
PIEDMONT . . . 463 NW
PIERCE . . . 462 NE
PINE HILL . . . 460 SW
PIPPIN CT. . . . 460 NW
PLAID . . . 461 SE
PLAYER . . . 461 SE
POE . . . 461 SW
POND RIDGE . . . 460 NW
POPLAR . . . 461 NE
PORTSMOUTH . . . 461 SE
POST . . . 461 SE
PREMIER . . . 462 SE
PRENTIS . . . 461 SE
PRIESTWICK . . . 461 SE
PRINCE . . . 461 SE
PRINCE . . . 461 SE
PROSPER . . . 460 NE

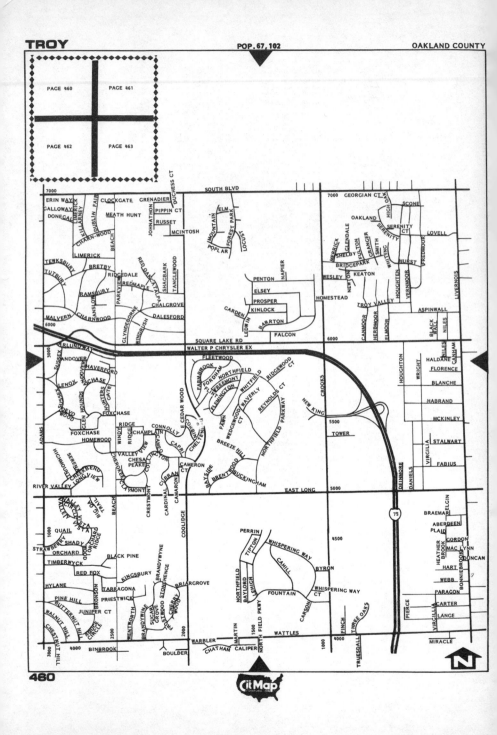

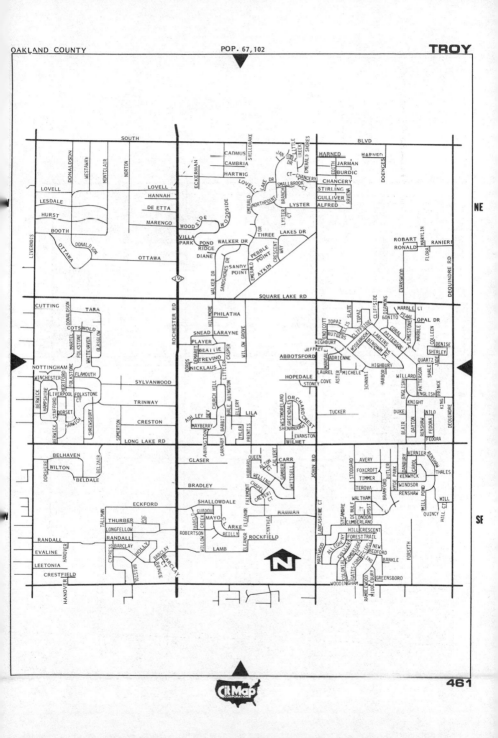

NE

SE

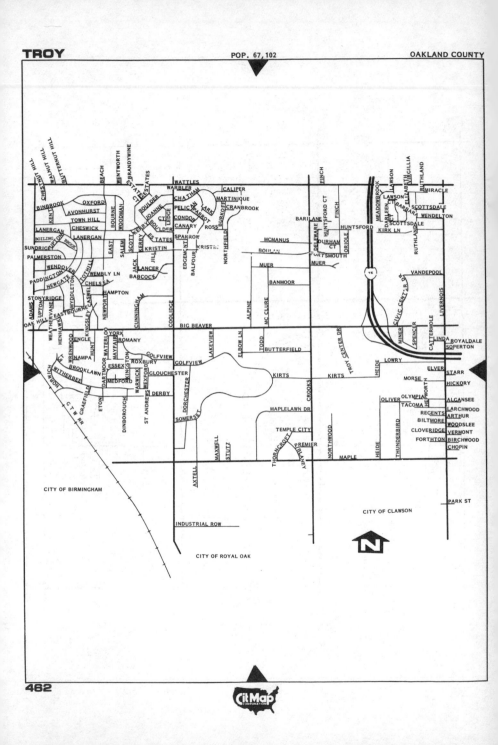

CITY OF BIRMINGHAM

INDUSTRIAL ROW

CITY OF ROYAL OAK

CITY OF CLAWSON

PARK ST

N

CitMap
CORPORATION

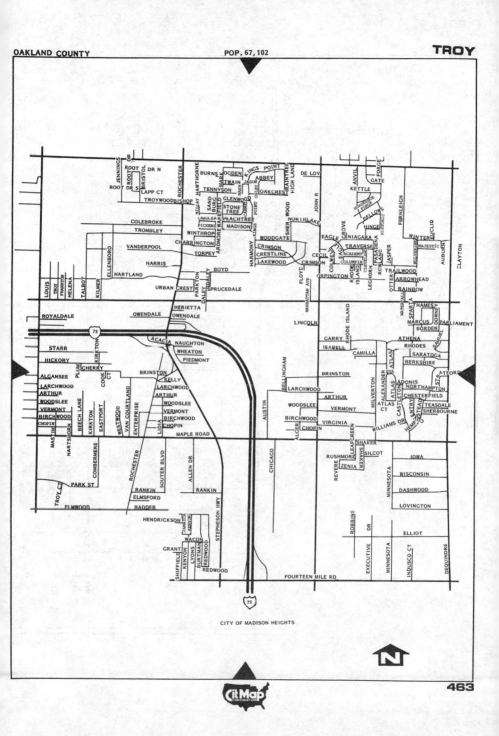

CITY OF MADISON HEIGHTS

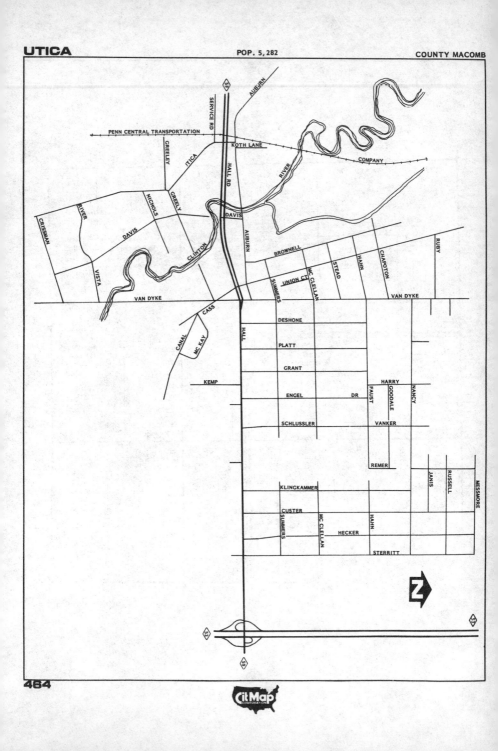

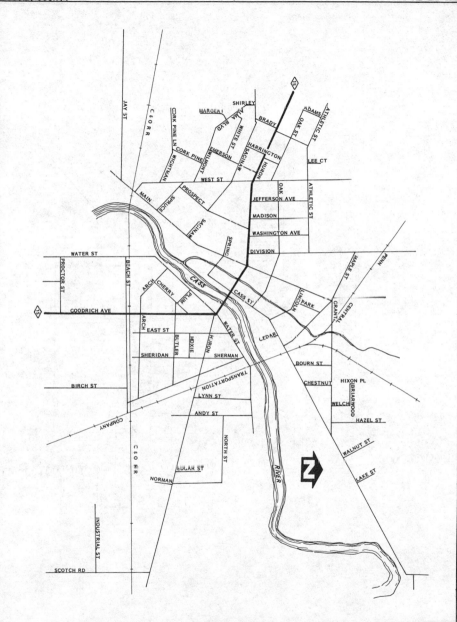

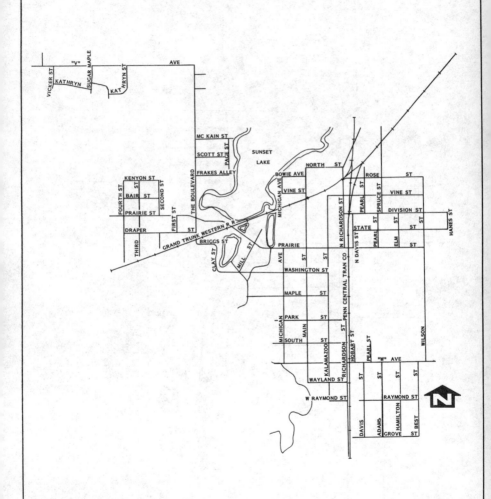

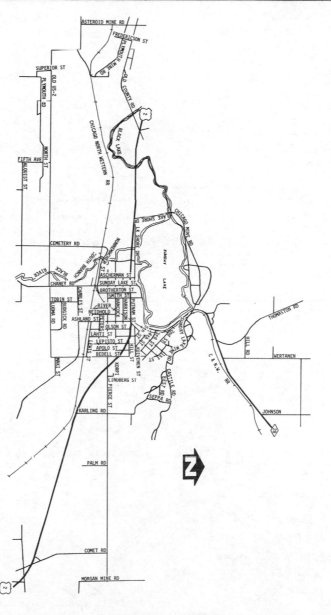

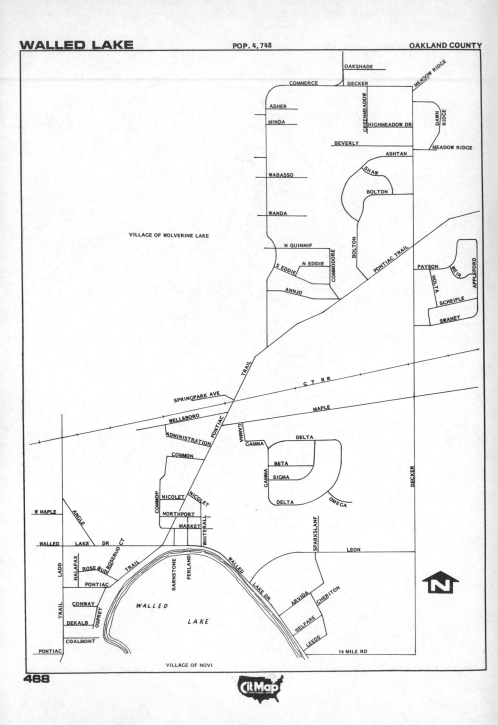

OAKSHADE

COMMERCE DECKER

ASHER

MINDA

GREENMEADOW

HIGHMEADOW DR

MEADOW RIDGE

DAWN RIDGE

BEVERLY

MEADOW RIDGE

ASHTAN

SHAW

WABASSO

BOLTON

WANDA

VILLAGE OF WOLVERINE LAKE

N QUINNIF

COMMODORE

BOLTON

PONTIAC TRAIL

PAYSON

WEIR

APPLEFORD

N EDDIE

S EDDIE

VLTON

ANNJO

SCHEIFLE

SWANEY

TRAIL

G T R R

SPRINGPARK AVE

WELLSBORO

PONTIAC

MAPLE

ADMINISTRATION

GAMMA

GAMMA

DELTA

COMMON

BETA

GAMMA

SIGMA

DELTA

COMMON

NICOLET

NICOLET

DELTA

OMEGA

DECKER

NORTHPORT

W MAPLE

ANGLE

MARKET

WHITERALL

SPARKSLANF

WALLED LAKE DR

LEON

WALLED LAKE DR

CT

ROSEBUD

TRAIL

BARNSTONE

FERLAND

WALLED LAKE DR

LADD

HALAFAX

ROSE BUD

PONTIAC

ARVIDA

CHERITON

TRAIL

CONWAY

OSPREY

WALLED

WELFARE

DEKALB

LAKE

LEEDS

COALMONT

14 MILE RD

PONTIAC

VILLAGE OF NOVI

CitMap

Street	Ref	Street	Ref
A CT.	470 SE	BUNERT	472 NE
A CT.	470 SE	BURGUNDY	470 SE
A CT.	470 SE	BURR	472 SE
AARON	472 SE	BUSCH	472 NW
ACHYL	472 NE	BUSKO	470 SW
ACTON	469 NW	BUSTER	470 SE
ADA	471 SW	C CT.	470 SE
ADAMS	460 NE	CADILLAC	471 SE
ADLER	470 SE	CALLAHAN	470 NE
AFTON	472 NE	CAMBELL	470 SW
ALBANY	471 SF	CAMBRIDGE	470 NW
ALDANY	469 SE	CAMPBELL	470 SE
ALETA	470 NW	CAPITOL	471 SW
ALGER	470 NE	CANTERBURY	469 NE
ALINE	471 SW	CAPRI	470 NW
ALKER	469 SW	CARLON	469 SW
ALLYN	472 SE	CARMODY	469 NW
ALPINE	469 SW	CARNEY	472 NW
ALVIN	469 SW	CAROL	470 SE
ALVINA LARK	471 SW	CAROL	470 SW
AMBER	472 SW	CARRIER	472 NW
AMBER	472 SE	CARRIER	472 NW
AMERICAN	469 SE	CARSON	472 SE
ANDREY	469 SW	CASMERE	469 NE
ANDRITHUS	471 NE	CASTLE	470 NE
ANITA	470 NW	CEDARS	470 NW
ANNA	470 SW	CENTER	472 SE
ANNA	470 SW	CHALEONTE	472 NE
ANTONETTE	472 NE	CHALMERS	472 SW
ANTONIA	471 NW	CHALMERS	471 NW
APOLONIA	470 SW	CHAMPAIGN	472 NW
APPLEWOOD	470 SW	CHAPP	472 SW
APRIL	470 NE	CHAPP	471 SE
ARDEN	469 NW	CHARD	469 SW
ARMANDA	470 SE	CHARLES	470 NW
ARNOLD	470 SE	CHARLOTTE	470 SE
ARSENAL	470 SW	CHASE	471 NW
ARTESIAN	469 NE	CHICAGO	470 SW
ASLENSION	472 SW	CHICAGO RD.	469 NW
ATLANTIC	471 SE	CHIPPENA	470 NE
AUDREY	471 NW	CHIPPEWA	471 SW
AUDREY	471 NW	CHIPPOWA	470 NW
AUGUHUN	469 NW	CHRISTINE	470 SW
AUGUSTINA	471 NW	CHRISTOPHER	471 SW
AUSTIN	470 SW	CIRCLE	470 NE
AUSTIN	469 NW	CIRCLE	470 NE
AUTOMOBILE	472 SW	CIVIC	470 NW
AUTUMN	470 NE	CIVIC CENTER	469 SE
AVONDALE	472 SW	CLAEYS	470 SW
B CT.	470 SE	CLARPOINTE	470 SE
BACH	471 SW	CLINE	471 SW
BACK	471 SW	CLORIA	470 NW
BADE	470 NE	CLOVERLY CIR.	469 NE
BAIRD	469 SE	COLEEN	472 SE
BALWIN	469 SE	COLMAN	472 NW
BARBARY	470 NW	COLPAERT	470 NE
BARFIELD	470 NE	COLUMBUS	472 SE
DARO	470 SE	COMMON	470 NE
BART	471 SW	CONNEL	469 NE
BART	471 SW	CONNER	471 SE
BARTHOLOMAEI	469 NW	CONTINENTAL	469 NW
BATES	469 NW	CONTINENTAL	472 SW
BATES CT	471 NW	COOLIDGE	477 NW
BAYLISS	471 NW	CORRAINE	469 SW
BECKER	472 SW	COSGROVE	469 NE
BEEBE	469 NE	COTTAGE LN.	472 NE
BEECHWOOD	471 SW	COUSINO	469 NW
BEHRENDT	471 SW	COWLIER	472 SE
BEIRMAN	470 NW	COVENTRY	469 NW
BELLEAU	469 NW	CRAIG	470 NE
BELMONT	472 SW	CROMIE	469 SW
BENNINGTON	470 NW	CRUNALT	471 SW
BERKSHIRE	470 SE	CRYSTAL	471 SW
BERNICE	470 SE	CUNNINGHAM	469 SW
BERRY	472 NE	CURIE	471 SE
BERWYN	469 NW	CURIE	471 NE
BETH	470 SE	CYMAN	469 SW
BICSAK	469 SW	DAHRAN	470 SE
BILLETTE	471 NW	DALE	472 NW
BINNEY	470 NW	DALLAS	471 SW
BIRCH	472 SE	DANN	472 NW
BLACKETT	472 SE	DARLA	471 NW
BLACKMAR	471 NE	DARLENE	470 SW
BLACKSTONE	473 SE	DARRYL	470 NE
BLAIR	469 NW	DAVY	469 NE
BLANCKE	470 NE	DAWN	472 NE
BLOOMFIELD	472 NE	DAWN	470 NF
BLOSSOM	470 NF	DAWSON	469 NW
BOLRE	469 SW	DEAN	471 SW
BOEWE	469 NW	DEARDEN	470 NW
BOLAM	469 SW	DEL CAPITIAN	470 NE
BOLAM	472 NE	DELL LANE	469 SW
BON BRAE	470 NE	DEMONT	470 SE
BON MAR	470 NE	DENMAR	470 SW
BONNIE	470 NE	DEQUINDRE	470 NE
BONNING	470 NE	DESMOND	470 NE
BRADNER	470 NE	DEWIGHT	469 SW
BRADNER	470 SE	DEXTER	470 NE
BRADNER	470 NE	DIEGEL	472 NE
BRAINWOOD	472 NE	DIENA	470 SE
BRAMBRIDGE	472 NE	DODGE	472 SW
BRETZ	470 NW	DOEPFER	471 SW
BRIARCLIFF	470 NW	DOLORES	471 NW
BRISTOL	470 SE	DOMINIC	470 NE
BROADMOOR	470 SE	DON	469 NW
BROHI	470 SE	DONNA	471 NW
BROWN	469 NW	DORMONT	470 SE
BRUCE	471 SW	DOUER	470 SE
BRUGEMAN	469 NE	DOVER	472 NE
BUCHANON	469 NW		

Street	Ref	Street	Ref
DOWLAND	472 NE	HARAM	469 NW
DOWLAND	470 SE	HARDER	469 SW
DOYLE	472 SE	HAROLD	472 SE
DUNDEE	472 NW	HAROLD	469 NW
DWYER	470 SW	HARRISON	471 NE
EARL	471 NW	HARTFORD	469 NE
EARL	470 SE	HARTILL	472 SF
EASTWOOD	471 SE	HARTILL	470 SE
EASY	470 NE	HARTLEIN	472 NE
EDGEMONT	470 SW	HARTLEIN	470 NE
EDGETON	470 NW	HARTLEIN	470 NE
EDISON	472 NE	HAVERHILL	469 SE
EDNA	469 NE	HAWTHORNE	470 SW
EDWIN	471 SW	HAYDEN	469 SW
EDWOOD	470 NW	HAYES	470 NE
EEGLOO	469 NW	HAYMAN	472 SE
EHLERT	472 SE	HEATHDALE	469 NE
EIFFEL	472 NW	HELEN	472 SW
EIFFEL	470 SE	HELEN	470 NE
EIFFEL CT.	470 SW	HELEN	470 NW
EIGHT MILE	469 NW	HENDRICKS	470 NE
EIGHT MILE RD.	472 SW	HERBERT	469 SW
ELDERWOOD	470 NE	HESSE	472 SW
ELEANOR	472 NE	HETTENBERGER	470 SW
ELEVEN MILE	470 NE	HEUSSNER	472 NE
ELLY	470 NW	HIGHLAND	472 NW
ELMER	472 SE	HILL	470 NW
ELMGROVE	469 SE	HILL	469 SE
ELROY	472 SE	HILLCREST	472 NE
ELZA	471 SE	HILLOCK	472 SE
ELZE	471 SE	HOBART	471 SE
EMMONE	471 SW	HOERNING	470 SE
ENGLEMAN	472 NW	HOLDEN	471 SW
ENGLEMAN	471 NE	HOLLY	472 NW
EPOM	472 SW	HOLMES	471 NE
ESCH	471 NW	HOLTWICK SHAWN	472 SW
ESSEX	471 SE	HOOVER	471 NW
ESSEX	471 NW	HOVEY	471 SE
EUREKA	470 NW	HUDSON	472 NW
EUREKA	471 NW	HUFF	470 SW
EVELYN	470 NE	HUGHES	471 NW
EXTER	469 NW	HUGHES	470 SW
FAIRFIELD	470 NW	HUNTINGTON	469 NW
FALMOUTH	470 SW	HUPP	472 SW
FARGO	472 NW	IMPERIAL	470 SW
FARNUM	470 SW	INDUSTRIAL HWY.	472 NE
FEDERAL	470 NW	IOWA	470 SW
FENWICH	469 SW	IOWA	470 NW
FIRWOOD	472 NE	IOWA	469 SW
FIRWOOD	470 NE	IRA	472 NE
FISHER	472 SW	IRENE	470 NE
FISHER	471 SE	IRMA	469 NW
FISK	472 SE	IRONWOOD	471 SE
FLANDERS	470 SW	IRVINGTON	470 SE
FORD	472 SE	IVANHOE	472 SE
FOURTEEN MILE RD.	469 NW	JACKSON	472 NW
FOX	471 NW	JACKSON	471 SE
FRAHO	470 NE	JADE CT.	469 NW
FRANCINE	469 NE	JAMES	469 SW
FRANGESCA	471 SE	JAN	470 SW
FRANK	470 NW	JANE	470 SW
FRANK	472 SW	JANET	469 SW
FRAHO	477 NW	JARVIS	471 SW
FRED	469 NW	JAY	470 SE
FREDA LUND	470 NW	JEAN	470 SW
FREEMAN	472 NE	JENNETT	469 NW
GAIL	469 NW	JENNY	470 NE
GAINBOROUGH	470 NE	JEWETT	471 SE
GANDER	472 SE	JIM PL.	470 NE
GARBOR	470 NE	JOANNE	471 SW
GARBOR	469 SW	JOHN B	472 SW
GARDEN COURT	471 NE	JOLIET	471 SW
GARRICK	471 SW	JONAS	471 NE
GEOFFRY	469 SW	JOY CT.	471 SW
GEOGIANA	472 SE	JOYCE	469 SW
GERALD	469 SW	JULIUS	472 SE
GERALDINE	472 SW	JUNE	469 SW
GIBSON	470 SE	KAISER	472 SE
GIBSON	472 NW	KALTZ	472 NW
GILBERT	471 SW	KARAM	470 NW
GILBERT	469 SW	KARAM BLVD.	470 SW
GIRARD	472 NW	KAREN	470 NW
GLENWOOD	470 SW	KAROS	470 NE
GLEDOE	470 NE	KATE	470 NE
GLOBE	469 NE	KATHLEEN	470 SE
GLOEDE	469 SW	KELSEY	472 SW
GOULSON	469 NW	HELSET	469 SW
GRABAR	469 NW	KELVIN	469 SW
GRACE	471 NW	KEN	472 SE
GRATH	470 NW	KENDALL	471 NW
GRAUM	470 SW	KENNEDY	469 SE
GREENBRIAR	469 NE	KENNEDY CIR.	470 NE
GREENBURG	472 NW	KENNEDY CIRCLE	469 SE
GREY	470 SW	KENNY	472 NW
GREY	469 SW	KENSINGTON	469 NW
GRIFFIN	470 NW	KIEFER	472 SE
GRINSELL	469 SW	KINGSLEY	469 SW
GROBBELL	472 SE	KNAPP	469 SW
GROBBELL	470 NE	KNOLLWOOD	469 NE
GROSEBECK HWY	470 SE	KNOXAL	472 SE
GRUENBURG	472 SW	KNOX	472 SE
GUNSTON	470 NW	LA ROSE	469 SW
GUY CT.	471 NW	LACHENE	472 NW
HAFF	470 NE	LACHENE CT.	470 NW
HALMICH	469 NE	LANCASTER	470 NW
HANFORD	471 NW	LARK CT.	471 SE
HANFORD	470 SE	LASALLE	472 SE
HANLEY	470 SE	LAUREN	470 SE
HANLEY	472 NE	LAWSON	472 SE
HANOVER	470 NW	LEBANON	470 NW
		LED	470 NW

Street	Ref
LEFEVER	471 SW
LEISURE	470 SE
LEONARD	472 SE
LIBERTY	469 SW
LILA CT.	471 NW
LILLIAN	471 NW
LINCOLN	471 NW
LINDA	469 SE
LINDERMAN	470 NW
LINVILLE	469 SW
LLOYD	471 SW
LOGUE	471 SW
LOIS	472 NW
LOIS CT.	470 SW
LONGVIEW	469 SE
LORETTA	471 NW
LORNA	469 SE
LORRAINE	472 NW
LOS ANGELES	471 SW
LOSCH	472 SE
LOSOLAS	470 SW
LOUISIANA	472 NW
LOUISE	470 NE
LOWE	470 NE
LOZIER	471 SE
LUND	470 NW
LUTE	470 NE
LUTZ	469 NW
LYNCH	470 NW
LYNN	470 NE
LYONS CIR.	469 NW
MAC ARTHUR	472 SW
MACKENZIE	469 SW
MACKENZIE W.	469 SW
MACKERSIE	471 NE
MADDOX	469 NW
MADELINE	472 NW
MAE	472 NW
MALVINA	472 NE
MARCIA	470 SW
MARCY	469 SE
MARAN	469 SE
MARIE	472 SW
MARIGOLD	472 NW
MARYLYN	470 NW
MARINO	472 SW
MARLA	470 NW
MARKLENE	469 NW
MARLIN	471 SW
MARLOW	469 SW
MARROROEO	470 NE
MARSHA	469 SW
MARSHALL	472 SE
MART CT	471 SE
MARTAN	470 SW
MARTIN	471 NW
MASCH	471 NW
MASE	470 NE
MASONIC	470 NE
MATILDA	469 SW
MAUKFTA	470 SE
MAVIS	470 SE
MAXWELL	471 SE
MC KINLEY	472 NE
MCMILLA	470 NE
MEADOW	471 SW
MEADOWBROOK	470 NW
MECKL	472 NE
MELODY	470 NE
MELVA	471 SE
MEMPHIS	471 NE
MENGE	471 NE
MERRICK	469 SW
MERRHUM	470 NW
METTER	472 SE
MEUTHEN	471 SW
MICHAEL	472 SE
MILTON	469 SW
MONTROSE	477 SE
MORGAN	470 NE
MOROSO	470 NE
MORRISSRY	472 SW
MOULIN	472 SW
MURIEL	469 SW
MURIEL	471 SW
MURTHUM	470 NE
MYRAND	472 SE
MYSTIC	470 NW
NAGEL	472 SW
NANCY	470 NE
NELSON	470 NE
NEW CASTLE	470 NW
NEWBERN	470 SW
NEWLAND	470 SW
NEWPORT	470 NE
NICLA	471 NW
NINE MILE	471 SE
NORBERT	470 SW
NORMA	470 SE
NORRID CIR.	470 NE
NORTH HAMPTON	470 NW
NORWOOD	469 NW
NOTTINGHAM CIR.	472 SW
NOTTINGHAM CIR. E.	469 SW
NOVAK	472 SE
NUMMER	472 SE
OAKLAND	472 SE
OAKVIEW	469 NW
OCALLA	472 NW

WARREN

Street	Grid		Street	Grid		Street	Grid
OHMER	469 NW		SHAVER	470 NW		WINIFRED	471 SW
OLIVE	470 NW		SHAW	470 NW		WINNIE	470 SW
ONGE CIR.	470 NE		SHAWN	470 NW		WINNIE	470 NW
ORCHARD	471 SE		SHEFFIELD	470 NW		WINSLOW	479 SE
ORR	471 NW		SHELBOURNE	470 SE		WINTERFIELD	469 SW
ORVYLLE	469 SW		SHELL	471 NW		WINTERS	469 SW
OTIS	471 SW		SHERICAW	470 SE		WINTERS CT.	469 SW
OTTER	469 NW		SHERMAN	472 SW		WIXSON	469 NW
PACKARD	471 SE		SHERWOOD	471 NE		WOGAST	470 NW
PAGELS	469 NE		SHOENHERR	470 NW		WONDER	470 SE
PAIGE	471 SE		SHORT	470 NW		WOOD	471 SE
PALAMINO	472 NE		SIAGKRIS	469 NW		WOODHOUSE	469 SW
PALL	469 SW		SIDONIE	472 SE		WOODINGHAM	471 NW
PALM BEACH	470 SW		SMITH	470 NW		WOODROW WILSON	471 SW
PANAMA	471 NE		ST. ANDREWS	472 SE		WOODRUFF	471 SW
PARENT	469 SW		ST. ANNE'S	469 NE		YACHT	471 SE
PARKER	470 NE		ST. CLEMENS	472 NW		YONKA	469 NW
PARKSIDE	470 NE		ST. VINCENT	469 NW		YOUNG	472 NW
PARKVIEW	469 SW		STAMFORD	470 SW		YUETTE	470 SE
PATRICIA	471 NW		STANLEY	470 SE		YVONNE	470 SE
PAUL	469 SW		STARTFORD	469 SW		ZAGAISKI	471 NE
PAULINE	469 SE		STATE PARK	472 NW		ZINK	470 NE
PEARL	471 SW		STEELE	470 SE		12 1/2 MILE RD.	469 SW
PECK	470 NE		STEPHEN	471 SE			
PECK	469 NE		STEWART	472 NE			
PEMBROKE	469 SW		STILWELL	469 SW			
PENROSE	470 SE		STOLZENFELD	471 SW			
PERRY	470 NE		STOUT	470 SW			
PETER KALTZ	470 NE		STRATHMOOR	469 SW			
PETERS	471 SE		STREEFKERK	469 NE			
PINE HILL	470 NW		STRICKER	470 NE			
PINEGREE	472 NE		STUDUBAKER	471 SE			
PINEVIEW	471 NE		SUBURBAN	470 SE			
PINEWOOD	471 SE		SUNBURST	471 NW			
PINTO	470 NW		SUNBURY	469 SW			
PLEASANT	470 SE		SUNNY	469 NE			
PLUMOFF	471 SW		SUNSET	470 NE			
POPLAR	471 SW		SUPERIOR	472 NW			
POTOMAC	472 NE		SUROW CHECK	470 NW			
POTOMAC	471 NW		SUSAN	470 SW			
PRAIRE	472 NE		SYLVAN	470 SW			
PRESCOTO	471 SW		SYRACUSE	471 SE			
PRIMROSE	470 NE		TALBOT	470 NE			
PROSPECT	472 SW		TALLMAN	472 NW			
PROSPECT	471 SE		TANNEY	471 SW			
RACINE	470 NE		TAYLOR	461 NW			
RACINE	469 SE		TECLA	472 NE			
RAY	470 SE		TEFFT	470 NE			
RAYBURN	472 NW		TEN MILE RD.	471 NW			
READER	469 NW		THEUT	471 SE			
READY	471 SE		THIRTEEN MILE RD.	470 NE			
RED RUN	470 NW		THOMAS	471 SW			
REGAL	470 NE		TIMKEN	471 SE			
REID	460 NW		TOEPFER	471 SE			
REPUBLIC	472 SW		TOM ALLEN	471 NW			
REPUBLIC	471 SE		TOWNSEND	469 SE			
REVERE	469 NW		TREMBLETON	470 NW			
REYNOLDS	471 SW		TROPEA	479 SE			
RICHARD	472 NW		TROQUIS	470 NE			
RICHARD	470 SW		TTECLA	470 NE			
RIDGEFIELD	472 NE		TUZEDO	469 NW			
RIDGEFIELD	470 SE		TWELVE MILE RD.	470 SE			
RIGGS	471 NW		UNDERWOOD	469 SW			
FINKE	471 NE		UNITY	472 NW			
RIO	470 NW		UNIVERSAL	469 SW			
RIVARD	472 SW		UNIVERSITY	469 SW			
RIVER	470 NW		URBANEK	471 SW			
ROAN	472 NW		VAGAS	470 NW			
ROBERTSON	469 SW		BALENTE	470 NE			
ROBIN	472 NW		BAN DYKE	471 NE			
ROBINETTE	469 NW		VANLAAN	469 SW			
ROBINWOOD	470 NW		VENTURA	470 NW			
ROLF	469 NW		VERMONT	470 SW			
ROMANO	471 NW		VERNON	471 SE			
ROME	471 SW		VICTORY	471 SE			
ROSE	470 NE		VILLA	470 NW			
ROSE MARIE	472 NW		VIRGINIA	471 SW			
GOSEBERRY	472 SE		VOERNER	471 NE			
ROSELAWN	470 NE		VULCAN	472 NW			
ROSENBUSCH	470 NE		WAGNER	470 NW			
ROSSELLO	470 NE		WALCO	472 NE			
ROY	470 NE		WALTER	470 NE			
RUEHLE	470 NW		WALTHAM	472 SE			
RUGBY	470 NE		WALTZ	471 SW			
RUNEY	469 SW		WARD	479 SW			
RVINGTON	470 SW		WAREHAM	469 NW			
RYAN	471 NW		WARKOP	470 NW			
SADDLER	469 SW		WARNER	471 SW			
SANKAVER	470 NW		WARNER	471 NW			
SANTA ANA	470 SW		WARREN BLVD.	472 NW			
SARATOGA	470 NW		WARREN BLVD.	472 NW			
SARSFIELD	472 SE		WASHINGTON	470 NW			
SCHMEMAN	472 SW		WASMUND	471 SW			
SCHOEN HERR	472 NE		WAURETA	469 NW			
SCHOENHERR	470 NE		WEIER	470 SE			
SCHOOL	469 NW		WELLER	472 SE			
SCHULTZ	471 SW		WELLINGTON	472 AW			
SCOTT	470 SW		WELLSTON	470 NW			
SCRIUO	469 NW		WELSH	469 SE			
SEBASTIAN	470 NE		WEST MINISTER	471 SW			
SENECA	470 NE		WESTBROOK	469 SW			
SERVICE RD.	470 SE		WESTMINSTER	471 SE			
SEVENTH	469 NE		WEXFORD	471 NW			
SEYBURN	460 SE		WHITLEY	470 NE			
SHACKETT	470 SW		WIEK	471 NW			
SHADY	460 SW		WILLARD	472 SE			
SHARON	470 NE		WILSON	472 NW			

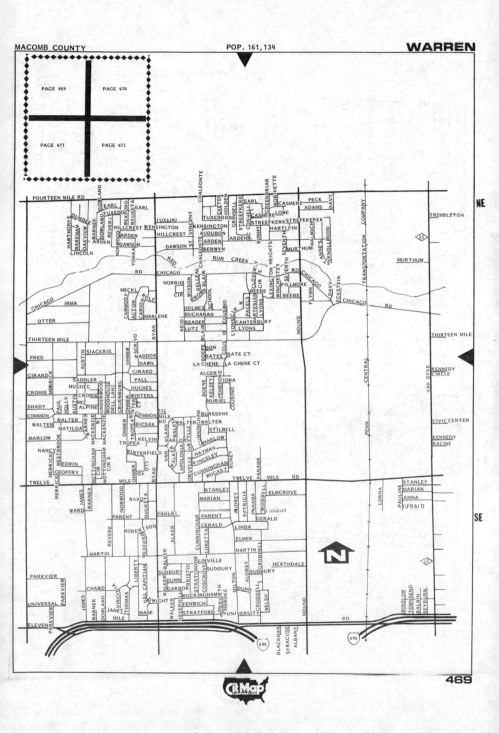

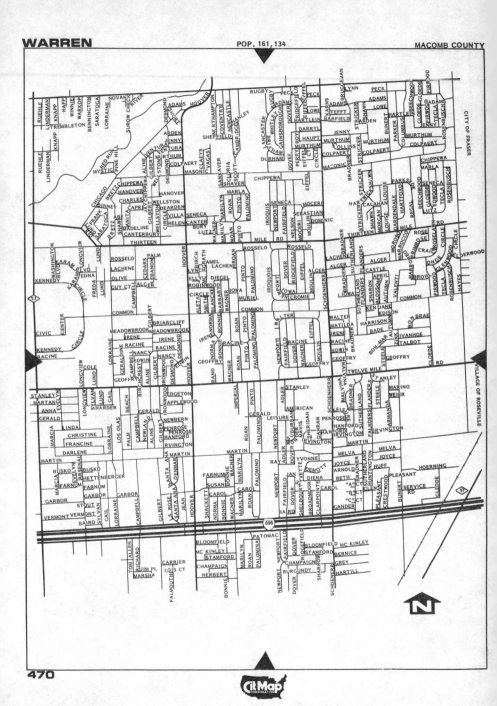

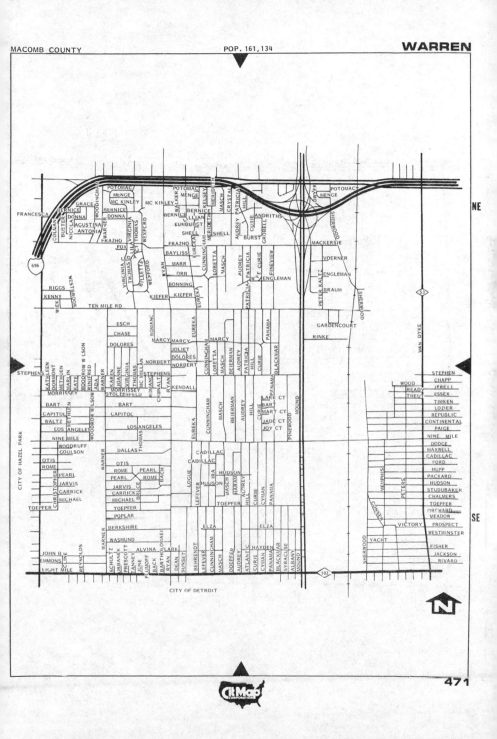

NE

SE

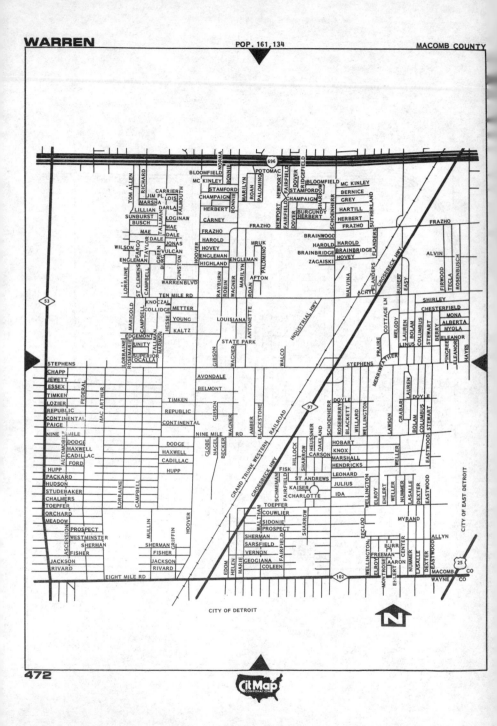

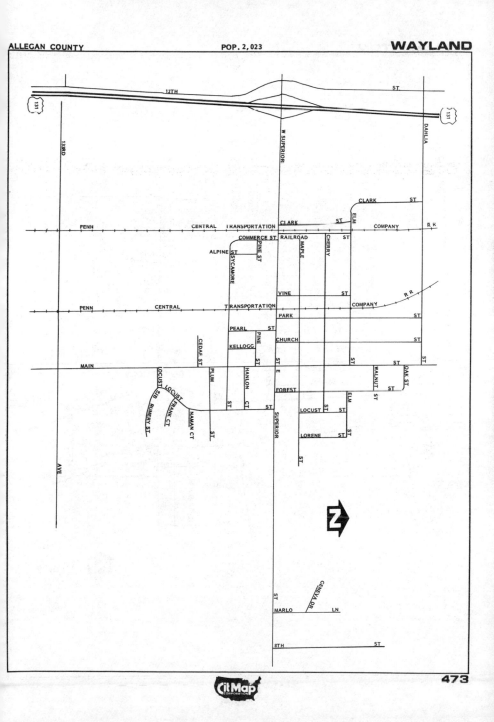

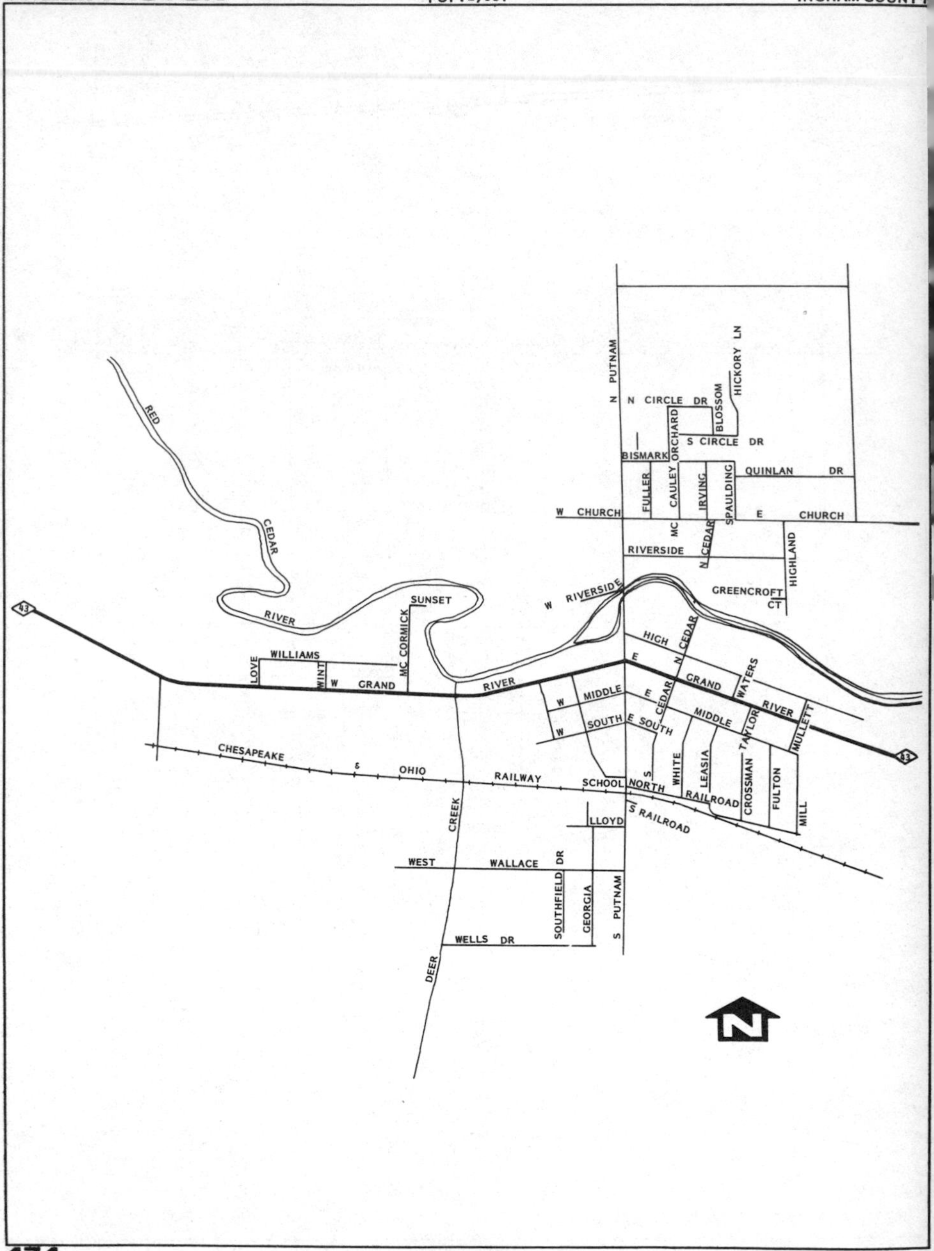
N PUTNAM
HICKORY LN
N CIRCLE DR
BLOSSOM
ORCHARD
S CIRCLE DR
BISMARK
QUINLAN DR
FULLER
MC CAULEY
IRVING
SPAULDING
W CHURCH
E CHURCH
N CEDAR
RIVERSIDE
HIGHLAND
RED
CEDAR
RIVER
W RIVERSIDE
GREENCROFT CT
SUNSET
MC CORMICK
43
HIGH
CEDAR
WILLIAMS
LOVE
WINT
W GRAND
RIVER
E GRAND
WATERS
RIVER
MULLETT
W MIDDLE
E MIDDLE
W SOUTH
E SOUTH
S CEDAR
TAYLOR
CHESAPEAKE & OHIO RAILWAY
SCHOOL
NORTH
WHITE
LEASIA
CROSSMAN
FULTON
RAILROAD
S RAILROAD
MILL
CREEK
LLOYD
WEST WALLACE DR
SOUTHFIELD
GEORGIA
S PUTNAM
WELLS DR
DEER
N

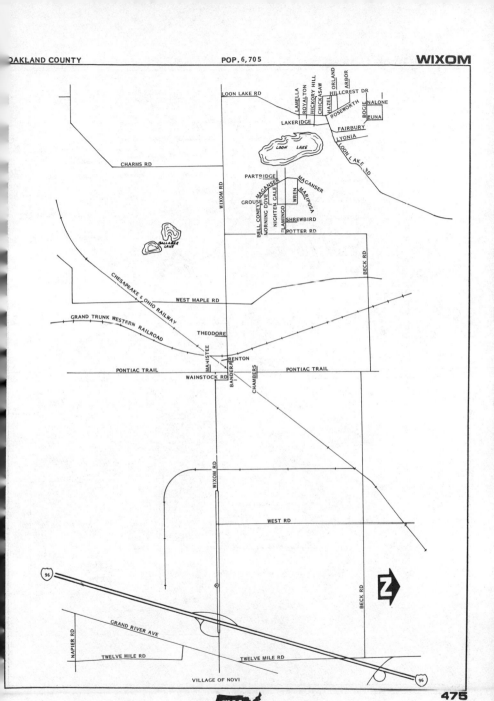

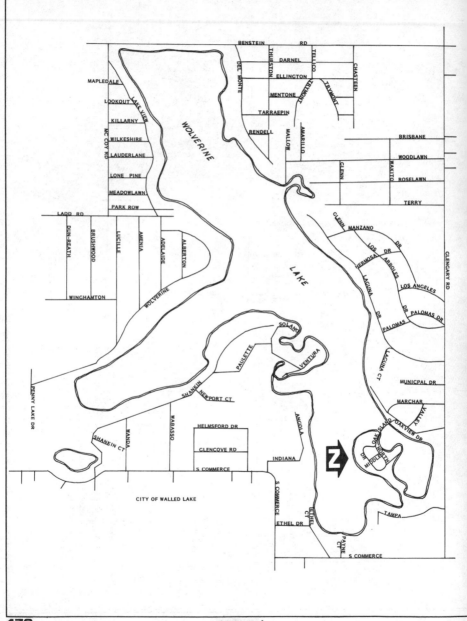

CITY OF WOODHAVEN

CITY OF RIVERVIEW

CITY OF TRENTON

75

KING RD

TOLEDO HWY

POPULAR
LILAC
LARCHE
TULLIWOOD
HALL
BIRCH
DR
BELLWOOD
NOTTINGHAM
CROSSWICK
QUAIL HOLLOW
BELLWOOD
CARTER
RD
WILLOW
ORCHARD
CHIPMUNK TRAIL
CHIPMUNK TRAIL
HILLCREST
LORETTA
REINHARDT
HILLCREST
CRANBROOK
OAK
NELSON
SOUTHPOINT
FOX CROFT
CANTERBURY
DEVONSHIRE
HUNTINGTON
OLDMILL
HALL

SHERWOOD
WELLINGTON
TIFFANY
MILLBURY
CAMDEM
WOODLAND
TIFFANY
DANBURY
MAYFAIR
TRUWOOD
TIFFANY
CARTER RD
MONTEREY DR
ZIEGLER AVE

ST
WEST RD

FAIRWAY
JUDITH
FAIRWAY
WOODSTOCK
OLD FORCE
FAIRWAY
KINGSTON
CHESTNUT
DORCHESTER
HERITAGE
KING
BEECHWOOD
WHITEHALL
FAIRWAY
GRIX RD
WESTWOOD
PROVINCIAL
RYGATE
INDEPENDENCE
HANOVER
CABOT
CABOT
HAMILTON
CHAPEL
CRESCENT
CAMBRIDGE
HAMPTON
COLONIAL
IRON GATE

DETROIT TOLEDO & IRONTON RR
DETROIT TOLEDO & IRONTON RR

VAN HORN RD

MONTEBELLO
RD
RD
RD
ORLEANS
GOODFELLOW
ARLINGTON
BRADFORD DR
ALBERT
SALEM
MAYWOOD
FAIRGROVE
REECK
FOREST HILL
OTTEBERGER
LANCASTER
LANCASTER
HYDE PARK CT
HYDE PARK
AMBER

MARTIN
MAYWOOD
COVE
BLAKLEY
KIM
WILLOW
DOVER
ANGELA
LAURIE
BODSFORD
BODSFORD
REECK
ALLEN
MAYWOOD
SANDRA

HALL RD
DETROIT–TOLEDO EXPRESSWAY
REAUME RD

85
85

VREELAND RD

75

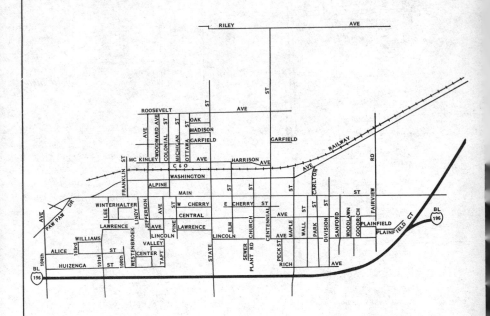

Jenison is the only unicorporated city in our book of Michigan city maps. Since it is a growing suburb of Grand Rapids, with a population of 16,339, we felt it necessary to include this section.

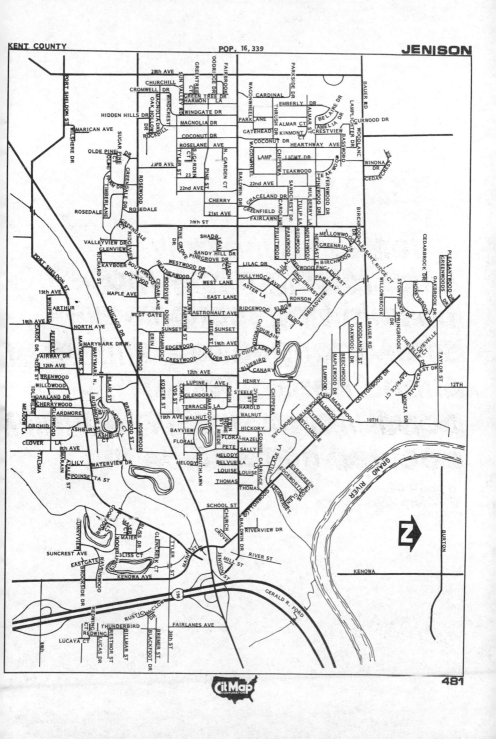

The Michigan city maps in the following section have been arranged two cities to a page. These cities have a population of one thousand to nineteen hundred.

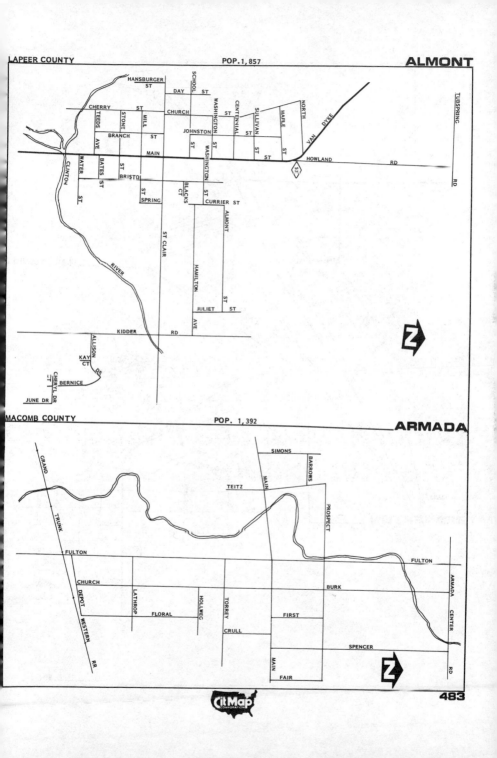

HANSBURGER ST

SCHOOL ST

DAY ST

TUBSPRING RD

CHERRY ST

TEEDS AVE

STONE

MILL ST

CHURCH ST

WASHINGTON ST

CENTENNIAL ST

SULLIVAN ST

MAPLE ST

NORTH ST

VAN DYKE

BRANCH ST

JOHNSTON ST

CLINTON

WATER ST

BATES ST

BRISTOL ST

MAIN ST

WASHINGTON ST

ST

HOWLAND RD

RD

SPRING ST

BLACKS CT

ST

CURRIER ST

ALMONT ST

ST CLAIR

HAMILTON

RIVER

JULIET ST

AVE

KIDDER RD

ALLISON

KAY CT

CHERYL ST

BERNICE

JUNE DR

Z

GRAND

SIMONS

BARROWS

MAIN

TEITZ

PROSPECT

TRUNK

FULTON

FULTON

CHURCH

DEPOT

LATHROP

HOLLWEG

TORREY

BURK

ARMADA CENTER RD

WESTERN

FLORAL

FIRST

CRULL

RR

SPENCER

MAIN

FAIR

Z

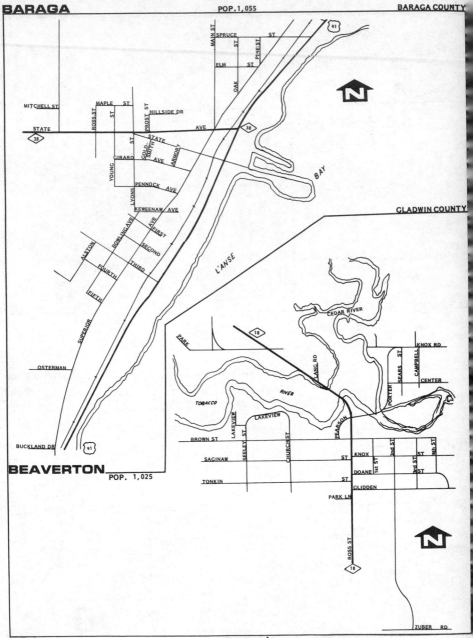

GLADWIN COUNTY

BEAVERTON
POP. 1,025

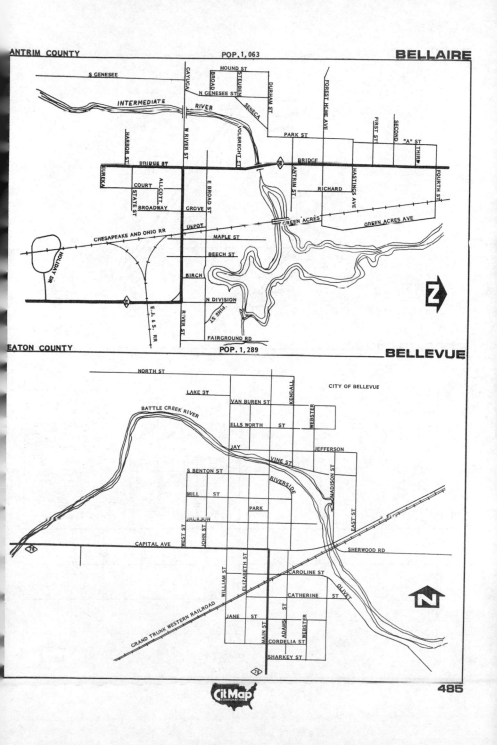

S GENESEE

INTERMEDIATE   RIVER

CAYUGA

MOUND ST

BROAD

STEUBEN

N GENESEE ST

DURHAM ST

SENECA

FOREST HOME AVE

VOLBRECHT ST

PARK ST

FIRST ST

SECOND

"A" ST

THIRD

HARBOR ST

W RIVER ST

BRIDGE ST   BRIDGE

ANTRIM ST

EUREKA

COURT

ALLCOTT

E BROAD ST

RICHARD

HASTINGS AVE

FOURTH ST

STATE ST   BROADWAY

GROVE

DEPOT   GREEN ACRES   GREEN ACRES AVE

CHESAPEAKE AND OHIO RR

MAPLE ST

BEECH ST

HOLIDAY DR

BIRCH

N DIVISION

E.A. & S. RR

RIVER ST

PINE ST

FAIRGROUND RD

NORTH ST

LAKE ST

BATTLE CREEK RIVER

VAN BUREN ST

KENDALL

CITY OF BELLEVUE

ELLS WORTH   ST

WEBSTER

JAY

JEFFERSON

VINE ST

S BENTON ST

RIVERSIDE

MADISON ST

MILL   ST

PARK

EAST ST

JACKSON

WEST ST

JOHN ST

CAPITAL AVE

SHERWOOD RD

WILLIAM ST

ELIZABETH ST

CAROLINE ST

OLIVET

CATHERINE   ST

ST

JANE   ST

ADAMS ST

WEBSTER

MAIN ST

CORDELIA ST

SHARKEY ST

GRAND TRUNK WESTERN RAILROAD

N

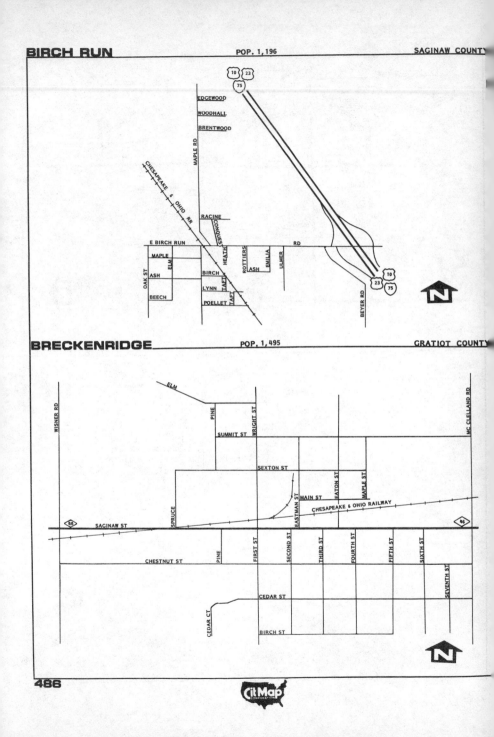

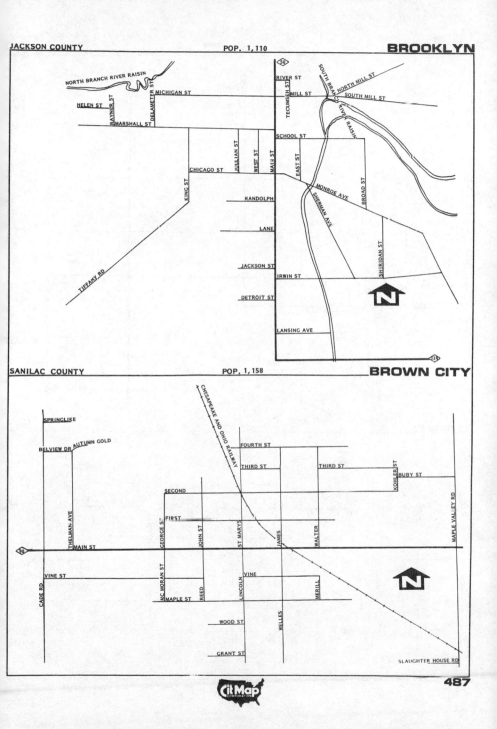

NORTH BRANCH RIVER RAISIN

HELEN ST

RAYNER ST

DELAMETER ST

MICHIGAN ST

MARSHALL ST

RIVER ST

TECUMSEH ST

MILL ST

SOUTH BRANCH

NORTH MILL ST

SOUTH MILL ST

RIVER RAISIN

SCHOOL ST

JULLIAN ST

WEST ST

MAIN ST

EAST ST

CHICAGO ST

KING ST

MONROE AVE

SHERMAN AVE

BROAD ST

RANDOLPH

LANE

SHERIDAN ST

TIFFANY RD

JACKSON ST

IRWIN ST

DETROIT ST

LANSING AVE

BROWN CITY

SPRINGLIKE

BELVIEW DR

AUTUMN GOLD

CHESAPEAKE AND OHIO RAILWAY

FOURTH ST

THIRD ST

THIRD ST

KOHLER ST

BUBY ST

SECOND

THELMAN AVE

FIRST

GEORGE S

JOHN ST

ST MARYS

JAMES

WALTER

MAPLE VALLEY RD

MAIN ST

CADE RD

VINE ST

MC MORAN ST

MAPLE ST

REED

LINCOLN

VINE

MERILL

WOOD ST

WELLES

GRANT ST

SLAUGHTER HOUSE RD

CitMap
CORPORATION

487

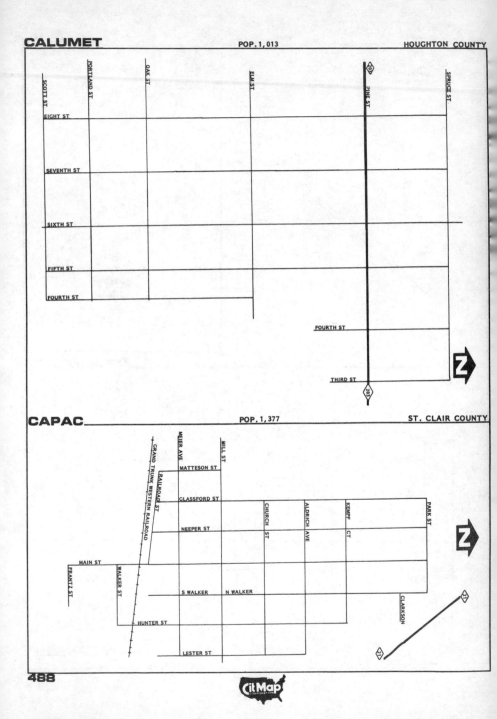

CALUMET

POP. 1,013

HOUGHTON COUNTY

CAPAC

POP. 1,377

ST. CLAIR COUNTY

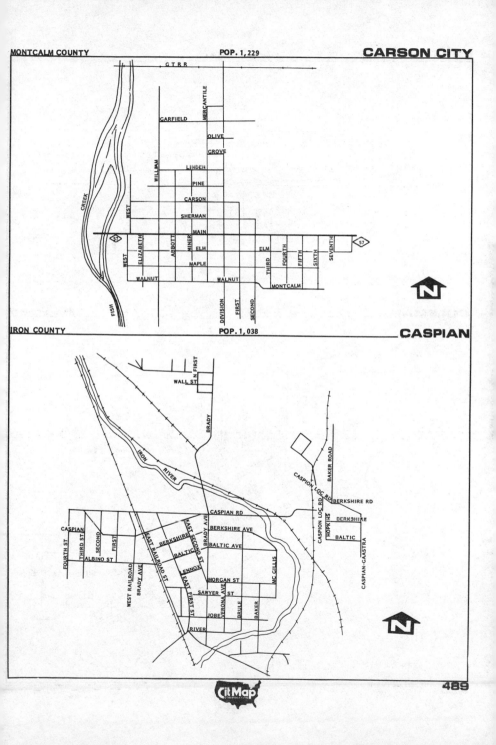

MONTCALM COUNTY   POP. 1,229   **CARSON CITY**

IRON COUNTY   POP. 1,038   **CASPIAN**

489

CENTREVILLE

POP. 1,202

ST. JOSEPH COUNTY

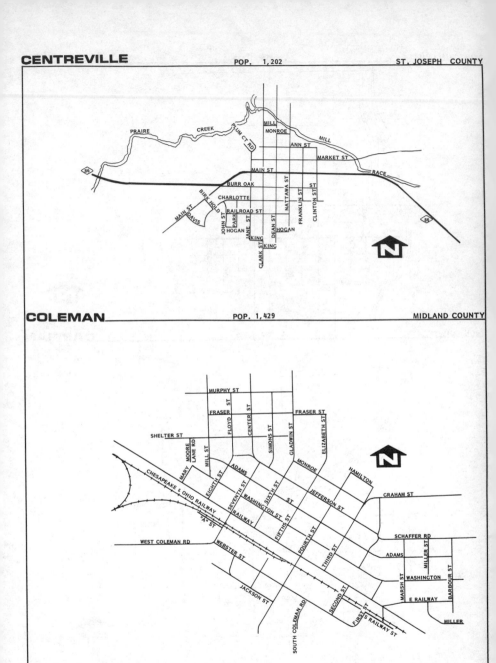

COLEMAN

POP. 1,429

MIDLAND COUNTY

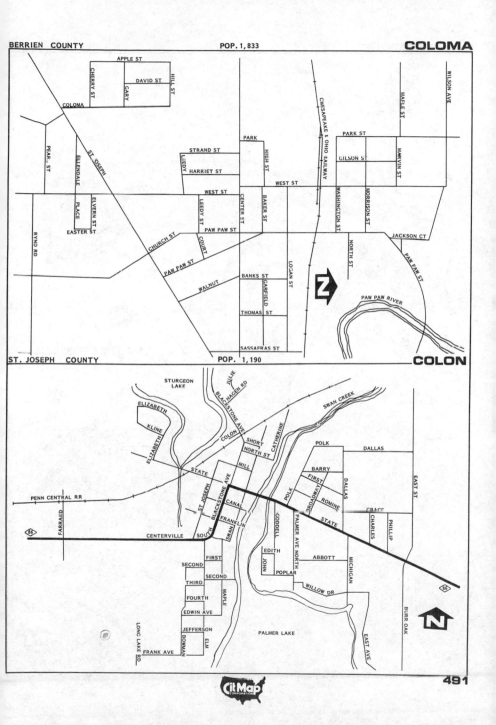

APPLE ST

CHERRY ST

DAVID ST

GARY

HILL ST

COLOMA

PEAR. ST

ST. JOSEPH

ELLENDALE

ELVERN ST

PLACE

EASTER ST

RYND RD

CHURCH ST

PAW PAW ST

LEEDY ST

COURT

WALNUT

STRAND ST

LEEDY

HARRIET ST

WEST ST

CENTER ST

PAW PAW ST

BANKS ST

GARFIELD

THOMAS ST

SASSAFRAS ST

PARK

HIGH ST

WEST ST

BAKER ST

LOGAN ST

CHESAPEAKE & OHIO RAILWAY

WASHINGTON ST

NORTH ST

PARK ST

GILSON ST

MORRISON ST

JACKSON CT

MAPLE ST

WILSON AVE

MARVIN ST

PAW PAW ST

PAW PAW RIVER

N

STURGEON LAKE

ELIZABETH

KLINE

ELIZABETH

JULIE

BLACKSTONE AVE

HAGEN RD

COLON

SHORT

NORTH ST

MILL

STATE

ST. JOSEPH

BLACKSTONE AVE

CANAL

FRANKLIN

SOUTH

CATHERINE

SWAN CREEK

POLK

BARRY

FIRST

POLK

SYCAMORE

ROMINE

STATE

GODDELL

PALMER AVE NORTH

EDITH

JOHN

POPLAR

ABBOTT

WILLOW DR

DALLAS

DALLAS

GRACE

CHARLES

PHILLIP

EAST ST

MICHIGAN

PENN CENTRAL RR

FARRAND

86

CENTERVILLE

FIRST

SECOND

SECOND

THIRD

FOURTH

EDWIN AVE

JEFFERSON

FRANK AVE

BOWMAN

MAPLE

ELM

LONG LAKE RD

PALMER LAKE

EAST AVE

BURR OAK

86

N

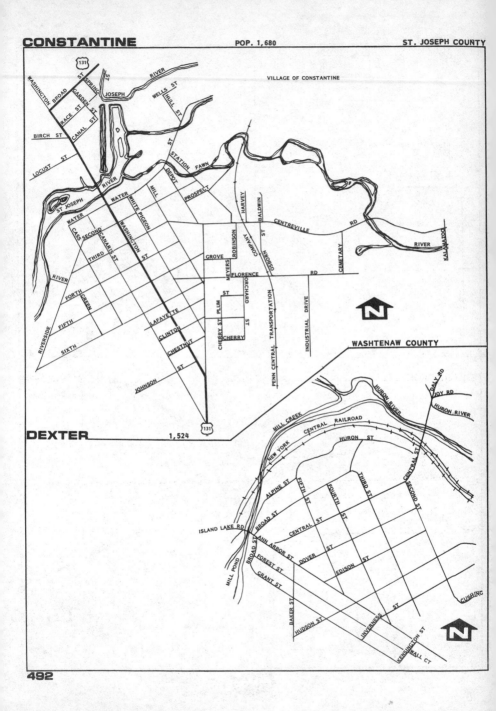

VILLAGE OF CONSTANTINE

DEXTER 1,524

WASHTENAW COUNTY

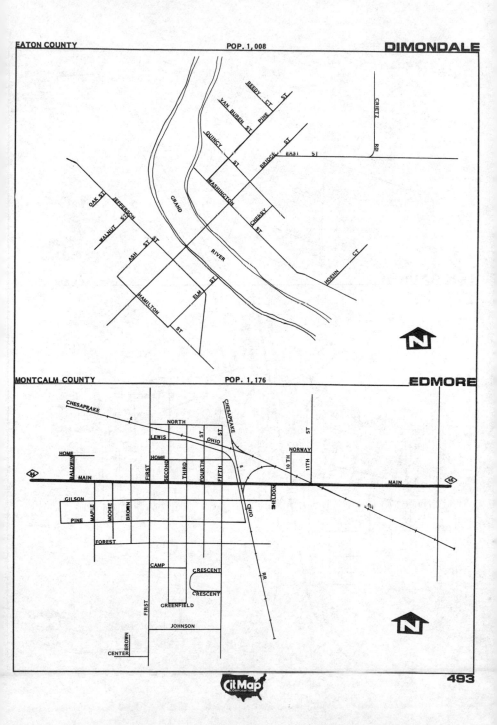

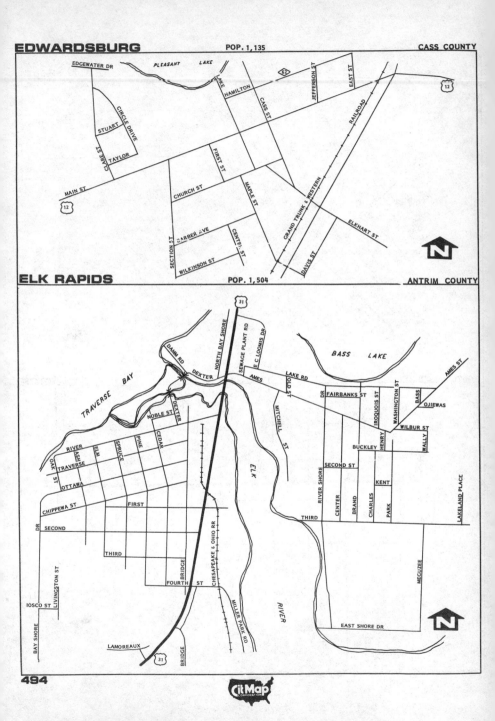

EDWARDSBURG

POP. 1,135

EDGEWATER DR
PLEASANT LAKE
62
12

CIRCLE DRIVE
STUART
TAYLOR
CLARKE ST
LAKE
HAMILTON
CASS ST
JEFFERSON ST
EAST ST
RAILROAD

MAIN ST
12
FIRST ST
CHURCH ST
MAPLE ST
SECTION ST
BARBER AVE
CENTER ST
WILKINSON ST
GRAND TRUNK & WESTERN
ELKHART ST
DAVIS ST

ELK RAPIDS

POP. 1,504

31
DAMM RD
DEXTER
NORTH BAY SHORE
SEWAGE PLANT RD
E C LOOMIS DR
AMES
LAKE RD
BASS LAKE
AMES ST

TRAVERSE BAY
NOBLE ST
DEXTER
OLD ST
DR
FAIRBANKS ST
IROQUOIS ST
WASHINGTON ST
BASS
OJIEWAS
WILBUR ST
WALLY

RIVER
ASH
ELM
SPRUCE
PINE
CEDAR
MITCHELL ST
BUCKLEY
HENRY

OAK ST
TRAVERSE
OTTAWA
ELK
RIVER SHORE
SECOND ST
KENT

CHIPPEWA ST
FIRST
CENTER
BRAND
CHARLES
PARK
LAKELAND PLACE

DR
SECOND
THIRD

THIRD

LIVINGSTON ST
FOURTH ST
CHESAPEAKE & OHIO RR
BRIDGE
MECUIZEE

IOSCO ST
BAY SHORE
MILLER PARK RD
RIVER
EAST SHORE DR

LAMOREAUX
31
BRIDGE

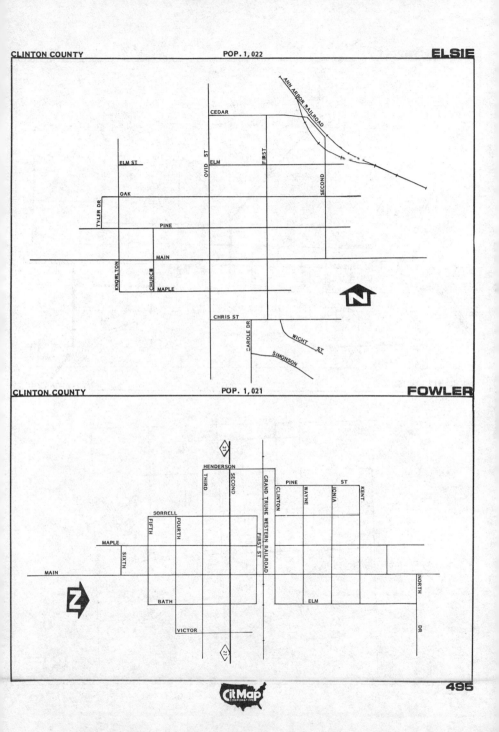

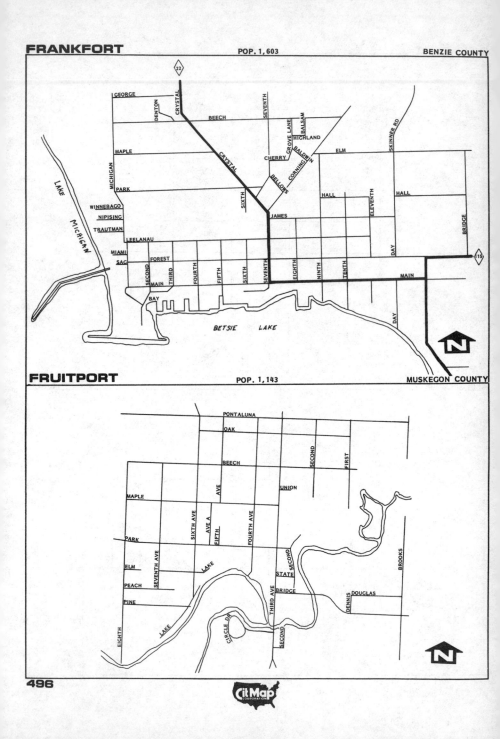

FRUITPORT

POP. 1,143

MUSKEGON COUNTY

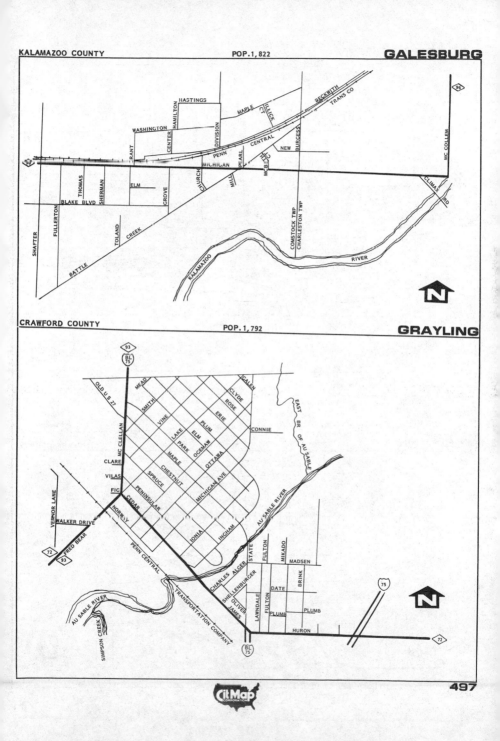

CRAWFORD COUNTY POP.1,792 **GRAYLING**

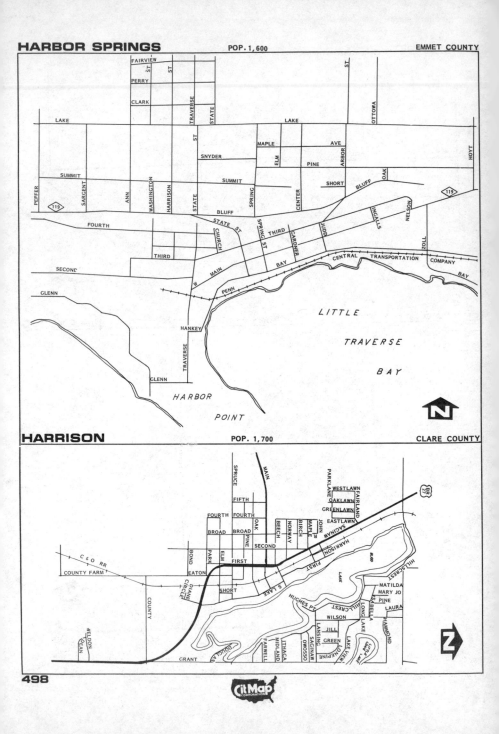

HARBOR SPRINGS

POP. 1,600

EMMET COUNTY

HARRISON

POP. 1,700

CLARE COUNTY

498

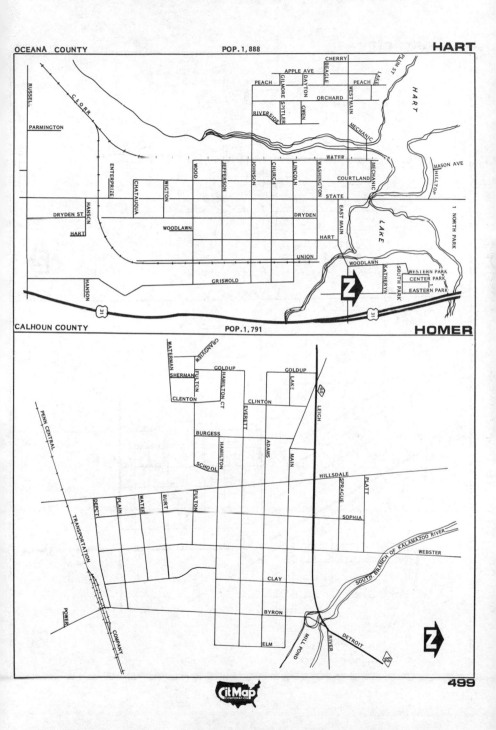

OCEANA COUNTY

POP. 1,888

CALHOUN COUNTY

POP. 1,791

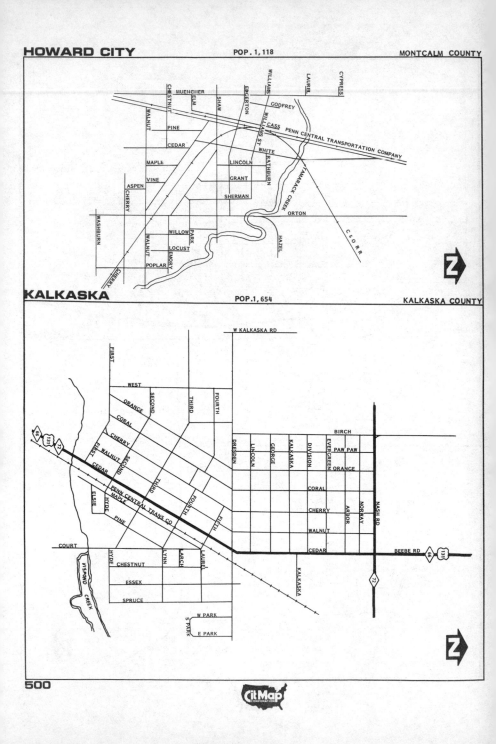

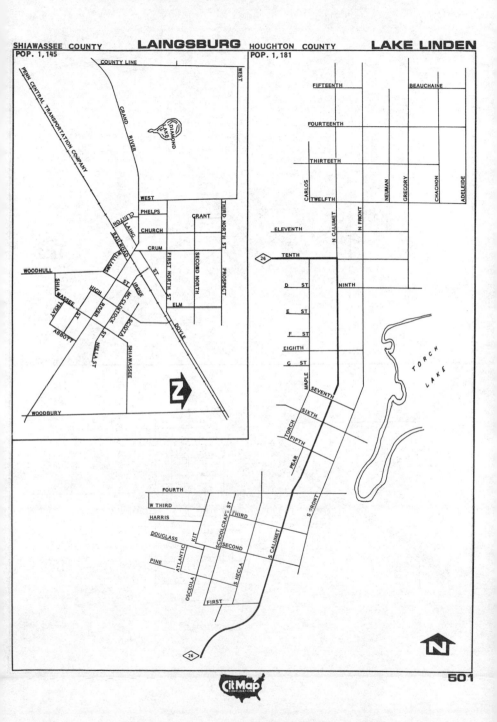

SHIAWASSEE COUNTY
POP. 1,145

LAINGSBURG

HOUGHTON COUNTY
POP. 1,181

LAKE LINDEN

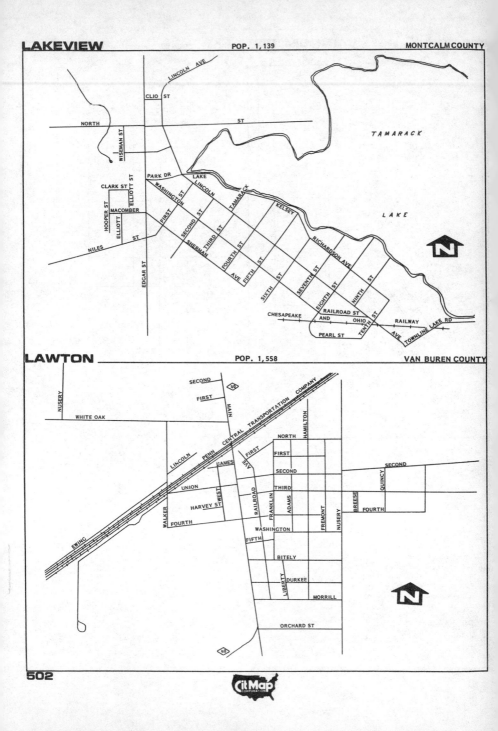

LAKEVIEW

LINCOLN AVE

CLIO ST

NORTH　　ST

TAMARACK

WISEMAN ST

PARK DR　LAKE

CLARK ST

HOOPER ST

ELLIOTT ST

MACOMBER

ELLIOTT

ST

NILES

EDGAR ST

WASHINGTON

LINCOLN

FIRST ST

SECOND ST

THIRD ST

SHERMAN

FOURTH ST

AVE FIFTH ST

SIXTH ST

TAMARACK

KELSEY

RICHARDSON AVE

SEVENTH ST

EIGHTH ST

NINTH ST

TENTH ST

LAKE

CHESAPEAKE

AND　OHIO

RAILROAD ST

PEARL ST

RAILWAY

TOWNLINE LAKE RD

AVE

LAWTON

SECOND

FIRST

NUSERY

WHITE OAK

LINCOLN

MAIN

PENN CENTRAL TRANSPORTATION COMPANY

HAMILTON

NORTH

FIRST

SECOND

THIRD

AVE FIRST

JAMES

UNION

WALKER

WEST

HARVEY ST

FOURTH

EWING

RAILROAD

FRANKLIN

ADAMS

WASHINGTON

FIFTH

BITELY

LIBERTY

DURKEE

MORRILL

ORCHARD ST

FREMONT

NUSERY

BREESE

QUINCY

SECOND

FOURTH

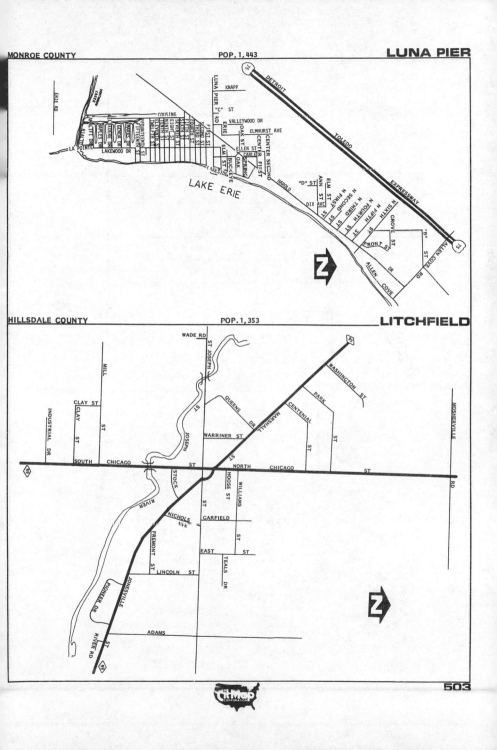

ERIE RD

DETROIT

TOLEDO

EXPRESSWAY

KNAPP

LUNA PIER RD

"C" ST

VALLEYWOOD DR

ELMHURST AVE

ERIE

OAK ST

ELLEN ST

CENTER

SECOND

FIRST

ELM ST

BUCKEYE

OAK

CARLE

SPRING

HAROLD

"D" ST

DIXIE

ANN ST

ELM ST

N FIRST AVE

N SECOND ST

N THIRD ST

N FOURTH ST

N FIFTH ST

N SIXTH ST

GROVE ST

FRONT ST

"B"

ALLEN COVE RD

ALLEN COVE

DR

75

75

COUSINO

BELLEVUE DR

OAKES DR

OAKS DR

SEVENTH ST

EIGHTH ST

NINTH ST

TENTH ST

ELEVENTH ST

FOURTEENTH ST

FIFTEENTH ST

CLIFF DR

LA PLAITTE

LA POINTE

FIRST ST

SECOND ST

THIRD ST

FOURTH ST

FIFTH ST

LAKEWOOD DR

PARKSIDE

LAKEWOOD DR

LAKE ERIE

Z

WADE RD

ST JOSEPH ST

39

WASHINGTON ST

MILL

CLAY ST

CLAY ST

QUEENS DR

MARSHALL ST

CENTENIAL

PARK

INDUSTRIAL DR

CLAY ST

WARRINER ST

JOSEPH ST

ST

MOSHERVILLE RD

SOUTH CHICAGO ST

NORTH CHICAGO ST

99

STOCK ST

HOOSE ST

WILLIAMS ST

RIVER

NICHOLS AVE

GARFIELD ST

FREMONT ST

EAST ST

TEALS DR

JONESVILLE DR

PIONEER DR

LINCOLN ST

ADAMS

RIVER RD

ST

99

Z

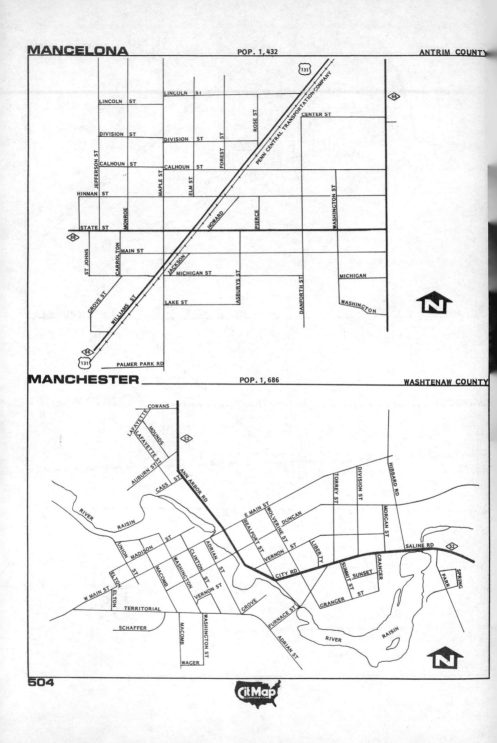

MANCHESTER   POP. 1,686   WASHTENAW COUNTY

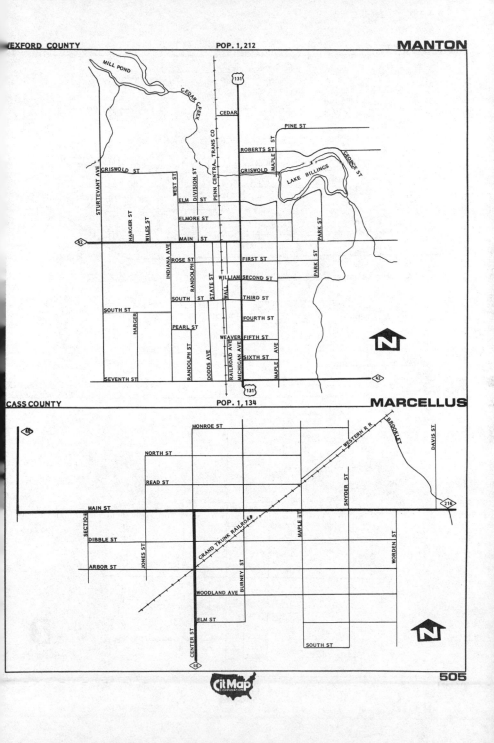

MILL POND

CEDAR CREEK

131

CEDAR

PINE ST

ROBERTS ST

STURTEVANT AVE

GRISWOLD ST

WEST ST

DIVISION ST

PENN CENTRAL TRANS CO

GRISWOLD

MAPLE ST

LAKE BILLINGS

GEORGE ST

ELM ST

ELMORE ST

HARGER ST

WILES ST

PARK ST

32

MAIN ST

INDIANA AVE

ROSE ST

RANDOLPH ST

FIRST ST

PARK ST

WILLIAM

SECOND ST

STATE ST

WALL

SOUTH ST

HARGER

SOUTH ST

THIRD ST

PEARL ST

FOURTH ST

RANDOLPH ST

DODDS AVE

WEAVER

FIFTH ST

RAILROAD AVE

MICHIGAN AVE

SIXTH ST

MAPLE AVE

32

SEVENTH ST

131

N

40

MONROE ST

WESTERN R R

BROOKLET

DAVIS ST

NORTH ST

READ ST

SNYDER ST

216

MAIN ST

SECTION

GRAND TRUNK RAILROAD

MAPLE ST

DIBBLE ST

JONES ST

WORDEN ST

ARBOR ST

BURNEY ST

WOODLAND AVE

ELM ST

CENTER ST

SOUTH ST

40

N

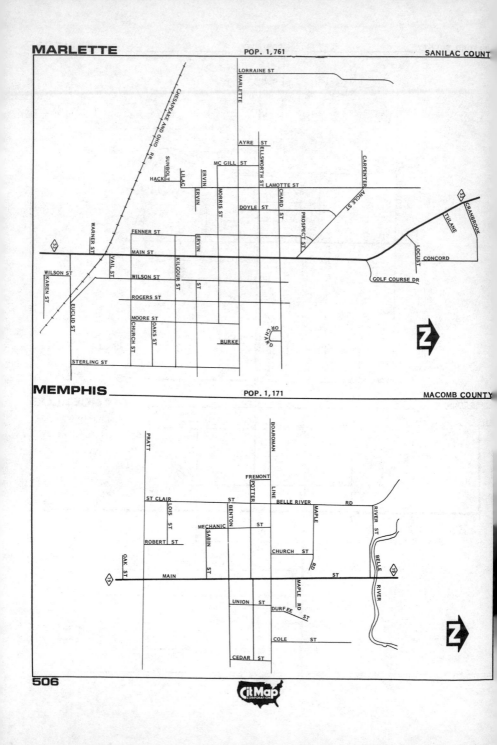

MARLETTE

SANILAC COUNT

LORRAINE ST

MARLETTE

CHESAPEAKE AND OHIO RR

AYRE ST

MC GILL ST

WELLSMORTH ST

SUNBOLT

LILAC

HACK

ERVIN

ERVIN

MORRIS ST

LAMOTTE ST

DOYLE ST

CHARD ST

PROSPECT ST

CARPENTER

ANGLE ST

CRANBROOK

TULANE

WARNER ST

FENNER ST

ERVIN

MAIN ST

VAIL ST

LOCUST

CONCORD

WILSON ST

KILGOUR ST

WILSON ST

ST

KAREN ST

ROGERS ST

GOLF COURSE DR

EUCLID ST

MOORE ST

OAKS ST

CHURCH ST

ORCHARD OR

BURKE

STERLING ST

MEMPHIS

MACOMB COUNTY

PRATT

BOARDMAN

FREMONT

POTTER

LINE

ST CLAIR

LOIS ST

ST

BENTON

BELLE RIVER RD

MAPLE

RIVER ST

MECHANIC

SABIN

ST

ROBERT ST

CHURCH ST

RD

OAK ST

MAIN

ST

BELLE RIVER

UNION ST

DURFEE ST

MAPLE RD

COLE ST

CEDAR ST

506

CitMap CORPORATION

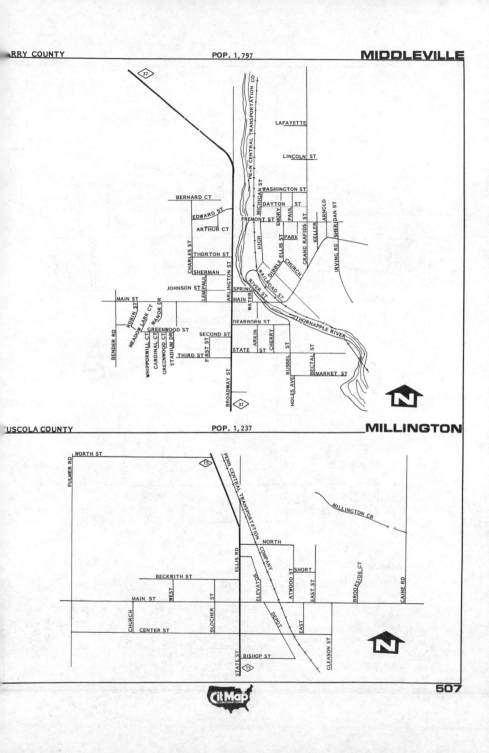

MIDDLEVILLE

37

LAFAYETTE

LINCOLN ST

PE-N CENTRAL TRANSPORTATION CO

BERNARD CT

EDWARD ST

ARTHUR CT

WASHINGTON ST

MICHIGAN
DAYTON ST

PAUL

FREMONT ST

EMORY

ARNOLD

KELLER

SHERIDAN ST

CHARLES ST

THORTON ST

HIGH

PARK

GRAND RAPIDS ST

IRVING RD

SHERMAN

LEM PAUL

ELLIS ST

DIBBLE

CHURCH

SECOND ST

JOHNSON ST

ARLINGTON ST

SPRING

RAILROAD ST

RIVER ST

MAIN ST

ROBIN ST

MEADOW LARK CT

MAJOR DR

MAIN

WATER

BENDER RD

CARDINAL CT

GREENWOOD CT

STADIUM DR

GREENWOOD ST

DEARBORN ST

SECOND ST

THORNAPPLE RIVER

WHIPPORWILL CT

FIRST ST

THIRD ST

STATE

ARKIN
ST

CHERRY

RUSSEL ST

BECTAL ST

MARKET ST

BROADWAY ST

HOLES AVE

37

N

MILLINGTON

WORTH ST

FULMER RD

15

PENN CENTRAL TRANSPORTATION COMPANY

MILLINGTON CR

NORTH

BECKWITH ST

ELLIS RD

ELEVATOR

ATWOOD ST

SHORT

EAST ST

BROOKSIDE CT

CAINE RD

WEST

ST

MAIN ST

CHURCH

CENTER ST

BLOCHER

DEPOT

EAST

GLEASON ST

N

STATE RD

BISHOP ST

15

CitMap
CORPORATION

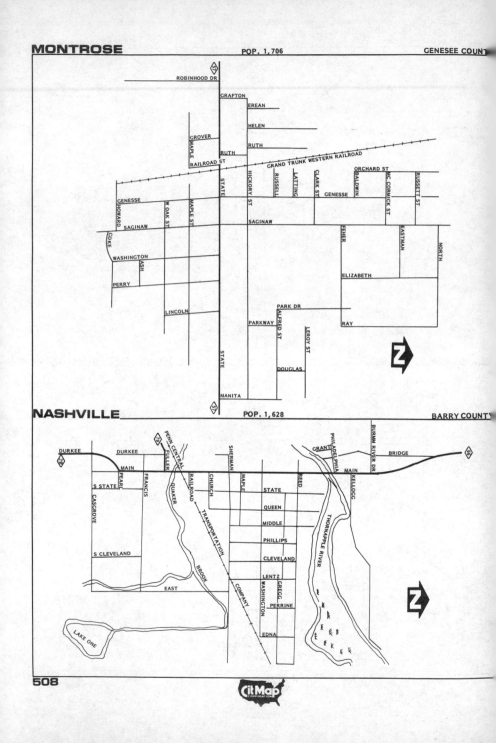

ROBINHOOD DR

GRAFTON

EREAN

HELEN

GROVER

RUTH

MAPLE

RUTH

RAILROAD ST

GRAND TRUNK WESTERN RAILROAD

ORCHARD ST

HICKORY ST

RUSSELL

LATTING

CLARK ST

BALDWIN

MC CORMICK ST

RUSSETT ST

STATE

GENESSE

GENESSE

HOWARD

W OAK ST

MAPLE ST

SAGINAW

SAGINAW

FEHER

EASTMAN

NORTH

COKE

WASHINGTON

ASH

ELIZABETH

PERRY

LINCOLN

PARK DR

ALFRED ST

PARKWAY

LEROY ST

RAY

DOUGLAS

MANITA

STATE

DURKEE

DURKEE

PENN CENTRAL

FULLER

SHERMAN

GRANT

PHILADELPHIA

BURMM RIVER DR

BRIDGE

MAIN

RAILROAD

CHURCH

MAPLE

REED

MAIN

KELLOGG

PEARL

S STATE

FRANCIS

QUAKER

STATE

CASGROVE

QUEEN

MIDDLE

THORNAPPLE RIVER

TRANSPORTATION

PHILLIPS

S CLEVELAND

CLEVELAND

LENTZ

GREGG

BROOK

WASHINGTON

EAST

COMPANY

PERRINE

LAKE ONE

EDNA

CitMap
CORPORATION

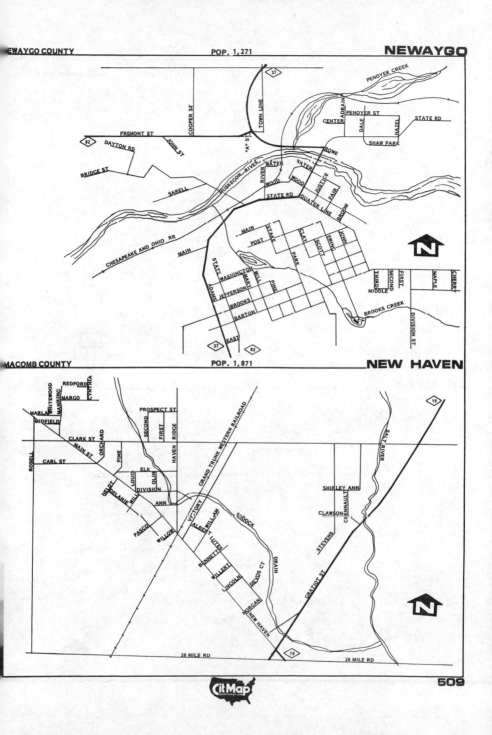

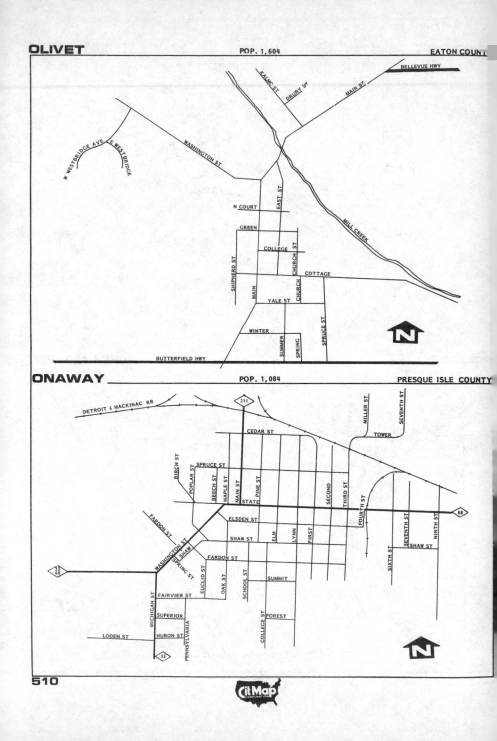

BELLEVUE HWY
KALMC ST
DRURY ST
MAIN ST
W WESTBRIDGE AVE
E WESTBRIDGE
WASHINGTON ST
EAST ST
N COURT
MILL CREEK
GREEN
COLLEGE ST
CHURCH ST
SHIPHERD ST
MAIN
COTTAGE
CHURCH
YALE ST
SPRUCE ST
WINTER
SUMMER
SPRING
BUTTERFIELD HWY

DETROIT & MACKINAC RR
211
MILLER ST
SEVENTH ST
CEDAR ST
TOWER
BIRCH ST
SPRUCE ST
POPLAR ST
BEECH ST
MAPLE ST
MAIN ST
PINE ST
SECOND
THIRD ST
STATE
FARDON ST
ELSDEN ST
FOURTH ST
68
WASHINGTON ST
SHAW ST
ELM
LYNN
FIRST
SEVENTH ST
NINTH ST
SPRING ST
SHAW
FARDON ST
SIXTH ST
SHAW ST
33
68
EUCLID ST
OAK ST
SCHOOL ST
SUMMIT
MICHIGAN ST
FAIRVIEW ST
SUPERIOR
COLLEGE ST
FOREST
LODEM ST
HURON ST
PENNSYLVANIA
33

CitMap CORPORATION

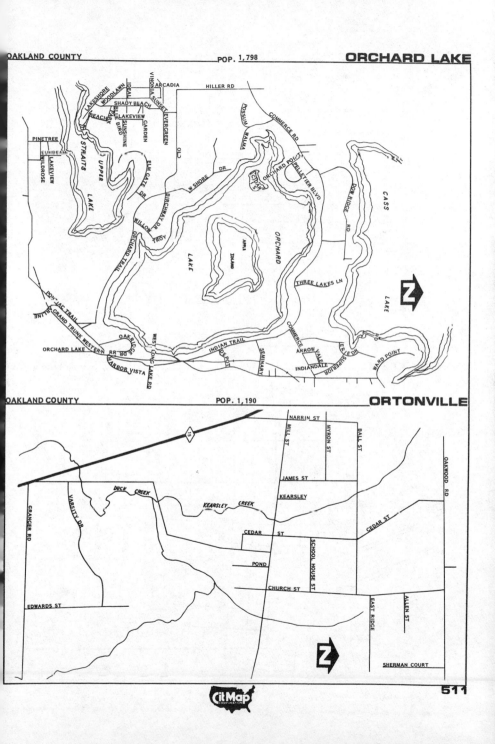

HILLER RD

COMMERCE RD

LAKESHORE
WOODLAWN
IDEAL
VIHONI
SUNSET
ARCADIA
SHADY BEACH
BLUE
BEACH
LAKEVIEW
EVERGREEN
SUNSHINE
BIRD
GARDEN
PINETREE
SUNBEAM
WILDROSE
LAKEVIEW
STRAITS
UPPER LAKE

POSSUM
WAMA
COMMERCE RD
ORCHARD POINT
PELLETIER BLVD
DON RIDGE RD

CASS

ELM GATE DR
BIRCHWAY DR
TROY
WILLOW DR
ORCHARD TRAIL
W SHORE DR
OLD ORCHARD

CITY 3/4

AMLI
ISLAND

ORCHARD
LAKE

LAKE

THREE LAKES LN

LAKE

PONTIAC TRAIL
AIRLINE
GRAND TRUNK WESTERN
OAK RIDGE
ORCHARD LAKE
HARBOR VISTA
WEST LONG LAKE RD
RR DR

INDIAN TRAIL
DE POIT
SEMINARY

COMMERCE
ARROW
VALLEY
INDIANDALE
LESLIE DR
SUPERIOR
WARD POINT

NARRIN ST
MILL ST
MYRON ST
BALL ST

JAMES ST

DUCK CREEK
VARSITY DR
KEARSLEY CREEK
KEARSLEY

GRANGER RD

OAKWOOD RD

CEDAR ST
CEDAR ST

SCHOOL HOUSE ST

POND

CHURCH ST

EDWARDS ST

EAST RIDGE
ALLEN ST

SHERMAN COURT

CitMap
CORPORATION

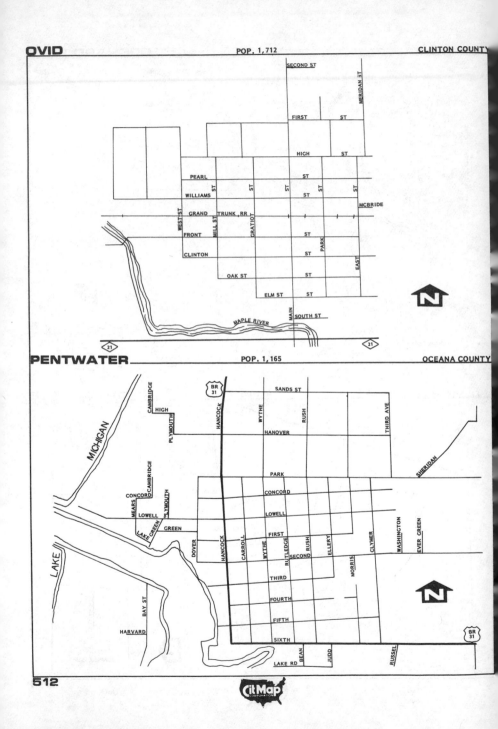

SECOND ST
MERIDAN ST
FIRST ST
HIGH ST
PEARL ST
WILLIAMS ST ST ST ST ST
WEST ST
MCBRIDE
GRAND TRUNK RR
MILL ST
GRATIOT
FRONT ST
PARK
CLINTON ST
EAST
OAK ST ST
ELM ST ST
MAIN
SOUTH ST
MAPLE RIVER
21 21

BR 31
SANDS ST
CAMBRIDGE
HIGH
PLYMOUTH
HANCOCK
WYTHE
RUSH
THIRD AVE
HANOVER
MICHIGAN
SHERIDAN
PARK
CAMBRIDGE
CONCORD
MEARS
PLYMOUTH
LOWELL
LAKE CREEK
GREEN
GREEN
LAKE
FIRST
DOVER
HANCOCK
CARROLL
WYTHE
RUTLEDGE
SECOND
RUSH
ELLERY
CLYMER
WASHINGTON
EVER GREEN
MORRIS
THIRD
BAY ST
FOURTH
FIFTH
HARVARD
SIXTH
BEAN
JUDD
RUSSEL
BR 31
LAKE RD

512

Cit Map
CORPORATION

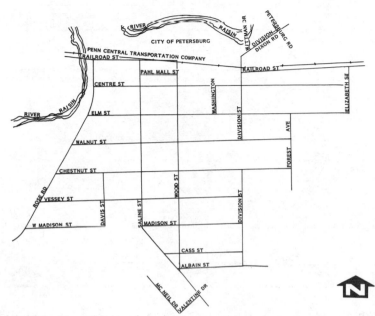

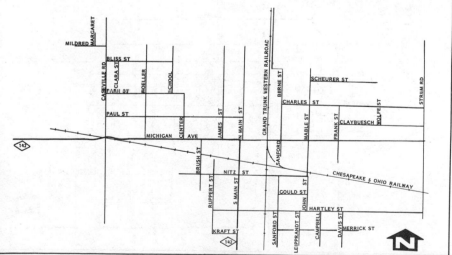

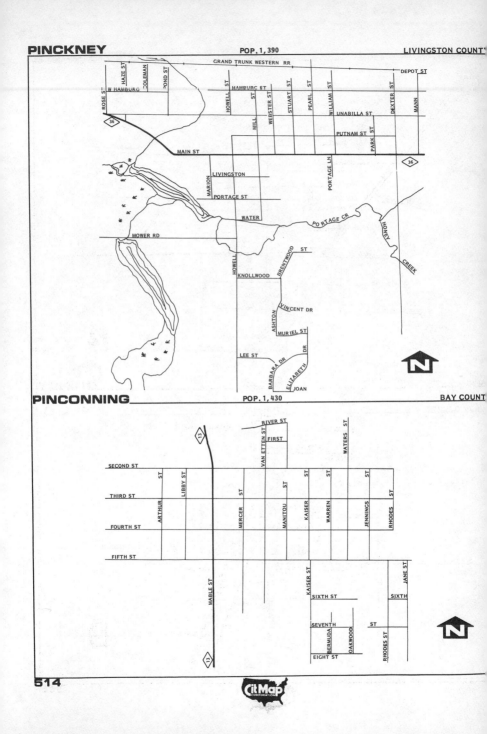

GRAND TRUNK WESTERN RR

DEPOT ST

HAZE ST
COLEMAN
POND ST
ROSE ST
W HAMBURG

HOWELL ST
HAMBURG ST
MILL ST
WEBSTER ST
STUART ST
PEARL ST
WILLIAM ST
UNABILLA ST
DEXTER ST
MANN

36

PUTNAM ST
PARK ST

MAIN ST

PORTAGE LN

36

LIVINGSTON
MARION
PORTAGE ST

WATER
PORTAGE CR

MOWER RD

HONEY CREEK

HOWELL
BRENTWOOD ST
KNOLLWOOD

VINCENT DR

ASHTON
MURIEL ST

LEE ST

BARBARA DR
ELIZABETH DR

JOAN

N

PINCONNING
POP. 1,430
BAY COUNTY

RIVER ST
FIRST
VAN ETTEN ST
WATERS ST

13

SECOND ST

LIBBY ST

MERCER ST
MANITOU ST
KAISER ST
WARREN ST
JENNINGS ST
RHODES ST

THIRD ST
ARTHUR ST

FOURTH ST

FIFTH ST

MABLE ST

KAISER ST

JANE ST

SIXTH ST
SIXTH

SEVENTH
ST
BERMUDA
OAKWOOD
RHODES ST

EIGHT ST

N

CitMap
CORPORATION

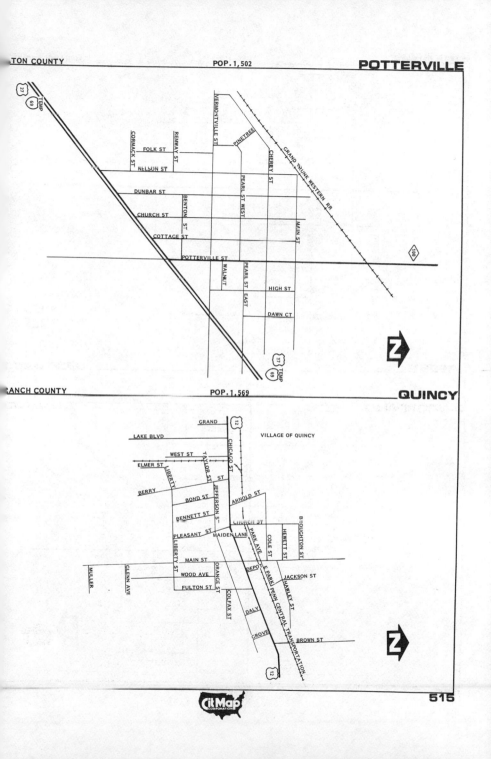

27 69 TEMP

VERMONTVILLE ST

CORMACK ST

FOLK ST

RENWAY ST

PINETREE

NELSON ST

CHERRY ST

GRAND TRUNK WESTERN RR

DUNBAR ST

PEARL ST WEST

BENTON ST

CHURCH ST

COTTAGE ST

MAIN ST

100

POTTERVILLE ST

WALNUT

PEARL ST EAST

HIGH ST

DAWN CT

27 69 TEMP

Z

GRAND

12

VILLAGE OF QUINCY

LAKE BLVD

CHICAGO ST

WEST ST

TAYLOR ST

ELMER ST

LIBERTY

BERRY

JEFFERSON ST

ARNOLD ST

BOND ST

BENNETT ST

CHURCH ST

BOUGHTON ST

PLEASANT ST

MAIDEN LANE

PARK AVE

COLE ST

HEWETT ST

LIBERTY

MAIN ST

DEPOT

E PARK

JACKSON ST

MULLER

GLENN AVE

ORANGE ST

WOOD AVE

HAWLEY ST

FULTON ST

COLFAX ST

DALY

PENN CENTRAL TRANSPORTATION

GROVE

BROWN ST

12

Z

Cit Map
CORPORATION

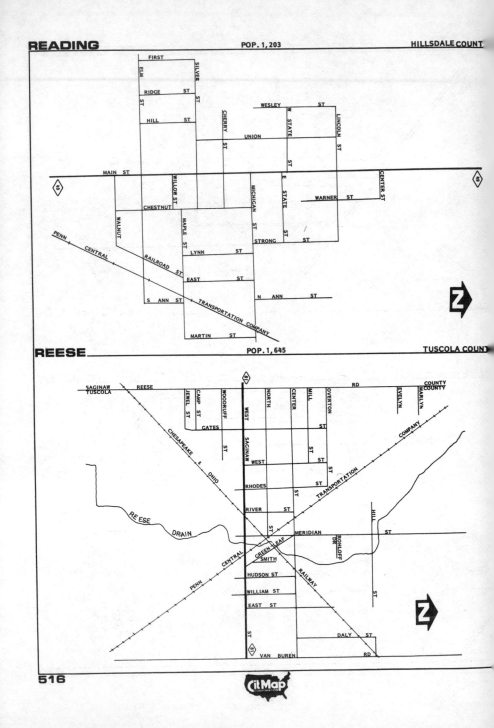

REESE
POP. 1,645
TUSCOLA COUNTY

CitMap
CORPORATION

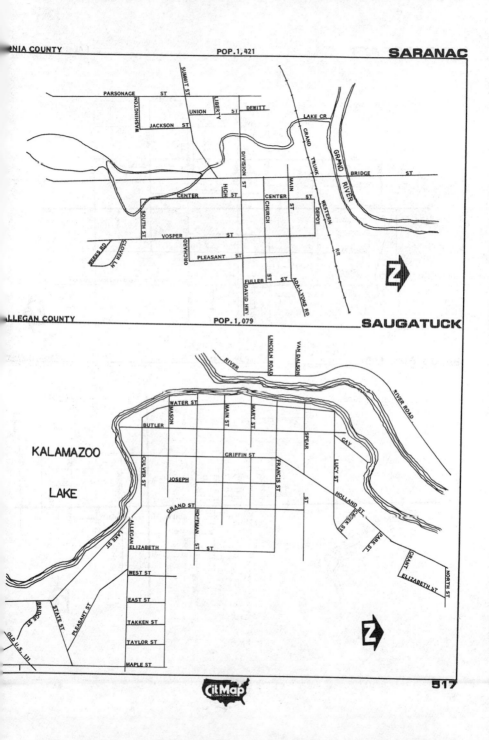

SUMMIT ST

PARSONAGE ST

WASHINGTON ST

LIBERTY ST

UNION ST DEWITT

JACKSON ST

LAKE CR

GRAND TRUNK

GRAND RIVER

BRIDGE ST

DIVISION ST

MAIN ST

WESTERN DEPOT

CENTER HIGH ST CENTER ST

CHURCH ST

SOUTH ST

VOSPER ST

WEEKS RD

CLOVER LN

ORCHARD

PLEASANT ST

RR

FULLER ST ST

DAVID HWY

ADA-LYONS RD

RIVER

LINCOLN ROAD

VAN DALSON

RIVER ROAD

WATER ST

MASON

MAIN ST

MARY ST

SPEAR

GAY

BUTLER

KALAMAZOO

CULVER ST

GRIFFIN ST

FRANCIS ST

LUCY ST

LAKE

JOSEPH

ST

HOLLAND ST

GRAND ST

HOFMAN ST

MOSER ST

PARK ST

ALLEGAN

LAKE ST

ELIZABETH

WEST ST

GRANT

ELIZABETH ST

NORTH ST

BRIDGE ST

STATE ST

PLEASANT ST

EAST ST

TAKKEN ST

OLD U.S. 131

TAYLOR ST

MAPLE ST

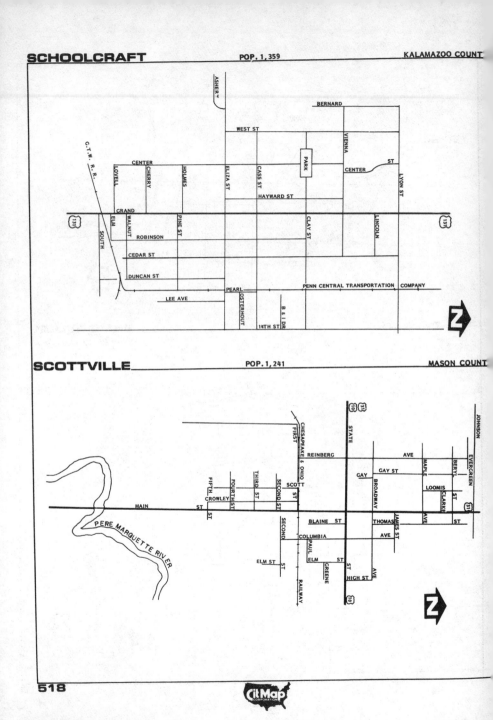

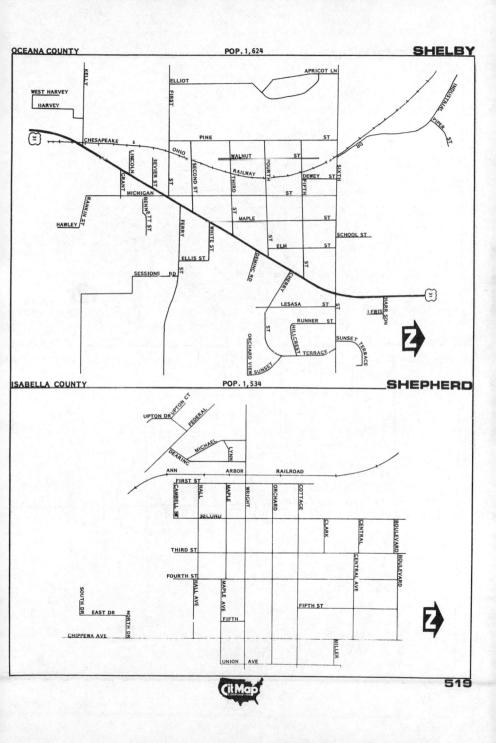

KELLY

WEST HARVEY

HARVEY

ELLIOT

FIRST

APRICOT LN

PINE   ST

CHESAPEAKE

OHIO

WALNUT   ST

RAILWAY

LINCOLN

BEVIER ST

SECOND ST

THIRD ST

FOURTH

FIFTH

DEWEY

SIXTH

GRANT

MICHIGAN

BENNETT ST

ST

RANKIN ST

HAWLEY

FERRY

WHITE ST

MAPLE   ST

SCHOOL ST

ELLIS ST

ELM   ST

DEMING RD

SESSIONS RD

CHERRY   ST

LESASA   ST

LEWIS

HARRISON

PIPER ST

TRANSTROM

RUNNER   ST

ORCHARD VIEW

HILLCREST

SUNSET TERRACE

SUNSET

TERRACE

31

Z

UPTON DR

UPTON CT

FEDERAL

MICHAEL

LYNN

DEARING

ANN   ARBOR   RAILROAD

FIRST ST

CAMBELL ST

HALL

MAPLE

WRIGHT

ORCHARD

COTTAGE

SECOND

CLARK

CENTRAL

BOULEVARD

THIRD ST

BOULEVARD

FOURTH ST

CENTRAL AVE

HALL AVE

MAPLE AVE

FIFTH ST

SOUTH DR

EAST DR

NORTH DR

FIFTH

MILLER

CHIPPEWA AVE

UNION   AVE

Z

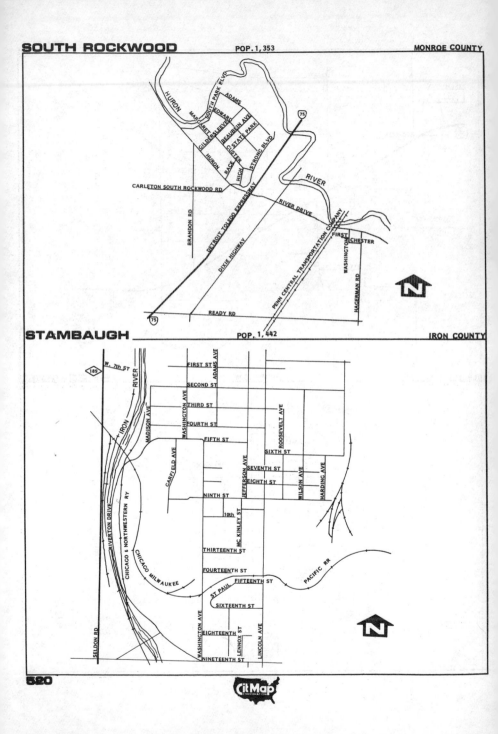

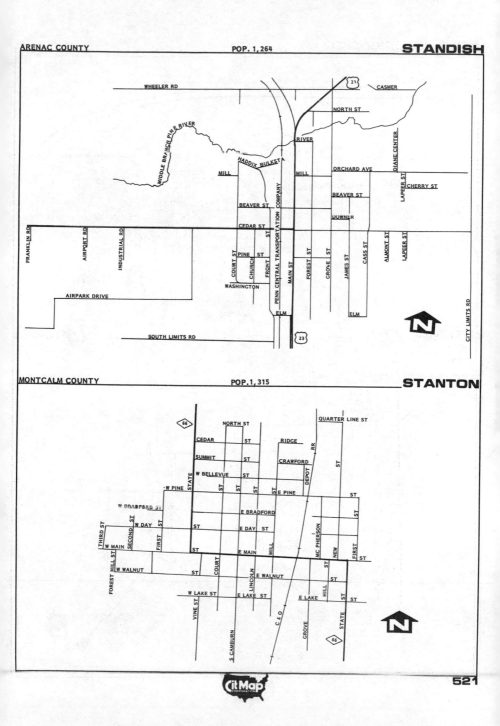

WHEELER RD

CASMER

NORTH ST

RIVER

DIANE CENTER

MIDDLE BRANCH PINE RIVER

HADDIX BULK STA

MILL   MILL   ORCHARD AVE

LAPEER ST   CHERRY ST

BEAVER ST

BEAVER ST

CEDAR ST   DOWNER

FRANKLIN RD   AIRPORT RD   INDUSTRIAL RD

COURT ST   PINE   ST   FOREST ST   GROVE ST   JAMES ST   CASS ST   ALMONT ST   LAPEER ST

CHURCH   FRONT ST   MAIN ST

WASHINGTON

AIRPARK DRIVE

PENN CENTRAL TRANSPORTATION COMPANY

ELM   ELM

CITY LIMITS RD

SOUTH LIMITS RD

QUARTER LINE ST

66

NORTH ST

CEDAR   ST   RIDGE   RR

SUMMIT   ST   CRAWFORD   DEPOT

W BELLEVUE   ST   ST

W PINE   ST   ST   ST   E PINE

STATE

W BRADFORD ST   E BRADFORD

THIRD ST   SECOND   ST   W DAY   ST   E DAY   ST

FIRST   ST   MC PHERSON   NEW   FIRST

W MAIN ST   ST   E MAIN   MILL

FOREST HILL ST   W WALNUT   ST   E WALNUT   ST

COURT   LINCOLN

W LAKE ST   E LAKE ST   E LAKE   HILL   ST   ST

VINE ST   C & O

S. CAMBURN   GROVE   STATE

66

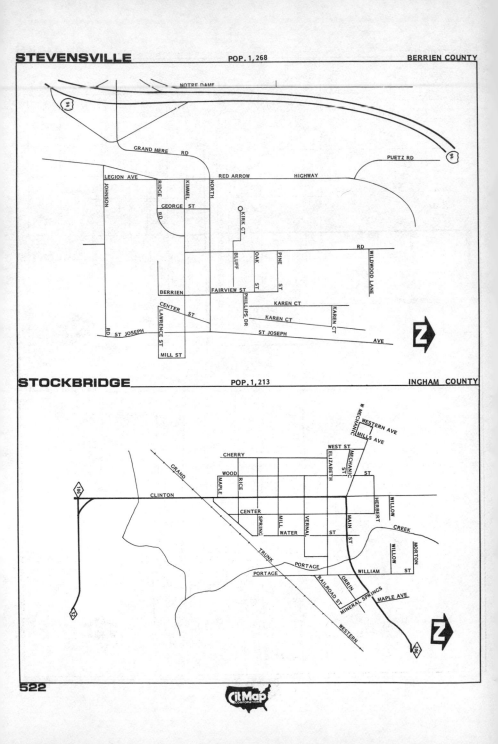

STEVENSVILLE

POP. 1,268

BERRIEN COUNTY

NOTRE DAME

94

GRAND MERE RD

PUETZ RD

94

LEGION AVE

RED ARROW HIGHWAY

JOHNSON

RIDGE RD

KIMMEL ST

GEORGE ST

NORTH

KIRK CT

RD

WILDWOOD LANE

BLUFF

OAK ST

PINE ST

BERRIEN

FAIRVIEW ST

PHILLIPS DR

KAREN CT

KAREN CT

KAREN CT

CENTER ST

LAWRENCE ST

RD ST JOSEPH

ST JOSEPH AVE

MILL ST

STOCKBRIDGE

POP. 1,213

INGHAM COUNTY

W MECHANIC

WESTERN AVE

MILLS AVE

WEST ST

CHERRY

ELIZABETH

MECHANIC ST

ST

106

CLINTON

WOOD

MAPLE

RICE

HERBERT

WILLOW

GRAND

CENTER

SPRING

MILL

WATER

VERNAL

ST

MAIN ST

CREEK

WILLOW ST

MORTON

TRUNK

PORTAGE

PORTAGE

RAILROAD ST

ORRIN

WILLIAM

106

MINERAL SPRINGS

MAPLE AVE

WESTERN

106

522

CitMap CORPORATION

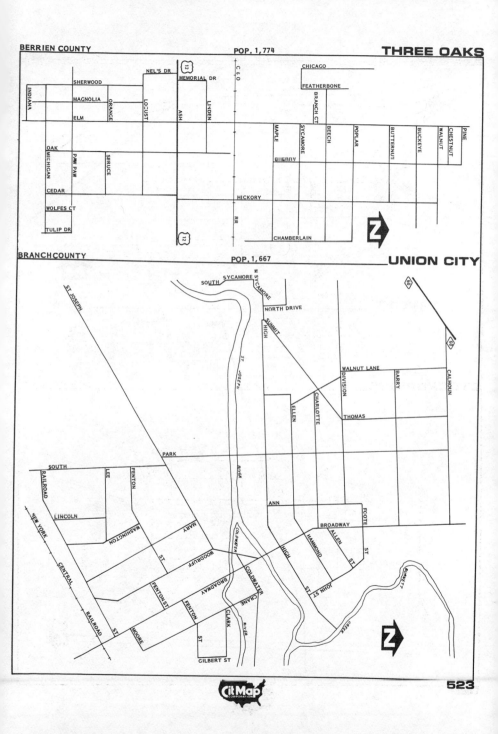

BRANCH COUNTY
POP. 1,667
UNION CITY

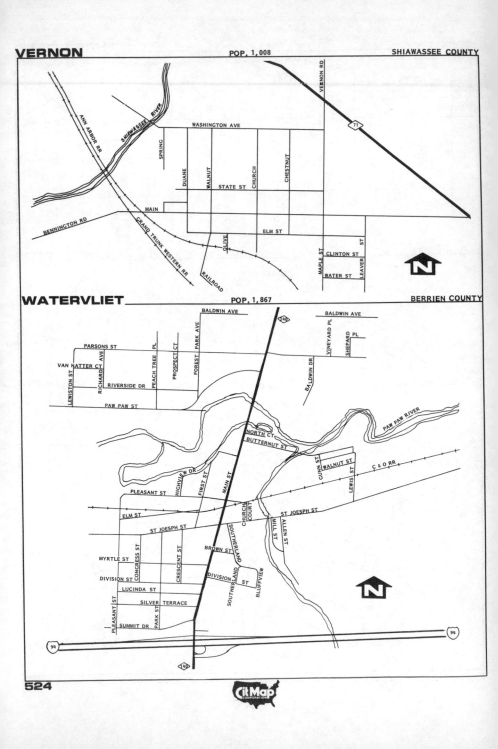

VERNON

POP. 1,008

VERNON RD

71

ANN ARBOR RR

SHIAWASSEE RIVER

WASHINGTON AVE

SPRING

DUANE

WALNUT

CHURCH

CHESTNUT

STATE ST

MAIN

BENNINGTON RD

GRAND TRUNK WESTERN RR

OLIVE

ELM ST

RAILROAD

MAPLE ST

CLINTON ST

LEAVER ST

WATER ST

N

WATERVLIET

POP. 1,867

BALDWIN AVE

BALDWIN AVE

PARSONS ST

VINEYARD PL

SHEPARD PL

FOREST PARK AVE

PROSPECT CT

PEACH TREE PL

VAN NATTER CT

RICHARD AVE

RIVERSIDE DR

BALDWIN DR

LEWISTON ST

PAW PAW ST

PAW PAW RIVER

NORTH CT.

BUTTERNUT ST

GUNN ST

WALNUT ST

C & O RR

HIGHVIEW DR

FIRST ST

MAIN ST

LEWIS ST

PLEASANT ST

ELM ST

CHURCH COURT

ST JOESPH ST

ST JOESEPH ST

MILL ST

ALLEN ST

MYRTLE ST

CONGRESS ST

CRESCENT ST

BROWN ST

SOUTHERLAND

DIVISION ST

DIVISION ST

BLUFFVIEW

LUCINDA ST

PLEASANT ST

SILVER TERRACE

PARK ST

SUMMIT DR

N

94

94

140

CitMap CORPORATION

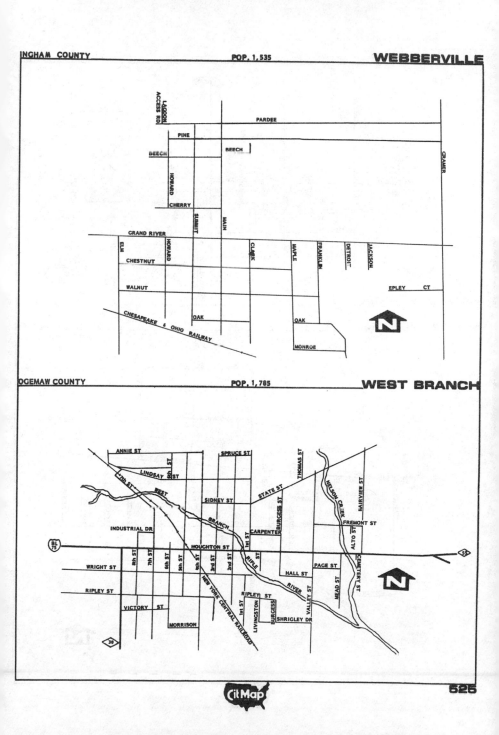

LAGOON ACCESS RD.

PARDEE

PINE

BEECH   BEECH

HOWARD

CRAMER

CHERRY

SUMMIT

MAIN

GRAND RIVER

ELM

HOWARD

CLARK

MAPLE

FRANKLIN

DETROIT

JACKSON

CHESTNUT

WALNUT

EPLEY   CT

CHESAPEAKE & OHIO RAILWAY

OAK

OAK

MONROE

ANNIE ST

SPRUCE ST

THOMAS ST

9th ST

LINDSAY

7th ST

WEST

SIDNEY ST

STATE ST

NELSON CREEK

FAIRVIEW ST

BRANCH

BURGESS ST

CARPENTER

FREMONT ST

ALTO ST

INDUSTRIAL DR

1st ST

BL 75

HOUGHTON ST

RIFLE ST

PAGE ST

CEMETERY ST

33

WRIGHT ST

8th ST

7th ST

6th ST

5th ST

4th ST

3rd ST

2nd ST

HALL ST

MEAD ST

RIVER

VALLEY ST

RIPLEY ST

RIPLEY   ST

1st ST

LIVINGSTON

BURGESS

VICTORY   ST

NEW YORK CENTRAL RAILROAD

SHRIGLEY DR

MORRISON

30

WHITE CLOUD
POP. 1,101
NEWAYGO COUNTY

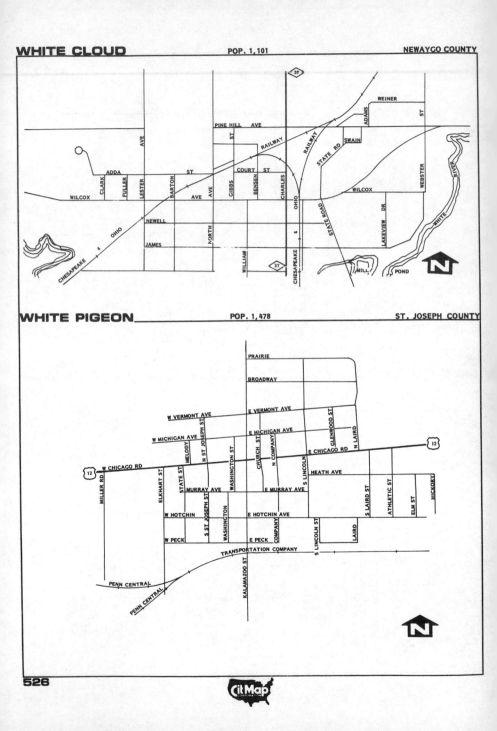

WHITE PIGEON
POP. 1,478
ST. JOSEPH COUNTY

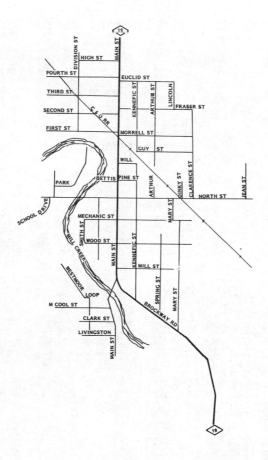

MICHIGAN - CITY ZIP CODES

ADRIAN CITY	49221
ALBION CITY	49224
ALGONAC CITY	48001
ALLEGAN CITY	49010
ALLEN PARK CITY	48101
ALMA CITY	48801
ALMONT VILLAGE	48003
ALPENA CITY	49707
ANN ARBOR CITY	48106
ARMADA VILLAGE	48005
AUBURN CITY	48611
BAD AXE CITY	48413
BANGOR CITY	49013
BARAGA CITY	49908
BATTLE CREEK CITY	49016
BAY CITY	48707
BEAVERTON CITY	48612
BELDING CITY	48809
BELLAIRE VILLAGE	49615
BELLEVILLE CITY	48111
BENTON HARBOR CITY	49022
BERKLEY CITY	48072
BERRIEN SPRINGS VILLAGE	49103
BESSEMER CITY	49911
BEVERLY HILLS VILLAGE	
BIG RAPIDS CITY	49307
BIRCH RUN VILLAGE	48415
BIRMINGHAM CITY	48025
BLISSFIELD VILLAGE	49228
BLOOMFIELD HILLS CITY	48013
BOYNE CITY	49712
BRECKEN RIDGE VILLAGE	48615
BRIDGMAN CITY	49106
BRIGHTON CITY	48116
BRONSON CITY	49028
BROOKLYN VILLAGE	49230
BROWN CITY	48416
BUCHANAN CITY	49107
BURTON CITY	
CADILLAC CITY	
CALUMET VILLAGE	49913
CAPAC VILLAGE	48014
CARLETON VILLAGE	48117
CARO VILLAGE	48723
CARSON CITY	48811
CASPIAN CITY	49915
CASS CITY VILLAGE	48726
CASSOPOLIS VILLAGE	49031
CEDAR SPRINGS CITY	49319
CENTER LINE CITY	48015
CENTERVILLE VILLAGE	49032
CHARLEVOIX CITY	49720
CHEBOYGAN CITY	49721
CHELSEA CITY	48118
CHESANING VILLAGE	48616
CLARE CITY	48617
CLAWSON CITY	48017
CLINTON VILLAGE	49236
CLIO CITY	48420
COLDWATER CITY	49036
COLEMAN CITY	48618
COLOMA CITY	49038
COLON VILLAGE	49040
CONSTANTINE VILLAGE	49042
COOPERSVILLE CITY	49402
CORUNNA CITY	48817
CROSWELL CITY	48422
CRYSTAL FALLS CITY	49920
DAVISON CITY	48423
DEARBORN CITY	48122
DEARBORN HEIGHTS	48127
DECATUR VILLAGE	49045
DETROIT CITY	
EASTLAND CENTER	48225
ECORSE	48229
FERNDALE (Oakland Co.)	48220
GROSSE POINTE	48236
HAMTRAMCK	48212
HIGHLAND PARK	48203
METRO AIRPORT SOUTH	48242
METROPOLITAN AIRPORT	48242
OAK PARK (Oakland Co.)	48237
REDFORD	48329/48240
RIVER ROUGE	48218
DEWITT CITY	48820
DEXTER VILLAGE	48130
DIMONDALE VILLAGE	48821
DOWAGIAC CITY	49047
DUNDEE VILLAGE	48131
DURAND CITY	48429

City	ZIP
EAST DETROIT CITY	48021
EAST JORDAN CITY	49727
EAST LANSING CITY	48823
EAST TAWAS CITY	49730
EATON RAPIDS CITY	48827
ECORSE CITY	48229
EDMORE VILLAGE	48829
EDWARDSBURG VILLAGE	49112
ELK RAPIDS VILLAGE	49629
ELSIE VILLAGE	48831
ESCANABA CITY	49829
ESSEXVILLE CITY	48732
EVART CITY	49631
FARMINGTON CITY	48024
FARMINGTON HILLS	48018
FENTON CITY	48430
FERNDALE CITY	48220
FERRYSBURG CITY	49409
FLAT ROCK CITY	
FLINT CITY	
HISTRCL CROSSROADS	48506
SOUTHEAST ANNEX	48519
FLUSHING CITY	48433
FOWLER	48835
FOWLERVILLE VILLAGE	48836
FRANKENMUTH CITY	48734
FRANKFORT CITY	49635
FRANKLIN VILLAGE	48025
FRASER CITY	48026
FREMONT CITY	49412
FRUITPORT VILLAGE	49415
GALESBURG CITY	49053
GARDEN CITY	48135
GAYLORD CITY	49735
GIBRALTAR CITY	48173
GLADSTONE CITY	49837
GLADWIN CITY	48624
GRAND BLANC CITY	48439
GRAND HAVEN CITY	49417
GRAND LEDGE CITY	48837
GRAND RAPIDS	
KENTWOOD	49508
LEONARD HEIGHTS	49504
NORTHGATE	49505
REEDS LAKE	49506
WALKER	49504
WYOMING	49509
WYOMING PARK	49509
GRANDVILLE CITY	49418
GRAYLING CITY	49738
GREENVILLE CITY	48838
GROSSE POINTE CITY	48236
HAMTRAMCK	48212
HANCOCK CITY	49930
HARBOR BEACH CITY	48441
HARBOR SPRINGS CITY	49740
HARRISON CITY	48625
HART CITY	49420
HARTFORD CITY	49057
HASTINGS CITY	49058
HAZEL PARK CITY	48030
HIGHLAND PARK CITY	48203
HILLSDALE CITY	49242
HOLLAND CITY	49423
HOLLY VILLAGE	48442
HOMER VILLAGE	49245
HOWARD CITY VILLAGE	49329
HOWELL CITY	48843
HUDSON CITY	49247
HUDSONVILLE CITY	49426
HUNTINGTON WOODS	48070
IMLAY CITY	48444
INKSTER CITY	48141
IONIA CITY	48846
IRON MOUNTAIN CITY	49801
IRON RIVER CITY	49936
IRONWOOD CITY	49938
ISHPEMING CITY	49849
ITHACA CITY	48847
JACKSON CITY	49201
JENISON	49428
JONESVILLE VILLAGE	49250
KALAMAZOO CITY	49004
KALKASKA VILLAGE	49446
KEEGO HARBOR CITY	48033
KENTWOOD CITY	49508
KINGSFORD CITY	49801

City	ZIP
LAINGSBURG CITY	48848
LAKE LINDEN VILLAGE	49945
LAKE ODESSA VILLAGE	48849
LAKE ORION VILLAGE	48035
LAKEVIEW VILLAGE	48850
L'ANSE	49946
LANSING CITY	
LAPEER CITY	48446
LATHRUP VILLAGE CITY	48076
LAURIUM VILLAGE	49913
LAWTON VILLAGE	49065
LESLIE CITY	49251
LINCOLN PARK CITY	48146
LINDEN VILLAGE	48451
LITCHFIELD CITY	49252
LIVONIA CITY	48151
LOWELL CITY	49331
LUDINGTON CITY	49431
LUNA PIER CITY	48157
MADISON HEIGHTS CITY	48071
MANCELONA VILLAGE	46659
MANCHESTER VILLAGE	48158
MANISTEE CITY	49660
MANISTIQUE CITY	49854
MANTON CITY	49663
MARCELLUS VILLAGE	49067
MARINE CITY	48039
MARLETTE VILLAGE	48453
MARQUETTE CITY	49855
MARSHALL CITY	49068
MARYSVILLE CITY	48040
MASON CITY	48854
MATTAWAN VILLAGE	49071
MELVINDALE CITY	48122
MEMPHIS CITY	48041
MENOMINEE CITY	49858
MIDDLEVILLE VILLAGE	49333
MIDLAND CITY	48640
MILAN CITY	48160
MILFORD VILLAGE	48042
MILLINGTON VILLAGE	48746
MONROE CITY	48161
MONTAGUE CITY	49437
MONTROSE VILLAGE	48457
MORENCI CITY	49256
MOUNT CLEMENS CITY	48045
MOUNT MORRIS CITY	48458
MOUNT PLEASANT CITY	48858
MUNISING CITY	49862
MUSKEGON CITY	49445
MUSKEGON HEIGHTS	49444
NASHVILLE VILLAGE	49073
NEGAUNEE CITY	49866
NEWAYGO CITY	49337
NEW BALTIMORE CITY	48047
NEWBERRY VILLAGE	49868
NEW BUFFALO CITY	49117
NEW HAVEN VILLAGE	48048
NILES CITY	49120
NORTH MUSKEGON CITY	49445
NORTHVILLE CITY	48167
NORWAY CITY	49870
NOVI CITY	48050
OAK PARK CITY	48237
OLIVET CITY	49076
ONAWAY CITY	49765
ONTONAGON VILLAGE	49953
ORTONVILLE VILLAGE	48462
OSTEGO CITY	49078
OVID VILLAGE	48866
OWOSSO CITY	48867
OXFORD VILLAGE	48051
PARCHMENT CITY	49004
PAW PAW	49079
PENTWATER VILLAGE	49449
PERRY CITY	48872
PETERSBURG CITY	49270
PETOSKEY CITY	49770
PIGEON VILLAGE	48755
PINCKNEY VILLAGE	48169
PINCONNING CITY	48650
PLAINWELL CITY	49080
PLEASANT RIDGE CITY	48069
PLYMOUTH CITY	48170
PONTIAC CITY	
AUBURN HILLS	48057
WEST BLOOMFIELD	
ORCHARD LAKE	48033

City	ZIP
PORTAGE CITY	49081
PORT HURON CITY	48060
PORTLAND CITY	48875
POTTERSVILLE CITY	48876
QUINCY VILLAGE	49082
READING CITY	49082
REED CITY	49677
REESE VILLAGE	48757
RICHMOND CITY	48062
RIVER ROUGE CITY	48218
RIVER VIEW CITY	48192
ROCHESTER CITY	48308
ROCKFORD CITY	49341
ROCKWOOD CITY	48173
ROGERS CITY	49779
ROMEO VILLAGE	48065
ROMULUS CITY	48174
ROOSEVELT PARK CITY	49441
ROSEVILLE CITY	48066
ROYAL OAK CITY	48072
SAGINAW CITY	48603
ST. CHARLES VILLAGE	48655
ST. CLAIR CITY	48079
ST. CLAIR SHORES	48080
ST. IGNACE CITY	49879
ST. JOHNS CITY	48879
ST. JOSEPH CITY	49085
ST. LOUIS CITY	48880
SALINE CITY	48176
SANDUSKY CITY	48471
SARANAC VILLAGE	48881
SAUGATUCK VILLAGE	49453
SAULT STE. MARIE	49783
SCHOOL CRAFT VILLAGE	49087
SCOTTVILLE CITY	49454
SEBEWAING VILLAGE	48759
SHELBY VILLAGE	49455
SHEPHERD VILLAGE	48883
SOUTHFIELD CITY	48076
SOUTHGATE CITY	48195
SOUTH HAVEN CITY	49090
SOUTH LYON CITY	48178
SOUTH ROCKWOOD	48179
SPARTA VILLAGE	49345
SPRING LAKE VILLAGE	49456
STAMBAUGH CITY	49964
STANDISH CITY	48658
STANTON CITY	48888
STERLING HGTS. CITY	48130
STEVENSVILLE VILLAGE	49127
STOCKBRIDGE VILLAGE	49285
STURGIS CITY	49091
SWARTZ CREEK CITY	48473
TAWAS CITY	48763
TAYLOR CITY	48180
TECHUMSEH CITY	49286
THREE OAKS VILLAGE	49128
THREE RIVERS CITY	49093
TRAVERSE CITY	49684
TRENTON CITY	48183
UNION CITY VILLAGE	49094
UTICA	
STERLING HEIGHTS	48077
VASSAR CITY	48077
VERNON VILLAGE	48476
VICKSBURG VILLAGE	49097
WAKE FIELD CITY	49968
WALKER CITY	49504
WALLED LAKE CITY	49088
WERVLIET CITY	49098
WAYLAND CITY	49348
WEBBERVILLE	48892
WEST BRANCH CITY	48661
WESTLAND CITY	48185
WHITE CLOUD CITY	49349
WHITEHALL CITY	49461
WHITE PIGEON VILLAGE	49099
WILLIAMSTON CITY	48895
WIXOM CITY	48096
WOLVERINE LAKE	49799
WOODHAVEN CITY	48183
WYANDOTTE CITY	48192
WYOMING CITY	49509
YALE CITY	48097
YPSILANTI CITY	48198
ZEELAND CITY	49464

CitMap
CORPORATION

Automobile Mileage
Between Michigan Cities

TO \ FROM	Alpena	Ann Arbor	Bay City	Cadillac	Charlevoix	Clare	Detroit	Flint	Grand Rapids	Lansing	Ludington	Mackinaw City	Marquette	Muskegon	Sault Ste. Marie	Traverse City
Adrian	264	40	136	199	279	153	68	95	133	73	227	297	463	172	354	244
Albion	251	53	123	165	245	121	91	90	86	40	171	264	431	123	322	209
Alma	89	110	52	80	159	33	132	73	80	49	123	177	344	95	235	124
Alpena	—	225	129	150	114	151	233	173	247	211	220	94	261	257	152	137
Ann Arbor	225	—	96	188	257	142	38	54	127	63	220	272	439	166	330	233
Bad Axe	188	140	59	155	223	109	108	86	181	134	199	238	405	196	296	200
Battle Creek	260	76	132	146	226	130	114	99	61	49	153	266	433	98	324	191
Bay City	129	96	—	96	164	50	104	44	128	82	140	179	346	143	237	141
Benton Harbor	327	145	202	178	262	181	183	170	83	120	145	302	469	90	360	220
Big Rapids	190	169	89	40	124	51	189	130	57	107	64	164	331	67	222	85
Brighton	207	18	78	170	240	124	40	36	109	45	203	254	421	148	312	215
Cadillac	150	188	96	—	84	46	197	137	97	127	73	124	291	107	182	49
Charlevoix	114	257	164	84	—	126	267	207	180	206	142	52	219	184	110	50
Cheboygan	79	262	169	126	59	135	272	212	223	216	197	16	183	233	74	109
Clare	151	142	50	46	126	—	151	91	99	80	90	143	310	114	201	91
Coldwater	279	81	151	181	261	149	109	119	99	69	190	292	459	135	350	226
Copper Harbor	408	585	492	437	365	457	595	535	534	537	507	313	147	544	311	415
Crystal Falls	324	502	409	353	282	373	511	451	450	453	424	230	72	460	237	332
Detour	156	334	241	186	114	205	343	284	282	286	256	62	207	293	59	164
Detroit	233	38	104	197	267	151	—	60	149	85	241	281	448	188	339	242
Escanaba	242	420	327	272	200	291	429	369	368	372	342	148	65	378	175	250
Flint	173	54	44	137	207	91	60	—	104	50	184	222	388	144	279	182
Frankfort	175	238	147	55	88	97	248	188	142	177	64	140	307	118	198	38
Gaylord	72	216	123	79	42	87	225	166	175	168	149	57	224	185	115	65
Grand Haven	266	158	152	116	194	123	180	136	32	96	67	240	407	13	298	144
Grand Rapids	247	127	128	97	180	99	149	104	—	65	95	221	387	40	278	139
Grayling	93	190	96	60	69	61	199	139	156	141	131	84	250	167	141	52
Hillsdale	278	69	149	194	274	150	96	117	116	70	207	294	460	152	352	239
Holland	274	140	155	124	207	126	172	132	29	88	90	247	414	35	305	165
Houghton	361	538	445	390	318	410	548	488	487	490	460	266	100	497	264	368
Imlay City	203	87	73	170	238	124	51	34	139	84	213	252	419	178	310	214
Ionia	226	100	99	97	180	80	122	71	33	38	127	217	384	72	275	141
Iron Mountain	294	472	378	323	252	343	481	421	420	423	394	200	79	430	227	302
Iron River	340	518	424	369	298	389	527	467	466	469	440	246	88	476	253	348
Ironwood	406	583	490	435	363	455	593	533	532	535	505	311	145	542	309	413
Ishpeming	273	451	358	302	231	322	460	400	399	402	378	179	12	409	177	281

CitMap
CORPORATION

Automobile Mileage
Between Michigan Cities

FROM / TO	Alpena	Ann Arbor	Bay City	Cadillac	Charlevoix	Clare	Detroit	Flint	Grand Rapids	Lansing	Ludington	Mackinaw City	Marquette	Muskegon	Sault Ste. Marie	Traverse City
Jackson	241	35	113	164	244	118	73	80	98	38	192	261	428	137	319	209
Kalamazoo	283	98	155	147	230	148	136	123	50	73	138	270	437	84	328	188
L'Anse	328	506	413	357	286	377	515	455	454	457	428	234	67	464	232	336
Lansing	211	63	82	127	206	80	85	50	65	—	158	224	391	104	282	171
Lapeer	189	75	60	156	224	110	56	21	126	71	200	239	406	165	297	201
Ludington	220	220	140	73	142	90	241	181	95	158	—	194	361	58	252	92
Mackinaw City	94	272	179	124	52	143	281	222	221	224	194	—	167	231	58	102
Manistee	196	232	141	49	112	91	242	182	119	171	31	164	331	85	222	62
Manistique	188	366	273	218	146	238	375	316	315	318	288	94	87	325	121	196
Marquette	261	439	346	291	219	310	448	388	387	391	361	167	—	397	165	269
Marshall	256	65	127	157	237	125	102	95	75	45	166	269	436	112	327	202
Menominee	296	474	381	326	254	345	483	424	423	426	396	202	120	433	229	304
Midland	145	110	19	79	159	33	120	60	111	86	122	174	341	126	232	124
Monroe	260	39	131	224	294	178	37	87	161	101	255	308	475	200	366	269
Mt. Clemens	234	57	104	197	267	151	21	60	158	94	241	282	448	197	339	242
Mt. Pleasant	167	127	46	62	142	16	147	87	84	65	106	159	326	99	217	107
Munising	218	396	303	248	176	267	405	345	344	348	318	124	43	354	122	226
Muskegon	257	166	143	107	84	114	188	144	40	104	58	231	397	—	289	134
Newberry	169	346	253	198	127	218	356	296	295	298	268	74	105	305	67	177
New Buffalo	354	171	231	204	287	207	206	198	109	148	170	328	494	116	387	247
Niles	338	144	210	194	277	196	181	178	98	128	160	317	484	106	377	237
Northport	164	260	168	76	77	118	269	210	166	199	120	130	295	162	187	27
Ontonagon	375	553	460	405	333	424	562	503	501	505	475	281	115	512	279	383
Owosso	180	69	53	127	207	81	83	25	79	31	170	224	391	119	282	172
Petoskey	101	251	158	88	16	122	260	200	185	202	158	36	203	195	94	67
Pontiac	209	48	79	173	242	126	25	35	133	69	216	257	423	172	315	217
Port Austin	196	157	67	163	231	117	124	103	195	149	207	246	413	210	304	208
Port Huron	237	96	108	204	272	158	59	69	174	119	248	287	454	213	345	249
Port Sanilac	204	127	75	172	239	125	90	85	186	134	215	254	421	200	312	216
Roscommon	91	177	83	59	84	60	186	126	156	141	132	98	265	166	156	67
Saginaw	141	86	13	102	173	55	96	36	116	70	145	188	355	131	246	146
St. Ignace	101	279	186	131	59	150	288	228	227	231	201	7	162	237	52	109
Sault Ste. Marie	152	330	237	182	110	201	339	279	278	282	252	58	165	289	—	160
Sturgis	302	107	174	189	269	172	134	141	93	91	181	309	476	126	367	231
Tawas City	64	161	65	105	147	89	169	109	189	146	178	159	325	204	216	131
Traverse City	137	233	141	49	50	91	242	182	139	171	92	102	269	134	160	—

CitMap

NOTES

NOTES

NOTES

NOTES

NOTES

NOTES

NOTES